The Fluid Borders of Europe

The Open University

The Fluid Borders of Europe

EDITED BY Mark
Pittaway

This publication forms part of an Open University course AA300 *Europe: Culture and Identities in a Contested Continent*. Details of this and other Open University courses can be obtained from the Course Information and Advice Centre, PO Box 724, The Open University, Milton Keynes MK7 6ZS, United Kingdom: tel. +44 (0)1908 653231, e-mail ces-gen@open.ac.uk

Alternatively, you may visit the Open University website at http://www.open.ac.uk where you can learn more about the wide range of courses and packs offered at all levels by The Open University.

To purchase this publication or other components of Open University courses, contact Open University Worldwide Ltd, The Open University, Walton Hall, Milton Keynes MK7 6AA, United Kingdom: tel. +44 (0)1908 858785; fax +44 (0)1908 858787; e-mail ouwenq@open.ac.uk; website http://www.ouw.co.uk

The Open University
Walton Hall, Milton Keynes
MK7 6AA

First published 2003

Edited, designed and typeset by The Open University

Printed and bound in the United Kingdom by The Bath Press, Bath

ISBN 0 7492 9610 0

1.1

27422B/aa300b2prei1.1

Contents

Contributors

Mark Pittaway, Lecturer in European Studies, History Department, the Open University

Suman Gupta, Senior Lecturer in Literature, the Open University

Colin Chant, Senior Lecturer in History of Science, Technology and Medicine, the Open University

Paul G. Lewis, Reader in Government and Politics, the Open University

Robert Fraser, Senior Research Fellow in Literature, the Open University

Readings

The readings that appear in this book are extracts from the following works.

Chapter 1

Christopher Hitchens, 'On the road to Timişoara'

Peter Sahlins, *Boundaries: the Making of France and Spain in the Pyrenees*

Slavenka Drakulič, 'Who is afraid of Europe?'

Michael Herzfeld, 'Theorizing Europe: persuasive paradoxes'

Edward Said, *Orientalism: Western Conceptions of the Orient*

Larry Woolf, *Inventing Eastern Europe: the Map of Civilization on the Mind of the Enlightenment*

Chapter 2

V. S. Naipaul, 'Jasmine'.

Louis Simpson, 'To the Western World'.

Mazisi Kunene, 'Europe'.

Václav Havel, 'Politics and conscience'.

Chapter 3

Alice F. A. Mutton, *Central Europe: a Regional and Human Geography.*

Jenő Szücs, 'Three historical regions of Europe: an outline'.

Timothy Garton-Ash, 'Does central Europe exist'.

Introduction

MARK PITTAWAY

The Fluid Borders of Europe, explores a range of issues that are fundamental to understanding contemporary Europe. The book considers borders in general and Europe's borders in particular by examining how they interact with and shape the identities of the people who live on either side of them. The approach adopted by the authors therefore problematizes the whole issue of borders. Rather than seeing a border as simply a physical reality or a clearly defined line on a map, the book examines borders as mental constructs both shaped by and, in turn, constitutive of identities. Consequently borders are approached as *fluid* entities shaped by the cultures, identities, histories and societies they seek to demarcate. This approach provides an extremely useful framework for looking at questions of *inclusion* and *exclusion* in relation to the continual making and re-making of contemporary Europe. This focus allows the student to explore patterns of inclusion and exclusion, not as universal truths but as a continuous process characterized by conflict and negotiation.

The book consists of a series of case-studies that reveal how patterns of inclusion and exclusion have been shaped by the construction of identities within and outside Europe. In so doing they aim to show that notions of who belongs in Europe are, and have been, intimately related to the identities that have formed along Europe's perceived borders. These issues are reflected in aspects of European history, societies and culture. Culture is taken to mean here, in Cristina Chimisso's definition, 'the totality of symbols and artefacts produced by human beings ... Modes of thinking, feeling and behaving ... values, customs, traditions and norms' (Chimisso, 2003, p. 14). The range of cultural identities through which the authors explore Europe's fluid borders is therefore very broad, from the literature of post-colonial migration into Europe to the writings of British women travellers in 'the Balkans', from the writings of a nineteenth-century Russian traveller and political observer to the political cultures of post-socialist Poland, from contemporary analyses of the roots of right-wing populism in Europe at the end of the twentieth century to critiques of European 'orientalist' thought. The importance attributed to the cartographic representation of European boundaries is reflected in the inclusion of a full visual essay dealing with how mental projections of both Europe in general, and southeastern Europe in particular, have shaped maps of those spaces. The essays in this book approach these issues from an interdisciplinary perspective, recognizing that their own disciplines alone are insufficient to explore the questions that surround borders and identities in European culture. The historical roots of many of the phenomena discussed here can be seen in the inclusion of, for example, discussion of the formation of Europe's national borders over the past three hundred years, the nineteenth-century formation of Polish national identities and the process of postwar decolonization across the globe. It would be impossible to consider the issues raised by borders without examining institutions as well as society. The modern border is itself both a product and a symbol of the power of modern state institutions, while patterns of inclusion and exclusion in contemporary Europe could not be discussed without reference, for example, to the policies of European states towards immigration or the practices of the European Union.

Chapter 1, 'Borders and identities', provides a theoretical discussion of the issues involved in exploring Europe's fluid borders, setting up a framework for the other essays in the book. I analyse the relationship between borders and identities in the context of modern national borders, examining the ways in which these borders are the products of history before moving on to consider how the mental, external borders of Europe have been shaped. I discuss a variety of texts, including extracts from two very different journalistic essays by Christopher Hitchens and Slavenka Drakulič, historical monographs by Peter Sahlins and Larry Woolf and theoretical works by Michael Herzfeld and Edward Said. I also introduce some of the themes to be discussed in depth in the following chapters: the relationship between the non-European world and European identities (Chapter 2), eastern European identities (Chapters 3, 4, 5 and 6) and migration and identity (Chapter 7).

In Chapter 2 'Outside perspectives of Europe after the Second World War' Suman Gupta provides a survey of how Europe has been seen from 'without' during the postwar period. He discusses the issues raised by both 'Eurocentric' and 'synecdochical' views for an analysis of the relationship between Europe and the wider world. He then shifts focus to consider the historical dimensions of these changing relations by examining Europe's relationship to the postcolonial world, its role in the cold war and briefly introduces issues raised by the role of Europe in a globalized world. He discusses extracts from the work of writer V. S. Naipaul, the poets Louis Simpson and Mazisi Kunene, and the playwright, essayist and politician Václav Havel.

Chapter 3 'Europe's borders, Europe's regions: eastern Europe, central Europe', investigates the nature of eastern European identity and its ambiguous relationship to broader European identities, expanding on themes introduced by Suman Gupta's discussion of the work of Václav Havel in the preceding chapter. I use postwar debates about the the regional division of the continent into 'central' and 'eastern' Europe as a means of exploring this issue. I discuss extracts from the work of a British-based political geographer (Alice Mutton), a Hungarian historian (Jenő Szücs) and a British observer of the 'dissident' opposition in eastern Europe during the 1980s (Timothy Garton-Ash). I argue that the saliency of concepts of 'central Europe' are based not so much on constructions of identity based on history and geography, but on an eastern European identity which sees eastern Europe as both part of and, at the same time, excluded from the rest of the continent.

The examination of debates around eastern European identities is developed in Chapter 4 'Exploring Europe's borderlands: "the Balkans"'. In this essay I investigate claims made by the Bulgarian-born historian Maria Todorova that the term 'the Balkans' is one that has been deployed to exclude the peoples of southeastern Europe and to define them as non-European. I discuss an extract from Todorova's work, but the bulk of the chapter is devoted to a consideration of two influential pieces of travel writing about the region – Edith Durham's *High Albania* and Rebecca West's *Black Lamb and Grey Falcon* – and the way in which they present the societies and cultures of Yugoslavia and Albania to their British readership.

Chapter 5, 'Alexander Herzen's Russia: between Asia and Europe' examines Russian identity and its ambiguous, problematic relationship to European identities. Colin Chant briefly sets this relationship in its historical context, before moving on to focus on the life and work of the nineteenth-century Russian political writer Alexander Herzen. Chant sets Herzen's work in the context of debates current in the nineteenth century about Russia's relationship with European societies to its west, while drawing out its relevance to contemporary Russian identities.

Chapter 6 reflects a shift of temporal focus though it is centrally concerned with issues of ambiguous relationships to ideas of Europe on the continent's eastern periphery. In 'Joining Europe: Polish parties and the European Union' Paul G. Lewis analyses the debates between Polish political parties about the country's future membership of European Union that were current at the end of the twentieth century. He links the contours of these debates to continuities in Polish political culture that stretch back to the genesis of Polish nationalism on Europe's eastern periphery during the second half of the nineteenth century. In his essay Lewis discusses the programmes of Poland's contemporary political parties and the work of political scientists (Tomasz Zarycki and Andrej Walicki).

In Chapter 7, '"A new condition?": European identities and the literature of migration' Robert Fraser considers another ambiguous set of identities within Europe; those of postcolonial migrants who have settled in western European nation states after those nation states have been formed. He does this through focusing on the work of the author Mehdi Charef, a leading figure in France's Beur movement, and the Indian-born yet German-resident writer Sujata Bhatt. Fraser's discussion leads him to conclude that the condition of migration is profoundly subversive of any hard-and-fast notions of borders or boundaries between 'cultures'.

This is the second of four books in the series *Europe: Culture and Identities in a Contested Continent*, which form the main texts of an Open University level 3 course of the same name.

Reference

Chimisso, C. (2003) *Exploring European Identities*, Milton Keynes, The Open University.

1

Borders and identities

MARK PITTAWAY

Introduction

On 7 February 1992 the ministers of finance and foreign affairs of the twelve member states of the European Community gathered at Maastricht in the Netherlands to create a 'European Union' into which the existing European Community was to be subsumed. The Maastricht Treaty was to mark 'a new stage in the process of creating an ever closer union among the peoples of Europe' (Council of the European Communities, 1992, p. 7). The negotiations on the treaty had been marked by protracted discussion over the nature of the union and particularly the role to be played by the nation-state within it, resulting in a messy compromise that diluted the intentions of those who sought to create a unified, federal European state. During these negotiations the question of who 'the peoples of Europe' were had been largely ignored. As the EC agreed to transform itself into a quasi-state that represented Europe, whose citizens were to be bound through common European citizenship, it sought to define the borders of 'Europe' as the external borders of the new European Union. A little over two years before the EC's ministers met in Maastricht, however, the cold war division of the continent had ended as socialist dictatorships to the east collapsed in the autumn of 1989. As political leaders in Paris, Bonn and Rome laid the foundations of a European state for western Europeans, new political leaders in Bucharest, Budapest, Prague, Sofia and Warsaw sought to 'rejoin Europe' after the fall of the previous regimes. Some warned as the socialist dictatorships collapsed 'that the one-dimensional definition of Europe peddled by Nato and the EC will shut out the Poles, Russians and Czechs, marginalize those groups which have settled in Europe over the last decades and extinguish their right to history' (Keane, 1989, p. 31). During the first half of the 1990s these predictions appeared to have been borne out as western European economies weathered recession and as the Maastricht Treaty was ratified. From the mid 1990s onwards the European Union changed policy and opened the door to former socialist countries that sought membership. By the end of the twentieth century little tangible progress had been made; no former socialist country had been admitted to the EU. Plans for future expansion were mired in debate over the possible consequences of economic migration, as well as regional assistance policies and agricultural support.

In the decade that followed the collapse of Soviet socialism and the signature of the Maastricht Treaty the borders of western Europe were tightened. In the minds of those who lived in the western part of the continent the eastern half was increasingly constructed as a zone of chaos, poverty, criminality, conflict and outward migration. In an essay on the meaning of the division between eastern and western Europe following the collapse of the dictatorships the writer Dubravka Ugrešič describes her experience of the external border of the European Union, from her perspective as a citizen of an east European state:

> At airports I stand in the queue for passport control. Signs over the booths behind which uniformed officials sit indicate my place. In some places it says *others*, in some there is merely an absence of the blue board with the ring of little yellow stars. My queue is long, it drags on slowly. The EU people in the parallel queue enter quickly. I notice that none of them looks in our direction. There is not a single glance expressing sympathy, curiosity or, if nothing else, contempt. They have no time, the queue is moving too quickly. But we, *others*, have plenty of time to observe them. We are different, our skin is often dark, our eyes dart suspiciously about or stare dully straight ahead, our movements are sluggish and subdued. No one chats or laughs in our queue, we are quiet, there is something surreptitious about us. The tension of our bodies testifies that we have only one thought in our heads: just to get across this frontier.

(Ugrešič, 1998, p. 237)

The experience of borders has long served to forge and shape identity in Europe. In an essay dealing with the construction of a European world view during the dying years of the eighteenth and the early years of the nineteenth centuries, historian Stuart Woolf argues that:

> boundaries have always assumed a symbolic importance for human identity greater than their practical reality. Those of Europe are no exception, as is reflected in the shifting of its geographical confines to demarcate whatever qualities were defined as 'European'.

(Woolf, 1992, p. 90)

The processes of creating boundaries inherent in building a European state during the 1990s, and then extending that state through enlargement in the first decade of the twenty-first century, represent the most recent of many attempts during European history to define the external borders of Europe – thus defining 'Europe' itself. The forces that have shaped these projects to fix the limits of the continent have been the subject of considerable historical investigation. In many accounts the area has been seen as the product of an idea of Europe, of the classical world, medieval Christendom or the Enlightenment, or as a combination of these (Bartlett, 1994; Davies, 1997; Leyser, 1992; Randsborg, 1992; Wilson and Van Der Dussen, 1993; Woolf, 1992). These complex and contested historical processes have left traces in the present that define contemporary perceptions of where the borders of Europe lie, thus shaping European identities.

All of the chapters in this book engage with the issues of where the borders of Europe lie and the consequences of these boundaries for identities within Europe. They approach these issues from different standpoints and explore different contexts. In this chapter I want to introduce some of the themes that run through the rest of the book. By the end of the chapter I shall have introduced you to the following issues:

- the relationship between borders and identities;

- that borders are not natural but the product of historical processes;

- that borders and boundaries can be as much mental constructs as they can be physical realities;

- that Europe's borders are fluid and are determined by interaction between Europeans and the wider world;

- finally, that divisions within Europe between east and west are as deeply ingrained in European identities as those between Europe and the wider world.

In the following six chapters you will be given the opportunity to engage in more depth with the issues that are raised here. I want to start this chapter by considering the question of borders, identities and their histories in terms of their 'symbolic significance', so that you may gain an appreciation of the more general issues involved. I shall then shift focus to bring Europe into the centre of this account and look at the issues that relate to the definition of the border between the European and non-European, before moving on to consider the division between east and west within Europe.

The symbolic significance of borders

In autumn 1989 borders lay at the heart of the events that shook
Europe. The opening that September of Hungary's road border with
Austria to citizens of the German Democratic Republic (East
Germany) wishing to emigrate triggered the momentous events of
the following months. They culminated in the dramatic opening of
the Berlin border of East Germany on 9 November 1989: the fall of
the Berlin wall. As socialist dictatorships across the region between
Germany and the Soviet Union were consigned to 'the dustbin of
history' western Europe was forced to confront east-central Europe
directly. These were societies that for four decades had been
organized along different principles to those that existed in western
Europe. Furthermore, east-central Europe was in an acute economic
crisis, one which would define the experiences of the majority of its
inhabitants for the whole of the following decade. The first reading
here is an account of the crossing of borders in east-central Europe in
December 1989. It was written by the British-born journalist and left-
wing commentator Christopher Hitchens and describes his journey
through Hungary into Romania in the first days following the
toppling of the dictatorship of Nicolae Ceaușescu (1965–89).

On Christmas night, stuck in freezing fog at the Austro-Hungarian
border, I had telephoned my best Budapest friend and spoken
across an insufferable line, fed with near-worthless *forint* coins
cadged from a friendly guard. 'Have you heard?' said Ferenc,
'Ceaușescu has been *assassinated.*' The choice of word seemed odd.
'Murdered' wouldn't do, of course, in the circumstances. 'Killed'
would have been banal. 'Executed' – too correct. And Ferenc
always chooses his terms with meticulous care. No, a baroque
dictator who was already a prisoner, and an ex-tyrant, had
somehow been 'assassinated'. I took the first of many resolutions
not to resort to Transylvanian imagery. Yes, there had been King
Vlad, known as the Impaler, reputed to drink blood as well as spill
it. Every writer and sub-editor in the trade was going to be dusting
him off. Still, I found myself wondering just how Ceaușescu had
been 'assassinated' after his capture. A stake through the heart? I
had read that the chief of Ceaușescu's ghastly Securitate was
named General Julian Vlad, but I was determined to make
absolutely nothing of it.

A sorry-looking shop-front, which was in one of the radial streets
off Calvin Square in Budapest, housed the Alliance of Free
Democrats (SDS), Hungary's main opposition party. It resembled
the headquarters of every 'movement' I'd ever visited. The stickers
and posters in haphazard pattern gave promise of an interior of

clanking duplicators, overworked telephones and bearded young men in pullovers. One of the stickers was fresh and blazing with colours – the national colours in fact. It read: TIMIŞOARA=TEMESVÁR. To any Hungarian, it summoned an immediate, arresting image. On the plains of Transylvania, near the town the world now knows as Timişoara, the Hungarian patriots of 1848 were scattered and cut down by the Czar's Cossack levies, lent as a favour to the Austrian emperor. Near Temesvár, as the Hungarians call it, the national poet Sándor Petőfi lost his life. At nearby Arad, the thirteen generals who had sided with the 1848 revolution were put to death. Now, under its Romanian name, this lost city so well-watered with patriotic Hungarian gore was again an emblem.

Today, the first day of the post-Ceauşescu era, the office was crowded to the doors with people of every class and category, standing around wearing intense expressions. Most wore buttons reading simply: TEMESVÁR. Others displayed the more reflective symbol of two ribbons, one in the Hungarian colours and one in the Romanian, arranged over a black mourning stripe. Nationalists and internationalists, they were all waiting for the Romanian border to be declared open so that they could get to the stricken field of Transylvania and the wounded city of Timişoara. A volunteer convoy was in formation, with taxi drivers, workers, housewives and students offering to donate, or to transport, food and medicine. As so often in the course of the astounding Eastern European revolution of 1989, people seemed to know what to do. And they seemed to know, what's more, without being told. My companion and I, who continually needed and sought advice and instruction, felt this keenly.

The Romanian Embassy in Budapest, scene of numerous protests (some of them cynically encouraged by the nearly defunct Hungarian Communist Party), had offered exactly the wrong kinds of reassurance. 'No problem,' said the greasy officials who had just run up a hand-stitched 'National Salvation' banner on the balcony. Had the border, sealed by Ceauşescu, been reopened by his death? 'No problem.' (I find these the two least relaxing words in the lingua franca.) Visas were said to be obtainable at the border. Or at the embassy, of course, with a wait on the cold pavement. And there would be a fee. In dollars. In cash. For some reason, we couldn't give hard currency to these soft, shifty figures, who were still dealing with the public through an insulting grille.

As the ten cars, one truck and one taxi that together comprised the Hungarian dissident convoy prepared to set off, I got an idea

Secu or Securitate refers to the internal security services of the Socialist Republic of Romania between 1948 and 1990. Both terms are short for Direcţia Generalā a Securitāţii Poporului (General Directorate of Popular Security). This organization acted as the political police for the dictatorships of Gheorghe Gheorgiu-Dej (1948–1965) and his successor Nicolae Ceauşescu (1965–1989). It played a central role in the violent defence of the regime during the revolution of December 1989, which resulted in its disbandment.

of how excited and intimidated they were by the whole idea of Transylvania. We got a short and cautionary talk from Tibor Vidos, an SDS organizer, who specialized in taking the romance out of things. 'There's to be no driving at night once we cross the border ... We pick up the blood supplies before we meet at the checkpoint ... No car is to pick up hitch-hikers, however innocent-looking they are. *Secu* men have been taking lifts and getting out while leaving plastic bombs behind ...' Carrying blood to Transylvania? No, too glib an image and indecent in the context. Dismissing Dracula once more, I went for a swift meal with Miklós Haraszti, author of *The Velvet Prison,* a book which relates the trials of writers and intellectuals in the 'goulash archipelago'. He had been to Timişoara/Temesvár years before, to see the now-famous Father László Tőkés, and had been detained and tortured by the *Secu.* Haraszti comes from Leninist stock; his Jewish watchmaker parents left Hungary for Palestine in order to escape fascism, but quit Palestine in 1948 – the year of the proclamation of Israel – in order to come back to a people's republic. His own disillusionment had taken him through Maoism before fetching him up with the majority of Budapest's 'urbanist' intellectuals into the ranks of the liberal SDS.

Haraszti told us of something that had just happened to the convoy in front of ours. 'One of the volunteers was pulled from his car, not by the *Secu* but by the Romanian crowd. They said he looked like an Arab, and that Arab terrorists had been helping Ceauşescu's gangs.' This was an instance of the *grande peur* that infected Romania in those days, and that was to poison the inaugural moments of the revolution. Not a single Arab corpse was found, nor a single prisoner taken. Yet the presence of Libyans, Syrians, Palestinians in the degraded ranks of the *Secu* was something that 'everybody knew'. The cream of the jest, as Haraszti went on to say, was that the 'Arab-looking' volunteer seemed exotic in appearance because he was a Budapest Jew. 'One of the few New Leftists we still have. He probably does sympathize with the PLO.' Nobody knew what had become of this hapless comrade, because the convoy had been too scared to stop. As we concluded our meal, the waiter brought us the last of several predictions about the time at which Hungarian TV would transmit video pictures of the Ceauşescus' execution. At that stage, excited rumour was calling for an actual sequence of the bullets hitting the couple. Neither he nor his customers could wait for the event. I vaguely recalled seeing television pictures of the dead General Kessem after a coup in Iraq in the colonial fifties, but couldn't otherwise think of a precedent for a prime-time 'assassination' of a fallen leader. 'The genius of the Carpathians', as Ceaușescu characterized himself, hogged the stage until the very last.

I describe this hesitation on the border of Transylvania because it shows, even in small details, the way that Hungarians felt Romania to be *in partibus infidelium*. Romania is much larger than Hungary, by virtue of having absorbed so much of it, and Ceaușescu was the perfect ogre neighbour from the point of view of the regime. Not only did he run a terrifying, hermetic police state, the weight of which was felt disproportionately by the Hungarian-speaking minority, but he flaunted a mad, grandiose, population-growth policy which overtopped the megalomania of a Mussolini. And, as he raved from his balcony, it seemed to ordinary Hungarians that the Bucharest crowd supported him, at least passively and at least in his 'Greater Romania' fantasy. I asked Haraszti if this had made him feel nationalist in turn. 'The fact that the Romanian revolution was started by Hungarians,' he said firmly, 'is a miracle.' Almost at a blow, the mutual xenophobia had been dispelled. Neither regime could ever again easily mobilize or distract its people by fear of the other. This is no small issue for Hungarian democrats, who remember that their country took the Axis side in the stupid, vainglorious hope of 'redeeming' lost Magyar territory, and instead lost most of its Jews and decades of its history as well as its national honour.

As the convoy got on the move, and as people were allocating and being allocated their tasks and their cars, I was brought the news that Queen Elizabeth II had rescinded her award of the Order of the Bath to Nicolae Ceaușescu. There were polite Hungarians who felt that I might wish to know this, and who added that the decision was taken not a minute too soon. Bloody hell, I think, it's like Chesterton's definition of journalism – telling the public that Lord X is dead when the public didn't know that Lord X had ever been alive. I'm sure most people didn't know that Ceaușescu was sporting a Windsor honour. And, by the way, for what was the Order bestowed? The brute got 'most favoured nation' status from the United States, the Order of Lenin from Moscow, the moist thanks of international bankers for exporting all his people's food, pay-offs from Israel and the Arab League and solidarity from Beijing. He was the perfect postmodern despot – a market Stalinist.

Departure was announced for two in the morning, so that all night-time driving could be done on Hungarian territory, and everyone was ready to move out on time, and did move out, without being told. Our car was the property of a man who normally drove a beer-truck, and looked like it, and drove like it (the image of the SDS as an intellectual and élitist party is misleading). The freezing fog had thickened. At first light, after frequent stops and regroupings, and a detour for the blood pick-up at the border town of Gyula, all the cars met again at the border-point. Here people started to get nervous. It would have been a good thing to have had a leader or a commander. We knew that the previous convoy had been shot up and had lost one of its Bohemian-looking members to the liberated populace.

The Romanian border guards were in the very act of revisionism when we turned up. A large blank space on the wall spoke eloquently of yesterday's *Conducator*, as Ceauşescu got himself called, and various party and state emblems were being hurriedly junked. Still, the place wore the dismal, dingy aspect of a little machine for the imposition of petty authority. Everything from the lavatories to the waiting-room was designed for insult, delay and humiliation and there was no one-day, quick-change cosmetic to disguise the fact. The unctuous, ingratiating faces of the guards who were 'making nice' for the first time in their lives, only reinforced the impression they were trying to dispel. Eager to please, they overdid their hatred of the *Secu* to whom they had deferred the day before. They even suggested that we not proceed. 'They are firing from cars. There is no law, no authority.' Without orders, they had no idea what to do. When I said, quite absurdly and untruthfully, that I was given 'clear instructions' from the capital that visas were free of charge today, they gladly waived the fee. There was a pathetic relief in the gesture of acquiescence.

Quitting the stranded, irrelevant guardhouse, and holding perhaps the last stamps that read 'Socialist Republic of Romania', we fell back a few decades. The Hungarian town of Gyula had amenities, as Americans say. Shops and telephones, restaurants, street lamps. Across the border there were herds of pigs and geese, horse-drawn wagons and wayside hovels. The first cars to be seen were waiting in an abject queue, not because of the upheaval but because today was the day when the exiguous petrol ration was issued. The people at the side of the road looked like caricatures of Eastern European misery, in their shapeless bundles of coats and scarves. But there was a palpable lift in the atmosphere even so, because every person raised a hand in a V-salute at the sight of the Hungarian flag (or was it our reassuring Red Cross?). These villages had been the target for 'systematization', perhaps the nastiest political neologism since 'normalization' in Czechoslovakia, and were saved from bulldozers and unheated tower-blocks where the water-pressure sometimes got as far as the first floor, and where the official cultural activity was praise for the *Conducator* and the denunciation of fellow sufferers.

At the city of Arad, our first major stop, we found what we were to find everywhere, which was that the centre of activity had shifted to the gates of the hospital. The *Conducator*'s cops had been vicious and thorough in their last stand, whether from panic or from sheer professional pride it is hard to say.

In the street an army lorry screamed to a halt and I heard the sound of boots hitting tarmac. This forbidding noise heralded a squad of uncertain young soldiers, steel casques reassuringly askew, who held up traffic with large gestures before entering the crowd and fraternizing. In the Romanian attitude to the army there was something of the Stockholm syndrome. The soldiery had changed sides at the last minute, and some of the brass (including the excellent-sounding General Militarescu) had been in touch with Party dissidents when it was dangerous to do so. Thus there was a popular willingness to smile, to repress unease, to cry, 'Army and People.' It became an article of faith that the soldiers who had fired on crowds on Christmas Eve were not really soldiers at all, but *Secu* devils in disguise. To have armed men on your side at long last, for whatever reason, seemed worth the sacrifice of pride. So the classic photograph became that of old women handing scarce food and drink to tank crews. Which indeed happened, showing in the oddest way that Brecht was right when he said that every tank had a mechanical weakness – its driver.

The beer-truck chauffeur, who seemed a stranger to exhaustion, had had the idea of stuffing his back seat with bales of Hungarian newspapers, including the daily organ of the Communist Party he despised. To stand in the streets of Arad and hand out free copies of yesterday's Budapest editions, was to court instant popularity. Every hand reached for a copy, probably because a good deal of Hungarian is spoken in these parts and probably because there hadn't been any newspapers for days, but also and undoubtedly because the front page bore the death-masks of Ceauşescu and his wife Elena. Watching people rivet themselves to this photo-exclusive, I again fought down the impulse to Transylvanian cliché. They had to see the dead monster, had to know he was dead. The Ceauşescus' 'trial' had been a shabby, panicky business with unpleasantly Freudian overtones (Elena: 'I was a mother to you all.' BANG!), conducted by a tribunal which feebly refused to show its members' faces; but their execution had a galvanic effect on the morale of Transylvania and a correspondingly lowering effect on the fighting spirit of the *Secu*.

All had been festivity on the way to Arad, and as we left we met bystanders who were happy and eager to point the way to Timișoara. Wayside saluting and waving seemed inexhaustible. It was like being in Orwell's Barcelona, or in Portugal in 1974, or even like being on the skirts of a liberating army. But everything changed as we approached Timișoara. There were fewer people on the roads, and they seemed less keen and animated. As we found the outlying bits of the town, we noticed that our salutes were not returned. All the window-glass in the city seemed to have gone. Except for some flags with the now famous hole cut in the centre (a borrowing from Budapest in 1956), there were no signs of anything except shell-shocked, sullen wretchedness. I felt almost cheated. Here was the town of the resistance, of the revolutionary epicentre; the town that had lived up to 1848 – and won this time. Where were the garlands, the proud slogans, the maidens in national dress, the gnarled old men with fierce tears in their eyes?

How could I have been so romantic and vulgar? Timișoara was the scene not of a triumph but of an atrocity – a sort of distillate of twentieth-century horrors. The inhabitants had been strafed from the air like the people of Guernica. They had been shot down in heaps like the victims of Babi Yar, and buried like refuse in mass graves in the forest on the pattern of Katyn. Many had been raped and mutilated like the villagers of My Lai. Before he left on a state visit to, of all places, Iran, Ceaușescu had given explicit orders that the city be punished. This was his Lidice; his Ouradour. At least the people who had been through such a digest and synopsis of horror could tell themselves that they were the last carnage of the last European dictator. But this obviously was not much of a consolation on the day after.

Again, it was at the hospital that everybody gathered. Timișoara is a superficially uninteresting town with a dull, routine Stalinist design. The box-like buildings even have generic names stencilled on the outside: 'Hotel', 'Restaurant', 'Cultural Centre'. It was a surprise to learn that the fateful, desperate demonstration in support of Father Tőkes had taken place in Opera Square, because Timișoara doesn't look as if it rates an Opera House. Opera Square, on the other hand, doesn't disappoint your imagination of what a Transylvanian provincial city might boast after twenty-five years of philistine despotism. What a terrible place to die, I thought grotesquely, especially if you feared you might be doing it for nothing. On the other hand, a perfect place for concluding that you had little or nothing to lose.

(Hitchens, 1990, pp. 130–7)

EXERCISE _____

I should like you to reflect on what this reading tells you about how borders are experienced. I suggest that you make notes considering the following questions.

1   Hitchens describes two borders, first that between Austria and Hungary and then that between Hungary and Romania. From his description, do you think the experience he records of the two borders is different? In what ways is it different, or the same? How far can you discern that Hitchens's experience of both borders is shaped by his identity as a western commentator?

2   I want you to think carefully about how Transylvania, the region of Romania to which Hitchens says he is travelling, is represented in the extract. You should focus your note taking around the differences between Hitchens's own representations of Transylvania and those of the Hungarian political activists with whom he travels from Budapest. What do you attribute these differences to?

DISCUSSION _____

1   Hitchens discusses his experience of crossing the border between Austria and Hungary less than he describes the experience of crossing that between Hungary and Romania. I felt when reading Hitchens's account that in both cases he was describing culture shock. In the very opening sentence of the reading Hitchens describes speaking to a friend by telephone on 'an insufferable line': a description of a westerner meeting the reality of Hungary's telephone system in 1989. This was characterized by outdated telephone exchanges, malfunctioning phone booths, low coverage relative to western Europe and frequent unreliability. As a former resident of Hungary I bristled a little at Hitchens's description of the forint as a 'near-worthless' currency, a choice of adjective which for me demonstrates his westernness. After all, I know that ordinary Hungarians worked and continue to work very hard for their forints.

As far as the Hungarian–Romanian border is concerned I want to draw your attention to the following sentences:

> The Hungarian town of Gyula had amenities, as Americans say. Shops and telephones, restaurants, street lamps. Across the border there were herds of pigs and geese, horse-drawn wagons and wayside hovels ... The people at the side of the road looked like caricatures of Eastern European misery, in their shapeless bundles of coats and scarves.

Hitchens's description of crossing into post-revolutionary Romania is written almost entirely through a western lens. Indeed he recognizes Romania's newly liberated citizens as 'caricatures of Eastern European misery'. Though differences between Hungary and Romania are discernible from his account, on my first reading of the piece I thought that both countries were very definitely treated as part of an east that was defined according to western norms. More specifically those western norms, ironically for an avowedly left-wing commentator, were those of capitalist consumerism.

2 You will have noted that despite Hitchens's 'resolutions not to resort to Transylvanian imagery' he does this frequently in the piece. Transylvania is widely known in the English-speaking world not as a region of western Romania, but for its place in the fiction of Bram Stoker and gothic horror. These perceptions are strongly suggestive of the eastern, exotic flavour of Transylvania and powerfully shape the image of the territory in the English-speaking world. Furthermore, they have nothing to do with the reality of Transylvania. Moving beyond the associations of Transylvania and Dracula, Transylvania is represented as a land of desperate poverty and a site of little more than communist dictatorship. Take, for example, Hitchens's description of his destination:

> Timișoara is a superficially uninteresting town with a dull, routine Stalinist design ... It was a surprise to learn that the fateful, desperate demonstration in support of Father Tőkes had taken place in Opera Square, because Timișoara doesn't look as if it rates an Opera House.

For the Hungarians in this account both the border and Transylvania itself carry different cultural meanings. The Hungarians Hitchens travelled with were activists in the **SzDSz** (misspelled in the extract as SDS), the most anti-nationalist and socially liberal of Hungary's parliamentary parties during the 1990s. It is notable that even for a group of anti-nationalist political activists attachment to Transylvania and pride in the actions of its Magyar minority during the revolution reflect their Hungarian national identity. For them both the border and their destination have a radically different meaning.

The SzDSz (Szabad Demokráták Szövetsége), or the Alliance of Free Democrats, was the second largest party in Hungary between 1990 and 1998. Formed by former dissidents, it was the junior partner in Hungary's governing coalition between 1994 and 1998 and again following the 2002 parliamentary elections. My point may seem pedantic, but Hitchens does misspell SzDSz. In Hungarian 's' and 'sz' are separate letters in the alphabet: 's' is pronounced like the English 'sh', while 'sz' is pronounced like the English 's'.

This brings me back to the point made above in the introduction, with the sentence I quoted from Stuart Woolf: 'boundaries have always assumed a symbolic importance for human identity greater than their practical reality' (Woolf, 1992, p. 90). I hope that by reading the extract and thinking about it you have gained some insight into how the 'symbolic importance' of boundaries is shaped by identities; after all Hitchens invests meaning in the borders he crosses by interpreting difference in the light of his western identity. For the Hungarian political activists with whom Hitchens travels the symbolic significance of Romania's revolution is the challenge the events posed to the Hungarian–Romanian borders and the symbolic significance of those boundaries for Hungarians.

EXERCISE

I want you now to think about your own reactions to the piece and particularly your own ideas of what the borders between western and eastern Europe mean. Try and write down in a few sentences what you think they signify. If you have visited this region you can base your observations on your direct experience of crossing these borders. Even if you have no direct experience of doing this, I want you to think about your own perceptions – whether these have come from novels, newspapers, films, television, the accounts of others you may know, or all or none of these things. Where do your perceptions come from? To what extent is your perception of a boundary a projection of your own personal identity? There are, I should stress, no right or wrong ways of completing this task.

DISCUSSION

I don't know what you wrote in response to this reflexive task. You might choose to review what you wrote in the light of what I am going to say about my perceptions of the border between eastern and western Europe. I hope that this will give you some appreciation of how your identity and experience inform your own standpoint and thus the symbolic significance you invest in boundaries. My own relationship to the border between eastern and western Europe is unusual. I write as a historian of Hungary, born and brought up in England with no family connections to Hungary at all. I first became aware of the divide between east and west as a teenager during the second cold war in the 1980s, a period of renewed superpower rivalry that followed the Soviet invasion of Afghanistan in 1979 and was associated with the hawkish policies of the United States under the administration of Ronald Reagan (1981–9). I saw eastern Europe as a part of my own continent that was unimaginably different; plagued by dictatorship, food shortages and badly made cars. Yet even at that time I was fascinated by it; for me it was deeply 'exotic', a region of writers and informers, dictators and protestors.

Solidarity or Solidarnošč was founded in September 1980 as a co-ordinating body of independent trade unionism in Poland; it became the first independent trade union confederation in socialist Eastern and Central Europe. Its first president Lech Wąesa, an electrician from the Lenin Shipyards in Gdansk, would later serve as President of Poland (1990–5). During 1981 it acted as a focus both of industrial unrest and of broader political opposition to the regime. The political crisis in the country during the year resulted in the imposition of martial law in December and the suppression of the organization. Solidarity continued to function as an underground organization for the rest of the decade until strikes in 1988 resulted in its legalization.

The Prague Spring refers to the attempts to reform and liberalize the institutions of socialist dictatorship in Czechoslovakia that were initiated by the publication of the Action Programme of the Czechoslovak Communist Party (KSČ) in April 1968. Associated with the party's secretary-general between 1968 and 1969 Alexander Dubček they aimed to create 'socialism with a human

I have crossed both the borders described by Hitchens in the reading several times. I first crossed the land border between Austria and Hungary in August 1989. I spent that summer as a student on a German-language summer course in Vienna; even in the comfort of the Austrian capital I could feel the rumblings further east. Every evening at 7:30 television news gave us a running total of the number of east Germans who had illegally crossed the border from Hungary the previous night. The week before I travelled Poland's communists had surrendered power to a transitional administration dominated by **Solidarity**. The Czechoslovak authorities were nervous, according to newspapers, about the twenty-first anniversary of the Soviet suppression of the **Prague Spring**. I bought my purple visa bearing the words 'The People's Republic of Hungary' from the Hungarian tourist office on Kärtner Straße. I packed my bags with chocolate and coffee bought in Viennese supermarkets for Hungarian friends (until the mid 1990s the quality of coffee and chocolate available inside Hungary was markedly inferior to that in western Europe) and set off for my train. My passport and visa were stamped by a border guard whose colleague trained his machine gun on the occupants of my carriage. Even looking through the window I experienced culture shock; Hungary looked so different and exotic. Like Hitchens, I looked at what I saw through my western European lenses.

As a result of living in Budapest for almost four years, having learned Hungarian and become used to the culture, today I invest a very different symbolic significance in that border. It was really unusual for me to cross the border from Austria after a day in Vienna in spring 1994 and feel that I was coming home, even though I am not Hungarian and have no Hungarian relatives. As a result of becoming a resident of post-socialist Budapest, changing one aspect of my identity, my relationship to the border changed completely. Yet when I first crossed the Hungarian–Romanian border to visit Transylvania for the first time in 1996 I still experienced culture shock. All my friends in Budapest had told me I should go to Transylvania, because only then would I understand Hungary. One friend, a geographer in a Budapest research institute, arranged for me to go on a trip with teachers of geography. We set off in our coach from Gyula – the place where Hitchens crossed the border in 1989 – a smart, turn-of-the-century spa town in southeast Hungary. We sat at the road border for about an hour and half. From the familiarity of Hungary I was catapulted into a landscape of industrial decay and environmental despoliation. Between the border and Oradea I finally saw 'communism' as it had been represented on British television – and I had been to the German Democratic Republic, Czechoslovakia, Hungary and the Soviet Union before communism's fall. This was Romania, seven years after the revolution. It seemed to me that the

face in the country'. Opposition from both the Soviet Union and hardliners within the party leadership proved fatal for the Prague Spring which resulted in a Soviet invasion of the country on the night of 20–21 August 1968. Dubček was removed as secretary-general of the party by Gustáv Husák (1969–1987), who reversed the policies of the Prague Spring.

The Paris peace settlement refers to the peace treaties signed in Paris and neighbouring towns that ended the First World War. These consisted of the Treaty of Versailles signed with Germany in 1919, the Treaty of Saint Germain signed with Austria in 1919, the Treaty of Trianon signed with Hungary in 1920, the Treaty of Neuilly signed with Bulgaria in 1919 and the Treaty of Sèvres signed with Turkey in 1920.

Burgenland is one of Austria's nine federal provinces (*Bundesländer*). Both Austria's First Republic (1919–38) and Second Republic (1945–) were formally federal republics, with considerable authority vested in provincial governments.

borders of western Europe had moved from Sopron (Hungary's westernmost major town) to Gyula in seven years.

These autobiographical reflections are profoundly subjective; an account of my personal standpoint. They are reflective of my identity and, above all, of the fact that my identity is constituted by my experience. The fact that Hungary became more familiar and less exotic had more to do with my greater experience of it than the fact that Budapest has become more obviously 'western' since the first time I crossed that land border in 1989. I speak the language; I feel at home there; at least half of my closest friends live within an hour of Budapest. My standpoint changed.

The symbolic significance invested in a boundary depends on standpoint. Mine shifted from being a British teenager fascinated by the exotic eastern other when I became an academic specialist or, more important, as a result of becoming both a resident and participant in the society that I studied. There is much more to standpoint, however, than the merely personal. The symbolic significance invested in a border or boundary depends on and is shaped by the identity of the people who experience that border. Furthermore, that symbolic significance can depend on national, cultural or ethnic identity. It is also historically variable.

I shall take a little time to develop these two points by concentrating on the two borders crossed by Hitchens in the extract. The first – that between Austria and Hungary – is perhaps most easily identified outside the two countries as the boundary between capitalist western and socialist eastern Europe prior to 1989 (the so-called Iron Curtain). The notion of that border as one between two distinct halves of Europe has persisted since 1989, and with the European Union's expansion to include Austria in 1995 it once again acquired concrete form, as the eastern border of the EU. Historically the border between Austria and Hungary has emerged relatively recently as a consequence of the break-up of the Habsburg monarchy and the creation of Austria and Hungary as two sovereign nation-states in 1918. Even though Austria and Hungary were defined territories within the monarchy and from 1867 onwards were treated as separate political entities, the current borders between the two are not the same as those that existed prior to 1918. As a result of the **Paris peace settlement** that drew the borders of the states formed out of the monarchy, Hungary was forced to give those of its northwestern territories largely populated by German-speakers to Austria. These lands formed the Austrian province of **Burgenland** In recognition of Burgenland's 'borderland' nature and historical connections to

Hungary, the state's new political rulers sought to integrate the territory into Austria by forging a distinctive regional identity. Many residents in western Hungarian towns along the border, like Sopron, continued to have close links to the territories that found themselves under Austrian rule (Haslinger, 2001; Romsics, 1999, p. 147).

With the disappearance of the first Austria in 1938 as a result of its incorporation into Nazi Germany, the border became that between Hungary and Germany until 1945. With the creation of a socialist dictatorship in Hungary in 1948 the symbolic significance of the border for those living on either side of it changed again. The border was closed to ordinary Hungarians, barbed wire and watchtowers were erected, and the state restricted travel within Hungary to towns in the western border region – an arrangement that remained in place until the 1970s. Consequently those living in the border regions with relatives in Austria were unable to visit them. The western border was the site of the escape of around 200,000 Hungarians in the aftermath of the 1956 revolution. Its opening to Hungarians in January 1988, with the lifting by the Hungarian government of the restrictions on its citizens leaving the country, was an early sign of the changes that were to sweep the region less than two years later. The boundary between Austria and Hungary was also the site of the first mass breach of the Iron Curtain when several hundred East Germans, taking advantage of a demonstration by members of the Hungarian opposition, forced their way through a border across which they could not legally travel (Litván et al., 1996; Gerő and Pető, 1997; see also Pan-European Picnic website).

The symbolic significances of the border between Hungary and Romania and the identities associated with them shifted as much since the nineteenth century as those relating to the boundary between Austria and Hungary. The current border between Hungary and Romania was established for the first time by the Treaty of Trianon in 1919 with the transfer of all of Transylvania and the Banat from Hungary to Romania. For Hungarians 'lost' Transylvania has played a central role in the creation and development of Hungarian national identity; consequently many Hungarians have failed and continue to refuse to accept the permanence of the current border (Kürti, 2001). For Romanians, however, in view of the ethnic Romanian majority in the territory, Transylvania was seen as an integral part of their nation even prior to its formal incorporation into the Romanian state after the collapse of the Habsburg monarchy (Hitchins, 1974; Livezeanu, 1995; Mitu, 2001).

Two national identities have been projected on to the Hungarian–Romanian border, investing it with a symbolic significance that has had explosive political consequences. The Hungarian desire

The photographs on this and the following pages are a record of a visit by western European students to Transylvania in 1998 organized by the Forum of European Students (AEGEE). This visual record is the work of Ralph Böhlke, a German co-ordinator in the organization's network for east–west relations. The aims of the trip, according to Ralph, were 'research for the future' and 'a discovery trip in a region relatively unknown in the western world'. The photographs concentrate on people. As well as documenting the trip they form 'an attempt to visualize the different ethnic influences in the region'. They depict a number of scenes in the Sibiu and Braşov counties of southern Transylvania. The images are revealing of the experiences of the students on the trip in crossing borders and encountering cultural difference. Photos: Ralph Böhlke.

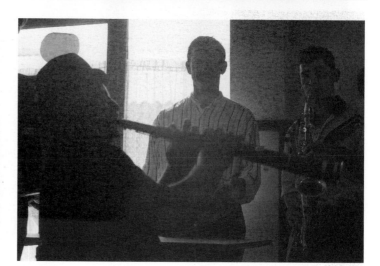

to 'reclaim' Transylvania played a central role in the revisionist politics that drove the country into the arms of Nazi Germany during the interwar years. Transylvania was then partitioned in 1940 as the result of an agreement brokered by Hitler; northern Transylvania was awarded to Hungary while the south of the region remained part of Romania. Forced exchanges of population resulted, while Hungarians and Romanians who found themselves on the wrong side of the partition faced routine persecution until Transylvania was returned wholly to Romania by the invading Red Army in 1944. Ethnic tension between Hungarians and Romanians inside Transylvania as well as between Romania and Hungary was skilfully exploited by Nicolae Ceauşescu as part of his bid to use nationalism to legitimate his dictatorship between 1965 and 1989 (Deletant, 1995; Gabanyi, 2000; Verdery, 1991). Since 1989 Transylvania has played a central role in the vocabulary of nationalist politicians in both countries and in the policies of nationalist governments. In 2001, for example, Hungary's right-wing prime minister Viktor Orbán (1998–2002) introduced a 'status law' to bind Magyar minorities living outside Hungary's borders to the Hungarian state, thus fuelling suspicion among Romanians about Hungary's intentions. Orbán's policies echoed those of the earlier right-wing governments of József Antall (1990–3) and Péter Boross (1993–4) and are thus indicative of the symbolic importance of Transylvania to supporters of the country's right-wing parties.

At this stage I want to pause for breath and recap a little before moving on. I have used the examples of two borders with which I am well acquainted to make the following points:

- The symbolic importance of borders is often more important than their physical reality.

- The symbolic importance invested in the border depends on the identity of the person or group that experiences the reality of the border.

- The symbolic importance of a border is neither natural, nor given for all time, but is shaped by history.

It is, however, not just the symbolic importance of a border that is shaped by history, but the physical reality of the border itself. Most obviously, you should be aware of the changing borders of nations or, prior to the advent of modern nationalism, to the boundaries of the various territorial states in Europe – over the course of several centuries. I want, however, to make a point that is much less self-evident: our contemporary notion of a border as marking the boundary of a discrete territory controlled by a state is also a product of history. In the European past other kinds of borders and boundaries have existed. These have shaped other kinds of identities. The second reading below should give you an appreciation of this issue. It is an extract from the introduction of Peter Sahlins's book *Boundaries: the Making of France and Spain in the Pyrenees* (1989). This is a historical monograph which deals with the development of French and Spanish national identities over two centuries in the Cerdanya – a borderland region in the Pyrenees. Sahlins argues that the formation of national identities along the border between France and Spain was fundamental to the formation of French and Spanish identities. Sahlins heads the preface of his book with a quotation from historian Pierre Vilar: 'The history of the world is best observed from the frontier.' I am not directly concerned with the validity of Sahlins's argument with reference to French and Spanish national identities; what I am more interested in is his historical account of the development of modern borders, or boundaries.

Boundaries and territory

The Pyrenean frontier of France and Spain is one of the oldest and most stable political boundaries in western Europe: it has not shifted location since France annexed the province of Roussillon and part of the Cerdanya valley in 1659–1660. Twentieth-century theorists consider the French–Spanish boundary a 'fossilized,' 'cold,' or 'dead' boundary, since it has rarely presented cause for major international contention.[1] Today, the official boundary of France and Spain has none of the political significance of the many contested borders throughout the Third World, or even the United States–Mexican boundary, to mention only the most newsworthy. Yet the reports of its 'death,' in the sense of the French–Spanish boundary's permanent lack of controversy, have been slightly exaggerated. The rights of fishermen near Hendaye, the protests of Roussillon wine-growers opposed to the entry of Spanish wines, and disputes over territorial competence in the repression of Basque terrorism are among the issues that continue to occupy the press and the foreign offices of Spain and France. For some, Spain's 1986 entry into the European Common Market may have revived echos of Louis XIV's claim that 'the Pyrenees are no more'; for others, 1993 means a Europe without boundaries; but the reality of the Spanish–French boundary in the Cerdanya suggests otherwise.

[1] For example, J. Brunhes and C.Vallaux, *La géographie de l' histoire* (Paris, 1921), 353; M. Foucher, *L'invention des frontières* (Paris, 1987), 128; for a typology of classes of tension in border areas, see R. Gross, 'Registering and Ranking of Tension Areas,' in *Confini e Regioni: Il potenziale di sviluppo e di pace delle periferie*) (Trieste, 1973), 317–28.

Still, border disputes in the Pyrenees are not the catalysts of military conflagrations or diplomatic entreaties as they are at other boundaries; and it is this relative 'fossilization' of the boundary that requires explanation. That the Spanish–French boundary in this century has become less of a source of political tension than others in Western Europe, such as the Rhine, is due in large part to shifts of European geopolitical concerns. But the explanation also lies in the dual appearance of an undisputed boundary line and an accepted opposition of nationalities in the borderland. This book is concerned with the historical development of these two structural components of the nation-state – a national community within a delimited state territory – as they took shape in one section of the French–Spanish borderland between 1659 and 1868.

The dates are derived from the history of the political boundary itself. By the Treaty of the Pyrenees in 1659 and its addenda the following year, the French crown acquired the province of Roussillon and a portion of the Cerdanya valley. Political geographers call this the 'allocation' of the boundary, the first step in a three-stage process of 'allocation, delimitation, and demarcation.'[2] The delimitation and demarcation of the Pyrenean border occurred more than two centuries later, when between 1854 and 1868 the Spanish and French governments agreed in the Treaties of Bayonne to mark an imaginary border line by posing officially sanctioned border stones. The French–Spanish boundary between 1659 and 1868 may have been stable, in the sense that no territories were exchanged between the two states. Yet in 1659 it was a boundary defined by the jurisdictional limits of specific villages. Much would happen before it became a delimited boundary defining national territorial sovereignty ...

Political geographers, following conventional usage, generally distinguish 'boundaries' and 'frontiers.' The first evokes a precise, linear division, within a restrictive, political context; the second connotes more zonal qualities, and a broader, social context. Though the linear/zonal distinction draws its connotations in English from the American experience of the western frontier, similar distinctions are made in most modern European languages,

---

[2] These distinctions are shared by such disparate approaches as P. de Lapradelle, *La frontière: Etude de Droit International* (Paris, 1928); and S. B. Jones, *Boundary-Making: A Handbook for Statesmen, Treaty Editors, and Boundary Commissioners* (Washington, 1945).

where they too are colored by particular historical experiences.[3] The fact of this dualism has often misled theorists into perceiving an evolutionary movement, necessary and irreversible, from a sparsely settled, ill-defined zone toward an uncontested, nonsubstantial, mathematically precise line of demarcation. Such was the model that nineteenth- and early twentieth-century theorists of the frontier adopted, including the father of modern political geography, Friedrich Ratzel.[4] Applied to the historical experience of state formation in Europe, and in particular to the paradigmatic example of France, the model fails to explain much of anything. As a schema, it ignores two critical dimensions of political boundaries: first, that the zonal character of the frontier persists after the delimitation of a boundary line; and second, that the linear boundary is an ancient notion. As a historical description, the model falls dramatically short of the evidence.

On one hand, the persistence of a zone after the delimitation of the boundary has long been noted by jurists and students of international law. The zonal character of the frontier is a political construction of each state independently and of two contiguous states together. The zone consists in the distinct jurisdictions that each state establishes near the boundary for the purposes of its internal administration – thus a military zone, a customs zone, and so forth. And the zone represents the area where contiguous states realize policies of international cooperation and friendship, or *bon voisinage*. Although forms of international cooperation often precede the delimitation – as was the case in the Pyrenean frontier – they are codified and given stature in international law as part of the delimitation proceedings.[5]

---

[3] On the French distinction of *frontière* and *limite*, see L. Febvre, '*Frontière*: The Word and the Concept,' in P. Burke, ed., *A New Kind of History: From the Writings of (Lucien) Febvre*, trans. K. Folca (London, 1973), 208–218; and D. Nordman, 'Des limites d'Etat aux frontières nationales,' in P. Nora, ed., *Les lieux de mémoire*, 2 vols. (Paris, 1986), 2 (pt. 2): 50–59; and his 'Frontiera e confini in Francia: Evoluzione dei termini e dei concetti,' in C. Ossola, C. Raffestin, and M. Ricciardi, eds., *La frontiera da stato a nazione: Il caso Piemonte* (Rome, 1987), 39–55. On the Spanish distinction of *frontera* (or *marca*) and *limite*, see A. Truyol y Serra, 'Las fronteras y las marcas,' *Revista española de derecho internacional* 10 (1957): 107; and J. M. Cordero Torres, *Fronteras hispanicas: Geografíca e historia* (Madrid, 1960).

[4] Febvre, '*Frontière*,' 212, citing F. Ratzel, *Politische geographie* (Paris and Munich, 1903); C. Vallaux, *Le sol et l'état* (Paris, 1910), chap. 10; and J. Brunhes and C. Vallaux, *La géographie de l'histoire* (Paris, 1921), 344 et seq.

[5] Lapradelle, *La frontière*, pt. 2; I. Pop, *Voisinage et bon voisinage en droit international* (Paris, 1968).

On the other hand, the concept and practice of a linear boundary is an ancient – perhaps the most ancient – part of the frontier, one that long preceded modern delimitation treaties of the eighteenth and nineteenth centuries. Techniques of delimitation were known to the Greeks and Romans, and the Treaty of Verdun in 843 involved 120 'emissaries' who worked more than a year to determine the boundaries of the parcels distributed to the three heirs of Charlemagne.[6] Historians once argued that the medieval polity in France had no conception of precise territorial boundaries. The division of Verdun remained without significance, it was claimed, not only because of the complete absence of topographical maps, but also because the extensive fragmentation of authority and the growth of feudal jurisdictions soon became the rule in western Europe.[7] More recently, medieval historians have recognized that the extension of feudal relations from the tenth to the thirteenth centuries did not mean the disappearance of questions over boundaries. The territorial extent of a *seigneurie* could be largely ignored, but it could also be precisely delimited, especially in areas where the seigneurie took shape within the limits of the ancient gallo-roman divisions, or *pagi*. Moreover, the kingdom's boundaries were in general well-defined, marked by stones, rivers, trees, and sometimes man-made trenches, even if these borders were often disputed.[8]

Yet in the eleventh and twelfth centuries, the political boundaries between kingdoms were fundamentally similar in kind to feudal limits within the kingdom. Only in the later thirteenth century did the two become different. The word 'frontier' dates precisely from the moment when a new insistence on royal territory gave to the boundary a political, fiscal, and military significance different from its internal limits. The 'frontier' was that which 'stood face to' an

[6] On the 'primitive' and 'sacred' character of linear boundaries, see Lapradelle, *La frontière*, 18–19; and A. Van Gennep, *The Rites of Passage*, trans. M. B. Vizedom and G. L. Caffee (Chicago, 1960), 15–25. On Roman and Greek conceptions of the linear boundary, see M. Foucher, *L'invention des frontières* (Paris, 1987), 63–96; and Lapradelle, *La frontière*, 20–25. On the Treaty of Verdun, see R. Dion, *Les frontières de la France* (Paris, 1947), 71–85.

[7] For example, R. Doucet, *Les institutions de la France au XVIe siècle*, 2 vols. (Paris, 1948), 1: 16; Lapradelle, *La frontière*, 29–31; and G. Dupont-Ferrier, 'L'incertitude des limites territoriales en France du XIIIe au XVI siècle', in *Académie des Inscriptions et Belles Lettres: Comptes Rendus* (Paris, 1942), 62–77.

[8] J. F. Lemarignier, *Recherches sur l'hommage en marche et les frontières féodales* (Lille, 1945); P. Bonenfant, 'A propos des limites médiévales,' in *Hommage à Lucien Febvre: Eventail de l'histoire vivant*, 2 vols. (Paris, 1953), 1: 73–79; and B. Guenée, 'Des limites féodales aux frontières politiques,' in P. Nora, ed., *Les lieux de mémoire*, 2 (pt. .2): 11–33.

enemy. This military frontier, connoting a defensive zone, stood opposed to the linear boundary or line of demarcation separating two jurisdictions or territories. But from the sixteenth century onward, and especially in the later eighteenth century, the two tended to overlap; and the notion of delimitation became one of finding the *limites de la frontière*, the 'boundaries of the frontier.'[9]

Yet the conception of a linear political boundary as it appeared in the early modern period was not identical to the border line that slowly emerged after the seventeenth century. Peace treaties of the sixteenth and seventeenth centuries sometimes included provisions for the delimitation and demarcation of boundary lines, but the Old Regime state was something less than a territorial one. The French monarchy continued to envision its sovereignty in terms of its jurisdiction over subjects, not over a delimited territory, relying on the inherited notions of 'jurisdiction' and 'dependency' instead of basing its administration on firmly delineated territorial circumscriptions.[10]

Thus the Treaty of the Pyrenees of 1659 named the Pyrenees Mountains as the division between France and Spain, and further stipulated that commissioners were to meet to define more precisely which were the Pyrenees. The commissioners used the word 'delimitation' and claimed to seek the 'line of division,' but they resorted to ideas of 'jurisdiction' and 'dependency' when dividing up the villages of the Cerdanya. Only in 1868 did the Bayonne commissioners 'delimit' the boundary by establishing an imaginary border of two national territories and 'demarcate' the division by means of boundary stones.

The history of the boundary between 1659 and 1868, then, can hardly be summarized as the simple evolution from an empty zone to a precise line, but rather as the complex interplay of two notions of boundary – zonal and linear – and two ideas of sovereignty – jurisdictional and territorial. The two polarities can be found at any given moment in the history of the boundary, although the dominant but hardly unilinear tendency was the collapse of separate jurisdictional frontiers into a single territorial boundary line. The French Revolution gave to the idea of territory a specifically national content, while the early nineteenth-century states politicized the boundary line as the point where national territorial sovereignty found expression.

---

[9] B. Guenée, 'Les limites,' in M. François, ed., *La France et les français* (Paris, 1972), 57–64; Febvre, '*Frontière*,' 210–211; and Foucher, *L'invention des frontières*, 104–110.

[10] Febvre, '*Frontière*,' 213–214; and Lapradelle, *La frontière*, 35–37 ...

Nations and national identity

The creation of the territorial state constituted one component of the modern nation-state; the emergence of national identity formed another. According to received wisdom, modern nations were built from political centers outward and imposed upon marginal groups or peripheral regions in a process of cultural and institutional 'assimilation' and 'integration.'[11] National identity, in this view, is the expression of cultural unity and national consciousness consolidated within the political framework of a centralized state. The paradigmatic experience is, of course, the French one. Though an older generation of scholars saw in the French Revolution a formative period in the creation of French unity, more recent scholarship suggests that France only became a unified nation at a surprisingly late date. For only during the early Third Republic (1870–1914) did the French state create the road and railway networks, policies of compulsory primary education, and the universal military conscription by which peasants became Frenchmen.[12]

The corollary idea is that peasants become national citizens only when they abandon their identity as peasants: a local sense of place and a local identity centered on the village or valley must be superseded and replaced by a sense of belonging to a more extended territory or nation. In the words of Arnold Van Gennep, the dean of French folklorists, nationhood is 'the extension of real or symbolic love felt for the corner of land which belongs to the commune, to an entire valley, an immense plain, the steppe, and

[11] Examples include K. Deutsch, *Nationalism and Social Communication: An Inquiry into the Foundations of Nationality* (Cambridge, Mass., 1953); K. Deutsch, 'Some Problems in the Study of Nation-Building,' in K. Deutsch and W. Foltz, eds., *Nation-Building* (New York, 1963), 1–16; C. A. Macartney, *National States and National Minorities* (Oxford, 1934); and R. Bendix, *Nation-Building and Citizenship* (New York, 1964). On the resistance of mountain regions to 'the establishment of the state, dominant languages, and important civilizations,' see F. Braudel, *The Mediterranean and the Mediterranean World in the Age of Phillip II*, trans. S. Reynolds, 2 vols. (New York, 1966), 1: 38–41; and C. Levi, *Christ Stopped at Eboli*, trans. F. Frenaye (New York, 1947), 37–38.

[12] H. Kohn, *Prelude to Nation-States: The French and German Experience, 1789–1815* (Princeton, N.J., 1967); E. Weber, *Peasants into Frenchmen: The Modernization of Rural France, 1870–1914* (Stanford, Calif., 1976); for critical reviews of Weber's use of modernization theory, see C. Tilly, 'Did the Cake of Custom Break?' in J. Merriman, ed., *Consciousness and Class Experience in Nineteenth-Century Europe* (New York, 1979), 17–41; and T. M. Margadant, 'French Rural Society in the Nineteenth Century: A Review Essay,' *Agricultural History* 53 (1979): 644–651.

the great city like Paris or Vienna.'[13] National identity means replacing a sense of local territory by love of national territory.

Focusing on how the nation was imposed and built from the center outward, and claiming that its acceptance meant giving up local identities and territories, this received wisdom denies the role of local communities and social groups in shaping their own national identities. This book argues that both state formation and nation building were two-way processes at work since at least the seventeenth century. States did not simply impose their values and boundaries on local society. Rather, local society was a motive force in the formation and consolidation of nationhood and the territorial state. The political boundary appeared in the borderland as the outcome of national political events, as a function of the different strengths, interests, and (ultimately) histories of France and Spain. But the shape and significance of the boundary line was constructed out of local social relations in the borderland. Most concretely, the boundaries of the village jurisdictions ceded to France were not specified in the 1660 division, nor were they undisputed among village communities. The historical appearance of territory – the territorialization of sovereignty – was matched and shaped by a territorialization of the village communities, and it was the dialectic of local and national interests which produced the boundaries of national territory.

In the same way, national identity – as Frenchmen or Spaniards – appeared on the periphery before it was built there by the center. It appeared less as a result of state intentions than from the local process of adopting and appropriating the nation without abandoning local interests, a local sense of place, or a local identity. At once opposing and using the state for its own ends, local society brought the nation into the village.

(Sahlins, 1989, pp. 1–2, 4–9)

EXERCISE

Take notes on the extract, organizing them around answers to the following questions.

1 Sahlins criticizes a dualistic model of conceptualizing borders around models of 'boundaries' and 'frontiers'. What are the characteristics of this model?

---

[13] A. Van Gennep, *Traité comparatif des nationalités: 1. Les éléments extérieures de la nationalité* (Paris, 1922), 144.

2   On what grounds does Sahlins criticize this dualistic model?

3   What did the 'boundaries' between states look like prior to the advent of the modern national territorial state, according to Sahlins?

4   What differences did modern nationalism make to the creation of the boundary, or border, between France and Spain in the Pyrenees, in Sahlins's account?

DISCUSSION

1   The boundary is characterized as 'a precise, linear division, within a restrictive, political context' – in other words it has all the characteristics of a physical border between two states; it is fundamentally uncontested. The frontier has 'more zonal qualities, and a broader, social context'. It is a borderland – a meeting point, between two cultures or communities. In terms of the territories I have already discussed in this chapter it would most closely resemble Transylvania, though it need not be so clearly politically contested.

2   For Sahlins, the fundamental problem with this model is that it 'has often misled theorists into perceiving an evolutionary movement, necessary and irreversible, from a sparsely settled, ill-defined zone toward an uncontested, nonsubstantial, mathematically precise line of demarcation'. In other words, it leads commentators to believe that the history of borders is the story of their unproblematic and natural creation. For Sahlins, this ignores several basic facts, such as the persistence of frontier regions after precise borders have been established. Furthermore, it ignores the fact that the history of state building and therefore of the construction of borders has been more complex than simply the story of progress towards the modern European nation-state.

3   You will have noted from Sahlins's account that the meaning of political boundaries changed radically between the eleventh century and the end of the seventeenth. In medieval Europe the 'political boundaries between kingdoms were fundamentally similar in kind to feudal limits within the kingdom'. In other words, the external border of a kingdom might be little different from the boundaries between the territories of knights or lords within the kingdom. The frontier, or boundary, emerged with the centralization of European monarchies. The boundaries that had emerged from the process of building centralized monarchical states in the early modern period did not resemble modern

borders. Note what Sahlins says about the mid-seventeenth century boundary between France and Spain:

> the Treaty of the Pyrenees of 1659 named the Pyrenees Mountains as the division between France and Spain, and further stipulated that commissioners were to meet to define more precisely which were the Pyrenees. The commissioners used the word 'delimitation' and claimed to seek the 'line of division,' but they resorted to ideas of 'jurisdiction' and 'dependency' when dividing up the villages of the Cerdanya. Only in 1868 did the Bayonne commissioners 'delimit' the boundary by establishing an imaginary border of two national territories and 'demarcate' the division by means of boundary stones.

4   According to Sahlins, national identity as experienced in borderland village communities helped place the border between the two states. As the identities of the villagers along the border became national identities the national boundaries were shaped at the local level along the border. Sahlins writes that

> the political boundary appeared in the borderland as the outcome of national political events, as a function of the different strengths, interests, and (ultimately) histories of France and Spain. But the shape and significance of the boundary line was constructed out of local social relations in the borderland ... The historical appearance of territory – the territorialization of sovereignty – was matched and shaped by a territorialization of the village communities, and it was the dialectic of local and national interests which produced the boundaries of national territory.

I hope that you have gained several things from working with this reading. The first is an appreciation that the modern national border, with its border posts, border guards, passports and customs searches, is a product of history. The second is that there have in the past been borders that have been much more fluid and contested on an everyday level than those that exist in Europe today. The third is that the modern European border has not emerged out of an inevitable historical process, but has been the product of history – of the highly contested construction of European territorial states and then of their shifts to become modern nation-states. The last point is that borders and boundaries are lived in actual social relations – in the case analysed by Sahlins (that of nineteenth-century France and

Spain) the creation of the present-day national border was the product of the adoption of villagers of either French or Spanish national identities.

When taking your notes you may have been drawn to the following two sentences. Sahlins writes, 'States did not simply impose their values and boundaries on local society. Rather, local society was a motive force in the formation and consolidation of nationhood and the territorial state.' This suggests that although physical borders can be imposed from the top down, the creation of borders can be also a process that occurs from the bottom up. For Transylvania Sorin Mitu has shown how the region came to be seen as Romanian territory during the nineteenth century, thus creating a mental border between Romania and Hungary in the minds of Romanians that served to establish their claim to the area (Mitu, 2001). This border existed in the minds of many Romanians prior to the movement of the physical border in 1919. These two cases demonstrate that a cultural and mental border can exist although it may have no physical embodiment and is not rooted in state boundaries. It can be as real for those standing on either side of it as any physical border. In short, the symbolic significance invested in a boundary point can shape physical borders, but it can become a border in itself. This notion of a mental border is one that I should like you to bear in mind, given its relevance to any consideration of the borders of Europe.

What about Europe?

EXERCISE _____

I want you to return to the introduction of this chapter and to re-read it. There I advanced an intentionally provocative argument. Try to summarize what you thought I was arguing and think of various ways in which you could argue against what I said there. Also I would like you to say what the implications of my argument might be if it was to be proved correct.

DISCUSSION _____

I argued that some of the signatories of the Maastricht Treaty aimed to give the then European Community some of the attributes of a territorial state. Because of the compromise necessary to create the treaty these intentions were diluted. The signatories, however, proclaimed that their new European Union would be a union of the peoples of Europe and gave concrete expression to this aspiration by agreeing to create a common European citizenship. I suggested that in this they were doing nothing more than laying claim to represent

Europe and deciding that membership of the EU would determine who was included and excluded from that Europe. I did argue in the fourth paragraph that the project of the EU was only the most recent of many political projects throughout the history of the continent that has claimed to represent 'Europe' and has sought to determine who belongs and who does not. Implicit in my argument is an assertion that there is far more to European identity than identification with the EU. What determines, or who determines, whether an identity is European or non-European? If identities respond to, are remade by and in turn produce borders, then what do the answers to these questions tell us about where the borders of Europe lie?

I am not going to pretend that there are any hard-and-fast answers to these questions; nor am I going to give you any attempts at definitive answers, though all the chapters in this volume explore these questions and should, I hope, provoke you to think about them in new ways. I have selected the third reading because it raises many of the issues that you will be asked to think about. It is an essay by the Croatian-born writer Slavenka Drakulič and is, above all, a comment on the state of Europe at the beginning of the twenty-first century. It was written in response to what she perceived as the rise of racist and xenophobic politics across the continent in the year 2000. Though I want you to bear in mind the temporal context of the piece as you read it, it does advance ideas that have relevance outside of that context.

I live in Sweden, Croatia, and Austria. Europe is my home. I remember when, a couple of years ago, the checkpoint at the border crossing between Austria and Italy was abandoned, and we passed the border near Klagenfurt, barely believing that we were not going to be stopped by the police. But there were no police, only empty booths. What a great feeling of relief it was! Especially because I remembered the strange sensation when I crossed the newly erected border post between Slovenia and Croatia in 1991 for the first time. Being an Eastern European, I also know how it feels to stand in line at the airport checkpoint that says 'non-EU citizens,' or sometimes, just bluntly, 'Others.'

Living on both sides of real and imagined European borders and crossing back and forth all the time, I have to say that only a year ago I believed in the project of constructing a united Europe much more that I do today. But, of course, that was before the elections in Austria, in Norway and Switzerland or in the city of Antwerp, before the referendum on the euro in Denmark – or incidents such as the one in Malaga where a mob, mobilized by a neo-Nazi web site, chased Moroccan workers for three whole days. The list of disturbing events all over Europe is much longer. It is as if there is suddenly a pattern of a different Europe emerging in front of my eyes, and when I look at it, it gives me goosebumps. It is not a *déjà vu* because I belong to a generation that did not experience fascism. But I can see growing xenophobia, nationalism, and racism everywhere. Moreover, because of where I come from, I can tell when the fear of the Other becomes something one must start to take into account. And I just wonder if these are isolated incidents or are perhaps already signs that the project of European integration is in danger of losing its momentum?

I was born after the second world war and grew up on a sleepy continent divided by the Iron Curtain, dwelling in the shadow of a possible nuclear war. As school kids, we would practice what we had to do in the case of such an attack. We learned to recognize its characteristics by heart: first a mushroom cloud would appear on the horizon, followed by a blast of heat and ashes. You should hide behind any barrier, pull the gas mask over your face, and under no circumstances drink water (the bit with the water was particularly strongly impressed upon us, and I always wondered why). Although only children, we understood that these preparations would give us little protection if such a horror as described in our textbooks should happen. Still, we practiced dutifully. It did not help us. When the next war, the war in the Balkans erupted much later, we were taken by surprise. Little did we know in the late fifties that the war we would witness would be local, limited, and of small intensity – a war that would catch us totally unprepared.

My generation grew up with the idea that such a war, with genocide, concentration camps, and forced resettlement of entire populations, was simply impossible in the world after the Second World War. Europe had learned its lesson, the history teachers told us, and such horrors could not take place any longer. Today, after the war in my country and in Bosnia and Kosovo, I no longer believe that Europe has learned that lesson. But perhaps I am wrong. After all, the last war happened not quite in Europe, but in the Balkans. Are the Balkans Europe? Today it seems so, although tomorrow it could be decided differently. But if this is so, what then is Europe and where does it end?

Back then, in my school days, even that was somehow clearer. Europe was where the Soviet Union was not. The big political changes during the last ten years have blurred that childish certainty. The Europe of today is no longer a question of geopolitics and defined borders to the east, not even of economic unity – but more of attitudes, definitions, institutions, of a certain mental *landscape*. There is no longer any Iron Curtain to make definitions easier. During the last ten years, the peoples of Europe have witnessed the collapse of communism and the disappearance of the common enemy, the speeding up of the integration process within the European Union (EU), its planned enlargement into the east, as well as the war in the Balkans. At the same time the globalization process seems to engulf the entire world. But these changes happened too fast for people to comprehend, to grasp them fully. They reacted as people always react to the unknown, with uncertainty and fear. While the known world is dissolving in front of their eyes, the new one taking shape is not yet comprehensive. What is Europe really and how far can it spread eastwards whilst still remaining Europe? Is Turkey Europe? In that case, what about Russia?

These are not abstract questions. The bottom line here is how these changes will influence the life of Europeans, their work, income, education, language, and so on. More and more people have the feeling of losing the possibility to control their own lives. Anxiety undermines their confidence in the world around them and their sense of security. This anxiety is vague, to be sure. But although it is not entirely identified or specified, often not even recognized as such, it is out there, palpable, measurable in opinion polls, referendums, election results, articulated as doubts about the necessity of a common currency, of integration and enlargement, or about the free circulation of a work force. That is to say, as vague as it is, this anxiety is already having effects on the political life of some countries and might soon bring substantial changes to the political landscape of Europe.

The mechanism of exploiting fear is simple and well known. As an individual, you may feel lost and confused, swept away by the speed and magnitude of historical events. Suddenly, there is somebody offering you shelter, a feeling of belonging, a guarantee of security. We are of the same blood, we belong to the same territory, our people first, so goes the rhetoric. To scared ears it is soothing to hear old-fashioned words like *blood, soil, territory, us, them*. Hearing that, you feel stronger, you are no longer alone, confronted with the Others – with too many immigrants, Muslims, Turks, refugees, Africans, asylum seekers, Gypsies, or too much big bureaucracy that wants to rule your life from Brussels. Once you have found the pleasure of belonging, Others don't frighten you any longer. From the fear of the unknown to the creation of the 'known' enemy is sometimes only a small step. It doesn't need much more than that vague sense of anxiety, plus a political leader who knows how to exploit it. The media will do the rest.

It looks as if the new, darker picture of Europe started to surface with the victory of the Freedom party and Jörg Haider in Austria a year ago. The truth, however, is that his electoral success only made the anxiety more visible. Haider has been the most successful, but others such as Umberto Bossi, Christoph Blocher, Karl Hagen, Edmund Stoiber, Filip Dewinter, Pia Kjersgaard, or Jean-Marie LePen are catching up as well ...

What emerges is not necessarily a pattern of brown and black shirts again – but a new pattern of the rising anxiety of people. The right-wing parties then whip up people's fear with populist rhetoric using this anxiety. However, the truth of the matter is that the right-wing parties are the only ones to have their fingers on the people's pulses, to recognize that feeling of anxiety. Of course, they use it for their own purpose – to come to power. But it would not be right to say that the anxiety is produced or invented by these parties. To say that would be to dismiss the anxiety in the easiest way. These parties, with the generous help of the media, only give shape to that vague feeling of dissatisfaction. Directing it towards xenophobia is easy, there are Others in every society. As long as this xenophobia expresses itself on the level of polemics about this or that proposed law regarding citizenship for immigrants (like in Germany in 1998), one can say that it is not alarming. But it is alarming that an opinion poll published in *Der Spiegel* last summer showed that the majority of Germans agreed with some opinions of the extreme right, especially regarding immigrants. And it is alarming that such rhetoric has produced concrete political results in elections – especially during the last year. After that, it is hard to dismiss it, and arrogant to consider it a mere marginal phenomenon.

Anxiety is sweeping postcommunist Europe as well. The enthusiasm of the first years after the fall of communism has been replaced with disappointment. Once more a united Europe looks distant, there are now walls different from the Berlin wall, conditions for joining the EU are hard to meet, and the date is pushed further into the future. This opens up room for nationalists and anti-Europeans who argue that the newly won sovereignty should not be yielded so easily. They spread fear of multinational companies that will buy their country, of the Americanization of their culture, of globalization. It is not surprising when somebody like Slobodan Milošević uses this kind of language. Yet, democrats like Václav Klaus, the former Czech prime minister, are speaking out against the EU as well: 'Europe is now fundamentally challenging the nation state, particularly its sovereignty' he said, speaking in Austria last June. He is right – but this is the very idea of an integrated Europe. Klaus, too, speaks of assimilation and the loss of national identity: 'We don't want to become Euroczechs!' The Hungarian prime minister Viktor Orbán is also skeptical about the EU, not to mention the Slovak populist Vladimír Mečiar, or the Hungarian nationalist and anti-Semite István Csurka. Postcommunist Eastern Europe is far away from a united Europe in another sense as well: 67 percent of Poles, for example, believe that when their country joins the EU they will become second-class citizens.

Success of right-wing nationalist, xenophobic, and anti-European parties and populist leaders seems to be a danger in both Western and Eastern Europe. By spreading their influence even further through the exploitation of anxiety and fears that no one else wants to address, they can really undermine the integration process. Their leaders tell people that they will lose their national sovereignty, their culture, their language, etc. Their national, cultural, and social identity is in jeopardy. Not only will foreigners take all their jobs, but also – and this seems more important – the society itself will be transformed beyond recognition. In the language of the right wing, a multicultural society means cultural disintegration. This does sound threatening to people. It is not important if we prefer to call this political egocentrism, regional nationalism, or new regionalism, the result is the same everywhere: homogenization, mobilization of defensive mechanisms, and isolationist politics.

In research done in March (at the Institut fur Demoskopie Allensbach) about the fear of losing their identity in a united Europe, over 50 percent of Germans that said yes, they thought German identity will be lost – compared to 35 percent in 1994. But what is the identity they would like to protect so much? Usually one is not often in a position to ask this question because the need arises only if this identity is in some way challenged or threatened. From the individual's point of view, national identity looks like something given and definite, something as natural as eye color. Culture, history, language, myth, memory, mentality, values, habits, food ... All are part of a national identity, and a national identity strongly dominates our sense of personal identity. Recently, in the small French town of Millau a man was imprisoned for destroying a local McDonald's restaurant. But the trial turned into a manifestation of support for José Bove. He became a national hero because he had managed to articulate the French fear of American domination. This time people protested against the globalization of taste, and the French are against McDonald's fast food just as they are defending their right to make cheese from non-pasteurized milk. Anything else would threaten their national identity. You cannot ask the Germans to stop drinking their beer or the Dutch not to grow tulips. When they were negotiating to join the EU, the Swedes were particularly keen to make sure that chewing tobacco would not be forbidden for them – it is a matter of their national identity.

On the other hand, in newly established states, like Croatia for example, one can actually observe how a national identity is constructed and symbols of national identity are invented – mostly out of myths and the re-interpretation of history. It only proves what modern anthropology argues, that national identities do not represent a set of eternal, ready-made cultural, historical, or social characteristics. In other words, what we believe to be a fundamental support for an individual is no more than a cultural construct – that is, invented, not natural. But the archaic populist rhetoric of **Franjo Tudjman** didn't want to know that identity is always constructed in relation to the Others, it only wanted to exclude these Others, that is Serbs. Yet from the examples of emigrants, mixed marriages, and people who live close to borders, anthropologists are proving that it is possible to identify with more than one nation and one culture.

When I met a Turkish *Gastarbeiter* on a train in Germany, he complained that 'When I am in Germany, they consider me a Turk, but when I visit Turkey, they don't take me as one of them, they consider me a foreigner, a German. I always feel that I have to choose between the two, and I don't like that.' 'Well, how do you feel, what do you think you are?' I asked him. He answered, 'I am both.' He himself did not have a problem with his identity – others did. Indeed, in a culture of nationalism, identity is made up of borders, territory, and blood, and one is forced to choose one nation. But forcing people to choose sometimes brings unexpected results. Some years ago, two small villages in Istria were caught in a dispute between two newly founded states, Croatia and Slovenia. When Slovene journalists asked people there if they were Slovenes, they answered positively. But when Croatian journalists asked them if they were Croats, they also answered positively. This, of course, was confusing, and journalists sought an explanation. Finally

Franjo Tudjman (1922–1999) was the President of Croatia from 1990 until his death. As president he presided over the republic's moves towards independence and the ensuing civil war (1991–5).

somebody told them that 'either/or' simply is the wrong question to put to them. They feel strongly about their identity, but they don't define it in national terms, they prefer a regional reference, they are Istrians. Indeed, in a 1991 census about 20 percent of people in that region declared themselves Istrians; according to the regulations, they should have declared themselves 'others.' This was a kind of anti-nationalist demonstration against Franjo Tudjman's government, and the message was clear: for Istrians, their nationality and their identity do not necessarily overlap. Nation, as a political category, is only one aspect of their identity. For them the transnational regional identity was stronger than the national one. Istrians were not willing to choose one nationality over the other, rather they preferred to experience their identity as a sum of the cultural, national, and political identities represented in their region. 'The EU will only achieve a solid basis of legitimacy when Europeans perceive a European political identity. This does not imply that they would no longer feel themselves to be Swedes, Finns, Frenchmen, Portuguese, Czechs, Poles or Hungarians, but that the sense of common European destiny had been added to these identities,' writes Ingmar Karlsson.

I recall the earlier census of 1981 in Yugoslavia when almost 10 percent of the population declared themselves Yugoslavs. Further analysis demonstrated that this was the voice of the postwar generation, the young urban population. Was this the beginning of the Yugoslav nation? I don't think so. I think people were still very much aware of their ethnic identities. In my experience, this was rather the case of simply adding one identity to another, a common Yugoslav identity had been added to a Serbian, a Croatian, or a Bosnian one.

If nations are not eternal and national and personal identities are constructed, then they can be re-constructed as well. Another kind of imagined community can be created. Perhaps this is the right time to think about a new paradigm for understanding identity in order to balance the growing anxiety in Europe. Instead of using cultural exclusion mechanisms, is it possible to create identities by summing up ethnic, regional, national, and transnational elements of identity? If identity can be reconstructed in terms of a multiple identity, is this a way to establish a European identity? Not as a standardized and globalized community, but as a non-hierarchical community of diverse cultures. People would feel that they belong to a specific culture but not to a state – just like the Istrians. Can transregionalism help to overcome the anxiety people feel towards integration?

Because of the way I live, a united but diverse Europe is a possibility that enriches me and gives me more freedom. But in order to create such a Europe, people need to be convinced that they, too, are gaining, not losing something. We are at the point when losing seems more obvious, when fear overtakes hope facing our future. Who is afraid of Europe? Bronislaw Geremek, the former Polish foreign minister, already answered that question beautifully when he said, 'Europe is afraid of itself!'

(Drakulič, 2001, pp. 1–4, 5–9)

EXERCISE

Your notes on the extract should refer to the following questions.

1 Some of the things that you learned about standpoints from my discussion of borders should be applied to your reading of this piece. What is Drakulič's standpoint on the Europe she describes? In other words what is her view of Europe? How far is it shaped by her identity – her relation as an 'outsider', an 'insider', or both?

2 How does Drakulič regard national identity in the Europe she describes?

3 What does Drakulič identify as being the preconditions for greater and more successful European integration?

4 How convincing do you find her argument?

DISCUSSION

1 Drakulič begins her essay with the two sentences: 'I live in Sweden, Croatia, and Austria. Europe is my home.' I felt when reading the piece that she places considerable weight on the issue of borders and freedom of travel in relation to Europe. Perhaps this is because as an eastern European the external borders of the European Union are where she feels a certain exclusion from a Europe she also simultaneously feels part of. You will have noted the parallel between Drakulič's sentence – 'Being an Eastern European, I also know how it feels to stand in line at the airport checkpoint that says "non-EU citizens", or sometimes, just bluntly, "Others"' – and the passage written by Dubravka Ugrešič quoted in the introduction. Furthermore her nationality, as a Croatian who grew up in Tito's Yugoslavia, affects Drakulič's standpoint. She describes the feeling of crossing new borders – that between Croatia and Slovenia in 1991 – at the beginning of her piece. Her experience of what happened in

former Yugoslavia between 1991 and 1999 plainly feeds her fear and enhances her sensitivity to the growing xenophobia she argues has arisen in Europe at the very end of the twentieth century. At numerous points she makes this explicit, for example in the sentence 'because of where I come from, I can tell when the fear of the Other becomes something one must start to take into account'.

> Her actual view of Europe is quite complex. She identifies two sides to Europe. The first is that of a Europe without borders, that exists between and beyond nations and, above all, is one in which real recognition of the multiple and complex nature of identity and all its layers becomes possible. The other side to Europe is darker; one that stems from Drakulič's experience of war in her own country. This is a Europe of fear, nationalism and xenophobia: a Europe which clearly defines itself in relation to perceived others, and one in which most Europeans live their lives behind the borders of nation-states and articulate their identities in terms of those nations.

2   Drakulič argues that 'national identity strongly dominates our sense of personal identity'. At one and the same time she argues that national identity is fundamentally a human creation and the product of a distinct set of historical circumstances; an argument that parallels the one I have made in relation to borders. Her experience as a citizen of a relatively young state, Croatia, which gained independence in 1991, has heightened her sense of the culturally constructed nature of national identity. For her, the experience of Croatia

> only proves what modern anthropology argues, that national identities do not represent a set of eternal, ready-made cultural, historical, or social characteristics. In other words, what we believe to be a fundamental support for an individual is no more than a cultural construct.

Drakulič seems to suggest that the predominance of national identity actually masks the multiple identities of many Europeans: 'from the examples of emigrants, mixed marriages, and people who live close to borders, anthropologists are proving that it is possible to identify with more than one nation and one culture'.

3   Drakulič argues that a 'united but diverse Europe' could be created, but only through '[a]nother kind of imagined community' from that of the nation, one that forms 'a non-hierarchical community of diverse cultures'.

4   I don't know how you chose to answer this question. I am attracted by the vision of a border-less, multinational and multicultural Europe that Drakulič proposes. I share her fears of

a Europe merely united in its commitment to nation-states and by its xenophobia. Drakulič is clearly right to draw our attention to the fact that national identities are not eternal; that they are merely cultural constructions and products of historical processes. I find her argument that identities are always plural and that their plural nature should be recognized to be fully persuasive. I am not wholly convinced, however, by some of the conclusions she draws from these arguments; for me, her preferred Europe seems to lack an ideal that can bind its 'imagined community' together.

Drakulič focuses – as do many commentators – on overcoming the internal national borders within Europe as a means of unifying Europe. Her own experience, shared with Dubravka Ugrešič, of standing at the external border of the European Union in a queue under a sign designating her as non-European is powerfully suggestive of other internal obstacles to the creation of an all-embracing European identity. In fact I felt that it was her throwaway observations about the external borders of Europe and where they lie that make her piece particularly interesting. In her argument she explicitly links racism and xenophobia to fear about what an inclusive, multinational Europe might mean. I would draw your attention to the passage where she writes:

> What is Europe really and how far can it spread eastwards whilst still remaining Europe? Is Turkey Europe? In that case, what about Russia?

> These are not abstract questions. The bottom line here is how these changes will influence the life of Europeans, their work, income, education, language, and so on. More and more people have the feeling of losing the possibility to control their own lives. Anxiety undermines their confidence in the world around them and their sense of security.

In the body of the essay Drakulič shows a strong but implicit awareness of the fact that borders and boundaries are in fact as much mental constructs as physical realities. She also implies that the borders of Europe are perceived by the people of Europe, and that these perceptions of where the external borders lie are shaped by both standpoint and history. In order to develop this point further I want to take you back to the text of her essay. Describing her mental map of Europe as a child in Tito's Yugoslavia, Drakulič writes that 'in my school days ... Europe was where the Soviet Union was not'. Drakulič grew up in a country that was a one-party socialist state, but at the same time not part of the Soviet bloc. Indeed the Yugoslav state's anti-Stalinism, following Tito's break with the Soviet Union in

1948, was one of the pillars on which a postwar Yugoslav identity was built (Lampe, 1996, pp. 241–64; Wachtel, 1998, p. 132). In the next few sentences Drakulič implies that the eastern border of Europe prior to 1989 was the 'Iron Curtain' – namely the western boundary of the Warsaw Pact states. She writes that the 'Europe of today is no longer a question of geopolitics and defined borders to the east ... There is no longer any Iron Curtain to make definitions easier.' You may find the notion startling that before 1989 Europe ended at Berlin and Vienna, but as I shall show in Chapter 3, when I describe shifts in the representation of central Europe during the last century, this notion was uneasily internalized by many eastern Europeans themselves prior to the collapse of state socialism. As late as 1994 Hungarian friends constantly asked me whether I thought Hungary was a European country. Even though, in the west, eastern Europe was definitely part of 'Europe' it was also, for many western Europeans, profoundly different. Witness the culture shock Christopher Hitchens experienced when crossing the borders of Austria and Hungary, and then of Hungary and Romania, that was recounted in the first reading above. Note also the mental image of 'eastern Europe' that I had before I lived in the region.

Drakulič seems to argue that this notion of the eastern border of Europe disappeared in 1989, to be succeeded by uncertainty about where the eastern border lay. This leads to her question: 'What is Europe really and how far can it spread eastwards whilst still remaining Europe?' She also demonstrates the uncertainty surrounding this issue with her rhetorical question about the wars in former Yugoslavia during the 1990s: 'After all, the last war happened not quite in Europe, but in the Balkans. Are the Balkans Europe?' (I shall discuss this issue in more depth in Chapter 4). Just like the physical borders of national territorial states that criss-cross the continent, the experience of borders and the symbolic significance invested in them are shaped by standpoint. Furthermore, just like the physical borders of national territorial states, the 'fluid' borders of Europe are shaped by history.

When I first read Drakulič's essay I was particularly struck by one passage:

> When I met a Turkish *Gastarbeiter* on a train in Germany, he complained that 'When I am in Germany, they consider me a Turk, but when I visit Turkey, they don't take me as one of them, they consider me a foreigner, a German. I always feel that I have to choose between the two, and I don't like that.' 'Well, how do you feel, what do you think you are?' I asked him. He answered, 'I am both.' He himself did not have a problem with his identity.

In the years following the Second World War capitalist western Europe experienced an economic boom. Unemployment, which had plagued the region in the interwar years, fell and in some parts of northwestern Europe all but disappeared until it re-emerged in the mid 1970s. Between 1955 and 1973 the Federal Republic of Germany (West Germany) sought to use workers from abroad to solve problems of labour shortage generated by the boom. By 1973 there were some 2.6 million 'foreign workers' in the country and though most came from southern Europe – Italy, Greece and Yugoslavia – the largest single national contingent, (around 600,000) came from Turkey (Herbert and Hunn, 2001). As Robert Fraser shows in Chapter 7, France experienced substantial migration from North Africa in the postwar period. Meanwhile, in Britain the arrival of *Empire Windrush*, carrying 492 migrants from Jamaica in 1948, heralded a wave of postwar Commonwealth migration. By 1958 some 125,000 people from the Caribbean region and 55,000 from India and Pakistan had settled in the UK (Fryer, 1984, pp. 372–3). The experience of postwar migrants into Europe, whose children and grandchildren have known no countries other than the UK or France, for example, suggests yet another side to the issue of Europe and its fluid borders, with the generation of new, historically unique European identities. These identities have also been shaped in part by the experience of European racism. The novelist E. R. Braithwaite wrote in 1967 that:

> In spite of my years of residence in Britain, any service I might render the community in times of war and peace, any contribution I might make or wish to make, or any feeling of identity I might entertain towards Britain and the British, I ... am considered an 'immigrant'. Although this term indicates that we have secured entry into Britain, it describes a continuing condition in which we have no real hope of ever enjoying the desired transition to full responsible citizenship.

(quoted in Fryer, 1984, p. 382)

Postcolonial migration into the UK, France and the Netherlands, as well as economic migration from Turkey to West Germany in the postwar period, opened up new and very fluid borders for the continent. Robert Fraser discusses the implications of this for the formation of European identities in France and Germany in Chapter 7.

If migration into Europe has influenced our understanding of the area's fluid borders, what are the implications of outward migration over the past four centuries? With western Europe's Atlantic expansion into the 'New World' migrants settled in a new continent. In South America from the sixteenth century onwards, forms of Spanish and Portuguese civilization were established throughout the Indies, as the territories were called, and these were modified to different extents by the surviving native cultures – although in some cases nothing of the latter remained, as in Hispaniola, where within thirty years of the arrival of the Spanish, the total native population had disappeared.

(Rowe and Schelling, 1991, p. 19)

By the mid eighteenth century both North and South America had been the site of considerable settlement from Europe and was seen by Europeans at the time as little more than an extension of the 'old' continent. The French intellectual and revolutionary politician Constantin François de Volney (1757–1820) in the 1780s commented that it would be 'a fanciful mistake ... to describe as a new and virgin people a gathering of inhabitants of old Europe' (quoted in Woolf, 1992, pp. 80–1n.). Only with the American Revolution of 1776 and the creation of independent states in much of Latin America during the first half of the nineteenth century did a process begin which would result by the late nineteenth century in Europeans seeing the Americas as more than extensions of the 'old' continent (Woolf, 1992, p. 80). The Americas continued, however, to absorb substantial numbers of migrants from across Europe, many of whom did not entirely leave their cultural identities behind when they crossed the Atlantic. According to one historian of nineteenth-century Irish migration to the United States, 'with its well-established Irish neighbourhoods ... Philadelphia's urban environment was not a complete contrast to life in Ireland' (Mageean, 1991, pp. 58–9). While these ceased to be identities within Europe, outward migration further shaped the fluidity of Europe's borders.

If the notions of these fluid borders and identities linked to and formed by them have been affected by patterns of postcolonial migration into Europe, as well as by outward migration, then such notions have been profoundly shaped by the experience of colonialism. This has almost certainly had an influence on the development of identities in former colonial states such as France and Britain. Europe's experience of colonialism and its relationship to the continent's fluid borders might be more ambiguous than a simple concentration on the western European colonial powers would suggest. In order to set you thinking about how this might be the case the next reading is an extract from an essay written by the American anthropologist Michael Herzfeld. This reading returns to the problematic and fluid eastern border of Europe. It is shorter than the previous reading yet it is also much denser.

Europe is often seen as the source rather than the destination of colonialism, yet Europe contains a number of sites that were colonized rather than colonizing even in Victorian times: Malta and Cyprus are clearly defined examples ... There are some less obvious cases as well; Begoña Aretxaga ... and Jane Nadel-Klein ... have argued for Ireland and Scotland, respectively, as the training grounds for the grand expansions of colonial rule in Africa, Asia, and elsewhere far from Europe ... Larry Woolf ... has suggested an analogous subordination of the former Eastern Bloc countries ...

There is an additional and perhaps equally instructive complication. Colonialism ... is often taken to be a primarily European, or at least Western, project ... Greece, however, and indeed much of the Balkans entered the family of nation-states, not through the breakup of a European empire but from the detritus of Ottoman suzerainty, as did much of the Arab world. It is thus important to ask whether Syrian, Greek, and Serbian complaints about 'the Turkish yoke' bear witness to 'another' colonialism or whether, as I suspect, they instead indicate a hegemony by certain specific Western powers that find it convenient to treat the Turkish past as a stain on these countries' occidental escutcheon. For these powers the orientalist argument has proved useful for reining in the lesser and more dependent European countries' frequent demands for greater control over their own destinies. It has perpetuated an uneven struggle over cultural capital at the global level, a struggle that is also reproduced ... in everyday life ...

In other words, we must confront two very different, but interrelated, variants of the usual sense of colonialism: the possibility of a non-Western variant and the distinct possibility that a more discreet and perhaps far more insidious Western colonialism, one that is primarily engaged today in the international politics of cultural distinction, is still very much alive and well.

(Herzfeld, 1997, p. 714)

EXERCISE

Having read the extract, make some notes around the following points.

1   In what ways does Herzfeld see Europe as the 'destination' rather than the 'source' of 'colonialism'?

2   What non-western forms of colonialism has Europe experienced, according to Herzfeld?

3   What is the 'more insidious' form of colonialism he describes?

4   Lastly I want you comment on the extract. How convincing do you find Herzfeld's argument and above all his definitions? Do you think his argument sheds any light on the way the fluid borders of Europe have been drawn?

DISCUSSION

1   Herzfeld gives a number of examples of European colonies, some of which you may find slightly strange. Malta, Cyprus, Scotland and Ireland are mentioned. So is the eastern part of Europe, which was captured in 'analogous subordination'.

2   In discussing non-western forms of colonialism Herzfeld focuses largely on the Ottoman empire. He argues – and this for me is one of the most interesting aspects of the case he presents – that the Ottoman legacy has had long-term implications in how its former territories were incorporated into Europe. He argues that the legacy of the Ottoman past has proved useful to western Europeans 'for reining in the lesser and more dependent European countries' frequent demands for greater control over their destinies'. While you may feel, and I would agree, that Herzfeld's argument seems a little too intentionalist, some obvious illustrations – such as western European definitions of 'the Balkans', which are discussed in depth in Chapter 4 – spring to mind.

3   The 'more discreet and perhaps far more insidious Western colonialism' is actually not a form of 'colonialism' at all, in that it does not involve the formal occupation and administration of one territory by another. It is a form of domination, however, that is exercised through culture – one that defines one culture, a 'western' one, as superior, and another, 'eastern', one as inferior.

4   As I have already indicated in this discussion I feel that Herzfeld misuses the concept of colonialism in order to advance a provocative argument about the nature of Europe and political power within it. Herzfeld's definition of 'colonialism' is so stretched as to render the concept almost meaningless; here it is simply a word to describe the domination of one part of Europe by another. Nevertheless I am much more convinced by two other elements of his argument. The first is that the history of Ottoman rule has shaped the experience of those territories in southeastern Europe that fell under it, and that this has had lasting implications for their incorporation into contemporary

Europe. The second is that the fluid borders of Europe on its eastern flank are determined by notions of a hierarchy between east and west that determine who is included and excluded, as well as the terms on which certain identities are included within 'Europe'.

The question of the former Ottoman territories of Europe and western reaction to them is explored in more depth in Chapter 4. Before I move on to talk about how notions of east and west have shaped notions of Europe's eastern borderland I shall briefly recap and summarize the complex argument advanced in this section.

Here I have made the following points:

- Borders can be mental constructs as well as physical realities – so mental borders can be invested with symbolic significance as much as physical borders are.

- Perceptions of the borders of Europe shape European identities in the same way as national or regional boundaries do.

- Europe's borders are fluid – they exist as much in people's identities as in actual geographical space.

- Notions of 'where' Europe's fluid borders lie are shaped by interaction between Europe and the wider world.

The invention of the east; the invention of eastern Europe

I end this chapter with the idea that started it. In the opening two paragraphs I described the attempts of the member governments of the European Community to forge a political union at Maastricht in 1992. Though I did not say it in so many words I implied that this European Union was to be a union of western Europe. I strongly suggested that its creation would serve to reproduce the divide between western and eastern Europe. The advocates of this union have planned a continual process of enlargement to incorporate the states of east-central Europe within the EU in order to overcome this division. In the provocative spirit in which I suggested that the building of the union would serve to reproduce boundaries between the eastern and western halves of the continent, it is worth posing the question of whether the ultimate effect of enlargement will be to eliminate this division, or simply to reproduce it in a new form. Paul Lewis in Chapter 6 discusses how the prospect of enlargement of the European Union has been received in post-socialist Poland, thus helping you to think in some depth about this question. Here, however, I pose the question more provisionally in order to help you develop ideas of your own at the outset of this book.

According to Stuart Woolf, at the end of the eighteenth century

> a European view of the extra-European world was consolidated which drew on earlier perceptions, but transformed them into a radically different unifying concept of European civilization and progress which allowed the classification, and justified the material exploitation, of the rest of the world.

(Woolf, 1992, p. 74)

It was at this time that divisions between east and west took hold within the European imagination and became central to European identity. The fifth reading should help you consider how conceptual divisions between west and east have helped shape European identities, while the sixth reading should help you reflect on how the same conceptual division has shaped notions of an east European identity and simultaneously served to define eastern Europe as a borderland. In Chapter 5 Colin Chant considers the development of Russian identity through examining the career of political philosopher Alexander Herzen, which should also help you to think about this issue.

The fifth reading is an extract from the introduction of Edward Said's *Orientalism: Western Conceptions of the Orient* (1978). The book's arguments have been much debated and in Chapter 2 Suman Gupta sets the book in its full intellectual context. It is about the discipline of oriental studies and the way in which 'the orient' has been constructed in the western mind. Some of the questions it raises, like the issue of whether it is possible to know or study another culture, have been hotly debated. Said's ambiguous relationship with theories associated with postmodernism – note his use of the concept of discourse formulated by the French philosopher Michel Foucault (1926–84) – has also provoked some controversy. I am not primarily interested in these issues for the purposes of this chapter; what I want you to focus on is the role Said argues that the orient has played in the creation of a European identity, and thus in determining where the fluid borders of Europe lie.

On a visit to Beirut during the terrible civil war of 1975–1976 a French journalist wrote regretfully of the gutted downtown area that 'it had once seemed to belong to ... the Orient of Chateaubriand and Nerval'.[14] He was right about the place, of course, especially so far as a European was concerned. The Orient was almost a European invention, and had been since antiquity a place of romance, exotic beings, haunting memories and landscapes, remarkable experiences. Now it was disappearing; in a sense it had happened, its time was over. Perhaps it seemed irrelevant that Orientals themselves had something at stake in the process, that even in the time of Chateaubriand and Nerval Orientals had lived there, and that now it was they who were suffering; the main thing for the European visitor was a European representation of the Orient and its contemporary fate, both of which had a privileged communal significance for the journalist and his French readers.

Americans will not feel quite the same about the Orient, which for them is much more likely to be associated very differently with the Far East (China and Japan, mainly). Unlike the Americans, the French and the British – less so the Germans, Russians, Spanish, Portuguese, Italians, and Swiss – have had a long tradition of what I shall be calling *Orientalism*, a way of coming to terms with the Orient that is based on the Orient's special place in European Western experience. The Orient is not only adjacent to Europe; it is also the place of Europe's greatest and richest and oldest colonies, the source of its civilizations and languages, its cultural contestant, and one of its deepest and most recurring images of the Other. In addition, the Orient has helped to define Europe (or the West) as its contrasting image, idea, personality, experience. Yet none of this Orient is merely imaginative. The Orient is an integral part of European *material* civilization and culture. Orientalism expresses and represents that part culturally and even ideologically as a mode of discourse with supporting institutions, vocabulary, scholarship, imagery, doctrines, even colonial bureaucracies and colonial styles. In contrast, the American understanding of the Orient will seem considerably less dense, although our recent Japanese, Korean, and Indochinese adventures ought now to be creating a more sober, more realistic 'Oriental' awareness. Moreover, the vastly expanded American political and economic role in the Near East (the Middle East) makes great claims on our understanding of that Orient.

[14] Thierry Desjardins, *Le Martyred u Liban* (Paris: Plon, 1976), p. 14.

It will be clear to the reader (and will become clearer still throughout the many pages that follow) that by Orientalism I mean several things, all of them, in my opinion, interdependent. The most readily accepted designation for Orientalism is an academic one, and indeed the label still serves in a number of academic institutions. Anyone who teaches, writes about, or researches the Orient – and this applies whether the person is an anthropologist, sociologist, historian, or philologist – either in its specific or its general aspects, is an Orientalist, and what he or she does is Orientalism. Compared with *Oriental studies* or *area studies*, it is true that the term *Orientalism* is less preferred by specialists today, both because it is too vague and general and because it connotes the high-handed executive attitude of nineteenth-century and early-twentieth-century European colonialism. Nevertheless books are written and congresses held with 'the Orient' as their main focus, with the Orientalist in his new or old guise as their main authority. The point is that even if it does not survive as it once did, Orientalism lives on academically through its doctrines and theses about the Orient and the Oriental.

Related to this academic tradition, whose fortunes, transmigrations, specializations, and transmissions are in part the subject of this study, is a more general meaning for Orientalism. Orientalism is a style of thought based upon an ontological and epistemological distinction made between 'the Orient' and (most of the time) 'the Occident.' Thus a very large mass of writers, among whom are poets, novelists, philosophers, political theorists, economists, and imperial administrators, have accepted the basic distinction between East and West as the starting point for elaborate theories, epics, novels, social descriptions, and political accounts concerning the Orient, its people, customs, 'mind,' destiny, and so on. *This* Orientalism can accommodate Aeschylus, say, and Victor Hugo, Dante and Karl Marx.

The interchange between the academic and the more or less imaginative meanings of Orientalism is a constant one, and since the late eighteenth century there has been a considerable, quite disciplined – perhaps even regulated – traffic between the two. Here I come to the third meaning of Orientalism, which is something more historically and materially defined than either of the other two. Taking the late eighteenth century as a very roughly defined starting point Orientalism can be discussed and analyzed as the corporate institution for dealing with the Orient – dealing with it by making statements about it, authorizing views of it, describing it, by teaching it, settling it, ruling over it: in short, Orientalism as a Western style for dominating, restructuring, and having authority over the Orient. I have found it useful here to employ Michel Foucault's notion of a discourse, as described by him in *The Archaeology of Knowledge* and in *Discipline and Punish*, to identify Orientalism. My contention is that without examining Orientalism as a discourse one cannot possibly understand the enormously systematic discipline by which European culture was able to manage – and even produce – the Orient politically, sociologically, militarily, ideologically, scientifically, and imaginatively during the post-Enlightenment period. Moreover, so authoritative a position did Orientalism have that I believe no one writing, thinking, or acting on the Orient could do so without taking account of the limitations on thought and action imposed by Orientalism. In brief, because of Orientalism the Orient was not (and is not) a free subject of thought or action. This is not to say that Orientalism unilaterally determines what can be said about the Orient, but that it is the whole network of interests inevitably brought to bear on (and therefore always involved in) any occasion when that peculiar entity 'the Orient' is in question. How this happens is what this book tries to demonstrate. It also tries to show that European culture gained in strength and identity by setting itself off against the Orient as a sort of surrogate and even underground self.

(Said, 1978, pp. 1–3)

EXERCISE

Your notes on the extract should be organized around the following two issues.

1   From Said's account, who created the orient and how did they create it?

2   What, according to Said, has been the relationship between the orient and European identity?

DISCUSSION

1   'The orient' has been created in the minds of Europeans out of their experience of civilizations and cultures to the east of them. For Said it 'was almost a European invention, and had been since antiquity a place of romance, exotic beings, haunting memories and landscapes, remarkable experiences'. In the European mind, the orient was an exotic other.

2   The orient, according to Said, marks the border of Europe, and has consequently been one of the influences under which European identity formed – as Said writes, 'the Orient has helped to define Europe'. For him it 'is an integral part of European material civilization and culture'. The relationship between the orient and Europe, according to Said, is 'orientalism' which, borrowing from the work of Michel Foucault, is defined as a 'discourse': a body of ideas or practices within which power is constructed. In the case of Said's orientalism the discourse constructs and reproduces the power of Europe, or the west, over the orient. During the post-Enlightenment period, Said argues, 'European culture gained in strength and identity by setting itself off against the Orient as a sort of surrogate and even underground self.' In short, the border of Europe established by orientalist ideas was a border between an assumed superior and an inferior.

You will have the opportunity to consider other aspects of Said's arguments later in this volume. For now, though, I want to move directly from the fifth to the sixth and final reading. This is an extract from the introduction to a historical monograph, Larry Woolf's *Inventing Eastern Europe: the Map of Civilization on the Mind of the Enlightenment* (1994). Woolf's intellectual debt to Said is obvious from this extract. It begins with a point similar to that made by Slavenka Drakulič in the third reading in this chapter, about 1989 destroying our perceptions of the internal borders of the continent. Woolf's contention is that the division of Europe into eastern and western halves is intimately connected to European identity and much more than the product of cold war division.

The revolution of 1989 in Eastern Europe has largely invalidated the perspective of half a century, compelling the reconsideration of Europe as a whole. The maps on the wall have always showed a continent of many colors, the puzzle pieces of many states; the dark line of the iron curtain, supplying the light and shadow in front and behind, was drawn on the maps in the mind. Those maps must be adjusted, adapted, reconceived, but their structures are deeply rooted and powerfully compelling. In the 1990s Italians are worriedly deporting Albanian refugees: *Albanesi, no grazie!* reads the graffiti on the wall. Germans are greeting visitors from Poland with thuggish violence and neo-Nazi demonstrations, while tourists form Eastern Europe are being arbitrarily stopped and searched in Paris shops, under suspicion of shoplifting. Statesmen, who once enthusiastically anticipated the unity of Europe, are looking away from the siege of Sarajevo, wishing perhaps that it were happening on some other continent. Alienation is in part a matter of economic disparity, the wealth of Western Europe facing the poverty of Eastern Europe, but such disparity is inevitably clothed in the complex windings of cultural prejudice. The iron curtain is gone, and yet the shadow persists.

The shadow persists, because the idea of Eastern Europe remains, even without the iron curtain. This is not only because the intellectual structures of half a century are slow to efface themselves, but above all because that idea of Eastern Europe is much older than the Cold War. Churchill's oratorical image of the iron curtain was powerful and persuasive, and its success was in part on account of its apparent aptness in describing the contemporary emergence of a Soviet sphere as the international cataclysm of the historical moment. Yet its aptness and prescience also concealed a part of what made Churchill's imagery so powerful, the traces of an intellectual history that invented the idea of Eastern Europe long before. Churchill's demarcation of a boundary line 'from Stettin in the Baltic to Trieste in the Adriatic' followed a line that was drawn and invested with meaning over two centuries, dating back to the age of his most famous ancestor, the warrior duke of Marlborough. The 'iron curtain' seamlessly fit the earlier tracing, and it was almost forgotten, or neglected, or suppressed, that an older epoch in the history of ideas first divided the continent, creating the disunion of Western Europe and Eastern Europe.

The distinction is older than Churchill and the Cold War, but it is by no means a matter of time immemorial, undiscoverably ancient. It was not a natural distinction, or even an innocent one, for it was produced as a work of cultural creation, of intellectual artifice, of ideological self-interest and self-promotion. Churchill might remove himself to Fulton, Missouri, to produce a semblance of external perspective, discerning from a distance the division of Europe. The original division, however, happened at home. It was Western Europe that invented Eastern Europe as its complementary other half in the eighteenth century, the age of Enlightenment. It was also the Enlightenment, with its intellectual centers in Western Europe, that cultivated and appropriated to itself the new notion of 'civilization,' an eighteenth-century neologism, and civilization discovered its complement, within the same continent, in shadowed lands of backwardness, even barbarism. Such was the invention of Eastern Europe. It has flourished as an idea of extraordinary potency since the eighteenth century, neatly dovetailing in our own times with the rhetoric and realities of the Cold War, but also certain to outlive the collapse of Communism, surviving in the public culture and its mental maps. One may begin to understand and confront the idea of Eastern Europe by exploring the intricate historical process that left it embedded and encoded in our culture.

In the Renaissance the fundamental conceptual division of Europe was between the South and the North. The city states of Italy were the almost unquestioned centers of art and learning, of painting and sculpture, rhetoric and philosophy, not to mention finance and trade. The Italian humanists did not hesitate to proclaim a perspective of cultural condescension, most dramatically expressed in Machiavelli's famous 'Exhortation to Liberate Italy from the Barbarians,' the last chapter of *The Prince*. He was looking back to the landmark event of his generation, for every Florentine and most Italians, the invasion of Italy in 1494 by Charles VIII, the king of France, which inaugurated a period of 'barbarian' invasions from the north, presaging the end of the *quattrocento*, the most glorious age of the Italian Renaissance. Even more traumatic was the great disaster of the next generation, the sack of Rome in 1527 by the German soldiers of the Holy Roman Emperor, Charles V. The Italian Renaissance saw itself battered by the blows of northern barbarians, and classically conscious humanists could look back a thousand years, from the sack of Rome by Germans in 1527, to the sack of Rome by the Goths in 476, to reinforce their directional perspective on the lands of barbarism. Ancient Romans and Renaissance Italians alike read Tacitus on the Germans to discover people who performed human sacrifices, wore wild animal skins, and generally lacked the refinements of culture: 'When not engaged in warfare they spend a certain amount of time hunting, but much more in idleness, thinking of nothing else but sleeping and eating.'[15] Tacitus knew of other barbarians further to the east, such as the Sarmatians and the Dacians, but his chief concern was the Germans in the north, and this classical perspective was marvelously suited to the Italians of the Renaissance. Indeed, Machiavelli seized upon the perspective of ancient Rome with the same splendid verve and rhetorical opportunism that Churchill demonstrated in exploiting the perspective of the Enlightenment for the foundation of the iron curtain.

[15] Tacitus, *Germania*, in *The Agricola and the Germania*, trans. H. Mattingly and S. A. Handford (London: Penguin, 1970), p. 114.

The polarization of Europe between Italy and the northern barbarians, so obvious to the ancient Romans, so convenient to the Renaissance Italians, survived into the eighteenth century as a rhetorical form. William Coxe, publishing in 1785 his *Travels into Poland, Russia, Sweden, and Denmark*, could still sum them up as 'my travels through the Northern kingdoms of Europe.'[16] Yet this geographical perspective had begun to appear seriously anachronistic, and it was the intellectual work of the Enlightenment to bring about that modern reorientation of the continent which produced Western Europe and Eastern Europe. Poland and Russia would be mentally detached from Sweden and Denmark, and associated instead with Hungary and Bohemia, the Balkan lands of Ottoman Europe, and even the Crimea on the Black Sea.

From the age of the Renaissance to the age of the Enlightenment, Europe's centers of culture and finance had shifted from the treasures and treasuries of Rome, Florence, and Venice to the now more dynamically important cities of Paris, London, and Amsterdam. Voltaire's perspective on Europe from eighteenth-century Paris was altogether geographically different from that of Machiavelli in sixteenth-century Florence. It was Voltaire who led the way as the philosophes of the Enlightenment articulated and elaborated their own perspectives on the continent, gazing from west to east, instead of from south to north. In so doing, they perpetrated a conceptual reorientation of Europe, which they bequeathed to us so that we now see Europe as they did; or, rather, we have passively inherited the Europe that they actively reconceived. Just as the new centers of the Enlightenment superseded the old centers of the Rennaissance, the old lands of barbarism and backwardness in the north were correspondingly displaced to the east. The Enlightenment had to invent Western Europe and Eastern Europe together, as complementary concepts, defining each other by opposition and adjacency.

Travelers were essential to this work of orientation, eighteenth-century travelers from Western Europe to Eastern Europe. The lands of Eastern Europe were sufficiently unfamiliar in the eighteenth century, still such unusual destinations, that each traveler carried a mental map to be freely annotated, embellished, refined, or refolded along the way. The operations of mental mapping were above all association and comparison: association

---

[16] William Coxe, *Travels into Poland*, from *Travels into Poland, Russia, Sweden, and Denmark: Interspersed with Historical Relations and Political Inquiries* (London, 1785; rpt. New York: Arno Press and New York Times, 1971), preface.

among the lands of Eastern Europe, intellectually combining them into a coherent whole, and comparison with the lands of Western Europe, establishing the developmental division of the continent. This book will begin with a traveler, the count de Ségur, one of the French heroes of the American Revolutionary War, entering Eastern Europe on his way to St. Petersburg in the winter of 1784–85 to serve as French ambassador to the court of Catherine the Great. When he passed from Prussia into Poland – roughly where the iron curtain would descend two centuries later – he was powerfully conscious of crossing an extremely significant border. He felt he had 'left Europe entirely,' and furthermore had 'moved back ten centuries.' This book will end with another traveler returning to Western Europe, an American, John Ledyard, who had traveled around the world with Captain Cook, and in 1788 was returning from a solo expedition to Siberia, which ended in his arrest by order of Catherine. Traveling west across the Russian empire, then through Poland, he did not consider himself to be back in Europe until he reached the Prussian border. There, between Poland and Prussia, Ledyard located 'the great barrier of Asiatic & European manners,' and he 'leapt' across with gushing enthusiasm: 'Once more welcome Europe to my warmest embraces.'[17] It is hardly necessary to consult an atlas to see that Ségur, when he felt he had 'left Europe entirely,' was nowhere near the boundary of Europe, and that Ledyard, traveling in the other direction, was all at once welcoming and embracing Europe in sheer defiance of the fact that he had already been traveling in Europe for more than a thousand miles.

Ledyard had a name for such freely constructed geographical sentiment; he called it 'Philosophic Geography.' Such was the Enlightenment's subordination of geography to its own philosophical values, its investment of the map with subtleties that eluded the stricter standards of scientific cartography. Ségur had a name for the space that he discovered when he seemed to leave Europe but still remained in Europe; eventually he located himself in 'the east of Europe,' which in French, as *l'orient de l'Europe*, offered also the potently evocative possibility of 'the Orient of Europe.' As late as the eve of World War I, French scholarship still alternated between two seemingly similar terms, *l'Europe orientale*

[17] Louis-Philippe, comte de Ségur, *Mémoires, souvenirs et anecdotes, par le comte de Ségur*, vol. I, in *Bibliothèque de mémoires: relatif à l'histoire de France: pendant le 18e siècle*, vol. XIX, ed. M. Fs. Barrière (Paris: Librairie de Firmin Didot Frères, 1859); and John Ledyard, *John Ledyard's Journey Through Russia and Serbia 1787–1788: The Journal and Selected Letters*, ed. Stephen D. Watrous (Madison: Univ. of Wisconsin Press, 1966).

(Eastern Europe) and *l'Orient européen* (the European Orient).[18]
Edward Said's *Orientalism* has proposed that the Orient was
constructed by the Occident 'as its contrasting image, idea,
personality, experience,' an image of otherness, while Orientalism
served as 'a Western style for dominating, restructuring, and
having authority over the Orient'.[19] The idea of Eastern Europe
was entangled with evolving Orientalism, for while Philosophic
Geography casually excluded Eastern Europe from Europe,
implicitly shifting it into Asia, scientific cartography seemed to
contradict such fanciful construction. There was room for
ambiguity. The geographical border between Europe and Asia was
not unanimously fixed in the eighteenth century, located
sometimes at the Don, sometimes farther east at the Volga, and
sometimes, as today, at the Urals.

Such uncertainty encouraged the construction of Eastern Europe
as a paradox of simultaneous inclusion and exclusion, Europe but
not Europe. Eastern Europe defined Western Europe by contrast,
as the Orient defined the Occident, but was also made to mediate
between Europe and the Orient. One might describe the invention
of Eastern Europe as an intellectual project of demi-
Orientalization. This was a process that could also work the other
way. Martin Bernal's *Black Athena* has proposed that purposeful
Hellenism purged our understanding of ancient Greece of its
African and Asian influences. It also helped to exempt modern
Greece from inclusion in the idea of Eastern Europe, and
Churchill still celebrated the salvation of its 'immortal glories'
from the shadow of the iron curtain in the twentieth century. The
parallel intellectual processes of Orientalism and Hellenism, both
dating back to the eighteenth century, created important points of
reference and influential parameters for the evolution of the idea
of Eastern Europe. Interestingly, the idea of Europe as a whole
came into cultural focus at the same time that the continent was
conceived in halves. The Italian historian Federico Chabod,
looking toward European unity after World War II, argued that the
idea of Europe emerged with a coherent character and secular
philosophical significance in the age of Enlightenment. Chabod
placed special emphasis on the writings of Montesquieu, on the
opposition between Europe and the Orient in the *Persian Letters*,

[18]   Abel Mansuy, *Le Monde slave et les classiques français aux XVIe–XVIIe siècles*, preface de
Charles Diehl (Paris: Librarie Ancienne Honoré Champion, 1912), pp. 8, 10.

[19]   Edward W. Said, *Orientalism* (New York: Vintage Books, 1979), pp. 1–3.

and between European liberty and Asiatic despotism in the *Spirit of the Laws.*[20] Those oppositions, however, allowed for an intermediary cultural space, in which the idea of Eastern Europe evolved.

(Woolf, 1994, pp. 3–7)

EXERCISE

Your notes on this reading should consider the following issues.

1   What, for Woolf, is the 'idea of Eastern Europe'?

2   When and how, according to Woolf, was Eastern Europe 'invented'?

3   What are the similarities between Woolf's 'idea of Eastern Europe' and Said's conception of 'the Orient'? How do you account for them?

DISCUSSION

1   The 'idea of Eastern Europe', according to Woolf, was a product of the Enlightenment and its notion of civilization and progress. The Enlightenment cast western Europe as the centre of its concept of progress and defined the east as 'shadowed lands of backwardness, even barbarism'. Eastern Europe was thus the flip-side of western Europe.

2   Eastern Europe was not an eternal idea. It was instead the product of history. According to Woolf, during the Renaissance 'the fundamental conceptual division of Europe was between the South and the North'. With the shift in the centre of gravity within early modern Europe 'from the treasures and treasuries of Rome, Florence, and Venice to the now more dynamically important cities of Paris, London, and Amsterdam' the conceptual map of Europe shifted. Eastern Europe became a zone of backwardness, western Europe of civilization and progress.

[20]   Martin Bernal, *Black Athena: the Afroasiatic Roots of Classical Civilization*, vol. I, *The Fabrication of Ancient Greece 1785–1985* (New Brunswick, N.J.: Rutgers Univ. Press, 1987); Federico Chabod, *Storia dell'idea d'Europa* (Bari: Editori Laterza, 1965), pp. 82–121; Denys Hay, *Europe: The Emergence of an Idea* (Edinburgh: Edinburgh Univ. Press, 1968), pp. 117–27; Jean-Baptiste Duroselle, *L'Idée d'Europe dans l'histoire* (Paris: Denoël, 1965), pp. 77–133; see also Janusz Tazbir, 'Poland and the Concept of Europe in the Sixteenth–Eighteenth Centuries', *European Studies Review* 7, no. 1 (Jan. 1977): 29–45.

3   There are close parallels between Said's notion of the orient and Woolf's idea of eastern Europe. Both concepts have been constructed by and to serve a western half. Both were substantially products of Enlightenment notions of civilization and progress. There are differences between the two ideas – eastern Europe is almost conceived in Enlightenment thought, according to Woolf, as a kind of transitional zone between the occident and orient.

You might account to some extent for the parallels between Said's and Woolf's arguments in terms of the influence of Said on Woolf. There is some truth in this, but if you stressed this aspect I would have hoped you mentioned that Said and Woolf are describing two different, yet mutually reinforcing dimensions of the same process. This is the definition of the Enlightenment view of Europe and its borders – a view which still shapes our contemporary understanding of where the borders of Europe lie. Both the notion of a Europe defined in part against an 'oriental' other and the notion of Europe's borderland region stem from this period.

Conclusion

At the beginning of this section I asked a rhetorical question about whether expansion of the European Union was likely to lead to the overcoming of Europe's fundamental divisions. I don't want to answer this question at this point, but leave it open. You could answer that the division in Europe between east and west is so much more deep-rooted than any short-term political project that it cannot be overcome. Or you might argue that such divisions are products of history anyway, and are therefore changeable. If you are minded to agree with the latter view then any political project that aims to overcome this division needs radically to reconstruct European identity. The processes that have determined borders within Europe, however – and indeed the borders of Europe itself, as well as how they are and have been experienced – are complex. They are far more rooted in a number of multiple histories and in particular identities than any one political project can determine. This chapter has only introduced you to the major issues necessary to think about the borders of Europe. In exploring specific dimensions of some of the issues I have raised here, this book should help you to think about where the borders of Europe lie, and what implications they have for European identities.

References

Bartlett, R. (1994) *The Making of Europe: Conquest, Colonization and Cultural Change 950–1350*, Harmondsworth, Penguin.

Council of the European Communities – Commission of the European Communities (1992) *Treaty on European Union*, Brussels/Luxembourg, Office for Official Publications of the European Communities.

Davies, N. (1997) *Europe: a History*, London, Pimlico.

Deletant, D. (1995) *Ceauşescu and the Securitate: Coercion and Dissent in Romania, 1965–1989*, London, Hurst.

Drakulič, S. (2001) 'Who is afraid of Europe?', *East European Politics and Societies*, vol. 14, no. 2, pp. 1–9.

Fryer, P. (1984) *Staying Power: the History of Black People in Britain*, London/Sydney, Pluto.

Gabanyi, A. U. (2000) *The Ceauşescu Cult: Propaganda and Power Policy in Communist Romania*, Bucharest, Romanian Cultural Foundation.

Gerő, A. and Pető, I. (1997) *Befejezetlen Szocializmus: Képek a Kádár-Korszakból*, Budapest, Tegnap és Ma Kulturális Alapítvány.

Haslinger, P. (2001) 'Building a regional identity: the Burgenland, 1921–1938', *Austrian History Yearbook*, no. 32, pp. 105–23.

Herbert, U. and Hunn, K. (2001) 'Guest workers and policy on guest workers in the Federal Republic: from the beginning of recruitment in 1955 until its halt in 1973' in H. Schissler (ed.), *The Miracle Years: a Cultural History of West Germany, 1949–1968*, Princeton, NJ/Oxford, Princeton University Press.

Herzfeld, M. (1997) 'Theorizing Europe: persuasive paradoxes', *American Anthropologist*, vol. 99, no. 4, pp. 713–15.

Hitchens, C. (1990) 'On the road to Timişoara', *Granta*, no. 31, pp. 129–40.

Hitchins, K. (1974) *The Rumanian National Movement in Transylvania 1780–1849*, Cambridge, MA, Harvard University Press.

Keane, J. (1989) 'Identikit Europe', *Marxism Today*, vol. 33, no. 4, pp. 30–1.

Kürti, L. (2001) *The Remote Borderland: Transylvania in the Hungarian Imagination*, Albany, NY, State University of New York Press.

Lampe, J. R. (1996) *Yugoslavia as History: Twice There was a Country*, Cambridge/New York, Cambridge University Press.

Leyser, K. J. (1992) 'Concepts of Europe in the early and high Middle Ages', *Past and Present*, no. 137, pp. 25–47.

Litván, G., Bak, J. M., Békés, C., Kozák, G., and Rainer, J. M. (1996) *The Hungarian Revolution of 1956: Reform, Revolt and Repression 1953–1963*, London/New York, Longman.

Livezeanu, I. (1995) *Cultural Politics in Greater Romania: Regionalism, Nation Building and Ethnic Struggle*, Ithaca, NY/London, Cornell University Press.

Mageean, D. M. (1991) 'From Irish countryside to American city: the settlement and mobility of Ulster migrants in Philadelphia', in C. G. Pooley and I. D. Whyte (eds), *Migrants, Emigrants and Immigrants: a Social History of Migration* London/New York, Routledge.

Mitu, S. (2001) *National Identity of Romanians in Transylvania*, Budapest, Central European University Press.

Pan-European Picnic, website: http://sopron.hu/paneu-piknik/

Randsborg, K. (1992) 'Barbarians, classical antiquity and the rise of western Europe: an archaeological essay', *Past and Present*, no. 137, pp. 8–24.

Romsics, I. (1999) *Magyarország Története a XX. Században*, Budapest, Osiris.

Rowe, W. and Schelling V. (1991) *Memory and Modernity: Popular Culture in Latin America*, London/New York, Verso.

Sahlins, P. (1989) *Boundaries: the Making of France and Spain in the Pyrenees*, Berkeley, CA/Oxford, University of California Press.

Said, E. W. (1978) *Orientalism: Western Conceptions of the Orient*, Harmondsworth, Penguin.

Ugrešič, D. (1998) *The Culture of Lies: Antipolitical Essays*, transl. C. Hawkesworth, London, Phoenix.

Verdery, K. (1991) *National Identity under Socialism: Identity and Cultural Politics in Ceauşescu's Romania*, Berkeley, CA, University of California Press.

Wachtel, A. B. (1998) *Making a Nation, Breaking a Nation: Literature and Cultural Politics in Yugoslavia*, Stanford, CA, Stanford University Press.

Wilson, K. and Van Der Dussen, J. (eds) (1993) *The History of the Idea of Europe*, London/New York, Routledge.

Woolf, L. (1994) *Inventing Eastern Europe: the Map of Civilization on the Mind of the Enlightenment*, Stanford, CA, Stanford University Press.

Woolf, S. (1992) 'The construction of a European world-view in the revolutionary-Napoleonic years', *Past and Present*, no. 137, pp. 72–101.

Outside perspectives of Europe after the Second World War

SUMAN GUPTA

Introduction

This chapter addresses the issue of how Europe and Europeans have been perceived from outside Europe since the Second World War. In an obvious sense, Europe is a geographical land mass, a continent, attached to Asia; Europeans are those who happen to live within this area and are considered as belonging to it; and those cultures, social organizations and histories that pertain to the area should be thought of as European cultures, social organizations and histories. While keeping these self-evident definitions in mind, in this chapter I suggest that when addressed from outside the geographical domain of Europe, issues such as who are the European people, what are European cultures or societies or politics or histories, and what is the status of Europe in the world are not determined by geography alone. Such issues are also influenced by the prevailing concerns of non-European cultures and societies; by the different histories of cultural and political contact between European peoples and those from outside Europe; and by the various modes of exchange and transmission (through common languages and translations, education and the academic interchange of knowledge, the media and so on) that occur between societies both within and outside Europe.

It is crucial to ask who addresses these issues from outside Europe and why. It is important to be specific about whether similar questions are asked in India, China, Nigeria and so on, and to have some understanding of the situations and histories of those particular countries. It is undoubtedly useful to know why such questions may be asked, whether for academic purposes, for the sake of political and economic negotiations, or in the interests of cross-cultural understanding. In this chapter, however, I do not undertake a detailed exposition of all these specific questions or contexts. Instead I offer certain general observations that may help you to formulate your ideas in this area. I do this with the understanding that these observations should not be taken as truisms or formulae, but rather should be used to approach such questions and contexts in a coherent and organized fashion, and assumed or discarded as necessary.

Two sorts of general observations are presented here. The first are those of a theoretical nature about certain factors that often influence studies in this area, focusing on the cultivation of eurocentric perspectives inside and outside Europe, and on the implications of thinking about Europe (and indeed other social, political and cultural locations) in a synecdochical fashion. I explain in some detail below, in the part of this chapter entitled 'Theoretical issues', what exactly I mean by both eurocentric perspectives and synecdochical thinking. Secondly there are general observations of a historical character concerning the position of Europe in the world after the Second World War. These are presented in three sections (which together form the second part of this chapter, entitled 'Social, political and historical perspectives'), each emphasizing different historical viewpoints: Europe in the postcolonial world, Europe and the cold war, and European integration and globalization. These viewpoints are actually not wholly distinct, for the postcolonial world is also the world during and after the cold war, and both impinge on the current period of globalization. There is, however, a certain chronological justification for approaching these sections in this order: the study of European colonialism and its aftermath necessarily draws upon a long historical perspective of several centuries, while the cold war is now readily understood as beginning and ending within the twentieth century, and the phenomenon of globalization is generally associated with the end of the twentieth century and thereafter.

Theoretical issues

Eurocentrism

The idea underlying the term 'eurocentrism' is that European cultural, social and political attitudes are often unwarrantably thought of as universal or natural, and are inappropriately applied as such to, or accepted as such in, societies outside Europe.

The prevalence of eurocentrism within and outside Europe is primarily because different European countries have systematically exerted not only administrative and economic control but also intellectual control through a long history of imperial expansion and rule in the rest of the world. From the fifteenth to the late twentieth centuries European imperialism extended to Africa, the Americas, and a significant part of Asia and Australasia. The intellectual control that followed the imperial venture was exerted through the development of educational and administrative policies and academic pursuits which were designed to consolidate and justify European domination. Briefly, the idea was that if the colonized peoples of the world were encouraged to think as Europeans do and to believe what Europeans believe they would be more compliant to European rule. This was also presumed to have the additional benefit of persuading both colonizers and colonized of the natural superiority of Europe, since in the process it could be suggested that the thinking and beliefs of the colonized peoples were wanting. Arguably, such attempts at intellectual domination were so successful that even after decolonization former colonized societies and former colonizer societies have found it difficult to escape the grip of eurocentrism.

Eurocentrism may also be attributed to the patterns of migration from Europe that have taken place in the wake of imperial expansion. Thus the fact that significant majorities today in such economically successful countries as the United States, Canada, Australia and New Zealand locate their ancestry and heritage in Europe no doubt has a role to play in the perpetuation of eurocentrism.

Another key factor which contributes to eurocentrism is that, for complex cultural and historical reasons, modern forms of industrialization and the development of industrial capitalism occurred first in Europe. Indeed there is little doubt that imperial expansion from Europe since the eighteenth century was essentially driven by commercial and industrial capitalism, in the search for new markets and raw materials, and to satisfy the desires of an increasingly wealthy capitalist class through the import of new commodities. The economic success of industrial capitalism and its association with European cultures have persuaded many countries, even those with distant historical links to Europe, to 'westernize' themselves and install political systems and initiate social changes to facilitate the development of technologies and capitalist processes in a more or less European mould. A good example of this is provided by the moves towards economic modernization and industrialization in Japan starting from the **Meiji restoration** in 1868, and especially in the economic recovery and growth after the devastation of the Second World War. An interesting, though ideologically questionable, account of the manner in which different societies outside Europe accommodated industrial capitalism can be found in Francis Fukuyama's *Trust* (1995).

What eurocentrism may mean is best understood by the contemplation of some examples of writers and thinkers who have reflected on this. I shall now look at three of these, who have found

The point in Japanese history when the last Shogun or military dictator was overthrown in a short civil war and the Meiji Emperor, Matsuhito (1852–1912), was restored to symbolic importance. Thereafter efforts toward transforming Japan into an industrial state began.

themselves self-consciously drawn into eurocentric ways of thinking, some of whom have sought to interrogate and resist such ideas.

The Trinidadian writer V. S. Naipaul, who moved to the United Kingdom in 1950 and eventually settled there, was given a scholarship by the government of Trinidad and Tobago in 1960 to travel to and write about the Caribbean. The result was a controversial account of his experience of visiting Trinidad and other Caribbean countries entitled *The Middle Passage*, first published in 1962. In this Naipaul argues that Caribbean cultures are no more than cultures that unsuccessfully mimic those of the European countries which ruled them in the past. Though this might appear to be a condemnation of eurocentrism it is in fact a curiously eurocentric argument itself: Naipaul implicitly suggests that a successful mimicry would be as good an option for the Caribbean as an attempt to develop an independent culture, and he also paradoxically implies that European cultures are in some sense true cultures as opposed to Caribbean mimic cultures. Reflecting on this in a later novel, *The Enigma of Arrival*, Naipaul says:

> I knew and was glamoured by the idea of the metropolitan traveller, the man starting from Europe. It was the only kind of model I had; but – as a colonial among colonials who were very close to me – I could not be that kind of traveller, even though I might share that traveller's education and culture and have his feeling for adventure. Especially I was aware of not having a metropolitan audience to 'report back' to. The fight between my idea of the glamour of the traveller-writer and the rawness of my nerves as a colonial travelling among colonials made for difficult writing.

> (Naipaul, 1987, p. 140)

However, Naipaul's later attempts to negotiate this conflict of affiliations, mainly British and Trinidadian – of which *The Enigma of Arrival* is a good example – in the light of such awareness have not been successful either. These attempts often involve a search for distinct and hidden essential cultures lying behind the obvious mimic cultures in various contexts outside Europe, and resulted either in similar kinds of failure as described in *The Middle Passage* or in absurdly reductionist and politically worrying generalizations that continue to smack of eurocentrism.

The most influential consideration of eurocentrism, which continues to be debated, appears in Edward Said's *Orientalism* (1978). This is an examination of mainly academic studies in the fields of anthropology or ethnology, history, politics and sociology, which have been conducted by scholars in various institutions devoted to that purpose (in Europe and some former colonies, particularly since the eighteenth century) and which have had a profound effect on the manner in which European peoples approach and understand cultures outside Europe and vice versa. These are ostensibly studies of societies and peoples outside Europe – covering such diverse contexts as Egypt, China, India, Japan, and other Far Eastern and Middle Eastern cultures – conducted in an objective scientific spirit. Said argues that in fact the field of oriental studies is not what it seems to be. He feels it is absurd to lump together a range of complex and highly developed societies in this fashion, and that doing so says little about such cultures except that they are approached as being different from Europe – are, therefore, defined from a European perspective. He also maintains that such studies are actually used to perpetuate and justify the exploitative domination of Europe (and later the United States and other 'western' powers) over other societies by generating disadvantageous stereotypes of other peoples and cultures. To his mind, evidence of this is available not only in directly repressive colonial situations but also in a more subtle fashion in the economic and political relationships that develop in postcolonial situations. Said's reflections on this are guided to some extent by an essay by Abdel Malek entitled 'Orientalism in crisis' (1963), in which Malek observed:

> One sees how much, from the eighteenth to the twentieth century, the hegemonism of possessing minorities, unveiled by Marx and Engels, and the anthropocentrism dismantled by Freud are accompanied by europocentrism in the area of human and social sciences, and more particularly in those in direct relationship with non-European peoples.
>
> (Malek, 1963, p. 108; quoted in Said, 1978, p. 97)

Said concludes that the field of orientalism is not so much informative about the so-called orient as revealing of a European imperial psyche. These views have spawned a series of efforts to analyse eurocentrism and try to find non-eurocentric spaces; renewed interest in the nature of the relationship between Europe (or the 'west' broadly) and other societies; and given birth to an academic area which passes as 'postcolonial studies'. Numerous critiques of Said are now available, some defending certain aspects of orientalist studies and imperial intercultural encounters, and others elaborating and refining his arguments. Interesting among these are views such as those expressed by Aijaz Ahmad in his book *In Theory* (1992), where it is argued persuasively that much of 'postcolonial studies' is itself, despite the best of intentions, located in or conducted at the behest of 'western' institutions and manifest insidious eurocentrism.

My third example is a well-known essay written by the historian Dipesh Chakrabarty entitled 'Postcoloniality and the artifice of history', originally published in 1992. This asserts that

> Insofar as the academic discourse of history – that is, 'history' as a discourse produced at the institutional site of the university – is concerned, 'Europe' remains the dominant theoretical subject of all histories, including the ones we call 'Indian,' 'Chinese,' 'Kenyan,' and so on. There is a peculiar way in which all these other histories tend to become variations on a master narrative that could be called 'the history of Europe.'
>
> (Chakrabarty, 1997, pp. 263–4)

Chakrabarty goes on to cite the specific instance of Indian history as evidence of his argument: the very construction of an Indian people is a eurocentric idea given the diversity of peoples and histories in the Indian sub-continent; such a construction is more than a little artificial and is inspired by ideas about history which pertain to Europe. His essay appeared in the context of efforts made by a group of historians to rewrite the history of colonial India and the Indian nationalist movement (which they felt was dominated by historians who subscribed to ideas of history rooted in Europe) not as something guided from above by administrators and political leaders and intellectuals, but as a series of spontaneous movements and ripples and responses *within* peoples of different parts of India. These efforts were published between 1986 and 1995 in a series of six volumes entitled *Subaltern Studies*, edited by Ranajit Guha, to which Chakrabarty was a frequent contributor. The term 'subaltern' here derives from the reflections of the Italian political theorist Antonio Gramsci (1891–1937) in his *Prison Notebooks*. Gramsci thought of marginalized social groups of working peoples as subaltern classes and outlined certain principles for writing a history of such classes in the context of the Italian *Risorgimento* (Gramsci, 1971, pp. 52–5).

Risorgimento: The Italian term for 'resurgence' which is used to designate the 19th century movement through which Italy achieved unity as a single state under Victor Emmanuel II (1820–78)

These examples give a sense of the content and scope of eurocentrism, as well as of efforts to resist eurocentric positions. I do not think the ideas underlying these examples need to be summarized: a careful consideration of them should render the basic ideas self-evident. To organize your thoughts on this have a look at the first reading, an essay entitled 'Jasmine' by V. S. Naipaul, first published in 1964. It is essentially a complaint about what Naipaul understands as being his disadvantages as a Trinidadian writer (rather than a scholar of English literature).

One day about ten years ago, when I was editing a weekly literary programme for the BBC's Caribbean Service, a man from Trinidad came to see me in one of the freelances' rooms in the old Langham Hotel. He sat on the edge of the table, slapped down some sheets of typescript and said, 'My name is Smith. I write about sex. I am also a nationalist.' The sex was tepid, Maugham and coconut-water; but the nationalism was aggressive. Women swayed like coconut trees; their skins were the colour of the sapodilla, the inside of their mouths the colour of a cut star-apple; their teeth were as white as coconut kernels; and when they made love they groaned like bamboos in high wind.

The writer was protesting against what the English language had imposed on us. The language was ours, to use as we pleased. The literature that came with it was therefore of peculiar authority; but this literature was like an alien mythology. There was, for instance, Wordsworth's notorious poem about the daffodil. A pretty little flower, no doubt; but we had never seen it. Could the poem have any meaning for us? The superficial prompting of this argument, which would have confined all literatures to the countries of their origin, was political; but it was really an expression of dissatisfaction at the emptiness of our own formless, unmade society. To us, without a mythology, all literatures were foreign. Trinidad was small, remote and unimportant, and we knew we could not hope to read in books of the life we saw about us. Books came from afar; they could offer only fantasy.

To open a book was to make an instant adjustment. Like the medieval sculptor of the North interpreting the Old Testament stories in terms of the life he knew, I needed to be able to adapt. All Dickens's descriptions of London I rejected; and though I might retain Mr Micawber and the others in the clothes the illustrator gave them, I gave them the faces and voices of people I knew and set them in buildings and streets I knew. The process of adaptation was automatic and continuous. Dickens's rain and drizzle I turned into tropical downpours; the snow and fog I accepted as conventions of books. Anything – like an illustration – which embarrassed me by proving how weird my own recreation was, anything which sought to remove the characters from the make-up world in which I set them, I rejected.

I went to books for fantasy; at the same time I required reality. The gypsies of *The Mill on the Floss* were a fabrication and a disappointment, discrediting so much that was real: to me gypsies were mythical creatures who belonged to the pure fantasy of Hans Christian Andersen and *The Heroes*. Disappointing, too, was the episode of the old soldier's sword, because I thought that swords belonged to ancient times; and the Tom Tulliver I had created walked down the street where I lived. The early parts of *The Mill on the Floss*, then; chapters of *Oliver Twist, Nicholas Nickleby, David Copperfield*; some of the novels of H. G. Wells; a short story by Conrad called 'The Lagoon': all these which in the beginning I read or had read to me I set in Trinidad, accepting, rejecting, adapting, and peopling in my own way. I never read to find out about foreign countries. Everything in books was foreign; everything had to be subjected to adaptation; and everything in, say, an English novel which worked and was of value to me at once ceased to be specifically English. Mr Murdstone worked; Mr Pickwick and his club didn't. *Jane Eyre* and *Wuthering Heights* worked; *Pride and Prejudice* didn't. Maupassant worked; Balzac didn't.

I went to books for a special sort of participation. The only social division I accepted was that between rich and poor, and any society more elaborately ordered seemed insubstantial and alien. In literature such a society was more than alien; it was excluding, it made nonsense of my fantasies and more and more, as I grew older and thought of writing myself, it made me despairingly conscious of the poverty and haphazardness of my own society. I might adapt Dickens to Trinidad; but it seemed impossible that the life I knew in Trinidad could ever be turned into a book. If landscapes do not start to be real until they have been interpreted by an artist, so, until they have been written about, societies appear to be without shape and *embarrassing*. It was embarrassing to be reminded by a Dickens illustration of the absurdity of my adaptations; it was equally embarrassing to attempt to write of what I saw. Very little of what I read was of help. It would have been possible to assume the sensibility of a particular writer. But no writer, however individual his vision, could be separated from his society. The vision was alien; it diminished my own and did not give me the courage to do a simple thing like mentioning the name of a Port of Spain street.

Fiction or any work of the imagination, whatever its quality, hallows its subject. To attempt, with a full consciousness of established authoritative mythologies, to give a quality of myth to what was agreed to be petty and ridiculous – Frederick Street in Port of Spain, Marine Square, the districts of Laventille and Barataria – to attempt to use these names required courage. It was, in a way, the rejection of the familiar, meaningless word – the rejection of the unknown daffodil to put it no higher – and was as self-conscious as the attempt to have sapodilla-skinned women groaning like bamboos in high wind.

With all English literature accessible, then, my position was like that of the maharaja in *Hindoo Holiday*, who, when told by the Christian lady that God was here, there and everywhere, replied, 'But what use is that to *me*?' Something of more pertinent virtue was needed, and this was provided by some local short stories. These stories, perhaps a dozen in all, never published outside Trinidad, converted what I saw into 'writing'. It was through them that I began to appreciate the distorting, distilling power of the writer's art. Where I had seen a drab haphazardness they found order; where I would have attempted to romanticize, to render my subject equal with what I had read, they accepted. They provided a starting-point for further observation; they did not trigger off fantasy. Every writer is, in the long run, on his own; but it helps, in the most practical way, to have a tradition. The English language was mine; the tradition was not.

Literature, then, was mainly fantasy. Perhaps it was for this reason that, although I had at an early age decided to be a writer and at the age of eighteen had left Trinidad with that ambition, I did not start writing seriously until I was nearly twenty-three. My material had not been sufficiently hallowed by a tradition; I was not fully convinced of its importance; and some embarrassment remained. My taste for literature had developed into a love of language, the word in isolation. At school my subjects were French and Spanish; and the pleasures of the language were at least as great as those of the literature. Maupassant and Molière were rich; but it was more agreeable to spend an hour with the big Harrap French-English dictionary, learning more of the language through examples, than with Corneille or Racine. And it was because I thought I had had enough of these languages (both now grown rusty) that when I came to England to go to university I decided to read English.

This was a mistake. The English course had little to do with literature. It was a 'discipline' seemingly aimed at juvenile antiquarians. It by-passed the novel and the prose 'asides' in which so much of the richness of the literature lay. By a common and curious consent it concentrated on poetry; and since it stopped at the eighteenth century it degenerated, after an intensive study of Shakespeare, into a lightning survey of minor and often severely local talents. I had looked forward to wandering among large tracts of writing; I was presented with 'texts'. The metaphysicals were a perfect subject for study, a perfect part of a discipline; but, really, they had no value for me. Dryden, for all the sweet facility of his prose, was shallow and dishonest; did his 'criticism' deserve such reverential attention? *Gulliver's Travels* was excellent; but could *The Tale of a Tub* and *The Battle of the Books* be endured?

The fact was, I had no taste for scholarship, for tracing the growth of schools and trends. I sought continuously to relate literature to life. My training at school didn't help. We had few libraries, few histories of literature to turn to; and when we wrote essays on *Tartuffe* we wrote out of a direct response to the play. Now I discovered that the study of literature had been made scientific, that each writer had to be approached through the booby-traps of scholarship. There were the bound volumes of the Publications of the Modern Language Association of America, affectionately referred to by old and knowing young as PMLA. The pages that told of Chaucer's knowledge of astronomy or astrology (the question came up every year) were black and bloated and furred with handling, and even some of the pencilled annotations (*No, Norah!*) had grown faint. I developed a physical distaste for these bound volumes and the libraries that housed them.

Delight cannot be taught and measured; scholarship can; and my reaction was irrational. But it seemed to me scholarship of such a potted order. A literature was not being explored; it had been codified and reduced to a few pages of 'text', some volumes of 'background' and more of 'criticism'; and to this mixture a mathematical intelligence might have been applied. There were discoveries, of course: Shakespeare, Marlowe, Restoration comedy. But my distaste for the study of literature led to a sense of being more removed than ever from the literature itself.

The language remained mine, and it was to the study of its development that I turned with pleasure. Here was enough to satisfy my love of language; here was unexpected adventure. It might not have been easy to see Chaucer as a great imaginative writer or to find in the *Prologue* more than a limited piece of observation which had been exceeded a thousand times; but Chaucer as a handler of a new, developing language was exciting. And my pleasure in Shakespeare was doubled. In Trinidad English writing had been for me a starting-point for fantasy. Now, after some time in England, it was possible to isolate the word, to separate the literature from the language.

Language can be so deceptive. It has taken me much time to realize how bad I am at interpreting the conventions and modes of English speech. This speech has never been better dissected than in the early stories of Angus Wilson. This is the judgment of today;

my first responses to these stories were as blundering and imperfect as the responses of Professor Pforzheim to the stern courtesies of his English colleagues in *Anglo-Saxon Attitudes*. But while knowledge of England has made English writing more truly accessible, it has made participation more difficult; it has made impossible the exercise of fantasy, the reader's complementary response. I am inspecting an alien society, which I yet know, and I am looking for particular social comment. And to re-read now the books which lent themselves to fantastic interpretation in Trinidad is to see, almost with dismay, how English they are. The illustrations to Dickens cannot now be dismissed. And so, with knowledge, the books have ceased to be mine.

It is the English literacy vice, this looking for social comment; and it is difficult to resist. The preoccupation of the novelists reflects a society ruled by convention and manners in the fullest sense, an ordered society of the self-aware who read not so much for adventure as to compare, to find what they know or think they know. A writer is to be judged by what he reports on; the working-class writer is a working-class writer and no more. So writing develops into the private language of a particular society. There are new reports, new discoveries: they are rapidly absorbed. And with each discovery the society's image of itself becomes more fixed and the society looks further inward. It has too many points of reference; it has been written about too often; it has read too much. Angus Wilson's characters, for instance, are great readers; they are steeped in Dickens and Jane Austen. Soon there will be characters steeped in Angus Wilson; the process is endless. Sensibility will overlay sensibility: the grossness of experience will be refined away by self-awareness. Writing will become Arthur Miller's definition of a newspaper: a nation talking to itself. And even those who have the key will be able only to witness, not to participate.

All literatures are regional; perhaps it is only the placelessness of a Shakespeare or the blunt communication of 'gross' experience as in Dickens that makes them appear less so. Or perhaps it is a lack of knowledge in the reader. Even in this period of 'internationalism' in letters we have seen literatures turning more and more inward, developing languages that are more and more private. Perhaps in the end literature will write itself out, and all its pleasures will be those of the word.

A little over three years ago I was in British Guiana. I was taken late one afternoon to meet an elderly lady of a distinguished Christian Indian family. Our political attitudes were too opposed to make any discussion of the current crisis profitable. We talked of the objects in her veranda and of the old days. Suddenly the tropical daylight was gone, and from the garden came the scent of a flower. I knew the flower from my childhood; yet I had never found out its name. I asked now.

'We call it jasmine.'

Jasmine! So I had known it all those years! To me it had been a word in a book, a word to play with, something removed from the dull vegetation I knew.

The old lady cut a sprig for me. I stuck it in the top buttonhole of my open shirt. I smelled it as I walked back to the hotel. Jasmine, jasmine. But the word and the flower had been separate in my mind for too long. They did not come together.

(Naipaul [1964] (1972), pp. 23–9)

EXERCISE

1 What exactly are the disadvantages that Naipaul complains about and how does this relate to the issue of eurocentrism?

2 Do you think Naipaul feels he has been able to overcome these disadvantages?

DISCUSSION

1 Like most Trinidadians Naipaul feels that the English language is his language. A complex series of population extinctions, transplantations and migrations in the course of Trinidad's colonial history has left it with English as a national language and the language of common usage. Naipaul accepts the language but, as an aspiring Trinidadian writer, feels that it imposes a literary sensibility, normalizes a literary idiom and naturalizes a literary history which are in fact extrinsic to Trinidad – which, for the Trinidadian, are rather uncomfortably located within Britain, or within Europe. This seems to the aspiring writer a serious dislocation, such that he constantly feels that 'it seemed impossible that the life I knew in Trinidad could ever be turned into a book'. Because of the very inheritance of the English language and the literary baggage that comes with it the Trinidadian feels the exclusion of his life and environment, of himself, from literary expression – and colludes, so to say, in a curious self-negation. Such exclusion and self-negation were instilled from childhood, when every act of reading had to be

conducted through a series of translations of images, and were only confirmed and clarified with further study and maturity, when the regional quality of English literature and its distance from Trinidad were fully revealed. The manner in which what is acceptable as English literary expression is dictated from within a European context even in a distant and quite different context like Trinidad, and the sense of self-negation and exclusion this creates in that country, is precisely what is understood as the prevalence of eurocentrism. This is neatly summarized by Naipaul in the central flower images: in Trinidad the daffodil of Wordsworthian fame (a flower that doesn't grow there) is much more familiar and vividly envisaged than the indigenous jasmine, which seems remote and exotic.

2   The last sentences of the essay suggest that as a writer Naipaul feels unable to overcome this prevailing eurocentric attitude: 'But the word and the flower had been separate in my mind for too long. They did not come together.' However, the essay is not entirely pessimistic. Just like the Trinidadian writer who is (rather sarcastically) mentioned in the first paragraph, Naipaul himself feels that an understanding of prevailing eurocentric attitudes and an attempt to come to grips with the Trinidadian context in their literary efforts would eventually (if not immediately) bring about an authentic Trinidadian literature in English: 'a nation talking to itself'. That Naipaul says he continues seriously to write himself is proof of this. It is also noteworthy that Naipaul finds at least some timeless and placeless elements in the English literary works of Shakespeare and Dickens.

The prevalence of eurocentrism inside and outside Europe and an awareness of this may have the following effects on perceptions of Europe from outside. First, societies which have been, and perhaps still are, subject to economic, political and cultural domination from Europe (especially former colonies), or those which have populations that locate their heritage in Europe, are likely to look to it for models of their social and political institutions. At a deeper level there might also be manifested a need to find recognition and validation from Europe in cultural and intellectual matters. Secondly, an awareness of prevailing eurocentrism both within themselves and in Europe is likely to raise a strong desire to resist it in such contexts. This might take several forms:

• a certain sensitivity to manifestations of eurocentrism, including possibly reading positions which are not in fact eurocentric as if they are;

- an often self-defeating determination to define themselves as different from Europe (self-defeating in that to *define against* is still to *define in terms of*);

- a particular hostility to Europe, expressed as grievance at its historical imperial role and the hypothetical lost possibilities in their own histories;

- an especial competitiveness with Europe in economic and international affairs.

Thirdly, the prevalence of eurocentrism might also mean that societies which have come to be dominant economic and military powers, or are in the process of becoming so, and have superseded the influence of Europe in world affairs, would still be happy to align themselves with and extend their patronage to Europe.

A warning: there is an all-too-often evident possibility that the association of eurocentrism with certain ideas may lead to the wholesale rejection of those ideas themselves. Thus it is possible that the appropriation of political and philosophical rationalism by certain European thinkers as something that is peculiarly European, and the association of rationalism with the European Enlightenment (examined most influentially in Adorno and Horkheimer, 1972), can lead to the rejection of political and philosophical rationalism (for example, in favour of traditional or religious social mores) by those who seek to resist eurocentrism. This would, it seems to me, be a grave mistake – there is no reason to consider political and philosophical rationalism to be Europe-specific, and plenty of evidence of long traditions of such rationalism in Asian and other societies is available. Similarly, such ideas as political freedom, the need for women's emancipation and the undesirability of communal or racial or religious discrimination are also not especially located in Europe or the 'west', or necessarily entail eurocentrism. There are sufficient grounds for considering these to be matters of universal import, and enough evidence that this is recognized in societies almost everywhere in the world. *It is vitally important to be very clear and precise about where evidence of eurocentrism is discerned and in what manner it appears.*

With these caveats I conclude these initial observations on eurocentrism, and move on to another area of theoretical interest in this context – the prevalence of synecdochical contructions of Europe (and other social, political and cultural locations). The links between these two areas will become evident, particularly in the second part of this chapter, 'Social, political and historical perspectives'.

Synecdochical views

A synecdoche is a figure of speech in which a part of something is used to represent the whole of that thing, or vice versa. Synecdoches are common in the use of continent names to designate social, cultural or political matters, or specific peoples and countries. For instance, one is accustomed to hearing about 'events in Africa' or 'events in Asia' when what is actually meant is 'events in a few specific regions and relevant to certain social groups in Africa or Asia'; in Britain groups of Indian, Pakistani and Bangladeshi people pass as 'Asians' (the Chinese and Japanese are even more absurdly thought of as 'oriental'); and so on. Similar synecdochical usage is common with regard to the terms 'Europe' and 'European' both inside and outside the continent. Such usage is usually a matter of convenience (it is more economical to say 'a group of Europeans' rather than, for example, 'a group of people from France, Germany, Norway and Spain'); but these apparently innocent synecdochical terms may also sometimes contain implicit – perhaps unconscious – political and social attitudes. In so far as this attaches to the use of 'Europe' and 'European', especially when this occurs from outside Europe, this is a matter of some interest in this chapter.

The politics of synecdochical usage arises from two sorts of false inferences that can be drawn. First, using synecdoche may lead to reductionist and inappropriate generalizations or stereotypifications. For example, if a particular instance of genocide by a certain group of people in a specific region of Europe is alluded to as a 'European phenomenon' one may, quite mistakenly but not irrationally, infer that all of Europe and all Europeans are culpable. Or if the cultural customs of a particular tribal group in the south of the continent of Africa are described as revealing something about 'African culture or the African psyche', one might erroneously credit all of Africa and all Africans with those cultural forms.

Secondly, it may also lead to simplistic polarizations. For example, if one talks of 'European rationalism' (the synecdoche of using certain instances of rationalistic thinking in particular quarters inside the continent of Europe as representing rational thinking *per se*) it might seem quite possible that its meaningless opposite, 'non-European irrationalism', is in fact meaningful.

The use of synecdoches is so convenient and so unconsciously a part of all languages, and the incidence of politically and culturally effective misconceptions arising from them is so frequent, that only the most careful examination of such usage reveals its implications. This cannot be emphasized enough: *it is crucial that appropriate distinctions be made as to where a synecdochical usage is merely a harmless matter of convenience, and where such usage gives rise to undesirable and irrational social and political misconceptions.*

The terms Europe and European have been and continue to be used in a synecdochical fashion, and often with misleading social and political effect, *within* Europe. What sort of image comes to mind when one hears the phrase 'European person'? *The Times Guide to the Peoples of Europe* (Fernández-Armesto, 1997) provides some information about 115 'historic communities' (including Magyars, Gypsies and Jews, but excluding such recent arrivals in Europe as people of African or Asian descent) – to how many of these does that amalgamated image of the 'European person' attach? Such a person is most likely to be imagined as white or Caucasian, Christian, with a variety of social and cultural attitudes which vaguely pertain to western Europe. This synecdochical image of the 'European' is not an accident: it has been gradually constructed since roughly the seventeenth century by certain dominant groups within the continent in keeping with their interests.

Behind this image lies a long tradition of understanding 'European history' as the history of certain dominant countries and social groups. It involved a fierce effort (in which the work of such eminent scholars as the French philologist and historian Ernest Renan (1823–92), the German psychiatrist Richard Krafft-Ebing (1840–1902), and the Italian physician and criminologist Cesare Lombroso (1836–1909) was implicated) in the nineteenth century to chart racial types and identities for Europeans and others. It continues to involve a significant academic strain of thinking that equates certain kinds of freedoms, rational philosophies and economic processes which pertain to a few parts of Europe as wholly 'European', as well as the habit of thinking of 'European colonialism' when what is actually referred to is the imperial initiative of a handful of dominant countries from the European continent (and often imposed on weaker countries within that continent). This image is also coherent with current observations such as that the European Union and European Monetary Union do not include several countries within the continent of Europe; that representatives of 'Europe' in influential alliances like the G8 and Nato in fact represent only a part of Europe; that emigration policies which seem to link Europe together are markedly nervous about such perpetual outsiders inside Europe as Gypsies; that there is an air of embarrassment in the media about acknowledging the unrest in the Balkan states as happening inside the continent of Europe.

To a large extent the synecdochical usage of terms like Europe or European that are available inside the continent of Europe has developed because it allows certain countries and social groups to assert political and cultural dominance *within* the continent. Furthermore, to some extent these views are also the product of the desire of such dominant groups and countries to differentiate themselves clearly (to play on the potential for polarization in synecdochical usage) from peoples *outside* the continent whom they hoped to dominate. To that extent synecdochical views complement eurocentrism. Polarization in this usage is particularly evident in racial stereotyping – in, for example, the juxtaposition of European 'whiteness' with African 'blackness', Asian 'darkness' or oriental 'yellowness'. There are several levels of synecdochical usage and polarization here: the synecdoche of using skin colour to represent the whole racial group; of using the whole racial group to represent the whole continent; of using colour by association with certain moral qualities (in most major European languages 'whiteness', 'blackness', 'darkness', 'yellowness' are suggestive of certain moral qualities). The polarization suggested by such synecdochical juxtapositions are clearly favourable to those who can unambiguously declare themselves to be 'European' in this fashion.

It is easily understandable that from outside Europe such synecdochical usage of the terms Europe or European may be exaggerated in certain ways and acquire different connotations. I shall demonstrate how this may occur by providing some more examples, beginning with an exercise, which involves reading the two poems below.

The first is by the Jamaica-born American poet Louis Simpson and the second is by South African poet Mazisi Kunene. Louis Simpson was a war hero and followed a successful academic career; in general much of his poetry builds a vision of American culture in terms of continuities from and reflections of European cultures. Mazisi Kunene has also had a successful academic career and has played a significant political role in South Africa (as director of education for the South African United Front, and later director of finance for the African National Congress); he has a particular interest in Zulu oral and written traditions, and his poetry is written first in Zulu and then translated.

To the Western World

A siren sang, and Europe turned away	1
From the high castle and the shepherd's crook.	
Three caravels went sailing to Cathay	3
On the strange ocean, and the captains shook	
Their banners out across the Mexique Bay.	5

And in our early days we did the same.
Remembering our fathers in their wreck   7
We crossed the sea from Palos where they came
And saw, enormous to the little deck,   9

A shore in silence waiting for a name.
The treasures of Cathay were never found.   11
In this America, this wilderness
Where the axe echoes with a lonely sound,   13
The generations labour to possess
And grave by grave we civilize the ground.   15

(Simpson [1957] (1972), p. 117)

Europe

Europe, your foundations
Are laid on a rough stone.
Your heart is like cobwebs
That are dry in the desert.

Your children fill us with fear:
They are like the young of a puff adder
Who devour the flesh of their parent.

Once I believed the tales.
Once I believed you had breasts
Over-flowing with milk.

I saw you rushing with books
From which the oracles derive their prophecies.
I heard you in the forest
Crying like wolves,
Breaking the bones of your clans.

I know the hardness of your visions:
You closed the doors
And chose the bridegroom of steel.

You chose her not to love
But because she alone remained
Dedicated to silence.

From her you made your prophecies
And summoned the oracles:
You laughed at the blind men
YBut you yourself were blind,
YStruggling in this great night.

Children have inherited the fire
YThey blow its flames to the skies
YBurning others in their sleep.

What will the sun say?
YThe sun will laugh
YBecause it burnt out cradles from age to age.

(Kunene [1970] (1975), pp. 20–1)

EXERCISE

With particular reference to the manner in which Europe is
personified, and the manner in which the poets locate themselves
apropos these personifications, discuss the kind of synecdochical
connotations that are given to Europe in these two poems.

DISCUSSION

The first stanza of Simpson's poem refers to the early history of the
'discovery' of America by Spanish and Portuguese sailors, from 1492
onwards (though it could just as well apply to the earlier and equally
accidental landing in America described in the **Vinland Sagas**), who
were in search of a sea route to east Asia. These early landings and
explorations did not lead to immediate colonial settlement but
symbolic conquests and failed searches for mythical riches (such as
the **El Dorado** explorations by the Spaniard Gonzalo Jiménez de
Quesada (1509–79) and England's Francis Drake (1540–96)) – hence
'Europe turned away'. This initial experience is compared to
Odysseus's (in Homer's *Odyssey*) careful measures against the sirens:
Odysseus had himself tied to a mast and had his sailors seal their ears
so that they might sail by the sirens without being lured by their song.
In the personification of 'Europe' Simpson does two things: he
synecdochically generalizes the explorers who came from specific
countries as being representative of all Europe; and by evoking the
Greek myth he makes this synecdochically personified 'Europe'
representative of an ancient, established and common 'European'
culture. The second and third stanzas of the poem describe the
colonial settlement of America by migrants from Europe – the

The Vinland Sagas are the
story of the Icelandic
landing in North America
around 1000 ce, told in
two different versions, the
Grœnlendinga saga and
Eiríks saga rauai.

El Dorado was the mythical
city built of gold believed to
exist in South America.

pioneers – who have attempted (and still do) to 'possess' and 'civilize the ground'. These stanzas are characterized by two significant features. First, the poet and his compatriots (the 'we' of 'we did the same') draw their ancestry from the synecdochical Europe of the first stanza (they are like 'our fathers'). Secondly, at the same time the poet contrasts the already civilized Europe and the still uncivilized America from within which he speaks: this establishes the distance from which the synecdochically constructed Europe is seen as the well of civilization from where the civilizing efforts of the settlers have derived.

In Kunene's poem 'Europe' is straightforwardly personified as the addressee, to whom the poet speaks. In contrast to Simpson's poem the distance of the African location from which Kunene addresses the personified Europe is not underlaid by any sense of continuity with Europe. Instead of the consistent 'we' of Simpson's poem, in Kunene's poem the clear 'you' that is Europe is set against the 'I' and 'us' who are not of Europe: Europe is the 'other' of the 'us' and 'I' who speak. The personified Europe is also distanced because its heritage is subtly disowned; the whole idiom of the poem is Zulu. The images derive from an environment and culture that are distinctly Zulu, attuned to the South African landscape and drawing upon proverbial wisdom. Indeed Kunene deliberately dissociates himself from any European influence, distancing himself from any conviction that 'you had breasts/Over-flowing with milk', and declaring that 'You laughed at the blind men/But you yourself were blind'. From this carefully imposed distance the personified 'Europe' can no longer be thought of as a complex and variegated social-cultural formation, but appears as a synecdochically homogeneous symbol of misdirected knowledge (with hardened 'visions' which consort with the 'bridegroom of steel') and destructive conflict ('Burning others in their sleep'). All Europe becomes synecdochically culpable in this distanced personification.

There are two points worth noting here. The first is that from a distance it becomes easier to see Europe in a more or less simplistic synecdochical fashion as a concrete representative part of some phenomenon or idea that is larger than itself (the synecdochical usage sits more easily in these because of the sense of perspective that the poets' locations outside Europe provide). The second is that both the perspectives so created are quite different from those available within the continent of Europe. In some sense Europe is seen from the perspective of the 'other', or Europe becomes the 'other' of the 'other'.

Decolonization and postcolonial migration have created new kinds of European identities and have reshaped perceptions of Europe's fluid borders. The images on these pages were taken by photographer Anaïk Frantz on a journey through the Paris suburbs accompanying writer François Maspero in 1989. They document the multicultural nature of the Paris suburb of Aubervilliers during the late twentieth century.

Figure 2.1 Aubervilliers. The hostel in rue Herault by Anaïk Frantz. Photo: Editions du Seuil

Figure 2.2 Aubervilliers. La Maladrerie I by Anaïk Frantz. Photo: Editions du Seuil

Representing Europe's border(land)s: maps, borders and identities

MARK PITTAWAY

Maps reflect choices made by their creators and are therefore very much cultural artefacts that reveal something of the identity of the map-maker. Maps, particularly political maps, can also have important legitimizing functions. They can be used to state and legitimize claims to territory and thus mark boundaries. With the rise of the territorial state the political map may acquire a particular political role too. It can also show who belongs and who is excluded. This map, which will be discussed in more depth later, was produced in Dublin in 1808 and depicts Europe. The territories it delimits were not those that actually existed in Europe at the time it was produced. It shows 'Europe' as a defined entity with clear political boundaries. This visual essay shows how maps may not only legitimize particular conceptions of borders; they have also proved extremely powerful in describing the characteristics of those regions which have been defined as 'borderlands'. In order to do this the essay considers two interlinked case studies; that of the definition of the eastern border of Europe and the description of 'the Balkans' – probably Europe's most contested 'borderland'.

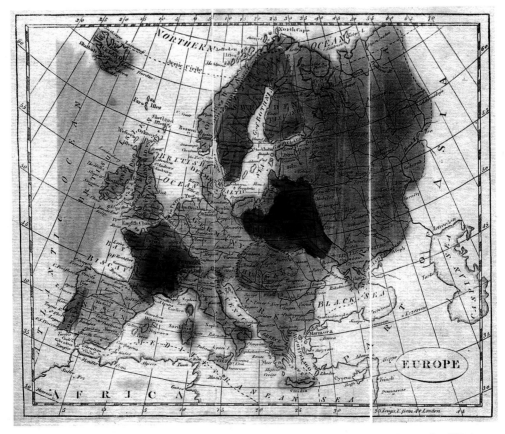

Map 1 *Europe 1808*, from R. Brookes, *The General Gazetteer; or, Compendious Geographical Dictionary*, revised W. Guthrie and E. Jones, 8th edn., Dublin, 1808. Image: University of Texas at Austin Libraries.

Our modern cartographic image of Europe dates back to the sixteenth century, the result of cartographers' responses to the growing demand among merchants for accurate maps to aid their pursuit of trade. The Flemish cartographer Gerardus Mercator (1512–94) provided the first 'modern' cartographic representation of Europe in 1554. The one displayed here, from 1569, is essentially similar. This representation marked a real break from medieval maps of Europe.

The map is not a political map, for the boundaries of territories can scarcely be discerned, though this may reflect the essential fluidity of boundaries in early modern Europe. If the border of Europe is defined at all it is implied by the right-hand edge of the map. This eastern border is further east than the one that appears on later maps; the geographical centre of Mercator's Europe, as shown here, lies in the western regions of modern-day Ukraine.

Map 2 G. Mercator, *Europa 1569*.
Image: Walking Tree Press.

As this map shows, others were thinking of Europe as a discrete territory with a definite eastern border. This 1570 map forms part of the pioneering atlas *Theatrum orbis terrarvm* produced by Mercator's contemporary and fellow Flemish cartographer Abraham Ortelius (1527–98). Europe is much more clearly demarcated from Asia on this map; neither modern-day Turkey nor much of Russia is seen as part of Europe.

Map 3 *Europa*, from A. Ortelius, *Theatrum orbis terrarvm*, 1570 edn. Image: Library of Congress, Washington, DC.

This map, also from Ortelius's *Theatrum orbis terrarvm*, depicts Russia in the late sixteenth century. It demonstrates that western European views of Russia as, at best, only ambiguously European stretch back to the early modern period. Russia here is depicted as a borderland between a civilized and settled Europe and a wilder Asia. This map seems, however, to depict the eastern border of Europe as much more fluid and ambiguous than Ortelius's map of Europe as a whole.

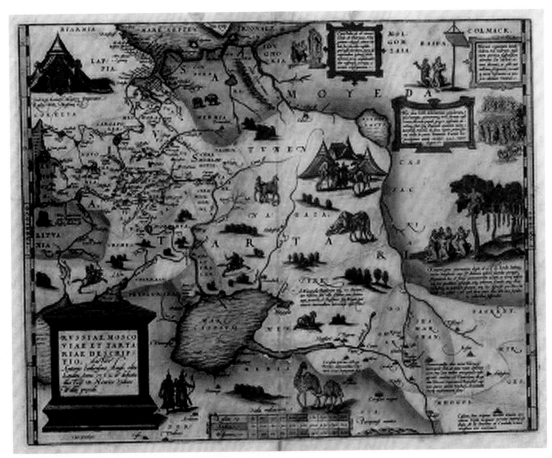

Map 4 *Rvssia aut potius magni dvcis Moscoviae imperivm*, from A. Ortelius, *Theatrum orbis terrarvm*, 1570 edn. Image: Library of Congress, Washington, DC.

If Ortelius explored one of Europe's eastern borderlands – Russia – when producing *Theatrum orbis terrarvm*, he neglected the other region that would become defined as one of Europe's borderlands in the modern era – southeastern Europe. Notions of southeastern Europe's problematic relationship to the rest of Europe were to emerge later.

Southeastern Europe had entirely different meanings for sixteenth- and seventeenth-century European map-makers from those that it has today. The Balkan peninsula, when represented at all, was depicted as the site of ancient Greece. Cartographic representations such as this one – which combines the depiction of both contemporary and ancient sites – reflect this.

Map 5 G. Mercator, *Macedonia Epirvis et Achaia*, special edn. of 'Asia Minor', Duisburg, 1628. Image: British Library.

Some maps of southeastern Europe were explicitly historical, as for example this seventeenth-century Dutch map which depicts the Macedonia of Alexander the Great (356–323 BCE).

Map 6 L. Laurenberg, *Macedonia Alexandri Magni Patria Illustris*, Amsterdam, 1647. Image: British Library.

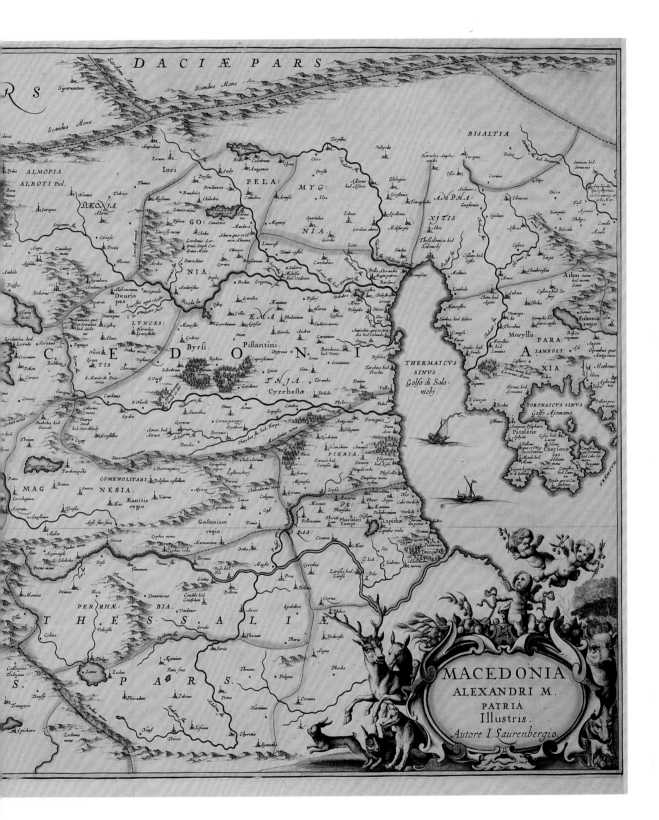

For much of the early modern period, from the beginning of the sixteenth century until the end of the seventeenth century, the Ottoman empire was the dominant power in what we now know as southeastern Europe. They ruled the whole of the Balkan peninsula. This was significant in that a large part of what was commonly recognized as part of 'Europe' had fallen under the rule of a non-European power. These territories included many of the sites of classical Greece, which had been carefully documented by western European map-makers throughout the sixteenth and seventeenth centuries.

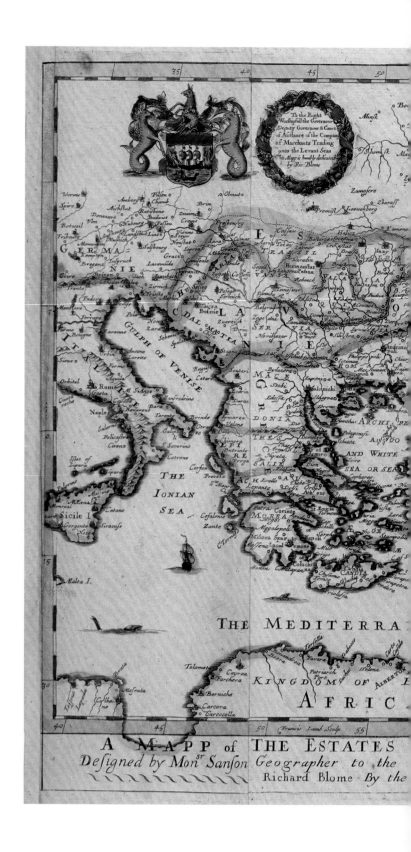

Map 7 R. Blome, *A Map of the Estates of the Turkish Empire in Asia and Europe*, London, 1669. Image: Walker Collection, University of Melbourne.

PART

OF GREAT

TARTARIE

MOSCOVIA

PETITE TARTARIE

ASTRACAN

COMANIE

CIRCAS

ZUI RI SES

THE SEA OF

BACU OR OF SALA

OF TABARESTAN

OF GILAN &c

OR THE CASPIAN

SEA

THE BLACK SEA

otherwise called

PONTUS   EUXINUS

MINGRELIE

GEOR GRE LIE

GISGEORGIA

GUR OR G

DERBENT als
BAB ALABUAB

ANATOLIE

AMASIE

TURCOMANS

TURCO

VAN

THE

EMPIRE

PERSIA

DIAR

CARAEMIT

BEK

SORIE

ORA

PHOENICE
ISTAN

BERIARA

ARABIE

DESERT

IUDEA

ARABIA
the
STONI

EGYPT   Red Sea

ALEXANDRIA

AN SEA

CAIRO

the TURKISH EMPIRE in ASIA, and EUROPE
nch King, and Rendered into English, and Illustrated with Figures By
Especiall Command,   Printed for Richard Blome. Anno 1669

By the end of the seventeenth century, as this French map of 1696 shows, southeastern Europe was increasingly defined by the fact of Turkish rule. Western European interest in the political governance of southeastern Europe was undoubtedly fuelled by the rolling back of Turkish power in central Europe with the breaking of the second Siege of Vienna (1683) and the Turkish wars that drove the Turks out of Hungary (1683–9).

Map 8 N. Sanson, *Estats de l' Empire des Turqs en Europe*, Paris, 1696. Image: British Library.

ESTATS DE L'EMPIRE DES TURQS EN EUROPE

Top border (longitude/letters): I · K Septentrion · L · M · N · O · P · Q · R · S · T · V

Left margin labels: IERES DES ESTATS DE POLOGNE · PARTIE · DE LA · PETITE

RUSSIE · POKUCIE · PODOLIE · UKRAINE ou PAYS DES COSAQUES

TARTARES NOGAI · SERA MORFI · MER DE ZABACHE olim MEOTIS PALUS

TRANSILVANIE · MOLDAVIE · BESSARABIE · TARTARES DU CRIM ou TARTARIE · PERECOP

VALAQUIE · olim Carcinites Sinus

MESWAR

SERVIE · BULGARIE · ROMELIE ou ROMANIE · DROMELIE

MER NOIRE autrefois PONT EUXIN

MACEDOINE · MER DE MARMORA olim PROPONTIS · STAMBOUL CONSTANTINOPLE

Golfe de Contessa

ESTATS DE L'EMPIRE DES TURQS EN EUROPE Subdivisés suivant l'estendue des BEGLERBEGLICZ ou GOUVERNEMENTS Dans lesquels sont Marqués les Residences des Sangiaes qui en dependent, Tirés de plusieurs Memoires et des Relations les plus Recentes.
Par le S. SANSON, Geographe Ordinaire de sa Majesté.
A PARIS, Chez N. Eaillet, Gendre aux grand Sangiaes sur deux Globes, avec Privilege du Roy pour Vingt ans. 1695.

ARCHIPEL ou MER BLANCHE autrefois MER AEGEE

Golfe de M. Santo · Stalimene I. · Lemno I.

ACHAIE · BEGLERBI · Golfe de Salonichi · THESSALIE

Scio I. · Scio · PARTIE DES ESTATS ou ASIE MINEURE · NATOLIE · DES TURQS en ASIE

Negrepont · Samo I. · Nicaria I. · Langa I.

PELO · ISLES · Golfe de Lepanto · Golfe d'Engia · Mora I.

CYCLADES · Zante · Golfe de l'Arcadia · Naxia I. · Stampalia I.

Isle de RHODES · GOLFE et · MER DE SATALIE · ISLE DE CIPRE

Sapienza I. · MER DE SAPIENZA · Cerigo I. · MER DE CANDIE · Scarpanto I. · MER DE SCARPANTO

ISLE DE CANDIE · Coos I.

ER DE LEVANT · RANEE

Scale cartouche: Milles Pas Geometriques ou Milles d'Italie · Lieues Communes de France · Lieues Communes d'Allemagne ou Grand Lieues de Pologne · Lieues de Hongrie · Lieues d'une heure de Chemin · Postes ou Journées Communes de 20 M.P. chacune · Residence des Beglerbeg · Residence des Sangiaes

Bottom border: K Midy · L · M · N · O · P · Q · R · S

As the title of this 1755 French map of southeastern Europe (the full map is reproduced over the page) makes clear, by the eighteenth century the definition of the region of 'European Turkey' was a common one. At the time this map was produced, Enlightenment thinkers in France were exploring apparent 'Turkish despotism'. The Ottoman Turkish state was described as non-European by virtue of this perceived despotism, which was contrasted with European, and particularly Enlightenment, ideals of government. Southeastern Europe may have been considered 'European' geographically, but it was governed by a power that was defined as very definitely non-European.

Map 9 Detail from G. R. de Vaugondy, *Turquie Européenne*, Paris, 1755. Image: British Library.

This map tells us more about late eighteenth-century French preoccupations with southeastern Europe than it does about southeastern Europe itself at that time. It is described as a map of 'European Turkey', but does not show the whole of southeastern Europe under Ottoman rule in 1755. Instead it shows Greece, thus reflecting Enlightenment interest in the classical roots of European civilization. It seeks to make the point, however, that these territories were under the rule of Turkey; a non-European power.

Map 10 G. R. de Vaugondy, *Turquie Européenne*, Paris, 1755. Image: British Library.

This map, published in Dublin in 1808, may seem familiar in that it delimits the borders of Europe and units that look like modern nation-states. It is, however, an idealized map of the continent and the divisions it represents were not the existing political divisions at the time of its creation. At the time the map of Europe was being re-made as a result of the French Revolution of 1789 and the policies of the French Emperor Napoleon Bonaparte (1804–15). Not only does the map clearly delimit the assumed eastern borders of the continent, but in identifying German and Italian units it anticipates the political nationalism of the nineteenth century. In some respects the map has blind spots – note that the whole of the Balkan peninsula is identified as Turkey. This is especially noteworthy because as the nineteenth century progressed European political nationalism was to undermine Ottoman rule in this part of the continent. The tension that resulted would serve to shape the modern definition of this borderland as 'the Balkans'.

Map 11 *Europe 1808*, from R. Brookes, *The General Gazetteer; or, Compendious Geographical Dictionary*, revised W. Guthrie and E. Jones, 8th edn., Dublin, 1808. Image: University of Texas at Austin Libraries.

EUROPE

The rise of nationalism in southeastern Europe undermined Ottoman rule throughout the nineteenth century, with the creation of new nation-states beginning with Greece in 1830. Struggles for statehood on the part of the peoples of 'the Balkans' were often represented as battles between Christian peasantries and a Turkish oppressor. By the late nineteenth century Europe's great powers, particularly Russia and Austria as well as Ottoman Turkey, were interested parties in these conflicts. This meant that political divisions in southeastern Europe were increasingly settled around the conference table. This 1884 map, taken from a British historical atlas, sought to explain the outcome of the Congress of Berlin (1878) and the subsequent Treaty of San Stefano that recognized the independence of Serbia, Romania and Bulgaria and granted Austria control over Bosnia-Hercegovina.

Map 12 *Eastern Europe 1878*, from R. H. Labberton, *An Historical Atlas*, E. Elaxton and Co., 1884. Image: University of Texas at Austin Libraries.

The modern image of 'the Balkans' is one of a zone of intense conflict sparked by the issues of ethnicity and nationality. According to this view, internecine 'Balkan' conflict has had the potential to spark war across Europe as a whole. This interpretation owes much to the political concerns of the early twentieth century, especially as conflict between Serbian nationalists and Austria–Hungary over Bosnia-Hercegovina provided the spark that ignited the First World War. This map was produced on the eve of that conflict in 1914 by the international commission set up by the Carnegie Endowment for International Peace which sought to ascertain the causes of the Balkan wars (1912–13). The first of these wars was fought between Serbia, Bulgaria, Montenegro and Greece on the one side and the Ottoman empire on the other. It secured the effective withdrawal of Turkey from all but a small part of southeastern Europe. The second war arose because Bulgaria sought to gain Macedonia at the expense of Serbia and Greece.

This map explains the Balkan wars in terms of the competing national aspirations of the peoples inhabiting the region. It is worth noting that competing nationalism has not only been used as an explanation for the Balkan wars; it has also been seen throughout the twentieth century as a fundamental characteristic of 'the Balkans'. It is worth remembering, too, that this explanation ignores the interests of other great powers in the region in fanning conflict from the mid nineteenth century onwards.

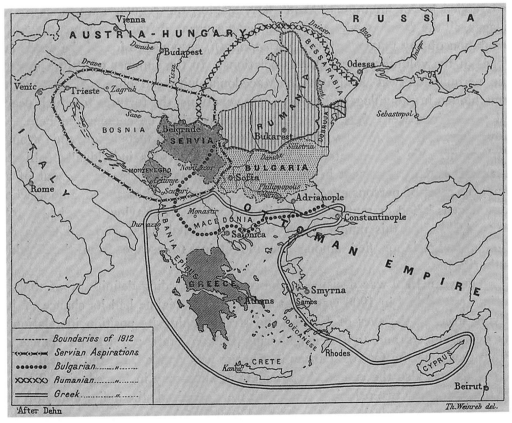

Map 13 *Balkan Aspirations* (showing boundaries of 1912), from 'Report of the International Commission to inquire into the causes and conduct of the Balkan Wars', Carnegie Endowment for International Peace, 1914. Image: University of Texas at Austin Libraries.

Ethnic identification has been central in establishing national claims to territory across Europe, and not merely in 'the Balkans'. The mapping of ethnicity has played a role in constructing these claims. This is a problematic process for a number of reasons, as the maps on these and the following pages illustrate. A central question is that of who defines the limits of an ethnic group. The example of early twentieth-century Macedonia, the cause of the second Balkan war, provides a case in point. This map, produced for the international commission of inquiry into the causes of the Balkan wars, is an ethnographic map of Macedonia showing the location of ethnic groups. The map was drawn up, however, according to Serb definitions of ethnic groups within Macedonia. Serbia was one of the combatants in both Balkan wars.

Map 14 *Carte Ethnographique de la Macedoine: Point de vue serbe* (Ethnographic map of Macedonia from the point of view of the Serbs), from 'Report of the International Commission to inquire into the causes and conduct of the Balkan Wars', Carnegie Endowment for International Peace, 1914. Image: University of Texas at Austin Libraries.

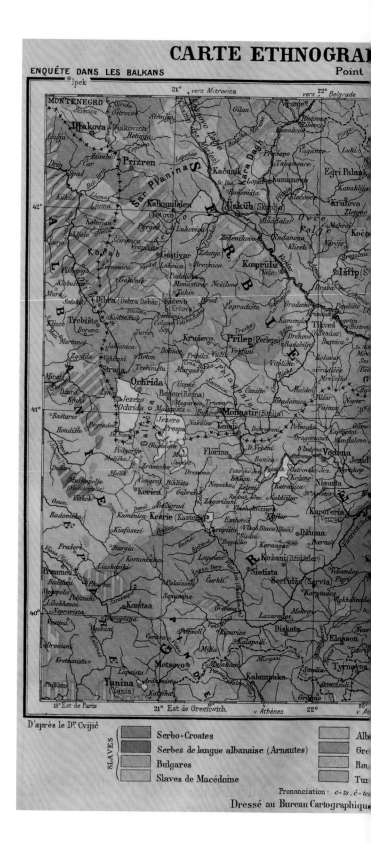

Dessiné par Th. Weinreb

------- Frontières anciennes
+·+·+·+ Frontières actuelles
Chemins de fer

Echelle de 1 : 1.500.000

10 0 20 40 60 80 100 km.

(Kutzovalaques)

,j=i, š=ch, u=ou, ü=u, ž=j

LIBRAIRIE HACHETTE ET Cie PARIS

Imp. Erhard frres Paris.

The Bulgarian view of ethnic identification in early twentieth-century Macedonia did not correspond with the Serbian view illustrated in the previous map. The Bulgarians claimed many of the Macedonian Slavs as Bulgarian. It is also interesting that no Serbian, or 'Serbo-Croat', population is identified on the ethnic map drawn up according to the Bulgarian standpoint. These two ethnographic maps, when taken together, raise an interesting question. How can ethnic identities be ascribed to populations at all when such identities are contested from outside and when ethnic or national identification among the populations themselves is far from well developed?

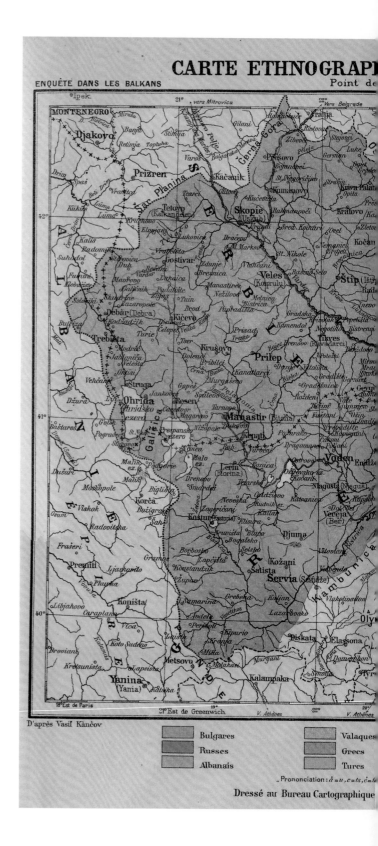

Map 15 *Carte Ethnographique de la Macedoine: Point de vue bulgare* (Ethnographic map of Macedonia from the point of view of the Bulgarians), from 'Report of the International Commission to inquire into the causes and conduct of the Balkan Wars', Carnegie Endowment for International Peace, 1914. Image: University of Texas at Austin Libraries.

UE DE LA MACÉDOINE
bulgare

DOTATION CARNEGIE

Dessiné par Th. Weinreb

- - - - - -   Frontières anciennes
+·+·+·+   Frontières actuelles
·············   Limites de la Macédoine

Echelle de 1: 1.500.000

10 0   20   40   60   80   100 km.

ur, j = i, š = ch, u = ou, ü = u, ž = j.

LIBRAIRIE HACHETTE ET Cᴵᴱ PARIS

Imp. Erhard fʳᵉˢ Paris.

There are other problems with reading ethnographic maps that are not directly raised by the two examples discussed here. These two maps represent the territory of each ethnic group as homogeneous, yet beneath the solid blocks of colour represented on the map reality was always more complex. Across southeastern Europe individuals with different linguistic, ethnic or national identities have in fact lived side by side. This is an issue I shall return to when discussing later ethnic maps.

The conflagration of the
First World War resulted in
the disappearance of
multinational empires from
the face of southeastern
Europe and their
replacement with nation-
states during the interwar
years. Haunted by the
memory of the period that
had immediately preceded
the First World War, many
people in interwar Europe
were concerned about the
uneasy relationship between
state borders and ethnic
identification, discerning in
them the roots of conflict.
This map, published in New
York in 1923, was produced
in this context and examines
this relationship. Here 'the
Balkans' are defined as a
potential trouble spot even
in the absence of direct
conflict.

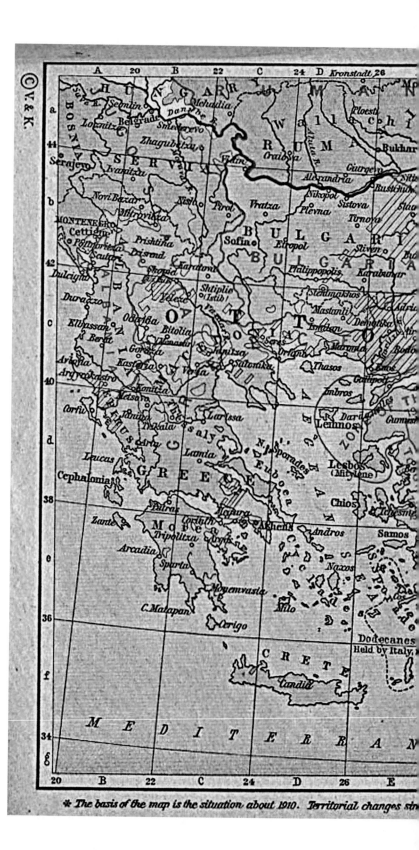

Map 16 *Distribution of Races in
the Balkan Peninsula and Asia
Minor*, from W. R. Shepherd,
Historical Atlas Henry Holt, New
York, 1923. Image: University of
Texas at Austin Libraries.

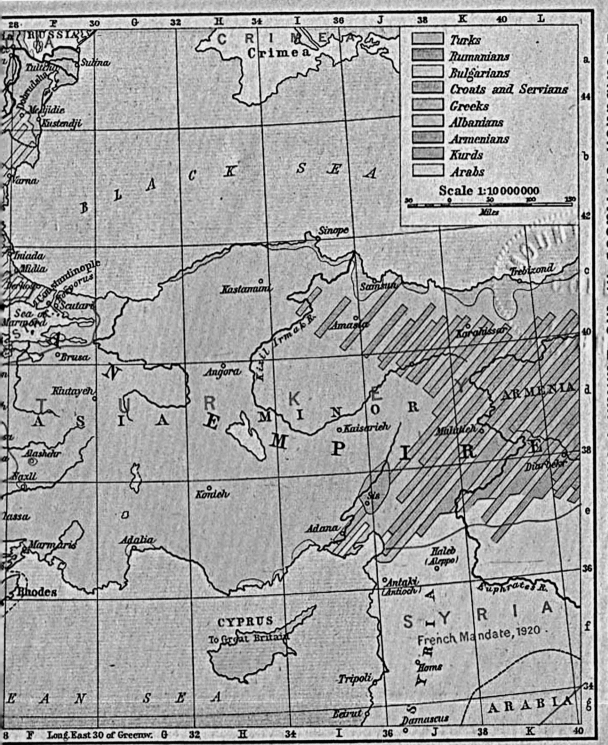

Distribution of Races in the Balkan Peninsula and Asia Minor.

Legend:
- Turks
- Rumanians
- Bulgarians
- Croats and Servians
- Greeks
- Albanians
- Armenians
- Kurds
- Arabs

Scale 1:10 000 000

Miles

RUSSIA

CRIMEA
Crimea

BLACK SEA

Tultcha
Sulina
Meljidie
Kustendji
Varna

Sinope

Iniada
Midia
Derkos
Constantinople
Bosporus
Scutari
Sea of Marmora
Brusa
Kastamuni
Samsun
Amasia
Trebizond
Karahissar

ASIA MINOR
TURKEY EMPIRE
Kiutayeh
Angora
Kizil Irmak R.
ARMENIA
Alashehr
Naxli
Kaisarieh
Malatieh
Diarbekr

Kordeh
Sis
Adana

Marmaris
Adalia
Haleb (Aleppo)

Rhodes
Antaki (Antioch)
Euphrates R.

CYPRUS
To Great Britain
SYRIA
French Mandate, 1920
Homs

Tripoli
ARABIA
Beirut
Damascus

EAN SEA

e War of 1914–1918 are indicated in red.

The National Socialist regime in Germany (1933–45) sought to radically remake the map of Europe. Its attempts to create a 'new order' in central and eastern Europe were focused on Russia and the territories that lay between it and Germany. These plans had their counterparts in southeastern Europe, which were to be implemented following the invasions of Yugoslavia and Greece (in 1941). They were informed by bodies of professional researchers within Germany concerned with the study of what they referred to as *Südosteuropa* (southeastern Europe). This map, produced in 1940 by one such researcher based in Graz, documents the distribution of the population of Yugoslavia according to ethnicity. The map was to be used as a tool to aid the creation of the 'new order' in Yugoslavia.

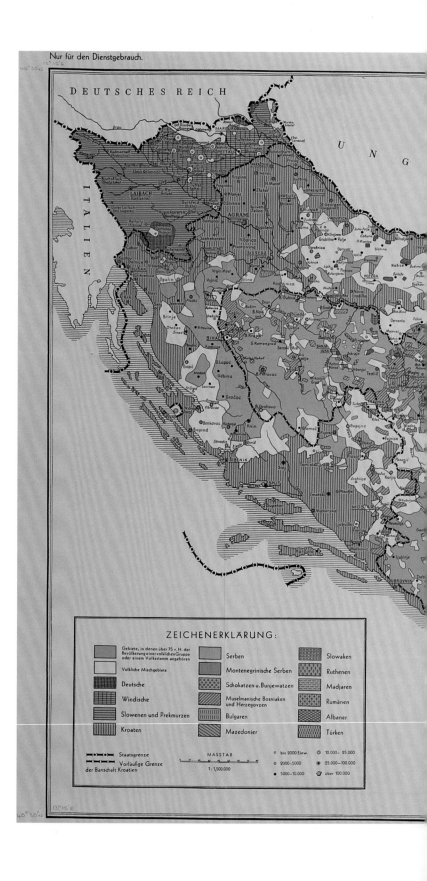

Map 17 M. Straka, *Jugolawien: Volkliche Gliederung Kerngebiete*, Südostdeutsches Institut, Graz, 1940. Image: British Library.

Jugoslawien: Volkliche Gliederung
Kerngebiete

Entworfen von Dr. Manfred Straka, Südostdeutsches Institut, Graz

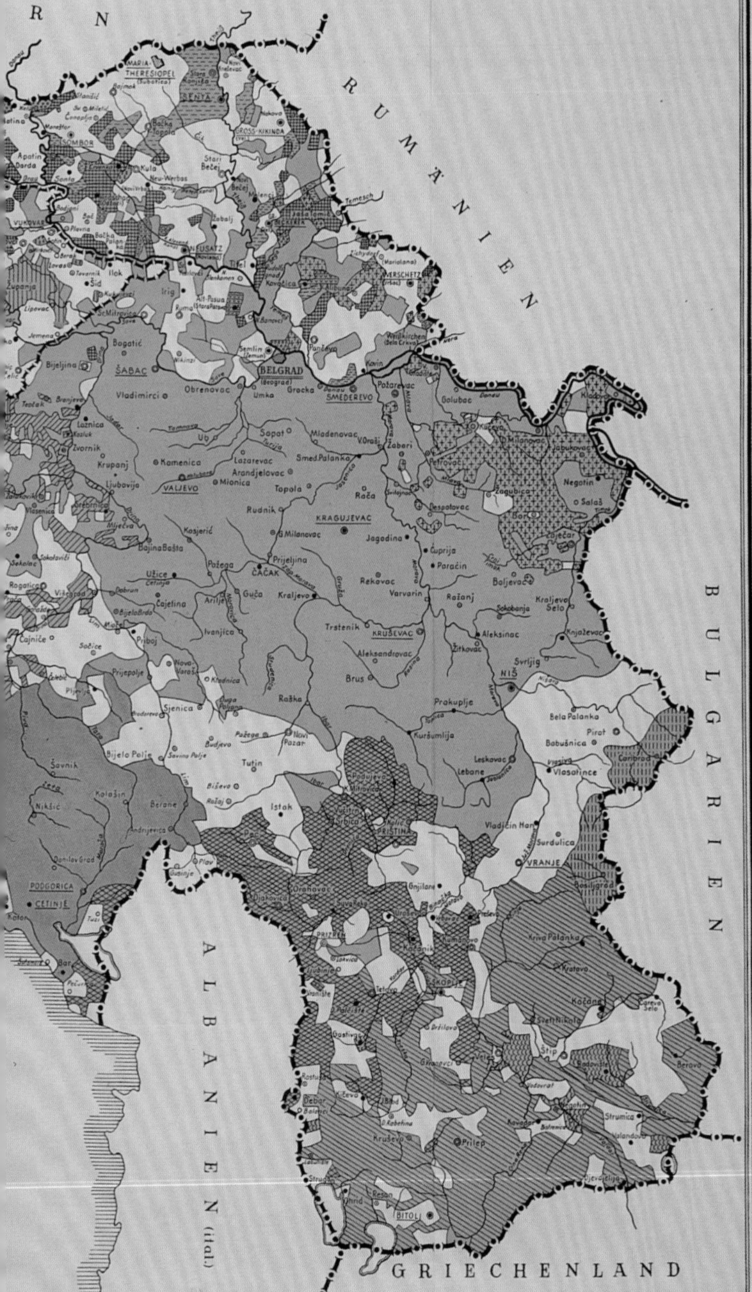

R N
RUMÄNIEN
BULGARIEN
ALBANIEN (ital.)
GRIECHENLAND
MARIA-THERESIOPEL (Subotica)
SENTA
GROSS-KIKINDA
SOMBOR
NEUSATZ
VUKOVAR
WERSCHETZ
BELGRAD (Beograd)
Semlin (Zemun)
ŠABAC
SMEDEREVO
VALJEVO
KRAGUJEVAC
ČAČAK
KRUŠEVAC
NIŠ
Zaječar
Negotin
Pirot
Leskovac
VRANJE
Priština
PRIZREN
SKOPLJE
Štip
Prilep
BITOLJ
Ohrid
Debar
PODGORICA
CETINJE

23°15'E 46°30'N
40°30'N

The fact of ethnic division in Yugoslavia was used by Nazi Germany to shape its 'new order' in southeastern Europe, along the lines of the way in which the country was dismembered between 1914 and 1945. The postwar restoration of Yugoslavia under the leadership of Marshal Tito and the communists was accompanied by a settlement between the constituent republics and nationalities, which was not without its tensions but which allowed for stability in the country between 1945 and the end of the 1980s.

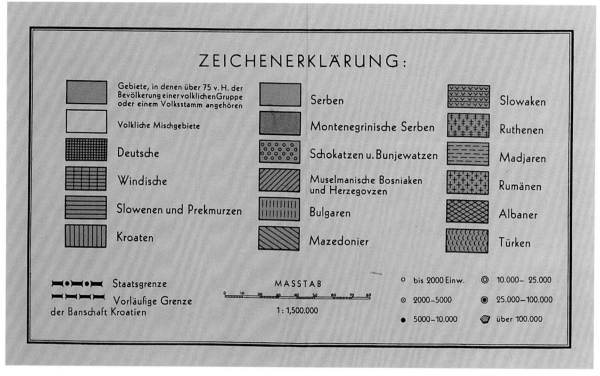

Map 18 Detail from M. Straka, *Jugoslawien: Volkliche Gliederung Kerngebiete*, Südostdeutsches Institut, Graz, 1940. Image: British Library.

The wars that accompanied the break-up of the second Yugoslavia (1991–2001) have led to the emergence of new nation-states in the region. Yugoslavia was reduced to those territories coloured in pink on this map, while Slovenia (set up in 1991), Croatia (1991), Bosnia-Hercegovina (1992) and the Former Yugoslav Republic of Macedonia (1991) all became independent states. Moreover, these wars have also revived the early twentieth-century image of 'the Balkans' as a war-torn borderland. In this revived image 'the Balkans' have become almost synonymous with the territories of Albania and former Yugoslavia. As the end of this visual essay shows, many of the issues embedded in early twentieth-century representations of 'the Balkans' re-emerged in the maps of the region at the very end of the century.

Map 19 *The Former Yugoslavia*, United Nations, 1998. Image: the United Nations.

As has been shown in Chapter 4, many commentators in western Europe and North America sought to explain the conflict in Yugoslavia in terms of the revival of 'ancient ethnic hatreds'. This map was created in 1998 by the United States Central Intelligence Agency to explain the conflict in Kosovo (1989–99). In the map, however, an explanation for the broader conflicts in Yugoslavia during the 1990s is implied. This implication is conveyed by reference to the national aspirations of Serbia and echoes to some extent Map 13 depicting national aspirations in the region from 1914. However, it differs in that it locates the roots of the conflict in the history of Serbia as a series of independent states and maps these histories onto contemporary political divisions in 'the Balkans'.

Map 20 *Boundaries of Serbia*, from *Kosovo: History of a Balkan Hot Spot*, Central Intelligence Agency, Washington, DC, 1998. Image: University of Texas at Austin Libraries.

The conflict of the 1990s in former Yugoslavia has seen a revival of the ethnic map, particularly in attempts to document the conflict in Bosnia-Hercegovina (1992–6) and to shape debate over its possible solutions. This map, produced by the Central Intelligence Agency in 1998 from 1991 Yugoslav census data, is more careful than most attempts to map ethnicity. It depicts 'ethnic majorities', rather than ascribing particular territories to specific ethnic groups. It also shows the substantial areas of the state where no one ethnic group constitutes a majority. Yet even this relatively careful approach is not without its problems. The ethnic groups are defined according to the official nationality categories of the former Yugoslav state. Furthermore, in areas where there are ethnic majorities, the minorities who share territories with them are not represented on the map.

Bosnia-Hercegovina during the 1990s also illustrates the political uses to which such representations can be put. Ethnic maps can serve to legitimize claims to territory. Most obviously, notions that Bosnia-Hercegovina's problems could be solved through 'cantonization', or the creation of sub-national units in which different ethnic groups are in the majority, formed part of many peace plans during the war and of the Dayton Accord (1995) that finally ended it. They have also been used to legitimize the two entities into which Bosnia was divided at Dayton. This echoes to some extent the political uses to which ethnic maps from earlier in the twentieth century have been put.

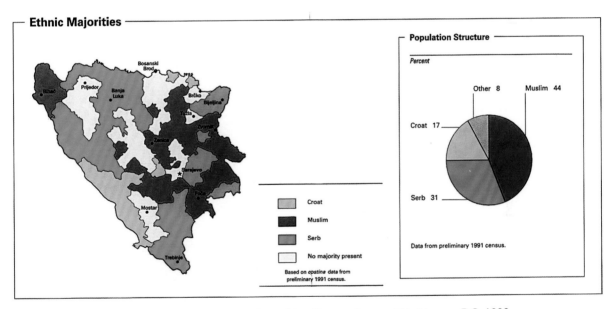

Map 21 *Ethnic Majorities in Bosnia-Hercegovina,* Central Intelligence Agency, Washington, DC, 1998.
Image: University of Texas at Austin Libraries.

Just as the mapping of 'the Balkans' in the 1990s reproduced ideas about the region that were far from unique to that decade, contemporary ways of thinking about Europe have deep roots. Although no eastern border of Europe is marked on this map, the border of the map itself suggests a border. The boundary of Europe is remarkably similar to that represented by Ortelius in 1570 or that depicted in 1808 (Maps 3 and 11). Turkey is excluded, as is much of Russia.

Map 22 *Political Map of Europe*, Central Intelligence Agency, Washington, DC, 2001.
Image: University of Texas at Austin Libraries.

Figure 2.3   Aubervilliers. La Maladrerie 2 by Anaïk Frantz. Photo:
Editions du Seuil

Figure 2.4   Blanc-Mesnil. Rachid Kimoune's Children of the World by
Anaïk Frantz. Photo: Editions du Seuil

Figure 2.5 Aubervilliers. La Maladrerie 3 by Anaïk Frantz. Photo: Editions du Seuil

Figure 2.6 Uncaptioned by Anaïk Frantz. Photo: Editions du Seuil

In the context of societies that have suffered the yoke of colonial exploitation by certain European powers, the synecdochical usage of 'Europe' to represent something tainted (as expressed by Kunene) is familiar. It can be seen, for example, in the words of the Martiniquean theorist and psychologist Frantz Fanon (1925–61) in his influential *The Wretched of the Earth*: 'Europe now lives in such a mad, reckless pace that she has shaken off all guidance and all reason, and she is running headlong into the abyss; we would do well to avoid it with all possible speed' (Fanon, 1961, p. 252). The idea recurs in *Discourse on Colonialism*, by the (also Martiniquean) writer and politician Aimé Césaire:

> What is serious is that 'Europe' is morally, spiritually indefensible.
>
> And today the indictment is brought against it not by the European masses alone, but on a world scale, by tens and tens of millions of men who, from the depths of slavery, set themselves up as judges.
>
> (Césaire [1955] 1972, p. 10)

Such statements are synecdochical in two ways. First, they do not distinguish sufficiently, at least at the general level, between the whole continent of Europe and all the people who live in that space, and the particular individual perpetrators of European imperialism who were born in specific dominant European countries (and bearing in mind that such imperialism was often imposed on certain peoples within Europe itself). This leads to Césaire's own polarization from the European in his understanding of African '**negritude**' (see interview with René Depestre in Césaire, 1972, pp. 73–4). Secondly, they present Europe as the concrete embodiment of phenomena which are not in fact necessarily manifest only in, or confined to, the continent of Europe. In such statements, for both Fanon and Césaire, Europe becomes the singularly representative context which is infected by imperialism and the inequities of industrial capitalism (for both writers these are part of one phenomenon). Thus 'Europe' itself comes to signify *all* that capitalism/colonialism connotes; other societies (the American, or those of the newly independent countries of Africa and Asia, for example) can only be infected by 'Europe' or by the emulation of 'Europe'. But as social-historical processes and political-economic concepts neither capitalism nor imperialism need be culture-specific or continent-specific to Europe.

Though the quotations above both date from an early phase of postcolonial thinking, the sentiments they express are still far from uncommon in formerly colonized societies.

Negritude: an affirmation of pride in black heritage and culture, especially in the New World. For Césaire this affirmation arises from the unity of black experience as it developed through the African slave trade and New World plantation system.

Even in societies which have not experienced colonization in the sense that Fanon and Césaire talk about, 'Europe' or 'Europeanness' may also synecdochically stand for broader notions of liberalism or the phenomenon of industrial capitalism. This occurs both in the tendency to see Europe as a homogeneous entity in these terms, and in thinking of Europe as particularly representative of something that is larger than it. This may have both positive and negative connotations. 'Europeanization' is closely associated with 'westernization' and 'Americanization', in that these terms conjure up some notion of turning to 'first world' riches and the enterprise of capitalism, becoming drawn into the 'free world' of individualism and liberal democracy, assuming the mantle of 'rationalism' and technological progress, and so on. 'Europeanization' in these senses is usually a positive synecdochical construction – there is a desirable air about such evocations. However, very similar terms can easily be given a negative edge. One example is the catchphrase of 1960s Iran, 'euromania', inspired by the writer Jalal Al-e Ahmad (1923–69) (actually the Iranian term was *gharbzadegi*, literally something like 'west-stricken-ness', which was easily and rather significantly condensed to 'euromania'). In his book of that name, published in 1962, Al-e Ahmad used the term to designate the all-encompassing hold of technology and consumerism in the modern world, which he felt had extended its grip to Iran and was diminishing the spiritual well-being of the Iranian people. A lucid discussion of Al-e Ahmad's views in this regard is available in Roy Mottahedeh's *The Mantle of the Prophet* (Mottahedeh, 1985).

The pre-eminence of synecdochical views of Europe both within and outside the continent, coupled with a certain fluidity about geographical and institutional definitions, has naturally led to some legalistic confusion regarding the precise status of what it is to be 'European' (or to be *within* 'Europe'), especially at the boundary areas. Thus, in the 1980s, it was a matter of debate whether or not Turkey was qualified to join the European Community – the question arose because, according to Article 237 of the Treaty of Rome of 1957, 'Any European state may apply to become a member of the European Community'. (Article 237 was repealed in the Maastricht Treaty of 1992.)

As a generalization it is worth keeping in mind that different synecdochical constructions of 'Europe' or 'European' may simultaneously be in use from different perspectives both inside and outside the continent. So, for instance, 'Europe' from the point of view of political geography and international relations, 'Europe' in a cultural and historical perspective, 'Europe' as an economic entity, 'Europe' from the point of view of demography, may each have somewhat different connotations. Significantly, such different connotations can overlap and become inappropriately confused with each other.

Social, political and historical perspectives

These theoretical issues can be brought to bear on more focused and context-specific examinations of postwar views of Europe from outside. In this section I present some thoughts on three broad categories within which such focused examinations may fall and to all of which the theoretical issues discussed above are relevant.

Europe in the postcolonial world

In the period between the two world wars, and especially after the Second World War, a large number of countries that were colonized by dominant European powers in Africa, Asia, South America and the Caribbean gained independence. The chronology of decolonizations in Africa and Asia between 1922 and 1964 (a rather limited view) conveys an idea of the scale of this world phenomenon (see Appendix). Several factors combined to initiate the move towards decolonization:

- the growth of nationalistic and other anti-colonial political alignments and emancipatory movements within the colonies;

- the changing fortunes of some of the colonial powers in the world wars (thus the fate of the German and Turkish colonies after the First World War was a matter of concern for the Allies, who were caught in the paradox of **mandating** them for decolonization while hanging on to their own colonies);

Mandating meant that interim trustee administrations were set up under international supervision to oversee the transition from colonial rule to self-rule.

- the fact that the emerging superpowers in the course of the two wars, the United States and Soviet Union, were unsympathetic to the continuing colonial domination of European powers;

- the evolution of new modes of economic influence which rendered the need to maintain a direct colonial administrative apparatus redundant.

In most instances decolonization was, however, far from smooth. In many colonies the process involved a brutal struggle against a repressive colonial administration. The scale of change from a condition of being colonized to a state of being independent is naturally enormous: it usually involves a complete reorientation and even the transformation of government, administrative, economic and, to some extent, social systems. In many instances extended periods of colonization had left the colonized peoples with little experience of self-government and under-developed economic infrastructures. During the period of decolonization different ideological formations and interest groups vied for power – which has led to lasting internecine and communal conflicts in many parts of the postcolonial world. This was complicated by the spheres of influence that European powers and the American and Soviet superpowers sought to maintain in the second half of the twentieth century, often in a blatantly interventionist fashion. The experience of decolonization has indubitably coloured perceptions of Europe from outside.

In *The Wretched of the Earth* Frantz Fanon observed that in the period following decolonization the reins of power in a newly independent country would be taken by the 'national bourgeoisie' – an indigenous middle class which had sustained itself during the colonial period by assuming the colonizer's values – who would perpetuate eurocentrism and betray their national credentials. Fanon anticipated that such a national bourgeoisie would rigidify class-based and implicitly racist colonial attitudes, would continue in colonial tradition to dispossess a large number of the people, and would continue to turn to former European colonizers for validation and paternalistic support. As he put it:

> With its wave-lengths tuned in to Europe, it continues firmly and resolutely to make the most of the situation. The enormous profits that it derives from the exploitation of the people are exported to foreign countries. The young national bourgeoisie is often more suspicious of the regime that it has set up than are foreign companies ... [The national bourgeoisie] acquires foreign securities in European markets, and goes off to spend the weekend in Paris or Hamburg.
>
> (Fanon, 1961, p. 139)

Fanon also anticipated a backlash against this situation, which would come either in the moves for revolutionary change on the part of the still dispossessed common people (the '*lumpen proletariat*'), or from certain conservative religious and sectarian alignments.

Arguably, Fanon overstated his case against the national bourgeoisie in former colonies: in many instances those fitting this description who came to power have, despite their reverence for certain European ideas and institutions (often as a matter of pragmatism rather than blind eurocentrism), been uncompromisingly nationalistic – for good or bad (frequently the latter). But the general truth of Fanon's reflections cannot be denied. The need for validation by 'Europe', the tendency to regard 'European' institutions and cultural forms as the ideal to aspire to, the desire to be 'European' in some sense – all these are experiences that many people in former colonial contexts would recognize. In most instances this need to turn to 'Europe' might have been replaced by a turning to the 'American way' – but that is not a particularly distinct position. Such synecdochical desire for 'Europe' (or 'America') is naturally filtered through the particular perception, from within the previously dominated colony, of the former colonizer (whether British, Dutch, French, and so on) as the dominant outsider.

Moreover, Fanon's anticipation of internal conflicts arising from this, initiated by dispossessed peoples or conservative alignments, has also been confirmed in many ex-colonies. Regretfully, these have more often taken the form of regressive religious and sectarian conflicts rather than attempts to install a more just order.

What Fanon's indictment of colonial influence after decolonization also manifests (rather than discusses) is the resentment against a synecdochical 'Europe' that may come to exist in such contexts. The postcolonial desire for 'Europe' and 'Europeanness' has its flip-side; it underlines the belief that the same 'Europe' and 'Europeanness' are responsible for the shortcomings of the former colonial context. This too can be over-determined: in the postcolonial world 'Europe' – and latterly 'America' – may synecdochically become the scapegoat for social and political phenomena which cannot be directly linked to the experience of being colonized.

The view of Europe that is available in different parts of the postcolonial world is necessarily mediated by the particular relationship that exists between the former colonial society and the specific former European colonizer. This is a complex matter that involves the manner in which political and economic alliances and negotiations have been conducted, the nature of their participation in international politics, the degree of cultural exchange that might exist, the patterns of migration between the countries (usually involving migration from the less developed and poorer previously colonized to the richer and more developed previously colonizer countries), and so on. An adequate examination of this is impossible in this space – it requires a close examination of specific contexts. (A reasonably recent and useful investigation, and one that is relatively broad-based (dealing primarily with the relationship of three Caribbean countries to their former colonizer France), is Helen M. Hintjens's *Alternatives to Independence* (1995).) The study of postcolonial relations has been a prodigious academic endeavour, especially in the last three decades. Works on the subject, however, often draw on sophisticated theoretical abstractions and a range of historical and cultural references which either lead to observations that are so general as to be difficult to apply to specific contexts, or so specifically located as to be difficult to generalize from.

An interesting element is the extent to which former European colonial powers have sought to maintain a cultural and economic presence in their erstwhile territories. One such venture is the British Commonwealth, initially an association of the United Kingdom and sovereign countries which were its former colonies – the Commonwealth Office in the UK grew out of the amalgamation of the Dominions Office and the Colonial Office. Its influence, however, has understandably progressively diminished. A similar Dutch Commonwealth was contemplated after the withdrawal of the Japanese occupation force in Indonesia in 1945. More potently, cultural organizations designed to promote specific European languages and cultures – usually those of former European colonial powers in the postcolonial world – have extended their scope of influence since the 1960s. Among these the most influential are the British Council for the United Kingdom, the Alliance Française for France and the Goethe Institute for Germany. These organizations have naturally been emulated by the postwar superpowers: American Centers and Houses of Soviet Cultures were founded wherever they were allowed to exist. These have succeeded in promoting academic and educational exchanges and in sponsoring educational visits and cultural events, thus ensuring a certain positive image of 'Europe' in many formerly colonized countries.

Former European powers have also sought to maintain economic influence in ex-colonies by negotiating special trade privileges and monopolizing the import and export of certain commodities, by offering collaboration, by continuing to maintain wherever allowed certain industrial sectors, and occasionally by providing aid where needed. Such European powers had hoped to capitalize on cultural affinities which had inevitably come to exist in the course of colonial rule – and in some cases have done so successfully. The economic influence of these special relationships between former colonizers and colonized is such that their removal could affect the economies of certain 'third world' countries adversely. A number of studies have expressed concern about the effects of a more integrated and protective European economy superseding the different multilateral agreements which exist between rich European countries and developing countries outside Europe. These include Marjorie Lister's *The European Community and the Developing World* (1988) and *The European Union and the South* (1997), and Michael Davenport and Sheila Page's *Europe: 1992 and the Developing World* (1992).

Another substantial mediating factor between Europe and the postcolonial world outside it is provided by religious institutions, especially the different Christian churches. The period of imperial expansion by European powers was attended (and sometimes preceded) by various hugely successful missionary enterprises across the colonized part of the world – though this was not always or necessarily ideologically linked to imperialism. But the spread of various forms of Christianity in the colonial world outside Europe has been coincident with imperial expansion to the extent of making an association of Christianity with Europe seem natural, and sometimes making the polarization of imperial European Christians against the colonized Islamic or Hindu (or other indigenous religious persuasions) seem plausible. This is obviously a false polarization, for significant numbers of people in the postcolonial world outside Europe are Christians and indubitably practise their religion in distinctively indigenous ways.

This again is a complex area that has been the subject of much discussion and debate. But in the context of this chapter the following two general points have a bearing on perceptions of Europe from outside the area as mediated by religion. First, it continues to be essentially the case that despite the status of certain Christian churches as established world institutions, their seats of power lie in European countries and North America, and the upper levels of their hierarchies are dominated by Europeans and North Americans. Where significant indigenous movements associated with a Christian church outside the sphere of European (or broadly western) influence have arisen – as, for example, in the development of liberation theology within the Catholic church, primarily in South American countries from the late 1960s onwards (especially associated with the **Medellin conference** of 1968) – these have had a difficult relationship with the European centre.

The Medellin conference is the general conference of Bishops of Latin America, held at Medellin, Colombia, in 1968, which spoke of the church 'listening to the cry of the poor and becoming an interpreter of their anguish'.

Secondly, despite this fact, Christian churches have tried to appear to be eradicating their eurocentric bias in order to present a more international and open character. Once again using the example of the Catholic church, this is demonstrated by the modernizing and liberalizing moves made by the second Vatican Council (1962–5), set up by Pope John XXIII (1958–63). The attempt to release the Catholic church from a eurocentric bias continues with the activities of Pope John Paul II (who became pope in 1978) as its rather conservative (anti-abortionist and homophobic) ambassador to such seemingly unlikely places as Cuba and Israel.

Europe and the cold war

The extended period of tension and hostility between the Soviet Union and United States and their respective allies within Europe (or between east and west) which followed a brief period of attempted cooperation between the superpowers after the Second World War is called the cold war because there was no direct ('hot') military conflict between the two powers or inside Europe. The geographical confrontation of west and east in this period was primarily an ideological confrontation between capitalism and a certain form of revolutionary socialism. Both sides were suspicious of the expansionist tendencies of the other; both sought to maintain spheres of influence in the rest of the world; both strove to gain the upper hand in terms of military armaments (starting an arms race and the rapid growth of nuclear arsenals) which eventually led to the control of militarization by mutually agreed self-restraint (*détente*) in the 1970s and after the late–1980s; both conducted a massive propaganda campaign against the other within their own territories and strove to expurgate those within who did not accept the dominant ideology. The main military alliance of the west in the cold war was the North Atlantic Treaty Organization (Nato) established in 1949; for the east it was the signatories of the East European Mutual Assistance Treaty (Warsaw Pact) of 1955.

The cold war divisions were drawn most clearly within the continent of Europe; the east–west boundary (the 'Iron Curtain', the line between the two blocs, symbolized by the Berlin wall – whose construction began in August 1961, as a consequence of the division of Germany in 1949 and whose fall began in 1989, more or less marking the period of the cold war) lay inside Europe. What is interesting with regard to outside perspectives of Europe is that the effectively divided continent led to a shrinking of the synecdochical connotations of 'Europe'. In some sense, in this period particularly (though the tendency can be traced earlier) eastern Europe seemed to lie outside 'Europe', and western Europe became 'Europe'. On the eastern side of the boundary the cultural-continental identity was diminished in favour of a social order which wished to eschew traditional social organizations and supersede nationalisms (unsuccessfully, as it turned out). The superpower of the east, the USSR, was itself a union of European and Asian geographical and cultural societies – its continental identity was mixed. On the other hand, on the western side of the boundary the US located its roots in western Europe and identified with western European traditions: western Europe naturally retained its continental identity, and indeed strengthened it by contrast to eastern Europe. To the outside world 'Europe' during this period was usually synecdochically western Europe, while the eastern bloc was particularly marked as 'eastern Europe', or more neutrally as the 'Soviet bloc' or 'communist bloc'. Either way, it was different from 'Europe'. Even within eastern Europe this perception was not unusual. The following reading is from the Czech writer and politician Václav Havel's essay 'Politics and conscience', first published in 1984, shortly after Havel's release from prison in 1983 (he had been imprisoned by the communist Czechoslovakian government as a political dissident in 1979). It is an examination of what he considered to be the growing prevalence of an impersonal and faceless exercise of power characterizing the modern (and not just communist) world.

The Czech philosopher Václav Belohradský has persuasively developed the thought that the rationalistic spirit of modern science, founded on abstract reason and on the presumption of impersonal objectivity, has its father not only in the natural sciences – Galileo, but also a father in politics – Machiavelli, who first formulated (albeit with an undertone of malicious irony) a theory of politics as a rational technology of power. We could say that, for all the complex historical detours, the origin of the modern state and of modern political power may be sought precisely here, that is, once again in a moment when human reason begins to 'liberate' itself from the human being as such, from his personal experience, personal conscience, and personal responsibility and so also from that to which, within the framework of the natural world, all responsibility is uniquely related, his absolute horizon. Just as the modern scientists set apart the actual human being as the subject of the lived experience of the world, so, ever more evidently, do both the modern state and modern politics.

To be sure, this process by which power becomes anonymous and depersonalized, and reduced to a mere technology of rule and manipulation, has a thousand masks, variants, and expressions. In one case it is covert and inconspicuous, while in another case it is entirely overt; in one case it sneaks up on us along subtle and devious paths, in another case it is brutally direct. Essentially, though, it is the same universal trend. It is the essential trait of all modern civilization, growing directly from its spiritual structure, rooted in it by a thousand tangled tendrils and inseparable even in thought from its technological nature, its mass characteristics, and its consumer orientation.

Rulers and leaders were once personalities in their own right, with particular human faces, still in some sense personally responsible for their deeds, good and ill, whether they had been installed by dynastic tradition, by the will of the people, by a victorious battle, or by intrigue. But they have been replaced in modern times by the manager, the bureaucrat, the apparatchik – a professional ruler, manipulator, and expert in the techniques of management, manipulation, and obfuscation, filling a depersonalized intersection of functional relations, a cog in the machinery of state caught up in a predetermined role. This professional ruler is an 'innocent' tool of an 'innocent' anonymous power, legitimized by science, cybernetics, ideology, law, abstraction, and objectivity – that is, by everything except personal responsibility to human beings as persons and neighbors. A modern politician is transparent: behind his judicious mask and affected diction there is not a trace of a human being rooted in the order of the natural world by his loves, passions, interests, personal opinions, hatred, courage, or cruelty. All that he, too, locks away in his private bathroom. If we glimpse anything at all behind the mask, it will be only a more or less competent technician of power. System, ideology, and apparat have deprived us – rulers as well as the ruled – of our conscience, of our common sense and natural speech and thereby, of our actual humanity. States grow ever more machinelike; people are transformed into statistical choruses of voters, producers, consumers, patients, tourists, or soldiers. In politics, good and evil, categories of the natural world and therefore obsolete remnants of the past, lose all absolute meaning; the sole method of politics is quantifiable success. Power is *a priori* innocent because it does not grow from a world in which words like 'guilt' and 'innocence' retain their meaning.

This impersonal power has achieved what is its most complete expression so far in the totalitarian systems. As Belohradský points out, the depersonalization of power and its conquest of human conscience and human speech have been successfully linked to an extra-European tradition of a 'cosmological' conception of the empire (identifying the empire, as the sole true center of the world, with the world as such, and considering the human as its exclusive property). But, as the totalitarian systems clearly illustrate, this does not mean that modern impersonal power is itself an extra-European affair. The truth is the very opposite: it was precisely Europe, and the European West, that provided and frequently forced on the world all that today has become the basis of such power: natural science, rationalism, scientism, the industrial revolution, and also revolution as such, as a fanatical abstraction, through the displacement of the natural world to the bathroom down to the cult of consumption, the atomic bomb, and Marxism. And it is Europe – democratic western Europe – which today stands bewildered in the face of this ambiguous export. The contemporary dilemma, whether to resist this reverse expansionism of its erstwhile export or to yield to it, attests to this. Should rockets, now aimed at Europe thanks to its export of spiritual and technological potential, be countered by similar and better rockets, thereby demonstrating a determination to defend such values as Europe has left, at the cost of entering into an utterly immoral game being forced upon it? Or should Europe retreat, hoping that the responsibility for the fate of the planet demonstrated thereby will infect, by its miraculous power, the rest of the world?

I think that, with respect to the relation of western Europe to the totalitarian systems, no error could be greater than the one looming largest: that of a failure to understand the totalitarian systems for what they ultimately are – a convex mirror of all modern civilization and a harsh, perhaps final call for a global recasting of how that civilization understands itself. If we ignore that, then it does not make any essential difference which form Europe's efforts will take. It might be the form of taking the totalitarian systems, in the spirit of Europe's own rationalistic tradition, for a locally idiosyncratic attempt at achieving general welfare, to which only men of ill-will attribute expansionist tendencies. Or, in the spirit of the same rationalistic tradition, though this time in the Machiavellian conception of politics as the technology of power, one might perceive the totalitarian regimes as a purely external threat by expansionist neighbors who can be driven back within acceptable bounds by an appropriate demonstration of power, without having to be thought about more deeply. The first alternative is that of the person who reconciles himself to the chimney belching smoke, even though that smoke is ugly and smelly, because in the end it serves a good purpose, the production of commonly needed goods. The second alternative is that of the man who thinks that it is simply a matter of technological flaw, which can be eliminated by technological means, such as a filter or a scrubber.

The reality, I believe, is unfortunately more serious. The chimney 'soiling the heavens' is not just a technologically corrigible flaw of design, or a tax paid for a better consumerist tomorrow, but a symbol of a civilization which has renounced the absolute, which ignores the natural world and disdains its imperatives. So, too, the totalitarian systems warn of something far more serious than Western rationalism is willing to admit. They are, most of all, a convex mirror of the inevitable consequences of rationalism, a grotesquely magnified image of its own deep tendencies, an extreme offshoot of its own development and an ominous product of its own expansion. They are a deeply informative reflection of its own crisis. Totalitarian regimes are not merely dangerous neighbors and even less some kind of an avant-garde of world progress. Alas, just the opposite: they are the avant-garde of a global crisis of this civilization, first European, then Euro-American, and ultimately global. They are one of the possible futurological studies of the Western world, not in the sense that one day they will attack and conquer it, but in a far deeper sense – that they illustrate graphically the consequences of what Belohradský calls the 'eschatology of the impersonal'.

It is the total rule of a bloated, anonymously bureaucratic power, not yet irresponsible but already operating outside all conscience, a power grounded in an omnipresent ideological fiction which can rationalize anything without ever having to come in contact with the truth. Power as the omnipresent monopoly of control, repression, and fear; power which makes thought, morality, and privacy a state monopoly and so dehumanizes them; power which long since has ceased to be the matter of a group of arbitrary rulers but which, rather, occupies and swallows up everyone so that all should become integrated within it, at least through their silence. No one actually possesses such power, since it is the power itself which possesses everyone; it is a monstrosity which is not guided by humans but which, on the contrary, drags all persons along with its 'objective' self-momentum – objective in the sense of being cut off from all human standards, including human reason, and hence entirely irrational – toward a terrifying, unknown future.

Let me repeat: totalitarian power is a great reminder to contemporary civilization. Perhaps somewhere there may be some generals who think it would be best to dispatch such systems from the face of the earth and then all would be well. But that is no different from an ugly woman trying to get rid of her ugliness by smashing the mirror that reminds her of it. Such a 'final solution' is one of the typical dreams of impersonal reason – capable, as the term 'final solution' graphically reminds us, of transforming its dreams into reality and thereby reality into a nightmare. It would not only fail to resolve the crisis of the present world but, assuming anyone survived at all, would only aggravate it. By burdening the already heavy account of this civilization with further millions of dead, it would not block its essential trend to totalitarianism but would rather accelerate it. It would be a Pyrrhic victory, because the victors would emerge from a conflict inevitably resembling their defeated opponents far more than anyone today is willing to admit or able to imagine. Just a minor example: imagine what a huge Gulag Archipelago would have to be built in the West, in the name of country, democracy, progress, and war discipline, to contain all who refuse to take part in the effort, whether from naivete, principle, fear, or ill will!

No evil has ever been eliminated by suppressing its symptoms. We need to address the cause itself.

(Havel [1984] (1991), pp. 256–61)

EXERCISE _____

Consider the following question: in the extract how precisely does Havel characterize Europe and locate himself apropos Europe?

DISCUSSION _____

In this extract Havel essentially argues that modern forms of totalitarianism do not, as is often alleged, derive from extra-European roots, but are actually rooted within Europe itself and especially western Europe. It is interesting that Havel uses Europe and western Europe interchangeably here, especially as he speaks from a location which lay within the eastern alignment in the cold war. This occurs quite naturally for Havel: 'it was precisely Europe, and the European West, that provided and frequently forced on the world all that today has become the basis of such power'; 'it is Europe – democratic western Europe – which today stands bewildered in the face of this ambiguous export'. Clearly the representation of 'western Europe' as simply 'Europe' is taken for granted in this context, and significantly in doing so Havel almost appears to locate the context he speaks within (and more immediately against) as lying outside Europe, as the victim of a 'European' imposition of rationalism. When he marks the expansion of the malaise of western rationalism as moving from 'first European, then Euro-American' to become 'ultimately global', this is a telling association that locates the ostensibly totalitarian states of the east, which neighbour Europe and turn their guns on Europe, in the rest of the world.

The whole argument of the extract is also of interest in terms of the theoretical issues of eurocentrism and synecdochical constructions discussed above. Not only does Havel subscribe to the synecdochical construction of 'western Europe' as 'Europe', he also synecdochically associates 'western Europe' with 'western rationalism' and therefore holds 'Europe' more or less exclusively responsible for the spread of the political rationalism which turns against its originator. This is something that should be looked at more interrogatively: the association of modern political rationalism with Europe as a whole from some location *outside* (in the east) is a kind of reversal of responsibility which was naturally pregnant with meaning in the context of the cold war. It was in fact an attempt to counter the eurocentrism which had in the first place encouraged the location of totalitarianism as anti-rational and of extra-European origin. The whole extract is an argument against a particular eurocentric position, which is actually synecdochically a western eurocentric position.

Cominform: the organization for joint communist propaganda in the eastern bloc

During the cold war neither the east nor the west was ever actually an ideologically uniform zone. Within the eastern area the president of Yugoslavia, Marshal Tito (originally Josip Broz), broke with Stalin and the **Cominform** in 1948, developed a distinct brand of socialist governance, and became one of the founding members of the Non-Aligned Movement, along with the prime minister of India, Jawaharlal Nehru (1947–64). Meanwhile, the cooling of China–Soviet relations in the 1960s was a matter of concern for the left movement generally. Then in the Prague Spring of 1968 the attempts of Alexander Dubcek (1968–9), the first secretary of Czechoslovakia, to reform communism had to be countered by a Soviet invasion. Finally, the end of the cold war came from within the east, initiated by the reform programme (*perestroika*) of President Mikhail Gorbachev and by popular protests within eastern European countries. Similarly, within the west a progressive socialist democratic Sweden and a rather precariously located Finland refused to join Nato during the cold war. At the same time, the course of internal political unrest (punctuated by military rule) until the socialist Andreas Papandreou (1981–9, 1993–6) first came to power, and conflict with Turkey over the fate of Cyprus, Greece kept slipping in and out of Nato. Moreover, the coup led by Major Otelo de Carvalho in Portugal, which led to the formation of a military government with socialist leanings during 1974–5, also caused political turmoil.

Perceptions of Europe from outside in the postwar period naturally changed during the cold war in more significant ways than the one mentioned above. From a dominant imperialist world power Europe (synecdochically representing dominant European powers) gradually came to be seen as a less coherent and self-possessed formation. It was perceived to be in the grip of forces larger than itself: ideological forces that were more powerful than its continental identity or its constituent (and formerly definitive) state identities, and military superpowers who were in a position to influence Europe in unprecedented ways from outside.

From a wider international perspective, to think of the cold war as 'cold' is peculiarly eurocentric. While it is true that this period was not marked by direct military conflict between the two superpowers, or between east and west inside Europe, it gave an overall coherence to numerous violent civil and military conflicts elsewhere. So while the cold war was 'cold' at the centre (at the meeting point of east and west in Europe) it was markedly 'hot' at the periphery. The situation can be characterized as one where the battlefields were not located where the conflict appeared to be. Cold war imperatives and different degrees of superpower involvement (mainly by the US and Nato countries, the USSR and Warsaw Pact countries, as well as China) determined the conduct of the Korean war (1950–3), the

Vietnam war (1964–75) (with direct American intervention in both), three Arab–Israeli wars (1956, 1967 and 1973) and the Angolan civil war (1975–87). Cold war tensions also underlay America's invasion of Nicaragua in 1984, American support and aid in the 1973 coup in Chile, the 1964 coup in Brazil, the 1954 coup in Guatemala, the 1953 coup in Iran (most of these attended by bloodshed and human rights violations) and the Soviet invasion of Afghanistan in 1979. In this larger world perspective the United States, with the support of its west European (or synecdochically European) allies, was far more aggressive in its bids to extend cold war spheres of influence than the USSR and its allies (and China came nowhere close to demonstrations of such aggressiveness). This has led the well-known linguistics scholar and commentator on American foreign policy Noam Chomsky to conclude in *World Orders, Old and New* (1994) that the role of the United States in the cold war was not so much to defend the ideology of liberal democracy and freedom, as it has claimed, as to serve its self-interests through a covert neo-imperialist policy of world domination.

European integration and globalization

The phrase European integration (the reasons and connotations of which continue to be widely debated) is *usually* applied to the process whereby European countries that can identify common economic and political interests hope to maintain and, if possible, maximize their position in the world by acting jointly in economic and political matters. This involves, first, the identification of such joint interests; secondly, the creation of common economic, legal and administrative structures to facilitate the further development of, and ability to act upon, these interests; and thirdly, the creation of European institutions to present a joint front in economic and political matters outside Europe. This was initially conceived as a move towards economic and political cooperation between certain western European countries. The executives of three communities which had been created for cooperation in such areas (the European Economic Community, European Atomic Energy Community, European Coal and Steel Community) merged to form a European Community (EC) in 1965, with a Council and Commission, while an Economic Monetary Union (EMU) between these countries started to be discussed in 1969. A unified political and legal framework in certain areas was created and assumed by EC members to give birth to the EU (effectively from 1993) by the Maastricht Treaty of 1992. The fall of the Soviet Union and the collapse of the Warsaw Pact have enabled an increase in EU membership and agreements between Russia and the Baltic states (which still remained outside this synecdochical 'Europe') since 1994. A new European single currency (the euro) came into effect in most EU member countries in January 2002.

The term 'globalization' refers (on the whole loosely) to the perception that a greater degree of economic cooperation and exchange has occurred in the world (especially after the cold war) through the liberalization of markets at an international level, the spread of capitalist multinational corporations and the development of international economic systems (such as stock exchanges); that this has been facilitated by and has facilitated developments in information and communications technologies which have effectively shrunk the world; and that the effects of all these have potentially opened up the possibility of greater cultural homogeneity across the planet. It has been observed that despite the upbeat tone of debates about globalization, these processes have also been attended by an escalation of internecine communal and nationalist conflicts, as well as by an increase in inequality across countries and between the haves and the have-nots.

It is usually understood that the moves towards European integration through the formation of the EU and the EMU have coincided with the phenomenon of globalization, and that such integration has enabled different European countries to achieve a substantial economic presence in an increasingly competitive and better coordinated world economy.

Under the Maastricht Treaty EU members adopted a Common Foreign and Security Policy (CFSP), in order to, as Julian Vassallo says in his chapter in the *Guide to EU Policies* (1998), 'give the Union a voice in international relations equal to its economic weight' (Vassallo, 1998, p. 297). In other words, it appears that the joint foreign policy which EU members are able to present through the CFSP is guided by economic considerations.

Throughout the 1980s the EC built up a network of foreign representations in countries outside Europe, which has expanded since the end of the cold war in the 1990s. However, this was conceived more as a mediatory framework between the individual member states than as an independent representative body and, in general, foreign policy decisions remain the prerogative of individual members acting as sovereign states. The view that these moves towards the political integration of Europe in foreign policy present from outside is probably best given in Christopher Hill and William Wallace's still pertinent words in *The Actors in Europe's Foreign Policy*:

> The member states of the European Union have established a collective 'presence' in the international arena, without achieving the ability to act collectively except through cumbersome consultative procedures and partially effective diplomatic, economic and military instruments. Even then

they depend on favourable conjunctions of external circumstances and operate largely in the longer term. True actorness requires not only a clear identity and a self-contained decision-making system, but also the practical capabilities to effect policy. In all of these dimensions the EU falls some way short. Its presence in the world is therefore real but incoherent, leaving third countries (which nonetheless seem to welcome it as a new 'pole' in the international system) to cope with relations with the European Community (through the Commission) alongside bilateral relations with the member states, to puzzle over the role and function of the WEU and over the duplication of national embassies by community representations which see themselves as playing an increasingly political role.

(Hill and Wallace, 1996, p. 13)

Incidentally, the WEU (Western European Union), originally formed in the late 1960s, was revived in the early 1980s as a forum for consultation about security matters among EC members. That 'true actorness' in Hill and Wallace's sense is on the the EU's agenda is evidenced by the changing prerogatives of the WEU. From the Treaty of European Union (TEU) at Maastricht in 1992 until 1997 its role was to 'elaborate and implement decisions and actions of the Union which have defence implications' (Article J.4.2 of the TEU). Since 1998, however, WEU and Nato mechanisms have gradually come to be used by the EU to provide a capacity for autonomous action, and the WEU's independent status has gradually been diminished in favour of new EU political and military bodies to which the crisis management responsibilities of the WEU have gradually been ceded.

In the initial stages moves towards European integration were made with American consultation and support; but increasingly since the end of the cold war and the removal of the so-called communist threat American interest in European integration has grown lukewarm. The perception inside Europe is that the role of the EU and EMU is to form a substantial economic force along with the United States and the rapidly growing East and Southeast Asian economies, and to be able to hold its own and contribute to the unravelling of the forces of globalization. The cultural changes that have come in the wake of globalization (following greater similarities of available commodities and informational, technological and economic infrastructures in different countries), however, can be perceived as the result of a continuing alignment of the US and Europe to extend ideological control out of economic self-interest. This argument is summarized trenchantly in an essay by John Tomlinson entitled 'Globalised culture: the triumph of the west?', as follows:

> [Globalized culture] is, in short, simply the global extension of *Western* culture. The broad implications – and the causes of critical concern – are that: (a) this process is homogenising, that it threatens the obliteration of the world's rich cultural diversity; (b) that it visits the various cultural ills of the West on other cultures; (c) that this is a particular threat to the fragile and vulnerable cultures of peripheral, 'Third World' nations; and (d) that it is part and parcel of wider forms of domination – those involved in the ever-widening grip of transnational capitalism and those involved in the maintenance of post-colonial relations of (economic and cultural) dependency.

> (Tomlinson, 1999, p.23)

Where 'westernization' is understood as:

> A whole range of things: the consumer culture of Western capitalism with its now all-too-familiar icons (McDonald's, Coca-Cola, Levi Jeans), the spread of European languages (particularly English), styles of dress, eating habits, architecture and music, the adoption of an urban lifestyle based around industrial production, a pattern of cultural experience dominated by the mass media, a range of cultural values and attitudes – about personal liberty, gender and sexuality, human rights, the political process, religion, scientific and technological rationality and so on.

> (Tomlinson, 1999, p. 23)

Such arguments about globalization as westernization (never too far from the synecdochical 'Europeanization' or 'Americanization') should not, however, be accepted too easily, and should be thought through carefully. Some of these values and attitudes, as I have maintained above, need not be considered as Europe-specific or west-specific. Tomlinson goes on to draw on arguments from the work of the sociologist Anthony Giddens suggesting that globalization may well portend the 'decline of the west' rather than 'the triumph of the west' (Tomlinson, 1999, p. 25–6). It may be argued, for instance, that globalization itself is far from a homogeneous phenomenon (it appears in different ways in different places); that the uniformity that is manifested by globalization may well lead to the diffusion of a strongly identifiable west; that the resources made available by economic and technological changes which are seen to be the results of globalization may allow new identities and political concerns to emerge. And yet, as I have also maintained above, at the same time the political and social misgivings and concerns which attend the so-called phenomenon of globalization should not be discounted.

Conclusion

To summarize, in this chapter I have examined at some length two theoretical issues that impinge on the manner in which Europe is perceived from outside: the prevalence of eurocentrism (considering ideas and attitudes which are primarily pertinent to European contexts to be natural or universal, and applying them inappropriately elsewhere); and the tendency towards synecdochical constructions (to think of the part as the whole or vice versa – for instance, to think of that which is pertinent to a small part of Europe as being 'European'). I have examined what sort of bearing these theoretical issues have had on three postwar outside perspectives of Europe: Europe in the postcolonial world, Europe in the cold war, and European integration and globalization. These three perspectives are a result of certain political, social and historical conditions which I have briefly discussed here, and regarding which I have offered a few general observations. Only more detailed analysis of the relationship between particular contexts inside and outside Europe can help us determine how far the theoretical formulations and general observations offered above are applicable and acceptable.

Notes

1 Ernest Renan (1823–1892), French philologist and historian. Among his many books are *Histoire générale des langues sémitiques* (1854), *Etudes d'histoire religieuse* (1856), *Vie de Jésus* (1863) and *Histoire du peuple d'Israël* (1887–1894).

Richard Krafft-Ebing (1840–1902), German psychiatrist. His work was mainly on forensic psychiatry and sexual pathology. His best-known work is *Psychopathia Sexualis* (1876).

Cesare Lombroso (1836–1909), Italian physician and criminologist. He specialized in forensic medicine, psychiatry and criminal anthropology. His best-known book is *L'uomo delinquente* (1875).

2, 3 Gonzalo Jiménez de Quesada (1509–79), Spanish conqueror of the Chibcha civilization of Columbia. He led several expeditions in search of the mythical city of gold, El Dorado.

Francis Drake (1540–96) explored the interior of the Orinoko Valley in quest of El Dorado.

References

Adorno, T. and Horkheimer, M. (1972) *Dialectic of Enlightenment*, London, Allen Lane.

Ahmad, A. [1962] (1977) *Gharbzadegi* [Weststruckeness], transl. J. Green and A. Alizadeh, Costa Mesa, CA, Mazda.

Ahmad, A. (1992) *In Theory: Classes, Nations, Literatures*, London, Verso.

Césaire, A. [1955] (1972) *Discourse on Colonialism*, transl. J. Pinkham, New York, Monthly Review Press.

Chakrabarty, D. [1992] (1997) 'Postcoloniality and the artifice of history', in R. Guha (ed.), *The Subaltern Studies Reader, 1986–1995*, Minneapolis, MN, University of Minnesota Press.

Chomsky, N. (1994) *World Orders, Old and New*, London, Pluto.

Davenport, M. and Page, S. (1992) *Europe: 1992 and the Developing World*, London, Overseas Development Institute.

Fanon, F. (1961) *The Wretched of the Earth*, transl. C. Farrington, Harmondsworth, Penguin.

Fernández-Armesto, F. (ed.) (1997) *The Times Guide to the Peoples of Europe*, London, Times Books.

Fukuyama, F. (1995) *Trust: the Social Virtues and the Creation of Prosperity*, New York, Free Press.

Gramsci, A. (1971) *Selections from the Prison Notebooks*, ed. Q. Hoare and G. Nowell-Smith, London, Lawrence & Wishart.

Grimal, H. [1965] (1978) *Decolonization: the British, French, Dutch and Belgian Empires 1919–1963*, transl. S. De Vos, London, Routledge & Kegan Paul.

Havel, V. [1984] (1991) 'Politics and conscience', in *Open Letters: Selected Prose, 1965–1990*, London, Faber & Faber.

Hill, C. and Wallace, W. (1996) 'Introduction: actors and actions', in Hill, C. (ed.), *The Actors in Europe's Foreign Policy*, London, Routledge.

Hintjens, H. M. (1995) *Alternatives to Independence: Explorations in Postcolonial Relations*, Aldershot, Dartmouth.

Kunene, M. [1970] (1975) 'Europe', in W. Soyinka (ed.), *Poems of Black Africa*, London, Secker & Warburg.

Lister, M. (1988) *The European Community and the Developing World: the Role of the Lome Convention*, Aldershot, Avebury.

Lister, M. (1997) *The European Union and the South: Relations with Developing Countries*, London, Routledge.

Malek, A. A. (1963) 'Orientalism in crisis', *Diogenes*, 44, winter.

Mottahedeh, R. (1985) *The Mantle of the Prophet: Religion and Politics in Iran*, Harmondsworth, Penguin.

Naipaul, V. S. [1962] (1969) *The Middle Passage: Impressions of Five Societies*, Harmondsworth, Penguin.

Naipaul, V. S. [1964] (1972) 'Jasmine', in *The Overcrowded Barracoon and Other Articles*, London, Andre Deutsch.

Naipaul, V. S. (1987) *The Enigma of Arrival*, Harmondsworth, Penguin.

Said, E. (1978) *Orientalism: Western Conceptions of the Orient*, Harmondsworth, Penguin.

Simpson, L. [1957] (1972) 'To the Western World', in D. Hall (ed.), *Contemporary American Poetry*, Harmondsworth, Penguin.

Tomlinson, J. (1999) 'Globalised culture: the triumph of the west?', in T. Skelton and T. Allen (eds), *Culture and Global Change*, London, Routledge.

Vassallo, J. (1998) 'Common foreign and security policy', in G. Glöckler et al (eds), *Guide to EU Policies*, London, Blackstone.

Summaries and notes to poems

'To the Western World'

The poem as a whole can be read as an imagistic history of America, from before the time of its 'discovery' by Europe to the present when it is still being settled and assuming its own identity (being 'civilize [d]').

Stanza 1

Lines 1–2. Here we have a past where America is no more than a mythical land (tempting and yet unknown). This shadowy pre-Colombian America is more myth than reality, more a surrealistic imagining than a place on the map – and is likened to the sirens, a symbol of temptation that might lead travellers (such as Odysseus) astray unless they restrain themselves (as Odysseus did). Europe is more concrete than the un-'discovered' America, but still in that distant past itself a land of romance ('high castle'), an idealized pastoral world ('the shepherd's crook') – and is likened to the traveller who is *not* led astray by the sirens, an Odysseus. In brief, in this distant past America is no more than a faint prefiguration in Europe's mind, no more than a longing for something new outside its world (a longing that is captured in the imagining of Odysseus' adventures) but one that it doesn't – perhaps daren't – explore.

(The sirens, and how Odysseus took himself and his comrades past their land without being tempted by their song, are described in Book 12 of Homer's *Odyssey.*)

Lines 3–5. These describe Christopher Columbus's 'discovery' of America (or, at least, Europe's 'discovery' of America) in 1492. This journey involved Columbus's flagship, the *Santa Maria*, and two small caravels, the *Pinta* and the *Niña*. In this first expedition Columbus explored an island of the Bahamas, as well as Cuba and Hispaniola – all lying around the Strait of Florida by the Bay of Mexico. Columbus was in fact searching for a sea route to India in this expedition, not 'Cathay' (an archaic name for China), which is mentioned here instead possibly to increase the sense of mystery traditionally associated with China and perhaps to evoke the spirit of adventure and wonder that took Marco Polo to China in 1275.

Stanza 2

Lines 6–10. America is now populated by those who emigrated in the wake of Columbus's explorations, and here the 'we' who speak are the voices of these early settlers. They draw their ancestry directly from Europe – they originate symbolically, as did Christopher Columbus's actual 1492 expedition, from the Spanish seaport of Palos. The settlers recall in lines 9 and 10 the first impression of this New World, an 'enormous' unnamed land, in direct counterpoint with the Old World Europe and its well-charted shores and seaports (like Palos).

Stanza 3

Lines 11–15. Here the old fantasies about the New World are dispensed with (so Cathay was 'never found'); the land acquires its own identity and the name 'America'. The acquisition of America's identity is seen as the fruits of the labour of descendants of European settlers, who gradually 'civilize the ground'.

'Europe'

Stanzas 1 and 2. Europe is personalized as the addressed object. These two stanzas are in the present tense and associate the personalized Europe with images of aridity in the first stanza and with cannibalistic self-consuming violence in the second.

Stanza 3. Here the addressee ('I') is introduced. This could be seen as the voice of someone who dissociates him/herself from Europe – who is the 'other' of Europe. This dissociation is enacted within the stanza: this is the voice of someone who once believed he/she was also the offspring of Europe (regarded Europe as the mother, with 'breasts/Over-flowing with milk'), but clearly erroneously since he/she now realizes that the true offspring of Europe are as described in stanza 2 ('Who devour the flesh of their parent'). This could well be the voice of the naive colonized continent of Africa, which had been led to regard Europe as the mother-continent.

Stanzas 4–7. These describe in an imagistic fashion the process through which the disenchantment, from that past naive outlook to the present sense of Europe's menace, developed. Stanza 4 sees Europe's learning itself ('rushing with books') leading it into the wilderness ('in the forest') and internal conflict ('Breaking the bones of your clans'). Stanza 5 briefly describes how Europe grew ideologically rigid ('hardness of your visions') and insular ('closed the doors') and turned to war ('chose the bridegroom of steel'). These are references to the hardening of ideological divides in twentieth-century Europe and the two world wars that were fought primarily within Europe or in terms of European interests. Stanzas 6 and 7 present a sort of moral evaluation of these developments within Europe. Stanza 6 observes that war in this instance was not motivated by any benign motive ('not to love'), but out of a lack of communication and understanding ('Dedicated to silence'). Stanza 7 elaborates on the self-deception ('laughed at the blind men/But you yourself were blind') and confusion ('Struggling in this great night') that followed.

Stanzas 8–9. Here 'I' comes back to the present. Europe has become tainted by the process described in stanzas 4–7. Her offspring continue the legacy of violent self-deception and confusion, only now it is directed outside Europe ('to the skies/Burning others in their sleep'). However, the now mature 'I' of the poem has outgrown his/her early naivety and has access to a larger viewpoint – a more universal viewpoint (like the sun's) – from which the violent concerns of Europe's offspring fade into insignificance ('The sun will laugh/Because it burnt out cradles from age to age').

Appendix

Chronology

Year	Country	Date of independence
1922	Egypt	28 February (British Declaration)
1932	Iraq	3 October
1941	Lebanon	26 November (proclaimed)
1945	Vietnam	2 September (Ho Chi Minh's declaration)

1946	Syria	17 April
	Transjordania (now Jordan)	25 May
1947	India	15 August
	Pakistan	15 August
	Ceylon (now Sri Lanka)	15 December
1948	Burma	4 January
1949	Laos	19 July
	Indonesia	27 December
1951	Libya	24 December
1953	Cambodia	9 November
1956	Sudan	1 January
	Morocco	2 March
	Tunisia	20 March
1957	Ghana	6 March
	Malaya (became Malaysia in 1963 with territories of North Borneo, Brunei and Sarawak)	31 August
1958	Singapore	3 June
	Guinea	2 October
1096	Cameroon	1 January
	Togo	27 April
	Madagascar	26 June
	Belgian Congo (later Zaire and Democratic Republic of Congo)	30 June
	Somaliland (Somalia)	
	Dahomey (now Benin)	1 July
	Niger	1 August
	Upper Volta (now Burkina Faso)	1 August
	Ivory Coast	5 August
	Chad	7 August
	Central African Republic	11 August 14 August
	Congo-Brazzaville (later Republic of Congo)	15 August
	Gabon	17 August
	Senegal	11 September
	Mali	23 September
	Nigeria	1 October
	Mauretania	28 November
1961	Sierra Leone	27 April
	Tanganyika (Tanzania)	9 December
1962	Western Samoa (now Samoa)	1 January

	Ruanda (Rwanda)	1 July
	Burundi	1 July
	Algeria	3 July
	Jamaica	6 August
	Trinidad-Tobago	31 August
	Uganda	19 October
1963	Kenya	12 December
1964	Nyasaland (now Malawi)	1 July
	Northern Rhodesia (now Zambia)	23 October

3

Europe's borders, Europe's regions:

eastern Europe, central Europe

MARK PITTAWAY

Introduction

The question of where Europe's eastern borders lie has exercised
commentators for over two and a half centuries. It is still an issue that
focuses the attention of politicians and scholars alike. These borders
are at best ambiguous; there is little consensus, for example, as to
whether Russia or Turkey is a European state. As Chapter 4
demonstrates, further west the states of southeastern Europe, often
known as 'the Balkans', are seen to have a similarly ambiguous
relationship to Europe, if only, to quote Maria Todorova, because
they have been both 'geographically inextricable from Europe, yet
culturally constructed as "the other" within' (Todorova, 1997, p. 188).
Throughout the cold war the socialist states (Albania, Bulgaria,
Czechoslovakia, the GDR (East Germany), Hungary, Poland,
Romania, the Soviet Union and Yugoslavia), with the partial
exception of Yugoslavia, formed an eastern bloc separated from
western Europe by walls, borders, travel restrictions and the denial of
political freedom. Even with the collapse of the socialist regimes the
notion of a difference between eastern and western Europe has
ceased to disappear, as discussed in Chapter 1. Even the richer of the
former socialist states remain significantly poorer than any of their
western neighbours. Moreover, images of war, of the desperate
poverty of nations such as Albania and Russia, of the spread of
corruption and organized crime, have allowed notions to develop
that eastern Europe, while geographically part of Europe, does not
quite belong. Intellectuals across eastern Europe have, since the later
decades of socialist rule, sought to claim their place in Europe by
asserting their identity as 'central Europeans' and not 'eastern
Europeans'. This has been attempted in Croatia, the Czech lands,

Hungary, Poland, Slovakia and Slovenia. It has excluded, explicitly and implicitly, Russia, Ukraine, Romania, Bulgaria and what is left of former Yugoslavia.

The purpose of this chapter is to explore how the boundaries of Europe are contested. It aims to show that the questions of where 'Europe' ends, of where 'eastern Europe' or 'central Europe' lie, are not simply questions of geography. They are tied to an idea of Europe as a conceptual space, as an area with a shared history, and to political programmes in certain states that aim for inclusion in a European space. These notions seek to exclude others from that Europe. Iver B. Neumann has shown that 'the East' has played a central role as 'the other' in forming contemporary ideas of Europe (Neumann, 1999). When notions of the east are superimposed on to notions of Europe, as in conceptual designations like eastern Europe, the result is to create a perceived region that is both simultaneously included and excluded from Europe. By the end of this chapter, therefore, you should have an understanding of the following issues.

1   The designation of a region is not simply a matter of geography. Ideas are superimposed on to physical geography in order to create regions.

2   Debates about where the borders of regions within Europe lie are the products of specific historical and political contexts. They are not fixed but shift over periods of time.

3   The eastern boundaries of Europe are therefore fluid and are determined in the same way as the boundaries of regions.

4   Eastern European identities are thus ambiguous; they are based on both inclusion and exclusion from Europe.

I introduced you to many of these issues in Chapter 1. Here I return to them in a little more depth by examining the debates about eastern European identity in the last two decades of the twentieth century. These debates have been dominated by two separate but related questions. The first and most important has concerned whether the countries that were part of the socialist bloc lying between Germany and the USSR were or are 'eastern Europe' or 'central Europe'. The second concentrates on the distinction made in the 1990s between central Europe and 'the Balkans'. Such discussions reveal a good deal about the nature of eastern European identity. In this chapter I outline the debates about central Europe, and then go on to examine the basis of these identities in geography before turning to history and to politics. I return to the issue of 'the Balkans' in Chapter 4.

The re-emergence of central Europe in intellectual discourse: historical background

Until 1989 Europe was divided into two politically defined blocs. Western Europe was made up of states that were either directly bound to the United States by military alliance or had some degree of commitment to capitalist economics and, from the mid 1970s onwards, to liberal democracy. The eastern part of the continent was dominated by states that were, with the exceptions of Yugoslavia and Albania, bound to the Soviet Union. All these states had largely socialized economies and were governed by political systems in which the leading role of a Marxist-Leninist party was constitutionally enshrined. This division was much more than a simple geopolitical one; these societies had very different kinds of industrial economies, and the nature of postwar social experience on both sides of the cold war divide was profoundly different. The revival of ideas of central Europe formed part of an intellectual revolt in some of the socialist states during the 1970s and 1980s that in many respects set the scene for the end of socialist eastern Europe in 1989.

During the 1970s tacit settlements between the regimes and peoples existed in most of the socialist states. In Czechoslovakia, Hungary and Poland the ruling Communist parties demanded political conformity from their populaces. In exchange the state aimed to pacify the population by guaranteeing them a rising standard of living and an ever-improving supply of consumer goods. In each of the countries the tacit settlements differed, as indeed did the historical circumstances from which they had arisen. These tacit settlements were more successful in some countries than others. In Hungary the memory of political turbulence in 1956 had long receded by the middle of the 1970s, and the consumerist model of socialism introduced during the 1960s succeeded in buying considerable political peace. In Czechoslovakia the settlement occurred in the context of the **normalization** that followed the end of the Prague Spring in 1968, when large numbers of the highly educated lost their jobs and the party was extensively purged. This meant that intellectual protest was more marked, yet throughout much of society there was considerable social peace. It was in Poland, however, where the settlement was at its shakiest, as considerable public protest shook the socialist state throughout the 1970s, culminating in the formation of **Solidarity** and the eventual declaration of martial law in 1981 (Ekiert, 1996; Tőkes, 1996; Šimecka, 1984).

The Polish events of 1980 and 1981 were one of the most important factors in exposing the bankruptcy of socialist regimes in eastern Europe. Upheaval in Poland was a symptom of a more general malaise that affected all of the socialist regimes during the 1980s. The

Normalization refers to the purges initiated by the secretary-general of Czechoslovak Communist Party, Gustáv Husák (1969–1987), designed to reverse the impact of the Prague Spring (see Chapter 1). The government and party were heavily purged of reformers. The impact of normalization was, however, most directly felt in intellectual and cultural life. Between 1969 and 1971 the writers' union and other bodies were extensively purged.

See Chapter 1.

Figure 1   Vacha, east/west German border, 1985. The images that accompany this chapter depict the landscape of a border that no longer exists; the so-called 'Iron Curtain', the cold war border that divided Europe into east and west. All of these photographs were taken by the American photographer Brian Rose. They form part of a project entitled 'The lost border', photographs taken between 1985 and 1996 that examine not only the reality of the cold war border but its afterlife. The images used here were produced between 1985 and 1987 when the cold war was very much a reality and some of the authors discussed in these chapters were rebelling against the continent's divide by articulating a central European identity.

The images taken together give an interesting perspective on that border. Rose has written that 'neither I nor anyone else foresaw how quickly the border would be erased, but the fatalistic notion that it was virtually permanent – part of the furniture of Europe – was something I was never able to accept' (Brian Rose website). This image, which contrasts the reality of the border in the background with an idyllic rural scene in the foreground highlights the unnatural nature of purely political division. Photo: Brian Rose

economic problems inherent in earlier strategies of socialist industrialization were becoming more apparent; poor quality goods produced by east European industry could not be sold on world markets. By the end of the 1970s, the debt levels of east European states had reached such heights that existing economic policies were unsustainable (Kopstein, 1997; Földes, 1995). Much of this was of course kept secret from eastern European populations. They did, however, experience this economic crisis through rising prices, longer working hours, more severe shortages of goods and services, and a declining quality of life. Throughout the 1980s public discontent increased.

The economic crisis and crumbling authority of the state formed the backdrop to growing intellectual interest in ideas of central Europe. It is important to note that this was by no means a mass phenomenon. The rediscovery of central Europe was largely restricted to small groups of intellectuals opposed to the socialist regimes. The core of these small groups was made up of the so-called dissidents; intellectuals who had broken with and had dared publicly to criticize the regimes during the 1970s. The assertion of a central European identity was marked in Poland, Czechoslovakia and Hungary within the Soviet bloc and to some extent in the then Yugoslav republic of Slovenia outside it. Those asserting such an identity argued that there was a central European space at the heart of Europe, distinct from both developed western Europe and undeveloped eastern Europe. Various advocates of this identity identified the roots of central European space in either history, geography or culture (Schöpflin and Wood, 1989). I shall examine some of these claims in a little more depth later in this chapter, but I want for now to identify the political meanings implicit in the rediscovery of a central European identity.

EXERCISE

Based upon this knowledge, why do you think that ideas of central Europe were so well received in 'dissident' circles during the 1980s?

DISCUSSION

First, and most obviously, the assertion of a central European identity challenged the notion that Hungarians, Czechs, Slovaks and Poles were east Europeans. In so doing it directly challenged the basis of the cold war division of Europe. Secondly, it represented an attempt to move the central European states from the periphery to the core. By claiming that they were central Europeans the advocates of this identity laid a claim to 'the heart of Europe'. This assertion has been repeated in scholarly works on countries in the region that make claims for the central European nature of Czechs, Poles, Slovaks or

Hungarians (for an example of the Czech case see Sayer, 1998). Thirdly, it differentiated these societies from other countries further to their east, particularly and most explicitly Russia. Fourthly, it gave anti-socialist intellectuals the framework to address serious social concerns. By the early 1980s the socialist states' low standard of living relative to the west, their poorer public services and their malfunctioning economies had become painfully apparent. Increasingly the opposition advocated 'joining Europe' as a solution to these problems, something that implied transforming bureaucratic economies into ones that resembled the developed welfare capitalisms of the west of the continent. Broader intellectual debate focused on previous missed opportunities to catch up with the west and sought to explain their countries' prior failure to develop truly 'modern', 'industrialized' economies, or proper liberal 'civil societies' (Gerő, 1996; Jedlicki, 1999). In this context intellectuals' rediscovery of a central European identity could be seen as part of staking a moral claim to 'join Europe': to achieve political democracy, freedom of speech and assembly, freedom of movement, a legally protected civil society and a higher standard of living.

Since 1989 Czechs, Hungarians, Poles and Slovaks as well as Slovenes and Croats have stopped referring to themselves as east Europeans; instead they identify with central Europe. Increasingly this designation has gained widespread acceptance, as the post-socialist states have been differentiated in the minds of many commentators and, above all, by the European Union. Hungary, Poland and the Czech Republic were marked out as candidates for the 'first wave' of EU enlargement in the mid 1990s, while Romania, Bulgaria, Russia and the countries of former Yugoslavia were placed behind in the queue for membership. Much more is therefore at stake than a term, or a definition of a given geographical space. Behind the assertion of central European identity is a series of claims about European identity, about who rightfully belongs, who is included and indeed who is excluded. It is therefore important to pause here to consider the bases on which a central European identity rests.

Defining eastern Europe and central Europe

There are many different definitions of both eastern Europe and central Europe. It has been defined as *Mitteleuropa*, a region under the effective domination of Germany, though the advocates of central Europe under discussion in this chapter have explicitly repudiated that vision. The question of where either eastern or central Europe lies is difficult to give a definitive answer to. Prior to 1989 the answer seemed clear – eastern Europe was made up of the states of the socialist bloc dominated by and including the western regions of the Soviet Union. Even this definition ignored the problem of how far Russia is a European society, an issue that is addressed explicitly by Colin Chant in Chapter 5. Not all definitions of central Europe include all of the former socialist states outside the Soviet Union. They also include states that were part of cold war western Europe. Lonnie R. Johnson, who has written probably the most up-to-date history of central Europe as a region, describes it as including

> contemporary Germany, Poland, the Czech Republic, Slovakia, Austria, Hungary, Slovenia and Croatia. The historical frontiers of Central Europe extend somewhat farther to the east and the south-east than the current borders of these states.

(Johnson, 1996, p. v)

Central Europe, in Johnson's definition, includes

> The Baltic states, western Belarus, and western Ukraine, because they were parts of Poland between the fourteenth and eighteenth centuries, as well as with Transylvania in Romania, parts of Serbia, and Bosnia-Herzegovina because they were territories of the kingdom of Hungary in the Middle Ages, the Habsburg Empire thereafter, or the Dual Monarchy of Austria-Hungary after 1867.

(Johnson, 1996, p. v)

Most commentators who use the term central Europe would accept something close to Johnson's definition, which is founded on the political history of the region. Although the overwhelming majority of the population of this central Europe shared an experience under socialism between the late 1940s and the early 1990s this is not the region's defining feature. Central Europe, therefore, does not include Albania, Bulgaria, Greece, most of Romania, or most of Serbia. Nor does it include Russia. Implicit in the definition and in Johnson's project of writing a history of the region stretching from 400 to 1996 is an argument that the area's twentieth-century experience is less important to its identity than the prior experience of several older political units. According to Johnson, what defines central Europe is the fact that its regions shared a common historical experience as parts of the Holy Roman empire – and its successors in the forms of Austria-Hungary and imperial Germany – and as part of early modern Poland. For Johnson the story of the post-Second World War years is not so much the failure of state socialism, but 'the failure of Eastern Europe' (Johnson, 1996, p. 249).

The question of what unites these regions and their peoples and divides them from others is important, for if central Europe has a meaning it has to be in a common experience of space or of history. It does not seem implausible that the traces of the shared experience of Habsburg rule have left their mark on these countries, or that Polish nationalism has shaped the aspirations of those living in the former kingdom of Poland. But both of those areas have seen such major political changes and enormous shifts of population during the twentieth century as to raise the question of how important that historical experience remains to the people living there and their identities. Furthermore, what makes the experience of living under Polish and Habsburg rule a common central European one? Lastly, there are areas that are both part of Johnson's central Europe and simultaneously part of states outside it. The experiences of Slovenia and Croatia as constituent elements of Yugoslavia between 1918 and 1991 are entirely ignored. Although Yugoslavia collapsed in 1991 one ought to pose the question of the extent to which there was a common Yugoslav experience and what effects it has had on Croatian or Slovene identities. The same applies to Transylvania which, since the end of the First World War, has been ruled from Bucharest as part of Romania. The twentieth century saw huge population changes in 1918. Poland regained its independence after over a century, only to be reoccupied in 1939. As a result of the Second World War around 17 per cent of Poland's population was killed (among them almost the whole of the country's Jewish population), its borders were shifted westwards and huge population transfers were experienced. The implications of the twentieth century for the notion of a historically defined central European space need to be addressed.

The question of whether central Europe is formed out of shared historical experience is one that will be returned to and explicitly discussed, as some commentators have argued that it constitutes one of three historical regions within Europe. Having defined central Europe, the question arises first as to whether it forms a geographical region rooted in the physical landscape or patterns of settlement that make it unique within Europe. Some commentators who advocate the use of the term central Europe have argued that although its identity is not solely located in geography, the region exists in a zone of transition between western Europe and Russia. George Schöpflin, for example, the London-based political scientist, argues that in terms of patterns of settlement and the natural environment, 'the contrast between Russia and Western Europe could hardly be greater. Central Europe, as might be expected, falls somewhere in between' (Schöpflin and Wood, 1989, p. 9)

The claim that Schöpflin makes about central Europe's geographic distinctiveness seems to me to be more than a little vague. Assessing his claim is difficult, if only because there are few recent surveys of central Europe as a geographical region. The first reading below, which is an extract from the writings of Alice F. A. Mutton, dates from the middle of the cold war and is a useful starting point for attempting to describe the region geographically.

Introduction: the concept of central Europe

Attempts to define Central Europe as a major geographical region seem to defy objectivity. While the physical environment provides a complex but constant set of pictures capable of analysis, the human scene has changed frequently, in fact kaleidoscopically, in modern times. It is no wonder then, that the concept of *Mitteleuropa* appears as the assessment of a particular writer, be he geographer, historian or politician, and recent attempts to find a common element have proved singularly unrewarding.[1] The term 'Central Europe' has been used in the present context to denote a rather more restricted area of Europe than that used in de Martonne's two great volumes, *Europe Centrale* (1931), for there is no coverage of the Danubian lands beyond Austria, nor is post-war Poland included. On the other hand, a description of the Benelux countries seems essential to complete the description of the Rhine basin, and some justification may be found in the classic line drawn by Sir Halford Mackinder when he demarcated the 'Latin Peninsula' of Europe along a line from Ostend, on the Belgian coast, to Trieste at the head of the Adriatic.[2] Although, on physical grounds, the Jutland peninsula and the Danish archipelago might be regarded as an extension of the Germano-Polish lowland between the North Sea and the Baltic, the fact that Denmark belongs to the cultural region of Scandinavia leaves its exclusion from this book in no doubt.[3] Attempts to include northern Italy within Central Europe, even on a basis of climate (Kendrew), seem to the writer far-fetched, and the lands south of the Alpine divide are relegated to the realm of the Mediterranean. On political grounds, the inclusion of Czechoslovakia may appear inconsistent,

[1] K. Sinnhuber: *Central Europe – Mitteleuropa – Europe Centrale, An Analysis of a Geographical Term*, Trans. Inst. Br. Geographers, Vol XX, 1954, pp. 15–39.

[2] Sir H. Mackinder: *Democratic Ideals and Reality*, 1919.

[3] See A. C. O'Dell: *The Scandinavian World*, 1956, in the same series as this book, and also C. B. Fawcett: 'The Nordic Region', *Scottish Geographical Magazine*, Vol. 48, 1932, pp. 78–83, and also W. R. Mead: *An Economic Geography of the Scandinavian States and Finland*, 1958, and A. Sømme (ed.): *The Geography of Norden*, 1960.

as indeed it would be if post-war 'Central Europe' is to be restricted to the 'free' states immediately west of the 'Iron Curtain'. The justification for the section dealing with the prolongation of Slavonic Europe westwards into the geometrical centre of the continent lies in the physical affinity between Bohemia-Moravia and the Hercynian uplands and basins of Germany, while the northern Carpathians of Slovakia have their counterpart in the Alpine system. The fact that the Czech lands were part of the Austrian Empire until 1919 is a further reason for their inclusion, for their economic development in the late 19th and early 20th century must be seen in relation to the Habsburg Empire, for Bohemia and Moravia were the most industrialized provinces of that Empire and their agriculture compared in progressiveness with that of the Vienna basin and Upper Austria. Poland, on the other hand, wiped off the map as an independent nation state after the partitions of 1772, 1793 and 1795, emerged anew in 1919, when Czechoslovakia was created a succession State, but her rate of economic progress in the twenty years between the wars was slight, especially in the Polish countryside, and the violent changes and land reforms since 1945 have seen in Poland, as in the other satellite states of eastern Europe, a new economy oriented towards the Soviet Union. Thus, although Poland has made a major advance westwards to the Oder-Neisse line, thus acquiring the Baltic port of Stettin (Szczescin), in addition to Danzig, she cannot be regarded in any sense a Central European state, but, like her tragic counterpart Hungary, she remains a member of the Soviet Communist *bloc* and part of East-Central Europe.

It has recently been suggested that Central Europe is a 'middle term', a region of transition, in a physical sense between the diversity of western Europe, the sharp local contrasts to be found in the Mediterranean lands, and the vast uniformity of eastern Europe.[4] Central Europe itself consists of a mosaic of regions but these may be classified into types, such as the regions of Alpine folding, the Alpine foreland, the Hercynian uplands and basins, the Jurassic scarplands of southern Germany and the delta lands of the Rhine-Maas. Only in the north does the Germano-Polish lowland recall the greater expanse of the Russian platform. The physical variety of Central Europe is also reflected in its fragmented history for, in spite of the centralizing tendency of the Habsburgs, *Mitteleuropa* remained a mosaic of duchies and principalities until the first steps towards economic unification

---

[4] P. George and J. Tricart: *L'Europe Centrale*, Vol. 1, 1954, p. 1.

were taken by the initiation of the *Zollverein* in 1819, to be followed by the emergence of Prussia as the dominant military and industrial power of Central Europe after the defeat of the Austrians at Sadowa in 1866. The regional contrasts between Bavaria, the Rhineland, and Prussia are today reflected in separatist tendencies. The northern lowland, so long a zone of conflict between the Teutons and the northern Slavs, has witnessed the re-advance of the Poles westwards to the Oder-Neisse line, at the expense of a defeated Germany and of the German minorities who formerly lived in the 'lost lands of the east' and who have now been added to the thousands of 'Displaced Persons' in West Germany. This post-war movement has reversed the advance of the Slavonic tribes to the line of the Elbe-Saale at the time of Charlemagne, when the *limes Sorabicus* was created, to be followed by the gradual reconquest of these infertile northern plains by the Teutonic Knights and the subsequent planting of German settlers in 'colonial' towns and villages in the Slavonic lands to the east of the Elbe, notably in Brandenburg, Pomerania and East Prussia. Siegfried describes this spread of Germanic 'civilization' over an originally heathen Slav substratum as being 'like piles in a marshland'. In Austria, the *Ostmark* of Charlemagne, there is no such vague limit to the culture of western Christerndom, for 'east of Vienna, the east begins',[5] or as Metternich expressed it: 'the Balkans begin at the eastern city gate of Vienna'.

Whereas, until recently, 'Central Europe was the axis of Europe; on the one side was Eastern Europe as a sort of march, and on the other was Western Europe, representing, together with Central Europe, the van of progress', today Central Europe tends to be 'a frontier rather than an axis'. As Fischer has recently written: '*Mitteleuropa* has contracted to a line'.[6] In so far as a united Germany was once the vital core of Europe, this heartland has indeed disappeared from the political scene. The two cities of Germanic Europe which have played a major political rôle in the past, notably Vienna, as the heart of the Holy Roman Empire, and subsequently Berlin, as the symbol of militant Imperialist and Fascist Germany, have both been forced to play a divided part, since 1945, in the affairs of Europe. Vienna is once more a free city but the persistent division of Berlin into a Western and an Eastern Sector symbolizes the fate of *Mitteleuropa*. It is difficult to envisage Bonn, the federal capital of the German Federal Republic, ever

[5] A. Siegfried: *Switzerland*, 1950, p. 13.

[6] W. G. East and A. E. Moodie: *The Changing World – Studies in Political Geography*, 1956, Chap. II – 'The Passing of Mitteleuropa' by E. Fischer, p 62.

playing a similar rôle to that of the traditional capital. An attractive city, on the banks of the Rhine, it lies excentrically and it has none of the political experience of Berlin. However, the impressive modern buildings of the *Bundeshaus* and of the embassies which have arisen to the south of the city mark the attempt of West Germany to begin again. It is all too symbolical of this post-war democracy that the Federal Parliament building bears a large phoenix in mosaic on its entrance wall.

It seems that the definition of *Mitteleuropa* must be regarded as just as much physical as political. De Martonne was clearly exhibiting Gallic prejudice when he wrote: 'Ainsi, l'Europe centrale n'est pas un mot'. In the early 19th century, German writers such as Carl Ritter recognized *Mitteleuropa* as a natural region in which relief was the dominant feature. In the first part of the present century, the expression came to be identified with the German Empire until 1919, and with the Third Reich of the 1930's. Compared with the term *Deutsches Reich,* that of *Deutschland* is much less precise and the pre-war expression *Deutschtum,* used to designate regions of German culture and speech, appears positively mystical[.][7] J. Partsch, with his inclusion of the lower Danubian lands, Switzerland, Belgium and the Netherlands, went far in this direction in 1905. In 1923, however, Hettner disagreed with the inclusion of the Danubian lands and with taking into account mainly cultural criteria.

Historically, the term 'Central Europe' is much more nebulous. The early division of Europe was on a tribal basis, the Celto-Roman west being distinguished from the lands of the Teutonic tribes of Central Europe and those of the Slavs of the East. The Roman *limes* marked a clear division from the lower Rhine to the Danube between the romanized West and the pagan East. After the time of Charlemagne, Austria stood out as the East March (*Österreich*) of western Christendom. The antagonism between Austria and Prussia in the 19th century for the hegemony of Central Europe was not resolved until the economic unity enforced by the 1914–18 War, which enabled Naumann to see Germany as the 'core' of *Mitteleuropa* (1915), at a time when Germany certainly served as the *lingua franca* of Central Europe. In the same year as Naumann's book, *Mitteleuropa,* appeared, A. Penck wrote of *Zwischeneuropa,* including no less than the Low Countries, Italy, Germany, Denmark, Sweden, Finland, Austria, Hungary, Poland and the Balkans. In 1917, H. Hassinger attempted to map Central Europe

---

[7] R. E. Dickinson: *Germany,* 1953, Chap 13.

on the basis of landscape features and he thus included the Low Countries, Denmark, Germany, Switzerland, and the Austro-Hungarian Empire. He labelled the lower Danubian lands as 'emerging Central Europe', as they clearly were at that time, but only in a political and economic sense, for the foodstuffs of south-eastern Europe were seen to be complementary to the industrial products of the north-west. It is clear that 'Central Europe' thus defined had been the realm of German influence for centuries but nonetheless it included a marked diversity of cultural and ethnographic elements. Later these ideas, developed by German geographers during the first world war, were revived and elaborated by geo-political writers under Hitler's Germany, notably by E. Banse and Karl Haushofer (1937), at the time of the annexation of Austria and Czechoslovakia.

The contraction and consolidation of the Germanic lands since 1945 has served to sharpen the definition of *Mitteleuropa*. It is also borne out by the refugee problem of modern Germany, whereby 20 million Germans have been 'liquidated' in the lost eastern provinces, notably East Prussia, East Pomerania, the Neumark of Brandenburg and Upper Silesia, all of which are now Polish territory (apart from the Soviet acquisition of the northern half of East Prussia). In all some 13 million Germans have fled into the German Federal Republic and West Berlin and 400,000 into Austria.[8] In East Germany, as well as in the Sudeten lands of Bohemia, deserted farms and villages bear witness to the number of political refugees who have escaped to the West. It is estimated that three million acres in the 'lost' provinces have reverted to wasteland and forests are reappearing where formerly there was cultivated land. In Czechoslovakia there are some 250 villages formerly occupied by German minorities, especially in the Sudetenland, which have been only partly re-settled by Slavonic peasants and gypsies. In all these eastern districts, under the present Communist régime, the former large estates of the *Junker* type have become the small-holdings of peasant cultivators or have been taken over as state farms, now increasingly mechanized.

Junker is a term used to describe Prussian aristocrats.

References

J. Partsch: *Central Europe* (trans.), 1905.

E. de Martonne: *Europe Centrale*, Géog. Univ. Vol. 4, Part I.

R. E. Dickinson: *The German Lebensraum*, Penguin Special, 1943.

[8] C. D. Harris and G. Wülker: 'The refugee problem of Germany', *Econ. Geog.*, Vol. 29, 1953, pp. 10–25.

H. R. Ormsby: 'The definition of Mitteleuropa and its relation to the conception of Deutschland in the writings of modern German geographers', *Scot. Geog. Magazine*, Vol. 51, 1935.

Sir H. J. Mackinder: *Democratic Ideals and Reality*, 1919, republished as a Penguin Special in 1944.

E. Fischer: *The Passing of the European Age*, 1948. *Idem:* W. G. East and A. E. Moodie: *The Changing World*, 1956, Chap. II, 'The passing of Mitteleuropa'.

K. A. Sinnhuber: *Central Europe–Mitteleuropa–Europe Centrale: An analysis of a geographical term*, Trans. Inst. Br. Geographers, Vol. XX, 1954.

(Mutton, 1968, pp. 3–8)

EXERCISE

I would like you to summarize the main points of the reading, paying particular attention to the following considerations.

1   The difference between Mutton's definition of central Europe as a region and that identified by Johnson in the discussion above.

2   The different definitions of the region that are discussed throughout the extract.

3   Whether, from the description given, you think that central Europe forms one coherent region.

4   The effect of postwar changes on the central Europe that Mutton describes.

DISCUSSION

1   It is clear from reading this extract that Mutton's definition of central Europe is very different from Johnson's. She argues that central Europe should be defined in terms of what are today Germany, Austria, Switzerland, the Czech Republic and Slovakia. She explicitly excludes Poland and Hungary from consideration, arguing that they form part of yet another region that she terms east-central Europe. I shall return to her reasons for adopting a narrow distinction in the discussion under point 4; here it is merely sufficient to note that at the time of writing she was wary about including any socialist country, making an explicit case based on physical geography for the inclusion of Czechoslovakia.

2   Mutton states in the extract that 'Historically, the term "Central Europe" is much more nebulous'. Her discussion of the history of this term naturally relies on earlier definitions of central Europe

than those used by intellectuals in socialist states during the 1980s – the first edition of her text was published in 1961. She quotes a range of analysts who have identified a central European region described either as *Mitteleuropa*, or in the case of one analyst, *Zwischeneuropa*. All the definitions discussed concede that central Europe is ethnically diverse, that its unity does not stem from a unity of culture. These definitions derive from the pre-1945 period, which, as you will see, is important. What these definitions identify is a common economic and geographical space centred on Germany. All argue that central Europe 'had been the realm of German influence for centuries but nonetheless it included a marked diversity of cultural and ethnographic elements'.

3   How you choose to address this point depends on the criteria you use. If you regard ethnic or cultural homogeneity as the defining characteristic of a coherent region you will be forced to concede that central Europe does not qualify on these terms. However, you might argue on the basis of economic links that central Europe did indeed form a coherent economic region centred on Germany. This existed, however, only in the period prior to 1945. The period following the Second World War was a different matter entirely.

4   That caveat neatly brings me on to a consideration of the effects of the cold war on the region. You will note that Mutton in her 1968 definition of central Europe is extremely cautious about including any of the socialist states. She argues, for example, that 'Poland ... cannot be regarded in any sense a central European state, but, like her tragic counterpart Hungary, she remains a member of the Soviet Communist *bloc* and part of east-central Europe'. Although Mutton rules Poland and Hungary out of her definition of central Europe by virtue of their forced integration into eastern Europe, she paradoxically includes Czechoslovakia in her definition. She concedes that this inclusion 'may appear inconsistent'. Indeed it is probably the most serious weakness of her definition, but the point to be borne in mind is that she does this explicitly, despite Czechoslovakia's cold war membership of the Soviet bloc. To Mutton, however, cold war central Europe is a German-centred space: 'The contraction and consolidation of the Germanic lands since 1945 has served to sharpen the definition of *Mitteleuropa*.' In short, the population shifts that followed the Second World War, with the expulsion of ethnic Germans from eastern Europe, has served to cut Germany's cultural and economic links to the lands around it, thus restricting the space that could be described as central Europe.

Figure 2   Blakenstein. east/west German border, 1985. Encounters with border guards, immigration officers, customs and police form part of the experience of crossing any border between states in contemporary Europe. The former 'cold war' border was no exception as this image shows. Photo: Brian Rose

Friedrich Naumann (1860–1919) described his concept of Mitteleuropa in his book of the same title in 1915. He argued that a union of Germany and Austria–Hungary would provide the basis for a German-dominated central European order in the event of a central powers victory in the First World War.

Alice Mutton's discussion of central Europe represents understandings of both the concept and the geographical region it was taken to cover before the term was revived in the socialist states during the 1980s. Her discussion also highlights the implications of the cold war and the effective creation of Soviet-type societies to the usefulness of the concept of central Europe. Notions of central Europe were influenced by Friedrich Naumann's concept of *Mitteleuropa* in 1915, which was based on a programme of German economic expansion into the countries immediately to its east that would integrate them into an economic region with industrial, imperial Germany at its heart. This idea of *Mitteleuropa* formed one key prong of German economic and foreign policy immediately prior to the First World War and later profoundly influenced Nazi policy too. It also influenced attempts to analyse central Europe as a distinct region, defining it as a German-dominated cultural and economic space. The formal division of Germany in 1949, as well as the sovietization of the political and social systems in many of the countries that had made up the *Mitteleuropa* envisaged by Naumann, led to the temporary death of the concept. For the years of the cold war therefore, eastern Europe formed a more useful category for the analysis of the region than did central Europe.

Central Europe as one of Europe's historical regions

If German-centred definitions of central Europe were the most common prior to the notion's revival in the 1980s, they were not the only ones. *Mitteleuropa* was not the only way in which people thought about the region. Furthermore, some of these ideas of a central European identity were located not in geography but in history. Notions of a space at the heart of Europe that was part of neither western nor eastern Europe, and that was defined by the circumstances in which Europe had entered the world economy, originated not in Germany but in Hungary. Before examining in some detail the most influential arguments for central Europe, or east-central Europe, as a 'historical' region I shall set the scene by paying some attention to the intellectual environment in which these arguments originated.

Hungary after the First World War was racked by two revolutions – one republican and the other socialist. The Soviet Republic had ruled Hungary for nine months before its violent overthrow in August 1919. Communist rule was followed by violent counter-revolution accompanied by substantial anti-semitic violence which resulted in the regency of Admiral Miklós Horthy (1920–44). Hungary had lost two-thirds of its pre-war geographic area and all of its ethnic minorities who preferred to join the new states of Czechoslovakia and Yugoslavia, or the expanded Romania. In Horthy's Hungary the door to even modest social reform was firmly closed, and the franchise was restricted to between one fifth and one quarter of the total population. Limited land reform at the beginning of the 1920s made little difference to a hugely unequal structure of landownership. Most of the population gained their living from agriculture – a sector dominated by an aristocracy that owned the majority of the land while most of the agrarian population laboured either as poor smallholders or as agricultural proletarians. The depression in the 1930s hit agriculture hard and many rural dwellers found themselves in desperate poverty during the first half of the decade.

The crisis induced by the depression in Hungary's rural areas was addressed by a loose movement termed the 'populist' movement (*népi mozgalom*) which was strong among groups such as schoolteachers and doctors who lived in rural areas and were shocked at the destitution of much of the agricultural population. They were represented most publicly by a group of writers who documented the poverty experienced by many in rural areas during the second half of the 1930s. Supporters of populist positions could be found on the

Mátyás Rákosi (1892–1971) was a leading figure in the Hungarian communist movement. He was most notorious as Hungary's leading communist during the country's Stalinist era (1948–1953). He served as general secretary of the Hungarian Communist Party (1945–1948) and of the Hungarian Workers' Party (1948–1956). He was also the country's Prime Minister (1952–3). Relieved of his party position in summer 1956, he was blamed by the new leadership for the political situation in the country that led to the 1956 revolution. He died in the Soviet Union in 1971.

János Kádár (1912–1989) was a leading figure in the Hungarian communist movement. He served as secretary-general of the Hungarian Socialist Workers' Party (the country's ruling party) between 1956 and 1988. During the 1956 revolution he sided with invading Soviet troops and suppressed the revolution. Despite this he created a liberal form of state socialism, known as gulyás communism. He was removed as general-secretary in 1988 and died in 1989.

political left, on the fascist radical right and among members of the liberal opposition to the Horthy regime. They were concerned with the declining population in rural Hungary – which they equated with the 'death of the nation' – and argued strongly for a radical land reform that would redistribute land from the nobility to those who worked on it. The more politically sophisticated of the populists developed well-worked programmes arguing for a 'third way' based on diffuse ownership of agricultural land that would represent a distinct Hungarian road of social development.

During the war years some of those on the left wing of the populist movement began to analyse the pattern of Hungary's development as one of incomplete integration into modern western Europe. Ferenc Erdei (1910–1971), a prominent writer on rural social issues during the 1930s who would later serve as a communist minister of agriculture, argued that Hungary's social structure stemmed from the incomplete development of a bourgeois, capitalist society. He argued that while capitalist social groups played a role in Hungarian social stratification, the influence of feudalism, particularly through the power of the landed aristocracy, remained strong (Erdei, 1988, pp. 9–93). Another populist thinker, the political theorist István Bibó (1911–1979), who belonged to the more democratic wing of the populist movement, began to analyse both Hungary and its neighbours in similar terms. He contended that the peculiarities of Hungarian social structure stemmed from its historical development: during the Middle Ages Hungary had belonged to the west but after 1526 its conquest by Ottoman Turkey had separated it from the rest of Europe. Its attempts, built on the role of the state, to rejoin western Europe from the mid eighteenth century onwards were thwarted. By the end of the nineteenth century Hungarian society was a 'blocked' society, consisting of a series of western and eastern elements (Bibó, 1994, pp. 311–27).

On both the left and the liberal wings of the populist movement at the end of the Second World War there was a consciousness that Hungary lay uncomfortably between the east and the west. The two wings, however, differed in terms of the remedies they proposed for the kind of social development that had occurred. Erdei and the left joined the project to build a socialist Hungary under the dictatorships of **Mátyás Rákosi** and **János Kádár**. Bibó, on the other hand, remained committed to political democracy. As a result of his brief period as a minister under Imre Nagy during the 1956 revolution he was imprisoned during the late 1950s and early 1960s. After his death in 1979 he was to become a hero to opponents of Hungary's socialist regime because of his uncompromising

Figures 3 and 4. Ratzeburg, east/west German border, 1987. Demarcating a border may often mean drawing a line that seems arbitrary to those that directly experience it. The sign that mars this winter scene warns visitors that the water is on the territory of the German Democratic Republic (former East Germany) and that its use for any reason is therefore dangerous. Photo: Brian Rose

commitment to political democracy and the fact that he bridged the divide between nationalists and liberals that characterized Hungary's 'dissident' opposition in the 1970s.

Among the Hungarian intellectuals who began to examine Bibó's ideas in order to assess Hungary's situation at the end of the 1970s, the historian Jenő Szűcs (1928–1988) applied Bibó's ideas about Hungarian development to Europe as a whole. He argued that Europe had been divided since the sixteenth century into three historically defined regions. The second reading consists of extracts from Szűcs's essay 'Three historical regions of Europe'.

The birth of European regions

Where do the internal boundaries of Europe lie? One very pronounced line runs southwards across Europe from the lower course of the Elbe-Saale, along the Leitha and the western border of ancient Pannonia: the eastern border of the Carolingian Empire around 800 AD. The region to the west of that line had witnessed, in the previous three centuries, an organic symbiosis between elements of late Antiquity and Christianity, on the one hand, and Barbarian Germanic elements on the other. The first (premature and transitional) synthesis of that symbiosis was the 'renovated' *Imperium* itself. The name often applied to that block even in those days was the West. Of course, the term *Occidens* did not refer originally to something removed from other parts of Europe, for example from 'Eastern Europe' – a term with little meaning or content before the turn of the millennium, even in retrospect. *Occidens* referred to the ancient 'world' that formed a belt around the Mediterranean in opposition to Byzantium and Islam, which had expropriated the southern half of that ancient world. Many consider that one can speak of European history as such from about 800, when the centre of historical development was shifted northwards to Europe by the Arab conquests, which robbed Graeco-Roman civilization of a southern swathe stretching from Syria through North Africa to Hispania. Europe, to the Ancients, had been a purely 'geographical' entity. At precisely this time a new type of structure was beginning to crystallize in its western parts. It was neither Ancient nor German, but a 'Christian and feudal society'. To express that new structure, the region began as early as the death of Charlemagne (814) to appropriate the term *Europe* exclusively to itself, although this was unjustified in that it represented only one pole of the Europe that was being born.

The other pole was Byzantium, although initially Byzantium entertained no European aspirations; and since its geographical centre was in Asia Minor it was not a European entity in the geographic sense either. Until the turn of the millennium, Byzantium's firm intention was to defend the eastern heritage of the 'Romans' (as they continued to call themselves) from the 'Barbarians', even at the expense of territorial losses, and to do so by carrying out thorough, ancient-style reforms and maintaining a defensive rigidity. Thus the history of Europe after the turn of the millennium started to develop out of those two poles by absorbing the intermediate region and the heterogeneous world that lay still further to the north: the *Occidens* had been transformed from a western pole of a putative Europe into 'Western Europe', and

Byzantium had abandoned its defensive rigidity. From that time onwards one can talk of European regions.

Particularly after the Great Schism of 1054, there was added to that dual radiation another, no less pronounced border running roughly parallel to it, but to its east. It stretched from the region of the Lower Danube to the eastern Carpathians and further north along the forests that separated the West Slavs from the East Slavs, reaching the Baltic regions in the thirteenth century. The comprehensive term used as early as the twelfth century for the region west of this line was *Europa Occidens (Occidentalis)*, the Elbe-Leitha lines obviously having been forgotten. Hardly had *Europa* advanced from being a mere geographical entity to being a synonym for Christendom than it was split into two by the influence of Rome and Byzantium. During the Middle Ages there were fewer and fewer scruples about speaking of Western Europe as the region that stretched from the Elbe to the curve of the Carpathians, and from the Baltic to the Adriatic: that is, the new region which had been annexed to the area of the former 'Carolingian Europe', including Scandinavia. Did that region really become Western Europe?

The workings of medieval Europe remained at their crudest and least complete in the east. The overwhelming majority of what was to become Russia (which would eventually occupy exactly half the entire territory of Europe), the area to the south and east of the Russian land, was not called either the 'Russian land' or 'Europe' until modern times. It formed a wedge-shaped western extension of the Euroasian steppe region and the world of nomads that extended like a wedge into geographical Europe, and which the predecessors of today's Hungarians and others had crossed to the Carpathians. But after the turn of the millennium the thin end of the wedge broke off and joined the area we are discussing. From the thirteenth century that huge wedge was acknowledged to be identical with the Mongol Empire. There was a succession of developments, starting with a loosening of dependence on the Golden Horde (1480), continuing with the Russian conquest of the khanates of Kazan and Astrakhan (in 1552 and 1556) and the annexation of the territories in the southern Ukraine under Polish rule (1667–86), and concluding with the annihilation of the Crimean Tatar khanate (in 1783). These have no less meaning in terms of European history than they have for the history of the Russian state, since they created (and simultaneously assimilated into the notion of Russia) the homogeneous formula of Eastern Europe *par excellence* out of the heterogeneous swathe between the Poles and the Ural mountains. These developments continued, in early modern times, the internal expansion of Europe and the conquest by the plough and towns, which in the Middle Ages had reached only to the Russian lands around Kiev and Moscow. This accomplishment in the eighteenth and nineteenth centuries in the region of the Dnepr, Don and Volga was similar to what 'Europeanized' Europe had accomplished (albeit in a more extensive way) 500 years earlier between the Rhine and the Vistula, Memel, Tisza and Maros. When comparing the structural models of European regions, one cannot disregard that final inclusion of the eastern half of Europe.

Nor can one disregard the penetration into Europe during the waning of the Middle Ages of another, Asian wedge. This particular invasion was stronger than ever before and entered from the south-east into South-Eastern Europe, where the process of 'Europeanization' was almost complete (if in a rougher form than elsewhere). This provided a whole area with the name of Rumelia, used for several centuries to refer to Byzantium, the Asia Minor portion of which had long before been swallowed up by the Seljuk advance, thereafter receiving the new name of Anatolia. Since the point of the wedge of the Ottoman Empire was blocked in its advance in Hungary, the latter's new role as a 'border area' became an important factor in the development of regions, at the same time releasing Eastern Europe from that role.

So, roughly speaking, the co-ordinates were as follows: the first expansion of the Barbarian peoples, having engulfed the western heritage of Rome, led to the birth of the notion of the 'West' (500–800); the first great eastward and northward expansion of the West (1000–1300) then enlarged the bounds of *Europa Occidens* (to include Northern and East-Central Europe), while in the meantime a 'truncated' Eastern Europe and South-Eastern Europe took shape under the sphere of influence of Byzantium, which had inherited Rome's mantle in the east. Since the latter area was to secede from the European structure (during the gradual decline of Byzantium) by the end of the Middle Ages, I shall disregard it.

Modern times arrived from two directions: one was the second great expansion of the West (1500–1640) which, by stretching over the Atlantic, connected America to itself (and later absorbed Scandinavia too); the other was the great expansion of 'truncated' Eastern Europe, which created a 'complete' Eastern Europe by annexing Siberia, which stretched to the Pacific. East-Central Europe became squeezed between these two regions. At the dawn of modern times, it was obliged to notice with some defensive amazement that while history had redrawn a border that had been thought to have faded, from the south the last (and strongest) wave of one thousand years of invasions from Asia Minor was lapping against its borders, and that it no longer knew whether it still belonged within the framework of *Europa Occidens*.

The original position of the regions, their movements and their responses to the challenges of history produced the structural models that have defined modern Europe ever since.

Western Europe

How did the original Western model look – at least from the viewpoint of István Bibó? His viewpoint (one of several possible) amounts to a search for the deepest roots of a 'democratic way of organizing society'. All that Bibó emphasized about these beginnings (the customary, personal and mutual obligations and rights; the balancing structure of 'narrow circles of freedom' that prevents a concentration of power and provides a counterweight to the 'brutally expedient' methods of unilateral subordination; and so on) were real and important elements, although they were shared with the successive structures of the Middle Ages. Yet something more comprehensive is at work. This can be shown by glancing backwards from the centuries of modern times to the Middle Ages in the West.

When considering concepts like natural law, social contract and popular sovereignty, the transfer of power or the separation of powers, most people will recall names such as Hobbes, Locke, Montesquieu and Rousseau, and, of course, the French Revolution and its aftermath. There are certainly few who know that these key problems were first pondered a good 500 years earlier in Bologna, Paris and Oxford, even if in a context fairly remote from and alien to the modern era. At the height of the Middle Ages, in the 'great' thirteenth century, such ideas were as much at the centre of political theory as they were in the great preparatory period of modern times, the eighteenth century. If one searches for the roots of 'social development in the Western sense' (as Bibó put it) or seeks to identify the 'original characteristics' of the West (as Marc Bloch would have put it), this consideration is important, since one such characteristic of the West is the structural – and theoretical – separation of 'society' from the 'state'.

This kind of separation is not an endogenous feature of human history. Of course, all states are built upon some society, but it is in the gravitational field of 5,000 years of high cultures that the emerging state finds a justification for itself 'beyond the bounds' of society, thus creating an operational mechanism in which society

Koinōnia means simply 'collectivity'.

appears to be the derivative of the state, and not vice versa. For any sector of society to exist autonomously, independent of the state (even when functionally connected with it) is a rare exception. And exceptions are the luxury products of history. A well-known example is the Greek *polis*, the primeval model of the autonomous society, in which the *koinōnia* of the free citizens is interpreted as a kind of 'natural' outcome. Another example is the Roman *res publica*, the form of the power of the *populus Romanus* expressed chiefly in the categories of public law. But like the Roman idea of the republic, the practice of Greek democracy was swamped by the Hellenistic empires and, having been transformed into a mere fiction, was confined to an imperial cul-de-sac. These early historical antecedents had no direct influence on the social development of Europe. Nothing, of course, was further removed from the medieval West than democracy; the republic was flirted with by only a handful of Italian city-states, and then in a very aristocratic style. Yet there remained an organic historical continuity that led from there to the development of modern Europe. The reason why Western feudalism was able to posit the category of *populus seu societas civilis* is not that feudalism in the West held itself to be the heir of Antiquity and had read the works of Aristotle; in these terms, Byzantium was a more faithful successor and, for a while, even Islam seemed a worthier one. The reason is that whereas this category was to some extent familiar to Western feudalism, it had nothing at all in common with the other two civilizations. To establish a correlation with the entirely new formula of the state at the dawn of modern times in Europe, the primeval form of 'civil society' had to be shelled out of its 'feudal context'. However, it is important to point out that that operation was not particularly unusual or entirely new since, much earlier, history itself had both created the category and established its relation to the state. No such thing had happened in Byzantium, in Islam, or in China: that is, in other cultures that for a long time had boasted higher 'indices of civilization'. Nor, indeed, had such a thing happened in Kiev ...

The West subordinated society to the state; the East 'nationalized' it. Absolutism everywhere strove to homogenize its 'subjects', and there was no difference in principle between, for instance, the views of Louis XIV (*mes peoples*) and that of the tsars concerning indivisible unity. But in practice the various local autonomies and 'freedoms' were not eliminated anywhere in the West. At most they were curtailed and subjected to state control. Corporate particularism and provincial variety were far more motley under every *ancien régime* than under the loose structure of a modern state. Periodically there would be a joint revolt of the nobility, the bourgeoisie and the peasantry in favour of restoring the various 'freedoms' of each, as in France from the period of the 'religious wars' to the *Fronde* (1648–53). Between these 'freedom movements' of the medieval type and the French Revolution some 150 years elapsed (punctuated in the main by local peasant movements against the burden of taxation). This gap was caused not by any strengthening of absolutism but by the fact that the earlier campaigns had become anachronistic. The new bourgeoisie, strengthened by mercantilism, had no need of any peculiar 'autonomies'. Centralization was not strong enough to homogenize the subjects thoroughly, but it was effective enough to encourage the relativized traditional 'freedoms' to begin to converge underneath the state; their content became more homogenous with the strengthening of the new bourgeoisie. István Bibó aptly observed that the early modern state 'administered together rather than annihilated' the colourful world of the existing traditional organizations. The first deed of Russian absolutism was in the spirit of unifying the Russian lands: Ivan III occupied Novgorod (1478), which had enjoyed an exceptional degree of autonomous government. He deported the entire leading strata, the boyars and the merchants, confiscated their property, and placed the city state under the tsarist governor. The pattern was taken from Moscow, the centre of administration and military power, which contained an agglomeration of boyars, civil servants, soldiers, merchants, artisans and agrarian people, each group (as was general in all towns in the Russian lands) depending separately on the principal power. Even the privileged rich merchants (*goshti*) were chiefly business agents of the tsar. In the ensuing centuries, all towns in the newly colonized territories, from Tsaritsyn to Archangelsk, and from there to Ufa and further to the East, adopted this model. The declining remnants of the local boyar self-government (*guba*) were eliminated by the first Romanovs, who annexed all territories to the central apparatus of state by organizing them into provinces. One of Western absolutism's contradictions was that its 'subjects' sooner or later began to turn their *libertates* into a unified *liberté* within the leeway remaining under the state. The direction taken by tsarist absolutism precluded that contradiction, such that the concept of 'society' meaning an amorphous mass of subjects, was consistently realized.

(Szücs, 1988, pp. 291–6, 318–19)

EXERCISE _____

I should like you now to answer the following questions.

1   How does Szücs define both the external and internal borders of Europe? Do you find anything unusual about how he draws the boundaries?

2   What are the characteristics of the region Szücs terms 'East-Central Europe'? What are the similarities and differences between this and the notions of central Europe that have already been discussed?

3   What factors – according to Szücs – have made the various 'regions' different from each other?

DISCUSSION _____

1   Szücs is unusual in that he adopts a broad geographical definition of Europe, arguing that it is what is often termed Eurasia. According to Szücs, Europe stretches from the Atlantic to the Pacific, expanding eastward with Russia's expansion into Siberia. The key point, however, is that he sees Europe as being divided into three distinct historical regions. The first of these is western Europe, which stretches from the Atlantic to include what was understood during the cold war as western Europe. The second region is the one termed east-central Europe, which includes what was understood for much of the cold war as eastern Europe, that is those states which were part of the socialist bloc but not part of the USSR. The third region, eastern Europe, consists of everything to the east of that. You might have noticed that while Szücs's historical regions bear a remarkable resemblance to political divisions in the late twentieth century, he traces their origins to the late Middle Ages.

2   The historical region that Szücs terms east-central Europe is, as I have noted above, broadly the same as that termed eastern Europe during the years of the cold war. It is defined as a transitional region and Szücs argues that it has been squeezed by two patterns of development – an eastern one and a western one. East-central Europe as defined by Szücs is very different to Mutton's definition of central Europe, rooted as the latter is in German-centred notions of _Mitteleuropa_. Szücs's east-central Europe bisects what is now Germany. Those areas which prior to 1990 formed the Federal Republic belong to historical western Europe, while the former German Democratic Republic belongs to east-central Europe. What is most striking, I think, about Szücs's argument is that it implicitly suggests that the geographic patterns that influenced cold war divisions within Europe have

deep historical roots that date back to Europe's entrance into the modern era. If you cast your mind back to the reading from Larry Woolf's *Inventing Eastern Europe* at the end of Chapter 1, you will realize that there are very real parallels between the arguments of these two authors in this regard at least.

3   Szücs advances a clearly historical explanation for why the different regions of Europe can be separated from each other. It is by no means the only available historical explanation – indeed Larry Woolf's argument about the origins of Europe's east–west split is one very clear alternative to this. It is possible to locate differences between regions in their levels of economic development, culture or changing patterns of settlement. Szücs has chosen to argue that in these three regions of Europe the relationship between the state and society was and is fundamentally different. In his view western Europe is characterized by an institutional split between the state and 'civil society'; that is, social organization is given some form of institutional legal protection from the encroachment of state power. By contrast, according to Szücs, in eastern Europe the state effectively nationalized society. Finally, Szücs regards east-central Europe as a transitional region between these two models.

The idea that the division of Europe into east and west has historical roots that go back to the dawn of the modern period is not unique to Szücs. As discussed in Chapter 1, the cultural historian Larry Wolff has argued that the division of Europe into two halves is a product of Enlightenment thought (Wolff, 1994). Others have located the origins of an eastern European region in notions of its inherent economic backwardness. Few analysts have actually suggested the existence of three historical regions. Furthermore, the interest of Szücs's argument lies in the period and the intellectual context in which it was written. It was originally published illegally in 1979 in Hungary in a *Festschrift* for István Bibó which contained essays from all wings of the country's intellectual opposition. Szücs's essay was intended to have an explicitly political meaning; in other words, it was a work of history that aimed directly to influence debates about Hungary's situation and its possible future. It is in this context that some of its historical claims should be considered. The first is that east-central Europe existed as a region separate from a Russian-dominated eastern Europe, a claim which in many ways anticipates arguments in the 1980s about central Europe. The second is that 'historical' east-central Europe corresponds to cold war eastern

Figure 5 West German/Czech border, 1987. This winter forest scene is disturbed by a sign warning that it lies near the cold war border between east and west; in this case the border between west Germany and Czechoslovakia. Photo: Brian Rose

Europe. The third claim worth bearing in mind is that differences between the regions of Europe can be located in the nature of their state–society relations.

Whether or not Szücs's historical analysis is correct, I am arguing that it was the product of a very specific political context and hidden behind the argument is the political programme of Hungary's non-socialist opposition during the latter decades of socialism. Szücs is suggesting, as Bibó did, that Hungary's and, by extension, east-central Europe's future lay in joining the west through emulating its pattern of development. To do this it had to eradicate the influence of eastern Europe within its society – in the late 1970s this meant an end to Soviet-imposed socialism in the region. It also meant joining western Europe by replicating the relationship between the state and civil society that, it was argued, existed there. In other words, Szücs was as much identifying a project for the future as analysing the past. His essay is, however, a specific product of Hungarian intellectual culture and clearly tells us something about Hungarian intellectuals' identities as Europeans. It tells us that in Hungary some kind of central, or east-central European identity existed in the 1970s and 1980s that was embedded in an ambiguous relationship to Europe. Hungarians wished to join the advanced west of the continent, which they did not feel part of.

Central Europe as a cultural or political space

The political programme which underpinned Jenő Szücs's analysis of Hungary's and east-central Europe's position at the end of the 1970s did not have resonance just in Hungary but also across the region during the 1980s. In that decade debate among intellectuals opposed to socialism across the Soviet bloc, in Slovenia and in exile employed a concept of 'central Europe' that, if it lacked the conceptual rigour of Szücs's magisterial historical analysis, was nevertheless remarkably similar in terms of the position it took and the identities to which to gave expression. In order to examine this version of central Europe and central European identity I want to focus on one debate and in particular one contribution to it.

In 1984 the Czech émigré writer Milan Kundera published an essay entitled 'The tragedy of central Europe'. His argument was explicitly directed against those who consigned certain countries – Czechoslovakia, Poland and Hungary – to the European periphery by defining them as eastern Europe. Instead he argued that central Europe was an entity unified by its cultural contribution to European civilization, thus asserting the claims of Czechs, Slovaks, Poles, and Hungarians to be considered 'full' Europeans. The tragedy of central Europe for Kundera was that it had been subsumed under the hegemony of Russia, which was not, in his view, a European nation. In other words, central Europe's tragedy was its exclusion from its natural place, which lay at the 'heart of Europe' (Kundera, 1984). The debate that this provoked among émigré intellectuals and some dissidents was tremendous, and also very revealing about the nature of the identities that were embodied in the concept. The third reading is an extract from an essay by the British historian and commentator on the region, Timothy Garton-Ash, entitled 'Does central Europe exist?', which provides a critical survey of the debates around central Europe during the 1980s.

Does Central Europe exist?

Central Europe is back. For three decades after 1945, nobody spoke of Central Europe in the present tense: the thing was one with Nineveh and Tyre. In German-speaking lands, the very word *Mitteleuropa* seemed to have died with Adolf Hitler, surviving only as a ghostly *Mitropa* on the dining cars of the Deutsche Reichsbahn. Even in Austria, as ex-Chancellor Fred Sinowatz has remarked, 'until ten years ago one was not permitted so much as to mention the word *Mitteleuropa*.' In Prague and Budapest, the idea of Central Europe continued to be cherished between consenting adults in private, but from the public sphere it vanished as completely as it had in 'the West'. The post-Yalta order dictated a strict and single dichotomy. Western Europe implicitly accepted this dichotomy by subsuming under the label Eastern Europe all those parts of historic Central, East Central, and South-eastern Europe that after 1945 came under Soviet domination. The EEC completed the semantic trick by arrogating to itself the unqualified title Europe.

In the last few years we have begun to talk again about Central Europe, and in the present tense. This new discussion originated not in Berlin or Vienna but in Prague and Budapest. The man who more than anyone else has given it currency in the West is a Czech, Milan Kundera, with his now-famous essay 'The Tragedy of Central Europe' (first published in French in 1983 and in English in 1984). Subsequently, the Germans and the Austrians have gingerly begun to rehabilitate, in their different ways, a concept that was once so much their own. The East German leader, Erich Honecker, talks of the danger of nuclear war in *Mitteleuropa*. The West German Social Democrat Peter Glotz says the Federal Republic is 'a guarantee-power of the culture of *Mitteleuropa*'; whatever that means. And Kurt Waldheim's Vienna recently hosted a symposium with the electrifying title '*Heimat Mitteleuropa*'. A backhanded tribute to the new actuality of the Central European idea came even from the central organ of the Polish United Workers' Party, *Trybuna Ludu*, which published a splenetic attack on what it called 'The Myth of "Central Europe"'.

There is a basic sense in which the term *Central Europe* (or *East Central Europe*) is obviously useful. If it merely reminds an American or British newspaper reader that East Berlin, Prague, and Budapest are not quite in the same position as Vladivostok – that Siberia does not begin at Checkpoint Charlie – then it serves a good purpose. So also, if it suggests to American or British students that the academic study of this region could be more than footnotes to Sovietology. But of course the voices from Prague and Budapest that initiated this discussion mean something far larger and deeper when they talk of Central Europe.

The publication in English[9] *Takie czasy ... Rzecz o kompromisie* by Adam Michnik, (London, Aneks, 1985). *KOR: A History of the Worker's Defense Committee in Poland, 1976–1981,* by Jan Józef Lipski, translated by Olga Amsterdamska and Gene M. Moore, (Berkeley, California: University of California Press, 1985). of the most important political essays of three outstanding writers, Václav Havel, György Konrád, and Adam Michnik, a Czech, a Hungarian, and a Pole, gives us a chance to examine the myth – and the reality. Of course it would be absurd to claim that any one writer is 'representative' of his nation, and anyway, Havel, Michnik and Konrád are different kinds of writers working in quite dissimilar conditions.

Havel comes closest to general recognition as something like an intellectual spokesman for independent Czech intellectuals, although there is a great diversity of views even within Charter 77 (as we can see from the other Chartist essays collected under Havel's title *The Power of the Powerless*). His 'political' essays are rich, poetic philosophical meditations, searching for the deeper meaning of experience, 'digging out words with their roots' as Karl Kraus once put it, but rarely deigning to examine the political

---

[9] The editions referred to in this essay are: *The Power of the Powerless: Citizens Against the State in Central-Eastern Europe* by Václav Havel et al., introduction by Steven Lukes, edited by John Keane, (London: Hutchinson, 1985). *The Anatomy of Reticence* by Václav Havel, Voices from Czechoslovakia No. 1, (Stockholm: Charta 77 Foundation, 1985). *Antipolitics: An Essay,* by György Konrád, translated from the Hungarian by Richard E. Allen, (New York: Harcourt Brace Jovanovich, 1984). *Letters from Prison and other Essays* by Adam Michnik, translated by Maya Latynski, foreword by Czesław Miłosz, introduction by Jonathan Schell, (Berkeley, California: University of California Press, 1985).

surface of things. (He nowhere so much as mentions the name of any of the present communist rulers of Czechoslovakia. Magnificent contempt!) He shows a great consistency, from his seminal essay 'The Power of the Powerless', written in the autumn of 1978, through his 1984 address on being awarded an honorary doctorate by the University of Toulouse, to his open letter to Western peace movements, published in 1985 as *The Anatomy of a Reticence*. You hear in his writing the silence of a country cottage or a prison cell – for his part in the Committee for the Defence of the

Unjustly Prosecuted (VONS), he was himself unjustly prosecuted and imprisoned from 1979 to 1983 – the quiet voice of a man who has had a long time for solitary reflection, a playwright catapulted by circumstances and the dictates of conscience into the role of 'dissident' but not at all by temperament a political activist. Yet his contempt for politics is also more generally characteristic of Czechoslovakia, where most people find it hard to believe that anything of importance will ever again change on the immobile, frozen surface of Husák's geriatric 'normalized' regime.

Michnik, by contrast, has seen the earth shake in Poland. Though a historian by training, he has spent most of his adult life actively engaged in political opposition. A central figure in the Committee for Social Self-Defence-KOR and then an advisor to Solidarity, he, unlike Havel or Konrád, writes with the knowledge that he will be read for immediate political advice. Activists of underground Solidarity, students involved in *samizdat* publishing, look to him (among others) for practical answers to the question 'What is to be done?' This gives a sharper political focus to his work, but also makes it more controversial.

Like Havel, he is a hero to many of his compatriots. Unlike Havel, his views are fiercely contested. The KOR tradition, of which he is perhaps the most articulate spokesman (and certainly the most lucid essayist), now vies for popularity in Poland with views that may be characterized, with varying degrees of inaccuracy, as Catholic positivist (in the very special Polish usage of that term), Catholic nationalist, liberal, libertarian, or even neo-conservative. Astonishingly, the greatest part of his work has been written in prison and smuggled out under the noses of General Jaruzelski's jailers. (Besides almost three hundred pages of political essays, he has also produced a 285-page book of literary essays.) His style is often polemical, full of rasping irony – the rasp of an iron file cutting at prison bars – but modulated by a fine sense of moral responsibility and a keen political intelligence. Like Havel, he also

Samizdat is a term derived from the Russian words *sam* or 'self' and *izdatelstvo* meaning 'publishing'. It refers to illegally produced banned and unofficial literature in the Soviet Union and eastern and central Europe, normally circulated by dissidents during the 1970s and 1980s.

displays a great consistency in his political thought, from his seminal 1976 essay 'The New Evolutionism' to his 1985 'Letter from the Gdańsk Prison' and his most recent essay '... On Compromise', which has so far appeared only in Polish.

Konrád is different again. He is writing not in and out of prison but in and out of Vienna or West Berlin. We hear in the background of his long excursive disquisitions not the slamming of prison doors but the clink of coffee cups in the Café Landtmann or the comradely hum of a peace-movement seminar. In his book *Antipolitics* (German subtitle: *Mitteleuropäische Meditationen*) and subsequent articles, Konrád, a distinguished novelist and sociologist, has developed what I might call a late *Jugendstil* literary style: colourful, profuse, expansive, and ornate. *Antipolitics* is a *Sammelsurium*, an *omnium gatherum* of ideas that are picked up one after the other, briefly toyed with, reformulated, then abandoned in favour of other, prettier, younger (but alas, contradictory) ideas, only to be taken up again, petted, and restated a few pages later. This makes Konrád's essayistic work both stimulating and infuriating. Contrary to a widespread impression in the West, one finds few people in Budapest who consider that Konrád is a 'representative' figure even in the limited way that Havel and Michnik are. On the other hand, they find it difficult to point to anyone else who has covered half as much intellectual ground, in a more 'representative' fashion.

So Havel, Michnik and Konrád are different writers, differently placed even in their own countries, neither fully 'representative' nor exact counterparts. Yet all three are particularly well attuned to the questions a Western reader is likely to raise, and concerned to answer them. And all three are equally committed to the dialogue between their countries. Havel's *The Power of the Powerless* was written specifically as the start of a projected dialogue between Charter 77 and KOR. In discussing the richness of Polish *samizdat*, Michnik singles out the work of 'the extremely popular Václav Havel' and both Havel and the Hungarian Miklós Haraszti have appeared alongside Michnik on the masthead of the Polish independent quarterly *Krytyka*. Konrád refers constantly to Czech and Polish experience, and in one striking passage he apostrophizes a Pole identified only as 'Adam' – but the 'Adam' is clearly Michnik. So if there really is some common Central European ground, we can reasonably expect to discover it in the political essays of these three authors. If we do not find it here, it probably does not exist.

In the work of Havel and Konrád there is an interesting semantic division of labour. Both authors use the terms *Eastern Europe* or *East European* when the context is neutral or negative; when they write *Central* or *East Central*, the statement is invariably positive, affirmative, or downright sentimental. In his *Antipolitics*, Konrád writes of a 'new Central European identity', 'the consciousness of Central Europe', a 'Central European strategy'. 'The demand for self-government,' he suggests, ' is the organizing focus of the new Central European ideology.' 'A certain distinctive Central European scepticism,' Havel comments in *The Anatomy of a Reticence,*

> is inescapably a part of the spiritual, cultural, and intellectual phenomenon that is Central Europe ... That scepticism has little in common with, say, English scepticism. It is generally rather strange, a bit mysterious, a bit nostalgic, often tragic and even at times heroic.

Later in the same essay, he talks of 'a Central European mind, sceptical, sober, anti-utopian, understated' – in short, everything we think of as quintessentially English. Or Konrád again:

> It was East Central Europe's historical misfortune that it was unable to become independent after the collapse of the Eastern Tartar-Turkish hegemony and later the German-Austrian hegemony of the West, and that it once again came under Eastern hegemony, this time of the Soviet Russian type. *This is what prevents our area from exercising the Western option taken out a thousand years ago, even though that represents our profoundest historical inclinations* (my italics).

In this last passage, history has indeed been recast as myth. And the mythopopic tendency – the inclination to attribute to the Central European past what you hope will characterize the Central European future, the confusion of what should be with what was – is rather typical of the new Central Europeanism. We are to understand that what was *truly* Central European was always Western, rational, humanistic, democratic, sceptical and tolerant. The rest was East European, Russian or possibly German. Central Europe takes all the *Dichter und Denker,* Eastern Europe is left with the *Richter und Henker.*

The clearest and most extreme articulation of this tendency comes from Milan Kundera. Kundera's Central Europe is a mirror image of Solzhenitsyn's Russia. Solzhenitsyn says that communism is to Russia as a disease is to the man afflicted by it. Kundera says that communism is to Central Europe as the disease is to the man afflicted by it – and the disease is Russia! Kundera's Central European myth is in frontal collision with Solzhenitsyn's Russian myth. Kundera's absurd exclusion of Russia from Europe (not endorsed by Havel or Konrád) has been most effectively criticized by Joseph Brodsky. As Brodsky observes, 'The political system that put Mr Kundera out of commission is as much a product of Western rationalism as it is of Eastern emotional radicalism.' But can't we go one step further? Aren't there specifically Central European traditions that at least facilitated the establishment of communist regimes in Hungary and Czechoslovakia, and traditions that those regimes signally carry forward to this day?

A superbureaucratic statism and formalistic legalism taken to absurd (and sometimes already inhuman) extremes were, after all, also particularly characteristic of Central Europe before 1914. That is one reason why we find the most exact, profound and chilling anticipations of the totalitarian nightmare precisely in the works of the most distinctively Central European authors of the early twentieth century, in Kafka and Musil, Broch and Roth. And then, what was really more characteristic of historic Central Europe: cosmopolitan tolerance, or nationalism and racism? As François Bondy has tellingly observed (in a riposte to Kundera), if Kafka was a child of Central Europe, so too was Adolf Hitler. And then again, I find myself asking: Since when has the 'Central European mind' been 'sceptical, sober, anti-utopian, understated?' For a thousand years, as Konrád seems to suggest? In 1948, when, as Kundera vividly recalls in The Book of Laughter and Forgetting, the most Central European of intellectuals joined hands and danced in the streets to welcome the arrival of heaven on earth? Or is it only since 1968?

The myth of the pure Central European past is perhaps a good myth. Like Solzhenitsyn's Russian myth, it is an understandable exaggeration to challenge a prevailing orthodoxy. Like the contemporary West German myth of the 20 July, 1944, bomb plot against Hitler (the myth being that the conspirators were true liberal democrats, proleptic model citizens of the Federal Republic), its effects on a younger generation may be inspiring. So shouldn't we let good myths lie? I think not. And in other moments, or when challenged directly, Havel and Konrád, among others, also think not.

In the late 1970s, the Czechoslovak historian J. Mlynarik (writing under the pseudonym Danubius) started a fascinating and highly fruitful discussion in Prague when he argued that the expulsion of the Sudeten Germans by the non-communist Czechoslovak government in the immediate aftermath of the Second World War was itself an inhuman and 'totalitarian' act – a precedent and path-breaker for the communist totalitarianism to come. 'Let us not forget,' the Czech writer Jií Gruša movingly reminded us at the unofficial cultural symposium in Budapest last year, 'that it was we (the writers) who glorified the modern state' and that 'our nationalist odes may be found in all the schoolbooks of Europe.' Havel goes out of his way to underline the lesson of his fellow intellectuals' 'post-war lapse into utopianism'. And Konrád declares bluntly: 'After all, we Central Europeans began the first two world wars.' So if at times they indulge the mythopoeic tendency, there is also, in this new discussion of Central Europe from Prague and Budapest, a developed sense of historical responsibility, an awareness of the deeper ambiguities of the historical reality; in short, an understanding that Central Europe is very, very far from being simply 'the part of the West now in the East.'

Besides these historical ambiguities there are, of course, the geographical ones. Like Europe itself, no one can quite agree where Central Europe begins or ends. Germans naturally locate the centre of Central Europe in Berlin; Austrians, in Vienna. Tomáš Masaryk defined it as 'a peculiar zone of small nations extending from the North Cape to Cape Matapan' and therefore including 'Laplanders, Swedes, Norwegians and Danes, Finns, Estonians, Letts, Lithuanians, Poles, Lusatians, Czechs and Slovaks, Magyars, Serbo-Croats and Slovenes, Romanians, Bulgars, Albanians, Turks and Greeks' – but no Germans or Austrians! As with the whole of Europe, the most difficult frontier to locate is the Eastern one. The reader may wonder why I have thus far talked so much of Prague and Budapest but not of Warsaw; of Havel and Konrád but not of Michnik. The reason is simple. Michnik never talks of Central Europe. His essays are full of illuminating references to European history and to the current affairs of other 'East European' countries, but in the whole corpus I have found not a single reference to Central Europe. And in this he is quite typical: the concept hardly surfaces in all the acres of samizdat produced in Poland over the last few years.

In the Polish part of old Galicia there is still more than a touch of nostalgia for the elegantly chaotic laxities of Habsburg rule – what Musil called the 'kakanische Zustände'. (At the offices of the Catholic weekly Tygodnik Powszechny in Kraków a portrait of the emperor Franz Josef hangs next to a row of popes.) For Michnik, as for most of the democratic opposition, it is self-evident that the small states between Russia and Germany contributed to their own destruction by the nationalistic rivalries of the inter-war years, and therefore that, were they ever to become independent again, they should co-operate as closely as possible – if not actually confederate. (The London-based Polish government-in-exile and the New York-based Council of Liberation of Czechoslovakia recently reaffirmed the 1942 Sikorski-Beneš declaration of intent to form a confederation of the Polish and Czechoslovak states.) But emotionally, culturally, and even geopolitically, the view eastward is still at least equally important to most Poles: the view across those vast eastern territories that for centuries were part of historic Poland. It is a lost half-mythical Lithuania that Czesław Miłosz celebrates in his poems and prose. And when Pope John Paul II talks of Europe he looks, with the eyes of a visionary and an exile, not just beyond the artificial, synthetic, truncated Europe of the EEC to Prague, Budapest and his beloved Kraków, but far, far beyond historic Central Europe, way across the Pripet marshes to the historic heartlands of Eastern Europe, to the Ukraine, to White Russia, even to the onion domes of Zagorsk; and when he preaches his European vision in Polish, he rolls an almost Lithuanian 'Ł'.

To say that Poland is to Central Europe as Russia is to Europe would be, no doubt, somewhat facile. But perhaps I have already said enough to indicate, however sketchily, just a few of the awesome historical, geographic, and cultural complexities, the rival memories and resentments that surround you, like a crowd of squabbling ghosts, the moment you revive the term Central Europe – let alone Mitteleuropa. If we treat the new Central European idea as an assertion about a common Central European past in the centuries down to 1945, as Konrád and Kundera seem to suggest we should, then we shall at once be lost in a forest of historical complexity – an endlessly intriguing forest to be sure, a territory where peoples, cultures, languages are fantastically intertwined, where every place has several names and men change their citizenship as often as their shoes, an enchanted wood full of wizards and witches, but one that bears over its entrance the words: 'Abandon all hope, ye who enter here, of ever again seeing the wood for the trees.' Every attempt to distil some common 'essence' of Central European history is either absurdly reductionist or invincibly vague. In this forest we find, with Stendahl, that 'all the truth, and all the pleasure, lies in the details.'

Fortunately, the new Central European idea is not only an assertion about the past. It is also, perhaps mainly, an assertion about the present. Put very baldly, the suggestion is that independent intellectuals from this part of the world today find themselves sharing a distinctive set of attitudes, ideas, and values, a set of attitudes they have in common but that is also, to a large degree, peculiar to them: just how common and how peculiar, they realize when they encounter Western intellectuals in Paris, New York, or California. This distinctive set of attitudes has, it is suggested, a good deal to do with their specifically Central European history – for example, the experience of small nations subjected to large empires, the associated tradition of civic commitment from the 'intelligentsia', the habit of irony that comes from living in defeat – but above all it has to do with their own direct, common, and unique experience of living under Soviet-type systems since Yalta. They are the Europeans who, so to speak, know what it is really about; and we can learn from them – if only we are prepared to listen. Central Europe is not a region whose boundaries you can trace on the map – like, say, Central America. It is a kingdom of the spirit.

'Compared to the geopolitical reality of Eastern Europe and Western Europe,' Konrád writes, 'Central Europe exists today only as a cultural-political anti-hypothesis (eine kulturpolitische Antihypothese) ... To be a Central European is a Weltanschauung not a Staatsangehörigkeit.' It is 'a challenge to the ruling system of clichés.'[10] (It is in this sense that Czesław Miłosz, too, has declared himself to be a Central European.) The Central European idea not only jolts us out of our post-Yalta mind-set, dynamiting what Germans call the Mauer im Kopf – the Berlin Wall in our heads. It also challenges other notions, priorities and values widely accepted in the West. What is more, it has something to offer in their place.

(Garton-Ash, 1991, pp. 161–70)

EXERCISE

Consider the following issues.

1 In what ways does Garton-Ash see the term 'central Europe' as useful?

2 What are the political backgrounds and positions of those Garton-Ash identifies as having being behind the revival of central Europe?

3 How does he treat the claims of advocates of central Europe that the region possesses some kind of cultural unity?

---

[10] Quotations in this paragraph are from his essay '*Mein Traum von Europa*', *Kurbuch* 81 (September 1985).

Figure 6 Gmünd. Austrian/Czech border, 1987. The 'Iron Curtain' not only split Germany in two and cut the country off from the rest of 'central Europe', it also divided Austria from territories that had also been part of the Habsburg monarchy at the beginning of the century. Photo: Brian Rose

4   What, according to Garton-Ash, motivates advocates of the term 'central Europe'?

DISCUSSION

1   Garton-Ash sees the term's essential usefulness as reminding the public that 'East Berlin, Prague, and Budapest are not quite in the same position as Vladivostok'. In other words the countries that belonged to the socialist bloc until the end of the 1980s, but were not part of the Soviet Union, were different from the Soviet Union. Furthermore, the term 'central Europe' is important in that it reminds people that the societies of what were at the time of writing called eastern Europe had only been cut off from those of the west by cold war division. There was therefore no necessary reason to lump them together with Russia as 'eastern Europe'.

2   All of the writers that Garton-Ash discusses were either 'dissident' or émigré authors who were opposed to continued socialist rule in their countries. You may have recognized the name of Václav Havel, the prominent dissident playwright who was rewarded for

The Velvet Revolution refers to events in Prague and other cities across Czechoslovakia in November and December 1989. These events led the Czechoslovak Communist Party (KSČ) to relinquish power and begin a transition to democracy in the country.

his central role in the **Velvet Revolution** of 1989 with the post of president of Czechoslovakia and later of the Czech Republic (and who wrote the final reading in Chapter 2). György Konrád, likewise a writer, served as a Hungarian member of parliament following the country's change of system in 1989–90. Adam Michnik too was a prominent dissident who became a respected political commentator following the fall of the socialist regime in Poland. You will note the association of the idea of central Europe with the opposition to continued communist rule in the countries discussed – something that is underlined by Garton-Ash's comments on the furious reactions of the official press to ideas of central Europe.

3   Garton-Ash does not explicitly raise the issue of the cultural unity of central Europe, but does see certain common elements in intellectual culture in the area. He writes about the 'distinctively *Central* European authors of the early twentieth century' and likewise, when the situation of the 1980s is discussed, states 'independent intellectuals from this part of the world *today* find themselves sharing a distinctive set of attitudes, ideas, and values'. When the focus is moved beyond the culture of intellectuals to consider whether central European societies were or are a broader cultural unity, then a note of scepticism is sounded. Garton-Ash describes central Europe in this sense as 'a forest of historical complexity – an endlessly intriguing forest to be sure, a territory where peoples, cultures, languages are fantastically intertwined'.

4   According to Garton-Ash the idea of central Europe, in the 1980s at least, was not primarily about asserting a unified identity rooted in geography, or in history, or for that matter in culture. Instead, as far as he is concerned, 'the new Central European idea is not only an assertion about the past. It is also, and perhaps mainly, an assertion about the present.' While it draws on the historical experience of intellectuals in the region – 'of small nations subjected to large empires, the associated tradition of civic commitment from the "intelligentsia", the habit of irony that comes from living in defeat' – it is very much focused around intellectuals' experiences of living under state socialism.

The definition of central Europe that emerged in the 1980s during the last years of socialist rule was very different from earlier notions of *Mitteleuropa*; of an ethnically diverse, yet German-dominated space in 'the heart of Europe'. Similarly, the discussion above of Hungarian definitions of east-central Europe as something rooted in history and

Figure 7 Austrian/Hungarian border, 1987. Though the landscape of this border may seem unremarkable, it has been the scene of some important historical events, as we saw in Chapter 1. Around 200,000 Hungarians crossed this border in 1956 to escape the suppression of the Hungarian Revolution. Photo: Brian Rose

the claims that dissident intellectuals made in the 1980s about their central European identity are also quite different. The central European identity as articulated by intellectuals was very much what might be described as a project identity – it rested on an aspiration to become something, rather than actually being rooted in history, geography or culture. The discussion here suggests that it represents the rejection by groups of intellectuals, opposed to the socialist regimes under which they lived, of an eastern European identity. Explicitly anti-Russian, it was about casting off a socialist vision of the future exported from Moscow and joining a western Europe characterized, according to the advocates of this identity, by notions of a state based on the rule of law, political democracy, and an institutional split between the state and civil society.

Conclusion

Why do the debates of intellectuals over where they belong matter? What I have tried to suggest here is that the notions of where Europe's borders – internal or external – lie are not fixed, but the product of struggle and indeed of a constantly shifting historical context. These shifts are above all about the idea of who belongs, who is an 'insider' and 'outsider', who is 'excluded' and who is 'included'.

During the early 1990s the socialist regimes of eastern Europe disappeared into history. Furthermore, since their disappearance terms such as 'eastern Europe' have all but vanished from the vocabulary of those studying the countries that made up that region. Instead articles in newspapers and academic journals speak of 'central Europe', 'east-central Europe', 'the Balkans' or 'southeastern Europe'. Notions of central Europe are said to describe the regional identity of societies such as the Czech, the Croat, the Hungarian, the Polish, the Slovene and the Slovak. They assert and underpin arguments that these societies are more advanced and more 'European' than, say, the Serb, the Romanian or the Russian. They underplay the common experiences that these countries had under Soviet-type socialism. In the case of former Yugoslavia which, much commentary suggests, is bisected by the division between central Europe and 'the Balkans', these notions ignore the experience that the component parts of that country gained in belonging to the same multinational state from 1918 to 1991.

Such shifting definitions therefore have important ideological implications – they are as much about 'including' and 'excluding', or 'remembering' and 'forgetting', as they are about describing the actual internal boundaries of Europe. Maria Todorova has argued persuasively that the notion of central Europe

> was harnessed as an expedient argument in the drive for entry into the European institutional framework. It is during this stage that the Balkans first appeared as a dichotomical opponent, sometimes alongside with, sometimes indistinguishable from Russia.

> (Todorova, 1997, p. 160)

In short, therefore, these definitions bring us back to the central themes of this book – namely that Europe's boundaries are not set in stone; they are matters of complex negotiation, shaped by historical context and defined by, while simultaneously defining, identities within the continent.

No one can accurately define where the actual borders of Europe lie, nor can they actually define Europe's internal regional boundaries. As you will have noticed, I have not even attempted to address these issues definitively. I have instead asked you to consider them in a different way, one which I hope helps you to come to your own conclusion about where Europe lies. I have done this by exploring one relatively current debate about the regional identities of the area known before 1989 as eastern Europe. I have examined this region because these debates underpin the way in which Europe's divisions are considered. I have also examined this region because the 'east' of the continent is one of the most important areas of contestation in defining a European identity. The former socialist states are both part of and outside Europe. Our own knowledge, however basic, tells us that these societies are different from ours. They are poorer, more unstable, racked with internal conflict, poverty and crime. Yet they share some aspects of a common cultural heritage. What the debates about central European identity show is that this ambiguous status is felt by, at least, many of the intellectuals in these societies themselves.

References

Bibó, I. (1994) *Demokratikus Magyarország: Válogatás Bibó István tanulmányaiból*, Budapest, Magvetö Könyvkiadó.

Brian Rose website: http://www.brianrose.com/Intro.htm

Ekiert, G. (1996) *The State against Society: Political Crises and their Aftermath in East Central Europe*, Princeton, NJ, Princeton University Press.

Erdei, F. (1988) *Ferenc Erdei: Selected Writings*, ed. T. Huszár, transl. P. Félix, S. Eszenyi and D. Biró, Budapest, Akadémiai Kiadó.

Földes, G. (1995) *Az eladósodás politikatörténete, 1957–1986*, Budapest, Maecenás Könyvkiadó.

Garton-Ash, T. (1991) *The Uses of Adversity: Essays on the Fate of Central Europe*, revised and updated edn, Cambridge/Harmondsworth, Granta/Penguin.

Gerő, A. (1996) *Modern Hungarian Society in the Making: the Unfinished Experience*, Budapest, Central European University Press.

Jedlicki, J. (1999) *A Suburb of Europe: Nineteenth Century Polish Approaches to Western Civilization*, Budapest, Central European University Press.

Johnson, L. R. (1996) *Central Europe: Enemies, Neighbors, Friends*, Oxford/New York, Oxford University Press.

Kopstein, J. (1997) *The Politics of Economic Decline in East Germany, 1945–1989*, Chapel Hill, NC/London, University of North Carolina Press.

Kundera, Milan (1984) 'The tragedy of central Europe', *New York Review of Books*, 26 April, p.33–8.

Mutton, A. F. A. (1968) *Central Europe: a Regional and Human Geography*, 2nd edn, London/Harlow, Longman.

Neumann, I. B. (1999) *Uses of the Other: 'the East' in European Identity Formation*, Manchester, Manchester University Press.

Sayer, D. (1998) *The Coasts of Bohemia: a Czech History*, Princeton, NJ, Princeton University Press.

Schöpflin, G. and Wood, N. (eds) (1989) *In Search of Central Europe*, Cambridge, Polity.

Šimecka, M. (1984) *The Restoration of Order: the Normalisation of Czechoslovakia*, London/New York, Verso.

Szücs, J. (1988) 'Three historical regions of Europe: an outline', in J. Keane (ed.), *Civil Society and the State: New European Perspectives*, London/New York, Verso.

Todorova, M. (1997) *Imagining the Balkans*, New York/Oxford, Oxford University Press.

Tőkes, R. (1996) *Hungary's Negotiated Revolution: Economic Reform, Social Change and Political Succession*, Cambridge/New York, Cambridge University Press.

Wolff, L. (1994) *Inventing Eastern Europe: the Map of Civilization on the Mind of the Enlightenment*, Stanford, CA, Stanford University Press.

4

Exploring Europe's borderlands:

'the Balkans'

MARK PITTAWAY

Introduction

The *Oxford English Dictionary* defines the term 'Balkan' as 'of or pertaining to the peninsula bounded by the Adriatic, Aegean, and Black Seas, or to the countries or peoples of this region'. When you scan down the page to examine the definition of the verb to 'Balkanize', you find the following: 'to divide (a region) into mutually hostile units, as was done in the Balkan Peninsula in the late 19th and early 20th centuries'. The earliest recorded use of this term in English, according to the *OED*, dates from 1920 and the aftermath of the First World War as observers grappled with the reality of the new nation-states that had emerged out of the carnage and confusion generated by war. In English, therefore, 'the Balkans' acquired a powerful pejorative meaning during the first half of the twentieth century. (It is to highlight this fact that I have chosen to place the term in quote marks throughout this chapter.) Despite the relative peace that was visible in southeastern Europe between the end of the Greek civil war in 1949 and the fall of socialist regimes at the end of the 1980s, 'the Balkans' still remained a by-word for conflict and division in English. In other languages it also carries pejorative meanings. In Germany the first to argue that the Balkan peninsula constituted a discrete geographical region was the geographer Johann August Zeune (1778–1853), writing in 1808. It was, however, during the second half of the nineteenth century that consciousness of its position on the borders of Europe interacted with growing political instability to generate a perception which became ingrained in popular consciousness (Hatschikjan, 1999, p. 9).

Since 1989 the meanings invested in the term 'the Balkans' that were shaped by events in the late nineteenth and earlier twentieth centuries have returned, influencing western European perceptions of the region ever more strongly than before. Southeastern Europe has once again come to be seen as 'the Balkans' – a territory characterized by intense ethnic conflict and severe poverty. As conflict in the territories of former Yugoslavia raged, growing academic fascination resulted in the publication of a number of academic histories of 'the Balkans' (Glenny, 1999; Mazower, 2000; Stavrianos, 2000). Despite this profusion of histories that suggested the timelessness of the region, one of these historians wrote that 'from the start the Balkans was more than a geographical concept. The term, unlike its predecessors, was loaded with negative connotations – of violence, of savagery, primitivism – to an extent for which it is hard to find a parallel' (Mazower, 2000, p. 4). Such connotations have led many of the peoples of southeastern Europe to deny that they form part of 'the Balkans' – seeing it as essentially a by-word for poverty, violence and conflict. In short, the designation of much of southeastern Europe as 'the Balkans' speaks to a considerable extent about identity.

This powerful negative stereotype has been constructed from outside of the region. According to one anthropologist and one political scientist, 'the very word "Balkan" in the English language has come to stand for confusion and fragmentation, and carries a definitely derogatory meaning' (Allcock and Young, 2000, p. xxi). The Bulgarian-born historian Maria Todorova, in a 1997 study of how the external image of southeastern Europe has changed during the past three centuries, argues that 'the Balkans' are both 'geographically inextricable from Europe, yet culturally constructed as "the other" within' (Todorova, 1997, p. 188). Like the western European definition of 'the orient' identified by Edward Said or the Enlightenment definition of eastern Europe described by Larry Woolf (both of which are discussed in Chapter 1), this image of 'the Balkans' has little to do with the reality of southeastern European societies. It instead speaks more to the concerns and ideas of western Europeans about southeastern Europe.

This chapter does not pretend to be a comprehensive treatment of the subject by any means. I am not going to provide a history of western perceptions of 'the Balkans'. Those wishing to pursue this further should turn to the books listed in the references section at the end of the chapter. Instead I shall focus on the development of views of 'the Balkans' in the English-speaking world. Because current stereotypes of the region owe much to concerns that stem from its role in European history during the first half of the twentieth century, I concentrate on two texts that have helped to shape these perceptions. The first dates from the period before the First World War – Mary Edith Durham's *High Albania* (first published 1909) – and the second from the interwar period – Rebecca West's *Black Lamb and Grey Falcon* (first published 1941). Both were reprinted in the 1990s following the renewal of interest in 'the Balkans' that came with the conflict in Yugoslavia. I shall not provide a complete treatment of these works but rather concentrate on how certain western perceptions of 'the Balkans' are embedded in both of them.

A collective term for the conflicts in the former Yugoslavia which consist of civil conflict in Slovenia, 1991; Croatia, 1991–5; Bosnia-Hercegovina, 1992–6; Kosovo, 1997–99 and Macedonia, 2001.

As a result of debate in western Europe about 'the Balkans' during the wars in former Yugoslavia between 1991 and 2001 there has been increased interest in how 'the Balkans' entered western consciousness during the first half of the twentieth century. Before I discuss the work of Durham and West I want to take you through some of the debate that occurred in the 1990s. This should help you think about the contemporary relevance of what you will work with later. I therefore start by introducing you to Maria Todorova's argument that western – by which she means both western European and North American – definitions of 'the Balkans' have projected a powerful negative stereotype on to the region. According to Todorova, this stereotype says more about western European and, more recently, North American anxieties about themselves.

'The Balkans': imagined? Constructed? Represented?

The profusion of books and articles on 'the Balkans' in the 1990s was closely connected to the tragic conflict in the territories of former Yugoslavia that raged throughout the decade. This should have been no surprise; according to one observer writing in 1940, 'the Balkans are usually reported to the outside world only in time of terror and trouble; the rest of the time they are scornfully ignored' (quoted in Todorova, 1997, p. 184). Much popular commentary on the wars in Yugoslavia – at least prior to Nato's intervention in Kosovo in spring 1999 – argued that the causes of the war lay deep in the history of 'the Balkans': a history that has been presumed to be one of profound ethnic conflict. In the words of the then British prime minister, John Major (1990–97), speaking in 1993, 'the conflict in Bosnia was a product of impersonal and inevitable forces beyond anyone's control' (quoted in Mazower, 2000, p. 128). According to one British-based commentator on events in former Yugoslavia, much informed comment on the causes of the war seemed to consist of statements such as 'ethnic cleansing is dreadful, but they all do it you know', or 'once the lid came off ... old ethnic passions ... Goes back to World War Two ... Goes back centuries ... warring factions ... competing nationalisms ...' (Magaš, 1993, p. xii). Such opinions reflected the re-emergence of older perceptions of 'the Balkans' current in both western Europe and North America earlier in the century. According to one American journalist, writing in 1940,

Figure 4.1 Mary Edith Durham, Montenegrin Shepherdess spinning. Plain of Banjani, Montenegro, 1905. Edith Durham not only wrote about her journeys through early twentieth century south-eastern Europe, but she also kept a photographic record. Because her interest was in patterns of dress her pictures provide a unique record of certain aspects of everyday life in the region. This chapter is illustrated with a selection of Durham's photographs taken not only on the 1908 journey through northern Albania which formed the subject of High Albania, but also contains images from Croatia, Macedonia and Montenegro. Photo: Mary Edith Durham/Bankfield Museum, Halifax

> it is an intolerable affront to human and political nature that these wretched and unhappy little countries in the Balkan peninsula can, and do, have quarrels that cause world wars … loathsome and almost obscene snarls in Balkan politics, hardly intelligible to a Western reader, are still vital to the peace of Europe, and perhaps the world.
>
> (Quoted in Glenny, 1999, p. xxiii)

When John Major described the conflict in former Yugoslavia as the result of ancient hatreds he was drawing upon a much older view of 'the Balkans' that had been current in western Europe and North America since the end of the First World War.

The first reading was written very much against the view of 'the Balkans' advanced by western governments and mainstream commentators as an explanation during the early years of the tragedy in former Yugoslavia. It is an edited section of the conclusion of Maria Todorova's book *Imagining the Balkans* (1997). In the extract Todorova is objecting to a view prevalent in the United States, where she teaches, that the conflict in former Yugoslavia was primarily 'a Balkan conflict'. Though her writing is focused around making a contribution to a contemporary political debate, her case is in fact far larger. She argues that 'the Balkans' has been misrepresented since the mid nineteenth century and that conclusions about the war in Yugoslavia having arisen from 'ancient ethnic hatreds' in fact represent views that have been held in the west about 'the Balkans' for far longer.

> Yet, like the poor, the Balkans shall always be with us.
>
> Konrad Berkovici[1]
>
> Perhaps the best solution would be to plow under every third Balkan.
>
> Howard Brubaker[2]

'The Balkans are usually reported to the outside world only in time of terror and trouble; the rest of the time they are scornfully ignored. Kipling epitomized this attitude by exclaiming in *The Light That Failed*: "Speaking of war, there'll be trouble in the Balkans in the spring."' This was the opening paragraph of a book written in 1940.[3] It can be the opening paragraph to a book written in 1995. To the ones who reproduce an essentialist image of the Balkans, it would be simply another proof that nothing has changed in the past fifty, one hundred, and even one thousand years. Yet, as I have argued, the Balkans have a powerful ontology that deserves serious and complex study, and it is an ontology of constant and profound change.

If one were to make more of the frozen vision of the Balkans than merely define it as the product of casual, dismissive, or hectoring journalism, one could argue that this image is more than a stereotype. It appears as the higher reality, the reflection of the

---

[1] *The Incredible Balkans*, 3.

[2] Gunther, *Inside Europe*, 437.

[3] Geshkof, *Balkan Union*, xi.

A distinction drawn from the work of the philosopher Immanuel Kant (1724–1804). Noumenon is a term used to refer to an object that exists only in the abstract, as opposed to a phenomenon which is something that the mind or the senses directly perceive.

phenomenal world, its essence and true nature, the 'noumenon' to the 'phenomenon,' to use the Kantian distinction. None of the politicians, journalists, or writers who have specialized in passing strictures on the Balkans have ever made a claim for a philosophical basis of their argument, yet this is what they have achieved. The frozen image of the Balkans, set in its general parameters around World War I, has been reproduced almost without variation over the next decades and operates as a discourse ...

It manifests an evolutionary belief in the superiority of orderly civilization over barbarity, archaic predispositions, backwardness, petty squabbles, unconforming and unpredictable behavior, that is, 'tribalism.' The very use of 'tribal' relegates the Balkans to a lower civilizational category, occupied primarily by Africans, to whom the term is usually applied. Africa and Asia have been classified by Elie Kedourie, according to their alleged political tradition, as the legacy of tribal rule and Oriental despotism. Tribal society's central feature is its primitiveness, lack of complexity and, implicitly, weakness, because when confronted 'with the demand of modernization for a sophisticated system of law and political representation, it merely collapses into tyranny.' It is also intrinsically passive, incompatible with initiative and enterprise. The classification of people according to notions of (social and technological) complexity and activity is a fundamental principle of the imperial discourse that has been inherited primarily by the press.[4] It also releases the 'civilized world' from any responsibility or empathy that it might otherwise bestow on more 'reasonable' people ...

It would do much better if the Yugoslav, not Balkan, crisis ceased to be explained in terms of Balkan ghosts, ancient Balkan enmities, primordial Balkan cultural patterns and proverbial Balkan turmoil, and instead was approached with the same rational criteria that the West reserves for itself: issues of self-determination versus inviolable status quo, citizenship and minority rights, problems of ethnic and religious autonomy, the prospects and limits of secession, the balance between big and small nations and states, the role of international institutions.[5] It is paradoxical to read American journalists bemoan the split of their society (which they call 'balkanization') while their politicians and their allies

[4] Spurr, *The Rhetoric*, 61–68, 71–73.

[5] Susan, L. Woodward, *Balkan Tragedy: Chaos and Dissolution after the Cold War*, Washington, D.C.: Brookings Institution, 1995.

sealed the virtual, not potential, balkanization of Yugoslavia by embracing unconditionally the principle of self-determination. This is not to deny the legitimate nature of processes of secession and self-determination, but to call on giving phenomena their proper names and on having a clear perspective of their repercussions. It is, of course, a sublime irony to observe leaders of the cleansed societies of Western Europe fifty years after their ugliest performance raise their hands in horror and bombard (in words and in deed, and safely hidden behind American leadership) the former Yugoslavs in preserving 'ethnic diversity' for the sake of securing a *Volksmuseum* of multiculturalism in a corner of Europe, after having given green light to precisely the opposite process.

There is another component, relevant in illuminating geopolitical choices and explicating balkanism as a discourse different from orientalism. As illustrated earlier, before the twentieth century, there existed an ambiguous attitude toward the Turks: an almost unconscious empathy with the rulers mingled with traditional sympathy for fellow-Christians. Britain, in particular, with its dominant anti-Russian attitude, upheld the Ottoman Empire as a barrier against further Russian expansion. This geopolitical configuration was in many ways inherited by the United States, and Turkey became an important element in the cold war anti-Soviet alliance. But there was no longer the admonishing figure of the suffering Balkan Christian. The former Christians were now all, with the exception of Greece, under the 'evil empire' of communism. Besides, the central discourse had shifted from religion to ideology.

Additionally, since World War II, it has become illegitimate to openly bash nonwhite races, non-Christian religions, and non-European societies. Kennan's introduction accordingly downplays the role of the Ottoman Empire and the Turks for the historical fate of the Balkans: current problems stem from their 'distant tribal past,' and have roots that 'reach back, clearly, not only into the centuries of Turkish domination.' Finally, 'one must not be too hard on the Turks'; after all, 'there was more peace when they were still under Turkish rule than there was after they gained their independence. (That is not to say that the Turkish rule was in all other respects superior to what came after.)'[6]...

By being geographically inextricable from Europe, yet culturally constructed as 'the other' within, the Balkans have been able to

---

[6] *The Other Balkan Wars*, 14–15.

absorb conveniently a number of externalized political, ideological, and cultural frustrations stemming from tensions and contradictions inherent to the regions and societies outside the Balkans. Balkanism became, in time, a convenient substitute for the emotional discharge that orientalism provided, exempting the West from charges of racism, colonialism, eurocentrism, and Christian intolerance against Islam. After all, the Balkans are in Europe; they are white; they are predominantly Christian, and therefore the externalization of frustrations on them can circumvent the usual racial or religious bias allegations. As in the case of the Orient, the Balkans have served as a repository of negative characteristics against which a positive and self-congratulatory image of the 'European' and the 'West' has been constructed. With the reemergence of East and orientalism as independent semantic values, the Balkans are left in Europe's thrall, anticivilization, alter ego, the dark side within. Reflecting on the European genius, Agnes Heller maintained that 'the recognition of the accomplishment of others has always been part and parcel of the European identity,' that 'the myth of Occident and Orient is not a juxtaposition of civilization with barbarism but rather of one civilization with another,' and that 'European (Western) cultural identity has been conceived as both ethnocentric and anti-ethnocentric.'[7] If Europe has produced not only racism but also antiracism, not only misogyny but also feminism, not only anti-Semitism, but also its repudiation, then what can be termed Balkanism has not yet been coupled with its complementing and ennobling antiparticle.

(Todorova, 1997, pp. 184–9)

EXERCISE

Your notes should be organized around responses to the following questions.

1   In this extract Todorova claims that there has been a timeless view of 'the Balkans' in the west. What does she see as the characteristics of 'the Balkans', according to this view?

2   At any point in the extract does Todorova contradict her earlier statement that notions of 'the Balkans' have been 'frozen' in time?

[7]   Agnes Heller, 'Europe: An Epilogue?' Brian Nelson, David Roberts, and Walter Veit, eds. *The Idea of Europe: Problems of National and Transnational Identity*, New York and Oxford: Berg, 1992, 14.

3   Do you think that there is an implied contrast between 'the Balkans' and western Europe in the view of 'the Balkans' that has been 'frozen' in time? To what extent and on what basis does Todorova challenge this implied contrast? Using your own knowledge, try to give reasons as to whether you find her challenge convincing, and why.

DISCUSSION _____

I am aware that I have given you quite a lot to think about in this extract and I hope that you have been able to take some useful notes. I also hope it has served to challenge some prevailing views of 'the Balkans'. Your notes, organized in the way suggested above, might contain the following points.

1   Todorova argues that, in essence, the timeless view of 'the Balkans' is an inherently imperialist one. You might have also remarked her suggestion that it contains racist undertones. You may have noted down some or all of the following sentences:

> It manifests an evolutionary belief in the superiority of orderly civilization over barbarity, archaic predispositions, backwardness, petty squabbles, unconforming and unpredictable behavior, that is, 'tribalism.' The very use of 'tribal' relegates the Balkans to a lower civilizational category ... The classification of people according to notions of ... complexity and activity is a fundamental principle of the imperial discourse that has been inherited primarily by the press.

2   At the beginning of the extract Todorova asserts the almost timeless nature of discourse about 'the Balkans'. She begins with a quote from another book about the link between attention paid to 'the Balkans' and concern about 'terror and trouble'. She then goes on to say that

> This was the opening paragraph to a book written in 1940. It can be the opening paragraph to a book written in 1995 ... The frozen image of the Balkans, set in its general parameters around World War I, has been reproduced almost without variation over the next decades and operates as a discourse.

You might, however, have noticed later in the extract a point that seems to conflict with notions of the unchanging nature of perceptions of the Balkans. Note the passage 'before the twentieth century, there existed an ambiguous attitude toward the Turks: an almost unconscious empathy with the rulers mingled with traditional sympathy for fellow-Christians'. Thus prior to the First World War not all the peoples of 'the Balkans' were represented as entrapped by Major's 'ancient ethnic hatreds'. It would, perhaps, be to make too much of this to claim that it is a contradiction in Todorova's arguments – it merely points to the importance of the First World War in creating the contemporary perception of the region in the west. This is, however, a point to which I shall return later in this chapter.

3   Your reflections on points 2 and 3 will have certainly alerted you to the fact that Todorova's 'frozen' view of 'the Balkans' implies a contrast between that region and western Europe. This contrast, according to Todorova, is expressed in attitudes to violence, in the existence of an assumed 'tribal' mentality and in the level of development. It is one that she effectively rejects as being both imperialist and racist. Her most polemical comments relate to her effective charge of hypocrisy against western Europe for seeking to accuse the peoples of 'the Balkans' of a kind of violence that has also been part of western European history. Note her comment:

> It is, of course, a sublime irony to observe leaders of the cleansed societies of Western Europe fifty years after their ugliest performance raise their hands in horror and bombard (in words and in deed, and safely hidden behind American leadership) the former Yugoslavs in preserving 'ethnic diversity' for the sake of securing a *Volksmuseum* of multiculturalism in a corner of Europe, after having given green light to precisely the opposite process.

I have deliberately not answered the last issue raised in point 3 because although I want you to think carefully about Todorova's arguments her tone is too polemical and controversial for a considered and clear answer to be given. Without providing a detailed examination of the history of southeastern Europe it would be impossible to present a thorough and clear response to her charge that 'the west' has sought to measure 'the Balkans' by a standard higher than its own and has thus found it wanting. It is, however, an issue you should consider in the back of your mind while reading this chapter. I would at this stage note, though, that the accusation Todorova makes against western Europeans is not entirely baseless. During the twentieth century three periods of conflict in southeastern Europe can be defined: that of 1912–19, that of 1939–49 (from the beginning of the Second World War to the conclusion of the Greek civil war) and finally that of Yugoslavia between 1991 and 2001. Some of these conflicts have engulfed the whole region; others, most notably in Greece between 1946 and 1949 and then in

Yugoslavia since 1991, have only involved parts of it. Most of the last 100 years have been characterized not by war, but by its absence. Even though this simplistic outline suggests that the region known as 'the Balkans' has been marginally more prone to conflict during the past century than Europe as a whole, the rest of Europe has been far from innocent where such violence has been concerned. To quote Mark Mazower:

> In 1994 an Austrian reader of my book *Inside Hitler's Greece* suggested that I had been too harsh in my judgement of German military behaviour in the Balkans in the 1940s, given that – as recent events again demonstrated, in his view – there was evidently a peculiar propensity to violence among the people of the region. To me, the wartime slave labour camp at Matthausen indicated that the Austrians did not have much to learn from the Bosnian Serbs about violence. But our argument was not really about violence so much as about cruelty – behaviour not numbers. It was, after all, neither the peoples of the Balkans nor their rulers who gave birth to the Gulag, the extermination camp or the Terror. Wehrmacht soldiers – not to mention other Nazi agencies – killed far more people in the Balkans than were killed by them.
>
> (Mazower, 2000, p. 129)

At the heart of Todorova's case is not merely the identification of a set of western European double standards with reference to an analysis of southeastern Europe, though this is important to her argument. She argues that west European views of southeastern Europe have produced what she terms a discourse of the Balkans – an idea of a region defined in a certain way because western observers have projected their concerns and notions on to social reality and have fundamentally defined it. This has ensured that 'the Balkans', though 'geographically inextricable from Europe', are 'yet culturally constructed as "the other" within' (Todorova, 1997, p. 188).

The argument Todorova presents raises questions that are fundamental to anyone from one culture who seeks to understand something about another. It also raises deep-seated questions about identity, power and definition. Can the reality of one region be represented to another? Can a people, or a region, be defined in opposition to another? How far does power shape the relationship between the representer and the represented? What implications does this have for a study of culture? These are important questions and I am not going to pretend that I have any definitive answers here.

Figure 4.2 Mary Edith Durham, Petar, his wife and son. Photo: Mary Edith Durham/Royal Anthropological Institute

You will also have noticed that while I have urged you not to dismiss Todorova's arguments I have also refrained from giving any kind of detailed commentary on them. I draw them to your attention merely to illustrate the political consequences of representation, before moving on to examine how a text written by an individual from one culture representing the reality of another can lead to the creation of the forms of discourse about a society, state or region.

Travelling in 'the Balkans'

In order to consider the question of representation further I shall now shift from the generalities of Todorova's polemic to some specifics of how certain forms of stereotype about the region have become embodied in culture. To do this I shall turn to the two pieces of travel writing mentioned in the introduction to this chapter, which have proved influential in forming what John Allcock has termed 'a particular image of the Balkan region' that 'has come to be accepted in the English-speaking world' (Allcock, 2000, p. 217). My ambitions are therefore considerably more modest than Todorova's – instead of presenting a comprehensive account of western European representation of 'the Balkans' I focus on how two writers represented certain aspects of reality in southeastern Europe during the first half of the twentieth century. The two texts, Edith Durham's *High Albania* and Rebecca West's *Black Lamb and Grey Falcon*, form part of a much broader body of work written by women about southeastern Europe. Issues of gender and identity shaped the experience of both of these British women in 'the Balkans', as is clear from their accounts. As some scholars have shown, these issues also shaped the way in which they wrote about and represented 'the Balkans' (Allcock and Young, 2000). Such concerns are beyond the scope of this chapter, which instead examines how their work contributes to and draws on notions of 'the Balkans'. Before moving on I want to provide a very brief introduction to both authors and to set their books in context.

Edith Durham's work 'had the most profound impact on the area she came to know and love' (Hodgson, 2000a). Born to wealthy middle-class parents in London in 1863, she came to travel in southeastern Europe at the age of 37 in 1900. Her original motivation for this had little to do with intrinsic attraction to 'the Balkans' as such, but was undertaken on medical advice. Her doctor had advised her to 'get right away, no matter where, so long as the change is complete' (quoted in Hodgson, 2000b). Her initial journey took her to Montenegro and began a fascination with the peoples and cultures of southeastern Europe that would last for the rest of her life. It is, however, for her work on Albania that Durham has become best known. She visited the country for the first time in 1903, after undertaking humanitarian work in neighbouring Macedonia following the revolt of that year.

At the time Durham first visited Albania it was still part of the Ottoman empire. In 1903, however, Ottoman power in southeastern Europe was placed under considerable pressure because of the growing power of the Christian nation-states (Bulgaria, Greece and Serbia) that had emerged in the region as a result of conflict during

Figures 4.3, 4.4 and 4.5   Mary Edith Durham, The Market in Agruar, Croatia.
Photos: Mary Edith Durham/Royal Anthropological Institute

the nineteenth century. Moreover, national feeling in the region was spreading, further undermining the hegemony of the Ottomans. The uprising in Macedonia in 1903 was one symptom of rising Slav nationalism conflicting with the power of the empire. Non-Slav and religiously heterogeneous Albania was not immune from the rise in national sentiment. During the last years of the nineteenth century nationalists in Albania had begun to raise money to found schools that taught the Albanian language, while Albanian-language newspapers were founded around the turn of the century (Vickers, 1999, pp. 44–5). Such expressions combined with rumbling instability in neighbouring Macedonia, the demands for territorial expansion on the part of Bulgaria, Greece and Serbia, the designs of the great powers and the internal crisis within the Ottoman empire to politicize Albanian national sentiment. Popular discontent and regional tension further fuelled political instability inside Albania during the first eight years of the twentieth century (Malcom, 1998, pp. 234–8; Vickers, 1999, pp. 50–1).

In 1908 Edith Durham undertook her journey into the mountains of northern Albania that formed the basis for her travelogue *High Albania*. She did so at a time of intense political crisis within the Ottoman empire. This was a year of revolution, as the 'Young Turks' who sought a modernization of the empire's institutions in order to arrest its growing crisis took power, curbing the authority of Sultan Abdülhamit II (1876–1909) and promising reform (Quataert, 2000, p. 64). Durham's book was written mindful of the political instability in southeastern Europe and, as the second reading shows, sought to present the people of Albania to her readers in this light. This reading is a short text, the opening passage *High Albania*. Durham's purpose is to introduce her subject to a British readership which was perhaps not knowledgeable about Albania itself, but which would have been preoccupied by the news of political crisis in Ottoman Turkey and the conflict in and around its southeast European territories.

The great river of life flows not evenly for all peoples. In places it crawls sluggishly through dull flats, and the monuments of a dim past moulder upon the banks that it has no force to overflow; in others it dashes forward torrentially, carving new beds, sweeping away old landmarks; or it breaks into backwaters apart from the main stream, and sags to and fro, choked with the flotsam and jetsam of all the ages.

Such backwaters of life exist in many corners of Europe – but most of all in the Near East. For folk in such lands time has almost stood still. The wanderer from the West stands awestruck amongst them, filled with vague memories of the cradle of his race, saying, 'This did I do some thousands of years ago; thus did I lie in wait for mine enemy; so thought I and so acted I in the beginning of Time.'

High Albania is one of these corners. I say High Albania advisedly, for the conditions that prevail in it are very different from those in South Albania, and it is with the wildest parts of High Albania alone that this book deals.

The history of Albania, a complicated tale of extreme interest, remains to be written – strange that it should be so. The claims of Greek, Bulgar, and Serb in the Balkan peninsula are well known; so are the desires of Austria, Russia, and Italy. But it has been the fashion always to ignore the rights and claims of the oldest inhabitant of the land, the Albanian, and every plan for the reformation or reconstruction of the Near East that has done so has failed.

'Constantinople,' says the Albanian, 'is the key of the Near East, and Albania is the key of Constantinople.'

The history of every people is a great epic, the writing of which is beyond me. The following brief sketch shows only the passing of the peoples that have swayed the fortunes of North Albania, but never yet subdued its stubborn individuality.

(Durham [1909] (2000), pp. 1–2)

EXERCISE

Now make some notes on the extract, bearing in mind the following issues.

1   What case does Durham make for the importance of the study of Albania?

2   More significantly, you will note that nowhere in this passage does Durham refer to southeast Europe, or to 'the Balkans'. Instead she uses another term for the region. What term is this? Why does she use it? Using information in the passage and your own knowledge try to jot down what implication her use of this term might have for the way in which 'High Albania' is represented to her predominantly British audience.

DISCUSSION _____

1   For Durham it is clear that Albania has been ignored and
     regarded as a backwater. She states as much in the extract by
     implying that Albania is one of the 'backwaters' of '[t]he great
     river of life'. This metaphor suggests a territory ignored and
     marginalized – peripheral to progress in the rest of Europe. She
     argues that the study of her 'backwater' is important if her
     readers are to understand the conflicts shaking the Ottoman
     empire, and thus southeastern Europe. She states that

> the claims of Greek, Bulgar, and Serb in the Balkan peninsula
> are well known ... But it has been the fashion always to ignore
> the rights and claims of the oldest inhabitant of the land, the
> Albanian, and every plan for the reformation or
> reconstruction of the Near East that has done so has failed.

You might have noted, casting your mind back to Todorova's
polemic, how Durham uses several arguments that have
characterized western discourse on 'the Balkans'. She concedes
the region's so-called backwardness, its separateness from where
what we might call 'real' history is made, with her metaphor of
the backwater and the river of life. In an echo of the view quoted
at the beginning of the first reading, which argues that outside
times of conflict 'the Balkans' have been ignored, Durham argues
that Albania is relevant because it holds the key to understanding
the conflict then taking place in southeastern Europe.

2   Though Durham employs the term 'the Balkan peninsula' once
     in this extract it is used only in its narrowest geographical sense.
     The political term she uses to describe the region in which
     Albania is located is 'the Near East'. This essentially denotes the
     fact that Durham is dealing with an Ottoman territory within
     Europe – in short, a part of what could alternatively be described
     as 'Turkey in Europe'. You might have noted that 'the Near East'
     is a far from neutral term as it implies that the territories ruled by
     the Ottomans are not themselves part of Europe. When
     combined with the use of the backwater metaphor it creates the
     impression that Albania itself is isolated and separated from
     Europe. Even in the work of an author as sympathetic to the
     peoples of southeastern Europe as Durham, certain aspects of
     what Todorova calls 'Balkanist discourse' are at work.

_____

Before moving on from Durham's introduction to northern Albania
and its people I shall pause briefly to consider the implications of the
Ottoman political heritage for an understanding of the region. You

will doubtless remember from Chapter 1 the argument advanced by
Michael Herzfeld that

> It is ... important to ask whether ... Greek, and Serbian
> complaints about 'the Turkish yoke' bear witness to 'another'
> colonialism or whether, as I suspect, they instead indicate a
> hegemony by certain specific Western powers that find it
> convenient to treat the Turkish past as a stain on these
> countries' occidental escutcheon.

(Herzfeld, 1997, p. 714)

Turkey, even today, is regarded in western Europe as a power that is
only ambiguously European, if it is regarded as European at all.
Describing the region of southeastern Europe as 'the Near East'
suggests that it is somehow not part of Europe. For much of the early
modern period the Ottoman empire was regarded within what is now
western Europe as an Islamic superpower, the antithesis of Christian
Europe. The lands under Turkish control could be described as being
outside Europe on the basis of a set of assumptions that rooted
European identity in religion (Kaser, 1999). With the onset of the
Enlightenment in the eighteenth century Ottoman Turkey
increasingly came to be seen as the archetype of 'despotism' – a

Figure 4.6 Mary Edith Durham, Catholic women of Maltsia e madhe
(Great Mountains) selling firewood at Scutari, Albania 1910. Photo: Mary
Edith Durham/Bankfield Museum, Halifax

political regime that represented the negation of the Enlightenment vision of progress (Kaiser, 2000). These notions of the non-Christian and despotic nature of Ottoman rule were to prove extremely powerful in the nineteenth century. Such arguments lay behind the attempts of Prime Minister William Gladstone (1868–74, 1880–5, 1886, 1892–4) during the 1870s to change British foreign policy towards the Ottoman empire. His statement that 'very nearly all ... now confess that in treating the question of the Ottoman Empire we cannot refuse to look at the condition of the subject races' (quoted in Todorova, 1997, p. 98) demonstrated the saliency of perceptions of Turkish 'despotism' throughout the nineteenth century.

By the time Rebecca West journeyed through Yugoslavia in 1937 and 1938 the map of southeastern Europe had changed utterly. 'Turkey in Europe' had disappeared as a result of the First World War. After that war existing nation-states were enlarged and new states were born out of the ruins of both Ottoman Turkey and Austria-Hungary. By the mid 1930s the liberal political systems in all of these states had been replaced by a series of authoritarian regimes, characterized by internal political conflict gathered around the poles of either class or ethnicity, or both.

West herself is considerably better known than Edith Durham. Born in 1892 of Anglo-Irish descent, she was a political activist and a writer of considerable note. She saw Yugoslavia on a journey through south-eastern Europe for the first time in 1936, and travelled through the country with her husband twice in 1937 and 1938. By this time, however, Yugoslav society was characterized by considerable political tension. The state of Yugoslavia had been created as a multinational democracy in 1918 out of the previously independent state of Serbia and the south Slav territories of Austria-Hungary. It promised to be a multi-ethnic state and a model for cooperation between peoples, but its democracy became paralysed by tension between Croat political parties seeking autonomy and their Serbian counterparts who sought a unitary state ruled from Belgrade (Banac, 1988). The political problems that this conflict generated led to increasing instability and to violence that eventually paved the way for royal dictatorship in 1929. This dictatorship was undermined, though not destroyed, by the assassination of King Alexander (1929–34) by a Macedonian terrorist in Marseille in October 1934 (Lampe, 1996, p. 176). Deep-seated political tension rumbled on in Yugoslavia throughout the late 1930s, though this was to explode into widespread conflict only with German invasion and occupation in 1941. It was against this background that West's *Black Lamb and Grey Falcon* was written. Just as the second reading was Edith Durham's attempt to introduce Albania to her British audience, the third is Rebecca West's introduction to Yugoslavia. Though West's book is presented as a travelogue, it is no simple account of a journey but, as Trevor Royle in his introduction to the 1993 edition points out, an attempt to show that 'the lands of the Balkans are not just places to visit; they need to be revealed so that the rest of the world can understand the historical forces which forged them into what they are today' (Royle, 1993, p.xvii).

I raised myself on my elbow and called through the open door into the other wagon-lit:

'My dear, I know I have inconvenienced you terribly by making you take your holiday now, and I know you did not really want to come to Yugoslavia at all. But when you get there you will see why it was so important that we should make this journey, and that we should make it now, at Easter. It will all be quite clear, once we are in Yugoslavia.'

There was, however, no reply. My husband had gone to sleep. It was perhaps as well. I could not have gone on to justify my certainty that this train was taking us to a land where everything was comprehensible, where the mode of life was so honest that it put an end to perplexity. I lay back in the darkness and marvelled that I should be feeling about Yugoslavia as if it were my mother country, for this was 1937, and I had never seen the place till 1936. Indeed, I could remember the first time I ever spoke the name 'Yugoslavia' and that was only two and a half years before, on October the ninth, 1934.

It was in a London nursing-home. I had had an operation, in the new miraculous way. One morning a nurse had come in and given me an injection, as gently as might be, and had made a little joke which was not very good but served its purpose of taking the chill off the difficult moment. Then I picked up my book and read that sonnet by Joachim du Bellay which begins '*Heureux qui, comme Ulysse, a fait un beau voyage.*' I said to myself, 'That is one of the most beautiful poems in the world,' and I rolled over in my bed, still thinking that it was one of the most beautiful poems in the world, and found that the electric light was burning and there was a new nurse standing at the end of my bed. Twelve hours had passed in that moment. They had taken me upstairs to a room far above the roofs of London, and had cut me about for three hours and a half, and had brought me down again, and now I was merely sleepy, and not at all sick, and still half-rooted in my pleasure in the poem, still listening to a voice speaking through the ages, with barest economy that somehow is the most lavish melody: '*Et en quelle saison Revoiray-je le clos de ma pauvre maison, Qui m'est une province, et beaucoup d'advantage?*'

I had been told beforehand that it would all be quite easy; but before an operation the unconscious, which is really a shocking old fool, envisages surgery as it was in the Stone Age, and I had been very much afraid. I rebuked myself for not having observed that the universe was becoming beneficent at a great rate. But it was not yet wholly so. My operation wound left me an illusion that I had a load of ice strapped to my body. So, to distract me, I had a radio brought into my room, and for the first time I realized how uninteresting life could be and how perverse human appetite. After I had listened to some talks and variety programmes, I would not have been surprised to hear that there are householders who make arrangements with the local authorities not to empty their dustbins but to fill them. Nevertheless there was always good music provided by some station or other at any time in the day, and I learned to swing like a trapeze artist from programme to programme in search of it.

But one evening I turned the wrong knob and found music of a kind other than I sought, the music that is above earth, that lives in the thunderclouds and rolls in human ears and sometimes deafens them without betraying the path of its melodic line. I heard the announcer relate how the King of Yugoslavia had been assassinated in the streets of Marseille that morning. We had passed into another phase of the mystery we are enacting here on earth, and I knew that it might be agonizing. The rags and tags of knowledge that we all have about us told me what foreign power had done this thing. It appeared to me inevitable that war must follow, and indeed it must have done, had not the Yugoslavian Government exercised an iron control on its population, then and thereafter, and abstained from the smallest provocative action against its enemies. That forbearance, which is one of the most extraordinary feats of statesmanship performed in post-war Europe, I could not be expected to foresee. So I imagined myself widowed and childless, which was another instance of the archaic outlook of the unconscious, for I knew that in the next war we women would have scarcely any need to fear bereavement, since air raids unpreceded by declaration of war would send us and our loved ones to the next world in the breachless unity of scrambled eggs. That thought did not then occur to me, so I rang for my nurse, and when she came I cried to her, 'Switch on the telephone! I must speak to my husband at once. A most terrible thing has happened. The King of Yugoslavia has been assassinated.' 'Oh, dear!' she replied. 'Did you know him?' 'No,' I said. 'Then why,' she asked, 'do you think it's so terrible?'

Her question made me remember that the word 'idiot' comes from a Greek root meaning private person. Idiocy is the female defect: intent on their private lives, women follow their fate through a darkness deep as that cast by malformed cells in the brain. It is no worse than the male defect, which is lunacy: they are so obsessed by public affairs that they see the world as by moonlight, which shows the outlines of every object but not the details indicative of their nature. I said, 'Well, you know, assassinations lead to other things!' 'Do they?' she asked. 'Do they not!' I sighed.

(West [1941] (1993), pp. 1–3)

EXERCISE

Make your notes on the reading with the following points in mind.

1   What event provokes West's interest in Yugoslavia?

2   From her explanation, why do you think she regards events in Yugoslavia as important?

3   How, with this extract, do you think West is trying to justify the relevance of her subject to a British audience?

DISCUSSION

1   The event that provokes West's interest in Yugoslavia is the assassination of King Alexander in Marseille, which she hears about on the radio in her London nursing home.

2   You might have noted that West sees the assassination of the Yugoslav king as an event of potentially world-shattering importance and one likely to provoke a major war. You might have remarked the passage where West says, 'So I imagined myself widowed and childless, which was another instance of the archaic outlook of the unconscious, for I knew that in the next war we women would have scarcely any need to fear bereavement'. She links the murder of King Alexander to the assassination of Archduke Franz Ferdinand in Sarajevo in 1914, drawing the conclusion that as war resulted from assassination then, it might have also been the result of a similar event in 1934. Your attention may have also been caught by the exchange with West's nurse at the very end of the reading: 'I said, "Well, you know, assassinations lead to other things!" "Do they?" she asked. "Do they not!" I sighed.'

3   West is trying to make a number of related points in this extract. She is attempting to overcome the insularity and ignorance of her audience as far as Yugoslavia is concerned. She does this by invoking the popular memory of the First World War, and its ignition in what was later to become Yugoslavia in 1918, to make a point about the relevance of conflict in southeastern Europe to the concerns of politics in western Europe. You might have said that West is seeking to stimulate interest by conceding to her readers that although they may know little of Yugoslavia, they ought to because political events there in the past have had earth-shattering consequences. If you thought of Todorova while reading this extract you might also have noted that West is trying to use certain elements of what Todorova terms 'Balkanist discourse' to make the case for the relevance of her subject to her British audience. In other words West might as well be arguing that because Yugoslavia has been the source of much conflict, her readership should be interested in her explanation of it.

EXERCISE

Go back at this point and have another look at the second and third readings, taking them together. Think of them both as the attempts of authors to present and argue for the relevance of their subjects to their British readerships. Think very carefully about the similarities and differences in how they approach their subjects. They obviously differ in style – West's presentation is much more literary than Durham's drier style. I am not so interested in the stylistic differences between the two extracts as in the arguments that are advanced. How do you explain these differences?

DISCUSSION

The most obvious similarity between the two pieces is that both have to make a case for the relevance of their subjects. Durham openly concedes that for most of her readers Albania will be a backwater of which they know little, and although West does not concede this point as directly as Durham does this is implicit in the way she introduces her subject. Both authors rely on 'Balkanist discourse' to make their pitch to their readers in the sense that they draw attention to the geopolitical consequences of events in southeastern Europe to argue for their relevance. There is, however, a marked difference in emphasis between the two introductions in their content as well as their style. Durham clearly identifies her subject – Albania – as a backwater and part of the 'Near East'. The notion therefore of large parts of southeastern Europe as 'Turkey in Europe' is marked. Yet

Durham was writing in 1909, when Albania was still part of the Ottoman empire and Turkey was still present in southeastern Europe even though the empire was ridden by crisis. In the late 1930s, when West began her travels, this was no longer the case. Instead 'the Balkans' impinged on popular consciousness in Britain largely as the place where conflict had ignited world war in 1914. Moreover, by the time *Black Lamb and Grey Falcon* was first published in 1941 Yugoslavia had been drawn into world war as a result of German invasion.

When comparing the two extracts you can see a parallel between an argument implicit in the piece by Todorova that she did not fully develop. She noted that what she termed the 'frozen image of the Balkans' was 'set in its general parameters around World War I' and 'has been reproduced almost without variation over the next decades'. In other words, the identification of 'the Balkans' with conflict has both defined it and set the terms within which it has been described as a region.

I would seek to argue that it is far from that simple, though. You will have noticed that I have quoted only from the very beginning of both Durham's and West's books. I have neither cited the works as a whole – that would be beyond the scope of this limited chapter – nor have I yet given you any of the meat of the two books to consider. Both of these passages serve one particular purpose: to argue for the relevance of the material within the books to their readerships, which was in both cases largely British, overwhelmingly English-speaking and exclusively English-reading. In order to do this both extracts in different ways seek to engage their readerships and thus reveal something of why they might be interested in the affairs of southeastern Europe. For Durham's readership the passage that you have read suggests that southeastern Europe only meant something in that it formed part of 'Turkey in Europe' and was the theatre of conflict that threatened the great power balance in the continent. West's readership seems to have had a darker view of 'the Balkans', as a region of inherent political instability, where the assassinations of virtually unknown monarchs could plunge the world into terrible conflict.

It would be both unfair and wrong to argue that either Edith Durham or Rebecca West sought to present a 'discourse' of 'the Balkans' that advanced or even constructed stereotypes of southeastern Europe. Durham's contribution to our knowledge of the history and culture of Albania has been enormous. Far from reinforcing stereotypes, her work can be said to have been motivated by a desire to promote greater understanding of the region and thus to have aimed at breaking down such stereotypes. West's book, rather than being a neutral travelogue, sought to explain Yugoslavia at the end of the 1930s and advanced a view of it as a society more complex than could be accounted for merely by presenting stereotypes of a country where royalty was routinely assassinated. My argument is that a text that seeks to explain a place should be read as a conversation between the readership, the author/traveller and the subject under consideration.

Representing Albania: Edith Durham and blood vengeance in northern Albania

My account of Durham and West cannot and does not pretend to develop an argument about their views of the societies they wrote about, or to give a comprehensive account of their books. I merely seek to explore the issues involved in the interrogation of texts that represent one society to another. In the rest of this chapter I shall narrow the focus and try to touch upon some of the issues raised by Edith Durham's description of her subject. In so doing I want to raise questions as to how far the representation of another culture might confirm or subvert stereotypes.

While Rebecca West's style and approach to her subject in the late 1930s were literary in nature, Durham's primary interest in Albania and in southeastern Europe as a whole was ethnographic. Writing many years after the trip through the mountains of northern Albania that resulted in *High Albania*, she justified her mission in writing about 'the Balkans' in these terms:

> It occurred to me that the vexed question of Balkan politics might be solved by studying the manners and customs of each district, and so learning to whom each place should really belong. I cheerfully started on this vast programme.

> (Quoted in Hodgson, 2000b, p. xi)

Behind her ethnography in *High Albania* lay an attempt to advocate the position of the Albanians to a British audience that was paying increasing attention to great power conflict at a time of intense instability in the region. Durham sought to use ethnography to argue that the aspirations of peoples should take precedence over the cynical diplomacy of the great powers. At the end of the epilogue to *High Albania* she wrote:

> 'Why,' I was asked on all sides, 'do the English people, who have a hundred times declared the Turk unfit to rule, believe he has changed his whole nature in twenty-four hours? Why after holding out hopes to the Balkan peoples, do they now rejoice to nail us once more under the Turk? Why should we suffer because it suits British politics that the Turk should remain?'

> (Durham [1909] 2000, p. 348)

Yet the ethnographic study of the culture and the customs of a people is not the same as political advocacy. Durham was studying a culture and a world that were deeply alien to her middle-class British readership. When compared with the most advanced countries in western Europe, Albania was economically peripheral – little of the infrastructure of a modern territorial state of any kind existed there. To borrow the phrase of two historians of economic development and social change in southeastern Europe during the nineteenth and twentieth centuries, it bore many of the characteristics of 'the third world on the borders of the first world' (Daskalov and Sundhaussen, 1999, p. 106). The fourth reading is a long extract where Durham describes the institution of blood feud in the mountain regions of northern Albania during the first years of the twentieth century.

The *fis* was the term for a tribe in early twentieth-century Albania. The *mehala* was a sub-division of the *fis*, often consisting of a group of blood relatives.

The most important fact in North Albania is blood-vengeance, which is indeed the old, old idea of purification by blood. It is spread throughout the land. All else is subservient to it.

'What profit is life to a man if his honour be not clean?' To cleanse his honour no price is too great. And in the mountains the individual is submerged tribe. He is answerable, too, for the honour of his **mehala**, sometimes indeed of his whole *fis*.

Blood can be wiped out only with blood. A blow also demands blood, so do insulting words. One of the worst insults is the marrying of a girl betrothed to one man, to another. Nothing but blood can cleanse it.

Abduction of a girl demands blood, as does of course adultery. This does not appear to be common. It entails so much blood that 'the game is not worth the candle.' The blood taken need not be that of the actual offender. It must be male blood of his house or tribe. The usage differs in various districts, and will be noted in the accounts of them.

A man is answerable, too, for his guest, and must avenge a stranger that has passed but one night beneath his roof, if on his journey next day he be attacked. The sacredness of the guest is far-reaching. A man who brought me water from his house, that I might drink by the way, said that I now ranked as his guest, and that he should be bound by his honour to avenge me should anything happen to me before I had received hospitality from another.

Blood-vengeance, slaying a man according to the laws of honour, must not be confounded with murder. Murder starts a blood feud. In blood-vengeance the rules of the game are strictly observed. A man may not be shot for vengeance when he is with a woman nor with a child, nor when he is met in company, nor when *besa* (oath of peace) has been given. The two parties may swear such an oath for a few weeks if they choose, for business purposes. There are men who, on account of blood, have never been out alone for years.

When the avenger has slain his victim, he first reaches a place of safety, and then proclaims that he has done the deed. He wishes all to know his honour is clean. That he is now liable to be shot, and, if the blood be taken within the tribe, to heavy punishment also, is of minor moment to him.

In the Dukaghini tribes the council has power not merely to burn his house, but to destroy his crops, fell his trees, slaughter his beasts, and condemn him to leave his land unworked. An incredible amount of food-stuff is yearly wasted, and land made desolate.

The house is perhaps not merely the home of himself, his wife and children, but that of a whole family community, forty or fifty people. The law is carried out to the last letter. It crushes the innocent along with the guilty; it is remorseless, relentless. But 'it is the Canon and must be obeyed.'

A man can save his house only if he can return to it and defend it successfully for three days, so that no one can approach near enough to set fire to it. A 'very brave man' was pointed out to me in Berisha, who has three times been condemned to have his house burnt, and each time saved it thus. A man can also save his property by inviting to the house the head of another *mehala*, who must then declare himself house lord and take command. The house is then, for the time being, his; he summons his own men to defend it, a regular battle may take place, and the house be saved. But it is usual at once to call a council of Elders to stop the warfare. In such a case it is usual to burn only the house, and spare the crop and other property (Berisha).

The Canon of Lek has but two punishments, fine and burning of property. Neither death nor imprisonment can be inflicted. Prison there is none. Death would but start a new feud. And Lek's object appears to have been to check feud.

In the case of a man accused of murder, and arraigned before the Elders, should it occur that they cannot come to any agreement as to whether he be guilty or not, a new trial can be made. But the Lord of Blood [the member of the deceased's family who has the right to demand blood] rarely waits for this. He prefers to shoot

Figure 4.7 Mary Edith Durham, North Albanian tribesman outside Scutari cathedral, Albania 1910. Photo: Mary Edith Durham/Bankfield Museum, Halifax

Figure 4.8 Mary Edith Durham, North Albanian tribesman in Scutari bazar, Albania 1903. Photo: Mary Edith Durham/Bankfield Museum, Halifax

the man that he accuses, and by so doing renders himself liable to house-burning, and to being shot in his turn. Sometimes the Ghaksur (taker of blood) flies and shelters with another tribe, leaving his burnt-out family to shift for themselves. Or his relations take him in, help pay his fine – for the honour of them all is cleaned by the blood-taking – give him, one a sheep, another an ox, and he helps work their land till free to work his own again, and so he makes a fresh start. I have met men burnt clean out three times, but now in fairly flourishing condition.

Any house to which a Ghaksur flies for shelter is bound to give him food and protection; he is a guest, and as such sacred. The Law of Blood has thus had great influence in mixing the population of all the western side (at least) of the Balkan peninsula, Montenegrins have for centuries fled from 'blood' into Albania, and Albanians into Montenegro. A large proportion of the Serbophone Moslems of Podgoritza are said to derive from Montenegrins, who refuged there from blood in the days when it was Turkish territory. According to the Canon a man is absolute master in his own house, and, in the unmodified form of the law, has the right to kill his wife, and any of his children. My informants doubted whether the killing of the wife would be tolerated now. She would be avenged by her own family. A man may, however, kill his wife with the consent of her family. A case in point took place, I was told, recently. The wife of a mountain man left him and went down to Scutari, where she lived immorally with the soldiers, thereby blackening the honour of her husband, and of her own family.

Her husband appealed to her brother (head of the family), who gave him the cartridge with which he shot her and cleaned the honour of them all. Had she eloped with a man, he would have been held guilty and shot. She would not be punished, as the man would be held to have led her astray. But in the above case her guilt was undoubted. It is very rare that a woman is killed. To kill a married woman entails two bloods – blood with her husband's and with her own family.

A woman is never liable for blood-vengeance, except in the rare case of her taking it herself. But even then there seems to be a feeling that it would be very bad form to shoot her. I could not hear of a recent case. I roused the greatest horror by saying that a woman who commits a murder in England is by law liable to the same punishment as a man. Shala is a wild tribe; it shoots freely. But a Shala man said, 'It is impossible. Where could a man be found who would hang a woman? No mountain man would do it.

It is a bad law. You must be bad people.' He was as genuinely shocked as is a suburban mission meeting over the sacrifices of Dahomey. The tribe cannot punish bloodshed within the family group, *e.g.* if one cousin in a communal house kill another. The head of the house is arbiter. A man said naïvely on this subject, 'How can such a case be punished? A family cannot owe itself blood?' To him the 'family' was the entity; the individual had no separate existence.

(Durham [1909] (2002), pp. 31–5)

EXERCISE

When you have read the extract, ask yourself how Durham interprets the institution of blood feud and attempt to sketch what you think, from her account, its role was in Albanian society. It might also be worth considering how Durham's readership might have considered this practice, especially in the light of what their attitudes to 'the Balkans' would have been.

DISCUSSION

One might have expected Durham, as an Edwardian British woman from a well-to-do background, to have been both appalled and shocked by the institution of blood vengeance in the mountains of northern Albania. Instead she is neither. Her description is cold and dispassionate; she refuses to either condone or condemn. Rather, her words rely on both the popular attitudes held by the people who believed in the institution as well as on actual cases where it occurred.

Durham's is an interpretation of blood vengeance as a form of customary law that takes precedence over civil law. It was plainly intended to establish a code of behaviour that sanctioned retaliation when the honour of individuals and families had been breached. One might say that Durham almost comes close to arguing that blood vengeance provided something approaching a kind of social cement in the northern Albania of the early twentieth century.

Obviously any attempt to guess the reactions of all Durham's readers to her description of blood vengeance can at best be informed speculation. You might have noted, however, that given widespread perceptions of southeastern Europe as a backwater isolated from the tide of mainstream European development, many of Durham's readers might have regarded the existence of the practice of blood vengeance as a sign of northern Albania's inherent backwardness.

Not entirely surprisingly, Durham's attempts to describe blood vengeance as part of a value system were missed by many of her readers, who saw it as evidence of Albanian backwardness and 'savagery'. One reviewer of *High Albania* indeed accused Durham of been taken up with the 'savagery' of her subjects:

> It is perhaps not too much to say that she has even acquired some of the savagery which is to her the most attractive quality of the Albanians. The blood feud seems to make an especial appeal to her. The book literally reeks of blood.
>
> (Quoted in Hodgson, 2000b, p. xiii)

In this light one may indeed wonder whether Durham's intention of promoting greater understanding of the tangled web of southeastern European politics through 'studying the manners and customs of each district' was always doomed to fail, as her ethnographic description of people a world away from her British Edwardian readers reinforced and fed dominant views of southeastern Europe rather than challenging them.

Rebecca West and the 'true' Yugoslavia

When writing *Black Lamb and Grey Falcon* West sought in part to engage with common stereotypes of 'the Balkans' among her British readership and to move beyond them, producing a more nuanced explanation of interwar Yugoslavia. Her discussion of commonly held western European stereotypes is well worth quoting:

> Violence was, indeed, all I knew of the Balkans: all I knew of the South Slavs. I derived the knowledge from the memories of my earliest interest in Liberalism, of leaves fallen from this jungle of pamphlets, tied up with string in the dustiest corners of junk-shops, and later from the prejudices of the French, who use the word *Balkan* as a term of abuse, meaning a *rastaquouère* [pejorative term for a 'flashy foreigner'] type of barbarian.
>
> (West, 1993, p. 21)

West's book uses the insights derived from three different trips to Yugoslavia during the late 1930s. Its narrative structure, however, is determined by one journey. In the book West travels to Yugoslavia by train from Austria, arriving in Zagreb, before going on to Dalmatia and through Bosnia to Sarajevo and Belgrade. From Belgrade she journeys south to Macedonia, in the far south of what was Yugoslavia, and on to neighbouring Kosovo, which she terms 'old Serbia' in her account. She then travels north through Montenegro to Dubrovnik and from there to Zagreb, before leaving Yugoslavia for Hungary. Her book is not simply a description of a journey, for an argument about

Bosnischer Holzverkäufer.

Bosnian wood seller . Serajevo market .
Planks were often entirely axe hewn , thus
wasting much wood as only a few could be hewn from one
tree trunk .

Figure 4.9 Postcard showing a Bosnian woodseller in Sarajevo market. Durham's own photographs were not the only ones which showed both everyday life and rural traditions in south-eastern Europe during the early part of the period. A wide range of postcards were commercially available that depicted such scenes. Photo: Mary Edith Durham collection, Bankfield Museum, Halifax

the nature of Yugoslavia is advanced in its pages even though 'it is difficult to discover a distinct narrative line, so sprawling is West's style and so disparate her thoughts about subjects as various as history, folklore, myth, archaeology and of course politics' (Royle, 1993, p. xiii). The book was shaped by the context in which it was written and published. In 1941 Hitler invaded Yugoslavia and began his attempt to integrate its territories into a 'new' European order. The country was dismembered – Slovenia was partitioned between Germany and Italy while an independent Croatian state was created under the rule of the fascist *Ustaše*. Montenegro was occupied by Italy and Macedonia by Bulgaria, while Serbia came under direct German military occupation (Lampe, 1996, pp. 201–4). In this context West took sides: she regarded German influence in the region as profoundly negative. Her antipathy to German influence is clear throughout her book and is most clearly expressed in the way she writes about one of her travelling companions – Gerda, the wife of her Serbian guide. Similarly, the Catholic Croats come out badly in her account. Her book advances a position that is certainly pro-Serbian, regarding the Orthodox peasantries as the backbone of Yugoslavia. Indeed West has been accused by critics of romanticizing this element of the south Slav population (Royle, 1993; Rosslyn, 2000).

It is impossible to do justice to a book that runs to well over 1000 pages in the limited space that is available to me here. I do, however, want to quote a passage that I think raises questions about the extent to which West romanticizes the Orthodox peasantries of Yugoslavia. It is an account of attending an Orthodox mass at the town of Ochrid in Macedonia, midway through her journey.

But the most exciting aspect of Ochrid relates to its more recent past, to events divided from us by a mere eleven hundred years. As the Slav tribes fell under the influence of Byzantium a considerable number of them were baptized but they were first converted to Christianity in mass by the Greek brothers, Cyril and Methodius, who translated part of the gospels into Slavonic languages about the year 870; and their mission was carried to Ochrid by their followers, Clement and Gorazd and Naum. That is what it says in the books. But what does that mean? How did these events look and sound and smell? That can be learned on the top of the hill at Ochrid, in the Church of Sveti Kliment, and the other churches up there which were built in that age. According to Serbo-Byzantine fashion they crouch low in the earth, outbuildings for housing something that should not be where people live, something that needs to be kept in the dark. Doubtless in those early days there were converts who went into the blackness of these churches hoping to find new gods like those they had worshipped in their heathen days, but bloodier. Such worship is commemorated in certain Balkan churches, which to this day are ill to enter, being manifestly bad ju-ju. But shadow is also a sensible prescription for good magic, and Christianity as a religion of darkness has its advantages over our Western conception of Christianity as a religion of light.

I remembered as I stood in the Church of Sveti Kliment what a cloak-and-suit manufacturer once said to me when he was showing me his factory on Long Island: 'Yes, it's a beautiful factory, sure it's a beautiful factory, and I'm proud of it. But I wish I hadn't built it. When I get a rush order I can't make my girls work in these big airy rooms the way they did in the little dark place we had down town. They used to get in a fever down there, their fingers used to fly. Up here you can't get them excited.' Though the domes of Sveti Kliment are bubbles the porch is of extravagant clumsiness,

Figure 4.10 Postcard: *Env. de Monastir. – Famille macedonienne* (The region of Monastir – A Macedonian family). Photo: Mary Edith Durham collection, Bankfield Museum, Halifax

Figure 4.11 Postcard: *Danses macedonniennes, le Jour de Pâques, sortie de la Messe* (Macedonian dancing, Easter day after leaving Mass). Photo: Mary Edith Durham collection, Bankfield Museum, Halifax

approached by squat steps and pressed by a wide flat roof, which is utterly unecclesiastical and might be proper in a cow-byre, and is supported by thick and brutal columns. Within the porch is a wide ante-room which is used as a lumber-room, full of spare chairs, ornate candles for festival use, broken models of other churches. Almost every Orthodox church looks as if the removal men have been at work on it, and that they have been inefficient. Beyond is another darker antechamber, where those sat in the early days of the Church who were not yet baptized or who were penitents; and beyond, darkest of all, is the church, a black pit where men could stand close-pressed and chanting, falling into trance, rising into ecstasy, as they stared at the door in the iconostasis, which sometimes opened and showed them the priests in dazzling robes, handling the holy things by the blaze of candlelight that is to the darkness what the adorable nature of God is to humanity.

It is a valid religious process; and it is the one that these people to this day prefer. Further down the hill is the Church of Heavenly Wisdom, of Sveta Sophia, which was built, it is said, at the same time as the Hagia Sophia of Constantinople and was restored by the Nemanyas. It is a glorious building, the size, I should think, of Steeple Ashton parish church, a superb composition of humble, competent brickwork achieving majesty by its sound domes and arches. It is decorated with some magnificent frescoes of the Nemanya age, one showing an angry angel bending over earth in rage against the polluted substance of those who are not angels, and another showing the death of the Virgin, where sorrowing figures drip like rain down the wall behind the horizontal body of a woman who is giving herself without reserve but with astonishment to the experience of pain, knowing it to be necessary. That the building should be now Christian is a victory, since the Turks used it as a mosque for five hundred years. But the church is full of light. It is built according to the Byzantine and not according to the Serbo-Byzantine fashion, and has no iconostasis but only a low barrier to divide the congregation from the priest. A makeshift iconostasis of chintz and paper and laths has been run up, but it is of no avail. Light stands like a priest over all other priests under the vaults that were raised high to cast out shadow. And this church is unbeloved. A fierce old nun keeps it fanatically clean and would give her life to defend it. But it is not the object of any general devotion. All the other churches in Ochrid have their devotees who can worship happily nowhere else and who speak of them with a passion which has something animal in it, something that one can imagine a beast feeling for its accustomed lair. But though Sveta Sophia was originally the Cathedral, the honour has been taken from it and given to the small dark Sveti Kliment; and nobody gives money or labour to mend the roof which is a sieve.

We left this rejected loveliness, and walked on through the town by a track which followed the top of a cliff beside the lake and took us at last to a church standing on a promontory covered with pale-yellow flowers. This I remembered well, for it was the Church of Sveti Yovan, of St John, where I had learned for the first time the peculiar quality of Eastern Christianity, that is dark and not light, and unkempt as only the lost are in the West. When I had been here with Constantine the year before he had heard that this church was having its annual feast, and that Bishop Nikolai was holding the service. So we took a rowing-boat from the hotel and travelled over the milk-white water, while the morning sun discovered green terraces high on the black Albanian mountains and touched the snow peaks till they shone a glistening buff, and on the nearest coast picked out the painted houses of Ochrid till the town was bright as a posy of pale flowers. As we came nearer to the promontory we heard a sound of voices, not as if they were speaking anything, but just speaking, as bees hum; and I saw that all the ground about the church, and all the tracks that led to it, were covered with people. They were right out on the edge of the promontory, where the rock fell in a sharp overhang, and it seemed as if at any moment some of them must fall into the water. There were also many people in boats who were rowing round and round the promontory, never going very far from it, who were singing ecstatically.

Our boat drew ashore. We climbed a flight of steps that ran upward through the yellow flowers, under bending fig trees; and on the cliff I found myself in the midst of a Derby Day crowd. They were talking and laughing and quarrelling and feeding babies, and among them ran boys with trays of rolls and cakes and fritters, and men selling sweet drinks. They sat or stood or lay in the grass as they would, and they were all dressed in their best clothes, though not all of them were clean. Some were pressing into the church, struggling and jostling in the porch, and others were pushing and being pushed through animal reek in the cave of darkness maintained by the low walls and doors in spite of the sunlight outside. There swaying together, sweating together, with their elbows in each other's bellies and their breaths on each other's napes, were people who had been lifted into a special state by their adoration of the brightness which shone extravagantly behind the iconostasis. After I had overcome the first difficulty of adapting myself to a kind of behaviour to which I was not accustomed, I found I liked the spectacle extremely.

The congregation had realized what people in the West usually do not know: that the state of mind suitable for conducting the practical affairs of daily life is not suitable for discovering the ultimate meaning of life. They were allowing themselves to become drunken with exaltation in order that they should receive more knowledge than they could learn by reason; and the Church which was dispensing this supernatural knowledge was not falling into the damnable heresy of pretending that this knowledge is final, that all is now known. The service was clear of the superficial ethical prescription, inspired by a superstitious regard for prosperity, which makes Western religion so often a set of by-laws tinged emotionally with smugness. Had the Eastern Church in the Balkans wished to commit this error, it has been prevented by history. For centuries it would have found it difficult to find a body of the fortunate sufficiently large to say with authority, 'Be like us, be clean in person and abstinent from sin, for of such is the kingdom of Heaven.' There were too few fortunate Christians, save among the phanariots, who had sold at least the better part of their souls; and the unfortunate were too poor to be clean, and were chaste perforce, since their women had to be enclosed in patriarchal houses against the rape of enemies, and could not wholly abstain from murder, since only by blood could they defend themselves against the infidel. The Church had therefore to concentrate on the Mass, on reiterations of the first meaning of Christianity. It had to repeat over and over again that goodness is adorable and that there is an evil part in man which hates it, that there was once a poor man born of a poor woman who was perfectly good and was therefore murdered by evil men, and in his defeat was victorious, since it is far better to be crucified than to crucify, while his murderers were conquered beyond the imagination of conquerors; and that this did not happen once and far away, but is repeated every day in all hearts.

So the crowd in the church waited and rejoiced, while the deep voices of the singing priests and the candles behind the iconostasis evoked for them the goodness they had murdered, and comforted them by showing that it had not perished for ever. The superb performance of the Mass, a masterpiece which has been more thoroughly rehearsed than any other work of art, rose to its climax and ceased in its own efficacy. Goodness was so completely evoked that it could no longer be confined, and must break forth to pervade the universe; and with it there poured into the open the priests and the congregation. They blinked their eyes, having become accustomed to the shadows and the candlelight. The sunshine must have seemed to them an incendiarism of the air, committed by the radiance that had rushed out from the iconostasis. Bishop Nikolai, a huge man made more huge by his veiled mitre, stood blindly in the strong light, gripping his great pastoral staff as a warrior might grip a weapon when it was difficult for him to see. The people surged forward to kiss his ring, having forgotten in the intoxication of the darkness what they might have remembered if they had stayed sober in broad day, that he was clean and they were dirty, that he was lettered and they could not read. They cried aloud in their gratitude to this magician who had brewed the holy mystery for them behind the screen and had made the saving principle visible and real as brightness. The people rowing on the lake, hearing the cries of those on the cliff, leaned on their oars, and gave themselves up to their singing. The flat brilliant waters trembled, and the snow peaks glittered. It was as if joy had permeated the whole earth.

(West [1941] (1993), pp. 710–14)

EXERCISE

I should like you to comment on this reading in the light of how I have described West's work. What do you think West is saying about the ceremony she witnesses? What do you think this says about her attitudes to what she witnesses? Do you think she romanticizes what she is seeing and, lastly, do you think this extract feeds or counteracts stereotypes of the Balkans?

DISCUSSION

I don't know how you chose to respond to this reading. Even if what Maria Todorova calls 'Balkanist discourse' is not explicitly contained in this extract, I think there is much here that might feed it. West's description of the religious ritual advances an argument about the difference between 'east' and 'west', defined according to the split between the western and eastern churches. For West the ceremony evokes a sense of spiritual purity and oneness with nature that she sees as absent in the western half of the continent. I think that she is certainly romanticizing both Orthodoxy and the Orthodox citizens of Ochrid participating in the ceremony.

This extract certainly doesn't contribute to notions that 'the Balkans' are violent but I think it contributes to another dimension of discourse: 'the Balkans' as a kind of exotic and romantic space set apart from western Europe. There may be closer parallels with the 'orientalism' identified by Edward Said, and discussed in Chapter 1, than with the kind of discourse that is described by Maria Todorova in this chapter. Nevertheless I would argue that this kind of description does contribute to a notion that sees 'the Balkans' as both 'geographically inextricable from Europe, yet culturally constructed as "the other" within' (Todorova, 1997, p. 188).

Conclusion

How far can 'the Balkans' be described impartially by western Europeans? Are 'the Balkans' nothing more than a construction of the western European mind? While I would argue that the societies and cultures of southeastern Europe can be described accurately from the outside, 'the Balkans' is so loaded a term, and so saturated with western stereotypes, as to hinder any serious study of the cultures of southeastern Europe. In this chapter I first introduced you to the fiery polemic of Bulgarian-born historian Maria Todorova, which should have alerted you to the fact that such processes of definition are important – they play a central role in how 'we' see other regions, and can be significant in decisions that are made about those regions. After using that reading to highlight the contemporary relevance of the topic under discussion I then narrowed my focus to examine how two British writers sought to argue for the relevance of their accounts of southeastern Europe to their audience. In doing so I suggested that powerful negative stereotypes of 'the Balkans' existed during the first half of the twentieth century within British intellectual culture – stereotypes that have been shaped by Britain's interaction with the region, first as part of the struggles in the last decades of the Ottoman empire and then, after 1914, as the region whose conflicts sparked a world war.

It has been often argued, and it is suggested by Maria Todorova, that negative stereotypes coalesce to form a 'discourse' about a region that prevents and distorts any impartial study of its culture and identity. The texts about that region simply reproduce the discourse in which people belonging to one culture construct those who belong to another as their 'other'. I have sought to suggest (and my conclusions in this regard are far from definitive) that this view of the text is too simplistic. I have certainly argued in this chapter for the existence of a western European or, more specifically, a British discourse of 'the Balkans' that constructs it as Europe's 'other'. The operation of that discourse and the way that it reproduces itself are quite complex. I have sought to suggest that a text written by one person about people living in another society or culture must be seen as a kind of conversation. The first partner in the conversation is the readership for which the text is intended; the second is the author; the third the society that is being studied, represented or described. Where a discourse operates these three are not equal partners in the conversation; the society that is being studied enters the conversation as a result of being represented by the author and that representation being understood by the readership. In the case of Durham's *High Albania*, the book may have had the effect of confirming negative stereotypes of southeastern European societies. This was, however, because of the prejudices of the audience of the book that existed prior to the text, not because of the text itself and still less because of the intentions of its author who believed that through representing reality she could promote greater understanding of the peoples of southeastern Europe. In the case of Rebecca West's *Black Lamb and Grey Falcon* the author sought to counteract stereotypes, but replaced them with a different set which defined 'the Balkans' almost as part of an exotic east. No one could therefore deny that 'the Balkans', as a result of the circumstances of history, has a central role in the mental geographies of western Europeans, or that notions of 'the Balkans' have, at best, only an imperfect relationship to the realities of southeast European societies.

References

Allcock, J. B. (2000) 'Constructing the "Balkans"', in J. B. Allcock and A. Young, (eds), *Black Lambs and Grey Falcons: Women Travellers in the Balkans*, New York/Oxford, Berghahn.

Allcock, J. and Young, A. (2000) 'Black lambs and grey falcons: outward and inward frontiers', in J. B. Allcock and A. Young (eds), *Black Lambs and Grey Falcons: Women Travellers in the Balkans*, New York/Oxford, Berghahn.

Banac, I. (1988) *The National Question in Yugoslavia: Origins, History, Politics*, Ithaca, NY/London, Cornell University Press.

Daskalov, R. and Sundhaussen, H. (1999) 'Modernisierungsansätze', in M. Hatschikjan and S. Troebst (eds), *Südosteuropa: Gesellschaft, Politik, Wirtschaft, Kultur: ein Handbuch*, Munich, C. H. Beck.

Durham, E. [1909] (2000) *High Albania: a Victorian Traveller's Balkan Odyssey*, London, Phoenix.

Glenny, M. (1999) *The Balkans 1804–1999: Nationalism, War and the Great Powers*, London, Granta.

Hatschikjan, M. (1999) 'Was macht Südosteuropa aus?', in M. Hatschikjan and S. Troebst (eds), *Südosteuropa: Gesellschaft, Politik, Wirtschaft, Kultur: ein Handbuch*, Munich, C. H. Beck.

Herzfeld, M. (1997) 'Theorizing Europe: persuasive paradoxes', *American Anthropologist*, vol. 99, no. 4, pp. 713–15.

Hodgson, J. (2000a) 'Edith Durham: traveller and publicist', in J. B. Allcock and A. Young, (eds), *Black Lambs and Grey Falcons: Women Travellers in the Balkans*, New York/Oxford, Berghahn.

Hodgson, J. (2000b) 'Introduction', in E. Durham, *High Albania: a Victorian Traveller's Balkan Odyssey*, London, Phoenix.

Kaiser, T. (2000) 'The evil empire? The debate on Turkish despotism in eighteenth century French political culture', *Journal of Modern History*, vol. 72, pp. 6–34.

Kaser, K. (1999) 'Raum und Besiedlung', in M. Hatschikjan and S. Troebst (eds), *Südosteuropa: Gesellschaft, Politik, Wirtschaft, Kultur: ein Handbuch*, Munich, C. H. Beck.

Lampe, J. (1996) *Yugoslavia as History: Twice There was a Country*, Cambridge/New York, Cambridge University Press.

Magaš, B. (1993) *The Destruction of Yugoslavia: Tracking the Break-up 1980–1992*, London/New York, Verso.

Malcom, N. (1998) *Kosovo: a Short History*, London/Basingstoke, Papermac.

Mazower, M. (2000) *The Balkans*, London, Weidenfeld & Nicolson.

Quataert, D. (2000) *The Ottoman Empire, 1700–1922*, Cambridge/New York, Cambridge University Press.

Rosslyn, F. (2000) 'Rebecca West, Gerda and the sense of process', in J. B. Allcock and A. Young (eds), *Black Lambs and Grey Falcons: Women Travelling in the Balkans*, New York/Oxford, Berghahn.

Royle, T. (1993) 'Introduction', in R. West, *Black Lamb and Grey Falcon: A Journey through Yugoslavia*, Edinburgh, Canongate.

Stavrianos, L. S. (2000) *The Balkans since 1453*, New York, New York University Press.

Todorova, M. (1997) *Imagining the Balkans*, New York/Oxford, Oxford University Press.

Vickers, M. (1999) *The Albanians: a Modern History*, London, I. B. Tauris.

West, R. [1941] (1993) *Black Lamb and Grey Falcon: a Journey through Yugoslavia*, Edinburgh, Canongate.

5

Alexander Herzen's Russia:

between Asia and Europe

COLIN CHANT

Introduction: Russia and Europe

Does Russia belong to Europe? The main question of this chapter is addressed in two ways: first, through a broad introductory survey of the geographical and historical contexts of Russia's ambivalent national identity; and second, through an extended case study of Alexander Herzen, a political writer who became the main focus of opposition to the Tsarist autocracy in the middle years of the nineteenth century. You will consider how his views on Russia's identity and its relationship with Europe were shaped initially by his experience as a dissident in Russia, looking to the west for inspiration and salvation; and then by his experience of Europe as a revolutionary *émigré*, looking back to his homeland to restore his shattered political hopes.

Russia's geography

This ambivalence is shared with the nations of the British Isles, which have often seen themselves as outside 'Europe', and with Turkey, a nation that extended its Asiatic dominion across southeastern Europe for nearly half a millennium. Some of Turkey's uncertainty extends to Cyprus, that historically mineral-rich Mediterranean island situated close to the Asiatic shores of Turkey and Syria, and long contested among European and Asian powers. Indeed, since the occupation of the northern part by Turkey in 1974, and the declaration of independence nine years later by the Turkish Republic of Northern Cyprus, the island is now divided into two parts, the south governed by its Greek Orthodox and the north by its Turkish Muslim inhabitants.

Russia's **ambivalence** about its relations with (the rest of) Europe resonates throughout its history and culture. A necessary, though not sufficient condition for this cultural-historical ambivalence is Russian geography. Russia, like Turkey, has territory that straddles the continents of Europe and Asia, though in Turkey's case the watery stretch of the Dardanelles, the Sea of Marmara and the Bosporus makes the distinction between its European and Asian territory unambiguous. In Russia, however, the European–Asian border is (ironically) more fluid, and perceptions of it have shifted over time. The view of the ancient Greek geographer Ptolemy (fl. 127–45 CE) that the river Don divided the continents was dominant in the early modern period (Neumann, 1999, p. 78). Today, the usually accepted north-to-south boundary between the continents is for most of its length a less sharply defined physical phenomenon: the Ural mountains, a chain of great length but relatively modest height. The boundary's southern extension is more distinct: the western bank of the Ural river, from its source in the Urals to its outlet into the

Caspian Sea. Or at least it was until the break-up of the Soviet Union in 1991: according to some recent atlases, the border of newly independent Kazakhstan to the west of the Ural river should continue the Urals divide.

Note in this respect the distinction between 'philosophic geography' and scientific cartography discussed by Larry Woolf in the final reading in Chapter 1.

In 2000 the press hailed the Indian chess grandmaster Viswanathan Anand as the first Asian male world champion (FIDE version), even though a recent predecessor, Garry Kasparov, was born south of the Caucasus mountains in Baku, the capital of Azerbaijan. Moreover, Anatoly Karpov, Kasparov's predecessor as champion, originates from Zlatoust, an industrial town on the eastern flank of the Urals, just inside Asiatic Russia. Israel is another case in point: clearly situated in the continent of Asia, but culturally and politically orientated to Europe and the wider 'west', it participates in football's European Nations Cup. It is also, using the term 'cultural' in its widest sense, a regular entrant in the Eurovision Song Contest, and in the case of its 1998 winner, Dana International, sexual rather than continental identities were the main talking point.

The problem of geographical definition resurfaces in the Caucasus, a term denoting both the great mountain range that runs east–west between the Caspian and the Black Sea, and also the much-contested territory to the north and south of this range. The Caucasus mountains conventionally marked the southernmost land boundary between European and Asiatic Russia, but again, following the break-up of the Soviet Union, the division between Europe and southwest Asia is even less clear. On the southern flank of the mountain range Orthodox Georgia, Christian (Gregorian) Armenia and Muslim Azerbaijan, former provinces of the tsarist Transcaucasian region and later constituent republics of the Soviet Union, all declared their independence in 1991. It is a moot point whether they are now to be regarded as Asian nations; here cultural orientation challenges the geographer's attempts at cartographic clarity. These new nations have recently been admitted to the Council of Europe; and football fans will be aware that, as members of UEFA (Union of European Football Associations), they take part in European national and club competitions.

The acquisition of a European identity by some of Russia's remoter erstwhile provinces is evidently a matter of some consequence for them. But quite where Europe ends and Asia begins in the vast Russian land mass is a mere debating point. Even if individual opponents of Russia's entry to the European Union have voiced doubts about the country's European pedigree, the member states would scarcely exclude their eastern neighbour on the grounds that most of its territory lies in Asia. The question of Russia's European identity is much deeper than the problematic geographical definition of its European territory: it goes to the heart of the Russian historical predicament, which has involved a very particular struggle with a unique environment and its other inhabitants, both European and Asian.

Russia's history: from Slavic thraldom to Soviet dominion

How 'European' was Russia's past? Ethnographers count Russians among the Slavs, one of the main Indo-European linguistic families, who become recognizable as such from the sixth century CE as agriculturalists settling the broad swath of the European plain above the Carpathian mountains, stretching from modern Poland down to Ukraine. The eastern Slavs first organized themselves into territorial states with fortified centres during the ninth century, and straight away there emerged what was to be a recurrent theme: the construction of Slavic identities in relation to other European identities, a process that complemented the forging of European identities in relation to marginal 'constitutive others', notably Russia and Turkey (Neumann, 1999). According to a hotly debated version of the origins of Russian statehood given in some of the chronicles (the earliest documents of Russian history), in 862 the eastern Slavic farmers invited Nordic Varangian warriors to become their rulers. These warriors policed an important trading route from the Baltic to Byzantium, by way of the river Dnepr and the Black Sea. At the end of the following century the eastern Slavs adopted Christianity from the Greek-speaking Byzantine relic of the Roman empire, along with the distinctive Cyrillic script, an adaptation of the Greek alphabet – further markers of emerging statehood and of a developing dialogue with older European civilizations.

The biggest emergent principality centred on Kiev in Ukraine, on the fertile 'black earth' region of the Russian steppes. By the eleventh century Kievan Russia was one of the largest states in Christendom, with around 100 towns. But again the vulnerability of states on the Eurasian plain was demonstrated, as it was exposed to equestrian nomadic incursions from the east across the treeless expanse of the steppes. By 1240 the Mongol successors of Genghis Khan (c.1165–1227) had absorbed most of the Russian principalities into their vast Asian empire, and though the power of the 'Mongol yoke' slowly waned after the first century of suzerainty, the princes continued to pay tribute until Ivan the Great (1462–1505) called a halt in 1480. Ivan, who was the first Russian ruler to use the title caesar, or 'tsar', had begun his reign as grand prince of the landlocked principality of Muscovy to the north of Kiev; its main centre, Moscow, was strategically situated between the fertile black earth region and the forest and woodland to its north: an agriculturally unyielding terrain, but compensatingly rich in exportable raw materials.

Muscovy spearheaded the liberation of Russian territory from the Mongols, and set Russia on a rebound course of conquest over the next half millennium. To the north, east and south the tsars met relatively little resistance in their push across the forests, steppes, marshes and tundra up to the farthest shore lines, the most inhospitable deserts and highest mountain ranges. But they also looked to the more challenging west for renewed access to prized European trading routes, and during the eighteenth century established footholds on the Baltic and Black Sea coasts, as well as absorbing much of dismembered Poland. From then on Russia asserted itself as a military power on the European stage, though there were periodic traumatic reminders of its vulnerability, as

Napoleon's armies entered Moscow in 1812 and Hitler's Wehrmacht laid devastating siege to Soviet cities during the Second World War. At the conclusion of that war, as its fullest insurance against the perceived dangers of 'encirclement' by hostile powers, the Soviet Union under Joseph Stalin (1879–53) effectively extended its dominion throughout eastern Europe. This point marked the apogee of Russian influence in Europe, but the strain of military competition with the west fully exposed the internal weaknesses of its command economy and precipitated a remarkably sudden collapse of the Soviet Eurasian empire.

Since the fall of the Soviet Union in 1991 Russia and its former dependent states have embraced western culture, in its contemporary commercial and popular forms, to a degree only paralleled during the reign of Peter the Great (1682–1725). Except for these periods, the attitude of Russian rulers and cultural leaders to the west was decidedly equivocal, an attitude fully reciprocated by other European states. The roots of Russia's ambivalence go back to the time of Asian (Mongol) domination, the main effect of which, underpinned by changes in European trade routes associated with the crusades, was to divert Russia from the cultural mainstream of Europe. This isolation was reinforced by the eleventh-century schism between the Roman Catholic and eastern Orthodox wings of the Christian church. This schism crystallized as dogma when, following the fall of Constantinople to the Ottoman Turks in 1453, the Russian Orthodox church designated Moscow the 'third Rome' and the tsar the true defender of the Christian Orthodox faith against western heresies, as well as Islam.

But the preservation of ideological purity in the face of heretical western ideas ran up against the pragmatic needs of the tsars to equip their expansionist drive through dealings with western traders and technicians. For a long time, however, those admitted to Moscow were quarantined in the city's 'German quarter'. For the remainder of the tsarist period the ruling elite oscillated between xenophobia and enthusiasm for the west. Though not the first tsar to be fascinated by western innovations, Peter the Great was the first to aspire to remake Russia as a European power. He trained himself in the dockyards of England and the Netherlands; introduced western-style scientific and educational institutions; built St Petersburg, a new capital on the Baltic designed by western architects; subordinated the xenophobic Russian Orthodox church to the state; and forced his nobility to don west European dress and shave off their beards. The process of Europeanization was taken further by the German-born Catherine the Great (1762–96). A fan of Enlightenment stars such as Voltaire (1694–1778) and Denis Diderot (1713–84), she flirted with the reform of Russia's illiberal institutions of serfdom and censorship and

Figure 5.1 Eighteenth-century engraving of a barber cutting off a beard on the orders of Peter the Great.
Photo: Novosti Photo Library

encouraged the adoption of western manners by an increasingly francophone nobility, only to recoil in horror at the excesses of the French Revolution. This pattern was repeated during the reigns of Alexander I (1801–25), whose liberal measures of educational and social reform turned to reaction and mysticism in the aftermath of the Napoleonic invasion; Alexander II (1855–81), the 'tsar-liberator' who emancipated the serfs in 1861 and relaxed censorship, only to crack down on further radical demands at home and preside over the ruthless suppression of the Polish revolt of 1863; and Nicholas II (1892–1917), under whom west European finance and technology were unleashed in a forced industrialization drive, but who fought against the concomitant demands of the rising professional and commercial classes for the curbing of the tsar's autocratic powers and for more representative political institutions. Although the implosion of the tsarist regime in 1917 was precipitated by the massive impact of the First World War upon its subjects, it can at a deeper level be seen as the price of its Faustian compact with western finance and technology, and the rending of the social and economic fabric that ensued.

Pre-Petrine Russia, then, had been isolated from the great sea changes in early modern European culture: the Renaissance, the Reformation, the rise of capitalism and the scientific revolution. Despite the generally westernizing and modernizing policies of the tsars during the eighteenth century, reaction set in after the French Revolution and the Napoleonic invasion; as a result, Russia's rulers responded to the innovations of the industrial revolution by erecting trade barriers. Only after the humiliation of its forces during the Crimean war (1853–6) did the Russian elite recognize the need to match the technological prowess of the west European powers. As Alexander Herzen, the main subject of this chapter, put it in 1857, 'The oil with which the engines of the new railways will be greased will anoint the Tsars more durably than the holy unguents of the Uspensky Cathedral' (Herzen, 1968, vol. 4, p. 1592).

Inevitably, the Russian autocrats attempted to have their western technological cake and eat it. But fears about the liberal institutions that underlay western innovations remained; the example of the west could threaten the Russian autocracy as well as strengthen it, as Herzen's career was to testify.

Alexander Herzen: Russian *intelligent* and *émigré*

This short chapter can hardly cover the development of Russia's ambivalent European identity over a millennium and more. Instead I have chosen one individual, albeit one of the most gifted and perceptive of Russian minds, to give a focus to the issues encapsulated in the introduction. Alexander Herzen (1812–70) has been lionized by the philosopher and historian Isaiah Berlin (1909–97) as the 'most arresting Russian political writer in the nineteenth century', and 'perhaps the greatest of European publicists of his day'; he considered Herzen's multi-volume autobiography *My Past and Thoughts*, originally published in instalments between 1852 and 1868, as 'a literary and political masterpiece, worthy to stand beside the great Russian novels of the nineteenth century' (Berlin, 1979a, pp. 186, 189; 1979b, p. xiii). Of particular relevance to the central concerns of this book is Herzen's re-evaluation of the issue of Russia's relationship to the rest of Europe, an issue that engaged him throughout his life, whether as distant youthful admirer of western politics and culture, or as first-hand critical interpreter on behalf of his compatriots.

Figure 5.2 Alexander Herzen. Photo: AKG London

Herzen was undeniably one of the most influential of the *intelligenty*, or members of the nineteenth-century Russian revolutionary intelligentsia. The 'intelligentsia' (a Russian neologism) was a tiny, socially heterogeneous group that self-consciously carried the torch of political opposition throughout the later imperial period. Its members struggled against the fate of so many gifted and independent-minded Russians under the repressive regime of Nicholas I (1825–55): the cynical existence of 'superfluous men' (*lishniye cheloveki*), in the phrase of the novelist Ivan Turgenev (1818–83). Herzen himself created a character of this type in his own novel of the 1840s, *Who is to Blame?* (a novel that also prefigured the love triangle that threatened his own marriage). The intelligentsia's existence was precarious; as Herzen put it, 'they were so insignificant and unnoticed that there was room for them between the soles of the great boots of autocracy and the ground' (Herzen, 1968, vol. 2, p. 415). Their ideas and actions, usually adaptations of west European exemplars, helped pave the way for the early twentieth-century revolutions that first weakened and then toppled the autocratic regime of the tsars, and finally set in train the radical assault upon the Russian political, economic and social structure conducted by the Bolsheviks, the intelligentsia's direct heirs. A range of interlocking identities – national, class-based, gender-based, cultural, ethnic, occupational, rural, urban and so on – was thereby challenged, overturned and recast. Many of these issues of identity are prefigured in the ideas and activities of Herzen and his contemporaries as they developed from the 1830s to the 1860s.

Herzen was born in Moscow in the momentous year of 1812. His encounter with western Europe was almost immediate, and highly dangerous: his autobiography *My Past and Thoughts* opens with his nurse's tale of the family's survival, including that of the six-month-old Herzen, during Napoleon's occupation of Moscow and the fires set by the city's authorities in response. The wider circumstances of Herzen's birth raised issues of personal as well as national identity. The Russian version of his name, transliterated from the Cyrillic script, is Alexandr Ivanovich Gertsen, but scholars outside Russia follow Alexander's own lead in using 'Herzen', as it was a surname deliberately manufactured from the German (implying 'of the heart') to convey the child's illegitimacy. He was the son of Ivan Alekseyevich Yakovlev, a Russian aristocrat, and Luisa Haag, the daughter of a minor German official, whom Yakovlev had met during a grand tour of western Europe. They were not married in the Russian Orthodox church and hence Herzen was not entitled to his father's noble surname. Was Herzen therefore a social outsider in a nation of European outsiders, whose subsequent career as a radical publicist can be rooted in bitterness about the circumstances of his birth? Although some scholars have attached some causal weight to his illegitimacy (Lampert, 1957, p. 172; Acton, 1979, p. 6; Berlin, 1979a, p. 187), this is open to question. Herzen does allude briefly to his 'false position' in his autobiography (Herzen, 1968, vol. 1, p. 23), but it was not unusual for aristocratic Russians such as Herzen's father to order their personal affairs in this casual way. Indeed Herzen's cousin and eventual wife Natalie was in a similar position, as the product of a union between one of Yakovlev's brothers and a household servant. There is no evidence that Herzen suffered socially through his illegitimacy – nor, as it turned out, financially. Though not his father's legal heir, he inherited a substantial share of his great wealth in 1846, a legacy that considerably eased his passage to the west the following year and his subsequent *émigré* life.

Yakovlev retired prematurely from his career of state service (on which Peter the Great had made noble status depend) and seems, from the amusing, affectionate and ironic portrait in Herzen's memoirs, to have spent the rest of his privileged life perfecting the role of a sarcastic and curmudgeonly hypochondriac. Herzen's father represented a type of westernized nobleman that became common from the reign of Catherine the Great onwards. He had a French tutor and a library of western works, and 'to the end of his days he wrote more fluently and correctly in French than in Russian' (Herzen, 1968, vol. 1, p. 76). Herzen records that after his prolonged grand tour of western Europe with an elder brother, 'they tried to arrange their life in the foreign style' (ibid. pp. 11–12), though he reckoned that the nature of the Russian landowner was stronger in them than their foreign habits. Herzen's aunt, Princess Mariya Alekseyevna Khovanskaya, however, decried 'the Western contagion that had infected her brothers and thrown them somewhat out of their native rut', as her nephew put it (ibid., pp. 297–8).

Herzen's own radical political views might well have been regarded by the authorities as foreign infection, but intellectual influences can never fully explain a given individual's philosophical outlook: there has to be some other explanation for that individual's receptivity to certain ideas. As a child Herzen was in daily contact with many west Europeans. Apart from his German mother, these included a German nurse and valet and various German and French tutors, one of whom Herzen portrayed as a supporter of the Jacobins, the most radical political faction of the French Revolution. But Herzen attributed his own radical sympathies more to his father's library, to sympathy with his father's house-serfs and to the aftermath of the 'Decembrist' rebellion. The Decembrists were young army officers who, languishing in the anti-climactic and reactionary wake of the Napoleonic wars, had formed secret societies dedicated to making Russia either a constitutional monarchy or a republic. On the death of Tsar Alexander I in 1825 they staged a revolt in St Petersburg; Alexander's brother Nicholas I, having survived the rebellion, ordered the five main conspirators to be hanged and sentenced hundreds of others implicated to penal servitude and exile in Siberia. Herzen and his lifelong friend the poet Nikolay Ogaryov (1813–77) took an adolescent oath on the Sparrow hills overlooking Moscow to sacrifice their lives to the struggle begun by the Decembrist martyrs (Herzen, 1968, vol. 1, pp. 52–3, 69–70).

The friends' initially liberal outlook took a more radical turn when, as students at Moscow University, they founded a student circle 'in the image and semblance of the Decembrists'. The circle studied French political writers, in particular the followers of the Comte de Saint Simon (1760–1825), precursors of socialism who preached 'the emancipation of women' and the 'rehabilitation of the flesh': 'Saint-Simonianism lay at the foundation of our convictions and remained so in its essentials unalterably'. Nicholas I and his advisers in St Petersburg regarded Moscow University with great suspicion, and

Figure 5.3 Nikolay Ogaryov and Alexander Herzen. Photo: Novosti Photo Library

although Herzen completed his studies in 1834 he was soon in trouble with the authorities because of the mildly subversive activities of his circle (which in the over-zealous and ill-educated eyes of the police included Ogaryov's possession of Georges Cuvier's treatise *Discours sur les révolutions des globes terrestres*, which was actually about geological not political revolutions). Herzen was arrested and spent the next five years in internal exile as a provincial official, first in Vyatka at the extremity of European Russia, and then rather nearer Moscow in the town of Vladimir, where he eloped with his cousin Natalie. His return to Moscow in 1839 was short-lived. First he was transferred in service to the 'unfriendly town' of St Petersburg, and then exiled again for no more than an indiscreet remark in a private letter to his father intercepted by the Tsar's secret police. This time he served as a councillor in Novgorod, 'the wretched little town with the great historical name' (it was indeed one of the main centres of Kievan Russia). His return to Moscow in 1842 was more secure. He established himself as leader of his friend Ogaryov's circle of 'westernizers' or 'westerners' (*zapadniki*) and made his name as an essayist, novelist and interpreter of west European thought (Herzen, 1968, vol. 1, pp. 149–50, 195; vol. 2, pp. 430, 468, 953).

During the mid 1840s rifts began to appear among the westernizers, some of whom found Herzen's increasingly withering critique of the west European bourgeoisie difficult to swallow. Herzen himself dated the end of the circle to an argument with Timofey Granovsky (1813–55), a liberal professor of history at Moscow University, when Herzen rejected the Christian belief in the immortality of the soul (Herzen, 1968, vol. 2, pp. 585–7; Roosevelt, 1986). In any case Herzen was a challenging friend; one of his circle spoke of 'the prodigal opulence of his intellect which astonished his audience' and his 'natural gift for criticism', qualities that inspired 'the most blind and passionate adoration' in some, but made his presence unbearable to others (Pavel Annenkov, quoted in Berlin, 1979a, pp. 189–90). Many of his acquaintances had lived abroad and Herzen, despite the range of his Russian experiences, was conscious of the bookishness on which so many of his ideas and attitudes were based, and was in any case tiring of the attentions of Nicholas I's police department. In addition his wife was ill and his young son Kolya suffered from deafness; it was to enable him to seek medical and educational help for the boy that Herzen was finally granted permission to travel abroad. As it turned out, in 1847 he left his homeland for good (he was granted Swiss citizenship by the canton of Fribourg in 1851).

Herzen's timing was impeccable. He arrived in France, and moved on to Italy, on the eve of the unprecedented spate of revolutions and uprisings against conservative monarchical rule that took place in Paris, Venice, Milan, Naples and Rome, as well as Vienna, Berlin, Dresden, Warsaw, Kraków, Prague and elsewhere in western and central Europe during 1848–9. Travelling between the two countries he was able to observe many of the leaders and key events at first hand. He even to some extent took part in these events: he was arrested in Paris during the 'June Days' of the 1848 Revolution in France, during which the new republican government that took over from King Louis-Philippe (1830–48) bloodily suppressed a left-wing revolt. Herzen left influential accounts of these events in his autobiography and in separate pieces later collected as *Letters from France and Italy* (Herzen, 1995) and *From the Other Shore* (Herzen, 1979). These have been described as 'the best personal documents about these events that we possess' (Berlin, 1979a, p. 186). He was disgusted and disillusioned by the failure of the revolutions, and by his own account his political outlook was profoundly affected. He remained a socialist, willing the destruction of the old political order that had once again survived; but it was socialism of a distinctly libertarian, indeterminist stamp. In *From the Other Shore* Herzen insisted that 'the liberty of the individual is the greatest thing of all', that individuals are ends in themselves and should not be sacrificed to the realization of some theoretical abstraction or distant historical end, that 'there is no eternal, immutable morality', that 'in history, all is improvisation, all is will, all is *ex tempore*' (Herzen, 1979, pp. 12, 39, 141).

His sense of political disillusionment developed and his faith in the wider European revolutionary movement diminished during a subsequent stay in Geneva among French, Italian, German, Hungarian, Bohemian and Polish exiles. It was compounded by the discovery of his wife's infidelity with his friend the radical German poet Georg Herwegh (1817–75), and converted to despair by successive personal tragedies. In November 1851 his deaf son and mother were drowned in a storm off Genoa when their steamer collided with another vessel, and in the following May his grieving wife died from pneumonia. Even so he refused, in characteristically tough-minded vein, to comfort himself over his wife's death with 'the stultifying thought of a meeting beyond the grave' (Herzen, 1968, vol. 2, p. 748). These extraordinary first years of Herzen's expatriate life have inspired two book-length studies by western historians (Carr, 1968; Zimmerman, 1989).

Herzen's life has also inspired *The Coast of Utopia*, a trilogy by the playwright Tom Stoppard, first performed at the National Theatre, London, in August 2002.

Many of Herzen's remaining years were spent in England, rather uneasily as he never warmed to his hosts nor to the 'thick, opaline fog' of London, 'the home of sore throats, bronchitis, asthma and speaking through the teeth' (Herzen, 1968, vol. 3, p. 1026; vol. 4, p. 1684). He lived until the mid 1860s in a succession of houses in and around the capital, where, anticipating the *samizdat* publications of the Soviet era, he used his considerable fortune to establish his Free Russian Press. He published two radical journals, the *Polar Star* from 1855) and *Kolokol* (the Bell) from 1857, which gave him a platform from which to hold forth like 'a Russian Voltaire of the mid-nineteenth century' (Berlin, 1979a, p. 189). Though banned in Russia, copies of these journals were smuggled in and devoured by friend and foe alike, as Herzen challenged the new administration of Tsar Alexander II to abolish serfdom and enact other liberal reforms. At this time Herzen was a prime focus of opposition to the Russian government, and Russian exiles and travellers beat paths to his various doors: '*we were the fashion*, and in a tourist's guide book, I was mentioned as one of the curiosities of Putney' (Herzen, 1968, vol. 3, p. 1295). But after he openly supported the Poles during the Russian

Казнены чрезъ повѣшеніе 13 іюля 1826 г. на валу Кронверкской куртины Петропавловской крѣпости въ Петербургѣ.

Figure 5.4 Title page of Herzen's journal the *Polar Star*, portraying the five Decembrist leaders (Pestel, Ryleyev, Bestuzhev, Murav'yov and Kakhovsky) who were hanged in 1826. Photo: Novosti Photo Library

Nihilism (from the Latin *nihil* meaning 'nothing') was originally a pejorative term applied to the young generation of radical *raznochintsy* (people of various ranks) that came to prominence during the liberal beginning of the reign of Alexander II (1855–81). Led by Nikolay Chernyshevesky (1828–89) and Nikolay Dobrolyubov (1836–61), they rejected out of hand the philosophical discourse and cultural values of Herzen's more aristocratic generation, substituting hard-nosed materialism and utilitarianism in philosophy, and an uncompromising social realist evaluation of art and literature.

suppression of their rebellion in 1863, the circulation of *Kolokol* plummeted and his influence rapidly waned. Attacks upon him by a more plebeian younger generation of '**Nihilists**' were part of a broader conflict of ideas and personalities that Turgenev immortalized in his novel of 1862, *Fathers and Sons*. Herzen resumed his travels on the west European mainland until his death in Paris in 1870; he was buried in Nice among some of his favourite European countryside.

'Nos amis les ennemis': westernizers *versus* Slavophiles

The great issue that divided the Moscow intelligentsia during the 1830s and 1840s was Russia's relationship with the rest of Europe. Herzen's westernizers were an alliance of radicals and liberals who saw it as a necessary step towards the attainment of nationhood

Note that the westernizers favoured a word of Latin derivation (from 'natio', or nation), and the Slavophiles a Slavonic word (Russian 'narod', or people).

(***natsial'nost'***) that the entire people should follow in the political, social, economic and technological footsteps of west Europe – a trail blazed by their hero Peter the Great, but now blocked by Nicholas I. Their opponents were the Slavophiles, who regarded Peter as the arch enemy and looked to the recovery of Russian nationhood (***narodnost'***) through the rejection of the European culture which he had forcibly implanted in Russia and which his successors continued to uphold. They saw this implant as alien to the Russian spirit, which for them was expressed in the communality (*sobornost'*) of the Russian Orthodox church and the ancient village way of life. In their respectively radical and reactionary ways both groups were critical of the regime of Nicholas I; it is therefore difficult to disentangle the intelligentsia's views on Russia's relationship with Europe from its self-defining political opposition to the Russian autocracy. The main point of this section of the chapter is to show that these intertwined debates developed with an imported, assimilated and reworked framework of western and central European philosophy.

Heightened interest in Russia's peculiar institutions and culture was part of the patriotic fervour kindled by the Napoleonic wars, though this experience did not lead everyone to a reverence for Russia's unique past. Peter Chaadayev (1794–1856), a veteran of the Napoleonic campaign, stayed on in western Europe and then published, in an 1836 issue of the Russian journal *Telescope*, an anonymous 'Philosophical letter', composed in French. For Herzen, then exiled in Vyatka, this was 'a shot that rang out in the dark night'; it was 'a turning-point in our understanding of ourselves'. Chaadayev, subsequently declared insane by Tsar Nicholas, derided Russia's oppressive history and deplored its isolation from the mainstream of European civilization. He nevertheless argued that this very isolation gave Russia the chance, as it had avoided some of the worst follies of recent European history, to assume the spiritual leadership of Europe on the basis of a universal, purified Christianity (though 'liked and respected' by Herzen, Chaadayev was a Catholic convert and politically conservative; Herzen, 1968, vol. 2, pp. 413, 516; vol. 3, p. 1582).

A Moscow University student circle of the 1830s led by Nikolay Stankevich (1813–40) was seminal to the Slavophile–westernizer controversy triggered by Chaadayev's letter. Unlike the contemporary student circle of Herzen and his francophile friends, it devoted itself to the abstract study of German idealist philosophy. Its membership included future Slavophiles, such as the Aksakov brothers, Konstantin (1817–60) and Ivan (1823–86) and future westernizers, notably Granovsky, the consumptive literary critic Vissarion Belinsky (1811–48) and the ex-artillery officer and future anarchist and pan-Slavist revolutionary Mikhail Bakunin (1814–76). The first German

Figure 5.5 Peter Chaadeyev. Photo: Novosti Photo Library

'Dialectic' is a philosophical term with a range of meanings going back to the ancient Greeks. It assumed central importance in the tradition of German idealist philosophy that flourished in the first half of the nineteenth century. In this tradition, philosophers aspired to attain absolute knowledge through a process of uncovering the contradictory nature of concepts, and finding a higher-order concept in which these contradictions were resolved. An abstract example from Hegel's *Science of Logic* is that the concept of 'being' (*Sein*), and its negation 'nothing' (*Nichts*) are transcended in the concept of 'becoming' (*Werden*), which contains the ideas both of existence and of non-existence (Inwood, 1992, pp. 44–6). Hegel's dialectical logic exerted a powerful influence on Karl Marx; hence the emphasis in Marxist analyses on the internal contradictions of capitalism, and their resolution under socialism, as society progresses dialectically to the perfect form of communism.

idealist philosopher to absorb the circle and wield influence in Russia was Friedrich Wilhelm Joseph Schelling (1775–1854), whose argument that each nation had its own peculiar pattern of development in the great unfolding of the 'World-Soul' (Bowie, 1993) had much to offer young Russians during the 1820s and 1830s. One such was Chaadayev, who was personally acquainted with the German professor and kept up a correspondence with him.

By the time of Herzen's return from exile in the early 1840s the vogue for Schelling among the Moscow intelligentsia had given way to a rage for George Wilhelm Friedrich. Hegel (1770–1831). The foremost exponent of the German idealist tradition, Hegel advocated that ultimate reality was an undivided, spiritual whole (the Absolute) that transcended all the divisions and imperfections of the phenomenal world of the here and now. It could be apprehended only by rational understanding of the **dialectical** process through which all separateness and contradiction were overcome and the Absolute realized itself. In Hegel's all-encompassing philosophical system, the dialectical process of the self-realization of the Absolute

Figure 5.6 Vissarion Belinsky. Photo: Novosti
Photo Library

offered a touchstone by which to judge progress in philosophy,
history, politics, art, religion and all other realms of human
endeavour. As was also true of Schelling's ideas, Hegel's world view
was fruitfully ambiguous, in that its dialectical logic could justify
diametrically opposed conclusions, such as those of the westernizers
and Slavophiles in Russia. Indeed the history of Hegelianism evinced
its own dialectical logic: after the master's death, his German
followers duly split into 'right-wing' and 'left-wing' Hegelians. The
former stressed the Hegelian formula 'all that is real is rational' and
drew the conservative conclusion that the status quo could always be
justified as a stage in the rational development of the Absolute Spirit.
The latter, who included the young Karl Marx (1818–83), stressed the
radical power of the dialectical process: the status quo was in an
unstable state of 'becoming', and the process of the dialectical
resolution of its contradictions would be led by those who understood
them.

Among the Russian westernizers, both Bakunin and Belinsky had
been briefly reconciled by the right-wing interpretation of Hegel to
the regime of Nicholas I and its official, anti-western ideology of

Michael Bakounine.

Figure 5.7 Mikhail Bakunin. Photo: Novosti Photo Library

'Orthodoxy, autocracy and nationality'. Herzen fell out with Belinsky while this lasted. Bakunin left Russia for Berlin in 1840 to pursue his purely abstract interest in idealist metaphysics, but soon allied himself with the leading left-wing Hegelians. In 1842 his pseudonymous article 'The reaction in Germany' appeared in a radical journal, and Bakunin was launched on his extraordinary trajectory of agitation, insurrection, incarceration, exile and flight: he famously ended his article with the flourish 'the passion for destruction is a creative passion' (Bakunin, 1934–5, vol. 3, p. 148). Herzen, who found Bakunin's article 'perfect from beginning to end', was obliged on his return from provincial exile to confront his distaste for speculative philosophy, which despite evidence to the contrary in Moscow he generalized as 'utterly opposed to the Russian temperament'. He applied himself to the esoteric writings of the German sage, struggling 'long and desperately in the squirrel's wheel of dialectical repetition' (Gertsen, 1954–65, vol. 2, p. 257; Herzen, 1968, vol. 2, pp.

397, 580). The result was two series of anonymous or pseudonymous articles in the Russian journal *Notes of the Fatherland* that conveyed the oblique, Aesopian form of opposition cultivated by the intelligentsia to fox Tsar Nicholas's censors: 'Dilettantism in science' (1843) and 'Letters on the study of nature' (1845–6), which represented 'the most important critique of Hegel from the Russian left' (Acton, 1979, p. 10). As he later wrote in his memoirs, 'The philosophy of Hegel is the algebra of revolution; it emancipates a man in an unusual way and leaves not one stone upon another in the Christian world, of the world of tradition that has outlived itself' (Herzen, 1968, vol. 2, p. 403).

The westernizers' belief that Russia should follow the west European example (including the ideas of its radical critics), and thereby transcend it, could readily be rationalized in Hegelian terms. Less easy to understand is the temporary coexistence of Orthodoxy and Hegelianism in the early views of the Slavophile Konstantin Aksakov, even though he could thereby justify growing his beard as a dialectical synthesis of bearded old and beardless new Russia (Lampert, 1957, p. 89). More representative of the Slavophiles' philosophical affinities was the choice of Ivan Kireyevsky (1806–56), who as a young man attended lectures by Hegel and Schelling and returned from Germany with a bust of the latter, judging him the greatest philosopher in the world. Overall, the Slavophiles were quicker than the westernizers to repudiate German idealism; as might have been expected, they turned away from western ideas to Russian Orthodoxy. Nevertheless, it says much about the construction of Russian identities in relation to European 'others' that their position was worked out through the experience of, and to some considerable extent through the categories of, German idealist thought (Walicki, 1975, pp. 334–5).

According to Herzen, at one time the westernizers were debating with the Slavophiles in Moscow two or three times a week. Herzen has left perceptive and sometimes ironic portraits of the Slavophiles, especially of Konstantin Aksakov, who 'wore a dress so national that people in the street took him for a Persian, as Chaadayev used to tell for a joke'. Ivan Kireyevsky even took Herzen to task over his west European name, urging that he change the first 'e' into its Slavonic equivalent. Despite the apparent chasm between their beliefs there was, in Herzen's view, considerable mutual respect and, in the end, important common ground between the two groups. Indeed in his memoirs Herzen was undecided whether to call the Slavophiles 'our friends the enemies' or 'our enemies the friends'. After the death of Konstantin Aksakov, he wrote in *Kolokol* that the westernizers and Slavophiles had a common love of the Russian people, way of life and cast of mind: 'and like Janus, or the two-headed eagle, they and we

Among the reforms of the Cyrillic script enacted by the Bolsheviks after the October Revolution was the abolition of this alternative Slavonic 'e'.

Figure 5.8 Konstantin Aksakov. Photo: Novosti Photo Library

looked in different directions while one heart throbbed within us'. And despite his respect for Peter the Great, in the end 'Petrograndism' took its place alongside Hegelianism, Christianity, nature and even the shibboleths of revolution, such as 'democracy', 'republic' and 'the idol of progress', as constructs too careless of the individual life. Herzen objected to the Slavophiles' Orthodox religion, and to their 'over-sensitive, exaggerated sense of nationality' which obscured what he took to be the essence of their thought: the village commune as the foundation of Russian life. But although Herzen rejected the Slavophiles' idealization of the Russian past, and their desire to return to it, he arrived at the conclusion that the institutions of the Russian village were seeds that could be fertilized by western socialism and help bring in a new phase of universal history. In a way, Herzen arrived at a Hegelian dialectical synthesis of westernism and Slavophilism (Herzen, 1968, vol. 2, pp. 511–12, 526–30, 545, 549; vol. 3, p. 1247; Christoff, 1982).

Was Russia a European nation, in Herzen's view? Perhaps appropriately, he was ambivalent. He routinely spoke of 'Europe' and 'European' as implicitly other than 'Russia' and 'Russian'. At one point in his memoirs he described the Russian people, 'extended so widely between Europe and Asia', as 'standing to the general family of European peoples somewhat in the relationship of a cousin'. At another he distinguished between the 'Russian Europe' of the court, nobility, higher clergy and officialdom, and the 'non-European Russia' of serfdom and the village. This is not to say that Herzen regarded non-European Russia as part of Asia: 'Asiatic', for him, went with 'quiescence' and the subordination of the individual to the mass; the 'locked-up, alienated, suspended form of existence' in China and Japan had no more attraction than the *petit bourgeois* state of western Europe as the destination of Russian history. At one point he defined Russia as a nation neither European nor Asian, but Slavic; at another he insisted that 'we Russians belong both by race and by language to the European family, *genus europaeum*, and consequently by the most immutable laws of physiology we are bound to follow the same path' (Herzen, 1968, vol. 3, pp. 1081; vol. 4, p. 1725, 1745, 1747). The following reading, an extract from the first of Herzen's *Letters from France and Italy*, written in Paris on 12 May 1847 contains Herzen's first published thoughts on this issue after leaving Russia.

In the East ... only the individuals, the generations change; the present life is the hundredth repetition of one and the same theme with slight variations introduced by chance – by the harvest, famine, pestilence, cattle plague, the character of the shah and his satraps. Such a life has no lived past, *keine Erlebnisse* – the way of life of the Asiatic peoples may be very significant, but their history is boring. We have taken a great step forward in comparison to Asia; by understanding our position, we can reject it ...

Our unsatisfactory past, its incompleteness and poverty, and our dim awareness of capacities we could not use – these explain the ease with which Russia obeyed Peter I's great command: 'Onto the European road, march!' Rus', with its mobile units, marched, and in fifty years it had separated itself so sharply from its former life that by the time of Catherine II it would have been incomparably more difficult for it to return to its old mores than to achieve European ways. However much people may declaim about our habit of imitation, it is nothing more than a readiness to accept and absorb forms without in any way losing our own character ...

On closer examination, Petrine Rus' could be indicted instead for its cunning; it is ready to shave and don new clothes, but despite the change always remains itself. The magnates of Catherine's day adopted all the civility and refinement of Versailles forms (they were far more successful at this than the German grandees ever were), and in consequence did they not always remain Russian lords in all respects, with all the boldness of the national character, with its failings, and with its breadth. There was nothing foreign about them except for the form they worked out, and they possessed *en maître*. Weren't their children, the heroes of 1812, Russian, completely Russian? ...

And yet the whole Catherinian epoch, which our grandfathers remembered with a shake of their heads, and the entire Alexandrian period, which our fathers remembered with a shake of their heads, belong to what the Slavophiles call the 'foreign period,' for they consider everything universal as foreign, everything educated as alien. They do not understand that the new Rus' was still Rus', they do not understand that with the Petrine break into two Russias our real history begins. For all that is grievous about this division, it is responsible for all we have – a bold state development, the emergence of Rus' on the scene as a political individuality, and the emergence of Russian individuals among the people. Russian thought becomes accustomed to express itself, literature appears, heterodoxy appears, questions trouble us, national poetry develops ...

Finally, our very consciousness of the break comes from that intellectual awakening. Being close to Europe encourages and develops faith in our own nationality, faith that the people who were left behind, for whom we now bear the historic yoke, and whom both our sorrow and our blessings passed by – that this people is not only emerging from its ancient way of life but is meeting us, having leapt over the Petrine period. The history of this people lies in the future; it has proved its capacity by the minority that truly followed Peter's order – it proved it with us!

(Herzen, 1995, pp. 18–20)

EXERCISE

Did Herzen see any contradiction between Peter the Great's command to march on 'the European road', and the development of Russian nationality? And how might the Slavophiles have responded?

DISCUSSION _____

Herzen squares this apparent circle by arguing that the European path, despite the division it created in Russian society, was necessary for Russian history to start and for Russian individuals to emerge. The Slavophiles would have rejected Herzen's notion of individualism as a western import at odds with the communality (*sobornost'*) of the Russian Orthodox tradition.

_____

It might seem paradoxical that the westernizer–Slavophile controversy about Russia's destiny was to some extent conducted within a framework provided by west and central European philosophers. But essentially the Russian disciples of Hegel and Schelling took from their works what they needed. Herzen's own dalliance with Hegel was bound to end in tears, as Hegel's views on the subordination of the individual personality to the impersonal logic of history, like the subjection of individual Russians to the tsarist autocracy, was the very antithesis of Herzen's mature political credo. This is an important interim conclusion to draw about Russia's relations with western Europe at this time, and perhaps at all times. Russia was not a passive recipient of western ideas and culture; there was a process of selection and modification, to the point in Herzen's case of an original contribution to Russian political thought.

From the other shore: a Russian Voltaire

Herzen's disillusionment over the failure of the 1848–9 revolutions ran deep. He joined the French peasant libertarian socialist Pierre-Joseph Proudhon (1809–65), and others of the French left, in scorning the French republican government's espousal of universal (male) suffrage, at a time when the peasants were uneducated and under the influence of the clergy, the rich landowners and the city bourgeoisie. In agreement with John Stuart Mill (1806–73), one Englishman that he did admire, he insisted that the 'arithmetic count of voices' required universal education at least; he opposed to the principle of universal suffrage, 'the right to persuade, the right of the more intelligent, the right of knowledge, even the right of energy and will' (Herzen, 1995, pp. 260–1). Although he was on good terms with leading radicals such as the Italians Giuseppe Mazzini (1805–72) and Giuseppe Garibaldi (1807–82), the Frenchmen Alexandre Ledru-Rollin (1807–74) and Proudhon, the Hungarian Lajos Kossuth (1802–94), the Swiss James Fazy (1794–1878) and the Pole Stanislaw Worcell (1799–1857) (like Herzen a fugitive from the Russian authorities), he felt increasingly alienated from the empty rhetoric and backbiting of the European revolutionary movement as a whole. More profoundly, his distrust of historical systems and grand historical goals requiring human sacrifice were increasingly accentuated in his writings. For all his despair at the outcome of the revolutions in western Europe, he remained deeply opposed to the new factory system of western industrial capitalism. This uncompromising rejection of bourgeois values and capitalism had set him apart from many of his fellow Russian westernizers, who argued that Russia needed to go through this stage of development to escape from autocracy. In order to reconcile his inveterate hatred of the tyrannies of monarchy, religion and profit with his new aversion to the inhumanity with which his socialist and liberal allies intended to realize their political ideals, the wounded expatriate now looked back to his homeland. There was an element of homesickness in this, as expressed in one of his *Letters from France and Italy*. Despite his love of the Savoyard countryside around Nice through which he passed *en route* from Paris to Rome, the high stone walls, strewn with broken glass, of its otherwise charming houses made the 'Slavic heart ache':

> It is impossible to imagine what a melancholy character these walls lend to the fields and the land; trees, like prisoners, gaze through them, and the most charming landscapes are spoiled. The Russian village does not exist in Europe. In Europe, the village commune is only an administrative unit; what is there in common between the hungry workers, to whom the commune grants le droit de glaner [gleaning rights], and the rich householders? Long live the Russian village, gentlemen – its future is great!
>
> (Herzen, 1995, p. 67)

Herzen went on to elaborate this vision of the future: he argued that Russia could avoid the evils of capitalism by pursuing an alternative path of 'Russian socialism', combining traditional notions of community found among the Russian peasants with the ideal of individual liberty that he imbibed from French socialism. Herzen presented these views in 'The Russian people and socialism', composed in French in 1851 as an open letter in riposte to the distinguished French historian Jules Michelet (1798–1874), who had recently published an article pronouncing the Russian people unfit for membership of the European nations because of their oppression of the Poles (Herzen, 1979, pp. 165–208). Partly on the basis of his Russian socialism, some scholars have portrayed Herzen as essentially a Russian nationalist (Malia, 1961; Greenfeld, 1992). According to Liah Greenfeld his was a distinctive kind of Russian nationalism characterized by *ressentiment*, a psychological reaction based on suppressed feelings of envy towards a model perceived to be superior (Greenfeld, 1992, pp. 15–17). The next reading is an extract from

Greenfield's *Nationalism: Five Roads to Modernity*. It is followed by an excerpt from Herzen's memoirs, which gives his own account of the westernizers' relations with the Slavophiles. Read both pieces and then turn to the exercise that follows them.

The terms 'Westernism' and 'Slavophilism' were coined to characterize an intellectual feud; this feud, however, occurred between friends, people moved by the same concerns, who forever remained sympathetic toward the seemingly opposing views of their opponents. Westernism and Slavophilism were very much alike; they differed in emphasis and in mood more than in anything else.

Both Westernism and Slavophilism were steeped in *ressentiment*. Both arose out of the realization of Russia's inferiority and a revulsion against its humiliating reality. In Slavophilism, this revulsion was transformed into excessive self-admiration. In Westernism, the very same sentiment led to the generalized revulsion against the existing world and to the desire to destroy it. Yet the difference was that of emphasis. Both were Westernisms, for as philosophies of *ressentiment* both defined the West as the anti-model. And both were Slavophilisms, for the model for them was Russia, which they idealized each in its own fashion and whose triumph over the West both predicted. Westernism saw the fulfillment of the ideal (Russia as anti-West) in the future, following the destruction of the old world and beyond the present splendor of the West, but it still accepted the direction in which the West developed as the only way. Slavophils, on the other hand, placed their ideal outside Western development and, in fact, outside history. They did not have to go beyond the West to prove to it Russia's superiority. It was proven, whether revealed or concealed, by its very nature. There was nothing to do about this. Slavophilism contained a streak of escapism, and thus it could seem conservative. The Slavophils were not conservative; many of them were critical of the reality which concealed Russia's brilliant – holy – self behind Western appearances, but they did not think that Russia had to develop to fulfill its mission. Westernism, on the other hand, was activist. Even though the final triumph was guaranteed, Westernists were never averse to helping it on the way. In its activism and orientation toward the future, Westernism retained some of the optimism of the eighteenth century.

The solution that Slavophils proposed to the harrowing problem of the difficulty and uncertainty of catching up with the West, so poignantly formulated by Chaadaev, was simple. On the one hand, not only the equality, but the superiority of Russia was already clearly achieved (it was inherent in the nation), and on the other, the West was rotten to the core and did not deserve imitation ...

The superiority of Russia derived from the fact that it was *not* a Western nation; indeed it embodied the principle opposed to that on which Western civilization was based. This – Russian – principle represented the true aspiration of man (or should we say: his species-being?) and made possible true freedom; it was the principle of the individual's dissolution in community, and thus the one that expressed itself in true – perfect – nations. For the nation was, of course, a moral individual endowed with a unique spirit. The principle was manifested with particular clarity in the Russian – Orthodox – Church, Eastern Christianity, and in the peasant commune. Eastern Christianity, now preserved for the world by Russia, was the original, and therefore the true, Christianity. The Russian Church, in contrast to the Western Churches, which emphasized the individual, was characterized by *sobornost'*, which Khomyakov, the Slavophil theologian, defined as the expression of 'the idea of unity in multiplicity' ...

The same redeeming qualities were found in the peasant commune. 'A commune,' wrote [Konstantin] Aksakov, 'is a union of the people who have renounced their egoism, their individuality, and who express their common accord; this is an act of love – in the commune the individual is not lost, but renounces his exclusiveness in favor of the general accord – and there arises the noble phenomenon of a harmonious, joint existence of rational beings (consciousness): there arises a brotherhood, a commune – a triumph of human spirit.' Freedom was freedom to live this principle; of course it was inner, of course it had nothing to do with the outward world of politics. This enabled Slavophils to accept, in fact uphold, the autocracy ...

The comparison between Russian and Western political structure underscored the idyllic character of the former: 'In the foundation of the Western State: violence, slavery, and hostility. In the foundation of the Russian state: free will, liberty and peace.'[1] And since the Russian people expressed the essence of humanity itself, it was not a people like any other. Like [Johann Gottlieb] Fichte [1762–1814] of Germany, Aksakov spoke of Russia as a universal nation. 'The Russian people is not a people; it is humanity; it is a people only because it is surrounded by peoples with exclusively

---

[1] Khomiakov, and Aksakov, quoted in Nicholas V. Riasanovsky, *A Parting of Ways: Government and the Educated Public in Russia 1801–1855*, Oxford, Clarendon Press, pp. 178, 187, 193.

national essences, and its humanity is therefore represented as nationality.'[2] What an easy way out this was! There was no need to catch up with the West; it was this pitiful opponent who had some catching up to do; Russia was the opposite of the West and so much better for that. Russia contained the salvation of the world within herself; she preserved and held high the torch of humanity, and the West was to watch her in amazement.

The Westernizers rejected the West without transferring their loyalties outside it and without defining Russia as a non-Western nation, or an embodiment of principles opposed to those of the West. They rejected the West in its current, present state, which was the state of betrayal of its own lofty principles, a decadent, rotting, aging state – and to it they opposed the young, exuberant Russia destined to bring these principles to fruition. The West was the only repository of history, it was the world ... This embodiment of world history was now leaving its task to Russia, 'the younger brother in the European family ...' opening before it 'a great and splendid field of activity.'[3]

The individualism of the Westernizers had nothing in common with Western – that is to say, Anglo-American – individualism: the commitment to the rights and liberty of the common man. Not for a moment did they doubt that 'a nation is collective in its nature' and that real freedom is inner freedom. But the spirit of the nation and the principle of freedom needed great, special individuals to reveal them, and it was the individualism of these special uncommon individuals, men like themselves, and their freedom unlimited by law and common sense, that Westernizers craved. They wished the glory of Russia, but they despised the 'masses.' And since the masses were expendable, the solution Westernizers proposed to the problem posed by Chaadaev, of the difficulty and uncertainty of catching up with the West, was that of a cataclysmic event, a purifying conflagration that would in one sweep destroy the West and the imperfections of Russian reality, and from which Russia, with its spirit finally liberated, would reemerge to enjoy its – crowning – share of historical greatness. The idea of a Revolution – not a Decembrist *coup d'état* – was the Westernizers' contribution to the Russian national consciousness. Undoubtedly, they were led to it by their activist, maniacal

[2] Askakov, in ibid., p. 192.

[3] T. N. Granovsky, quoted in Leonard B. Schapiro, *Rationalism and Nationalism in Russian Nineteenth-Century Political Thought*, New Haven: Yale University Press, 1967, p. 79.

temperament. Unlike the Slavophils, they were unable to sit with their arms folded and tolerate the spectacle of Western superiority; and under the crafty influence of *ressentiment*, Revolution was the form taken by their wishful thinking ...

Finding expression under the most diverse guises and names, the two traditions have formed the substance of Russian national sentiment ever since. There was no clear demarcation in the minds of people between Slavophilism and Westernism. Before the split Ivan Kireyevsky was a devoted admirer of the West and edited a journal entitled *The European*. Herzen ended as a Slavophil. [Nikolay] Chernyshevsky was a Westernizer; *Narodnichestvo*, a reincarnation of Slavophilism, sprang out of his ideas. The first Russian Marxists – the arch-Westernizers – were disillusioned Narodniks. The two currents, united by the spirit of Holy Russia and the rejection of the West, were one. They continued to exist side by side, upheld interchangeably in an unending oscillation between hope and withdrawal. And in the best Romantic tradition of striving toward unity in multiplicity, one could be a Westernizer in the morning, a Slavophil in the afternoon, and criticize after dinner.

(Greenfeld, 1992, pp. 265–71)

Side by side with our circle were our opponents, *nos amis les ennemis,* or more correctly, *nos ennemis les amis*[4] – the Moscow Slavophils.

The conflict between us ended long ago and we have held out our hands to each other; but in the early 'forties we could not but be antagonistic – without being so we could not have been true to our principles. We might have been able not to quarrel with them over their childish homage to the childhood of our history; but accepting their Orthodoxy as meant in earnest, seeing their ecclesiastical intolerance on both sides – in relation to learning and in relation to sectarianism – we were bound to take up a hostile attitude to them. We saw in their doctrines fresh oil for anointing the Tsar, new chains laid upon thought, new subordination of conscience to the servile Byzantine Church.

The Slavophils are to blame for our having so long failed to understand either the Russian people or its history; their

---

[4] From P. Béranger: *L'opinion de ces demoiselles.* (*Note from Soviet edition of Herzen's works*)

ikon-painter's ideals and incense smoke hindered us from seeing the realities of the people's existence and the foundations of village life.

The Orthodoxy of the Slavophils, their historical patriotism and over-sensitive, exaggerated feeling of nationality were called forth by the extremes on the other side. The importance of their outlook, what was true and essential in it, lay not in Orthodoxy, and not in exclusive nationalism, but in those elements of Russian life which they unearthed from under the manure of an artificial civilisation.

The idea of nationality is in itself a conservative idea – the demarcation of one's rights, the opposition of self to another; it includes both the Judaic conception of superiority of race, and the aristocratic claim to purity of blood and to the right of primo-geniture. Nationalism as a standard, as a war-cry, is only surrounded with the halo of revolution when a people is fighting for its independence, when it is trying to throw off a foreign yoke. That is why national feeling with all its exaggerations is full of poetry in Italy and in Poland, while in Germany it is vulgar.

For us to display our nationalism would be even more absurd than it is for the Germans; even those who abuse us do not doubt it; they hate us from fear, but they do not refuse to recognise us, as [the Austrian statesman Prince Klemens Fürst von] Metternich [1773–1859] did Italy. We have had to set up our nationalism against the Germanised government and our own renegades ...

Chaadayev and the Slavophils alike stood facing the unsolved Sphinx of Russian life, the Sphinx sleeping under the overcoat of the soldier and the watchful eye of the Tsar; they alike were asking: 'What will come of this? To live like this is impossible: the oppressiveness and absurdity of the present situation is obvious and unendurable – where is the way out?'

'There is none,' answered the man of the Petrine epoch of exclusively Western civilisation, who in Alexander's reign had believed in the European future of Russia. He sadly pointed to what the efforts of a whole age had led to. Culture had only given new methods of oppression, the church had become a mere shadow under which the police lay hidden; the people still tolerated and endured, the government still crushed and oppressed. 'The history of other nations is the story of their emancipation. Russian history is the development of serfdom and autocracy.' Peter's upheaval made us into the worst that men can be made into – *enlightened* slaves ...

From the point of view of Western civilisation in the form in which it found expression at the time of restorations, from the point of view of Petrine Russia, this attitude was completely justified. The Slavophils solved the question in a different way.

Their solution implied a true consciousness of the *living soul* in the people; their instinct was more penetrating than their reasoning. They saw that the existing condition of Russia, however oppressive, was not a *fatal disease* ...

'The way out is with us,' said the Slavophils, 'the way out lies in renouncing the Petersburg period, in going back to the people from whom we have been separated by foreign education and foreign government; let us return to the old ways!'

But history does not turn back; life is rich in materials, and never needs old clothes. All reinstatements, all restorations have always been masquerades ...

More than this, we have nothing to go back to. The political life of Russia before Peter was ugly, poor and savage, yet it was to this that the Slavophils wanted to return, though they did not admit the fact; how else are we to explain all their antiquarian revivals, their worship of the manners and customs of old days, and their very attempts to return, not to the existing (and excellent) dress of the peasants but to clumsy, antiquated costumes? ...

They took the return to the people in a very crude sense too, as the majority of Western democrats did also, accepting the people as something complete and finished. They supposed that sharing the prejudices of the people meant being at one with them, that it was a great act of humility to sacrifice their own reason instead of developing reason in the people. This led to an affectation of devoutness, the observance of rites which are touching when there is a naïve faith in them and offensive when there is visible premeditation. The best proof of the lack of reality in the Slavophils' return to the people lies in the fact that they did not arouse in them the slightest sympathy ... To go back to the village, to the workmen's guild, to the meeting of the *mir*,[5] to the Cossack system is a different matter; but we must return to them not in order that they may be fixed fast in immovable Asiatic crystallisations, but to develop and set free the elements on which they were founded, to purify them from all that is extraneous and distorting, from the proud flesh with which they are overgrown – this, of course, is our vocation ...

---

[5]   Village council. *(translator's note)*

The mistake of the Slavophils lay in their thinking that Russia once had an individual culture, obscured by various events and finally by the Petersburg epoch. Russia never had this culture and never could have had it. That which is now reaching our consciousness, that of which we are beginning to have a presentiment, a glimmer in our thoughts, that which existed unconsciously in the peasants' hut and in the open country, is only now beginning to grow in the pastures of history, manured by the blood, the tears and the sweat of twenty generations.

The foundations of our life are not memories; they are the living elements, existing not in chronicles but in the actual present; but they have merely *survived* under the difficult historical process of building up a single state and under the oppression of the state they have only been preserved not developed. I even doubt whether the inner forces for their development would have been found without the Petrine epoch, without the period of European culture ...

Only the mighty thought of the West, with which all its long history is united, is able to fertilise the seeds slumbering in the patriarchal mode of life of the Slavs. The workmen's guild and the village commune, the sharing of profits and the partition of fields, the meeting of the *mir* and the union of villages into self-governing *volosts*,[6] are all the corner-stones on which the mansion of our future, freely communal existence will be built. But these corner-stones are only stones – and without the thought of the West our future cathedral would not rise above its foundations ...

The receptive character of the Slavs, their *femininity*, their lack of initiative, and their great capacity for assimilation and adaptation, make them pre-eminently a people that stands in need of other peoples; they are not fully self-sufficing. Left to themselves the Slavs readily 'lull themselves to sleep with their own songs' as a Byzantine chronicler observed, 'and doze'. Awakened by others they go to extreme consequences; there is no people which might more deeply and completely absorb the thought of other peoples while remaining true to itself. The persistent misunderstanding which exists to-day as it has for a thousand years, between the Germanic and the Latin peoples does not exist between them and the Slavs. The need to surrender and to be carried away is innate in their sympathetic, readily assimilative, receptive nature.

---

[6] Administrative districts which each contained several villages. *(translator's note)*

To be formed into a princedom, Russia needed the Varangians, to be formed into a kingdom, the Mongols.

Contact with Europe developed the kingdom of Muscovy into the colossal empire ruled from Petersburg ...

There was a time when the half-free West looked proudly at a Russia crushed under the throne of the Tsars, and cultivated Russia gazed sighing at the good fortune of its elder brothers. That time has passed. The equality of slavery has been established ...

Meanwhile Europe has shown a surprising incapacity for social revolution.

We believe that Russia is not so incapable of it, and in this we are at one with the Slavophils. On this our faith in its future is founded, the faith which I have been preaching since the end of 1848 ...

[O]ne thing we have discovered for certain and it will not be eradicated from the consciousness of the coming generations; this is: that the *free and rational development of Russian national life coincides with the aspirations of Western socialism.*

(Herzen, 1968, vol. 2, pp. 511–12, 525–30)

EXERCISE _____

Does Herzen's mature political outlook really have so much in common with Slavophilism?

DISCUSSION _____

Greenfeld regards westernism and Slavophilism as essentially interchangeable forms, and Herzen's own eventual synthesis of the two lends some support to her analysis. What you have to decide is whether it follows from the identity of *motivation* that Greenfeld ascribes to the two groups that they held fundamentally the same *views*, given that many of their respective beliefs and values were clearly antithetical to each other. You need in particular, in the light of these extracts and the evidence in the next paragraph, to decide whether Herzen can indeed, like the Slavophiles, be classified as a nationalist.

_____

The nationalist interpretation has been rejected by other Herzen specialists (Acton, 1979, pp. 15, 27–9, 45). It sits ill with Herzen's own rejection of what he described elsewhere as the 'insufferably sensitive patriotism' of the Swiss, the 'obstinate patriotism' he detected beneath the cosmopolitan rhetoric of the German revolutionaries and the 'counterfeit nationalism' he ascribed to the Slavophiles. He also denounced the 'jealous patriotism' of the ancients, 'that ferocious virtue which has shed ten times more blood than all the vices put together'. In 'Ends and beginnings', his series of open letters to the novelist Turgenev first published in 1862–3, he lamented that 'the classification of men by nationalities becomes more and more the wretched ideal of this world which has buried the Revolution'. Nevertheless, Herzen drew the line at emigration to the United States, 'the last well-produced edition of the same Christian-feudal text and, what is more, in a crude English translation', which despite its republican, democratic form of government and proclamation of the 'rights of man' was tainted by slavery in the south and by Puritan intolerance in the north. He agreed with Garibaldi that the US was a 'land for forgetting one's own' for those who had no faith in their homeland (Herzen, 1968, vol. 2, pp. 711, 722, 786, 821; vol. 3, p. 1226; vol. 4, pp. 1561, 1730; 1979, p. 78).

Whether or not he was a nationalist, Herzen had a highly developed sense of nationality, believing that 'every people has a strongly defined physiological character that even foreign conquests rarely alter'. His experiences of a number of west European countries and nationals emboldened him to make regular generalizations of a kind that might well now be seen as national stereotypes. During his exile in Vyatka he came under the influence of the disgraced architect and mystic Alexander Vitberg (1787–1855), though in the end he preferred the 'daylight of thought' to the 'moonlight of fantasy' and attributed Vitberg's mysticism to his 'Scandinavian blood'. Half German himself, Herzen was acutely conscious of the 'Germanizing' effect of the St Petersburg government:

> The German lymph has matured in the coarse Russian blood; the healthy organism has given it fresh strength and, while infected by it, has not lost one vice of its own. The inhuman, narrow ugliness of the German trooper and the petty vulgarity of the German official have long ago blended in Russia with the broad cheekbones of the Mongol, the savage, remorseless cruelty of the oriental slave and of the Byzantine eunuch.

He wrote of the Germans' 'military mind', their diligence and philistinism, their yen for 'theories *sub specie aeternitatis*', and listed other qualities 'that the Russian temperament detests in the German – *gaucherie*, a coarse heartiness, a vulgar tone, a pedantry and a haughty self-complacency bordering on contempt for everything Russian'; he facetiously attributed their philistinism to the national cuisine and preoccupation with the stomach. His years of residence in

England left him with little warmth for its ill-mannered inhabitants, 'always seeming half asleep and not being able to wake up properly'. The Englishman 'has been accustomed physically and morally to do up all the buttons of his overcoat and turn up his collar, which protects him from damp winds and harsh intolerance'. But despite the 'closed, inaccessible society of the English aristocracy', he valued 'the Englishman's proud independence and unwavering confidence in the basis of law' and the fact that in England, as in Switzerland, the least restriction on personal freedom and speech was associated with the greatest tranquillity. Moreover, 'that refined corruption of soul, that envious hunger for enjoyment, power, and acquisition, which I have so well learned to read on West European faces ... is completely absent from those of the English'. In general he regarded the 'Anglo-Germanic race' as much coarser than the 'Franco-Roman', though in particular he blamed the penal servitude of factory life for the savage drunkenness of the English worker (Herzen, 1968, vol. 1, pp. 26, 68, 274; vol. 2, pp. 447, 706, 710–11, 715, 721, 746, 767–8; vol. 3, pp. 1079, 1114; vol. 4, pp. 1556–7, 1595, 1681; 1995, pp. 13–15).

Herzen was generally critical of the French, though much of this vituperative passion was surely an expression of the dashing of his youthful francophilia and idealization of the 1789 French Revolution by his experience in Paris of the events of 1848–9. The aristocratic Herzen objected to the 'tone of condescending superiority' that the French assumed with Russians, and excoriated them for their 'national stinginess' and 'habitual French bloodthirstiness'. His observation of one revolutionary's 'typically Gallic skull, not spacious but obstinate', shows in particular the contemporary cultural influence of phrenology and, more generally, Herzen's 'scientific' approach to the issue of national identities. More substantially, he rejected the despotism that resulted from the centralizing and equalizing Gallic subjection of individuality to the herd: 'In his soul, every Frenchman is a police commissar, he loves regularity and discipline; everything independent or individual maddens him ... The French in general love to oppress people.' He denounced their 'lack of any intellectual boldness or true initiative', 'political chatter' and adolescent, capricious 'political *gaminerie*', though he also took them to task for their preoccupation with ideas, for erecting 'every truth into a dogma':

> The French are the most abstract and religious people in the world; with them fanaticism for the idea goes hand in hand with lack of respect for the person, with disregard for one's neighbour ... Communism is close to the soul of the French people, which feels so deeply the great injustice of social life and respects so little the individual personality.

Herzen often analysed his contemporaries into their national or regional elements: 'like a Frenchman, [the socialist Louis Blanc (1811–82)] talks a great deal, yet, like a Corsican, he never says a word too much'. He spilt much ink, too, on national comparisons: 'the Englishman is always asking questions, the Frenchman is always giving answers. The Englishman is always wondering, always thinking things over, the Frenchman knows everything for certain' (Herzen, 1968, vol. 2, pp. 664–5, 746, 811, 834, 837; vol. 3, p. 1059; 1995, pp. 129, 159–61, 176, 182).

He was sympathetic to his fellow Slavs, the Poles, despite their understandable antipathy to their historic oppressors the Russians and his own distaste for their mysticism, spiritualism and Catholicism, which he found 'so alien to the Slavonic genius'. He was fondest of the Italians, 'a beautiful, attractive race of people, musical and artistic by nature', whom he considered 'badly slandered'; he found them most akin to Russians in their spontaneity and admired their 'proud sense of personal dignity and the inviolability of the person': 'the peasant of central Italy is just as unlike a repressed rabble as the Russian muzhik [peasant] is unlike property'. Herzen also identified with the Italians in having missed out on industrialization and a middle-class revolution, and in being measured by the dominant currency of France, Germany and England. He empathized with their distaste for centralized authority and Germanic administration: 'there is no people less fitted for discipline, a police system, a monarchical order'. Their long tradition of independent towns and cities appealed to him too: it was Italy's strength and its weakness (Herzen, 1968, vol. 2, pp. 651, 669, 698–9; vol. 3, pp. 1133, 1152, 1460; 1995, pp. 68, 88–90, 92).

He also happily generalized about his fellow Russians, though acutely conscious of the great cultural 'split' between the peasantry and the nobility created by the 'wedge' of Peter's reforms. However, even in the case of the educated Russian, Herzen saw how thinly the veneer of western manners and dress concealed the 'barbarian' within. He regretted his compatriots' 'provincial' deference to west European luminaries and decried the 'Russian disease of ambition' that underlay the national characteristics of servility to authority and oppression of subordinates. He admitted his own indulgence in 'the Russian weakness of drowning one's sorrows in drink', after the discovery of his wife's infidelity. But he was proud of the recklessness in the national temperament, and he celebrated the eccentricity and folly that resulted from 'the stifling emptiness and torpidity of Russian life, strangely combined with the liveliness and even turbulence of the Russian character' (1968, vol. 1, pp. 113, 229, 237, 253, 288; vol. 2, p. 886; vol. 4, p. 1576; 1995, p. 202).

Herzen's dismissal of entire nations will now read uncomfortably to Europeans who have learned from the twentieth century to be careful about the feelings of other national and cultural groups, even if they recognize some stability in the cultural stereotypes that Herzen invoked with such gusto. The final reading is an extended example from his memoirs of Herzen's national stereotyping.

The relationships formed between the different *émigrés* and the English might furnish by themselves wonderful data for the chemical affinity of various nationalities.

English life at first dazzles the Germans, overwhelms them, then swallows them up, or rather breaks them down into inferior Englishmen. As a rule, if a German undertakes any kind of business, he at once shaves, turns his shirt collar up to his ears, says *yes* instead of *ya* and *well* where there is no need to say anything at all. In a couple of years, he writes his letters and his notes in English, and lives entirely in an English circle. Germans never treat Englishmen as equals, but behave with them as our workpeople behave with officials, and our officials behave with noblemen of ancient standing.

When they enter English life, Germans do not really become Englishmen, but affect to be English, and partly cease to be Germans. The English are as whimsical in their relationships with foreigners as they are in everything else; they rush at a new arrival as they do at a comic actor or an acrobat and give him no peace, but they hardly disguise their sense of their own superiority and even a certain aversion they feel for him. If the foreigner keeps to his own dress, his own way of doing his hair, his own hat, the offended Englishman jeers at him, but by degrees grows used to recognising him as an independent person. If in his first alarm the foreigner begins to adapt his manners to the Englishman's, the latter does not respect him, but treats him superciliously from the height of his British haughtiness. Here it is sometimes hard, even with great tact, to steer one's course so as not to err either on the minus or the plus side; it may well be imagined what the Germans do, who are devoid of all tact, are familiar and servile, too stiff and also too simple, sentimental without reason and rude without provocation.

But if the Germans look upon the English as upon a higher species of the same genus, and feel themselves to be inferior to them, it by no means follows that the attitude of the French, and especially of the French refugees, is any wiser. Just as the German respects everything in England without discrimination, the Frenchman protests against everything and loathes everything English. This peculiarity sometimes, I need hardly say, is pushed to the most comically grotesque extreme.

The Frenchman cannot forgive the English, in the first place, for not speaking French; in the second, for not understanding him when he calls Charing Cross Sharan-Kro, or Leicester Square Lessesstair-Skooar. Then his stomach cannot digest the English dinners consisting of two huge pieces of meat and fish, instead of five little helpings of various ragouts, fritures, salmis and so on. Then he can never resign himself to the 'slavery' of restaurants being closed on Sundays, and the people being *bored to the glory of God*, though the whole of France is bored to the glory of Bonaparte for seven days in the week. Then the whole *habitus*, all that is good and bad in the Englishman, is detestable to the Frenchman. The Englishman pays him back in the same coin, but looks with envy at the cut of his clothes and like a caricature attempts to imitate him.

All this is of significance for the study of comparative physiology, and I am not describing it in order to amuse. The German, as we have observed, recognises that he is, in a civilian capacity at any rate, an inferior specimen of the same breed to which the Englishman belongs, and subordinates himself to him. The Frenchman, belonging to a different breed, not so distinct that he may be indifferent, as the Turk is to the Chinese, hates the Englishman, especially because both nations are each blindly convinced of being the foremost people in the world. The German, too, is inwardly convinced of this, particularly *auf dem theoretischen Gebiete*, but is ashamed to own it.

The Frenchman is really the opposite of the Englishman in every respect. The Englishman is a solitary creature, who likes to live alone in his own lair, obstinate and impatient of control; the Frenchman is a gregarious animal, impudent but easily shepherded. Hence two completely parallel lines of development with the Channel lying between them. The Frenchman is constantly anticipating things, meddling in everything, educating everybody, giving instructions about everything. The Englishman waits to see, does not meddle at all in other people's business and would be readier to be taught than to teach, but has not the time: he has to get to his shop.

The two corner-stones of the whole of English life, personal independence and family tradition, hardly exist for the Frenchman. The coarseness of English manners drives the Frenchman frantic, and it really is repugnant and poisons life in

London, but behind it he fails to see the rude strength with which this people has stood up for its rights, the stubbornness of character which makes it impossible to turn an Englishman into the slave who delights in the gold lace on livery and is in raptures over his chains entwined with laurel, though by flattering his passions you may do almost anything else with him.

The world of self-government, decentralisation, expanding capriciously, of its own initiative, seems to the Frenchman so savage, so incomprehensible that, however long he lives in England, he never understands its political and civic life, its rights and its judicial forms. He is lost in the incongruous multiplicity of precedents on which English law rests, as in a dark forest, and does not observe the immense and majestic oaks that compose it, nor see the charm, the poetry, and the significance of its very variety. His little Codex, with its sanded paths, its clipped shrubs and policemen-gardeners in every avenue, is a very different matter.

Shakespeare and Racine again.

If a Frenchman sees drunken men fighting in a tavern and a policeman looking at them with the serenity of an outsider and the curiosity of a man watching a cock-fight, he is furious with the policeman for not flying into a rage and carrying someone off *au violon*. He does not reflect that personal freedom is only possible when a policeman has no parental authority, when his intervention is reduced to passive readiness to come when he is summoned. The confidence that every poor fellow feels when he shuts the door of his cold, dark, damp little hovel transforms a man's attitude. Of course, behind these jealously guarded, strictly observed rights, the criminal sometimes hides – and so be it. It is far better that the clever thief should go unpunished than that every honest man should be trembling like a thief in his own room. Before I came to England every appearance of a policeman in the house in which I lived gave me an irresistibly nasty feeling, and morally I stood *en garde* against an enemy. In England the policeman at your door or within your doors only adds a feeling of security.

(Herzen, 1968, vol. 3, pp. 1047–9)

EXERCISE

Can Herzen be excused these views? Consider this question in the light of both the extract you have just read and the following apologia:

This kind of sweeping prejudice, these diatribes against entire nations and classes, are characteristic of a good many Russian writers of this period. They are often ill-founded, unjust and violently exaggerated, but they are the authentic expression of an indignant reaction against an oppressive milieu, and of a genuine and highly moral vision which makes them lively reading even now.

(Berlin, 1979a, p. 205)

DISCUSSION

You might well agree with Berlin that Herzen's perceptions of his west European contemporaries say little about objective ethnic or cultural characteristics. But you might doubt whether *as such* they reflect 'a genuine and highly moral vision'. It might be more enlightening to relate such attitudes to the cluster of Herzen's own identities as a dissident Russian nobleman abroad: these identities are the focus of the rest of this section of the chapter.

Herzen's ready opinions about national identity were assuredly informed by a very strongly developed sense of class. He mixed the two in offering his Russian readers advice on the best choice of foreign servant: German or English were much to be preferred to the temperamentally non-servile French, though he was glad of the Parisian worker's proud refusal to ask for tips, unlike their German or English counterparts. In such ways his attitudes surely remind us as much of his noble birth as of his radical political allegiances; though, in fairness to him, he also described the relationship between master and servant as the most 'degrading and offensive' form of social inequality. Although he abhorred his own class's frequently brutal and debauched treatment of serfs, when he was obliged to work in the 'signature factory' of government service he also disdained the corruption of his fellow officials and the drunkenness of the head clerks. He was aware of the class backgrounds of the Moscow circles, describing that of Stankevich as a 'mixed proletariat', and dealt uncomfortably with the effect on the westernizers of the 1840s when Nikolay Ketcher (1809–86), one of the circle, married an uneducated Russian woman: 'our pure, shining, mature circle began to be invaded by the tittle-tattle of servant girls and the bickerings of provincial governments clerks'. His young, plebeian Nihilist critics of the 1860s did most to bring out the aristocrat in him: they 'were lacking in the deportment which is given by breeding' and 'displayed the manners of the low-class pettifogger, the shop-boy and the flunkey' (Herzen, 1968, vol. 2, pp. 243, 458, 462, 481–2, 620; vol. 3, pp. 1348–50; 1995, pp. 25–6, 41).

He carried his great wealth easily, admitting that it turned him into a west European *rentier* but grateful that it gave him a weapon in his political struggle, enabling him to fund radical ventures such as Proudhon's newspaper *Le voix du peuple*, and his own press in England. He looked after his assets with the help of the Rothschild banking family, whose international clout was such that it could dissuade Tsar Nicholas from sequestering Herzen's mother's share of her husband's estate. Nevertheless, the French bourgeoisie was the class that incurred the lion's share of Herzen's contumely. This group combined the 'worst defects' of the 'brilliant nobility' and the 'crude plebes', without their good qualities; although the bourgeoisie appeared to share Herzen's supreme concern with the 'holiness of the rights of the personality', he considered that its members only played with the notion as long as it was to their own advantage and did not threaten their own exploitation of the proletarian. The essential value of 'the mean and squalid atmosphere which covers the whole of France like a green scum' was the greedy, stingy, money-grubbing pursuit of profit, and he ironically thanked God that *petite bourgeoisie* was 'incompatible with the Russian character' (Herzen, 1968, vol. 2, p. 490; 1979, p. 56; 1995, pp. 29, 56).

It is clear that gender as well as class identities were also an issue for Herzen, the lifelong Saint-Simonian dedicated to the emancipation of women. He admitted in his memoirs to an affair with a married woman during his provincial exile, and to an ungracious retreat when her husband's sudden death made her available; and also to a casual fling with a young servant after his own marriage, which he felt obliged to confess to a mortified Natalie. A passage in one of his letters from Paris contains his ruminations on feminine beauty in the various countries of Europe, including the considered view that women were better-looking beyond Russia, because they were less oppressed and better able to 'take care of themselves'. He commented on the wife of one of his circle that 'in her I learned for the first time how little can be done with logic in discussion with a woman, especially when the discussion relates to practical affairs'. His views on child-rearing were also traditional: a child saves a woman from 'crude egoism' and

> trains its mother in sacrifice, in subordinating her will, in eagerly spending her time not on herself, and trains her to indifference to all external reward, recognition, gratitude ... Without taking her out of the home, the baby transforms her into a citizen.
>
> (Herzen, 1968, vol. 2, pp. 986–7)

Nevertheless, he was proud that women had equality before the law in Russia, when in western Europe they were bound to their husbands. He penned this admiring portrait of Princess Yekaterina Romanovna Dashkov (1743–1810), president of the Russian Academy of Sciences under Catherine the Great:

> In Princess Dashkov, the personality of the Russian woman, awakened by the havoc wrought by Peter, emerges from her seclusion, displays her capacity, demands her share in politics, in science, in the reformation of Russia, and boldly takes her stand beside Catherine the Great.
>
> (Herzen, 1968, vol. 4, pp. 1585–6)

He was appalled by the attitude of French bourgeois men to their wives, in particular for regarding their pregnancies as 'improper', and by the coarseness of Englishmen which 'helps to explain how it is that women are nowhere beaten so often and so badly as in England'. Despite his admiration for Proudhon, he deplored the 'Bluebeard' attitude that the socialist displayed towards his wife, and reckoned that the choice for the bourgeois woman in Paris was 'either be a courtesan, or be bored and lost in banality and endless busyness'. He also deplored the inequality of Christian marriage, which 'delivers the wife in slavery to the husband', and the general attitude to women and sex of 'the celibate religion of Christianity' with its 'accursed immolation of the flesh'; this was taken to the limit by Protestantism, which had even cast the Virgin Mother out of its 'barn-like chapels, its factories of God's word'. However, Herzen's generally enlightened views on marriage and the relationship between the sexes were put severely to the test by his wife Nathalie's affair with Herwegh, a liaison that may well also have had some bearing on the mature views on the German national character of this youthful admirer of the land that produced Schiller and Goethe (Herzen, 1968, vol. 1, pp. 367, 372, vol. 2, pp. 474–7, 716, 822, 826, 975; 1995, p. 31, 48).

Conclusion

Herzen's stance on Europe reflected his own predicament, but surely also captures much of Russia's ambivalent European identity. He spent his Russian youth and early manhood looking to the west for inspiration and solutions to the problems he saw about him. Having escaped to the west, he became disillusioned and looked back to Russia for an alternative path to the realization of his radical social vision. His intellectual odyssey underlines a vital point: although Russia's relations with the rest of Europe are undeniably a dominating theme in its history, Russia's identity is not reducible to a set of imported west European influences. Even to the extent that the construction of the range of Russian identities is associated with such influences, the process of westernization has been a dialogue, in which ideas, techniques, mores, culture and institutions are selected, discarded, resisted, shaped and given a form that matches Russia's unique geocultural environment. Unquestionably, the balance of that dialogue has shifted. Russian culture in the eighteenth century was often imitative and deferential, but during the nineteenth century a more vigorous and independent culture became established, however uncongenial its political context, as evidenced by its most visible peaks: the poetry of Pushkin; the novels of Turgenev, Dostoevsky and Tolstoy; the plays of Chekhov; the music of Musorgsky, Rimsky-Korsakov, Borodin and Tchaikovsky; the science of Mendeleyev and Pavlov; and the mathematics of Lobachevsky.

After his death, Herzen's ideas helped inspire the Russian populism (*narodnichestvo*) of the 1870s and 1880s. The first Marxist groups were formed among the populists, and in due course Lenin, the leading Russian Marxist, raised Herzen to the pantheon of the progenitors of the Bolshevik Revolution – though whether he would have thanked Lenin for the honour is open to doubt. Herzen's antipathy for the German Marxists with whom he shared his London exile finds full expression in his memoirs, and he and Marx himself apparently managed to avoid each other. Were relations with the west any clearer after the end of the regime that Herzen and the Russian intelligentsia conspired to overthrow? In many respects the Soviet regime that succeeded the tsars faced a similar dilemma. Lenin saw 'large-scale capitalist engineering' as necessary for the realization of socialism (Lenin, 1960–80, vol. 27, p. 339), while his successor Stalin oversaw the transfer of western plant and technical expertise in the do-or-die attempt to catch up with the more advanced nations. A similar uneasy relationship with western culture persisted in the Soviet era: just as the tsars had opposed a Russian variant of an east European religion to heretical ideas from the rest of the continent, the Communist party of the Soviet Union preached hostility to the west in the name of a Russian variant of a central European critique of capitalism (Marxism-Leninism), an ideology that served to smother the culture and beliefs of the various peoples of the vast Soviet empire.

There were, then, in the Soviet era echoes of some of the main themes of Russia's ambivalent European identity encapsulated in the introduction, and to some extent reflected in Herzen's life and writings: a geographical position engendering a sense of insecurity on its European and Asian sides, and a consequent imperative to conquer or be conquered; periods of marginalization from the economic, technological, military and intellectual European mainstream, followed by uneasy accommodations with western European culture on one side, and its transmission, through the Russification of the non-Slavic peoples of its vast empire, on the other. For 500 years, Russia has been 'perpetually seen as being in some stage of transition to Europeanization' (Neumann, 1999, p. 111). It is striking that the fall of the Soviet Union was accompanied by a debate between 'westernizers' and 'nationalists' redolent of the Slavophile–westernizer controversy of the 1840s (Neumann, 1999, pp. 163–70). It remains to be seen whether the embrace of western neo-liberal economics and consumerism by the post-communist political and economic elite will generate a permanent 'insider' European identity for Russia, or whether a synthesis of 'westernizing' and 'nationalist' values will be adumbrated by some twenty-first-century Herzen, continuing Russia's ambivalent European role as a dominant 'constitutive other' in the construction of a European identity.

References

Acton, E. (1979) *Alexander Herzen and the Role of the Intellectual Revolutionary*, Cambridge, Cambridge University Press.

Bakunin, M. A. (1934–5) *Sobranie sochinenii i pisem 1828–76* [Collected Works and Letters 1828–76], 4 vols, Moscow.

Berlin, I. (1979a) *Russian Thinkers*, Harmondsworth, Penguin.

Berlin, I. (1979b) 'Introduction' to A. Herzen, *From the Other Shore* and *The Russian People and Socialism*, transl. M. Y. Budberg and R. Wollheim, Oxford, Oxford University Press.

Bowie, A. (1993) *Schelling and Modern European Philosophy: an Introduction*, London, Routledge.

Carr, E. H. (1968) *The Romantic Exiles: a Nineteenth-century Portrait Gallery*, Harmondsworth, Penguin.

Christoff, P. K. (1982) *K. S. Aksakov: a Study in Ideas*, Princeton, NJ, Princeton University Press.

Gertsen, A. I. (1954–65) *Sobranie sochinenii v tridtsati tomakh* [Collected Works in Thirty Volumes], Moscow.

Greenfeld, L. (1992) *Nationalism: Five Roads to Modernity*, Cambridge, MA/London, Harvard University Press.

Herzen, A. (1968) *My Past and Thoughts: the Memoirs of Alexander Herzen*, 4 vols, transl. C. Garnett, rev. H. Higgens, London, Chatto & Windus.

Herzen, A. (1979) *From the Other Shore* and *The Russian People and Socialism*, transl. M. Y. Budberg and R. Wollheim, Oxford, Oxford University Press.

Herzen, A. (1995) *Letters from France and Italy, 1847–51*, ed. and transl. J. E. Zimmerman, Pittsburgh, PA, University of Pittsburgh Press.

Inwood, M. (1992) *A Hegel Dictionary*, Oxford, Blackwell.

Lampert, E. (1957) *Studies in Rebellion*, London, Routledge & Kegan Paul.

Lenin, V. I. (1960–80) *Collected Works*, 47 vols, Moscow, Progress Publishers.

Malia, M. (1961) *Alexander Herzen and the Birth of Russian Socialism: 1812–1855*, Cambridge, MA, Harvard University Press.

Neumann, I. B. (1999) *Uses of the Other: 'the East' in European Identity Formation*, Manchester, Manchester University Press.

Roosevelt, P. R. (1986) *Apostle of Russian Liberalism: Timofei Granovsky*, Newtonville, MA, Oriental Research Partners.

Walicki, A. (1975) *The Slavophile Controversy: History of a Conservative Utopia in Nineteenth-century Russian Thought*, Oxford, Clarendon.

Zimmerman, J. E. (1989) *Midpassage: Alexander Herzen and European Revolution, 1847–52*, Pittsburgh, PA, University of Pittsburgh Press.

6

Joining Europe:

Polish parties and the European Union

PAUL G. LEWIS

Introduction

This chapter is about the nature of contemporary Poland and its
changing relationship with the expanding European Union. It
examines the mix of modern and traditional influences that affect
the attitudes towards EU membership held by both the Polish
population in general and the political parties that play a central role
in its new democratic order. The contemporary European Union
might be predominantly 'western' in terms of origin and
geographical location, but it is central and 'core' in terms of its
dynamic economic processes and political dominance over the
western portion of the Eurasian land mass. While many central and
east European countries spoke of 'returning to Europe' in general
terms following the end of Soviet domination in 1989, it was the
European Union rather than any more broadly constituted European
entity that they were increasingly concerned with. Poland itself is a
country that has a major claim to be regarded, in the title of one
major history, as *Heart of Europe* (Davies, 1986). But it is also part of
that more ill-defined border region whose relationship with 'Europe'
is generally regarded as problematic in terms of the marginal and
peripheral status of the eastern countries as discussed by Mark
Pittaway in Chapters 1 and 3 of this book. Poland (with nearly 40
million inhabitants) is the largest of the current EU **accession
countries** and in several respects poses some of the greatest problems
to the enlargement process as a major example of such marginality in
contemporary terms.

States that began to
negotiate their membership
of the EU in 1998.

The problematic status of the central and eastern countries within
Europe as a whole can be traced back through the centuries and has
been expressed in various ways. As far as Poland is concerned, this
does not play a part in the contemporary situation simply in terms of
the challenging accession procedures involved in the enlargement of
the present EU and the economic and political conditions imposed
on prospective members. It is also expressed in the ambivalence of

the Polish population towards the EU in terms of the combination of promise and threat that incorporation within the powerful western body can be understood to imply. Membership of the liberal-democratic, economically dynamic and wealthy European Union was enthusiastically pursued by Poland after the end of communism in 1989. In this respect its position was similar to that of most other countries of central and eastern Europe, although the intensity of this early enthusiasm was somewhat reduced as the realities of the free market and the nature of practical democratic politics became more apparent. But the development of modern Europe is not just a matter of concrete economic and political processes. Deeper-rooted questions of national identity are also involved – contestations of culture and identity within Europe – and these bear closely on the nature of the contemporary state and the conceptions of political life that have emerged in post-communist eastern Europe. The end of the highly restrictive Soviet influence over Polish national life had immediate political consequences, but also created conditions for a more gradual reconstruction of Polish identity that involved a return to older conceptions of history and religion and reconsideration of their relevance to the new circumstances of eastern Europe. As discussed in *Exploring European Identities* (Chimisso, 2003), especially Chapter 1, such features are particularly important elements in the construction of identity. They have a direct bearing on how Poles view themselves as part of a Europe critically engaged in new processes of integration.

As well as the more practical difficulties involved in the process of negotiating Poland's accession to the EU, the way in which Polish identity has evolved in the modern period also influences the rather mixed way in which 'Europe' is viewed both by the political class and by the public at large. By the time of the presidential elections of 2000, for example, the issues surrounding Poland's accession to the EU barely served to differentiate between any of the major candidates or leading political forces involved, although it was becoming clear that negotiations were encountering major problems on both sides and that sections of the Polish population were increasingly sceptical about membership. Nevertheless, the issue of Polish EU membership remained the subject of an overwhelming consensus among the main political parties, groupings and elites (Szczerbiak, 2001a, p. 109). In this respect Poland was not so different from many countries of western Europe, where voters showed considerably less enthusiasm for the EU than did governing elites and party leaders across the political spectrum as a whole (the UK constituted something of an exception to this general rule). Important to this outcome, however, was also the way in which democratic parties have developed in post-communist Poland, the way in which their organizational identities have evolved and the relation they have established with the electorate. Poland's place in Europe is therefore influenced by the specific way in which the post-communist state has developed as a modern democratic entity. But this in turn, it will be argued, has been influenced by Poland's lengthy experience in a particular location on the margins of Europe. Peripherality has not just affected Poland's relations with the rest of Europe but also represents a critical dimension of its contemporary domestic life.

This chapter focuses on the nature of Poland's national identity in modern Europe, the way in which contemporary political parties have confronted the issue of EU membership, and the attitude that the Polish people as a whole have taken towards the process of 'joining Europe'. More specifically it looks at:

1   The particular conditions under which Poland's modern national identity was formed in the nineteenth century and the specific form – or forms – it subsequently took.

2   The evolution of general Polish attitudes to EU membership.

3   The position taken by the main parties with regard to Poland's membership of the European Union.

4   The overall structure of party politics in post-communist Poland.

5   The linkage of contemporary political processes and accession issues with the evolution of Poland's peripheral status in Europe in historical and contemporary terms.

Poland's place in Europe

Poland has formed part of Europe throughout its long history (the origins of the Polish state are conventionally dated from 966), but it has been fully included in the European community only to varying degrees and has occupied different statuses within Europe as a whole. To this extent, it has also at times been excluded from what are regarded as the core processes of European development. Poland's contemporary position as an applicant for membership of the EU is just one more reflection of the country's ambiguous and peripheral status. Its identity as a member of a modern European community was particularly affected by the country's loss of statehood at the end of the eighteenth century and its recovery of national independence only after the First World War. Naturally enough, the Polish state experienced different fortunes across the centuries (including a period as a major European power of considerable wealth and cultural achievement in the sixteenth and early seventeenth centuries), but it succeeded in surviving as a political entity until its partition in 1795 at the hands of Russia, Prussia and Austria.

The loss of statehood at this critical juncture, just after the French Revolution and precisely as the tide of modern nationalism was beginning to swell, exerted a profound influence on the Polish national consciousness (or, more precisely, was a critical factor in its modern formation) and provided the basis for the stereotype of the modern Pole as strongly nationalist, fervently Catholic and continually struggling against superior powers. In distinction to the major territorial changes occurring during this period there was substantial continuity in terms of national tradition and ideas of nationhood, although the forms they took were subject to extensive change and major development. All this took place, moreover, in a socioeconomic context increasingly marked by the industrial breakthrough first seen in Britain at the end of the eighteenth century which then rapidly took root in the core areas of western Europe. One consequence of this for Poland, and eastern Europe more generally, was the growing economic tendency in the early nineteenth century towards disinvestment which became, in Andrew Janos's words, the 'starting point for the "downward drift" of the peripheries' (Janos, 2000, p. 61). Particularly badly affected were the middling classes of rural society (when, of course, urban growth in the east remained extremely limited), involving not just the *szlachta*, or petty gentry, of Poland, but also members of the aristocracy such as Prussian *Junkers*, the 'common nobility' of Hungary and Romanian *boyars* (Janos, 2000, p. 65). In Poland it was certainly the fate of such people that came to typify what many saw as the tragedy of the nation as a whole, a perspective further strengthened by the wave of nineteenth-century romanticism and the internationally renowned creations of Adam Mickiewicz (1798–1855), Poland's greatest poet.

As a modern Polish national identity developed through the nineteenth century these experiences exerted a profound influence on the process and imbued the Polish character with what were seen as very specific traits, by no means all positive. In the words of Polish historian Jerzy Jedlicki:

> Since the time of Napoleon, this culture had lived on memories, enveloped in a cocoon of nostalgia. Both gentry traditionalism and rebellious romanticism consolidated this bias. It survived for a long time, becoming a characteristic constituent feature of Polish spiritual life. The intellectual, pictorial and mythological wealth of Polish historical literature in all its genres is astounding when we compare it with the poverty and schematism of futuristic thinking and visions. Disputes about the future never reached such a high emotional temperature as disputes about the past, because Poles felt themselves to be the lords and masters only of their past.
>
> (Jedlicki, 1999, p. 213)

Another major component of this outlook was the strengthening conception of a specifically Polish-Catholic intellectual formation which served as a 'stronghold of nationality and faith, joined in a single, sacred bond'. In this view, Polishness and the church were threatened not so much by the Russification and Germanization policies of the major occupying powers (in the nineteenth century, just as in the twentieth), but more by 'Frenchifying' and 'materializing' influences. Later in the nineteenth century it was west European Protestanism, seen (as the historian Max Weber (1864–1920) was later also to argue) as the driving force of capitalism, that was perceived as a particularly virulent threat and a source of coarse materialism. Such reactionary distaste for modern western developments came close to rejecting the trajectory of contemporary European civilization as a whole (Jedlicki 1999, pp. 208, 215–17).

The romanticization of Polish gentry culture and the fondness for historical nostalgia are by no means just things of the past. Amid the tide of Americanization in the post-communist 1990s and after the withering of state-funded film production, it has been striking in more recent years how successful the home-grown historical epics derived from literary classics have been in Polish cinemas. *Pre-Spring* set in the early years of the modern Polish state, by Stefan Żeromski (1864–1925), and Mickiewicz's *Pan Tadeusz* (dealing with the fate of the early nineteenth-century gentry) and *By Fire and Sword* (depicting the Ukrainian wars of the seventeenth century) have all formed the basis of major popular productions, as has *Quo Vadis* by Henryk Sienkiewicz (1846–1916), which is set in Roman times but has – or at least had at the time of its first appearance – a strong Polish resonance in its focus on early Christian heroes in combat with a decadent pagan empire. A distinct variety of national masochism has been noted in this context (discussed in the Warsaw-based newspaper *Polityka*, 31 March 2001). But the romantic nationalism of the nineteenth century had its own critics and, as a basis for Polish national identity, was at least partly supplanted in the twentieth century by the ideas elaborated by Roman Dmowski (1864–1939), who (among other roles) was Poland's representative at the Versailles Peace Conference of 1919.

Dmowski developed a new form of Polish nationalism and identified roots for it that were quite separate from those of the old gentry tradition, of which strong traces could be seen in the views of his great competitor of the early twentieth century, Józef Piłsudski (1867–1935; generally hailed as the restorer of Poland's independence in 1918 and its president after the coup d'état of 1926). A man of urban working-class origins, Dmowski developed a 'new, plebeian nationalism that was highly critical of the defeated insurrections and fed on ethnic rivalry in a hard struggle for survival' (Walicki, 2000, pp. 14).This too has a distinct resonance in the post-communist Poland of the early twenty-first century and engages, as discussed below, with several of the currents in contemporary Polish policy in a significant way. Dmowski's nationalism had several characteristics. It was:

- mass-based and reflected the experiences of the lower classes rather than those of the gentry or aristocratic circles;

- anti-romantic and decidedly opposed to idealism and what was seen as political immaturity, appealing to more modern views about the struggle for social survival;

- an integral nationalism that placed great emphasis on the national bond as a primary form of social integration and later, after the 1926 coup, came to see this as primarily embedded in Polish Catholicism;

- associated with ideas of a homogeneous ethno-cultural nation and undivided ethnic loyalty.

From the outset, then, Dmowski 'perceived the Warsaw Jews and Germans as hostile aliens' (ibid., pp. 14–16). and by the 1930s the Dmowskiite tradition had become strongly identified with anti-semitism, an association which now makes his contribution to the evolution of the modern Polish identity a sensitive and troublesome one to explore.

Nevertheless, the twenty-one years following the restoration of Polish independence in 1918 represented the only period of independence the country enjoyed for much of the twentieth century. It was in this context yet more unfortunate that major currents in the development of Polish national identity were increasingly associated with overt sentiments of anti-semitism. Such tendencies were, however, hardly absent from any European country in the 1930s (the UK included) and were of course yet more strongly apparent in Hitler's Germany. Polish independence was in any case short-lived, as 1939 saw invasion and defeat by the German and Soviet armies. This was followed by occupation by the Nazi authorities and lengthy domination by Soviet and communist forces after the Germans were defeated. Poland's status changed once more in a fundamental way with the collapse of the Soviet empire in eastern Europe in 1989. The demise of Polish communism had been prefigured in 1980 by the welling up of a tide of popular opposition and the formation of a multi-million strong independent trade union, Solidarity, that challenged the whole basis of communist rule. Under strong influence from the Soviet Union and heightened military support for the authorities, ideological orthodoxy and communist dominance were nevertheless maintained for a few more years. But under the leadership of Mikhail Gorbachev (1985–91) from 1985 the Soviet Union decided that it would no longer maintain its outer empire by military force, and by 1989 the Polish communist authorities were prepared to re-legalize Solidarity and permit semi-contested parliamentary elections, events that paved the way for the end of Soviet domination and communist rule throughout central and eastern Europe.

This brought to the fore radically new perspectives on Poland's place in Europe. The end of communist rule saw the rapid opening up of Polish public and cultural life, the establishment of full parliamentary rule structured by competition between independent political parties, the popular election of the president (who was, between 1990 and 1995, Solidarity leader Lech Wałęsa), major reforms of economic institutions and processes that were increasingly associated with a fundamental restructuring on capitalist lines, and growing integration with the European and global economies – as well as extensive social mobility and general upheaval. Much of this broad process of transformation and social change was summed up by the idea of 'rejoining Europe' (increasingly identified in concrete terms with membership of the EU) as part of a general reorientation of Polish national life away from the interests and values embodied in Soviet Russia towards those of the Euro-Atlantic west. Another phrase commonly employed in this context was indeed that of 'integrating with the Euro-Atlantic community', reflecting the strong Polish interest in reinforcing ties with the United States. Whatever the precise form of this new western orientation, though, it was a transformation that promised both to reaffirm the strength of Poland's European roots and to provide further scope for the expression of the country's authentic national identity, rather than one imposed and modified by more powerful neighbours and broad structures of continental *Realpolitik*. Little attention, however, was initially paid to the possibility that there might be some tension or even major incompatibility between these two objectives.

The release of Poland from Soviet Russian control and the general reorientation of Polish national policy towards western Europe represented a change and redirection that enjoyed enormous popular support. The attempt to achieve EU membership was, for much of the early 1990s, endorsed by a good four-fifths of the Polish population. Even when a downturn in Polish support could be seen in the late 1990s (see Table 6.1), it was still only Romania (a country where the prospects of EU membership were, to say the least, less than immediate) that produced higher levels of approval for EU accession than those seen in Poland (Szczerbiak, 2000, p. 407).

Table 6.1 Polish support for EU membership in public opinion surveys, 1994–2000: per cent

June 1994	May 1995	May 1996	March 1997	Aug. 1997	May 1998	Dec. 1998	May 1999	Nov. 1999	May 2000	Sept. 2000
77	72	80	72	72	66	64	55	59	44	50

Source: Szczerbiak, 2000, p. 408

The politics of EU membership

Towards the end of the 1990s support in Poland for EU membership began to fall as the nature of the conditions for membership began to emerge more clearly. Leading factors in this were:

- doubts about the future of Poland's large but backward agricultural sector;

- demands for the restructuring of heavy industry, leading to fears of unemployment;

- the opening of Polish markets to relatively cheap EU imports;

- growing uncertainty about the likelihood of Poland gaining advantages from Common Agricultural Policy benefits and structural funds;

- the sheer length of the accession process and growing scepticism about western commitment to Polish membership;

- doubts about the implications for the country's national autonomy;

- growing suspicion on the part of substantial sectors of Poland's traditional and highly conservative Catholic church about west European religious liberalism and associated secular tendencies.

The early conviction that Poland's exclusion from Europe had been conclusively ended with the disappearance of the 'Iron Curtain' now seemed less secure. Poland's full inclusion was partly obstructed by the nature of the processes that governed the expansion of the EU, but it was also conditioned by aspects of Polish national culture and the nature of modern Polish identity.

The growing popular scepticism about EU membership, or even the outright rejection of the idea in some quarters, was hardly reflected in government policy, formal political processes or even the range of options expressed in the policies of the different parties. This was perhaps not so surprising at the time of the parliamentary elections of 1997, but the more sceptical tendencies were still not particularly prominent when presidential elections took place in 2000. The president, Aleksander Kwaśniewski (supported by the post-communist but now thoroughly social democratic Union of the Democratic Left), won an overwhelming victory in the first round of these elections, gaining 54 per cent of the vote. He was strongly in favour of EU membership. So too were both his main competitors, Andrzej Olechowski (an independent candidate with centre-right credentials, who won 17 per cent of the vote) and Marian Krzaklewski (the candidate of the Solidarity-supported electoral coalition that dominated parliament, who gained 16 per cent). Subsequent analysis of each candidate's supporters showed that they held remarkably similar views on the European issue, being 'equally, albeit lukewarmly, supportive of Poland's entry to the European Union' (Jasiewicz, 2001, p. 14).

It is necessary to look to the fourth-placed candidate to find someone with more sceptical inclinations. Jarosław Kalinowski, leader of the Polish Peasant Party and thus representative of a parliamentary body (albeit one of the minor opposition groups), gained 6 per cent of the vote. He contended that EU membership posed some threat to Polish identity and sovereignty, although he qualified this position with the view that the 'level of threat could be limited by the pursuit of wise domestic policies' (reported in *Polityka*, 7 October 2000). It was only among the other eight candidates, none representative of the party groups in parliament and only gaining 7 per cent of the vote between them, that more strongly articulated anti-EU views could be found. Fifth place in these elections (with 3 per cent of the vote) was taken by Andrzej Lepper, leader of the Peasant Self-Defence movement and organizer of widespread and sometimes violent demonstrations in support of peasant interests and against the consequences of EU agricultural policies in the Polish countryside. Similarly, Jan Łopuszański (with a 0.8 per cent share of the vote) was a former member of the Christian National Union group in parliament who had formed his own organization, Polish Accord, in April 1999 to campaign explicitly against membership of the European Union.

The growing euroscepticism among the Polish public was thus poorly reflected in the votes cast for presidential candidates, and most of these went to Lepper as an extremist non-parliamentary representative of a large, though still essentially marginal group (by the mid 1990s only 27 per cent of Poles were mostly employed in agriculture). The Polish parliament remained strongly pro-European and the government firmly committed to joining the EU at the first possible opportunity. From a broader political perspective there was just no alternative to 'Europe' or to Poland's integration into the expanding EU. An isolationist future was hardly realistic and held few attractions, while greater dependence on the east was scarcely a viable option for a number of very obvious reasons. Relations with the

United States were highly regarded, but the Americans also favoured a more integrated Europe and encouraged Poland to seek its future in that arena. Thus there remained a powerful view in parliament and among the political elite more generally in favour of EU membership.

Party policies and European integration

Following the 1997 elections the government comprised a right-wing coalition of Solidarity Electoral Action and the Freedom Union, who together commanded a majority of the parliament's 460 seats. This replaced the left-wing coalition of the Union of the Democratic Left and the Polish Peasant Party that had governed from 1993 to 1997. Members of parliament were drawn from five main groups, most of which were broadly pro-European but with varying degrees of enthusiasm and support for Poland's accession effort. The general consensus in the presidential contest of 2000 was thus based on an existing parliamentary agreement and a broad lack of differentiation between the leading parties. As there had undoubtedly been some shift in public opinion during the three years between elections, this agreement tended to mask the differences that did exist and to minimize the uncertainties emerging about EU membership.

Table 6.2 Majority representation in the Polish parliament, 1997

	Percentage of vote	Number of seats
Solidarity Electoral Action	33.8	201
Union of Democratic Left	27.1	164
Freedom Union	13.4	60
Polish Peasant Party	7.3	27
Movement for Polish Reconstruction	5.6	6

Source: Markowski, 1999, p. 234

The policy of the Polish government, whether dominated by left- or right-wing forces, barely shifted on European issues after 1997 and there remains a strong consensus in elite circles that Poland's future lies with the European Union. Indeed the whole idea of contemporary Polish politics as structured around a division between right- and left-wing parties is itself open to question. Issues of political structures and the nature of the processes by which concerns surface and are addressed in the political arena remain uncertain in Poland, as in other countries of post-communist eastern Europe. The quality and character of the democratic process in this part of Europe remain open to some question, as indeed they do (although often for rather different reasons) in other parts of Europe.

Nevertheless, there are divergences of orientation and emphasis on European issues between the major political actors. Although there was a broad consensus on the desirability of Poland's membership of the European Union in the parties' manifestos for the 1997 elections (a slightly later programme of the Peasant party has been used for this purpose), some different orientations and certain variations of emphasis can be identified. A survey of the parties' statements on the issue of 'Europe' or, more generally, Polish membership of the European Union suggests some key characteristics:

- any mention of European issues invariably occurs at the end of the party's programme or election manifesto; as it is preceded and generally overshadowed by issues of domestic policy the European dimension appears as something of an addendum to these;

- the approach of the main parliamentary parties is emphatically positive but couched in relatively broad terms;

- certain common features and references recur, but there are also differences in emphasis.

Samples of the parties' statements are presented in the extract below. You should try to identify some of their major features in the light of the discussion above.

Documentary extracts

For the antecedents of Solidarity Electoral Action see note on p. 18 of Chapter 1.

[The victor of 1997 was **Solidarity Electoral Action**, an electoral coalition of over forty different bodies, the largest and most important of which was the Solidarity trade union. It was a broadly right-wing force that stood for traditional values such as those of nation, religion and the family, but it also supported workers' interests and was by no means opposed to state intervention in the economy. Its electoral programme in 1997 contained the commitment that:]

> We shall be an active participant in processes of international cooperation; we shall aspire to the creation of a united Europe as a Europe of the Fatherlands composed of free nations. We are emphatically in favour of the most rapid acquisition possible by Poland of full Nato membership. Integration with the European Union creates the real possibility for us to achieve on equal terms a direct

influence on how a new order will be formed in Europe. In this way we shall preserve our own identity and cooperate in the unity of a continent based on the Christian roots of our civilization.

Entry into Nato and the European Union will dynamize Poland's development and economic growth. Support from democratic and market reforms will strengthen our position in the international arena and assist in the stabilization of central Europe. In creating permanent foundations for a solid community of the countries of Europe and the Atlantic area, Poland and the world will be able to enter the twenty-first century in safety.

(Translated from Gebethner, 1997, p. 252)

[The **Union of the Democratic Left** was the main left-wing force in the election and was composed of some thirty different political and social organizations. Its main component was the Social Democracy of the Polish Republic, a party formed in 1990 and largely comprising at that time members of the former ruling Communist party. It made several points as follows:]

Poland in the European family

- completion of the process of ensuring compliance of the law with that of the European Union;

- development of a pro-export economic policy; ...

- modernization and restructuring of Polish agriculture (as described in earlier sections), and in particular:

- integration of the Agricultural Market Agency with the intervention system of the European Union;

- aid for the Agricultural Chambers and farmers' branch organizations engaged in the promotion of Polish farm products in the EU market;

- broadening the range of access to pre-accession EU funds for the development of rural infrastructure and the processing of farm produce;

- measures for the effective long-term restructuring of heavy industry, including armaments, steel and mining;

- opposition to unfair competition and measures against dumping and excessive imports;

- organization and support of educational measures with the framework of the 'Poland in Europe' campaign.

  The above activities will ensure that Poland integrates with Nato and prepares its economy for integration with the European Union. Entry into a European 'Fatherland of Fatherlands' will allow Poles to live better and more securely.

  (Translated from Gebethner, 1997, pp. 327–8)

[The **Freedom Union** was a centrist party formed by old Solidarity activists and supporters of the first post-communist prime minister and presidential candidate Tadeusz Mazowiecki. It maintained its distance from the contemporary Solidarity Trade Union, the politically active representatives of the church establishment and former president Lech Wałęsa. Its leader was the rigorously liberal economist Leszek Balcerowicz, who was also greatly disliked by the more economically protectionist elements within Solidarity Electoral Action. It emphasized:]

- preparation for Polish entry into the European Union in accordance with Poland's national interests and with assurance for the protection of the economic sectors which might be threatened by operations during the first phase of EU membership;

- efforts to ensure that the enlargement of Nato and the European Union also encompasses Poland's neighbours and countries with which we have been linked for centuries of history ...

  Reform activities essential for the success of our foreign policy are also necessary if we wish to pull Poland away from decades of relative backwardness. These efforts will bring us greater international security and a faster rate of development if we bring a reformed Poland into Nato and the European Union. Without the completion of domestic reform the achievement of national goals may not be possible ...

  It will be a priority for the Freedom Union to restore Poland's authority and credibility in the international arena and to take all necessary steps to achieve proposals for Nato membership in 1999 and the quickest possible membership of the European Union. A matter of fundamental importance is the assurance that Poland enters Nato and the European Union in an economic, military and systemic condition that guarantees the achievement of all benefits accessible to a 40 million-strong sovereign state located in the heart of Europe and deriving its strength from the centuries' old traditions of ties with a Christian and democratic Europe ...

We aim to prepare for Poland's entry into the European Union in accordance with the Polish national interest while ensuring the protection of those sectors of the economy for which entry into the EU offers major opportunities for long-term development but for which there are certain threats in the initial period.

(Translated from Gebethner, 1997, pp. 294–6)

[The **Polish Peasant Party** was, as its name clearly indicates, the prime representative of the farming community which continued to represent a substantial proportion of Polish society. Unlike extra-parliamentary forces, it remained largely committed to the government and broad parliamentary consensus that EU membership was a desirable objective and that Polish agriculture was in need of a major transformation. Understandably, however, it was sympathetic to the needs of the largely backward Polish agricultural sector and the serious grievances of the farming population. This duality was clearly expressed in its programme and overall view of European integration, as set out in 2000:]

Polish membership of the European Union creates a long-term perspective for national development and participation in processes of global progress, but requires an enormous effort on the part of the whole society based on a sensible economic policy. The two-year experience of negotiation for Polish membership of the Union, as well as the practice of implementing the European Agreement about Polish associate membership of the EC, confirms this position and directs attention to the importance of the Polish government securing membership conditions guaranteeing a positive balance of benefits from the outset as well as taking advantage of the pre-membership period to strengthen the potential of the Polish economy and raise the level of its competitiveness ... We reaffirm the position that the aspiration of achieving Polish membership of the European Union, like our earlier entry into Nato, is a choice that should serve several objectives: making up for delays in 'civilizational development', catching up in levels of economic development and assuring conditions for all-round Polish development ...

We speak out for a model of the European Union that secures the maintenance of the national identity of member states and their equal participation in the taking of the most important decisions for their future, building at the same time a Europe of the Fatherlands. We must also remind people that by joining the European Union Poland will reclaim its due position in the family of European nations in accordance with the words of our great countryman [Pope] John Paul II: 'Poland always was part of Europe, is still and always will be.' We bring to a common Europe our own traditions, national identity and wealth of national values, the legacy of more than 1000 years of statehood, as well as a considerable human, social and cultural potential. With its market of nearly 40 million consumers, great reserves of untapped socioeconomic potential, and centuries' long culture Poland will make a solid contribution to European integration ...

The Peasant Party's area of particular interest thus remains agriculture ... Our evaluation of the state of preparedness of Polish agriculture and its institutional structures for EU membership is critical. It is in a dangerous state, and its role in the national economy remains underestimated both by the government and by broader social circles.

(Translated from 'Documents of the Peasant Party's VII Congress', 2000)

[The **Movement for Polish Reconstruction** was a fairly small and politically marginal party founded by Jan Olszewski after his relatively good results in the 1995 presidential elections. The party's general position was right wing and quite nationalist, little different from a number of the groups involved in Solidarity Electoral Action. Its reasonable success in the 1997 parliamentary elections was based on Olszewski's personal reputation, but his poor prognosis in the run-up to the 2000 presidential elections led him to withdraw before the ballot was held. In 1997 the party's programme included the following on European integration:]

Poland cannot remain in a grey zone between Russia and western Europe. Poland's participation in European economic structures will require time and money. This must be prepared for by modernizing agriculture, regaining self-sufficiency in agricultural production and achieving a positive balance in the foreign trade of farm produce; modernization of the production sector, the

> radical elevation of enterprise productivity, and the development of strong export sectors.
>
> We shall strengthen economic cooperation with the countries of east-central Europe, with particular emphasis on the development of a common agricultural market. We shall conduct an economic policy directed to ... the creation of a highly qualified negotiating team capable of representing effectively Polish interests in the process of European integration.
>
> (Translated from Gebethner, 1997, p. 344)

EXERCISE

Draw up a checklist of the major features these statements contain and try to compare the five parliamentary parties on this basis. An example of how the conclusions might be presented appears in Table 6.3 below.

DISCUSSION

The key points are:

- Most parties' statements include an emphasis on the Christian roots of European civilization, although this does not appear in the statement of the Union of the Democratic Left. The Movement for Polish Reconstruction does not mention this in its relatively brief statement on European integration, although the general preamble to the party's programme does emphasize that its programme is based 'on the Christian tradition and the principles of the church's social teaching'.

- In the programme of the Union of the Democratic Left this feature is replaced by a more general reference to a 'European family'.

- The principles alluded to by several parties include that of Polish sovereignty and a 'Europe of the Fatherlands' (a relatively neutral term, it should be added, and more reminiscent of the 'Europe des patries' invoked by former French president Charles de Gaulle (1958–69) than conveying any aggressive overtones that the German word 'Vaterland' might have).

Table 6.3   Checklist of parties' views on European integration

	Solidarity Electoral Action	Union of Democratic Left	Freedom Union	Polish Peasant Party	Movement for Polish Reconstruction
Christian roots of Europe highlighted	✓		✓	✓	(✓)
Poland as member of European family		✓			
'Europe of Fatherlands'	✓	✓		✓	
Equality of EU member states	✓			✓	
Importance of central European links			✓		✓
Primacy of socioeconomic reform	✓	✓	✓	✓	✓

- There is a stress on the need for Poland to join the European Union on equal terms. This is associated with a general concern for Poland's national identity and the fairness with which the central and east European countries might expect to be treated in the process of European integration.

- The statements emphasize Poland's intrinsic strength, the significance of its national legacy and the extent of its potential contribution to the European community.

- There is a universal acknowledgement of the need for modernization and socioeconomic reform, accompanied by a particular emphasis on agriculture and its clear need for reform in association with or prior to membership of the EU, and whatever further change and economic arrangements are necessary to ensure that Polish interests are not disadvantaged.

A study of the policies and activities of the parties in the 1997 elections (Kucharczyk, 1999, p. 220) has thus drawn three broad conclusions:

1   Behind the public consensus for Poland's entry lay a range of attitudes which fell into two broad groups representing different philosophies of integration. The first (characteristic of the Freedom Union) was that domestic reforms should proceed apace to secure EU membership at the earliest possible opportunity, while the second (represented by the Polish Peasant Party) expressed the view that the overall success of the project

was totally dependent on the strong determination and unyielding approach that should be adopted by negotiators in order to secure the most advantageous position for Poland.

2   A form of political correctness nevertheless dictated that substantive differences of view were disguised as matters of technical detail, particularly in the emphasis placed on the pace of integration.

3   The two groups that could be described as euro-enthusiasts were the Freedom Union and the Union of the Democratic Left, although the latter was particularly strong in terms of rhetoric and paid relatively little attention to the compatibility of its programme with the stated opinions of the European Commission.

In the context of Poland's dominant left/right-wing cleavage, then, it is not difficult to see how 'Europe' and issues of European integration fitted in with the consensus of the broad elite. While parties and their supporters might have differed on their appraisal of the past and the assessment of the communist period, the question of a European future was considerably less contentious – particularly as the main issues requiring government decision had yet to emerge. As in other respects, however, the position of the Polish Peasant Party emerges as somewhat different. This was clearly reflected in surveys of the views of potential supporters of the main parties (see Table 6.4). In line with the views of the population overall, between January 1999 and September 2000 there was a distinct drop in the level of support for EU membership, although it remained considerably higher among the identifiable supporters of three of the four main parties than among Poles as a whole. The exception was the Peasant Party, where EU support was waning fast. But there was also a significant drop among supporters of the Democratic Left, although such views diverged from the formal statements of the party's leaders on this issue.

Table 6.4 Parties' (potential electorate) supporters in agreement with Polish membership of the EU

	January 1999	September 2000
Freedom Union	82	79
Solidarity Electoral Action	74	67
Union of Democratic Left	73	60
Polish Peasant Party	51	35

Source: Stadtmüller, 2000, p. 39; Szczerbiak, 2001b, p. 21

Visions of Europe and, more specifically, of the European Union have nevertheless been sufficiently diverse to encompass the various parties' contrasting views of the continent not just as a traditional, Christian and civilizational whole but also as a modern, economically dynamic, reform-orientated social entity. Certain Polish parties clearly find particular elements of the European conception more appealing than others, but there has been little as yet that forces them to choose between the various components of the European vision. The ways in which political cleavages and the orientations of particular parties have developed in post-communist Poland also play a part in this.

The structure of Polish politics

The supporters of the main right- and left-wing forces in Poland as a whole were distinguished primarily by their ideological self-placement (where people place themselves on the political spectrum), itself largely derived from attitudes towards the communist past and views on moral and cultural issues. Such views cut across different social groups and encouraged parties to take a relatively undifferentiated approach to the electorate. With one partial exception, it was difficult to see any party claiming to represent just one specific social group in Polish society. Rather, the main parties' electoral strategy was to win over as much of the electorate as possible. Differences were more strongly expressed in terms of attitudes to the church and the communist period, with the Union of the Democratic Left arguing for the principle of separating church and state and for a balanced assessment of the communist period. Only the Polish Peasant Party, understandably enough, focused its attention on the interests of a distinct group and sought to favour rural interests. During the election campaign the Democratic Left, for example, stressed its economic competence and pragmatism, as well as the need for broad-based reform to hasten the process of integration with Europe. On the other hand, Solidarity Electoral Action placed an emphasis on the youth vote in its campaign and organized a number of pop concerts; it generally played down issues of economic policy and stressed the need for a full break with communism, the symbolism of the early Solidarity movement and the spirit of national unity, while its emphasis on the slogan of 'Poland, Freedom, Family' reflected old-fashioned simplicity as well as an appeal to 'traditional values'.

In terms of electoral profiles, the various parties drew their support from all identifiable segments of the population – with the significant exception of the Peasant Party, which gained 7 per cent of votes overall, but 38 per cent of the farmers' vote and 17 per cent of the rural electorate as a whole. The only other party to see a similar concentration of its voting support was the Freedom Union, which gained 13 per cent of votes overall but received 25 per cent of the votes cast by the better educated, 25 per cent of those of economic specialists and 21 per cent of those of managers (Szczerbiak, 1999, pp. 1405–20).

The character of Poland's recently established parties has also played a role in maintaining the somewhat superficial consensus on the issue of EU membership. Political parties in the traditional sense are only partly developed in much of post-communist central and eastern Europe, and while they generally appear as the main actors on the political scene they are not strongly institutionalized (Lewis, 2000, pp. 119–22). For example, both Solidarity Electoral Action and the Union of the Democratic Left were electoral coalitions rather than permanent political organizations and included a number of small, though formally constituted parties.

The concept of left and right in political terms is also diffuse in contemporary Poland (although it should be acknowledged that it is not easy to distinguish, in particular, much of an ideologically coherent left in contemporary west European politics either). Left and right generally emerge as a weakly defined line of cleavage throughout central and east European politics where market processes and capitalist economies are still being constructed after decades of state control and public ownership of most significant economic assets. Broadly speaking, in the west left-wing forces are perceived as favouring principles of social equality and a higher level of state intervention in economic and social processes (and are thus seen as reformist), while the right is associated with a more *laissez-faire* approach to economic organization and the social structure as a whole (and is thus more 'conservative' in nature). However, the issue is more confused in Poland and other central and east European countries emerging from decades of communist rule. Here, is the 'right' that is reformist and radical in the post-communist context as it intervenes to privatize state assets and construct a capitalist economy, while the 'left' remains associated with the personnel, institutions and processes of the former communist system, and is to this extent conservative. On the other hand, historically, the west European left has also been associated with positions that are socially more liberal, and while this linkage has not always emerged in contemporary central and eastern Europe it has become generally characteristic of positions adopted by Polish parties. Moreover, generally speaking, in western Europe stances on European integration have not been split along the left/right division and it is even less likely that this has been the case in central and eastern Europe. Nevertheless, the left/right distinction remains an important one in the analysis of Polish politics and is one of the key ways in which the different political forces are identified.

The precise components of left- and right-wing political identities vary throughout central Europe. Detailed investigation, using extensive social surveys, has suggested that among the post-communist countries in this area the established left–right distinction where the economic dimension of political choice remains dominant is particularly prominent in the Czech Republic. However, this dimension has been far less prominent in Poland; in particular, there were considerable differences in the economic policies of the various groups that made up the centre-right governing coalition after 1997.

Until it fell apart in June 2000, the governing coalition was composed of forces associated with the Solidarity trade union, together with the Freedom Union party led by Leszek Balcerowicz. The Solidarity grouping, as well as other interests identified with broad nationalist and traditional religious perspectives, generally supported state intervention to protect the old working class, mitigate the effects of heavy industrial decline and cushion the effects of market forces on traditional farming groups. But Balcerowicz, who was also a vice-minister, had overseen the economic shock therapy introduced in 1990 which provided for the rapid introduction of market forces and radical transformation of the Polish economy along capitalist lines, and gave as little support as possible to declining industries and the unproductive sectors of the former communist economy. Moreover, the traditional, nationalist component of the right was generally more eurosceptic, but such views did not dominate the governing coalition as a whole. While government in Poland was not especially ineffective, lines of policy were often confused and some issues simply fudged. It terms of EU accession too, such divergences between political allies had not been that important: 'rhetoric to one side, in the early and mid 1990s, the question of Poland's relationship with the EU was not of fundamental concern to either parties or their supporters and voters' (Antoszewski, 2000, p. 82).

However, while the diversity of economic perspectives often made coherent government a hazardous affair and the formulation of economic policy a particular difficulty after 1997, it was not necessarily a source of confusion for Polish voters in electoral terms and was not in itself seen as especially problematic. Such issues of structure and political orientation were more comprehensible in the light of the broad trajectory of Poland's historical and political development. In the Polish context 'left' and 'right' were generally understood to refer 'more to a set of ideological and moral-cultural attitudes – which were, in turn, often rooted in, and derived from, different assessments of the communist past – rather than to attitudes to a number of socio-economic issues' (Szczerbiak, 1999, p. 1420). The strength of the religious commitment, its close association with a historically rooted national identity and the ease with which such orientations coalesced with blanket, and rather superficial, appraisals of the communist period all contributed to the emergence of a specifically Polish pattern of party politics in the relatively short post-communist period.

The significance of these somewhat diffuse value orientations in determining the main lines of cleavage that separate right and left in contemporary Poland should not simply be identified with political nostalgia or the influence of a backward-looking national culture. Polish national identity has been sharply marked, as I have pointed out, by the conditions of its modern formation and the path of its subsequent turbulent development. The great strength of Polish nationalism and the population's attachment to the Catholic faith have been widely commented on, and are notable even against the background of strong nationalist currents throughout Europe as a whole in the nineteenth and twentieth centuries. Such features can be understood to exert a special influence on contemporary political alignments and the particular place that European issues occupy in Polish discourse.

Traditions of peripherality and contemporary party politics

Poland's historical status as part of the European periphery can thus be clearly seen to impinge on the structure and content of contemporary politics. The particular experience of Poland's peripheral status – from historical, cultural and political perspectives as well as the obviously geographic – affects not just the country's external relations but also the internal pattern of party politics and the way it has responded to the demands of post-communist democracy. In this respect the discussion in the following reading, from Tomasz Zarycki's 'Politics in the periphery' (2000), throws a certain light on the dynamics of the contemporary situation and explores issues of Polish identity in relation to broader questions of European development.

In the following section I will try to show how and why the Polish 'Left–Right' axis can be interpreted as a centre–periphery cleavage.

The 'Left–Right' cleavage as a form of the 'centre vs. periphery' cleavage

Using the 'international' perspective, we can look at the countries dominating Poland during the past two centuries as political and cultural centres. Polish national culture should be seen in this perspective as a peripheral one, resisting the Russian, Prussian and Austrian occupation in the 19th century, later the Soviet and German supremacy and, finally, a broadly defined Western domination. As far as the interpretation of the structure of the political scene is concerned, the centre–periphery cleavage would have the form of a conflict over the attitude towards the central culture. The divide would run between hard-liners defending the 'peripheral' Polish culture and softliners ready for compromise and a partial or total acceptance of the dominant culture. In other terms, we could speak about a conflict between those accepting the peripheral status of the country and those contesting it. During the entire 19th century, i.e. the period of the partitions, the Polish territory could be seen as composed of peripheral regions belonging to three different states. The occupied Polish land was in most cases distant from the centres of the dominating states (Berlin was the closest), distinct in languages (Russian and Polish belong to the Slavonic family of languages but they are quite different and most of their speakers find them mutually incomprehensible, while German is not understood at all), distinct in religion (with the exception of Austria), distinct in cultural and political traditions and in several other respects.[1]

During the communist period Poland could be regarded as the periphery of the Soviet empire. Moscow decided not to impose the predominant Russian culture on Poland directly but chose instead to use its local communist version based on the Polish language and selected Polish national traditions.[2] The Communists reinterpreted most of Polish history and embarked on a cultural homogenisation of the country based on a Polish version of the Soviet model. Moreover, Moscow had to give up its early ambition to eradicate the influence exerted in Poland by the Catholic

---

[1] For a synthetic discussion of the development of distinct political cultures in three different occupational zones see [Hubert] Tworzecki, *Parties and Politics in Post-1989 Poland* [Boulder, 1996], pp. 83–89. See also for an analysis of the social and economic policies of the three empires occupying the Polish territory Norman Davies, *God's Playground. A History of Poland: Volume II: 1795 to the Present* (Oxford, 1981).

[2] See for example Wojciech Roszkowski, *Historia Polski 1914–1990* (Warsaw, 1992), pp. 194–196 and elsewhere.

Church. Although the Church was restricted in its public activities during the entire period of communist rule, it remained independent of the state. In Poland, the outer periphery of the Soviet empire and one of the most liberal countries of the communist block, the anti-communist opposition, although banned and persecuted, acted in organised forms, sometimes openly, at least from the mid-1970s. The anti-communist 'Solidarity' trade union can be viewed in this context as a form of movement of peripheral resistance against the central culture. On the other hand, the Communist Party and its members and proponents can be viewed as supporters of the centre, more susceptible to the Soviet nationalisation process.

The attitude towards the occupying powers (or, in other words, the centre) was one of the main issues dividing Poles during the 19th and 20th centuries. The period of the partitions was marked by dramatic uprisings and internal conflicts over the strategy of behaviour towards them. The main political cleavage during the inter-war period had its roots back in the late 19th century and dominated the Polish political scene until 1939. It was symbolised by the two leading political figures of that period – Roman Dmowski and Józef Piłsudski. They represented two completely different models of the reconstruction of the Polish state. Their strategies may seem incoherent if we do not take into account the peripheral status of Poland. Piłsudski, originally the leader of the Polish Socialist Party, advocated the separation of church and state, compulsory secular education for all and equal rights for all citizens irrespective of their nationality (ethnicity). Dmowski, the leader of the National Democrats, advocated construction of a modern nation-state and cultural unification, but 'viewed the church as the director of the nation's moral life and sought "an appropriate position" for the church in the state'.[3] One may notice here an apparent paradox. While the construction of modern nation-states in most Western countries implied efforts at reducing the influence of the Catholic Church, Dmowski saw it as the main tool of cultural consolidation. This can be explained by the fragility of the Polish state and, earlier, absence of statehood, for which the Catholic Church was viewed as a substitute. This notwithstanding, the crucial difference between Piłsudski and Dmowski concerned international politics.[4] Dmowski saw Germany

---

[3]   [Sharon Werning] Rivera, 'Historical cleavages or transition mode? [*Party Politics*, 2, 2, 1996, pp. 177–208], p. 185.

[4]   Henryk Wereszycki, *Historia polityczna Polski 1864–1918* (Wroclaw, 1990), pp. 230–233 and elsewhere.

as the most powerful neighbour of Poland and hence the most dangerous. In his view, Germany had not only economic and military superiority over Poland but, even more importantly, cultural prevalence. Therefore, Dmowski viewed Russia as a better potential partner because, although more powerful than Poland economically and militarily, it did not exert the same influence as Germany and was at least Poland's equal culturally. Dmowski did not see the Russian culture as menacing, unless imposed on Poles by force. On the other hand, he perceived the German culture as a danger to Polish national identity. In some ways, Piłsudski's vision was the opposite. He could not imagine Russia as a Polish ally but neither did he believe in Poland's ability to challenge Germany without assistance. His solution to this problem lay in the idea of a federation of nation-states along the Russian and German borderlands (the region between the Black Sea and the Baltic). Of course, this project alluded to the old Polish–Lithuanian Commonwealth. In Piłsudski's idealistic vision, Poles, Lithuanians, Ukrainians, Belarussians and, possibly, other nations should establish a federation based on an equal status of all member-nations and a common interest in defence against Germany, Russia and other potential enemies. Thus, we could say that the socialist Piłsudski, seemingly more 'progressive' than the nationalist Dmowski, was nevertheless much more old-fashioned and backward-looking in his geopolitical views.

I would argue that the crucial difference between Dmowski and Piłsudski resided in their international rather than domestic programmes. To some extent, one could see domestic policy as being determined by foreign circumstances. Dmowski saw Russia as a lesser centre than Germany and hoped for a peripheral alliance between Russia and Poland against the 'predominant centre'. Undoubtedly, even if more powerful than Poland, Russia has been and still is a peripheral country in relation to the Western 'centre'. This is best manifested by an analysis of the Russian political scene, always dominated by the conflict concerning the country's attitude toward Europe and Western culture (earlier 'Westernisers vs. Slavophiles', today 'Democrats/Liberals vs. Communists/Statists').[5] Piłsudski, instead of an alliance with Russia, advocated weakening the Romanov empire (later the Soviet Union) by creating new states (which would form a federation) on its peripheries. Hence

This debate is discussed in Chapter 5 above.

---

[5] For discussion of the importance of attitudes towards the West in modern Russian politics see Vladimir Shlapentokh, '"Old", "New" and "Post" Liberal Attitudes Toward the West: From Love to Hate', *Communist and Post-Communist Studies*, 31, 3, 1998, pp. 199–216.

he was less optimistic about the strength of the Polish culture and state than Dmowski, who believed in Poland's cultural homogenisation and the nationalisation (i.e. polonisation) of the Ukrainian, Lithuanian and other ethnic groups located within its borders.

Today, the cleavage described above is only a historical memory. Both concepts – a federation with Ukraine and Lithuania and an alliance with Russia – are purely abstract. The change in the international situation after World War II completely redefined Polish politics. However, one element of it remains intact and deserves more attention. It is the alliance between the Roman Catholic Church and the national opposition in their struggle against foreign centres. Rokkan[6] sees it as a part of a larger process, in which the 'Catholic Church played a major role in the development of peripheral nationalism in some of the territories of the Counter-reformation Europe'. He mentions Poland and Lithuania as examples of the alliance between the Church and nationalist or secessionist leaders against the rulers at the centre. The same phenomenon is also noted by Martin[7] in his 'general theory of secularisation'. He quotes Poland, Malta and Eire as the best examples of the influences of external domination on religiosity. He argues that 'the historic role of the church as guardian of a culture and as a substitute state leads to the accretion of further roles and these are carried forward in a relatively undifferentiated form with the onset of independence and/or industrialisation. Even the advent of classic internal tensions, such as affected Poland between the wars and Malta in the 1960s, does not break this indissoluble union and compromises have to be arrived at much more favourable to the church than in countries like France or Italy'.

In the 19th century the strongest conflicts between the Catholic Church and the state appeared, of course, in the Prussian and Russian partition zones. The German cultural unification project led by Bismarck was a classic case of the construction of a modern nation-state. The aggressive 'Kulturkampf' (struggle for culture) in the Prussian part of Poland (mainly in the province of Wielkopolska), which included a range of anti-Catholic policies, resulted in the domination of this part of occupied Poland by

---

[6] Stein Rokkan, with Angus Campbell, Per Torsvik & Henry Valen, *Citizens, Elections, Parties; Approaches to the Comparative Study of the Processes of Development* (New York, 1970), pp. 128.

[7] David Martin, *A General Theory of Secularisation* (Oxford, 1975), pp. 55.

ardent supporters of the National Democrats (Dmowski's party).[8] Russia sought to russify the Catholic Church on its Polish territory and isolate it from Rome. These efforts, however, ended in complete failure.[9] Only in the Catholic Austro-Hungarian empire was the role of the Church more ambiguous and the national policy of Vienna far from the 'nation-state' model. It could be seen rather as an attempt at building an alternative Habsburg model.[10]

In general, the alliance of the Catholic Church and the Polish traditionalist camp was responsible for the very strong connection between national and religious identity and for the obvious dependence today between level of religiosity and support for the hard-liner (traditionalist/anti-communist) option. The religious setting of the Left–Right conflict has introduced a related element of moral judgement. As examples of this phenomenon one could point to the accusations by the hard-liners (anti-communists) that the post-communists had betrayed the national interest during the communist period (by cooperating with the Soviet occupiers) and that they appropriated state assets when the period of privatisation began. On the other hand, the Social Democrats, who deny any connection with communist ideology, see the anti-communists (cultural traditionalists) as parochial and authoritarian nationalists and dangerous religious fanatics. Consequently, the Left–Right cleavage has acquired a very emotional and persistent character. Today, although the Soviet domination over Poland is over, the Left–Right conflict has not ceased to dominate the political scene and discussions over the moral interpretation of the communist period still remain the central element of the political dispute. In Lipset–Rokkan language, we could probably speak of a 'freezing' of this cleavage.

Viewed from this perspective, the Left–Right cleavage could be compared with the main political conflict in Ireland, which is also largely dominated by attitudes towards foreign domination. Just like Poland, Ireland has experienced the alliance of the Catholic Church with the peripheral national culture. Consequently, there is an exceptionally high level of religiosity in both countries compared with the rest of Europe and the social and political meaning of religiosity is very pronounced. The Polish post-communist Social Democrats (SLD) and the anti-communist Solidarity (AWS [Solidarity Electoral Action]) could be compared

[8] Wereszycki, *Historia polityczna Polski 1864–1918*, pp. 100–109.

[9] Wereszycki, *Historia polityczna Polski 1864–1918*, pp. 61–64.

[10] See for example Ernest Gellner, *Nations and Nationalism* (Oxford, 1983).

with [the Irish parties] Fine Gael and Fiana Fail respectively. On the basis of such a comparison we can predict that the Left–Right conflict over historical issues will dominate Polish politics for a long time to come, just as happened in Ireland, where it has been continuing already for several decades since independence.

However, the prediction of the continuation of the Polish Left–Right conflict in its present form on the basis of the Irish experience can be misleading. While in the Irish case the British culture remains the central culture, the international context of the situation in Poland, which, as I said earlier, has been the political determinant, has changed completely with the collapse of the Soviet Union. The centre has moved to the broadly defined West. Although the post-communist vs. anti-communist cleavage still dominates, a new axis of political conflict is in the process of developing, based on the attitude toward the West. Sosnowska[11] considers that the attitude toward the West is already the main Polish political cleavage. Kitschelt[12] also notices an international dimension to the libertarian–authoritarian axis. He argues that 'libertarian positions embrace integration in the Western economic civilisation and sphere, whereas authoritarians insist on national autonomy to protect a unique cultural heritage that provides a line of defence against the libertarian civilisation'. I believe that this unequivocal interpretation is premature. At least in Poland, issues like decommunisation and the interpretation of the communist past still dominate the dispute over the attitude toward the West.

The emerging cleavage can be viewed as a product of the gradual transformation of the traditional Left–Right conflict. The new peripheral (traditional) option will be represented by peasants (left authoritarians) and, to some extent, AWS (anti-communist/ cultural traditionalists). The AWS coalition may even break up over the mounting importance of this cleavage. There is also a growing division within the Catholic Church over the attitude toward the West. The 'Westernisers' will be represented by the liberal Freedom Union (UW) (right libertarians), but also, to a large extent, by the Social Democrats (left libertarians). As we can see, the former Polish Communists represent the option of co-operation with the centre both in the old and in the new international configuration. One of the reasons for such a smooth transformation from supporting the 'old' Eastern centre to supporting the 'new'

---

[11] Anna Sosnowska, 'Tu, Tam–pomieszanie', *Studia Socjologiczne*, 1997, 4, pp. 61–68.

[12] [Herbert] Kitschelt, 'Formation of Party Cleavages in Post-Communist Democracies' [*Party Politics*, 1. 4. 1995, pp. 447–472], p. 462.

Western one by the Social Democrats is their acceptance of a secular order inherited from their communist ideology. In contrast, the Right (cultural traditionalists), although formally more 'Western' than the post-communist Social Democrats, often see the secularised West as falling into a moral decline and as aggressively propagating a cosmopolitan culture which threatens Polish national identity based on religious values.

(Zarycki, 2000, pp. 857–61)

EXERCISE

After reading the extract, consider the following questions.

1 Reflect on the themes you were introduced to by Suman Gupta in Chapter 2, and on the discussion in the first part of this chapter. Can you identify, in Zarycki's discussion, the particular features of Poland's peripheral status?

2 During the early twentieth century which strategies emerged in Poland for the restoration of Polish independence? What different elements did these strategies involve?

3 Which features of the strategies for Polish independence seem to recur most strongly in contemporary Polish politics?

DISCUSSION

1 Many countries of central and eastern Europe had chequered and complex experiences of statehood, empire and independence but Poland was distinctive in losing its independence and being partitioned between Russia, Prussia and Austria at the end of the eighteenth century. Until the early 1700s it had been one of the major European powers – and still emerges today as the largest of the countries currently seeking EU membership. It lost its statehood as the Ottoman empire in southeastern Europe was weakening, and just as countries such as Greece, Romania and Serbia were beginning to gain elements of national independence and starting off on the path to modern statehood. The partition of Poland therefore took place as the contours of a modern Europe with specific forms of national independence were beginning to develop. This has lent a particular significance to Poland's peripheral status in contemporary Europe, and produced a basic divide between hardliners and softliners in their response to the culture of an external 'centre'.

2   Contrasting strategies towards the occupying powers were developed by Józef Piłsudski and Roman Dmowski. They differed most clearly in their international policies and in their view of which power – Russia or Germany – should be regarded as the main enemy of Polish national independence. There was strong evidence to support both views in the twentieth century, and for a lengthy period until the collapse of the Soviet empire between 1989 and 1991 it was Piłsudski's conception, with its strong opposition to Russian power, that was most influential in Poland. The two also differed in their conception of the political form in which modern Polish nationhood would find its best expression (that of the culturally unified nation-state or the multinational federation) and in the role of church and state in relation to Polish nationhood. Dmowski saw Catholicism as the main tool of cultural consolidation and as having the particular relation to modern statehood that Zarycki suggests is replicated in other parts of the European periphery.

3   The most obvious legacy of this path of Polish national development concerns the continuing centrality of the church in the modern conception of national identity and the conflicting views on the appropriate relation between church and state. The particular trajectory of Poland's development has thus left religious issues at the centre of contemporary politics, bound up with the sharp antagonism between hardliners and softliners that developed during the communist period. This helps explain the strong salience of judgements on the communist period in Polish electoral and party politics compared with other central European polities, as well as the overt politicization of issues surrounding the Catholic church. Both aspects impinge on the views taken of current European issues, and provide a direct link between contemporary discussions of Poland's place in Europe, the conditions of its membership of the European Union and earlier manifestations of the country's peripheral status during the eighteenth and nineteenth centuries.

In Zarycki's view, though, it remains debatable how far the European Union emerges as a new centre against which Poland's peripheral status should be judged. While attention has shifted in terms of international policy, he is uncertain whether western Europe is now a focus of or even a target for cultural nationalism – and to this extent is held responsible or even blamed for Poland's continuing 'subaltern' status (as such positions were termed by Suman Gupta in Chapter 2 of this book). These perceptions clearly enter into contemporary party politics although, as I have pointed out, they were not strongly articulated in policy terms during either the 1997 elections or the more recent (2000) presidential contest. There was little evidence that the EU membership issue produced a major division in Polish politics in 2000, or indeed that it would do so in the parliamentary election year of 2001. It is, in one observer's view, likely to become divisive in a central sense only when voters focus less on the desirability of membership *per se* and more on the *kind* of European Union that they want to be a member of (Szczerbiak, 2001b, p. 16).

Nevertheless, broadly conceived European issues certainly contributed to the continuing tensions and instability of Polish right-wing forces. The governing coalition of Solidarity Electoral Action and the Freedom Union came to an end in June 2000. Moreover, as the 1997 parliament neared the end of its term, and after the poor performance of its candidate in the presidential elections, the Solidarity coalition also began to break up, providing the Polish right as a whole with bleak prospects in the parliamentary elections of September 2001 (see the next section of this chapter). In this context, increasing attention has been paid to the Dmowskiite legacy. Roman Dmowski's continuing influence on conceptions of Polish identity, contemporary Polish parties and their underlying views of Europe was underlined in a parliamentary vote in 1999 to mark the sixtieth anniversary of his death. It highlighted the fact that the overwhelming parliamentary consensus on Polish membership of the European Union is associated with an implicit endorsement of traditional religious values and a particular view of nationalism that in some ways contradict current understandings of contemporary processes of European integration.

The reading below is an extract from 'The troubling legacy of Roman Dmowski' by Andrzej Walicki. As you read it, consider what this tradition means for contemporary Polish politics and its attitude to European issues.

The emphasis here is to better understand Dmowski as one of the seminal nationalist thinkers of East Central Europe at the beginning of the twentieth century, and to shed light on the phenomenon of his continuing influence in contemporary Poland. The most telling testimony of this influence is the resolution of the Polish Sejm of 8 January 1999 that celebrated the sixtieth anniversary of Dmowski's death by paying tribute to him as an outstanding Pole who had rendered great service to his country.[13] The initiative belonged to the right wing of the ruling coalition but the resolution was supported by an overwhelming majority of deputies including many from the postcommunist Alliance of the Democratic Left. Though different groups clearly joined this celebration for different reasons, opposition was weak to nonexistent ...

[T]he current trends in the reception of Dmowski's ideas are increasingly anti-liberal, cynical about democracy, and more and more exposed to the fatal influences of political irrationalism. Gone is a selective use of Dmowski's ideas to serve geopolitical realism, as opposed to 'political heroism', or the cause of political rationalism, as opposed to the anti-politics of symbolic gestures. Instead, we are witnessing numerous attempts to create and consolidate a right-wing fundamentalism and an inward-directed nationalism, sharply distinguishing between good, Catholic Poles and different kinds of de-nationalized groups – Polish-speaking, but alien to Polish national values.

Two obvious issues seem at the root of this sad development. First is the deep frustration of the post-Solidarity political elite, caused by the spectacular successes of postcommunist forces. The policy of totally isolating the post-communist Democratic Left Alliance failed to prevent this party's winning the parliamentary elections in 1993; the anticommunist hysteria that followed failed to prevent Aleksander Kwaśniewski from winning the presidential elections in 1995. It became clear that the liberal-democratic rules of the game are not enough to eliminate the post-communists from the Polish political scene. It could be argued, of course, that nothing threatened systemic reforms, because the former communists had been reborn as convinced supporters of liberal democracy. But this was not an argument for power-hungry politicians, thinking in terms of 'we' (the former anticommunist opposition) against 'them' (the former supporters of the communist regime). For such people, the failure of democratic mechanisms to secure their own political domination became the reason to accuse democracy of moral relativism and, thereby, of an inner affinity with communism. This paved the way for an increased popularity of the

---

[13] See below, n. [5].

right-wing anti-liberal rhetoric – including, of course, Dmowski's version of Catholic nationalism.[14]

Second is the growing awareness among Catholic traditionalists of the anti-traditionalist implications and social consequences of Poland's policy of integration with the West. From this perspective, closely resembling Dmowski's views on the desirable third way between capitalism and socialism,[15] the enemy is not the alleged sovietization of a large part of the population of Poland, but the secularism and cosmopolitanism (real or alleged) of the liberal elites. The latter, however, cannot effectively defend their stand without breaking their anti-communist alliance with Krzaklewski's AWS – an alliance based upon the false assumption that past ideological divisions are more important than present political choices.

Thus, the current cold civil war in Poland helps to make more and more room for the right-wing anti-liberalism in Polish politics.

We can now return to the resolution of the Sejm of 8 January 1999. What was the meaning, who voted for it and why? Why it was passed so easily and without a wave of criticism in the liberal-democratic press?[16] The text of the resolution reads as follows:

> In connection with the 60th anniversary of Roman Dmowski's death the Sejm of the Republic of Poland expresses its appreciation of the struggle and work of this great statesman for the restoration of independent Poland. Dmowski rendered great services to his fatherland. He formulated the notion of national interest and stressed that the development of the Nation requires the possession of its own state. This meant the unification of all lands of the former Commonwealth, inhabited by a Polish majority, and

[14] See B. Grot, *Nacjonalizm chrzescijański* (Kraków: Ostoja, 1996). Stefan Niesiołowski [a major contemporary Catholic politician] combines a leading role in the 'anti-communist' crusade with an outspoken allegiance to Dmowski's Catholic nationalism. Dmowski himself was very far from a hysterical anti-communist. He interpreted Russian communism in terms of Russian historical development, refused to treat communist ideology seriously, and predicted its inevitable collapse.

[15] See T. Włudyka, *'Trzecia droga' w myśli gospodarczej II Rzeczpospolitej* (Kraków: Universitas, 1994). In the last elections to self-governing bodies (October 1998), the radical right, questioning Poland's integration with Europe, won 9 percent of the votes; 230,000 votes more than in 1997. See J. Paradowska, 'Ciasto czteropartyjne,' *Polityka*, 19 December 1998, 24–25.

[16] Explicit criticism of this resolution was expressed only in my own article 'Testament Dmowskiego,' *Przegląd Tygodniowy*, 10 March 1999, 15.

> raising the national consciousness of all strata and groups of Polish society. He created a school of political realism and responsibility. As a representative of the resurrected Poland at the Versailles Conference he made a decisive contribution to the establishment of national frontiers, especially in the West.
>
> Particularly important was Dmowski's role in emphasizing a close linkage of Polishness with Catholicism – a linkage which was indispensable for the survival of the Nation and the restoration of the State.
>
> The Sejm of the Republic of Poland expresses its appreciation for an outstanding Pole, Roman Dmowski.[17]

Most surprising is that the text makes no distinction between Dmowski's genuine services to the national cause before the emergence of independent Poland and the content of his ideological testament. It may seem proper for patriotic Poles to acknowledge Dmowski's positive contribution to the activism and nationalization of the masses in partitioned Poland, his brilliant analysis of the geopolitical aspects of the Polish question before the First World War, or his able and energetic defense of Polish territorial interests at the Peace Conference in Paris. But is it proper to remain silent about his role as spiritual father of the most anachronistic, xenophobic and anti-liberal tradition in Polish nationalism? Is it normal for the parliament of a democratic country in 1999 to pay an *unreserved* tribute to a politician who played with the idea of a 'national revolution' that would end 'the system based upon the Declaration of the Rights of Man'?[18] A politician who, in the last period of his activity, saw western democracies as instruments of an all-pervasive Judeo-Masonic conspiracy, and proclaimed a veritable war-to-death against the Jewish citizens of Poland?

Perhaps the deputies to the Polish Sejm were not aware of all the implications of their decision to celebrate Dmowski as an exemplary Pole. Almost certainly most had no idea about the content of his last works. Nevertheless, it is not possible to assume a total ignorance of Dmowski's ideological legacy. If so, the results of the voting are curious and intriguing, and require explanation.

---

[17] See 'Uchwała Sejmu Rzeczypospolitej Polskiej z dnia 8 stycznia 1999 o uczczeniu pamięci Romana Dmowskiego,' *Monitor Polski*, 15 January 1999, No. 3, pos.12.

[18] See R. Dmowski, *Przewrót*, 438.

As expected, the small parties of the extreme right – like Jan Olszewski's Movement to Rebuild Poland (ROP), or Adam Słomka's Confederation of Independent Poland (KPN-O) – unanimously supported the resolution. For somewhat different reasons, the same was true of the Polish Peasant party (22 votes 'for,' nobody voted against or abstained from voting, four deputies did not vote). Almost unanimous also was the main force of the ruling coalition – Krzaklewski's Electoral Action Solidarity (AWS): 171 of its deputies voted for, one deputy voted against, one abstained, and 14 did not vote. The reasons are, unfortunately, quite clear: AWS wants to unite the Polish right and, therefore, tries to present itself as the best guardian of the 'national and Catholic values.' Its political pragmatism, or opportunism, is combined with ideological militancy, directed against postcommunists and sees no enemy on the right.

Unlike AWS, the Union of Freedom (UW) is, of course, deeply committed to western-style liberal democracy. But it is a part of the coalition dominated by AWS and must avoid conflicts with the ideology of its more powerful ally. Its liberalism makes it open to allegations of cosmopolitanism and moral relativism; hence the need for ideological concessions – especially if they have no direct relevance to the program of market reforms, seen by the party as more important than ideological quarrels. This awkward situation partially explains why 36 deputies of UW (including Tadeusz Mazowiecki) voted for the resolution. However, five deputies abstained from voting, and 18 (among them Leszek Balcerowicz, Bronisław Geremek, and Jacek Kuroń) did not vote at all.

The deputies of the opposition, that is, members of the post-communist Democratic Left Alliance (SLD), were divided on the issue: 60 persons (including the leader of SLD, Leszek Miller, and the former prime minister, Józef Oleksy) voted for the resolution, 34 (among them the former prime minister, Włodzimierz Cimoszewicz) voted against, 48 deputies abstained, and 22 did not participate in the voting. Thus, the majority of the SLD deputies distanced themselves from the celebration of Dmowski's achievements. It is reasonable to believe that those SLD deputies who supported the resolution were motivated by political pragmatism, minimizing the importance of ideology, and by the desire to manifest their readiness to embrace what is perceived to be the mainstream patriotic tradition. The other SLD deputies, especially those who voted against, proved more attached to leftist values – or perhaps were simply more aware of the sinister aspects of Dmowski's legacy.

Anyhow, one thing is obvious. As far as ideology is concerned, the Polish political scene has moved so much to the right that liberals (UW) and, of course, social democrats (SLD) have found themselves on the defensive. They lack self-confidence and defend their values half-heartedly, thus showing symptoms of ideological intimidation. In such an ideological climate, the official unreserved celebration of the main representative of Polish right-wing nationalism was simply natural, almost unnoticed, and unworthy of serious public discussion.

(Walicki, 2000, pp. 14, 42–6)

EXERCISE

1 How has Dmowski's legacy impinged on contemporary Polish politics?

2 How should its implications for Poland's integration with the European Union be assessed?

DISCUSSION

1 An initial view of the 1999 vote in the Polish *Sejm* (or parliament) commemorating Dmowski's death and celebrating his contribution to the foundation of modern Poland confirms the ambivalence in Polish attitudes towards Europe. The vote was taken by a parliament almost wholly in favour of EU membership but represented, in Walicki's view, a strengthening of inward-directed nationalism and right-wing fundamentalism (which only a minority of left-wing deputies actually voted against). This reflects a growth of political irrationalism, as well as ideas about democracy that are increasingly anti-liberal and cynical (it might be worth considering how far these tendencies can also be detected in Britain, whose attitude towards 'Europe' is in some ways equally uncertain and about whose contemporary identity major doubts have also been raised). In more concrete terms, it also reflects the 'deep frustration' of the post-Solidarity political elite and the Polish right more generally. The vote exposed the weak basis of the governing coalition in terms of underlying values as well as overt policy, placing the western-orientated liberals of the Freedom Union in a particularly sensitive position (it is easy to understand why its leading figures chose not to vote at all). From a broader perspective, the episode raises questions about the nature of political cleavages in post-communist societies more generally, as well as the character of the contemporary

political right and the resources available to it for use in democratic electoral competition.

2   In terms of specifically European issues the vote reflects the growing perception among Catholic traditionalists of the negative consequences of integration with the west. The question of the precise terms of Polish EU accession (with respect to the impact of the Common Agricultural Policy, access to structural funds, labour mobility, terms of trade,and so on) are not raised here at all, and these of course, will also have an important bearing on the integration process and domestic judgements on how Poland is treated by the European Union and its existing members. At issue here are the underlying tendencies of cultural sentiment and the emotive bases of political judgement. Their role will be to strengthen or moderate popular responses to the practical outcome of negotiations in either a positive or a negative direction. Walicki's view is clearly that it is the negative responses that will be strengthened in this context.

The 2001 elections

The parliamentary elections held in September 2001 clearly served to confirm the negative responses of which Walicki wrote, and voter preferences certainly reflected the nationalist, anti-liberal tendencies he saw strengthening in Polish society. The main features of the results can be summarized as follows.

1   A swingeing defeat for the governing Solidarity party and the failure of what remained of its political supporters to gain any seats in parliament at all (see Table 6.5).

2   A further example of what Walicki termed the 'spectacular success' of post-communist forces, which gained a clear majority (although not an absolute one) in parliament.

3   The elimination from parliament of the Freedom Union, the prime representative of the western-orientated liberal tendency and the strongest supporter of entry to the European Union.

4   The entry into parliament of outright anti-liberal and anti-EU forces: on the one side the Catholic fundamentalist League of Polish Families (which included presidential candidate Jan Łopuszański and representatives of the former Movement for Polish Representations) and, on the other, Andrzej Lepper's

populist Self-Defence party, which had now dropped its 'Peasant' identification and strengthened its political position by appealing to a wider electorate.

5   The bare maintenance by the Polish Peasant Party, hitherto the most eurosceptic group, of its parliamentary position and its decision to form a governing coalition with the post-communist Left Alliance.

6   The persistence on this basis of a government policy that was – somewhat paradoxically – still decidedly in favour of Poland's entry to the European Union and which could, further, generally count for its implementation on the support of the Civic Platform as a moderate right-wing force. While the balance of opinion in the Polish parliament had clearly changed as a result of the 2001 elections, then, it was by no means clear that government policy would be greatly modified.

Table 6.5   Election results, 2001

	Number of seats	Percentage of vote, 2001	Percentage of vote, 1997
Union of Democratic Left/Union of Labour	216	41.0	27.1/4.7
Civic Platform	65	12.7	–
Self-Defence	53	10.2	0.1
Right and Justice	44	9.5	–
Polish Peasant Party	42	9.0	7.3
League of Polish Families	38		–

Conclusion

Poland's place in Europe has been an ambiguous and peripheral one for much of the modern period, and it is not difficult to see how closer European integration has emerged as a very attractive option for the country now that the Iron Curtain has disappeared. Despite the growth of some popular scepticism towards the European Union, official and governmental attitudes to EU membership have been overwhelmingly positive. The particular way in which political cleavages have developed in post-communist Poland, and the way in which left- and right-wing affiliations have come to be expressed in the party system, nevertheless helped to mask differences over current policy options until the elections of September 2001 when popular doubts and opposition received greater parliamentary expression. They in turn may be traced to the way in which Poland's national identity developed during the nineteenth century under the specific conditions of the country's peripheral status. This included the strong association between Polish national identity and traditional Catholic faith that developed under the influence of Roman Dmowski, persisted through the communist period and has manifested itself in post-communist Poland, with implications that are by no means wholly positive for the country's eventual integration into a broader European community.

But it would be misleading to regard in too negative a light the attitudes taken by Polish parties and their approach to membership of the European Union. A more robust and quite convincing appraisal of Poland's contemporary position is provided by Karl Cordell in the conclusion to his informative volume:

> Contemporary Poland is in fact a remarkably normal society possessed of a political system and culture that has more in common with Western Europe than it does with a majority of former communist states. We have noted how it pursues foreign policy goals that are not marked by either extreme demands or unrealistic expectations. We have also noted that the majority of Polish society supports the primary objective of the government's foreign policy, namely accession to the EU. Similarly, although some political parties, politicians, members of the clergy and the agricultural lobby remain deeply wary of the whole process ... neither they nor their supporters have any real chance of bringing it to a halt.
>
> (Cordell, 2000, p. 200)

To the extent that the national–clerical lobby constitutes, as Walicki suggests, the most strongly entrenched core of opposition to EU membership and the 'Europeanization' of Poland more generally, it is also instructive to pay some attention to mainstream Catholic policy and opinion in the country as a whole. A degree of early scepticism towards EU membership was overcome in 1997 when a more determinedly positive approach was adopted by the Catholic leadership, while Pope John Paul II (himself of course Polish) has also expressed a resolutely pro-accession attitude – not least in his visit to his homeland in 1999. A survey of the clergy's attitude to this issue in 1998 revealed an overwhelmingly positive view, with 84 per cent of clerics in favour, a level of support far higher than that in the population as a whole (Stadtmüller, 2000, p. 37). The very low proportion of the vote gained by Jan Łopuszański, the most resolutely anti-European of the presidential candidates in 2000, should also be borne in mind even though a rather different picture emerged in the parliament elected in 2001. This of course does not mean that Polish membership of the EU will be easily achieved or that the process of accession will not on occasion be troublesome or bitterly fought. But existing EU member states and the union's negotiators will play a large part in these developments. If there are problems it is very unlikely that they will all stem from the Polish side – and certainly not just from attitudes shaped in past centuries, or indeed from entrenched but by no means immutable dimensions of cultural and national identity.

References

Antoszewski, A. (2000) 'Political competition in Poland: traditionalisation or westernisation?', in K. Cordell (ed.), *Poland and the European Union*, London, Routledge.

Chimisso, C. (ed.) (2003) *Exploring European Identities*, Milton Keynes, The Open University.

Cordell, K. (ed.) (2000) *Poland and the European Union*, London, Routledge.

Davies, N. (1986) *Heart of Europe: a Short History of Poland*, Oxford, Oxford University Press.

Documents of the Peasant Party's VII Congress (2000): http//www.psl.org.pl

Gebethner, S. (ed.) (1997) *Wybory '97: Partie i programy wyborcze*, Warsaw, Dom Wydawniczy Elipsa.

Janos, A. C. (2000) *East Central Europe in the Modern World: the Politics of the Borderlands from Pre- to Postcommunism*, Stanford, CA, Stanford University Press.

Jasiewicz, K. (2001) 'Pocketbook or rosary? Economic and identity voting in the 2000 presidential election in Poland', paper presented to the annual conference of the British Association for Slavonic and East European Studies, Cambridge, April.

Jedlicki, J. (1999) *A Suburb of Europe: Nineteenth Century Polish Approaches to Western Civilization*, Budapest, Central European University Press.

Kucharczyk, J. (1999) '"Za, a nawet przeciw": partie polityczne wobec perspektywy integracji europejskiej w wyborach '97', in L. Kolarska-Bobińska (ed.), *Polska Eurodebata*, Warsaw, Instytut Spraw Publicznych.

Lewis, P. G. (2000) *Political Parties in Post-communist Eastern Europe*, London, Routledge.

Markowski, R. (ed.) (1999) *Wybory parlamentarne 1997*, Warsaw, Instytut Studiów Politycznych/Ebert Stiftung.

Stadtmüller, E. (2000) 'Polish perceptions of the European Union in the 1990s', in K. Cordell (ed.), *Poland and the European Union*, London, Routledge.

Szczerbiak, A. (1999) 'Interests and values: Polish parties and their electorates', *Europe-Asia Studies*, vol. 51, no. 8, pp. 1401–32.

Szczerbiak, A. (2000) 'Spadek i stabilizacja: Zmieniające się wzorce poparcia dla członkostwa Polski w Unii Europejskiej', in E. Popławska (ed.), *Konstytucja dla rozszerzającej się Europy*, Warsaw, Instytut Spraw Publicznych.

Szczerbiak, A. (2001a) 'Explaining declining Polish support for EU membership', *Journal of Common Market Studies*, vol. 39, no. 1, pp. 105–22.

Szczerbiak, A. (2001b) 'Europe as a realigning issue in Polish politics? Evidence from the October 2000 presidential election', paper presented to the annual conference of the Political Studies Association, Manchester, April.

Walicki, A. (2000) 'The troubling legacy of Roman Dmowski', *East European Politics and Societies*, vol. 14, no. 1, pp. 12–46.

Zarycki, T. (2000) 'Politics in the periphery: political cleavages in Poland interpreted in their historical and international context', *Europe-Asia Studies*, vol. 52, no. 5, pp. 851–73.

Figure 6.1 Victory day in Moscow near Red Square by Robert Kowalewski, May 1996. Just as central and eastern Europe has undergone enormous political change, as this chapter reminds us, it has also undergone tremendous social and economic change. Central and eastern Europe has become more integrated into the global capitalist economy and western consumer culture has permeated the region. Photo: Robert Kowalewski

Figure 6.2 Wheel clamping, Prague/Czech Republic by Yiorgos Nikiteas, March 1993. The changes associated with economic transformation have permeated daily life in a number of different, unexpected ways. In this photograph a flower delivery man watches his car clamped by a German contractor enforcing the Czech capital's parking regulations. Photo: Yiorgos Nikiteas

Figure 6.3 Kladno coal mine, the Czech Republic by Dana Kyndrova, 1994. State socialism prior to 1989 celebrated productive industrial labour, indeed the industrial working class was regarded ideologically as the foundation of the state. The economic changes of the 1990s brought huge de-industrialization in their wake, destroying countless jobs. Establishments like Kladno, once a flagship of the state-run industrial sector, have been swept away or pushed into crisis by the winds of economic change. Photo: Dana Kyndrova

Figure 6.4 Untitled, Bucharest, Romania by Roger Lemoyne, 1999. In other aspects of daily life, like housing, there have been real continuities with the state socialist recent past. Photo: Canadian International Development Agency

Figure 6.5   At the train station, Bucharest, Romania by Yiorgos Nikiteas, March 1991. The photographer remembers that as the train came to a stop the conductor became 'aware of me and smiled kindly. A few minutes later inside the station a frustrated rail employee shouted in favour of Ceauşescu, and how good the country was when he was around, and to my amusement nobody tried to shut him up'. Photo: Yiorgos Nikiteas

Figure 6.6   Couple dancing, Jewish community centre, Prague Czech Republic by Yiorgos Nikiteas, March 1993. The photograph was taken in the Jewish community centre in Prague at the Passover festival. It shows a newly engaged couple dancing to a jazz/blues tune. Photo: Yiorgos Nikiteas

Figure 6.7   Another day, Tetovo, Former Yugoslav Republic of Macedonia by Miklós Teknős, 2001. In the midst of civil conflict between Albanian rebels and the forces of the government of the Former Yugoslav Republic of Macedonia in 2001, normal life still continues. Photo: Miklós Teknős/ Népszabadság

7

'A new condition?' European identities and the literature of migration

ROBERT FRASER

Migration and identity

Whether considered as an individual or a collective phenomenon, identity is seldom a straightforward affair. In her introductory chapter to *Exploring European Identities*, the philosopher Cristina Chimisso explains a number of ways in which this complex question has been interpreted in a European context (Chimisso, 2003, Chapter 1). She writes, for example, about the notion of personal identity that we have inherited from the French thinker René Descartes (1596–1650) and about the proliferation of identities that have been, and are being, adopted in an increasingly diverse world. She then goes on to consider how under these circumstances individuals often respond by constructing a sense of belonging to a group or sub-group defined by its history, geography or religion. Her contention – which draws on the thinking of Benedict Anderson (1991), Manuel Castells (1997) and Alain Touraine (2000) – is that such 'imagined' communities represent reactions to the problems of globalization. Confronted with a society where barriers of communication appear gradually to be breaking down, and ties to be loosening, people tend to associate with a particular social and mental environment, either inherited or of their own choosing, which makes sense of their lives as citizens and as private beings.

On the face of it, few tendencies have contributed more to such conditions in modern Europe than widespread migration, within nation-states, across national frontiers, or from beyond the continent itself. Migration of course has been a regular feature of the scene since before the Romans. By the time of the *Germania* of the historian Tacitus (55–c. 117CE) successive waves of population were arriving from the east to diversify that area known to certain twentieth-century intellectuals – as Mark Pittaway has already pointed out in Chapter 3 – as *Mitteleuropa*. Migration across the narrow straits from North

Africa has frequently replenished Iberia, especially in the period of the Arab occupation between the eighth and fifteenth centuries CE. More recent times have seen large movements of population from Turkey into Germany and from the North African Maghreb into France, resulting in both instances in a substantial migrant presence. It might be argued that in the long term such shifts of population have contributed more than any other single factor to the political map of Europe. Seen from that point of view, the 'nation-states' which Clive Emsley discusses in his contribution to *Exploring European Identities* (Chimisso, 2003, Chapter 3) may well have formed over the centuries partly as a result of – or, in any case, as a willed superimposition upon – such slow accretions of people upon people, culture upon culture: a fact at least as important as the network of settled agrarian communities described by Ernest Gellner in his book *Nations and Nationalism* (1983). To that extent, Chimisso's thesis may be applicable in a special retrospective sense: nationhood and collective identity may very well, at definable periods in the past, have cohered as bulwarks against social and demographic flux.

A question therefore arises at to what happens when migration continues or intensifies after national boundaries have been drawn up. The period of national consolidation in Europe – the coalescence, for example, of Germany and Italy as nation-sates in the mid to late nineteenth century – was preceded by an era of overseas adventure and territorial acquisition, resulting in the mercantile trading system that dominated the economic scene throughout the eighteenth century. It was followed by an age of high imperialism in which Britain, France, Germany, Italy and the Netherlands acquired overseas empires. In the mid twentieth century, after these conglomerations had collapsed and the overseas territories acquired their independence, there frequently occurred an influx of population from erstwhile colonies to the former metropolis: from Algeria to France, from Jamaica to Britain, from Indonesia to Holland and from Eritrea to Italy, for instance. Opportunities in the burgeoning workshops of western Europe also attracted economic migrants in increasing numbers, both from the old colonies and from other economically disadvantaged countries, a prime example being the Turkish workforce that since the Second World War has supplied a significant portion of the labour needs of Germany. With whom or with what, to employ Chimisso's terms of reference, do such relative newcomers 'identify'? And what are the consequences of their presence for the sense of national 'identity' espoused by the host countries? How much light does imaginative literature – fiction and poetry in particular – shed on these concerns?

Migration and settlement in France

Such questions are difficult to resolve in the abstract. In this chapter I want to examine two contrasted examples from France and Germany which may help to suggest parameters for thought. I begin with a cultural movement that, though containing unique elements, also possesses distinct advantages as a body of articulate, clear-sighted opinion: one, what is more, that since the late 1980s has expressed these characteristics in an energetic and growing corpus of literature.

Migration to France from the coastal area of North Africa known as the Maghreb – particularly from Algeria but also from Morocco and Tunisia – has been a marked feature of the last 100 or so years. As Alec G. Hargreaves – a perceptive British commentator on shifts of population in the francophone world – has noted, this excursus and incursus has occurred in successive waves, each with a somewhat different socioeconomic pattern (Hargreaves and Heffernan, 1983). Until the Second World War migration from North Africa was seldom permanent. A common procedure was the so-called rotation system whereby one man of working age from a given family would travel to an urban industrial centre in France to work for a few years, sending back money to his extended kin in, say, Algeria before returning home. His role overseas was then taken over by a male relative. A certain amount of this 'rotating' migration originated from Arabic-speaking regions of Algeria. Much of it, however, came from Berber areas such as the mountainous Kabylie (Kable) region east of Algiers, where the traditional family system suited such arrangements and where travelling beyond the village to work had been an accepted way of life since well before the French conquest. With very few exceptions, the wife and children of such migrants stayed behind in the village. Resettlement as such – and with it the possibility of a second generation growing up overseas away from the sustaining influences of family, religion and regional tongue – was in most cases out of the question.

'*Harkis*': from the Arabic word 'harka' or 'movement'.

'*Maquis*': the underground resistance (from the French word for Corsican scrubland).

This state of affairs lasted up to the bitter Algerian war of independence of 1954–62. Not only did this conflict poison the relationship between France and Algeria, it also split opinion within local communities in North Africa. In some rural areas, such as the Grande et Petite Kabylie (Kable mountains), recruitment into the ranks of the French army proved an attractive option, at least in the financial sense. Those who accepted it – widely reviled as *harkis* – were understandably distrusted by the majority of their fellow nationals who supported the independence struggle being waged by the guerrilla fighters of the *maquis*. At the end of the war the *harkis* and their families were automatically offered French citizenship for their own protection, whereupon they and their families moved to

France. In some areas in France *harki* families still form a distinct group, though with the passage of time hostility between them and other Algerian residents has necessarily abated. There are tragic exceptions to this rule.

Meanwhile, the increasing prosperity of France – and the uncertain political future of Algeria in the 1960s and 1970s – had another, complementary effect. The transitory and shifting rotation system of labour was gradually replaced by a pattern of more permanent migration. No longer did *maghrébin* workers return to their villages of origin in such large numbers. Instead they tended to settle in France, with the more or less conscious design of staying on. Since, at least to begin with, they could not afford even standard rented accommodation, shanty towns known as *bidonvilles* or *cités de transit* grew up in some urban conurbations to accommodate them. Such districts were generally situated in the *banlieu*, or suburbs, and they consisted of lean-tos with no running water and the most basic facilities. After several years the tendency was for the labourer, who had been sending a portion of his wages back home, to call his wife and family to join him. If this reunited family was fortunate, after some years in a *bidonville* it found a small apartment in an HLM – '*une habitation à loyer modéré*' – a tower block resembling those on some British council estates (Begag, 1987). Return visits to North Africa became less and less frequent, if they happened at all. The children went to local schools.

The presence of growing numbers of newcomers caught the wider French community on the hop. Since the French Revolution immigration policy had been based on a desire to bolster the prestige and labour power of *la patrie* (the fatherland) and ensure that any newcomers were well and truly integrated into society, learning to formulate their loyalties in appropriate terms. To ensure cohesion within the French empire this policy – known as *assimilation* – operated in different ways inside and outside the home country. In French possessions abroad, colonial subjects who had achieved a recognized level of education were entitled to certain privileges tantamount to French citizenship: to represent their country in the *Assemblée Nationale* in Paris, for example; to vote; or to take certain reserved examinations (such as the *agrégation*, the qualification needed by all university teachers of humanities or law).

Within France itself the rights of all residents were determined by two criteria enshrined in the constitution of 1791: the *jus soli* (right of the land), based on place of birth, and the *jus sanguinis* (right of the blood), defined by kinship. Originally the balance was in favour of the *jus soli*, giving identical rights to children of French parents and to children born to immigrant parents on French soil. By the time

Napoleon came to revise the constitution in 1804 there had been a tide of emigration to other European countries, so the provisions were changed to emphasize the *jus sanguinis*: citizenship was now offered as a matter of course, for example, to all children born to French citizens living abroad. While the resulting laws seemed liberal, in practice a certain cultural uniformity was preserved by an education system intolerant of deviation from national norms. When in 1883 the celebrated *loi Ferry* made secondary education compulsory and free throughout France, the freedom of citizens of whatever ethnic origin to depart from nationally defined patterns of thought and conduct diminished considerably.

In the first two decades after the Second World War the presence of growing numbers of immigrants determined to cling on to distinctive traditions made little impact on this state of affairs. While *maghrébins*, for instance, tended to collect together in informally organized groups, any more formal representation of their interests and point of view was prohibited under a law of 1901 denying foreign groups freedom of association. Many migrants, both young and old, considered this state of enforced conformity unfortunate. At the same time, anxieties about the high level of immigration were frequently expressed in the community at large. This in turn gave rise both to a resurgence of the political right and to a certain amount of what we would now call 'institutional racism' in society at large. During the *été meurtrier* (bloody summer) of 1973, for example, police brutality

Figure 7.1 Young Maghrébin residents on the playground of an HLM in Les Minguettes district of Lyon, 1985. Photo: Abbas/Magnum Photos.

291

against young *maghrébins* was widely reported. So far, however, these aspirations, worries and atrocities had failed to give rise to a concerted movement of opposition. As the 1980s wore on, this was to change in many ways.

The Beur movement

In 1980, in reaction to continuing police brutality against adolescents of *maghrébin* origin, a rock concert called 'Rock the Police' was held in the Paris suburb of Nanterre. The one-off event, held in defiance of the measure of 1901 forbidding association by ethnic groups, was itself symptomatic of a wider shift of opinion. The following year President François Mitterand (1981–95) repealed the offending law. This sequence of events was to a certain extent a reflection of developments elsewhere in Europe. You might like to compare the British police's revival in the late 1970s of the dreaded 'Sus' laws dating back to the Napoleonic wars, which was succeeded by the Brixton riots of 1981 and the gradual replacement of the 'Sus' provisions after 1984 by powers of 'stop and search'. In France, however, the change in the atmosphere was particularly significant because of the prescribed cultural attitudes – the narrow national self-definition – that for at least two centuries had been so marked a feature of French life.

A new activism soon seized the *maghrébin* community. On 15 October 1983 forty protestors left Marseille for Paris on a 'March for Equality and against Racism'. By the time it reached the Paris suburbs the column – now referred to as '*La Marche des beurs*' – had swollen to 100,000 (Bouzid, 1984). This was in effect the first manifestation of 'Beur' culture: the term can be used either as a noun or as an adjective, and has since become synonymous with a variety of cultural forms expressive of *maghrébin*, migrant, or more broadly dissident identity in Paris and other French conurbations. That year also saw the publication of a book that is examined in more detail below: Mehdi Charef's novel *Le thé au harem d'Archi Ahmed*, widely considered as the foundation text of the Beur movement. A related phenomenon was the establishment in 1981 of a radio station – Radio Beur or Beur FM – devoted to news, views and popular music emanating from the North African community. Not surprisingly, the new activism asserted itself most dramatically in places where traditional French cultural identity was strictly enforced, notably in the school system. Cristina Chimisso has referred to the notorious *affaire des foulards* (headscarves affair) of September 1989 in which three Muslim schoolgirls were excluded from their secondary school for wearing the traditional head-dress on the premises (Chimisso, 2003, Chapter 1); the incident was widely seen as an expression of *maghrébin* cultural resistance, though the girls were in fact Turkish.

Their cause was taken up by a vocal group of *maghrébine* women – '*les nanas-beurs*' – who persuaded the ministry of education to reverse its decision, provided the headscarves in question were not being worn for propaganda purposes. The new ruling of course presupposed that the motives behind such incidents can unambiguously be ascertained.

Thus summarized, the Beur movement appears to be – at least in origin – a clear instance of what Chimisso, following Castells, describes as 'resistance identity' (Chimisso, 2003, Chapter 1; Castells, 1997). A slightly different spin on it, however, is obtained if you consider the very meaning of the term 'Beur'. It is a versatile example of that variety of French street slang known as *verlan*. This inventive proletarian argot operates through the reversal of words within the conventional lexicon. *Verlan* itself is a reversed reading of '*à l'envers*', meaning back-to-front. In other words, it is 'backwards' backwards. As the director of Beur FM told Hargreaves in 1997, a similar reversal of the word *rebe* (Arabic for Arab), slightly re-transliterated, gives you 'Beur' (Hargreaves, 1997, p. 29). However, he went on to stress that this typical piece of streetwise word play accounts only for the origin of the concept, not its application. The word Beur is now claimed as a badge by a broad spectrum of French society, for whom its ethnic connections are of relatively minor significance. By the late 1980s, as the director explained, the concept had already come to describe 'a geographical and cultural space'. He defined this space as consisting of 'the suburbs and the French

Figure 7.2 Pro-immigration hunger strike, Vincennes, Paris, 4 September 1996. Photo: Martine Franck/Magnum Photos.

working class', an inclusive formulation bounded more by economics and sociology than by ethnic or religious factors. Even on the level of word play, one might add, it is clear that the term Beur potentially reaches beyond ethnic or even national frontiers, since as well as 'Berber' it encodes 'Europe' and even the EU. Its very eclectic quality, its tendency to attract to itself a diversity of meanings, affiliations and connotations, is profoundly revealing of the nature of urban social dynamics, and not only in France.

Bearing these facts in mind, take a look at the first reading. It is an extract from a conversation between the part-Sudanese novelist Jamal Mahjoub and Mehdi Charef, the Algerian-born author, Paris resident and architect of the Beur movement, recorded in November 1997 at Majhoub's flat in Barcelona. Charef grew up in a *bidonville* in Nanterre and has been involved in the Beur movement since its inception. In this extract Mahjoub asks Charef to define the movement. He replies that it corresponds to 'a new condition'.

Jamal Mahjoub   How would you describe the *beur* movement?

Mehdi Charef   As an explosion of expression that was born at the beginning of the 1980s. That is to say that our parents who arrived in France after the war comprised a generation who came solely with the intention of working. They could not speak and they could not express themselves. It was work and nothing more. They sent money back to the family and that was it. But later on their children came along and they wanted another life, a life which was not only working and having a job and going to school, but also included the possibility of expressing themselves culturally, in dance, cinema, literature, music, painting, sculpture ... and that is what the *beur* movement is.

JM   In your first novel, *Le thé au harem d'Archi Ahmed*, you tell the story of the experiences of this generation brought up in France.

MC   Yes, it is the story of two adolescents, teenagers 17 to 18 years old – one Arab, the other French – who are friends. It tells their story, their hopes, their dreams, and also it tells of the universe in which they live. It is a world that I know, which I grew up in. I wanted to talk about this universe, the city, the *banlieu* (the suburbs). In that sense there is a lot of autobiography in the novel. But I also wanted to talk about things that were being ignored. I had the impression that our community, in the city, in the *banlieu*, that is to say the French

Figure 7.3 Still from *Le Thé au Harem d'Archimède*, 1985, directed by Mehdi Charef. Photo: BFI Collections

as well as the immigrants, was something that was being ignored. People knew hardly anything about it, and what they knew was bad. They said bad things about us, our city, our *banlieu*. I had a small wish to say that the things that they said about the city about the violence, many things, were false. I wanted to say what I thought. They said for example that it was a universe in which one might happen to be born, but where you could not live. But actually you can live there, because there is a lot of tenderness. When there is no hope on the outside you are all the more reliant on the affection of family and friends. That is what I felt the need to say, that I did not believe them, that we were not savages, that we also had hopes, that we were not living an empty existence, the way people used to think. That is why I wrote the book. It is the story of the generation which came of age in the early 1980s.

JM The novel was a great success. Was that a surprise to you? To suddenly find yourself fêted by literary Paris in that way?

MC Well it is true that in a single stroke I managed to show that there was more to the *banlieu* than simply immigration, factories and so on. People said that it was a new thing, that a different form of expression had been born. That wasn't my

295

idea when I wrote the book. I was not thinking of that, I had enough to think about with writing the book itself. But it did lead to changes, in particular in terms of literature, of expression. There was an opening up at that moment.

JM Perhaps also at the personal level, for you yourself?

MC Absolutely, because I had always had the sense of living without existing, and this form of expression liberated me, personally. I was liberated because it was one of the things I had wanted to do for a long time, but I had the idea before this was out of the realm of possibility. You look around you and you see people working in the factory, washing cars, cleaning the streets. And that was the beginning of the *beur* movement, realising that there were other things in France that we could do. People began to look beyond the confines of the *banlieu*, beyond immigration. We came here originally to do other things. But now the younger generation accepts that we are going to die in France, that we were born in France.

JM You once said that your country was in the *banlieu* of Paris. I am curious about whether you feel that your work is addressed in any way to Algeria. Does the generation brought up in France feel a connection with young people growing up in Algeria today. Is there any connection at all?

MC I don't know if there is. No, on the contrary. When the book came out, ten, or twelve years ago, I did not have the impression that I was writing for Algerians. I always had the impression that I was writing ... I felt that I was an immigrant more than anything. I did not have a sense of nationality. I was an immigrant. And now I don't think that way any more, although I don't feel as though I belong to either France or Algeria. I feel as though a new nationality was created for me.

JM A new condition?

MC Yes, a new condition, although I cannot say where France begins and Algeria ends. It was as though a new condition had been discovered, in which I could work and express myself. It was a breakthrough for me to realise that I felt neither French nor Algerian.

(Fraser (ed.), 2000, pp. 37–41)

EXERCISE

1   In Charef's view, how essential to the self-presentation of the Beur movement is it that it originated in the Algerian, or more broadly in the North African, community?

2   How important to Charef is the fact that the Beur movement started in, and continues to reflect life in, certain urban or suburban localities?

3   How important to Charef is the movement as a reflection of reality as experienced and articulated by a certain social class? Would a Marxist analysis of the movement, for example, make any sense?

4   How relevant to the understanding of the Beur movement as outlined by Charef is Chimisso's model of 'resistance identity'? If Castell's model is employed, who might be taken as resisting whom or what?

5   As Charef characterizes it, the movement obviously has some connection both with social or political protest and with socially transgressive behaviour. Does this connection seem to be coincidental or an aspect of the movement's nature?

6   Can you think of similar movements elsewhere in Europe?

7   How, going on Charef's words, would you characterize in general terms the 'new condition' of which he speaks?

DISCUSSION

Whilst thinking about Charef's rejoinders, it is unnecessary to make them out to be more consistent than they in fact are. You might well conclude that they embrace a spectrum with 'resistance' at one end and integration at the other. The responses of interviewees are frequently influenced both by the setting of the conversation and the perceived motives of the interviewer. In conversation recorded in May 1983 with the journalist Farida Ayari, for example, Charef speaks of the Beur movement as a product of an identity crisis, a collision between worlds (quoted in Hargreaves, 1997, p. 20). By contrast when talking to a fellow novelist like Mahjoub, he drops this conflictual vocabulary. In fact Charef hardly uses the word 'identity' at all, describing instead a wide-ranging and integrative movement, a mouthpiece for all socially excluded people from the outer suburbs, no matter where they happen to originate from. Thus, though he begins by talking about 'our parents', meaning first-generation Algerian immigrants, he goes on to speak defiantly about 'our community', typifying this as 'the city, ... the *banlieu*, that is to say the French as well as the immigrants'. You might consider the force of his phrase 'as well as'.

You might also like to think here about the eclectic nature of much popular culture as manifested in the forms that Charef mentions – dance, cinema, literature, music, painting, sculpture – but also in such areas as fashion and speech. It has already been noted that *verlan* is broadly used across French urban society. Beur events, moreover, are attended by a wide range of people from well beyond the *maghrébin* community, out of choice rather than from any altruistic motive. A wide spectrum of listeners from very different backgrounds regularly tunes in to Radio Beur. Besides, versatile and eclectic street-languages, alternative idioms and styles of dress are not unique to French society. In many European societies, though such expressions often originate from one ethnic group, they rapidly become part of a playful social transaction by means of which aesthetic and social tastes are transferred in all directions, eventually becoming part of a general cultural pool. When a Bangladeshi woman from the East End of London converses in cockney rhyming slang, or when a Welsh woman from Tiger Bay (the traditionally 'immigrant' area of Cardiff) wears an Afro hairdo, whose 'identity' exactly is being expressed? Under such circumstances, might it not be better to drop the notion of 'identity' altogether and speak instead of a field of cross-cultural improvization, endlessly borrowing, transposing, parodying both other social landscapes and itself? Using a metaphor from popular music, you might call this field of play 'cultural riff'.

Archimedes' harem

This brings me to the second reading, taken from the foundation text of the Beur movement: Charef's novel of 1983, *Le thé au harem d'Archi Ahmed*. Interestingly, this book began as a draft cinematic treatment but was then published as a novel in the same year as the historic *Marche des beurs*. Afterwards the film director Michel Ray-Gavras persuaded Charef to return to his first idea and direct a film version, *Le Thé au harem d'Archimède*, which won the Prix de Jeune Cinéma Française at the Cannes festival in 1985. Some stills are included here as illustrations. As Charef says in his interview with Mahjoub in the first reading, the plot concerns a group of young people in the *banlieu*, the most vocal of whom are an Arab youth from North Africa (Majid) and his best friend, a French boy called Pat. In this extract they go out on the town together on Saturday night, first to the

Figure 7.4 *Still from Le Thé au Harem d'Archimède*, 1985, directed by Mehdi Charef. Photo: BFI Collections

cinema and then to a café-bar, before taking to the streets, discovering a cache of booze and getting well and truly drunk. The whole point of the work – both written text and film – is the inseparability of the two, their mutual support, their reciprocal mockery and the jokes that they share, both with one another and their wider, multi-racial peer group.

One of these jokes gives the book its title. As Ruth Bernard Yeazell has illustrated in a recent study, the penetration of the harem has been a baffling preoccupation of the male western mind for at least three centuries (Yeazell, 2000). Against this background, many readers open Charef's novel in the expectation of finding something exotic yet somehow sedate. Instead there is a scene set in a suburban Paris schoolroom where a bored schoolboy of Caribbean origin, a member of Majid's gang, is attempting to follow – or more precisely to resist – the maths master as he expounds Archimedes' principle (*'le théorème d'Archimède*). The resentful boy doodles in his exercise book a mangled version of this theorem's name – it comes out as '*le thé au harem d'Archi Ahmed*'. The English translator has lamely rendered this cheeky and deliberate malapropism as 'Tea in the Harem', which largely misses the joke. A more faithful attempt might be 'Archy Mehdi's Harem'. Bearing in mind that the whole point of the student's insolent inventiveness is a scribbled protest against maths, a compulsory component of the baccalauréat examination endured by French schoolchildren from all backgrounds, a more spirited and streetwise effort might be 'Up yours, Archimedes!'

For Pat and Majid, Saturday is a day like any other – except for the evenings, when they get together with their friends.

At the Alhambra, the midnight session is usually a porno film. Every hooligan for miles around makes it their rendezvous. The scene is indescribable – an appalling racket of shouting, insults, cheers and jeers. The usherette tries to get them to shut up, but no chance – they call her every name under the sun. The owner of the cinema keeps well out of the way. He's been roughed up on too many previous occasions ... And in the auditorium, they smoke, they spit, they hold conversations between the balcony and the stalls ... and they swap the latest news:

'Hey – Maxie's been sent down!'

'Oh?'

'He did over a jeweller's ...'

'He'll get a good stretch for that.'

'You know James – the one with the limp?'

'The blond kid with the spotty face?'

'That's the one. Well, he killed himself coming off his bike on the Pontoise motorway. On the way to see his girlfriend.'

'Too bad.'

Then all of them gather in the corner café. You usually find two rival gangs in there, scuffling at the bar. They've got nothing better to do, so they fight. Sometimes it turns really nasty, especially for the poor sod who ends up on the floor getting a kicking. One Bastille Day, the local neighbourhood dance was broken up by a mass brawl – the biggest the estate had ever seen – easily fifty of them, going at one another with bottles, knives and knuckle-dusters. The cops wouldn't even come near it ...!

Maggy really liked the gang, and they felt the same about her. She used to call them her 'little ones'. In her bar you'd always find a bit of human warmth, a pal, a cigarette, or a couple of francs to tide you over. There was never any trouble at Maggy's either: if they wanted to fight, they did it off the premises. Her son Noel was inside for robbery. He was usually part of the gang. She didn't blame the gang, though. That particular evening, there was a raid by the police. The familiar routine: produce your wage packet, your ID papers, your dole card ... Those who weren't students and who couldn't produce a wage slip – in other words the majority –

Figure 7.5 Still from *Le Thé au Harem d'Archimède*, 1985, directed by Mehdi Charef. Photo: BFI Collections

got the 'treatment'. The cops took their ID cards and went to the car outside to radio the station, to check you out, to see if you were on the wanted list, see if you had a record ...

One of the cops asked Pat for his papers. Pat refused. The cop was furious. He repeated his request:

'Your papers!'

Pat continued drinking his beer, casually, to show his pals that he wasn't afraid. He replied:

'I'm French. This is my country. What do you take me for, an Arab?'

'Mind who you're talking to.'

Pat put his glass on the bar and replied, cockily:

'So why do you want to see my papers, then?'

'There's going to be trouble if you refuse.'

Pat wasn't particularly keen on being taken for a spin in the paddy-wagon, so he pulled out a dirty, dog-eared ID card. The cop held it gingerly, as if he was afraid of getting infected. He asked Pat for his name and address, and then returned his card. They still dragged off two of the local lads, though, for looking shifty. What had they done? Nobody knew.

Once the cops had gone, Bibiche pulled out a couple of grammes of hash that he'd stashed in the goal of the table football machine. Maggy was furious.

Pat cursed the police as he heard their car start.

'Bastards.'

Majid paid for everyone's drinks before he left – which prompted Thierry to comment:

'You been fishing today, then?'

'I pay for your drinks, and you start asking questions?!'

'No need to get ratty: I was only joking.'

'Well don't.'

The four of them went out together – Majid, Pat, Bengston and Thierry. It was already dark, and there was a chill in the air. Just as they were arriving at the entrance to the estate, they saw a young Arab lad by the name of Lousef – nicknamed Lulu. He was completely drunk, and was more or less unsuccessfully trying to piss against the railings. He could hardly stand up. There were surprised at the state of him. As they came towards him, he was pissing on his boots. They waited behind him until he finally noticed there was someone there. Without even putting his cock back in his fly he grabbed at the railings with both hands. He was breathing heavily. Pat said:

'Lucky they put those railings there.'

The others smiled.

Lulu turned round with difficulty. He was still more or less holding onto the railings with his left hand. He looked at them, peered more closely, and finally recognized them. 'Oh, it's you ... bunch of wankers ...'

Bengston laughed, and said:

'Close your shop. You're showing your tools.'

'What?'

'Put your dick away, or someone might cut it off.'

Lulu looked down and saw his cock hanging out. He put it away. 'What you been up to, dum-dum?' Majid asked.

Lulu tried to speak, but the effort just made him throw up. The others laughed and dived out of the way as he vomited all over the railings. He wiped his mouth with his shirt-sleeve and confided:

'It's old Malard's wine ... and ... ha ... ha ... it's good stuff!!'

He laughed along with the others. 'I got it from his basement, the old bastard ... Ha, ha ...!'

The others took him by the arm and led him off.

'We're going to check if you're talking rubbish or not.'

They walked round the parking-lot and went through the hallway of Poppy House. Thierry turned on the light in the basement corridor. He found Malard's cellar door wide open. Several empty bottles were lying on the floor. There were five whole crates of wine sitting there! Good stuff, too. They set to, drinking straight from the bottle. Lulu laughed as he watched them. 'Hmm ... Not bad at all,' said Pat, with the air of a connoisseur.

(Charef, 1983, pp. 114–19)

EXERCISE _____

1   In the extract, what is the racial constitution of the gang to which Majid and Pat belong?

2   What do you gather about this group's social base? It is clearly, for example, very unlike the rival gangs portrayed in two well-known Americanized film versions of Shakespeare's *Romeo and Juliet* – *West Side Story*, set in 1950s New York, or the more recent version, set in Los Angeles. It is also quite different from any of the rival gangs of 1960s London, in the days of 'Mods' versus 'Rockers'. There is no indication anywhere of a rival grouping, and no sense of what used to be known as 'gang warfare'. If there's an enemy it is the older generation, or perhaps the housing estate – the HLM – as physical environment and instrument of social control.

3   When the French boy Pat is questioned by the policeman in Maggy's bar he snarls 'I'm French. This is my country. What do you take me for, an Arab?' This information is true enough but, given the social context, what is the point of the remark? Under other circumstances it would be a racist jibe; after all, both Pat and his interrogator are 'French'. But remember Pat's best friend is 'an Arab', and they are standing side by side. The gendarme responds with the reprimand, 'Mind who you're talking to.' Well, who *is* Pat talking to? Everything that he says can be quite clearly overheard by Majid. If there is a racist element to his behaviour, it is one that Majid accepts with good humour. Who then is joking, and about whom or what?

4   Going out into the night air, the group encounters an inaccurately micturating and very drunk 'Arab' called Lousef or 'Lulu'. His behaviour is hilarious, but who 'identifies' him as an Arab? Can it be the novelist who is, after all, an Arab himself? Charef was born in Maghnia, Algeria in 1952 and came to France with his parents when he was ten years old. In this respect he is untypical of the Beurs in general, who are by definition second-generation *maghrébins* born in France. Throughout the novel the narrative focus is on Majid, a young man of a not dissimilar background to the author's. Is there any suggestion that he experiences an affinity with the inebriated Lulu, or are his feelings so sunk in the group's that in the scene in question he briefly sees this 'Arab' through the others' eyes?

5   They then go off and get drunk themselves: Pat, Majid and everybody. But remember Majid is from a Muslim household, quite a devout one as it happens where alcohol is strictly outlawed. Is this something that occurs to him as he tucks into old Malard's wine? Who is breaking which taboos, and for whose benefit? Is the narrator's reticence about this moral issue telling in itself?

DISCUSSION

To assist you in contextualizing and interpreting this passage it might be helpful to think about the cohesive or divisive effect of certain kinds of wit and humour. Charef is quite explicit about the role of such levity in his work. The bald concrete HLM estate where the action is set, for example, is known as Fleursville (Flower City), and its individual tower blocks are named Azalea House, Rose House and so on. Needless to say, there is not a shrub in sight: an anomaly that is a sardonic comment both on the unimaginativeness of planners and on the clumsy sentimentality of bureaucrats. Lightness of touch is integral to the mood of the book and the film. In a later scene featured in both, an unemployed single mother is persuaded out of jumping from the balcony of her second-floor flat when concerned neighbours confront her with her little boy. The episode was based on a real-life incident in which the mother died. After the film's release, *Cinématographe* magazine asked Charef why he had altered the original experience. In his reply he coined a highly personal neologism:

> 'Surtout,' je n'ai pas voulu faire un drame social et misérabiliste. J'avais grand peur de cet adjectif: misérabiliste. J'ai préféré une chronique allègre plutôt qu'un film accusateur conçu pour choquer sysématiquement le spectateur. [Above all, I didn't want to create a miserabilist social drama. I was very apprehensive of that adjective:

> miserabilist. I preferred a light-hearted story to an accusatory film intended to shock the spectator.]
>
> (*Cinématographe*, July 1985, p. 11, quoted Hargreaves, 1997, p. 86)

The extemporized adjective was another joke, of course, this time at the expense of the nineteenth-century 'realist' novel of philanthropic concern, of which Victor Hugo's *Les Misérables*, first published in 1862, is such an outstanding example. So, up yours too, Monsieur Hugo!

There are a great many jokes in this novel, and their trajectories are both diverse and unpredictable. One fairly consistent effect, however, is to dissolve ethnic divisions and cement social ties within a generational socio-economic sub-group that in turn functions as a microcosm of a society whose composition is slowly being transformed.

Seen from one perspective this process, involving a blending of cultures among several other influences, approximately corresponds to what the cultural critic Homi Bhabha has called 'hybridity' (Bhabha, 1994, pp. 5–6, 112–16, 118–20, 251–2). For Bhabha, who is supplying a more contestatory, hence single-minded, version of readings of the early medieval world by the Russian critic Mikhail Bakhtin (1895–1975), culture tends to advance through a process of cross-fertilization. This has been the case since time immemorial; at certain moments, however, an acceleration in this process takes place. Culture then becomes hybrid as old alignments, affinities and lines of descent break down, bringing into being fresh formations that challenge earlier group definitions.

Arguably, this is an international phenomenon that can be illustrated from the history of France, Germany and the UK. One case may have been the fusion of 'Anglo-Saxon' and 'Norman' elements in the centuries following the 'invasion' of England in 1066, which gradually formed modern English identity, including the English language that was then exported worldwide. Particularly since the mid twentieth century, a slow influx of population from former colonies has brought about a similar fusion in the modern UK. Among those who have described this process are the historian Ron Ramdin (1999) and the sociologist and cultural critic Paul Gilroy. This, for example, is what Gilroy has to say in his book *Small Acts: Thoughts on the Politics of Black Cultures* (1993) about the assimilation of 'black' cultural forms in the contemporary UK. He is speaking of 'diasporic culture', in other words the spreading out of social and cultural forms from an original homeland:

> From the dawn of post-war settlement, diasporic culture has been an ambiguous presence in the autonomous institutions of the [British] working-class. Two generations of whites have appropriated it, discovering in its seductive forms meanings of their own. It is now impossible to speak coherently of black culture in Britain apart from the culture of Britain as a whole. This is particularly true as far as music is concerned. Black expressive culture has directly shaped youth culture, pop culture and the culture of city life in Britain's metropolitan centres. The white working class has danced for forty years to its rhythms. There is, of course, no contradiction between making use of black culture and loathing real life black people, yet the informal long-term processes through which different groups have negotiated one another have intermittently created a 'two-tone' sensibility which celebrates its hybrid origins and has provided a significant opposition to 'common-sense' racism.
>
> (Gilroy, 1993, p. 34–5)

In Gilroy's analysis, imported cultural forms spread outwards and upwards: from initially marginalized migrant groups to the indigenous working class, then to the wider urban community, and thence to society at large. Charef's fiction tends to support this theory. It also tends to suggest that humour and language, word play and literary expression have a significant role to play, alongside other cultural forms such as music, in the process described.

Migration and language: dilemma or opportunity?

Mark Pittaway has called attention to the fact that language can be a 'key "marker" of identity', but also a 'means of inclusion' that acts simultaneously as a 'means of exclusion' (Chimisso, 2003, Chapter 4). I have just examined a cultural movement whose inclusiveness and exclusiveness are defined by a number of contingent factors, including ethnic group, generation, economics and class.
(To 'identify' with this movement you do not, for example, have to be North African, and many North Africans would dissociate themselves from it. Nor do you have to be poor, though it helps. By the same token, many members of the working class have no contact with the movement at all.) Among these factors, language plays a typically complicated part. There is no one language that defines membership of such a group, but rather a spectrum of language use, ranging from French or Arabic to street slang or *verlan* with an admixture of

American slang as well. There is also a great deal of switching between these various languages or argots, even within a single conversation. Moreover, they can be combined or alternated for tactical reasons, as in the home for instance. At the beginning of *Le Thé au harem d'Archi-Ahmed* there is a scene where Majid is quarrelling with his mother. He puts a Sex Pistols album on the record-player and, when she refuses to be drowned out, pretends that he doesn't understand her Arabic. He does of course: that is a major point in the episode.

An almost defining characteristic of migrant groups is that they have at least two, or more usually a number of, languages at their disposal. For the writer who originates from such a background, this versatility can be a curse or a blessing. There are various ways in which he or she may deal with this. One common approach is for an author to centre the text in one fairly standard register of the language, and occasionally to inflect from it into others. Charef, for instance, goes backwards and forwards between French, *verlan* and conversations supposedly in Arabic. However, he never quotes Arabic directly, but just informs us that his French version of the relevant dialogue is a translation.

This is a feasible method when *what* a character is saying is more important to the author than the *sound* of what they are saying. When writing fiction, it is a practical way of conveying the feel of life within a multilinguistic environment. In the composition of poetry the choice of medium is more difficult. To start with, the voice heard is usually the poet's own. Furthermore, the poet is likely to want to convey the aural quality of the verbal music he or she is hearing inside his or her head. If that verbal music is Arabic or Turkish, say, no translation can convey this faithfully.

These generalizations are especially pertinent to a writer such as Sujata Bhatt, born in Ahmedabad in India, educated in Maryland and Iowa, and resident for some years in Bremen, Germany. Bhatt's mother-tongue is Gujarati; she was educated principally through the medium of English; her husband is the German writer Michael Augustin, and she has a daughter with German nationality. One view of her circumstances would be that she has a choice between three different linguistic identities, the use of which is determined situationally: she uses German in her everyday existence, writes in English for an English-speaking audience and communicates in her mother-tongue mainly when she returns to India or meets members of her birth family. If this is the case, her choice of language medium would be deliberate at every point and she would have complete control over the result. There would be a 'clash' of 'identities', but at least these identities could be separated out.

To work out whether this is indeed the case, it is necessary to consider Bhatt's poems. Each of the next three readings involves looking at one of these, but the three do not necessarily yield the same answer to the questions that I have put. I begin with the opening section of Bhatt's poem 'Search for My Tongue' (Bhatt, 1988, pp. 63–70). You will immediately notice that some of the lines are in unfamiliar notation (unless, that is, your own first language happens to be Gujarati). For non-Gujarati speakers – the majority of the poem's envisaged audience, I suspect – the problem is lessened by the fact that Bhatt has carefully transliterated each Indian line into the Roman alphabet, reproducing the sounds phonetically, and then translated it into English.

Days my tongue slips away.
I can't hold on to my tongue.
It's slippery like the lizard's tail
I try to grasp
but the lizard darts away.

મારી જીભ સરકી જાય છે
(mari jeebh sarki jai chay)
I can't speak. I speak nothing.
Nothing.

કાંઇ નહિ, હું નથી બોલી શકતી
(kai nahi, hoo nathi boli shakti)
I search for my tongue.

પરંતુ ક્યાં શોધું ? ક્યાં ?
(parantu kya shodhu? Kya?)

હું દોડતી દોડતી જાઉં છું.
(hoo dhodti dhodti jaoo choo)
But where should I start? Where?
I go running, running,

નદી કિનારે પ્હોચી છું, નદી કિનારે.
(nadi keenayray pohchee choo, nadi keenayray)
reach the river's edge.
Silence

એકદમ શાંત.
(akedum shant)

નીચે પાણી નહિ, ઉપ્પર પક્ષી નહિ.
(neechay pani nahi, oopur pakshi nahi)
Below, the riverbed is dry. Above,
the sky is empty: no clouds, no birds.
If there were leaves, or even grass
they would not stir today,
for there is no breeze.
If there were clouds
then, it might rain.

જો વાદળ હોત   તો કદાચ વરસાદ આવે,
(jo vadla hoat   toh kadach varsad aavay)

જો વરસાદ પડે તો નદી પાછી આવે,
(jo varsad puday toh nadi pachee aavay)

જો નદી હોય, જો પાણી હોય, તો કાંઈક લીલું લીલું દેખાય.
(jo nadi hoy, jo pani hoy, toh kaeek leelu leelu daykhai)
If the rains fell
then the river might return,
if the water rose again I might see something green
at first, then trees enough to fill a forest.
If there were some clouds that is.

જો વાદળા હોત તો.
(jo vadla hoat toh)
Since I have lost my tongue
I can only imagine
there is something crawling
beneath the rocks, now burrowing down
into the earth when I lift the rock.

જ્યારે પથ્થર ઉપાડું .
(jyaray patther oopadu)
The rock is in my hand, and the dry
moss stuck on the rock
prickles my palm.
I let it drop
for I must find my tongue.
I know it can't be here
in this dry riverbed.
My tongue can only be
where there is water.

પાણી, પાણી,
(pani, pani)

હજુ યાદ છે પેલી છોકરી.
(hujoo yad chay paylee chokri)

"ઠંડા પાણી, મીઠા પાણી," બોલતી બોલતી આવતી.
("thunda pani, meetha pani, bolti bolti aavti)
માથે કાળું માટલું , હાથમાં પીત્તળનો પ્યાલો.
(mathay kallu matlu, hathma pittulno pyalo)

ઉભેલી ગાડી બાજુ આવતી.
(oobhaylee gaadi baju aavti)

બારી તરફ હાથ લંબાવીને પાણી આપતી.
(bari taraf hath lumbaveenay pani aapti)

અને હું , અતિશય તરસી,
(unay hoo, ateeshay tarsi)

મોટા મોટા ઘૂં ટડા લેતી પી જતી.
(mota mota ghuntada layti pee jati)

હજુ યાદ છે પેલી છોકરી.
(hujoo yad chay paylee chokri)
Even water is scarce.
There was a little girl
who carried a black clay pitcher on her head,
who sold water at the train station.
She filled her brass cup with water,
stretched out her arm to me,
reached up to the window, up
to me leaning out the window from the train,
but I can't think of her in English.

(Bhatt, 1988, pp. 63–5)

EXERCISE

The task here is to write an analysis of the poem, addressing as many of the following issues as you can.

1   Why has Bhatt set the poem out in this manner? What need has she to feature Gujarati at all? What are the effects on you of this bilingual technique?

2   Give its linguistic multidimensionality, will the poem have the same effect on all of its readers as it has on yourself? Will readers from all countries and social groups react in the same way, or in different ways depending on their background? Read the poem several times to envisage the possible range of reactions. (Your ability to do this, of course, will be circumscribed by your own linguistic range; that does not mean that it is a worthless exercise.) What, for instance, might be its effect on:

    (a) A poetry lover from Gujarat who either does or does not read English.

    (b) A Gujarati-speaker from Bradford who also speaks English, assuming that this person also reads both languages. (He or she might read only one of them: it is quite possible to be able to speak a language without being able to read it.) I suppose you should discount people who read neither English nor Gujarati, though it might be amusing to imagine the result.

(c) Gujarati speakers from Turin or Grenoble or Karlsruhe who fall into the same categories as in (b). For a number of reasons the range of reactions might be quite different here, the most likely being that such a person might well be able to manage the Gujarati but not the English.

(d) Any other likely categories of reader that you can think of.

3   Once you have followed through these possibilities, tackle this issue: is 'Search for My Tongue' a poem with one possible interpretation or several? What in either case does it consist of: the poem as intended by the writer, or the poem as experienced by its reader(s)? If these alternatives differ markedly, does it matter?

4   The first line (corresponding to the first sentence) of the text has a finite verb – 'slips' – and a subject (in both the grammatical and semantic sense) – 'tongue'. In other respects, its syntax is quite odd because incomplete. Make as many different attempts as you can manage to fill out the syntax so as to form a complete, conventional prose sentence. You can be as imaginative as you like, provided the result makes grammatical and social sense. I'll give you a most improbable one to get you going: 'I always listen to a CD of Mahler's Sixth Symphony on days when my tongue slips away.' It is not a very convincing one, I agree. How many *likely* completions can you think up? Once you have written them out, try to work out the effect of each on the way that the reader approaches the poem in the first place; and on its total effect.

5   What, in any case, does Bhatt mean by the word 'tongue'?

6   In the second stanza does the statement 'I can't speak' mean the same as the next statement ('I speak nothing')? Bhatt then repeats the word 'nothing' as a one-word grammatical unit. Why? If you have a *Collected Works of William Shakespeare* to hand, you might like to compare *King Lear* Act 1, scene 1, lines 89–92. It would be better still if you read the whole of that scene. Do you think that there is a valid parallel (note the repetition in both cases)? If so, and given that both Bhatt and Cordelia are women in a divided world, do you think that the parallel enriches the poem? I may as well say that, in the light of Bhatt's educational background, an allusion to Shakespeare is very likely. Despite the alliteration *nahi ... nathi* there is no exact verbal repetition in the Gujarati, though it is there five lines further down in *kya ... kya?* (where ... Where?)

7   The rest of the poem tells a story about going in search of a tongue along a dried-up riverbed. At one point the tongue seems to have transformed into a reptile, something like a lizard. Bhatt is obviously playing with symbols, but what do you think is the

point of each? What specifically is the significance of the dried-up riverbed; the rock; the lizard-like reptile; and the search in general, and its outcome?

8 Do you notice any sort of a contradiction in the last eight lines?

DISCUSSION

Remember this is a poem, not a series of statements in support of a certain position, or even a discussion of a problem. If Bhatt were merely discussing an issue, or proposing a solution to it, she would probably not be writing poetry at all, but giving us an essay or chatting on the radio. A very simple (or simplified?) interpretation of the poem might run like this. An Indian poet has been educated through the medium of a European language (English, the *lingua franca* of the British raj in India that came to an end in 1947). Moreover, this poet lives in Germany, so she is a migrant placed in a strange society who has to converse day by day in German, a third 'tongue', with her neighbours and family. She is worried that she is losing contact with Gujarati and the poem expresses her anxiety about her linguistic 'identity'. In it, she experiences a kind of waking nightmare in which she goes in search of her mother-tongue, eventually finding it hiding behind some kind of obstacle, symbolized by the rock.

This is an entirely feasible reading of the poem, but it does not follow that it is the correct one (it does not even follow that there *is* a correct reading, either). For example, the state of affairs in the second line – 'I can't hold on to my tongue' – could mean that the poet has lost contact with one of her languages; it could just as well, however, be a reference to uncanny fluency, as in the phrase 'my tongue ran away with me'. Bhatt could mean that she has been rendered symbolically inarticulate, but she could equally well mean that she finds herself saying (or writing) what she does not mean. In the latter case, the poem would be an expression of quite a different anxiety from that indicated in the summary given above: a sense that her thoughts are in some sense being controlled by the medium through which they are expressed. Those of you who speak more than one language may well have had the experience of hearing yourself saying something and then wondering (either in that language or in another one), 'Did I say that?' 'Did I mean that?' 'Would I have expressed that thought if I was speaking in Urdu/Polish/Serbo-Croat/Greek?'

In Bhatt's poetry there is often a carefully worked out contradiction between what the poem says and what it enacts. There is a example of this at the end of 'Search for My Tongue' where Bhatt confesses of the young girl at the Indian railway station that 'I can't think of her in English' and yet somehow manages to convey her impression of the girl's presence using exclusively that language. This could mean that Bhatt has overcome her difficulty; it could also, however, mean that she has been betrayed by her fluency into giving an English-language version of her experience that is at variance with the subjective truth.

One final thought, then, expressed again as a sequence of questions. Do people think in words? If they do, are the thoughts that they think – and thereby arguably their sense of who they are and the opinions they hold – influenced by the language that they are using? If so, or if not so, what in a European context are the implications for our ongoing discussion of that mysterious phenomenon of 'identity'? When a doctor from, say, the Philippines thinks and speaks in Danish, who or what is expressing himself/herself/itself: the doctor, the Danish language with its characteristic thought set, or both? Do we speak languages, or do languages speak us?

The second reading is the second half of a poem published in 1991, titled by Bhatt 'Devighen Pathak' after her Indian grandmother. In the first section, set in Ahmedabad in 1938, the granny commissions a necklace from a goldsmith. She wonders what design to choose and eventually settles on one of the most ancient sacred symbols in Hindu art: the swastika. In the second section the poet, who has inherited the ornament, ponders what her attitude should be towards this hallowed object in the light of everything that has happened in world history in the meantime and the dreadful significance acquired by this once revered design. Should she hand it on to her own, half-German daughter? What would the daughter make of it? Was it, the poet wonders, a culpable error of judgement – or worse – for her grandmother to have ordered the heirloom in the first place?

She was right
and she was wrong.
Why else do I keep this necklace
in a box? Why else
am I suddenly unable to wear
this yellow gold snake heavy symbol?
I'm unable to believe the swastika
is untouched by history.

I remember practicing drawing swastikas
as a child, with other children ...
we also practiced drawing circles
and squares, perfect triangles
and five pointed stars.

Triangular Parvati
    pointing earthward.
Triangular Shiva
    pointing skyward.

Their bodies, sharp –
pared down to pure form.
Is that where truth lies?
In the shadow of a shoulder blade,
the corner of a triangle?
But the swastikas were always in red
and as I drew them
I always thought
this is holy
    holy
    holy – as I tried to steady my hand
always believing there was pure goodness
branching out from the centre.

I remember drawing swastikas everywhere
in so many notebooks, and outside
    even in the mud –
thinking this is beauty
this is true wisdom – while the difficult circles
and stars filled the background.

What does a circle mean?
What does a triangle mean?
Who knows the true meanings?

Oh didn't I love the Hindu swastika?
And later, one day didn't I start wishing
I could rescue that shape from history?

But how shall I begin?
What shall I say?
    Oh my German-born daughter,
    innocent girl with a Lübecker
    Baltic-eyed innocent father ...

Look at those neat rows of swastikas
        in red
plastered across the temple grounds, look
at the swastikas framing every wedding invitation.
The dowry determines
the paper's quality

the quality of the print.
Even that motion of the hand, that gesture
sweeping across the temple floor

is not always holy, not always innocent.
Something is wrong:
So many old religions fatten
on arguments, on fresh murders
or do they call that offerings?
Someone's blood, someone's money
someone's wife, someone's son
should not have been touched.

Meanwhile, the shape of the swastika remains:
Hakenkreuz, fylfot,
and when you slant your head
           towards the sun
also St Brigid's plaited fancy cross ...
And my daughter born
on the first of February,
           the first day of an early Springtide ...

स्वस्ति, स्वस्ति
(swasti, swasti,)   they used to say
meaning: Be well, be well!

Oh my German-born daughter,
arriving during a spell of bright Spring weather –
          lucky girl
          to be born on St Brigid's day ...
What will you say? What colours will you
prefer? In what language
      will you speak?

(Bhatt, 1991, pp. 49–51)

EXERCISE

1   How much responsibility does the poet seem to think that her grandmother bears for the ideological reverberations of her choice? Remember that she ordered the ornament in 1938, the year of the Munich Agreement that ceded the German-speaking parts of Czechoslovakia to Nazi Germany. Hitler's ambitions, his dislike of the Jewish and other non-Caucasian peoples and the iconography of his party were all well known to politically aware people. On the other hand, the public horizon in India was dominated at the time by the growing independence movement. Though many Indians – including as it happens Bhatt's

Figure 7.6 Migration of a symbol

(a) Maharastra, India: Khim Ashram: swastika with figures of the Hindu deities Ganesh and Trimurti. Photo: Trip/ H. Rogers

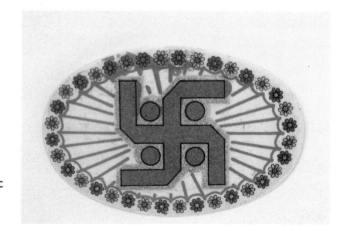

(b) India; swastika as contemporary domestic ornament. Photo: Trip/ H. Rogers

(c) Lullingstone Roman Villa, Kent: fourth century CE, geometric panel with swastikas in mosaic floor of audience chamber. Photo: English Heritage Photo Library

(d)   Echternach, Luxembourg: eleventh century CE, Golden gospel book of Henry III, St Mark's gospel, illumination with swastika motifs. Photo: AKG London

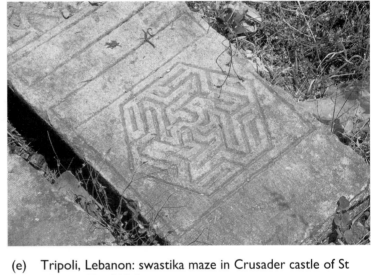

(e)   Tripoli, Lebanon: swastika maze in Crusader castle of St Giles. Photo: Trip/ H. Rogers

(f)   Unter den Linden, Berlin, 1 May, 1938, Nazi banners with Hakenkreuz design. Photo: AKG London

grandmother – supported the non-violent methods of Mahatma Gandhi (1869–1948), other more militaristically minded nationalists saw Germany as a potential ally against the British.

2   In Hindu art, as Bhatt herself explains, the swastika depicts the union of the gods Parvati and Shiva. The word itself comes from the Sanskrit *svastika*, taken from *svasti* (well-being), which is in turn derived from *su* (good) and *asti* (being). It implies a state of inner serenity and can still be used as a greeting. During the Middle Ages the swastika migrated to Europe, where it found a place in Christian art. In medieval churches it was sometimes found at the base of stained-glass windows, for which reason it was referred to as 'fyflot', or 'fill-foot' The Crusaders also carried the symbol with them wherever they went; several examples are to be seen in Crusader castles in the Middle East. In the 1930s the Nazis adopted the clockwise form of the swastika known as the *Hakenkreuz*, or 'hook-cross', turning it into a by-word for race hatred, genocide and war. How able or willing is the poet to separate her grandmother's adornment from the meanings that its shape has acquired in successive periods and cultures? Is there ever such a thing as an abstract design? Are all shapes ideologically loaded?

3   What is the religious orientation of this poem? Bhatt, like her grandmother, was brought up as a Hindu. Her daughter, as she carefully notes, was born in nominally Christian Bremen on 1 February, the feast day of the sixth-century Irish abbess St Brigid. Throughout much of Europe, including the Catholic parts of Germany, this saint is revered for her compassion and ability to perform healing miracles. Is this, do you think, a Hindu poem, a Christian or ecumenically minded piece, or a statement of humanism? What, in any case, should determine the answer to that question: the inferred attitude of the poet, or the reactions of the reader(s)?

4   Read the last seven lines carefully. In the light of what has gone before, do you think that this is just a poem about visual representation and its cultural implications, or are other forms of communication entailed?

DISCUSSION

Though the Hindu and the Nazi interpretations of the swastika seem to be polar opposites, one historical factor links them: the debate that raged in Europe during the nineteenth and twentieth centuries over the identity and movements of the Aryans. During the mid to late nineteenth century it was thought that this diverse ethnic grouping had spread out across Europe from a common homeland that was often placed in India, though other cradles of diffusion were also suggested. Furthermore, philologists followed Sir William Jones

(1746–94) in suggesting that most European languages had branched out from an Indo-European source common to both Greek and Sanskrit. The two theories often went hand in hand: tides of migration were supposed to have swept westwards from some Aryan homeland, bringing the Indo-European languages with them.

The Nazis perverted these ideas to make Aryan identity – which by the 1930s was academically questionable in any case – synonymous with a Caucasian or, more narrowly, Teutonic people. The eastern origins of this grouping were largely ignored, or placed so far back in time as to be innocuous. The Aryans were portrayed as a civilized, stable, and healthy elite, fully justified in mastering and even in exterminating other peoples.

The swastika is therefore connected with two radically different views of demographic history. The first holds that people habitually move, carrying symbols, ideas and languages with them. All identities are arbitrary, and authenticity is a myth or a wilful projection of what has been called an imagined community. In the opposing view, peoples are essentially fixed in location and in their characteristics. Such stable, defined populaces form the basis of nations, each of which possesses an inherited identity setting it apart from those in other areas of the continent or the world. Demographic facts that depart from this pattern are regarded as exceptions that validate the rule. Which of these two views does the poem seem to advocate?

Lastly, you should consider the poet's implied analogy between visual symbols and other forms of communication, pre-eminently language. Many critics would see this poem as being about semiotics, or the science of signs. According to the Swiss linguist Ferdinand de Saussure (1857–1913) all signs, including words, are arbitrary, their meaning depending on convention and use. (de Saussure, 1996) The poem suggests that migration intensifies this process, since signs and words travel along with peoples and are transformed in the process. This metamorphosis of symbols can itself be looked at in two different ways: as impartial change or as appropriation. The swastika, for instance, can be regarded as an ideologically neutral figure that has been endowed over time with varying signification by different cultures, or else as possessing an authentic Sanskrit meaning that has since been *appropriated* (and twisted) by extremists. Which of these two understandings, do you think, prevails in Bhatt's poem?

In her short poem 'The Undertow' Bhatt describes her small family – herself, her German husband and their daughter – running with dogs along a wave-tossed beach. The text bristles with images, the investigation of which provides an effective route into its many meanings.

There are at least three
languages between us.
And the common space, the common dream-sound
is far out at sea.
There's a certain spot, dark
far out where the waves sleep
there's a certain spot
we always focus on,
and the three languages are there
swimming like seals fat with fish and sun
they smile, the three languages
understand each other so well.

We stand watching, jealous
of the three languages, wishing
we could swim so easily.
But the waves keep us back,
the undertow threatens;
so we take one word at a time.
Take 'dog' for example,

કૂતરો (kootro) in Gujarati, *Köter* in Low German
Hund in High German, like hound in English.

Dog   કૂતરો   (kootro)   *Köter*   *Hund*

hound   *dog*   *Köter*   કૂતરો   (kootro)

કૂતરો   કૂતરો   કૂતરો
(kootro   kootro   kootro)

The waves come chasing
the dogs on the beach
the waves come flooding the streets
listen to the seals swimming
through the bookstores, listen
the words spill together,

the common sounds:
ક ખ ગ

શ ક્ષ સ
kö   kh   ga

sh   ksh   ß   spill together

spill together
filling our shoes,
            filling our love with salt.

(Bhatt, 1988, pp. 89–90)

EXERCISE

1   In the second line, does the preposition 'between' indicate a barrier or some kind of a conduit?

2   Where, and what, is the 'common space' described in line 3?

3   Can you say anything light about the thematic relevance of the wallowing seals?

4   Can you shed any light on the significance of the cavorting dogs?

5   In lines 20–5, Bhatt plays with the Gujarati, German and English words for 'dog', in that order. She then transposes the order, not once but twice. Why?

6   In lines 33–6, Bhatt breaks these words down into shorter phonemes (individual units of sound). Why?

7   In between the complete words and the phonemes there is another description of the skin-dipping seals. Why is it placed there and what effect does it have?

8   Apart from a general soothing oceanic sense, what is the effect of the sea at the end of the poem? What do you suppose is the effect of the sea salt in the last line?

DISCUSSION

Perhaps it might be helpful to think again about the theories of linguistic diffusion mentioned in connection with the previous poem. While the study of linguistics has now progressed far beyond the stage represented by William Jones, or even de Saussure, there is still a sense in which the interdependence of languages is fundamental to our understanding of, for example, etymology. In 'The Undertow' Bhatt allows the sea to pound and rend her words – her words in three languages – so as to reveal the common fragments from which they are composed. Language then becomes a synecdoche for the whole of culture, made out of similar transferable elements.

'[L]isten to the seals swimming/through the bookstores' exhorts the poet, with pardonable hyperbole, at lines 29–30. This imaginary and amphibious vision is much more than surrealistic excess. The seals here are oblivious or intolerant of human differences, recognizing no boundaries – geographical, cultural, linguistic or personal. In this respect they are, in the poet's eyes, like language and literature that owe no allegiance. Their natural habitat is the sea, which acts in the poem as an image of the 'new condition' alluded to by Charef in the first reading.

Notice how the poem progresses. It starts by looking at entities – people, words – and the differences between them. By the end, these divergences have dissolved under the relentless attrition of the ocean. No longer are there – to revert to the imagery of the third extract – three separate tongues, three separate personal and collective identities: Indian woman, German man and mixed-race daughter. Instead there is a ceaseless spilling, swilling and filling, an interchange and becoming.

In the poem this integrative process should be described in the context of a close family bond. It is interesting that in the works discussed in this chapter Charef and Bhatt both concentrate on intimate personal relationships: friendship, gang fraternity, parenthood, marriage. This preoccupation with the personal may seem a private affair, but its repercussions are revolutionary and far-reaching.

Conclusion

The example of the Beur movement suggests that ethnic origin constitutes an important but far from overwhelming ingredient in national 'identity'. Many other factors also come into play, including economics, class, religion and language. Under certain circumstances (of which urban deprivation is an example) money or the lack of money, social ambition or frustration all prove stronger cohesive forces than 'race'. The example of Sujata Bhatt goes further to suggest that under other circumstances – love, a profound feeling of personal affinity – economic and social catalysts do not even have to be present for integration to take place, either on the general or on the individual level. The limitation of some discussions about identity, and the politics based upon it, is that it concentrates exclusively on the very real crises and conflicts experienced by individuals or broad social groups. But as the theories of Paul Gilroy, the fiction of Mehdi Charef and the poetry of Sujata Bhatt all tend to suggest, in between there is also a network of informal ties where the set descriptions and distinctions – and the conflict models based on them – continually break down. The result can often be a readjustment in the cultural idiom, even in the identity, not just of contiguous groups, but of the national – even arguably of the continental – community as a whole. In that common country, where people exchange customs, words and tastes just as friends swop clothes, Charef's 'new condition' is a recurrent and energizing state.

References

Anderson, B. (1991) *Imagined Communities: Reflections on the Origin and Spread of Nationalism*, London/New York, Verso.

Begag, A. (1987) *L'Immigré et sa ville*, Paris, Transport Espace Societé.

Bhabha, H. K. (1994) *The Location of Culture*, London/New York, Routledge.

Bhatt, S. (1988) *Brunizem*, Manchester, Carcanet.

Bhatt, S. (1991) *Monkey Shadows*, Manchester, Carcanet.

Bhatt, S. (1995) *The Stinking Rose*, Manchester: Carcanet.

Bouzid, K. (1984) *La Marche*, Paris, Sinbad.

Castells, M. (1997) *The Power of Identity*, Oxford, Blackwell.

Charef, M. (1983) *Le thé au harem d'Archi Ahmed*, Paris, Mercure de France (filmed as *Le Thé au harem d'Archimède*, dir. Mehdi Charef, 1985; transl. as *Tea in the Harem*, London, Serpents Tale, 1989).

Chimisso, C. (2003) *Exploring European Identities*, Milton Keynes, The Open University.

de Saussure, F. (1966) *Course in General Linguistics*, eds C. Bailly and A. Riedlinger, transl. W. Baskin, New York, McGraw-Hill.

Fraser, R. (ed.) (2000) 'The long march: migrant writing in Europe', special issue of *Wasafiri*, no. 31, London, Queen Mary and Westfield College.

Gellner, E. (1983) *Nations and Nationalism*, Oxford, Blackwell.

Gilroy, P. (1993) *Small Acts: Thoughts on the Politics of Black Cultures*, London, Serpents Tail.

Hargreaves, A. G. (1997) *Immigration and Identity in Beur Fiction: Voices from the North African Immigrant Community in France*, 2nd edn., Oxford, Berg.

Hargreaves, A. G. and Heffernan, M. J. (eds) (1983) *French and Algerian Identities from Colonial Times to the Present: a Century of Interaction*, Lampeter, Edwin Mellen.

Ramdin, R. (1999) *Reimaging Britain: 500 Years of Black and Asian History*, London, Pluto.

Touraine, A. (2000) *Can We Live Together?*, Cambridge, Polity.

Yeazell, R. B. (2000) *Harems of the Mind: Passages of Western Art and Literature*, New Haven, CN/London, Yale University Press.

Acknowledgements

Grateful acknowledgement is made to the following sources for permission to reproduce material in this book:

Chapter 1

Hitchens, C. (1990) *On the Road to Timişoara,* Vol.31, Granta Books. Copyright © Christopher Hitchens.

Sahlins, P. (1989) 'Introduction', *Boundaries. The Making of France and Spain in the Pyrenees,* University of California Press. Copyright © 1989 The Regents of the University of California.

Drakulić, S. (2001) 'Who is afraid of Europe?', *East European Politics and Societies,* vol. 15, no. 1, Spring 2001, pp.1–9. Copyright © 2001 by the American Council of Learned Societies. All Rights Reserved. By kind permission of the University of California Press.

Said, Edward W. *Orientalism.* Copyright © 1978 by Edward W. Said. Used by permission of Pantheon Books, a division of Random House, Inc.

Wolff, Larry, *Inventing Eastern Europe.* Copyright © 1994 by the Board of Trustees of the Leland Stanford Junior University.

Chapter 2

Naipaul, V. S. (1972) 'Jasmine', *The Overcrowded Barracoon and Other Articles,* André Deutsch Limited. By permission of Gillon Aitken Associates. Copyright © 1972, V. S. Naipual.

Simpson, L. (1957) 'To the Western world', *A Dream of Governors,* Wesleyan University Press.

Kunene, M. (1975) 'Europe', *Poems of Black Africa,* Martin Secker & Warburg Limited. By permission of André Deutsch Limited.

Havel, V. (1991) 'Politics and conscience', *Open Letters,* Faber & Faber.

Chapter 3

Mutton, A. F. A. (1961) 'Introduction: the concept of Central Europe', *Central Europe: A Regional and Human Geography,* Longmans, Green & Co. Ltd. Reprinted by permission of Pearson Education Limited.

Szűcs, J. (1988) 'Three historical regions of Europe: an outline', in Keane, J. (ed.) *Civil Society and the State. New European Perspectives,* Verso.

Garton Ash, T. (1991) 'Does Central Europe exist', *The Uses of Adversity: Essays on the Fate of Central Europe,* London, Granta Books. Reproduced by permission of Penguin Books Ltd. Also by permission of Rogers, Coleridge and White.

Chapter 4

Todorova, Maria, *Imagining The Balkans.* Copyright © 1997 by Oxford University Press, Inc. Used by permission of Oxford University Press.

West, Rebecca, *Black Lamb and Grey Falcon: A Journey through Yugoslavia,* first published in 1942 and in 1993 by Canongate Publishing, Edinburgh.

Durham, E. (2002) 'High Albania', *High Albania: A Victorian Travellers Balkan Odyssey,* Phoenix Press. By permission of Orion Publishing Group. First published by Edward Arnold in 1909.

Chapter 5

Garnett, C. and Higgens, H. (trans.) (1968) 'Our "opponents"', *My Past and Thoughts: The Memoirs of Alexander Herzen,* Vol.2. Chatto & Windus. By permission of A. P. Watt Ltd.

Greenfeld, Liah, *Nationalism: Five Roads To Modernity,* Cambridge, Mass., Harvard University Press, Copyright © 1992 by Liah Greenfeld. Reprinted by permission of the publisher.

Garnett, C. and Higgens, H. (trans.) (1968) 'England', *My Past and Thoughts: The Memoirs of Alexander Herzen,* Vol.3. Chatto & Windus. By permission of A. P. Watt Ltd.

Chapter 6

Gebethner, S. (1997) *Wybory '97. Partie i Programy Wyborcze.* Dom Wydawniczy Elipsa.

Zarycki, T. (2000) 'Politics in the periphery: political cleavages in Poland interpreted in their historical and international context', *Europe-Asia Studies,* vol. 52, no. 5, University of Glasgow. By permission of Taylor & Francis Ltd.

Walicki, A. (2001) 'The troubling legacy of Roman Dmowski', *East European Politics and Societies,* vol. 14, no. 1, University of California Press. Copyright © by The American Council of Learned Societies.

Chapter 7

Mahjoub, J. (1997) 'An interview with Mehdi Charef', in Nasta, S., (ed.) *Wasafiri,* no. 31. Queen Mary Westfield College.

Charef, Mehdi. (1989) in Emery, E, (ed.) *Tea in the Harem,* Serpent's Tail.

Bhatt, S. (1998) 'Search For My Tongue', *Brunizem,* Carcanet Press.

Bhatt, S. (1991) 'Devighen pathak', *Monkey Shadows,* Carcanet Press.

Bhatt, S. (no date) 'The Undertow', *Point No Point,* Carcanet Press.

Index

Mac OS® X
Snow Leopard™
Just the Steps™

FOR

DUMMIES®

by Keith Underdahl

WILEY

Wiley Publishing, Inc.

Mac OS® X Snow Leopard™ Just the Steps™ For Dummies®

Published by
Wiley Publishing, Inc.
111 River Street
Hoboken, NJ 07030-5774
www.wiley.com

WILEY

About the Author

Keith Underdahl is a video producer, training coordinator, graphic designer, and freelance writer from Oregon. He has written numerous books, including *Digital Video For Dummies*, 4th Edition, *Adobe Premiere Elements For Dummies*, *Wi-Fi Home Networking Just the Steps For Dummies*, and more.

Author's Acknowledgments

First and foremost, I wish to thank my family for their patience and help as I completed this exciting project. My children had to give up their homework computer to become a Snow Leopard test machine, and my wife Christa provided unwavering support during an extremely challenging work schedule.

I want to thank Bob Woerner and Wiley for bringing me on for this book, and the Wiley publishing team who helped put it all together. Paul Levesque and Virginia Sanders turned my cocktail napkin scribblings into something readable, and Dennis Cohen made sure that it was all technically accurate.

Publisher's Acknowledgments

We're proud of this book; please send us your comments through our online registration form located at `http://dummies.custhelp.com`. For other comments, please contact our Customer Care Department within the U.S. at 877-762-2974, outside the U.S. at 317-572-3993, or fax 317-572-4002.

Some of the people who helped bring this book to market include the following:

Acquisitions and Editorial

Senior Project Editor: Paul Levesque

Executive Editor: Bob Woerner

Copy Editor: Virginia Sanders

Technical Editor: Dennis R. Cohen

Editorial Manager: Leah Cameron

Editorial Assistant: Amanda Foxworth

Sr. Editorial Assistant: Cherie Case

Cartoons: Rich Tennant (`www.the5thwave.com`)

Composition Services

Project Coordinator: Patrick Redmond

Layout and Graphics: Samantha K. Allen, Carl Byers, Reuben W. Davis, Joyce Haughey, Ronald Terry, Christine Williams

Proofreaders: Caitie Copple, Lisa Young Stiers

Indexer: Ty Koontz

Publishing and Editorial for Technology Dummies

Richard Swadley, Vice President and Executive Group Publisher

Andy Cummings, Vice President and Publisher

Mary Bednarek, Executive Acquisitions Director

Mary C. Corder, Editorial Director

Publishing for Consumer Dummies

Diane Graves Steele, Vice President and Publisher

Composition Services

Debbie Stailey, Director of Composition Services

Contents at a Glance

Mac users have always been a loyal group, and for good reasons. Since Apple first started producing Macintosh computers in the 1980s, the company has placed an emphasis on quality, ease of use, and stability. Modern Macs running the latest operating system, OS X, are among the most powerful and dependable personal computers you can buy, and they're versatile enough to meet virtually any personal or professional need you may have.

About This Book

Macs are user friendly, but they're still computers, so you must follow certain steps to complete tasks, like setting up an e-mail account, accessing a Wi-Fi hotspot, transferring music to an iPod, customizing the OS X interface, creating a network, and almost any other computer task you can imagine. This book provides the steps you need to get up and running quickly, without having to pore through extra narratives or examples that you probably don't need anyway. And because a picture is worth a thousand words, all the steps in this book are accompanied by figures that walk you visually through each task.

Why You Need This Book

Whether you're new to Macs or you just want a handy quick reference to OS X Snow Leopard, this book helps you get to work quickly and efficiently. Each task covers a specific subject, and most steps take only a minute or two to follow. This book also provides crucial tips that you won't find in your Mac's built-in help system.

Introduction

Conventions used in this book

➡ When you have to access a menu command, I use the ➪ symbol. For example, if you have to open the File menu and then choose Open, I say choose File➪Open.

➡ Internet addresses are presented like this: www.dummies.com. I leave off the http:// part of Web addresses because you usually don't have to type it anyway.

 When you see this icon, the text includes helpful tips or extra information relating to the task.

How This Book Is Organized

I organized the chapters of this book into several basic parts:

Part I: Using OS X

The Mac OS X operating system is accessible and easy to use right out of the box. But if you want to customize the way OS X looks and behaves, the chapters in this part show you how. Chapters also show you how to manage system preferences and work with files and folders, which is especially helpful if you're new to Macs.

Part II: Getting to Work in OS X

Macs aren't all about iPods and movies. This part shows you how to use some of the handy programs that are included with OS X, as well as how to use productivity programs, such as word processors and presentation programs. I show you how to use and customize the OS X *Dashboard*, an innovative tool that gives you instant access to notepads, calculators, weather updates, sports scores, and more. And I show you how to clean up desktop clutter with another great OS X Snow Leopard feature called *Spaces*.

Part III: Going Online with Your Mac

If you're like most people, the Internet is one of the main reasons you use a computer in the first place. In this part, I show you how to browse the Web, exchange e-mail, chat, and even create your own Web pages.

Part IV: Using Multimedia

A modern Mac running OS X Snow Leopard is one of the most powerful multimedia devices you can buy. With iLife programs that come bundled with new Macs, you can watch DVDs; manage and play your music library; send music to iPhones, iPods, and other MP3 players; organize and improve digital photos; and make your own movies.

Part V: Networking Your Mac

If you have more than one computer, you'll probably want to connect those computers at some point so that they can share files, printers, Internet connections, and other resources. This part shows you how to set up networks between all your computers, even if some of those computers are Windows PCs.

Part VI: Extending Your Mac's Capabilities

As powerful and versatile as most Macs are right out of the box, they can be even more so. In this part, I show you how to use Bluetooth peripherals with your Mac, and how to upgrade your Mac with more memory and storage. One chapter even shows you how to install the Microsoft Windows operating system on your Mac.

Get Ready To . . .

If you're ready to fire up your first Mac or you're a long-time user and need quick steps to access advanced features, a task in this book is ready to help you.

Part I
Using OS X

The 5th Wave   By Rich Tennant

AFTER INSTALLING OSX 10.6, NED AND LORETTA SELECT THE COMPUTER'S BACKGROUND

"Oh – I like this background much better than the basement."

Customizing OS X

Chapter 1

Apple is rightfully proud of the user interface design incorporated into the Macintosh OS X family of operating systems. The interface is easy to use, and it's also easy to customize so that your Mac looks and behaves the way you want.

This chapter shows you how to customize various parts of the OS X interface, including

→ **Desktop:** You can change the color scheme of your Desktop or use a picture as your background.

→ **Display:** You can also change the size of the Desktop display, use a custom screen saver, and adjust the way the clock appears.

→ **Dock:** The OS X Dock normally resides at the bottom of the screen and gives quick access to your most commonly used programs. You can move the Dock, add or remove items, and change the way the Dock appears.

→ **Keyboard and accessibility:** Mac OS X can accommodate most accessibility needs, and you can change common keyboard shortcuts.

→ **Exposé:** Switch quickly between programs with this OS X tool.

→ **Spaces:** If you're tired of constantly re-arranging your Desktop, create and easily move between multiple virtual workspaces using Snow Leopard's Spaces feature.

Get ready to . . .

Access System Preferences

1. Open the Apple menu by clicking the Apple icon in the upper-left corner of the screen.

2. Choose System Preferences from the Apple menu to reveal the System Preferences window, as shown in Figure 1-1.

 You can also open System Preferences from the Dock.

3. Click a preference icon to open a group of settings.

 To return to the main System Preferences window, click the Show All button at the top of any individual preferences pane.

Modify the Desktop Appearance

1. Open System Preferences and then click the Appearance icon.

2. In the Appearance preferences pane (see Figure 1-2), click the Appearance pop-up menu and then choose a color scheme for the overall appearance of the interface.

3. Click the Highlight Color pop-up menu and choose a highlight color for selected text.

4. Use the Place Scroll Arrows radio buttons to choose whether you want scroll arrows right next to each other or placed at the top and bottom of scroll bars.

5. Select other scroll bar options as desired.

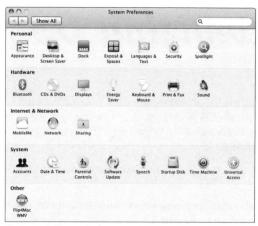

Figure 1-1: System Preferences

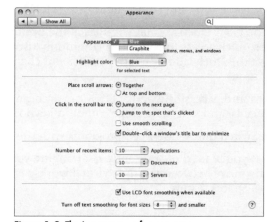

Figure 1-2: The Appearance preferences pane

 If you find that your computer freezes momentarily or responds slowly when scrolling through documents, deselect the Use Smooth Scrolling option.

6. Next to Number of Recent Items, choose the maximum number of items that are displayed from the pop-up menus for Applications, Documents, and Servers.

7. Click the Show All button to return to the System Preferences menu pane.

8. Click the Desktop & Screen Saver icon.

9. In the Desktop & Screen Saver pane that appears, click the Desktop tab to bring Desktop settings to the front (see Figure 1-3), if they aren't shown already.

10. Click a picture folder on the left side of the Desktop tab and then choose an image or swatch on the right to use as your Desktop background. Choices include

- **Desktop Pictures:** These are standard background graphics supplied with OS X.

- **Themed images:** OS X also includes stock photos of nature scenes, plants, black and white images, as well as abstract images, which can be used as desktop backgrounds.

- **Solid Colors:** Choose a color swatch to make your Desktop background a solid color.

- **iPhoto:** Select an image from a picture event in your iPhoto library, as shown in Figure 1-4.

- **Pictures Folder:** Here you can choose any image from your Pictures folder, even if it isn't in your iPhoto library.

11. Using the pop-up menu at the top of the Desktop tab, choose whether you want to tile smaller images or stretch them to fill the whole screen.

 Select the Change Picture check box at the bottom of the preferences pane to automatically change the background image periodically. By using this feature, you can turn your Desktop into a slideshow using the pictures in the currently selected folder.

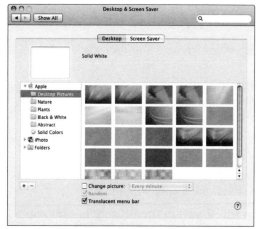

Figure 1-3: The Desktop settings

Figure 1-4: Picking your Desktop background

Change the Display Size

1. Open System Preferences and then click the Displays icon.

2. In the Displays pane that appears, click the Display tab to bring Display settings to the front, if they aren't shown already.

3. Choose a resolution on the left side of the window, as shown in Figure 1-5.

4. If your Mac has a built-in monitor, use the Brightness slider to adjust the display brightness.

5. Choose a refresh rate in the Refresh Rate pop-up menu.

 In general, you should use the highest available settings in the Refresh Rate pop-up menu. Reduce it only if you see distortion or other display problems.

 If you connect a second display to your computer — for example, an external monitor or a multimedia projector — open the Displays settings and then click the Detect Displays button. OS X detects the new display and allows you to adjust its settings as well.

6. Click the Color tab to bring the Color settings to the front, as shown in Figure 1-6.

7. Choose a Display Profile on the left side of the screen.

 Which display profile you use depends primarily on your hardware. See Chapter 4 for more on choosing display profiles.

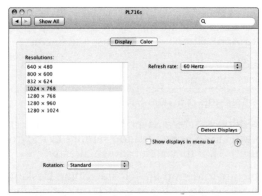

Figure 1-5: Changing the display resolution and refresh rate

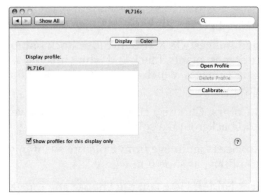

Figure 1-6: Choosing a color profile

Customize Keyboard Shortcuts

1. Quit any open applications by using ⌘+Q.

2. Open System Preferences and then click the Keyboard & Mouse icon to open the Keyboard & Mouse preferences pane, as shown in Figure 1-7.

3. Click the Keyboard Shortcuts tab to bring the Keyboard Shortcut settings to the front, as shown in Figure 1-8.

4. Choose a shortcut category from the menu on the left. Categories are organized into major OS X features.

5. Double-click the shortcut you want to change. Make sure you double-click the actual shortcut listed on the far right, not the command listed in the middle.

6. Press the new keyboard shortcut that you want to use for the command.

 If the shortcut you want to use is already assigned to a different command, a yellow warning triangle appears next to the duplicated shortcuts. If you see the yellow warning triangles, at least one shortcut must be changed.

7. To disable a keyboard shortcut, remove the check mark next to it.

8. Close the Keyboard & Mouse preferences pane to save your changes.

 If you're unhappy with the keyboard shortcuts you've customized or if you're using a pre-owned computer that was customized by someone else, open the Keyboard Shortcuts settings and click the Restore Defaults button. This restores all keyboard shortcuts back to their factory defaults.

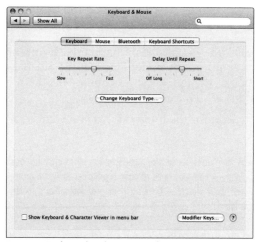

Figure 1-7: The Keyboard & Mouse preferences pane

Figure 1-8: Customizing keyboard shortcuts

Add and Remove Dock Icons

1. Double-click the desktop icon for your hard drive and then click Applications under Places in the Sidebar on the left side of the Finder. This action opens the Applications folder, as shown in Figure 1-9.

2. Locate the icon for the program that you want to add to the Dock.

    In some cases — such as Apple iWork or Microsoft Office applications — you may need to open a subfolder to find a program's icon. Look closely at the icon; if the icon looks like a folder, it's a folder.

3. Click and drag the program's icon to the Dock, as shown in Figure 1-9. The place where you drop the icon on the Dock will be that icon's location. (Keep in mind that applications must be to the left of the divider.)

4. To launch an application from the Dock, simply click the appropriate icon. The application launches.

5. To remove an icon from the Dock, click and hold the mouse button on the icon until a pop-up menu appears, as shown in Figure 1-10.

    If you're using a two-button mouse, simply right-click the Dock icon you want to remove instead of clicking and holding.

6. While still holding down the mouse button, move the pointer over Remove from Dock and then release the mouse button. The icon disappears from the Dock.

Figure 1-9: Clicking and dragging application icons to the Dock

Figure 1-10: Removing an icon from the Dock

Move and Hide the Dock

1. Open System Preferences and then click the Dock icon.

2. In the Dock preferences pane, as shown in Figure 1-11, move the Size slider to change the Dock size.

    You can also change the Dock size at any time by clicking and dragging up or down on the thin vertical line near the right side of the Dock.

3. If you want to use Dock magnification — a useful feature that magnifies icons when you hover the mouse pointer over them — place a check mark next to Magnification and adjust the slider as desired.

4. Choose a Dock position by clicking the Left, Bottom, or Right radio buttons. Figure 1-12 shows the Dock on the left side of the screen.

    If you have a widescreen monitor, you may find that putting the Dock on the left or right side of the screen makes more efficient use of screen real estate.

5. If you don't like the bouncy feedback provided by Dock icons when you launch a program, remove the check mark next to Animate Opening Applications. An arrow still shows you when the program is launching.

6. To automatically hide the Dock when it isn't in use, place a check mark next to Automatically Hide and Show the Dock. To reveal the hidden Dock, simply move the mouse pointer to the bottom (or left or right, as appropriate) of the screen.

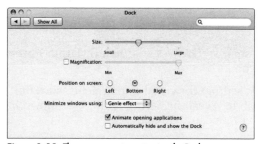

Figure 1-11: The many ways to customize the Dock

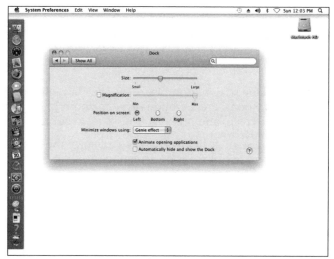

Figure 1-12: Repositioning your Dock to the side

Make OS X Accessible

1. Open System Preferences and then click the Universal Access icon.

2. To adjust settings for visual impairments, click the Seeing tab to reveal the Seeing settings, as shown in Figure 1-13.

3. To enable *VoiceOver* — a basic screen-reader program built-in to OS X — select the On radio button below VoiceOver.

 If you aren't happy with how VoiceOver sounds, click the Open VoiceOver Utility button. There you can change the voice, pitch, speed, and other characteristics of VoiceOver.

4. To enable screen zooming, select the On radio button below Zoom. Press Option+⌘+= to zoom in on an area of the screen, and press Option+⌘+− to zoom back out.

5. Use the settings below Display to change the appearance and use of color on-screen.

6. Click the Hearing tab to reveal audio options, as shown in Figure 1-14.

7. If you can't hear alert sounds from the computer, place a check mark next to Flash the Screen When an Alert Sound Occurs.

 Click the Flash Screen button to test the screen flash.

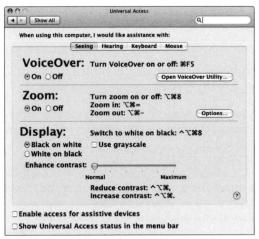

Figure 1-13: Settings that help you see your Mac

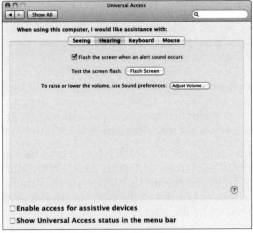

Figure 1-14: The Hearing tab and its audio options

8. Click the Keyboard tab to adjust keyboard options, as shown in Figure 1-15.

9. To enable Sticky Keys, select the On radio button next to Sticky Keys. The Sticky Keys feature allows you to use modifier keys, such as Shift, Function, Control, Option, and ⌘, without simultaneously pressing multiple keys.

 If you need Sticky Keys only occasionally, place a check mark next to Press the Shift Key Five Times to Turn Sticky Keys On or Off. This option gives you an easy way to quickly enable or disable Sticky Keys.

10. To create a delay between when a key is first pressed and when it's accepted by the computer, select the On option next to Slow Keys. Use the Acceptance Delay slider to change the length of the delay.

11. Click the Mouse (or Mouse & Trackpad if you have a laptop) tab to open pointer device settings, as shown in Figure 1-16.

12. If you want to use a numeric keypad in place of a mouse, select the On option next to Mouse Keys.

 If your keyboard doesn't include a dedicated keypad — this is usually the case with laptops — you can purchase a USB (Universal Serial Bus) keypad at most computer and office supply stores.

13. Use the Initial Delay and Maximum Speed sliders to fine-tune the behavior of the Mouse Keys feature.

14. If the mouse cursor is too small, use the Cursor Size slider to change the size of the cursor. The Cursor Size slider works with Mouse Keys as well as a conventional mouse or trackpad.

 If you're giving a presentation with your Mac and a digital projector, you may want to increase the size of the mouse cursor so that the cursor can be used as an on-screen pointer during the presentation.

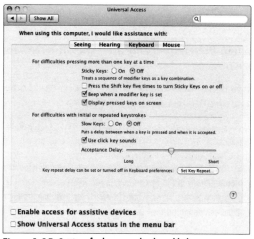

Figure 1-15: Settings for how your keyboard behaves

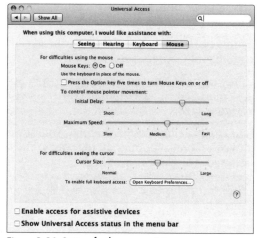

Figure 1-16: Settings for the mouse pointer

Activate a Screen Saver

1. Open System Preferences and then click the Desktop & Screen Saver icon.

2. Click the Screen Saver tab to reveal screen saver settings, as shown in Figure 1-17.

3. Scroll through the list of screen savers and click a screen saver to preview it in the area to the right.

 To create a screen saver with photos from your iPhoto library, choose Library in the Screen Savers list. Alternatively, scroll down the Screen Savers list and click Choose Folder and then browse to a folder containing pictures you want to use.

4. Use the Start Screen Saver slider to change when the screen saver appears. If you choose 15, for example, the screen saver appears only after the computer is inactive for 15 minutes.

5. To configure a hot corner for activating your screen saver, click the Hot Corners button.

6. Decide which corner you want as the hot corner and then choose Start Screen Saver in that corner's menu, as shown in Figure 1-18.

7. Click OK to close the hot corner options. To test the hot corner, move the mouse pointer all the way to the corner you selected. The screen saver begins.

 If you don't want to use a screen saver, move the Start Screen Saver slider to Never.

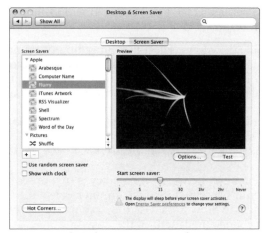

Figure 1-17: The Desktop & Screen Saver preferences pane

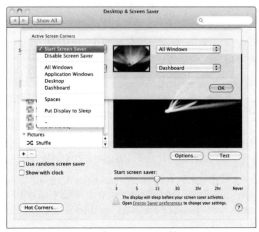

Figure 1-18: Creating a hot corner to quickly activate a screen saver

Display 24-Hour Time

1. Open System Preferences and then click the Date & Time icon.

    You can also open the Date & Time control panel by clicking and holding the clock in the upper-right corner of the screen and then choosing Open Date & Time from the contextual menu that appears.

2. Click the Clock tab to bring Clock preferences to the front, as shown in Figure 1-19.

3. Select the Use a 24-Hour Clock check box to display time in 24-hour format.

    If you're displaying time in 24-hour format, the Show AM/PM option is automatically disabled.

4. Adjust other clock options as desired and then click the Date & Time tab to show the calendar and time setting options, as shown in Figure 1-20.

    Some clock options — such as Analog display — aren't compatible with a 24-hour clock.

5. If you want the computer to automatically synchronize its clock with an online date and time source, make sure that Set Date & Time Automatically is selected. Choose a source based on your geographical location.

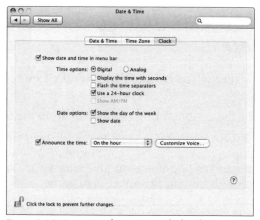

Figure 1-19: Customizing the way time is displayed on your computer

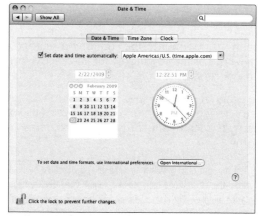

Figure 1-20: Letting your computer automatically check and set the time

Access Programs Quickly with Exposé

1. Open System Preferences and then click the Exposé & Spaces icon.

2. Click the Exposé tab to bring Exposé settings to the front.

3. Select a hot corner that you want to use for switching between open programs and then choose All Windows from that corner's pop-up menu. In Figure 1-21, I've chosen All Windows in the upper-right corner.

 You can assign different functions to each corner of the OS X desktop. For example, you may want to assign the screen saver to one corner, and the Dashboard to another.

4. Close the Exposé & Spaces preferences pane.

5. Move the mouse pointer to the corner you selected as the Exposé hot corner. A window for each active program appears, as shown in Figure 1-22.

6. Click the program window you want to bring to the front. The selected program becomes active as its space fills the screen; meanwhile, those other programs are still running.

 You can also quickly switch between open applications by holding down the ⌘ key and then pressing Tab. A small window appears in the middle of the screen with an icon for each open application. Keep pressing Tab until the desired program is highlighted and then release the ⌘ key.

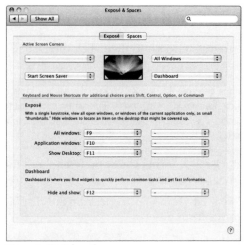

Figure 1-21: Select a hot corner

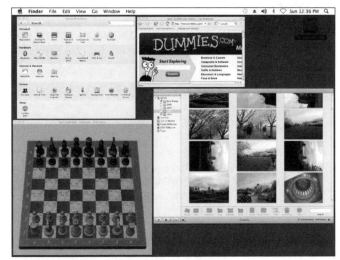

Figure 1-22: Click the program window you want to open

Set Up Spaces

1. Open System Preferences and then click the Exposé & Spaces icon.

2. Click the Spaces tab to view the Spaces options, as shown in Figure 1-23.

3. Place a check mark next to Enable Spaces.

 To switch between Spaces more easily, place a check mark next to Show Spaces in Menu Bar. A Spaces icon and number appear in the menu bar. Click the Spaces icon and then select a new space from the menu that appears to jump to that space.

4. To add spaces, click the plus sign next to either Column or Row. In Figure 1-23, a row and column have been added.

5. If you want to use only a certain program in a certain space — for example, you may set up a separate space just for the DVD player — click the plus sign under the Application Assignments list and then choose Other from the menu that appears.

6. In the Selection dialog that appears, as shown in Figure 1-24, select an application and then click Add. The application is added to the Application Assignments list.

7. In the Application Assignments list of the Spaces window, click the Space number corresponding to the added application and choose a space to which the application should be assigned.

 You can create assignments for any application, but they're most effective for multimedia applications that might compete with each other, such as iTunes and the DVD Player. If iTunes is in Space 3, audio from iTunes goes away when you switch to the DVD Player in Space 4 and vice versa.

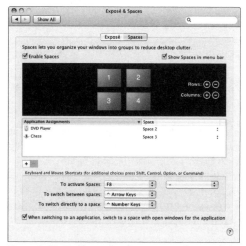

Figure 1-23: Enabling and configuring Spaces for your desktop

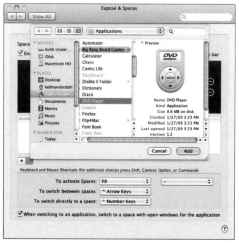

Figure 1-24: Assigning applications to specific spaces

Switch between Spaces

1. To switch between spaces, use one of the following techniques:

   • Press F8 to activate Spaces, as shown in Figure 1-25, and then click the space that you want to open.

    You can change the Spaces hot key by opening the Spaces preferences pane and selecting a different function key from the To Activate Spaces pop-up menu. (Refer to Figure 1-23.) F8 is the default hot key for Spaces.

   • Click the Spaces number in the menu bar (if shown) and then select a Space number from the menu that appears.

   • Launch a program that has a dependency to a specific space. The previous section shows you how to set up dependencies.

2. To move an application window from one space to another, activate the Spaces feature and then click and drag a window to a new space, as shown in Figure 1-26.

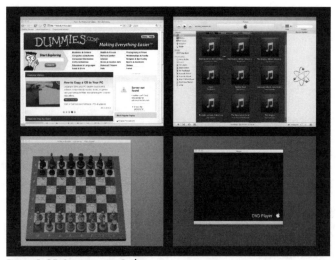

Figure 1-25: Spaces on your Desktop

Figure 1-26: Drag windows between spaces

Creating and Managing User Accounts

A fter you get a new computer, you'll probably want to customize it to fit your needs and personality. You may tweak the Desktop appearance, add favorite programs to the Dock, and set up e-mail and chat programs for your personal accounts. But what if your computer is shared by other people?

The Macintosh operating system allows you to easily set up multiple user accounts on your computer, and this chapter shows you how. Personal user accounts have several advantages:

➡ Each user can customize the way the operating system looks and behaves without affecting other users.

➡ Users can set up and use their own e-mail and Internet accounts. Private files and communications stay private.

➡ User accounts can help prevent unauthorized persons from using the computer.

➡ Parents can control how their children use the computer.

 Most security and account-related settings require an administrator password. If you see a lock icon in the lower-left corner of a preferences pane, click it to enter your administrator account name and password.

Disable Automatic Login

1. Open System Preferences and then click the Accounts icon.

2. In the Accounts preferences pane, click Login Options in the left pane.

3. In the Automatic Login pop-up menu, choose Off, as shown in Figure 2-1.

4. Next to Display Login Window As, select one of the following options:

   • **List of Users:** A list of users appears in the login window. Users click a name and then enter a password to log in.

   • **Name and Password:** The login window simply shows empty Name and Password fields. This option is less convenient but slightly more secure.

Require a Password to Wake the Computer

1. Open System Preferences and then click the Security icon.

2. In the Security preferences pane, select the Require Password check box.

3. Choose a time interval, as shown in Figure 2-2. This interval is sort of like a grace period between when the computer goes to sleep and a password is required.

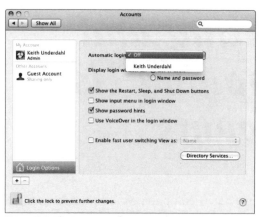

Figure 2-1: The Accounts preferences pane

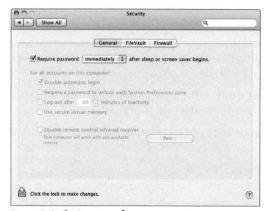

Figure 2-2: The Security preferences pane

 If you haven't already disabled Automatic Login, a warning message suggests that you do so if you require a password to wake the computer from sleep or a screen saver.

Create a New User Account

1. Open System Preferences and then click the Accounts icon.

2. In the Accounts pane, click the plus sign in the lower-left corner — just above the Lock icon. The new account dialog appears, as shown in Figure 2-3.

3. Enter a name and a short name for the account.

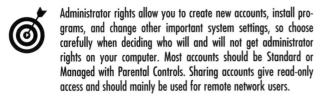 The short name is used for system folders. If you don't like the short name that's generated automatically, change it now because you can't change the short name after you create the account.

4. Enter a password twice and add a password hint for the new user.

If you're not sure whether your password is secure enough, click the key button next to the Password field to open the Password Assistant. The Assistant grades the quality of your password and suggests alternatives if necessary.

5. Choose an account type in the New Account menu.

Administrator rights allow you to create new accounts, install programs, and change other important system settings, so choose carefully when deciding who will and will not get administrator rights on your computer. Most accounts should be Standard or Managed with Parental Controls. Sharing accounts give read-only access and should mainly be used for remote network users.

6. Click Create Account. The new account appears in the accounts list, as shown in Figure 2-4.

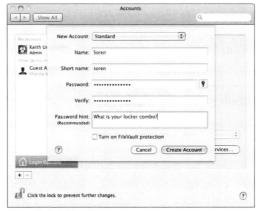

Figure 2-3: Adding the new account

Figure 2-4: The new Soren account

 If the user has a MobileMe (formerly known as .Mac) account, you may enter the MobileMe account name in the Accounts preferences pane shown in Figure 2-4.

Change Account Settings

1. Open System Preferences and then click the Accounts icon.

2. Click the account name for which you want to change settings in the pane on the left.

3. Adjust basic account settings, such as administrator rights.

4. To change the account's picture, click the picture.

5. Choose a picture from the menu that appears, as shown in Figure 2-5.

 If you want to use your own picture, click Edit Picture and then click the Choose button in the Images window that appears. Browse to the photo you want to use. If your computer has an iSight or a built-in camera, you'll also be given the option to take a picture using it.

Change a Password

1. Open System Preferences and then click the Accounts icon.

2. In the left pane, click the account name for which you want to change the password and then click the Reset Password button.

3. In the Reset Password dialog that appears, as shown in Figure 2-6, enter a new password twice and add a hint.

4. Click the Reset Password button to set the new password.

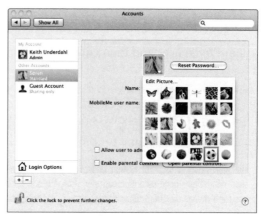

Figure 2-5: Many possible account pictures

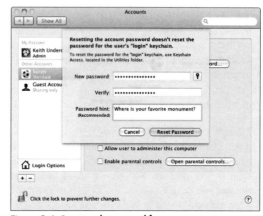

Figure 2-6: Resetting the password for a user account

 Click the key button if you need suggestions for a secure password.

Switch Quickly between Accounts

1. Open System Preferences and then click the Accounts icon.

2. Click Login Options at the bottom of the accounts list in the pane on the left.

3. In the login options that appear, select the Enable Fast User Switching check box, as shown in Figure 2-7.

4. From the View As pop-up menu, choose how you want users to appear on the switching menu — Name, Short Name, or Icon — and then close the Accounts window.

 Fast user switching makes it easier to switch between users, but it isn't necessary. Don't enable fast user switching if your computer has limited memory or you don't want to allow multiple users to log in simultaneously.

5. To switch to a different user, click the username in the upper-right corner of the menu bar.

6. In the User Switching menu that appears, as shown in Figure 2-8, choose a username to switch to that user. (The user's password may be required to log in.)

Figure 2-7: The Login Options pane

 If you don't enable fast user switching, you must log out of the current account before switching to a new user. Choose Apple➪Log Out to log out of the current account and then use the standard OS X login screen to log in to a different account.

Figure 2-8: Switching to a new user

Set Up Parental Controls

1. Open System Preferences and then click the Parental Controls icon.

2. Click the account name for which you want to set up parental controls, select the Enable Parental Controls check box, and then click the Enable Parental Controls button.

    You can't set up parental controls on administrator accounts.

3. To control what applications the user can access, click the System tab, select the Only Allow Selected Applications check box, and then select or deselect applications in the list box, as shown in Figure 2-9.

4. Place check marks next to system features that the user is allowed to use. In Figure 2-9, the user isn't allowed to burn CDs and DVDs or administer printers but can modify the Dock.

5. To limit who the person can correspond with by e-mail or iChat, click the Mail & iChat tab and then place a check mark next to the services you want to limit.

6. In the e-mail address list, click the Add button (it looks like a plus sign) and then type the name and e-mail address that you want to allow into the new dialog that appears.

7. Click the dialog's Add button to add the user to the list of allowable iChat or Mail partners, as shown in Figure 2-10.

Figure 2-9: The System tab of the Parental Controls window

Figure 2-10: The Mail & iChat tab

8. Select the Send Permission Requests To check box and then enter your e-mail address, as shown in Figure 2-10. You will be notified if your child attempts to contact someone you haven't allowed, and you'll have the option to authorize or decline the contact.

9. To limit your child's access to offensive Web sites or content, click the Content tab.

10. Select the Hide Profanity in the Dictionary check box to block access to offensive words in the OS X Dictionary program.

11. Select an option for limiting Web sites:

   - **Allow Unrestricted Access to Websites:** This option places no limits on Web site access.

   - **Try to Limit Access to Adult Websites Automatically:** Safari attempts to identify and limit access to adult Web sites. This works most of the time but not always.

   - **Allow Access to Only These Websites:** This reveals a list of Web sites, as shown in Figure 2-11. The user can visit only sites in this list. Click the plus sign under the list to add more Web sites.

12. To manage the amount of time your child spends on the computer, click the Time Limits tab.

13. Select the Limit Computer Use To check boxes under Weekdays and Weekends and then use the sliders to set the maximum time, as shown in Figure 2-12.

14. Under Bedtime, select the School Nights and Weekends check boxes and then use the clock menus to set a bedtime for computer use.

Figure 2-11: The Content tab of the Parental Controls window

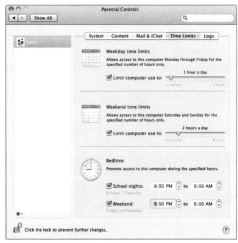

Figure 2-12: The Time Limits tab

Delete a User Account

1. Back up any important files and data that may be stored in the user's personal folders.

    To back up the user's files, you need to either log in to the computer as that user or use your administrator password to access the account.

2. After you back up any important files, open System Preferences and then click the Accounts icon.

3. Click the user account name that you want to remove.

4. Click the Delete User button, which is located under the accounts list and looks like a minus sign.

5. In the dialog that appears, confirm that you actually want to delete the account, as shown in Figure 2-13.

    If you choose to save the user's home folder in a disk image, the user's files are retained in a disk image that can easily be backed up to a recordable DVD or external hard drive. If you choose to delete the home folder, all the user's files and settings are deleted immediately.

Figure 2-13: Deleting an account

Managing Files and Folders

Consider all the things for which you use your computer: You compose e-mail, browse the Internet, edit photos, play music, type memos, and more. Many of these tasks involve files that are stored on your hard drive.

The Macintosh operating system makes managing your files easy. The Mac OS X component that helps you browse and manage files is the *Finder*. The Finder runs at all times in the background, and you can open Finder windows from the Dock or any time you double-click the icon for a hard drive or folder. The Finder lets you quickly perform basic tasks, like creating folders and moving or deleting files. The Finder also lets you perform more advanced tasks, such as customizing a file's icon or changing the default program you use to open a file.

This chapter shows you how to manage files with the Finder. It also shows you how to use other OS X file management tools, including

➡ **Spotlight:** This is a powerful tool for searching files, programs, and even system settings.

➡ **Trash:** Deleted files are sent to the Trash. If you accidentally delete a needed file, you can usually recover it from the Trash.

➡ **Burn folders:** Back up important files to recordable CDs or DVDs by using Burn folders.

➡ **Time Machine:** Time Machine makes it easy to back up your entire computer on a regular basis.

Get ready to . . .

Search Your Computer with Spotlight

1. Click the Spotlight icon in the upper-right corner of the OS X menu bar. The Spotlight icon looks like a magnifying glass.

2. Type a query. When you type, top results appear in a menu below Spotlight. Choose a result in the menu to open it.

3. To view a more detailed list of results, choose Show All from the Spotlight menu to open the Spotlight window, as shown in Figure 3-1.

 To search a specific location (such as an external hard drive or your Pictures folder), select the location in the sidebar on the left side of the Spotlight window.

4. If Spotlight searches resources that you prefer not to search, open System Preferences and click the Spotlight icon.

 You can also open Spotlight Preferences by choosing Spotlight Preferences in the Spotlight menu.

5. In the Spotlight pane, remove check marks next to resources that you don't want searched.

6. To block certain folders from being searched, click the Privacy tab near the top of the Spotlight pane.

7. Click the Add button (it looks like a plus sign) near the bottom of the Privacy tab and then browse to the folder you want to block from being searched.

8. Select the folder and click Choose. The blocked folder appears in the list, as shown in Figure 3-2.

Figure 3-1: The Spotlight window

Figure 3-2: Settings in the Spotlight pane

Associate Files with Different Programs

1. Open the Finder and browse to a file for which you want to change the program association.

2. Click the file once to select it but don't double-click the file or open it.

3. With the file selected, press ⌘+I.

 You can also open the Info window by selecting the file and then choosing File⇨Get Info, or right-click the file and choose Get Info from the menu that appears.

4. In the Info window, click the small arrow to the left of Open With to expand the file opening options, as shown in Figure 3-3.

5. Click the pop-up menu under Open With and choose a different program.

 If you don't see the desired program listed in the menu, choose Other from the bottom of the menu and then browse the Applications folder to find the program you want to use to open the file.

6. If you want to change program association for all files of a given type, click Change All below the Open With menu.

7. Click Continue in the dialog shown in Figure 3-4 to apply the global change.

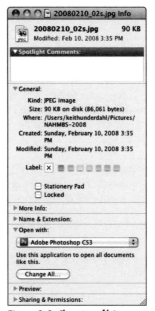

Figure 3-3: Changing a file's program association

 Make sure you select a program that's appropriate for opening the file. For example, if the file is a picture, you probably want to associate it with a graphics program like iPhoto or Adobe Photoshop. A word processing program, like Apple Pages, isn't the best program to open and edit photos in.

Figure 3-4: Making global program associations

Change a File's Icon

1. Open an image file containing the image you want to use as a file's icon.

    Ideally, the icon image should have some relevance to the document. For example, if the document is a PDF file containing information about your company, you may want to change the file's icon so that it uses your company logo.

2. Select the image and then copy it. If you're viewing the image in the OS X Preview program, click and drag a box around the image and then choose Edit⇨Copy, as shown in Figure 3-5.

3. Close the image.

4. Open Finder and browse to a file for which you want to change the program association.

5. Click the file once to select it but don't double-click the file or open it.

6. With the file selected, press ⌘+I.

7. Click once on the current icon image in the upper-left corner of the Info window to select it.

8. With the old icon selected (a border appears around the icon when it's selected), press ⌘+V to paste in the new icon image, as shown in Figure 3-6.

9. Close the Info window. As you can see in Figure 3-6, the new icon image appears immediately in the Finder.

Figure 3-5: Copy an image

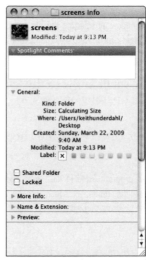

Figure 3-6: Paste the image onto a file's icon

 You can follow these same steps to change a folder's icon as well as a file's icon.

Customize the Finder

1. Click the Finder button on the Dock to open the Finder.

2. Click the Actions menu in the toolbar (it looks like a toothed gear) and choose Show View Options.

    Make sure that no folder or file in the Finder is selected. If an item is selected, the Action menu lists commands specific to that item, and the Show View Options choice isn't available.

3. In the View Options dialog that appears, customize appearance settings, such as icon sizes and labeling.

4. Close the View Options dialog, and with the focus still on the Finder, choose Finder➪Preferences.

5. Click the Sidebar icon at the top of the Finder Preferences window that appears and then deselect items that you don't want to appear in the Finder Sidebar, as shown in Figure 3-7. For example, if you don't use Apple's MobileMe service, you may want to deselect the iDisk check box so it doesn't needlessly take up Finder space.

6. Close the Finder Preferences window and then, with the focus still on the Finder, choose View➪Customize Toolbar.

7. In the Toolbar Customization dialog that appears, as shown in Figure 3-8, click and drag buttons to the Finder toolbar. In Figure 3-8, I added the Separator, New Folder, Path, and Get Info buttons to the toolbar. Click Done after you're finished making changes.

    To remove items from the toolbar, simply click and drag them from the toolbar to the Toolbar Customization dialog. You can easily add them back later if you want.

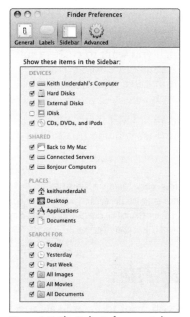

Figure 3-7: The Finder Preferences window

Figure 3-8: The Toolbar Customization window

Create Folders

1. Open the folder in which you want to create a sub-folder. If you want to create a new folder on the Desktop, click in an empty area of the Desktop to ensure it has the current focus.

2. Press ⌘+Shift+N to create a new folder. As you can see in Figure 3-9, the new folder is named Untitled Folder.

3. Type a new descriptive name for your folder.

 To keep sensitive files secure, store them in subfolders that you create on the Desktop or in the Documents folder under Places in the Finder Sidebar. Folders created on external hard drives may be accessible to anyone who uses your computer.

Rename Groups of Files

1. Make sure all the files you want to rename are together in a single folder. The folder should contain only the files you want to rename.

2. Open the Finder and then open the Applications folder.

3. In the Applications folder, open the AppleScript folder, open the Example Scripts folder, and then open the Finder Scripts folder. A list of Finder scripts appears, as shown in Figure 3-10.

 OS X comes with many handy scripts to help you automate various tasks. Poke around the AppleScript folder to find others that may be useful to you, but read the instructions for each script carefully to make sure you don't cause some damage.

4. To trim text from filenames, double-click `Trim File Names.scpt`. The Script Editor launches.

Figure 3-9: A new, untitled folder

Figure 3-10: Several Finder scripts

5. Open the folder containing the files you want to modify.

 Make sure that the folder containing the files you want to rename is in front of all other windows. The front-most window is the one to which the script is applied. If no folder window is open, the script renames files on the Desktop.

6. Click the Run button in the Script Editor window.

7. Enter the text string you want to trim from the file-names, as shown in Figure 3-11.

8. If the text string is to be removed from the beginning of each filename, click Trim Start. Click Trim End if you want to trim the end of each filename.

9. To add text to the filenames, open the Add to File Names.scpt script.

10. Confirm that the folder containing the files you want to rename is in front of all other windows.

11. Click Run in the Script Editor window.

12. Type the text string you want to add to the filenames, as shown in Figure 3-12.

13. To add the string to the beginning of each filename, click Prefix. To add the string to the end, click Suffix.

14. After you're done running scripts and renaming files, click the Script Editor window and then press ⌘+Q to quit the Script Editor and ensure that scripts are not inadvertently run later.

 If you're renaming files for use on a Web site, use the underscore character instead of spaces in the names. Also, remember that filenames on the Internet are usually case sensitive.

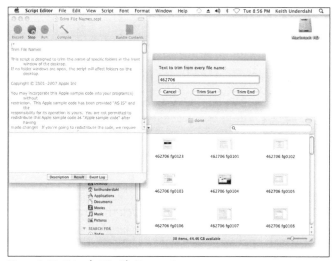

Figure 3-11: Using the Trim File Names script

Figure 3-12: Using the Add to File Names script

Trash Files or Folders

1. Locate a file or folder that you want to delete.

2. Click and drag the file to the Trash icon on the Dock.

 If you have a two-button mouse, you can also right-click a file and choose Move to Trash from the contextual menu that appears.

 You can immediately undo an accidental trashing by pressing ⌘+Z or choosing Edit⇨Undo.

3. To see what's in the Trash, click the Trash icon on the Dock. A Finder window displaying the contents of the Trash appears, as shown in Figure 3-13.

4. If you want to restore an item from the Trash, click and drag the item to a new, safe location.

5. To empty the Trash, press ⌘+Shift+Delete or choose Finder⇨Empty Trash. You can empty the Trash only when the focus is on the Finder. If the focus is on another application, the ⌘+Shift+Delete command won't work.

6. When you see the confirmation warning, as shown in Figure 3-14, click OK. Items in the Trash are deleted permanently.

Figure 3-13: The contents of the Trash window

Figure 3-14: A warning that emptying the Trash is permanent

 If you're tired of always confirming yes, you actually do want to empty the Trash, open a Finder window and choose Finder⇨Preferences. Click Advanced in the Preferences window that appears and then deselect the Show Warning before Emptying the Trash check box.

Back Up Files to a CD

1. In the Finder or simply on the Desktop (the menu bar at the top of the screen must say Finder), choose File➪New Burn Folder. A new Burn folder appears.

2. Type a name for the Burn folder. The name will be the disc volume name when the disc is recorded.

3. Click and drag files and folders to the Burn folder.

4. To review the items in the Burn folder, double-click the folder to open it.

5. To find out how much space will be required to store the files in the Burn folder, look at the Minimum Disc Size reading at the bottom of the Burn Folder window, as shown in Figure 3-15.

 Remember, most CDs can hold 700MB of data and most DVDs hold up to 4.7GB of data. To burn DVDs, your computer must have a SuperDrive or external DVD burner. Dual-layer DVDs can hold up to 8.5GB of data and require a dual-layer DVD burner. Most Apple SuperDrives produced since 2007 support dual-layer discs.

6. After you're done adding files, click the Burn button in the top-right corner of the Burn Folder window.

7. When you're prompted to do so, insert a blank, recordable disc of the appropriate size.

8. Choose a burn speed, as shown in Figure 3-16, and then click Burn.

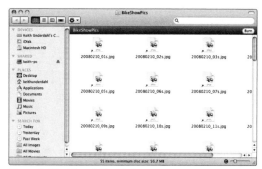

Figure 3-15: A Burn Folder window

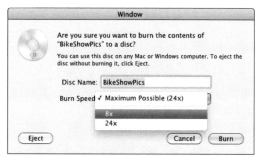

Figure 3-16: Setting your burn speed

 Recording errors are less likely to occur at slower burn speeds. Unless you're in a hurry, choose the slowest burn speed possible.

Back Up Your Computer with Time Machine

1. If you have an external hard drive, connect it to your computer and prepare it for use, as I describe in Chapter 22.

    An external drive isn't required for using Time Machine, but files that are backed up to an external drive will be safer in case a component inside your computer fails. Without an external hard drive, you must create a second partition on your internal hard drive to use Time Machine.

2. Open System Preferences and then click the Time Machine icon.

3. Next to Back Up To, click Select Disk.

4. Select a drive to which you want backups to be saved, as shown in Figure 3-17.

    If storage space is a major concern, select the Automatically Delete Backups Older Than check box and then select a time frame. Shorter time frames use less disk space.

5. Click Use for Backup to return to the main Time Machine preferences pane.

6. If you have a folder containing large files that don't need to be backed up, click Options, click the Add button (it looks like a plus sign) on the Do Not Backup tab that appears, and then browse to the desired folder. Select the folder and click Exclude, as shown in Figure 3-18.

7. To start a backup immediately, click Back Up Now and then close the Time Machine preferences pane. Backups occur silently and don't interfere with your other work.

Figure 3-17: Selecting a volume to which backups are saved

Figure 3-18: Determining what's backed up by Time Machine

Restore Files with Time Machine

1. Click the Time Machine icon on the Dock.

2. In the Time Machine screen that appears, as shown in Figure 3-19, click the arrows in the lower-right corner of the screen to move to earlier backups.

 You can also click a screen in the main window to jump directly to it. Each screen in the background represents a different backup time. You can also move through backups by clicking the graduated scale along the right side of the Time Machine screen.

3. Use the Finder window and its Sidebar to browse to the file that you want to restore. If you can't find the desired file, go back in time to an earlier backup.

 Click Only Show Changes to display only those files that have changed since the backup was performed. For example, if you edited a file yesterday, backups of that file from two or three days ago don't contain your edits.

4. When you find the file that you want to back up, select it and click Restore in the lower-right corner of the Time Machine window.

 Click Cancel if you want to close Time Machine without restoring a file.

5. Check the restored file to make sure it's the one you want. If the restored file has the same name as an item that's currently on your computer, the restored file assumes the proper name and the existing file has *(original)* tacked onto its name, as shown in Figure 3-20.

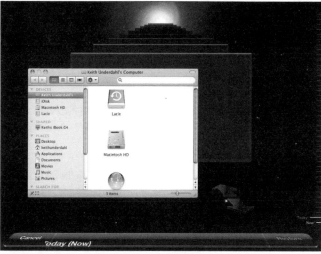

Figure 3-19: Moving back in time using Time Machine

Figure 3-20: Comparing current and restored versions of files

Suppress Desktop Icons for CDs and iPods

1. Open the Finder (or click an empty area of the Desktop) and choose Finder⇨Preferences.

2. Click the General tab and then remove the check mark next to CDs, DVDs, and iPods, as shown in Figure 3-21.

3. Close the Finder Preferences window.

 You can still eject discs and iPods by using the Eject commands in iTunes and DVD Player, by pressing the Eject key on your keyboard, or by clicking the Eject symbol next to the item in a Finder Sidebar.

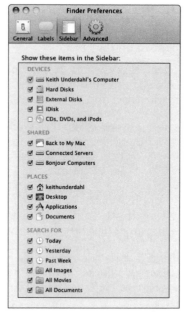

Figure 3-21: Suppressing certain Desktop icons

Adjusting System Preferences

*T*he Macintosh computer is known for its ease of use, but "easy" doesn't mean simplistic. Beneath the friendly exterior of OS X is a powerful operating system that you can configure for almost any task, and it doesn't hurt that you can use your Mac with a wide variety of peripheral hardware as well.

This chapter shows you how to configure the system software for your specific needs and hardware. Tasks show you how to take command of both the internal hardware in your Mac and the peripherals attached to it. Specific tasks include

➡ **Internal components:** Operating system tools help you make the most efficient use of your laptop's batteries, decide which disk is used to boot the system, and update the OS X software.

➡ **Peripherals:** Your Mac can work with a variety of printers, monitors, keyboards, and audio devices. Configuring peripherals in OS X is easy.

The tasks in this chapter show you how to control your computer's hardware with OS X software tools. The final task also shows you more about the specifications and performance of your computer, which is important if you decide to make some upgrades. If you want to upgrade the actual hardware of your Mac, see Chapter 22.

Chapter

4

Get ready to . . .

Save Energy with Power Settings

1. Open System Preferences by choosing Apple⇨System Preferences.

2. Click the Energy Saver icon.

3. If you have a laptop, choose Battery from the Settings pop-up menu and then choose a power saving profile from the Optimization pop-up menu.

4. Adjust the sliders to change when the computer and monitor will go to sleep, as shown in Figure 4-1.

    The monitor uses a lot of power, so it's a good idea to let the display sleep after a few minutes of inactivity. This is especially true if you have a laptop running on battery power. When the computer sleeps, the hard drive, memory, and processor turn off.

5. If other computers on your network use printers or hard drives on your computer, select the Wake for Network Access check box. This allows network computers to use shared printers and resources even if your Mac has gone to sleep.

    If you have a portable Mac, review additional laptop-specific options such as whether to display the battery icon in the menu bar and whether you want the monitor to dim slightly before going to sleep.

6. Click the Schedule button. If you want the computer to wake or start at a certain time each day, select the Start Up or Wake check box and then choose dates and times for automatic startup, as shown in Figure 4-2.

7. If you have a laptop, choose Power Adapter from the Settings For pop-up menu and then repeat Steps 3–6 to adjust settings for when your computer is plugged in to wall power.

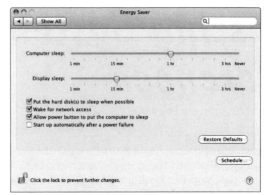

Figure 4-1: The Energy Saver preferences pane

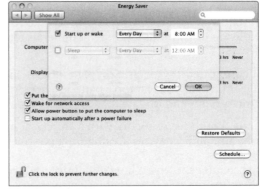

Figure 4-2: Scheduling your computer to start or sleep automatically

Update System Software

1. Make sure that your computer is connected to the Internet and close all open applications.

    Look at the Dock and make sure that you quit all programs. Running programs have a small, bluish-white dot below their icons. You can't quit the Finder, but you can quit everything else.

2. Choose Apple⇨Software Update. The Software Update application launches and checks the Internet for updates, as shown in Figure 4-3.

3. When a list of available updates appears, as shown in Figure 4-4, review each item and remove check marks next to items that you don't want to update.

   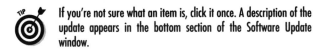 If you're not sure what an item is, click it once. A description of the update appears in the bottom section of the Software Update window.

4. Click the Install button at the bottom of the Software Update window to begin downloading the updates.

5. Enter your administrator password in the dialog that appears and then click OK.

6. Read and accept any license agreements that appear. After you accept all the agreements, a status window shows you the download progress of your updates.

    When you review the list of updates, look for ones that say they must be installed separately. These should be downloaded individually, which means you may have to run Software Update a couple of times.

    Software Update runs automatically when you restart your Mac, but not when you sleep or hibernate the computer. If you don't restart your Mac very often, manually run Software Update at least once a week to ensure that you get critical updates to OS X and your other software.

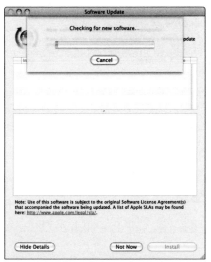

Figure 4-3: Software Update seeking updates

Figure 4-4: A list of available updates

Select a Startup Disk

1. Open System Preferences and then click the Startup Disk icon.

2. Select the disk you want to use when the computer starts up, as shown in Figure 4-5.

3. If you want to restart the computer right now using a different disk or operating system, click Restart. Otherwise, simply close the Startup Disk window.

Manage Printers

1. Open System Preferences and then click the Print & Fax icon.

2. To add a printer, click the Add button (it looks like a plus sign) below the list of available printers.

3. At the top of the dialog, click the button that corresponds to the type of printer that you want to add, as shown in Figure 4-6. For example, click Windows if you're adding a printer connected to a Windows PC on your network, or click IP to add a network printer with an IP address.

 Workplace printers are often connected directly to a network. Check the printer's control panel or a wall placard near the computer for the printer's IP address.

4. If you're connecting to a network printer, select the name of the computer to which the new printer is connected. In Figure 4-6, keith-pc is a network computer.

Figure 4-5: Selecting the startup disk

Figure 4-6: Selecting the computer to which the printer is connected

 Normally, it's necessary to manually add network printers only. Printers installed directly to your computer following the printer manufacturer's instructions should already appear in your list of printers.

5. When you're prompted to enter a name and password, enter a username and password that are valid on the computer to which you're trying to connect. Click OK.

6. Select the name of the printer that you want to add.

7. From the Print Using pop-up menu, choose Select a Driver and then choose the model name in the list that appears, as shown in Figure 4-7. Click OK and then click Add to return to the Print & Fax window, as shown in Figure 4-8.

 If your printer's manufacturer or model isn't listed in any menu, choose Generic PostScript Printer from the Print Using pop-up menu.

8. In the list of printers, as shown in Figure 4-8, check the status of your newly added printer. A green dot next to the printer's name means that the printer is ready to use.

9. To set a specific printer as your default printer, choose that printer in the Default Printer pop-up menu, as shown in Figure 4-8.

10. To adjust printer-specific settings, select the printer and click Options & Supplies. The Printer Options and Supplies utility runs, with options and settings tailored to the printer. Here you can change the name and model of the printer, its location, and other details.

Figure 4-7: Selecting a printer to add

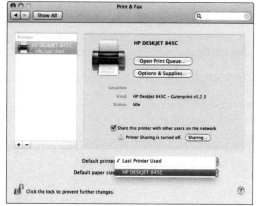

Figure 4-8: The Print & Fax window

Calibrate the Display Color

1. Open System Preferences and then click the Displays icon.

2. Click the Color tab to open the color preferences for your monitor.

3. In the list box on the left, select a profile that matches your monitor or display, as shown in Figure 4-9.

    If you're not sure which profile is compatible with your monitor, place a check mark next to Show Profiles for This Display Only. Incompatible profiles disappear from the list.

    Color calibration is usually necessary only if you have special color needs — for example, you're editing video for broadcast or performing professional graphics production — or if you're not satisfied with the color performance of your monitor.

4. Click the Calibrate button.

5. Read the instructions in the Display Calibrator Assistant and then click Continue.

    Don't use the Expert mode unless your monitor performs poorly and you're experienced with color calibration.

6. Follow the Assistant's instructions to calibrate colors. Slider controls such as the Select Gamma slider, shown in Figure 4-10, help you fine-tune the color calibration for your monitor.

7. On the last screen of the Display Calibrator Assistant, click Done to create your new calibrated color profile.

Figure 4-9: Selecting a color profile

Figure 4-10: Calibrating your display

 If your Mac is connected to a TV monitor as part of a home media center, select 2.2 Gamma on the Select Target Gamma screen of the wizard.

Change Keyboard and Mouse Settings

1. Open System Preferences and then click the Keyboard icon.

2. Click the Keyboard tab to bring keyboard settings to the front, as shown in Figure 4-11.

3. Adjust the Key Repeat Rate and Delay Until Repeat sliders to change how characters repeat when you press and hold keys.

4. Click the Show All button to return to System Preferences, and then click the Mouse icon (or the Trackpad icon if you have a laptop).

 If you're using a laptop, the Mouse button appears only if a mouse is connected to the computer.

5. Use the sliders to adjust the tracking speed, double-click speed, and scrolling speed (if appropriate), as shown in Figure 4-12.

6. Adjust other device specific settings, including

   • **Two-button mouse:** If you have a two-button mouse, you can choose whether the right or left button is the primary button.

   • **Trackpads:** Newer Apple trackpads incorporate multi-fingered scrolling. You can also enable clicking by tapping on the trackpad.

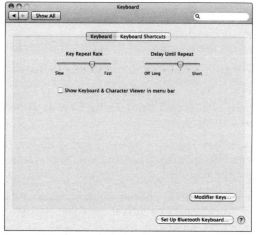

Figure 4-11: Changing the keyboard repeat rate

If you want to customize the modifier keys, click the Modifier Keys button and use the menus to change how the modifier keys are mapped. For example, if you use a keyboard originally designed for Windows PCs, you may need to swap the Control and Option keys.

Figure 4-12: Fine-tuning the mouse or trackpad

Adjust Audio Settings

1. Open System Preferences and then click the Sound icon.

2. Click the Sound Effects tab to bring sound effect settings to the front.

3. Select a new alert sound from the list box, as shown in Figure 4-13.

4. Choose whether you want interface sound effects, Front Row sound effects, or audible feedback to play when you adjust the volume.

5. Click the Output tab to choose which speakers are used for audio output and to adjust the speaker balance, as shown in Figure 4-14.

    In some cases, an operating system bug can cause audio balance to change inadvertently when you adjust volume with the function keys. If your speakers don't seem to be balanced properly between the left and right channels, open the sound output settings and double-check the volume.

6. Click the Input tab if you need to adjust the input volume for your computer's microphone. Speak normally and watch the Input Level indicators to fine-tune the microphone level.

    The Input Level indicators light up to the middle and upper part of the scale during speech. If the level is too low, your voice will be too quiet. If the level is too high and the indicators routinely bounce off the top of the scale, audible distortion may occur.

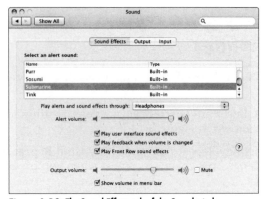

Figure 4-13: The Sound Effects tab of the Sound window

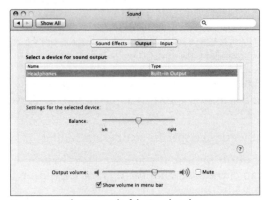

Figure 4-14: The Output tab of the Sound window

Check System Specifications and Performance

1. Choose Apple⇨About This Mac and then click More Info.

2. In the System Profiler window that appears, click Disc Burning under the Hardware heading in the Contents listing on the left.

 If you're not sure whether your computer has a Combo drive for burning CDs or a SuperDrive for burning both CDs and DVDs, check the Disc Burning properties. If you see a DVD-Write section, your Mac has a SuperDrive. If +R DL is listed next to DVD-Write, your drive supports dual layer DVDs.

3. In the Contents pane on the left, click the Memory item under the Hardware heading to check the size and status of your system memory, as shown in Figure 4-15. The Status column lists the status of each memory slot.

 The processor in Intel-based Macs performs best when each memory slot has a memory module of the same size and speed.

4. Click AirPort Card under the Network heading to see what kind of AirPort card (AirPort or AirPort Extreme) you have.

5. Click Applications under the Software heading as shown in Figure 4-16, and note the system listed in the Kind column. Most applications are one of four kinds:

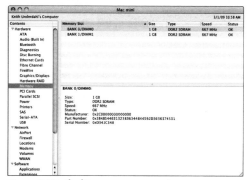

Figure 4-15: Checking out your computer's memory

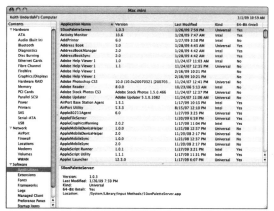

Figure 4-16: Checking the system compatibility of your applications

- **Classic:** Requires OS 9 to be installed

- **PowerPC or Native:** Compatible with OS X running on PowerPC-based Macs

- **Intel:** Compatible with OS X running on Intel-based Macs

- **Universal:** Universal binary, compatible with PowerPC- and Intel-based Macs

6. Review other categories as needed.

Part II
Getting to Work in OS X

Utilizing OS X Applications

Personal computers first became popular in the 1980s, well before the days of iPods and social networking Web sites. Why did people spend hundreds or even thousands of dollars on primitive computers like the Apple II, TRS-80, IBM PC, and early Macintosh? Even before digital multimedia and the online world came into power, computers were powerful tools to help organize data, type reports, and store information.

Today, most people take it for granted that computers help them compose letters, track schedules, and manage contacts. And with a Mac, you really *can* take these things for granted because new Macintosh computers come with an array of free programs to help you accomplish common tasks. These handy programs live in the OS X Applications folder, and this chapter shows you how to use some of them. This chapter shows you how to

➡ Keep a personal schedule with iCal.

➡ Manage names, addresses, and other contact information with the Address Book.

➡ Edit text files with TextEdit.

➡ Store and organize pictures with iPhoto (a free program on most new Macs, or available as part of iLife).

➡ Expand your vocabulary with the built-in dictionary.

➡ Save any file as a PDF for easy online sharing.

Chapter

5

Get ready to . . .

Open the Applications Folder

1. Open the Finder: Click the Finder icon on the Dock or double-click the hard drive icon on your Desktop.

2. Click Applications under Places in the Finder Sidebar to open the Applications folder, as shown in Figure 5-1.

3. To launch an application, simply double-click its icon in the Applications folder.

 In some cases, you may need to open a subfolder before launching an application. For example, if you have Microsoft Office installed, you may need to open the Office subfolder in the Applications folder before opening a program, such as Word or Excel.

Figure 5-1: The Applications folder in OS X

Plan Your Life with iCal

1. Open the Applications folder and then double-click the iCal icon.

 You may also be able to launch iCal from the Dock.

2. In the Calendars menu on the left side of the iCal window, select the check boxes next to the calendars you want to display. For example, if you want only your home schedule to display, remove the check marks next to all the other calendars.

3. To create a new calendar (in addition to the default calendars), choose File⇨New Calendar and then type a name for the calendar, as shown in Figure 5-2.

4. To add a calendar event, first select the calendar to which it should be added.

Figure 5-2: The iCal application

5. In the month calendar shown in the lower-left corner of the iCal window, click the day on which you want to create the event.

 Use the arrows above the calendar to move to a different month. Click the Day, Week, or Month tab at the top of the window to change how calendar events are displayed.

6. In the main calendar window, double-click a day or click and drag a box around the time of your event or appointment and then type a name for the event, as shown in Figure 5-3.

7. To see details of an event, double-click the event in the main calendar and then choose Edit from the menu that appears. Information about the event appears in a pop-up window, as shown in Figure 5-4.

8. To invite other people to the event, click in the Invitees text box and enter an invitee's e-mail address, as shown in Figure 5-4.

 After you enter an e-mail address, click the e-mail address to change options such as making the meeting optional or removing the attendee. Type additional e-mail addresses in the Invitees text box to invite multiple attendees.

9. Click Done or Send to close the Event window.

 Use the Calendar pop-up menu in the Event window to move events from one of your calendars (such as Home) to another calendar (such as Work).

10. To remove an event from iCal, simply click the event once to select it and then press the Delete key.

Figure 5-3: Adding events to the calendar

Figure 5-4: Easily view by month and invite attendees

 If you delete an event by accident, you can undo the deletion by choosing Edit⇨Undo.

Add Contacts to Your Address Book

1. Open the Applications folder and then double-click the Address Book icon to launch the Address Book.

    You can also launch the Address Book from other applications, such as iCal and Apple Mail or from the Dock.

2. To add a new person to the Address Book, click the Add a New Card button, which looks like a plus sign and is located below the list of names.

3. Type the person's name, company, phone numbers, addresses, and other information, as shown in Figure 5-5.

4. To edit an entry later, simply click the name of the person you want to change and then click the Edit button under his or her card information.

5. To add a picture to a person's Address Book card, click the name in the list and then double-click the picture icon next to the name.

6. In the picture chooser that appears, as shown in Figure 5-6, click Choose. Use the Open dialog that appears to find and select an image on your hard drive.

7. Zoom in on the image by using the Zoom slider below the picture and then click and drag the image left or right and up or down to reposition it. The area in the central box will be used in the Address Book.

8. Click the Set button.

9. To remove a person from your Address Book, select the name in the Name list and then choose Edit➪Delete Card.

Figure 5-5: Adding a contact to the Address Book

Figure 5-6: Adding personal photos to Address Book cards

Edit Text with TextEdit

1. Open the Applications folder and then double-click the TextEdit icon.

2. Begin typing text, as shown in Figure 5-7.

3. To change the size or formatting of text, click and drag over a passage of text to select it and then choose Format⇨ Font. Make a selection from the Font panel to change the size of text or apply characteristics, such as **bold** or *italics*.

You can change alignment and spacing of text by choosing Format⇨Text.

4. To save your work, choose File⇨Save. Choose a folder in which to save the file, enter a name, and then click Save.

5. To print your text, choose File⇨Print. Select a printer, specify the pages to print and the number of copies of each, and then click Print.

6. If you're not happy with the default text size or appearance, choose TextEdit⇨Preferences to open the Preferences window, as shown in Figure 5-8.

7. Choose whether you want the default format to be Rich Text or Plain Text. Rich Text allows you to format text so that it looks nice, but Plain Text is required for certain types of files, such as Hypertext Markup Language (HTML) files.

8. To change the default text appearance, click the Change button next to either Plain Text Font or Rich Text Font. In the Font picker, choose different default fonts, styles, and sizes, as desired.

Figure 5-7: The TextEdit application

If you ever need to edit raw HTML markup, TextEdit is a better choice than other word processing programs such as Apple Pages or Microsoft Word.

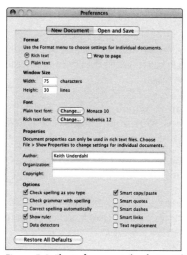

Figure 5-8: The Preferences window for TextEdit

Organize Pictures with iPhoto

1. Open the Applications folder and then double-click the iPhoto icon. If you're launching iPhoto for the first time, you're asked whether you want to use iPhoto when you connect a digital camera to the computer. Click a button to make a choice.

    You may also open iPhoto from the Dock.

2. Connect your digital camera to your computer's Universal Serial Bus (USB) port and turn on the camera. The camera should be in picture viewing mode, not picture taking mode.

3. When iPhoto detects photos on your camera, as shown in Figure 5-9, type a name and description for the event.

4. Click Import All to begin importing all photos from your camera, or select certain images and click Import Selected to only import certain photos.

    To import pictures that are already on your hard drive into iPhoto, choose File➪Add to Library. Use the Open dialog that appears to browse and import photos.

5. To create a new album in which to organize certain pictures, choose File➪New Album and then type a descriptive name for the album.

6. Click and drag photos from the Library window to the new album, as shown in Figure 5-10.

    To copy multiple photos, first click and drag a box around the photos you want to move. After a group is selected, you can click and drag that group to a new album.

7. Click the name of an album to view its contents.

Figure 5-9: The iPhoto application

Figure 5-10: An album with several pictures

Create PDF Files

1. Create a document in any application. The document can be text, a picture, or almost anything else, and it can be created in a bundled OS X application or a third-party application.

2. After you're done editing the file, choose File⇨Print.

3. Click the PDF button and then select Save as PDF from the drop-down menu that appears, as shown in Figure 5-11.

4. Type a filename for the PDF file in the Save As text box.

5. Choose a location in which to save the PDF file from the Where menu.

6. Click the Save button.

7. Locate the saved PDF file and double-click it to open it. If you have a PDF reader program (such as Adobe Reader) installed, the PDF file might open in that program, as shown in Figure 5-12. Otherwise, the PDF file opens in Preview.

 If you don't have Adobe Reader installed on your computer, visit www.adobe.com to download it for free. Although the OS X Preview program can open and display PDFs, Preview isn't compatible with some PDF features, such as cross-document links and multi-volume searching.

Figure 5-11: Creating a PDF file

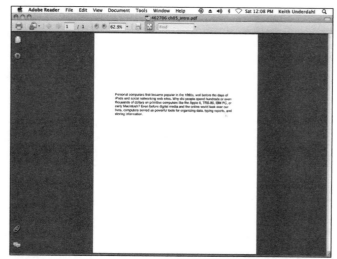

Figure 5-12: Viewing a PDF file

Look Up Words in the Dictionary

1. Open the Applications folder and then double-click the Dictionary icon.

2. Start typing a word in the search box of the Dictionary window, as shown in Figure 5-13. Type slowly and note the list of words that appears and is narrowed down with each letter you add. If the word you type isn't in the dictionary, you see a warning and suggestions, as shown in Figure 5-13.

3. Double-click a word in the list to view its definition, as shown in Figure 5-14.

4. Scroll down the page to find derivatives, etymology, and synonyms.

5. To return to the previous Dictionary window, choose History⇨Back.

 The Dictionary is interactive. If you see a word in a definition that you don't understand, simply double-click the word. That word's Dictionary entry appears.

 To change the preferred reference tool (Dictionary, Thesaurus, Wikipedia, or others) or pronunciation guide, choose Dictionary⇨Preferences. In the Preferences window, you can change these and other Dictionary settings.

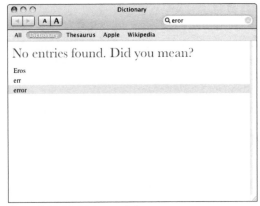

Figure 5-13: The Dictionary window

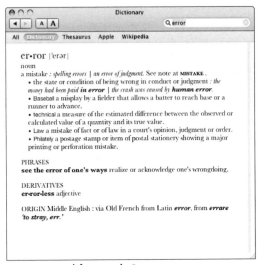

Figure 5-14: A definition in the Dictionary

Quit an Application

1. To see whether an application is still running, look at the Dock. Icons with arrows below them — such as TextEdit and Preview, as shown in Figure 5-15 — are still running, even if you closed all documents in that program.

2. To quit an application, first click the application's icon on the Dock to make the application active.

3. Click the name of the application (for example, TextEdit or Preview) on the menu bar and choose Quit from the menu that appears, as shown in Figure 5-16.

 You can also press ⌘+Q to quickly quit an active program.

 Make a habit of quitting programs after you're done using them. Each program that's left running uses up some memory and other system resources. Unlike Windows programs, most Macintosh applications don't quit when you simply click a window's red Close button.

Figure 5-15: Applications on the Dock

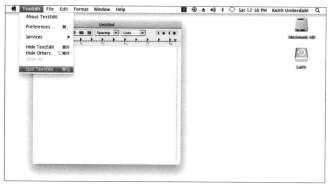

Figure 5-16: Quitting an application

Using Productivity Software

You probably have some Windows-using friends who say things like, "I would use a Mac, but the programs I need aren't available for OS X."

Given this perception, it comes as a surprise to many people that, in fact, a lot of applications *are* available for OS X, including ubiquitous Microsoft Office applications like Word, PowerPoint, and Excel. If you have work to get done, your Macintosh is up to the task.

Applications, such as word processors, spreadsheet programs, and presentation programs, are often called *productivity* programs. Apple offers its own suite of productivity programs — *iWork*. iWork is more affordable than Microsoft Office and includes *Pages* (a word processor), *Keynote* (a presentation program), and *Numbers* (a spreadsheet program).

This chapter shows you how to use iWork applications, but many of the basic techniques apply to Microsoft Office as well. To order iWork, visit your local Apple retailer or see www.apple.com/iwork. Tasks show how to create and edit new presentations and word processing documents with iWork applications.

 Free trials of Apple iWork and Microsoft Office are pre-installed in the Applications folders of most new Macs. For more on using Microsoft Office applications for OS X, check out *Microsoft Office 2008 for Macs For Dummies* by Bob LeVitus (Wiley Publishing, Inc.).

Get ready to . . .

Create a New Pages Document

1. Launch Pages from the iWork subfolder in the Applications folder.

 If this is your first time launching iWork, click Try to evaluate iWork free for 30 days.

2. Choose a template for your new document, as shown in Figure 6-1. To choose a template, click a document category in the list on the left and then scroll through the available templates on the right. When you find the template you want to use, click the template to select it and then click the Choose button.

 To create another new document at any time in Pages, choose File➪New.

3. Begin typing text, as you would in any word processor or text editing program.

4. To save the document, choose File➪Save.

5. In the Save As dialog that appears, type a name for the document. If you want to choose a different folder as your Save location, click the arrow to the right of the Save As field to display a small Finder-like pane, as shown in Figure 6-2.

6. After you name the file and select the folder where you want to save it, click Save.

 Save your document frequently while you work. To quickly save a document, press ⌘+S.

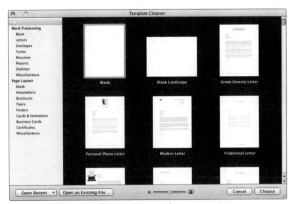

Figure 6-1: Many helpful document templates

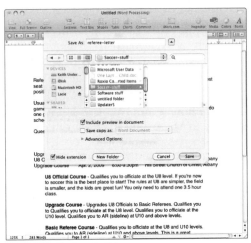

Figure 6-2: The Save As dialog

Style Text in Pages

1. Click to place the cursor in the paragraph to which you want to apply formatting.

2. Click the Style menu and choose a style, as shown in Figure 6-3.

3. To change the alignment of text, place the cursor in the desired paragraph and choose Format⇨Text. Choose an alignment option, such as Center or Justify.

 The Formatting toolbar also includes alignment buttons to help you quickly align text left, right, centered, or justified.

4. To create a bulleted or numbered list, select each line of text in the list and then click the List button on the far-right end of the Formatting toolbar — directly under Fonts. Choose a list style from the submenu that appears.

5. To change the style of a smaller passage of text, click and drag over the text to select it. Figure 6-4 shows some text selected.

6. Choose font face, style, size, and color options using the Formatting toolbar menus. In Figure 6-4, I'm about to make the selected text bold.

 You can also access font properties and other appearance settings by choosing Format⇨Font.

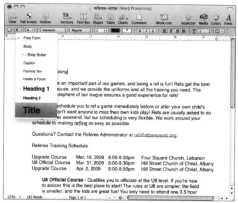

Figure 6-3: The Style menu

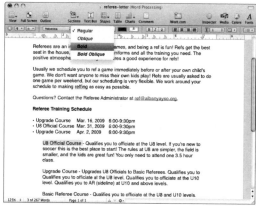

Figure 6-4: Applying bold to text

Insert a Photo into a Pages Document

1. With Pages open, create a document into which you want to insert a photo.

2. Place the cursor where you want to insert the photo.

3. Choose Insert⇨Choose.

4. In the dialog that appears, browse to the photo you want to insert.

5. Click the photo to select it, as shown in Figure 6-5, and then click the Insert button to include it in the document.

 If the image doesn't fit well into your document, click and drag the corner handles of the image to resize it.

Figure 6-5: Choosing the photo to insert

 To create a PDF file of your document, click the PDF button in the lower-left corner of the Print window and then choose Save as PDF from the drop-down menu that appears.

Print a Pages Document

1. Compose a document in Pages, as I describe earlier in this chapter.

2. Choose File⇨Print.

3. In the Print dialog that appears, click the down arrow to expand the print options.

4. Enter the number of copies and select other print options, as shown in Figure 6-6.

5. Click the Print button to begin printing.

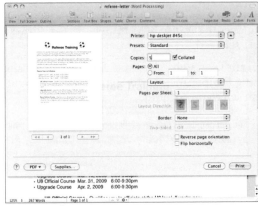

Figure 6-6: Choosing printing options

Start a New Keynote Presentation

1. Open the iWork subfolder in the Applications folder and then double-click Keynote to launch the program.

     If this is your first time launching iWork, click Try to evaluate iWork free for 30 days.

2. Choose a template for your new presentation from the Theme Chooser window, as shown in Figure 6-7. Scroll through the list of available templates. When you find the template you want to use, click the template to select it.

3. Select a size for your slides from the Slide Size pop-up menu, located in the lower-right corner of the Theme Chooser window.

     If your presentation will be viewed in a large room via a projector with average lighting and resolution, stick with a relatively small slide size, such as 1024 x 768 or 800 x 600. Larger slide sizes may result in text that's hard to read from the back row.

4. Click the Choose button to create a new presentation by using your chosen template and slide size.

5. Type a title and subtitle for your presentation in the provided text boxes on the first slide.

6. Choose File➪Save.

7. In the Save dialog that appears, enter a filename for your presentation, as shown in Figure 6-8.

8. Choose a folder in which to save the presentation in the Where menu and then click Save.

Figure 6-7: The Theme Chooser window

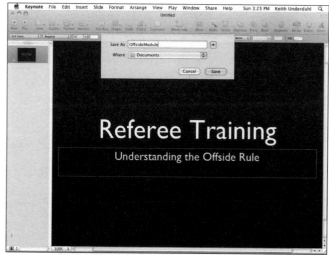

Figure 6-8: The Save dialog

Insert Slides

1. Open a Keynote presentation.

2. Click the New button in the upper-left corner of the Keynote window to insert a new slide, as shown in Figure 6-9.

3. To open a specific slide, click the slide in the Slides list on the left side of the screen.

4. To change the order of slides, click and drag slides up or down to new positions. Slides at the top of the list appear first when the slideshow is played.

5. To quickly change the layout or format of a slide, click the Masters button and choose a new master, as shown in Figure 6-10. Choosing a new master quickly reformats the appearance and styling of all your slides.

6. Click in the text areas and type text for your new slide.

 To delete a slide, select the slide and choose Edit⇨Delete. If you have a two-button mouse, you can also right-click a slide and choose Delete from the contextual menu that appears.

 To quickly create a new slide based on an existing slide, open the existing slide and choose Edit⇨Duplicate. An exact copy of the slide is added to the presentation.

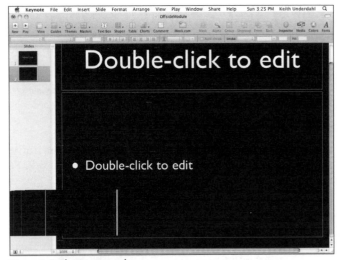

Figure 6-9: The Keynote window

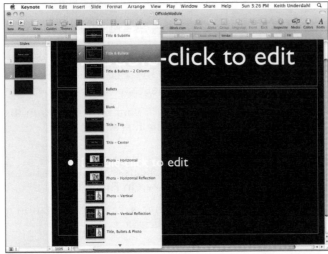

Figure 6-10: The Masters menu

Format Text

1. Enter text into a text box on a slide.

    To add a new text box to a slide, click the Text Box button on the Keynote toolbar. Click and drag the text box to the desired location and resize the box by using the handles on the sides and corners.

2. Click and drag over a passage of text to select it.

3. To change the size or style of the text, choose a font, style, and size from the menus on the Formatting toolbar, as shown in Figure 6-11.

    For more advanced control over text formatting, select some text and click the Fonts button on the Keynote toolbar. The Font panel opens with menus and options to control virtually every aspect of the font's appearance.

4. To change the color of text (or any object), select the text and then click the Colors button on the Keynote toolbar.

5. Use the Color picker, as shown in Figure 6-12, to select a new color.

    If you prefer to adjust color with sliders or specific numeric values rather than the circular color picker, click the Sliders button (the second button from the left) near the top of the Color picker.

    Remember to maintain strong contrast between text and background colors. Text that looks okay on your computer monitor may be unreadable on a dim projector in a bright room. White text on a dark background works best on most projectors.

6. Close the Color picker after you're done changing colors.

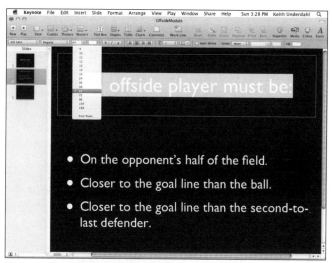

Figure 6-11: Formatting text in a text box

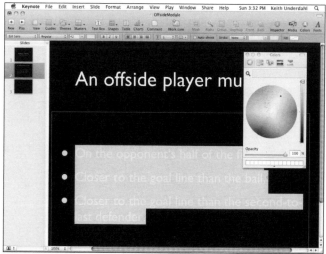

Figure 6-12: The Color picker

Add Graphics to Presentations

1. Open a Keynote presentation and select a slide on which you want to draw some basic graphics.

2. Click the Shapes button, as shown in Figure 6-13, and choose a shape that you want to draw.

3. When the shape appears on the screen, click and drag the corner and side handles to change the shape size.

4. To insert a photo, choose Insert➪Choose.

5. Browse to the image file that you want to insert. Select the image file and then click the Insert button.

6. Click and drag the image to a new location, as shown in Figure 6-14.

7. Click and drag the corner handles of the image to resize it.

 Don't make pictures too small because the people sitting in the back row must be able to see them, too.

8. If a shape or image blocks part of another image or object, select the image and choose Arrange➪Bring Forward or Arrange➪Send Backwards, as appropriate. Repeat until all graphics and objects on the slide are stacked in the proper order.

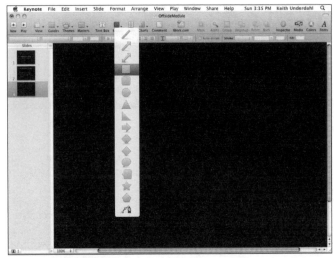

Figure 6-13: The Shapes menu

Figure 6-14: An image placed on a slide

Present a Keynote Presentation

1. Connect your Mac to a projector, if needed.

    You may need to use a special VGA adapter between your Mac and the projector cable. Apple offers VGA adapters, which allow you to connect most Macs to analog computer monitors or multimedia projectors.

2. Open the presentation that you want to play in Keynote.

3. Click the first slide in the presentation so that it's selected.

4. Click the Play button or choose Play➪Play Slideshow to play the slideshow. (Figure 6-15 shows a slideshow in progress.)

5. Press Return, the spacebar, the right arrow key, or the mouse button to move to the next slide.

6. To move to the previous slide, press the left arrow key.

7. To end the presentation, press the Esc key.

8. To export the presentation in a different format, choose Share➪Export.

9. In the Export dialog that appears, choose an export format and follow the instructions on-screen to export the presentation, as shown in Figure 6-16. The most useful formats include

   • **QuickTime:** Plays on any computer with QuickTime

   • **PowerPoint:** Exports a presentation that is compatible with Microsoft PowerPoint

   • **PDF:** Exports slides that can be viewed statically on any computer that has Adobe Reader

   • **HTML:** Produces an HTML file that can be viewed in a Web browser such as Safari or Firefox

   • **iPod:** Creates a movie that plays on a video-capable iPod

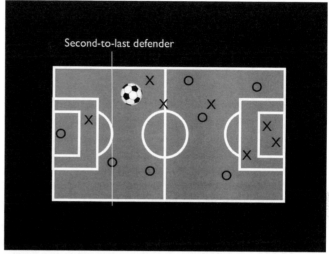

Figure 6-15: A slideshow in progress

Figure 6-16: The Export tab

Calculate Expenses Using Numbers

1. Open the iWork subfolder in the Applications folder and then double-click Numbers to launch the program.

     If this is your first time launching iWork, click Try to evaluate iWork free for 30 days.

2. Select a template for your new document and then click Choose.

3. Enter some numbers you want to add up in a column or row, as shown in Figure 6-17.

     If you're working from a new blank document, use Column A and Row 1 for labels. Columns are oriented vertically and rows stretch horizontally.

4. When you're done entering numbers, click and drag over all of the values to select them.

     Notice that a summary of the selected numbers is displayed in the lower-left corner of the Numbers window. This is a handy feature for calculating quick, at-a-glance sums and averages.

5. Click the Function button on the Numbers toolbar and then choose a function, as shown in Figure 6-18. The function is displayed in the next available cell.

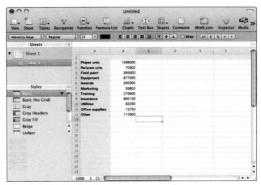

Figure 6-17: The Numbers program at work

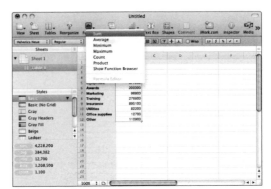

Figure 6-18: The Function menu

Using Dashboard

Computers are supposed to be labor-saving devices, but it seems to take an awful lot of mouse clicks, menu commands, and keyboard inputs to get anything done. This is what makes computers less intuitive than, say, a car, where every important control is immediately at hand and critical information is within your peripheral view.

The engineers at Apple must have been thinking about computer usability problems, too. When they released OS X version 10.4 Tiger, they included a new tool — *Dashboard*. Like the instrument panel in your car, the OS X Dashboard puts important information and tools within easy reach. Dashboard isn't quite in peripheral view — if it was it would be in the way — but it is just a single mouse click or keypress away, and Dashboard doesn't affect your other applications.

This chapter shows you how to open Dashboard and how to add and remove Dashboard items, which are also called *widgets*. Dashboard widgets covered in this chapter include

➠ Web Clips

➠ Weather

➠ Sticky Notes

➠ Flight Tracker

➠ Translation

➠ Unit Converter

➠ Movies

Open Dashboard

1. To open Dashboard, simply click the Dashboard icon on the Dock. The screen dims slightly, and Dashboard widgets zoom into view, as shown in Figure 7-1. You can also open Dashboard by two additional methods:

    - Double-click the Dashboard icon in the Applications folder.

    - Press F12 on your keyboard (F4 on newer Apple keyboards).

2. To change the way Dashboard opens, open System Preferences and then click the Exposé & Spaces icon.

3. To create a hot corner for Dashboard, click the Exposé tab and then select Dashboard from one of the Active Screen Corner menus. (In Figure 7-2, the lower-right corner has been set to Dashboard.) Then, to open Dashboard, simply move the mouse pointer to the corresponding corner of the screen.

4. To change the keyboard shortcut used for opening Dashboard, make a different selection in the Hide and Show menu.

 If you want to use a modifier key, such as ⌘ or Control, simply hold down that key (or keys) while making a selection in the Hide and Show menu.

 You can't quit Dashboard like other OS X applications. To close Dashboard, simply click a blank area of the screen. Although a blue and white dot remains under the Dashboard icon on the Dock, very few of your computer's resources are dedicated to Dashboard.

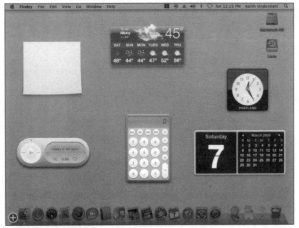

Figure 7-1: Dashboard

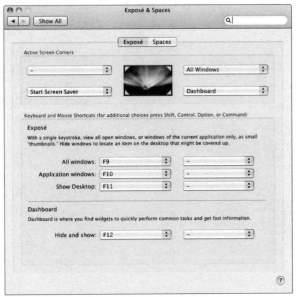

Figure 7-2: Setting a hot corner for launching Dashboard

Add Items to Dashboard

1. Open Dashboard.

2. Click the plus sign in the lower-left corner of the Dashboard screen. A list of widgets appears along the bottom of the screen, as shown in Figure 7-3.

3. Click the arrow buttons on the far right or left of the list of widgets to scroll through the list.

4. To add a widget, simply click the widget in the list. The new widget is plopped onto your Dashboard. In Figure 7-4, the widget for showing movie times was added.

5. Click and drag widgets to move them to new locations on the Desktop.

6. To remove a widget from Dashboard, click the X button in the upper-left corner of the widget. You can always add the widget back later if you want.

7. After you're done adding, moving, and removing widgets, click the X button in the lower-left corner of the screen, just above the horizontal list of widgets. The list disappears, and the X turns back into a plus sign.

 You can click and drag widgets to new locations at any time; the widget list at the bottom of the screen need not be visible when moving widgets. You need the widget list open only when you're adding and removing widgets.

 Dashboard lets you add multiple copies of the same widget. So for example, you can have one clock showing local time and another showing GMT, or you can display weather widgets for multiple cities.

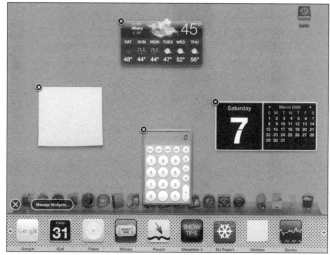

Figure 7-3: The widget list

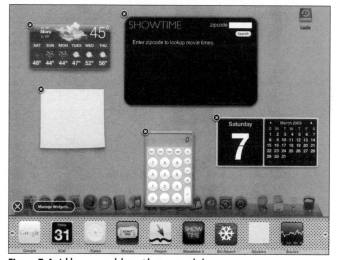

Figure 7-4: Add, move, or delete widgets as needed

Create Web Clip Widgets

1. In Safari, open a Web page containing the item you want to place in a widget.

2. When the page is loaded, choose File⇨Open in Dashboard.

 You can also click the Open This Page in Dashboard button on the Safari toolbar. The button looks like a dotted square with scissors. However, if the item is in a pop-up window, the Safari toolbar may not be visible, making it necessary to choose File⇨Open in Dashboard.

3. Click the general area of the page containing the item that you want to add to Dashboard. A clear box appears around the area.

4. Click and drag the handles at the corners and sides of the box so that the box surrounds only the area that you want to add to Dashboard. In Figure 7-5, I'm selecting a picture and some text in a pop-up window.

5. Click the Add button. A Web Clip containing the area is added to Dashboard, as shown in Figure 7-6. The Web Clip widget automatically updates whenever the web content it contains is updated. The Web Clip in Figure 7-6 is a highway cam image that updates every ten minutes.

6. Open Dashboard and reposition the Web Clip.

7. To remove a Web Clip from your Dashboard, open Dashboard and then click the plus sign in the lower-left corner of the screen. Click the Web Clip's close button to remove it.

Figure 7-5: Selecting the area to add to Dashboard

Figure 7-6: A Web Clip on Dashboard

Check Weather

1. Open Dashboard. If the Weather widget isn't already part of your Dashboard, add it, as described earlier in this chapter.

2. Hover the mouse pointer over the lower-right corner of the Weather widget and then click the *i* button when it appears.

3. In the City, State, or ZIP Code field, enter your city, state, or ZIP code.

    If you live in a suburb of a larger city, make sure you enter the name of your suburb and not the big city nearby. For example, if you live in Aurora, Colorado, enter **Aurora** and not Denver. This ensures that your weather report is as accurate as possible for your specific location.

4. Choose whether you want the temperature to display in Celsius (°C) or Fahrenheit (°F) in the Degrees menu.

5. If you want the weather outlook to display daily low temperatures as well as daily highs, select the Include Lows in 6-Day Forecast check box.

6. Click Done and then check your weather outlook, as shown in Figure 7-7.

7. For a compact display of the Weather widget, click the sun or moon (depending on the time of day). The widget display gets smaller, like the upper widget in Figure 7-8. Click the sun or moon again to expand the display, like the lower widget in Figure 7-8.

    If you want to monitor the weather in multiple locations, open multiple occurrences of the Weather widget simply by adding the Weather widget again, as described earlier in this chapter. You can then set each widget to a different geographic location.

Figure 7-7: Your weather outlook

Figure 7-8: The Weather widget

Leave Sticky Notes

1. Open Dashboard. If the Stickies widget isn't already part of your Dashboard, add it, as described earlier in this chapter.

2. Hover the mouse pointer over the lower-right corner of the Stickies widget and click the *i* button when it appears.

3. Choose a paper color, font, and font size, as shown in Figure 7-9.

    For best results, keep the Font Size menu set to Auto. When the size is set to auto, the text size adjusts automatically when you type notes.

4. Click Done.

5. To compose a note, simply click the Stickies widget and start typing, as shown in Figure 7-10.

6. To delete the text on a note, click and drag over text with the mouse to select it and then press Delete on your keyboard.

    If you want to save text in a Sticky Note, select the text and then press ⌘+C on the keyboard to copy it. Open another program (such as TextEdit) and then press ⌘+V to paste the text into that program. You can then save the text with that program. You can't save text by using the Stickies widget.

Figure 7-9: Paper color and font options for the Stickies widget

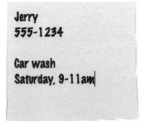

Figure 7-10: A quick note

Track Flights

1. Open Dashboard. If the Flight Tracker widget isn't already part of your Dashboard, add it, as described earlier in this chapter.

2. If you want to track flights for a specific airline, choose the airline from the Airline pop-up menu.

3. Select the departure city from the Depart City pop-up menu, as shown in Figure 7-11.

4. Select the destination from the Arrive City pop-up menu, as shown in Figure 7-11.

 If you know the three-letter airport code (for example, LAX for Los Angeles International Airport or MSP for Minneapolis-St. Paul International Airport) for either city, click in the relevant menu and type the code.

5. Click the Find Flights button.

6. Review the list of flights matching your results, as shown in Figure 7-12.

7. To perform another search, click the arrow next to the Track Flight button.

 Flight Tracker automatically refreshes its data every time you open Dashboard. If you plan to track a flight in the near future, set up Flight Tracker to monitor those flights beforehand.

Figure 7-11: The Flight Tracker widget

Figure 7-12: Flight status info in Flight Tracker

Translate Foreign Languages

1. Open Dashboard. If the Translation widget isn't already part of your Dashboard, add it, as described earlier in this chapter.

2. Select languages in the From and To pop-up menus to decide how the translation is made.

3. Enter a phrase, including punctuation, in the From field. A translation appears automatically in the To field, as shown in Figure 7-13.

 You can copy and paste text into the Translation widget from other programs or Web pages.

Convert Units of Measure

1. Open Dashboard. If the Unit Converter widget isn't already part of your Dashboard, add it, as described earlier in this chapter.

2. Choose the kind of unit you want to convert in the Convert menu. You can choose among Weight, Volume, Energy, Currency, Time, and many other categories.

3. Select a specific unit of measure from the menu on the left and then enter a value, as shown in Figure 7-14.

4. Choose a specific unit of measure in the right menu. This unit should be the one to which you want to convert the original value.

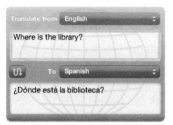

Figure 7-13: The Translation widget

Figure 7-14: The Unit Converter widget

Check Movie Times

1. Open Dashboard. If the Movies widget isn't already part of your Dashboard, add it, as I describe earlier in this chapter.

2. Click on the Movies widget to enlarge its window size.

3. Hover the mouse pointer over the lower-right corner of the Movies widget and click the *i* button when it appears.

4. Enter your postal code, as shown in Figure 7-15. Click Done to return to the main window.

5. Click the name of a movie under Movie Theaters to view a description of the movie. A list of local theaters that are showing the movie appears to the right.

6. Click a theater in the list to view a list of show times, as shown in Figure 7-16.

7. To view a trailer for the movie, click the Trailer icon in the lower-left corner.

8. To purchase tickets online, click Buy Tickets in the lower-left corner.

 By default, all movies and show times are displayed for the current day. To view a different day, click Today in the upper-right corner of the Movies widget and choose a different day from the menu that appears.

Figure 7-15: The Movies widget

Figure 7-16: Movie theaters, titles, and show times

Download New Dashboard Widgets

1. Open Dashboard and then click the plus sign in the lower-left corner to open the list of widgets along the bottom of the screen.

2. Click the Manage Widgets button in the lower-left corner, just above the widget list.

3. In the Widget Manager window that appears, as shown in Figure 7-17, click More Widgets.

4. In the Apple Web site that appears, as shown in Figure 7-18, browse the extensive list of available widgets.

 Make sure you read the terms of use for any widget before you download. Widgets listed as Freeware can be downloaded for free, but you should still click the More Info link if one is available. The More Info link also usually contains special installation instructions.

5. After you find a widget you want to install, click Download.

6. Click OK to save the widget.

7. After the download is complete, click the Downloads icon on the Dock and follow the on-screen instructions to extract the widget and finish installation.

Figure 7-17: The Widget Manager window

Figure 7-18: The Apple Web site and its many widgets

Part III

Going Online with
Your Mac

The 5th Wave · By Rich Tennant

"...so if you have a message for someone, you write it on a piece of paper and put it on their refrigerator with these magnets. It's just until we get our e-mail fixed."

Sending E-Mail and Browsing the Internet

8

*P*ersonal computers have been available since the 1970s, but in the early years they were mainly used by businesses, gamers, and hardcore computer geeks. With the advent of the World Wide Web in the 1990s, more people came to see personal computers as necessities. Today the computer is an indispensable tool for communication, information, and entertainment.

Your Macintosh is ready to communicate, entertain, and retrieve information as soon as you take it out of the box. It comes with all the software applications you need to send and receive e-mail, browse the Web, or download multimedia. Your Mac even comes with the hardware needed to connect to the Internet in the form of AirPort and an Ethernet network adapter. (An Ethernet port is optional on some models.) If you need a modem for dial-up Internet, Apple sells one that plugs into your Mac's USB port.

This chapter shows you how to get started with e-mail and Web browsing. In addition to the applications that come with OS X, this chapter also shows you how to download and use *Firefox*, a popular third-party Web browser.

 Before you can use e-mail and the Internet, you must have an Internet service account. These accounts are provided by Internet service providers (ISPs), of which many are probably in your area. If you don't already have Internet service, check with your telephone and/or cable company to see what services they offer, or look in the phone book under Internet Service. Once you are signed up, your ISP should provide specific instructions for connecting its service.

Get ready to . . .

Go Online with Safari

1. Launch Safari by clicking the Safari icon on the Dock or by double-clicking its icon in the Applications folder.

    The first time you launch Safari, you're shown the Top Sites screen. Click a thumbnail on this screen to open a Web page. As you browse the Internet, Safari remembers your favorite Web sites and automatically replaces the generic top sites with your personal favorites. Click the Top Sites button (it looks like a grid of squares) on the Safari toolbar to view the Top Sites screen.

2. Type a Web address — a *uniform resource locator* (URL) — in the address bar, as shown in Figure 8-1, and then press Return to visit the address.

3. Use these buttons on the Safari toolbar to navigate Web pages:

   • **Back:** Click the Back button to return to the previously viewed Web page.

   • **Forward:** If you click the Back button, you can click the Forward button to return to the page you just left.

   • **Bookmark:** Click this button (it looks like a Plus sign next to the Web address box) to bookmark a Web page. Edit the name of the bookmark and select a location from the pop-up menu, such as the Bookmarks bar, as shown in Figure 8-2. You can easily return to the bookmarked page by selecting it from the Bookmarks menu on the menu bar.

   • **Reload:** Use this button — located on the right side of the Web address bar — to reload the current page.

4. To change the size of text on the screen, open the View menu and choose to make text either bigger or smaller.

Figure 8-1: The Safari Web browser

Figure 8-2: Bookmarking a Web page

5. Choose Safari⇨Preferences.

6. In the General pane that appears, find the Home Page text box and enter the URL for the page you want to use as your home page, as shown in Figure 8-3.

 The *home page* is the Web page that opens first whenever you launch Safari. To use the current Web page as your home page, click Set to Current Page.

7. Click the Security icon at the top of the pane to open Security preferences.

8. Choose the Never option next to Accept Cookies if you don't want to accept cookies from Web sites.

 Cookies are files that Web pages save to track your Web browsing habits. This may sound bad, but the real risks are minimal. Some Web pages may not function correctly when cookies are disabled.

9. Close the preferences pane when you're done adjusting Safari preferences.

10. To browse anonymously, choose Safari⇨Private Browsing.

 Private browsing stops Safari from remembering which Web pages you've visited. This setting is especially valuable if you're using Safari on a public computer, such as in a library or school.

11. To return to a Web page in History, choose a page from the History menu, or click the Show All Bookmarks button (it looks like an open book) on the far-left side of the Bookmarks bar and then choose History in the list that appears, as shown in Figure 8-4. Click a page in the History to view it.

12. To clear the history, choose History⇨Clear History.

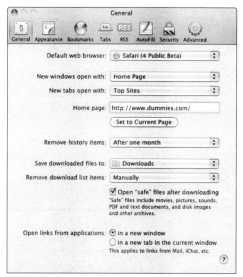

Figure 8-3: Setting your home page

Figure 8-4: Digging into your browsing history

Install Firefox

1. Use any Web browser (like Safari) to visit www.getfirefox.com.

2. Follow the instructions on the Mozilla Web site — home to the Firefox developer team — to download Firefox.

3. When the installer download is finished, click the Downloads folder on the Dock, and then double-click the icon for the disk image (the icon has the .dmg file-name extension) to extract and mount the disk image.

4. When you see the Firefox window, as shown in the upper-left corner of Figure 8-5, click and drag the Firefox icon onto the Applications folder icon right next to it. The Applications folder automatically opens, as shown in Figure 8-5. Drop Firefox in the Applications folder to install it.

 After you copy Firefox to the Applications folder, you can delete the downloaded Firefox disk image.

 To access Firefox more easily, add it to the OS X Dock. See Chapter 1 for more on adding items to the Dock.

Browse the Web with Firefox

1. Launch Firefox from the Applications folder.

2. Type a Web address in the address bar, as shown in Figure 8-6.

Figure 8-5: Installing Firefox

Figure 8-6: Typing a URL in the address bar

3. Use the navigation buttons on the Firefox toolbar to browse Web pages. From left to right, the buttons are

- **Back:** Click the Back button to return to the previously viewed Web page.

- **Forward:** If you click the Back button, you can click the Forward button to return to the page you just left.

- **Reload:** Use this button to reload the current page. The Reload button is especially helpful if a wireless connection drops momentarily and the page fails to load completely.

- **Stop:** Click this button to stop loading the current Web page.

- **Home:** Click the Home button to quickly return to your home page.

 Click and hold the Back and Forward buttons to reveal a longer list of visited pages.

4. Choose Firefox⇨Preferences.

5. On the Main tab, enter the URL for your desired home page in the Home Page text box, as shown in Figure 8-7, or click the Use Current Page button to set the current Web page as your home page.

6. Click the Advanced icon and then click the Check Now button to see whether Firefox is your default browser. If not, you may set Firefox as the default when you're prompted to do so. Close the Preferences window.

7. To view your browsing history, choose History⇨View All History. Use the History library, as shown in Figure 8-8, to browse previously visited Web sites.

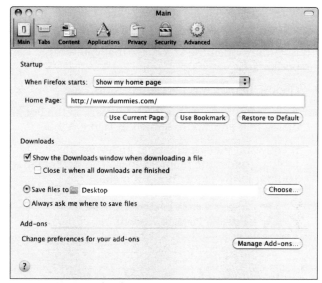

Figure 8-7: Setting Firefox's home page

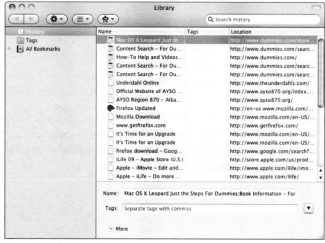

Figure 8-8: The History library

Bookmark Your Favorite Web Pages

1. In Firefox, open the Web page that you want to bookmark.

2. Choose Bookmarks⊏>Bookmark This Page.

3. Type a simple name for the bookmark in the Bookmark dialog that appears, as shown in Figure 8-9.

4. If you want the bookmark to appear on the Bookmarks toolbar (under the main toolbar), choose Bookmarks Toolbar in the Folder pop-up menu.

 To delete or update old bookmarks, choose Bookmarks⊏>Organize Bookmarks.

Search with the Google Widget

1. Add the Google widget to the Dashboard, using the steps I describe in Chapter 7 for adding new widgets to Dashboard.

2. Open Dashboard and type a search query in the Google widget, as shown in Figure 8-10.

3. Press Return to begin the search. Your default Web browser opens and displays a list of results.

 Your Web browser doesn't need to be open when you use the Google widget. The browser launches automatically when you begin the search.

Figure 8-9: A dialog for bookmarking a Web page

Figure 8-10: The Google widget

Set Up an E-Mail Account

1. Obtain an e-mail account from your ISP, an e-mail account provider, or MobileMe. See Chapter 9 for more on getting and using a MobileMe account.

2. Launch Mail from the OS X Dock or from the Applications folder. Make sure your computer is connected to the Internet.

3. Enter the e-mail address and password for your e-mail account when you're prompted to do so, and then click Continue. Mail searches for mail servers for your e-mail address.

4. Choose the account type (such as POP, IMAP, or Exchange) and enter the incoming mail server address, as shown in Figure 8-11. (The e-mail service provider should give you all of these details.)

5. Type a description for the account and enter the user name and password.

6. Click Continue and then enter the outgoing mail server address, as shown in Figure 8-12.

7. If your server requires SSL authentication, select the Use Authentication check box and enter the username and password, as shown in Figure 8-12.

8. Click Continue, verify the account summary that appears, and then click Create. Your Inbox launches and mail is downloaded.

 If Mail is unable to verify or create the account because you enter an invalid address, username, or password, you're asked to repeat the necessary steps. Addresses, usernames, and passwords are provided by the e-mail service provider.

Figure 8-11: Choosing the type of mail account to create

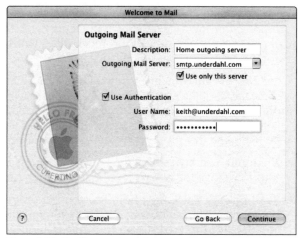

Figure 8-12: Handling outgoing mail server authentication

Compose and Send E-Mail

1. Open the Mail application and click New Message.

2. In the message window that appears, type the e-mail address of the recipient in the To field. If you aren't sure of the address, click the Address button and choose a name from your Address Book, as shown in Figure 8-13.

Figure 8-13: An Address Book

 To include a third party in on your e-mail, enter another address in the Cc field. You can enter multiple addresses in the To and Cc fields.

 When you receive an e-mail message, you can add the sender to your Address Book by selecting the message and choosing Message⇨Add Sender to Address Book.

3. Type a subject for your message in the Subject field. Make it descriptive so the recipient can easily identify the topic.

4. Compose your message, as shown in Figure 8-14. The mail composition window works much like a word processor. Composition options include

   - **Sending file attachments:** If you want to e-mail a file to someone, click the Attach button and browse to a picture or other file that you want to send with the e-mail. Try to keep attachment sizes small (usually 1MB or less) and keep in mind that some people can't receive attachments.

   - **Changing text styles:** Use the Fonts and Colors buttons to change the appearance of text in your e-mail.

   - **Send photos:** Click the Photo Browser button to browse your iPhoto library. To send a photo, click and drag it from the browser to your e-mail message, as shown in Figure 8-14.

5. After you're done composing your message, click Send. The message is sent.

Figure 8-14: Embedding photos by using the Photo Browser

Download and Read E-Mail

1. Launch Mail and make sure your computer is connected to the Internet.

2. If mail doesn't download automatically, click the Get Mail button on the Mail toolbar.

3. Review the list of downloaded e-mail in the Inbox. Unread e-mail is marked with a blue dot to the left of the message.

4. Click a message to view it in the Preview pane near the bottom of the window, as shown in Figure 8-15.

     To view an e-mail message in a separate window, double-click the message in the Inbox.

5. When you're done reading an e-mail, you can do one of several things with it:

    *   **Reply:** Select a message and click the Reply button to compose and send a reply back to the original sender.

    *   **Delete:** Click the Delete button on the toolbar to delete the message.

    *   **Junk:** If the message is spam or junk mail, select the message and click the Junk button. This action trains Mail to recognize and trash junk mail automatically.

    *   **Organize:** To organize e-mails that you want to keep, choose Mailbox⇨New Mailbox, type a name for the mailbox, and click OK. Click and drag messages to the new mailbox, as shown in Figure 8-16.

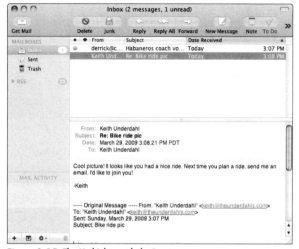

Figure 8-15: The Mail Inbox with the Preview pane open

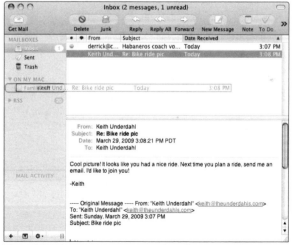

Figure 8-16: Organizing messages into sub-mailboxes

Adjust Mail Settings

1. Open the Mail application and choose Mail⇨Preferences.

2. On the General tab of the preferences pane that appears, select a time span from the Check for New Messages pop-up menu. In Figure 8-17, Mail was configured to check for mail every 15 minutes.

3. Click the Accounts icon at the top, click the Mailbox Behaviors button, and use the pop-up menu to choose how long you want to wait before deleted messages are emptied from the Trash. The default interval is one week.

4. Click the Junk Mail icon at the top and review junk mail filtering settings.

5. Click the Fonts & Colors icon and choose default fonts and colors for e-mail composition and viewing.

 Stick to basic fonts and contrasting colors so that your mail is easy to read.

6. Click the Composing icon. If you participate in e-mail lists that require plain text (with no formatting), choose Plain Text from the Message Format pop-up menu, as shown in Figure 8-18.

 If you want to reply to rich text messages in rich text format, select the check box labeled Use the Same Message Format as the Original Message.

7. Close the Preferences window after you're done making settings adjustments.

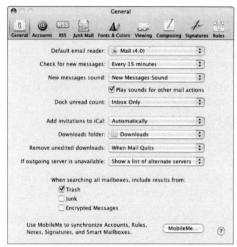

Figure 8-17: The General tab of the preferences pane for Mail

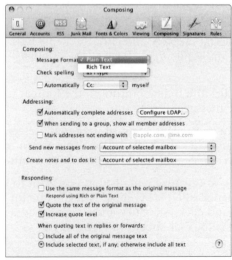

Figure 8-18: Configuring Mail for plain text mail

Using MobileMe

*O*ne of the coolest things about the Internet is that anyone can publish photos, blogs, and other stuff for the whole world to see. If you'd like your own online home page, you're going to need some online real estate on which to build it. Many different companies offer online server space, but such servers are often costly or difficult to use.

Apple offers online server space, too, and it's much easier to use than many other online services. The Apple online service is MobileMe, and you can use MobileMe for both public and private purposes. On the public side, you can use MobileMe to publish photos, videos, calendars, and Web pages. On the private side, you can use MobileMe to archive important data, as well as synchronize your calendars, contacts, and e-mails between multiple Macs, PCs, iPhones, and other devices.

An individual MobileMe account costs about $100 per year. This price is close to what other online server space companies charge, but with MobileMe you get user friendliness and seamless OS X integration for no extra charge. You can also try MobileMe for free for 60 days. This chapter shows you how to get started with a MobileMe account and how to start using some popular MobileMe features.

 MobileMe is the successor to Apple's earlier online service, .Mac. Apple transitioned .Mac accounts over to MobileMe accounts in 2008. MobileMe adds support for devices such as the iPhone, iPod touch, and even Windows PCs.

Create a MobileMe Account

1. Visit Apple's MobileMe Web site at `www.apple.com/mobileme`.

2. Click the link to sign up for a free trial.

3. Follow the on-screen instructions to create your account, as shown in Figure 9-1. Choose your member name carefully because you can't change it later. It will also become your @me.com e-mail address.

    If the member name you choose is already taken, the MobileMe Web site prompts you to enter a different one.

4. When you come to the MobileMe Setup page, as shown in Figure 9-2, click a link for a device (such as iPhone or Mac) to start setting it up. If you're working from your Mac, most MobileMe features will be configured automatically.

    The link for setting up Windows PCs contains addresses for incoming and outgoing e-mail servers (Simple Mail Transport Protocol, or SMTP), which you'll need when setting up MobileMe in Outlook or other Windows e-mail programs.

5. To log in to your MobileMe account from any Internet-connected computer, simply visit `www.apple.com/mobileme` and then click the Log In link in the upper-right corner.

    If you access MobileMe from a computer other than your own (especially a public computer), don't accept the browser's offer to remember your password and make sure that you log out when you're done.

Figure 9-1: The MobileMe sign up page

Figure 9-2: The MobileMe Setup page

Configure MobileMe on Your Mac

1. Open System Preferences and then click the MobileMe icon to open MobileMe preferences.

2. On the Sign In screen that appears, enter your MobileMe member name and password, as shown in Figure 9-3, and then click Sign In.

    Do not append @me.com to your MobileMe member name.

Figure 9-3: Signing in to MobileMe

3. In the MobileMe preferences pane that appears, click the Sync tab to open the Synchronization options.

4. Select the Synchronize with MobileMe check box, as shown in Figure 9-4.

5. In the Synchronize with MobileMe pop-up menu, choose whether you want synchronization of e-mails, contacts, and other items to happen automatically, manually, or at specific intervals. In Figure 9-4, synchronization happens automatically.

6. Select the check boxes next to the items you want to synchronize.

7. If you chose Manual or Specific Interval synchronization from the Synchronize with MobileMe pop-up menu, click the Sync Now button. Your MobileMe content synchronizes.

8. Repeat Steps 1–7 on other computers that you want to synchronize through MobileMe.

    If you receive an error message on other computers stating that they're not registered to synchronize through MobileMe, click Advanced in the MobileMe System Preferences window and then click Register This Computer.

Figure 9-4: The MobileMe preferences pane

Back Up Files

1. Configure your MobileMe account on your Mac, as described in the previous section. Also, make sure your computer is connected to the Internet.

2. Use the Finder to locate some important files you want to back up.

3. Click and drag the files to the iDisk icon in the Finder Sidebar, as shown in Figure 9-5. The files are copied from your computer to the iDisk online component of MobileMe. The copying process may take a few minutes depending on the size of the files and the speed of your Internet connection.

4. Click iDisk in the Finder Sidebar to browse iDisk contents.

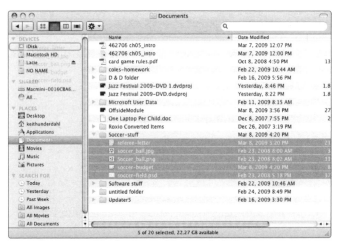

Figure 9-5: Dragging files directly to iDisk by using the Finder

 Files in iDisk can be organized into folders and subfolders, just like files on your hard drive. See Chapter 3 for more on creating and using folders in Finder and on iDisk.

5. To access your files on iDisk from any computer, use a Web browser to visit www.apple.com/mobileme, click the Log In link, and then log in using your member name and password.

6. Click the iDisk icon (it looks like a folder) near the top of the browser window.

7. Browse iDisk contents, as shown in Figure 9-6. Click a file to select it and then click the Download button to download it to your current computer.

 To share a file with anyone, click the file on iDisk once to select it and then click the Share File button. Enter a list of e-mail addresses, add a message, and click Share. iDisk automatically sends a link to the file to the e-mail addresses you entered.

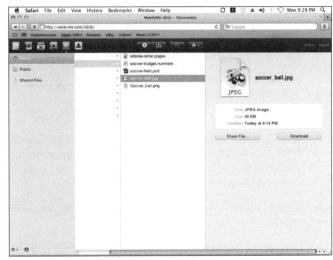

Figure 9-6: Browsing iDisk files by using a Web browser

Read and Send @me.com E-Mail

1. Log in to MobileMe and then click the Mail link.

> You can log in to MobileMe and check your MobileMe e-mail by using almost any Web browser on any computer connected to the Internet. You can also use the Apple Mail program (and some other e-mail clients) to access a MobileMe e-mail account. See Chapter 8 for more on using Apple Mail.

2. To download e-mail, click the Get New Mail icon (it looks like an envelope) near the top of the MobileMe Inbox, as shown in Figure 9-7.

3. To read a message, click it in the Inbox. The message opens in a preview pane, as shown in Figure 9-8.

4. Use the controls at the top of the screen to delete, reply to, or forward the message.

5. Click the Compose icon (next to the Get Mail icon) to compose a new e-mail message. In Figure 9-8, I'm composing a reply. This window works much like an e-mail composition window in Apple Mail.

6. After you're done composing your e-mail, click Send.

> Click the Attach a File link in the composition window to attach a file to the e-mail. When the attachment window appears, click Choose File and browse to the file that you want to attach. Select the file, click Choose, and then click Attach in the attachment window. Click Apply when you're done attaching files. Remember, some people are limited on the size of file attachments they can receive in e-mail, so avoid e-mailing large files.

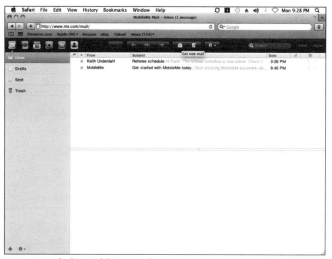

Figure 9-7: Checking MobileMe e-mail

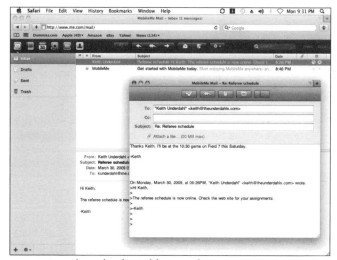

Figure 9-8: Reading and sending MobileMe e-mail

Publish Photos Online

1. Launch iPhoto. (See Chapter 15 for more on using iPhoto.)

    Make sure your computer is connected to the Internet and that your MobileMe account is configured, as described earlier in this chapter.

2. Open a Library or an Album that you want to publish online.

3. Choose Share➪MobileMe Gallery.

4. In the resulting dialog, use the Album Viewable By pop-up menu to determine who will be able to view the pictures, as shown in Figure 9-9. You can share the album with Everyone, or create usernames and passwords so your friends can log in.

5. Click the Publish button. A status bar near the top of the iPhoto window shows the progress of the file upload.

6. When the pictures are done uploading, a Web address for the gallery is displayed. Enter that address in a Web browser to view your gallery online, as shown in Figure 9-10.

    The Web address for your public galleries is `http://gallery.me.com/` followed by your account name.

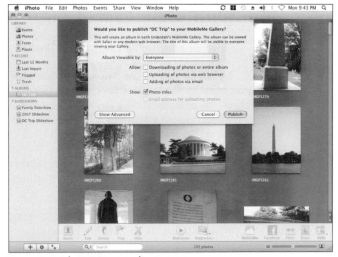

Figure 9-9: Selecting pictures to share

Figure 9-10: Viewing your photo album online

Web Designing
with iWeb

Not so long ago, keeping in touch with distant friends and family meant writing letters, stuffing envelopes, and licking stamps. And if you wanted to share some favorite photos, you had to get expensive film duplicates made by a photo processor.

The Internet has revolutionized the way people keep in touch. E-mail is one great way to communicate with distant relations, and you can also create your own Web site. When you create a Web page and put it online, anyone with Internet access can read your story and see your pictures. And you don't have to be a trained Internet engineer to produce your own Web site, because Apple produces a good Web design program called *iWeb*. iWeb is bundled with new Macs, or you can purchase it as part of the iLife suite from your favorite Apple retailer.

This chapter shows you how to create and share Web content with iWeb. Tasks also show you how to create and share

- ➡ **Web pages:** On Web pages, you can share stories, blogs, and photo galleries on any subject that interests you.

- ➡ **Podcasts:** A *podcast* is like a mix between a blog and a radio or TV show. You can record your own podcasts, which can then be shared with others through iTunes.

Get ready to . . .

Your Web pages must be uploaded to a Web server before others can view them. This chapter assumes that you use MobileMe as your Web server. For more on creating and using a MobileMe account, see Chapter 9.

Create a Web Page

1. Launch iWeb from the Dock or from the Applications folder.

 The first time you launch iWeb, you may be asked to confirm *keychain access* (where iWeb uses your MobileMe password to automatically log in) for your MobileMe account. Choose Allow to log in to MobileMe only this time, or choose Always Allow if you always want iWeb to connect to your MobileMe account.

2. In the Template dialog that appears, as shown in Figure 10-1, select a theme for your Web site from the list of themes on the left.

3. After you select a theme, select a page style from the list of pages.

4. Click the Choose button.

5. On the page that's created, click in a text area to replace placeholder text with your own, as shown in Figure 10-2.

6. To change text formatting, click and drag over the text you want to change and then click the Inspector icon on the iWeb toolbar at the bottom.

7. When the Inspector window appears in the upper-right corner of the screen, as shown in Figure 10-2, click the T button to open the Text Inspector.

8. Use the menus and options in the Text Inspector to change text formatting. If you want to create a numbered or bulleted list, as shown in Figure 10-2, click the List tab in the Text Inspector and then choose a list style from the Bullets & Numbering pop-up menu. Click the Close button in the upper-left corner of the Inspector to close it.

Figure 10-1: The Template dialog

Figure 10-2: Replacing the placeholder text

9. To replace a placeholder picture with a photo of your own, click the Photos tab in the upper-right corner of the iWeb screen.

10. Use the Photos pane to browse your iPhoto library or other photos on your hard drive, as shown in Figure 10-3. Click and drag a photo from the pane on the right to the iWeb page.

 You can also click and drag pages from iPhoto into your iWeb pages.

11. To change the name of a page, double-click it in the list of pages on the left side of the screen and then type a new name. Don't use spaces in page names.

12. To add a new page to your Web site, choose File➪New Page and then choose a page template for the new page. (Refer to Figure 10-1.)

13. To create a hyperlink, click and drag to select some text on which you want to create a link.

14. Open the Inspector if it isn't already open and then click the Link Inspector button (a blue circle with an arrow).

15. Select the Enable as a Hyperlink check box.

16. In the Link To pop-up menu, choose whether you want to link to one of your own pages, an external page, a file, or an e-mail message.

17. Choose a specific target for the link in the second menu or field. If you're linking to one of your own pages, choose the page, as shown in Figure 10-4.

 Don't forget to save your work periodically. Choose File➪Save to save your changes.

Figure 10-3: Selecting photos to add in iWeb

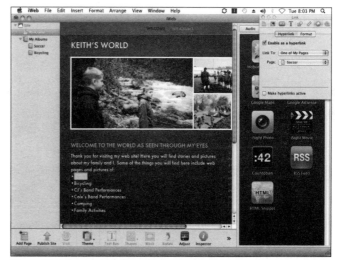

Figure 10-4: Using the Link Inspector to create hyperlinks

Publish the Web Page to MobileMe

1. After you're done creating your Web site, choose File➪Save to save your work.

2. Choose File➪Publish Entire Site, as shown in Figure 10-5.

    If you don't want to re-upload your entire site (it can take a while if your site gets big) just choose File➪Publish Site Changes to upload only things that have changed.

3. Read the warning message that appears about copyrighted content and then click Continue when you're sure that your Web site is in compliance with copyright laws.

4. If iWeb tells you that Publish will work in the background, click OK. Your Web site takes longer to publish if it includes many pictures.

5. When the site is completely uploaded, make a note of the Web address listed in the notification dialog that appears. This is the address that others can use to visit your Web site.

6. Click Visit Published Site in the notification dialog.

7. Test your Web site in your Web browser, as shown in Figure 10-6. Make sure that links function and that images display properly.

    If possible, test your Web site in several different Web browsers, such as Safari and Firefox. If possible, also test the site with Internet Explorer on a Windows PC.

Figure 10-5: Publishing a site to MobileMe

Figure 10-6: Testing the Web site in multiple Web browsers

Add a YouTube Video to Your Site

1. Launch iWeb and create a Web site, as described earlier in this chapter.

2. Create a page to which you want to add an embedded YouTube video.

3. Click the Widgets tab in the Media pane on the right side of the iWeb screen.

4. Enter the URL for a YouTube video in the YouTube dialog that appears, as shown in Figure 10-7.

    YouTube URLs are usually complex and difficult to type. It's easier to copy them from a YouTube Web page that you visit in Safari or another Web browser.

5. Click the Apply button to save the URL and add the YouTube widget to your site.

6. Click and drag the YouTube movie window to a spot on the page where it doesn't cover up other Web page elements.

7. Preview the video, as shown in Figure 10-8.

8. Click the close (X) button in the upper-left corner of the YouTube dialog box when you have the video window positioned where you want it on the page.

    YouTube videos are copyrighted, so only add YouTube videos to your Web site if you have permission to do so. You can easily make your own movies using iMovie (see Chapter 16) and then upload your movies to YouTube.

    You can add your iMovie videos directly to iWeb pages by clicking the Movies tab in the Media pane on the right. This avoids the YouTube step, but you use up your own MobileMe storage space and monthly transfer quota to host the video.

Figure 10-7: Adding a YouTube movie to a Web page

Figure 10-8: Positioning and previewing the YouTube movie

Link to MobileMe Galleries

1. Upload a photo gallery to MobileMe, as described in Chapter 9.

2. Create or open an iWeb page to which you want to add a MobileMe gallery.

3. Click the Widgets tab in the Media pane on the right to display a list of iWeb widgets, as shown in Figure 10-9.

4. Click and drag the MobileMe Gallery widget icon from the Media pane and drop it on a spot on your iWeb page.

5. In the MobileMe Gallery dialog that appears, choose a gallery from the Display menu, as shown in Figure 10-10.

6. Position the widget where you want it on the screen.

7. Save and upload your changes in iWeb. Changes you make to galleries in MobileMe are automatically incorporated into your iWeb site.

 You can also create photo galleries right in iWeb. Add a page to your site using the My Albums template. This page should be a landing page for all of your photo galleries. Create individual gallery pages using a Photos template.

Figure 10-9: Adding a MobileMe Gallery widget to your page

Figure 10-10: The MobileMe Gallery dialog

Record a Podcast

1. Launch GarageBand from the Dock or the Applications folder. (Like iWeb, GarageBand is part of the iLife suite.)

2. Click the Podcast icon in the GarageBand splash screen that appears. Then click Choose.

3. In the New Project from Template window, type a file name for the podcast and click Create.

4. In the list of audio tracks, click the Male Voice or Female Voice (as appropriate) track and make sure that a microphone is connected to your Mac.

5. Click the Record button and start recording your podcast. Click Stop when you're done.

 Try to record in as quiet an area as possible. Even things like noisy computer fans or air blowing through heat ducts can foul the quality of your audio recording. Also, consider hanging blankets or drapes on the walls to minimize sound reflection.

6. Choose Share➪Send Podcast to iWeb, as shown in Figure 10-11. A tab with sharing options appears.

7. Choose compression (AAC or MP3) and quality (Good, High, or Higher) settings and then click Share. iWeb opens automatically and inserts your podcast into a new page.

8. In iWeb, choose a template for your new page and then edit the page as described earlier in this chapter.

9. When the podcast appears on a new page in iWeb, as shown in Figure 10-12, edit the text of the page. The text should describe the subject of the Podcast.

10. Choose File➪Publish All to MobileMe to upload your podcast and other changes.

Figure 10-11: Sending your podcast to iWeb

Figure 10-12: Editing the text on the Podcast page

Chatting on Your Mac

Although the Internet has been in widespread use for only a little over a decade, its roots go all the way back to the late 1960s. One of the earliest uses for the Internet was *live chat* — distant parties typed messages to each other in real time. This chat tradition continues today and is made easy by instant messaging programs, such as AOL Instant Messenger (AIM), MSN Messenger, ICQ, and Apple's iChat. Not only does iChat give you access to the MobileMe network of chat users, but it can be configured to work with some other popular instant messaging networks as well. iChat also allows you to do screen sharing, which is sometimes used for online meetings or technical support.

In addition to typed text messages, some chat programs now offer voice chat as well. Real time voice chat may not seem revolutionary to anyone who has ever used a telephone, but the free or nearly free cost of Internet-based voice chat appeals to anyone who has ever paid a long distance phone bill. iChat can be configured to work with popular voice networks, including Skype and Google Talk.

This chapter shows you how to chat via iChat. It also shows you how to configure iChat for use with the Google Talk voice networks. Finally, this chapter also shows you how to use two third-party chat programs — Skype and Adium. Skype is a popular Voice Over IP (VOIP) service, and Adium can be used with many of the most popular instant messaging networks, including AOL Instant Messenger, MSN, ICQ, Yahoo!, and more.

Get ready to . . .

Set Up iChat

1. Launch iChat from the Dock or the Applications folder.

2. If this is the first time you're launching iChat, click Continue and enter your MobileMe or AIM account information, as shown in Figure 11-1, and then click Continue.

    If you don't yet have a MobileMe or other iChat-compatible account, click the Get an iChat Account button and follow the instructions on-screen to create a free account. If you would like to create a MobileMe account, see Chapter 9.

3. Click Done when you're done setting up your iChat account.

4. If you use a Jabber chat account, choose iChat⇨ Preferences, click the Accounts icon, and then click the Add Account button (it looks like a plus sign) in the lower-left corner of the preferences pane. Choose Jabber in the Account Type menu and enter your Jabber account information.

    Google Talk — which is covered later — is a Jabber account.

5. If you want to be able to easily chat with other people on your local network, click the Accounts button in iChat Preferences, click Bonjour under Accounts, and select the Make Bonjour Instant Messaging Active check box. Close the Preferences pane when you're done.

6. To add a chat partner, choose Buddies⇨Add Buddy and then click New Person.

7. Enter an account name or an e-mail address in the dialog that appears, as shown in Figure 11-2, and then click Add.

Figure 11-1: The Account Setup screen for iChat

Figure 11-2: Adding chat buddies to your Buddy List

Chat Using iChat

1. To chat with someone, double-click the person's name in your list of chat buddies.

2. Type a message, as shown in Figure 11-3, and then press Return to send the message.

 If you receive a chat message from a buddy, click in the chat window that appears automatically to begin chatting.

3. To add a smiley to your chat message, click the smiley icon on the right side of the text box and choose a smiley from the menu that appears.

4. If you're leaving the computer for a while, choose iChat⇨My Status and then choose a status (such as Out to Lunch or On the Phone) from the menu that appears.

5. To change your account picture, choose iChat⇨Change My Picture. In the Buddy Picture window, as shown in Figure 11-4, click the Choose button and browse to a new picture. Click Open to select the picture and then click Set to close the Buddy Picture window and set your new picture.

6. To change the font or chat balloon colors used when you chat, choose iChat⇨Preferences and then click the Messages icon. Use the color menus to change the color of your balloons or text and click Set Font to choose a different font and size.

 If incoming text is too small or too hard to read, select the Reformat Incoming Messages check box and then click Set Font to choose a bigger, easier-to-read font.

Figure 11-3: A chat in progress

Figure 11-4: The Buddy picture window

Share Screens with iChat

1. Launch iChat from the Dock or Applications folder.

2. Begin a chat with a buddy, as I describe earlier in this chapter.

3. To access your chat partner's screen, choose Buddies⇨ Share My Screen With and choose the buddy's name.

4. If you receive a request to share your screen, as shown in Figure 11-5, click Accept to accept the request or Decline if you don't want to allow sharing. If you accept, a Screen Sharing window appears as shown in Figure 11-6.

Figure 11-5: A request to share your screen

Figure 11-6: Controlling screen sharing

 Click Text Reply if you want to ask the buddy a question or send a message before you start screen sharing.

5. To control screen sharing, use the Screen Sharing window to perform the following tasks:

- **Stop:** Click the X (Stop) button to stop screen sharing.

- **Screen:** Click the Screen button (it looks like a cube) to view your buddy's screen.

- **Audio:** Click the Audio button (it looks like a microphone) to toggle audio on and off. You can also adjust volume using the volume slider under the Audio button.

 To immediately stop screen sharing at any time, press Control+Esc.

Use Google Talk with iChat

1. Launch iChat from the Dock or Applications folder.

2. Choose iChat➪Preferences to open the preferences pane.

3. Click the Accounts icon at the top of the preferences pane and then click the Add button (it looks like a plus sign) in the lower-left corner of the Accounts pane.

4. In the Account Type pop-up menu, choose Jabber, as shown in Figure 11-7.

5. Enter your Gmail e-mail address in the Account Name field, as shown in Figure 11-7.

     A Gmail account is required to use Google Talk.

6. Enter your Gmail password in the Password field and enter **gmail.com** in the Server field.

7. Click Add to create the account and then close the Accounts preferences pane.

8. In iChat, choose Window➪Show Jabber List to view your list of Google Talk buddies, as shown in Figure 11-8.

9. To start an audio chat with a Google Talk buddy, click the name of the buddy in your Jabber List and then click the Audio Chat button (it looks like a telephone) at the bottom of the Jabber List window.

Figure 11-7: Creating a new Jabber account with a Google Talk account

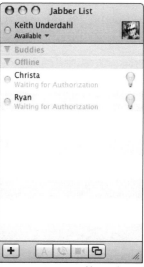

Figure 11-8: Using Jabber to chat with your Google Talk buddies

Install Skype

1. Visit `www.skype.com` and follow the instructions on the Skype Web site to download Skype for Mac.

2. After Skype is done downloading, double-click the downloaded disk image (`.dmg`) file to mount the installer's disk image. Click Continue if you see an application warning.

3. In the Finder that appears, click and drag the Skype icon to the Applications folder shortcut, as shown in Figure 11-9.

4. Open the Applications folder and then double-click the Skype icon to launch the program.

 If you want to add Skype to the Dock, open the Applications folder and then click and drag the Skype icon to the Dock.

5. Read and accept the Skype license agreement.

6. If you already have a Skype account, enter your Skype name and password, as shown in Figure 11-10.

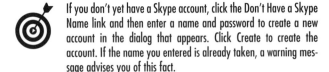 If you don't yet have a Skype account, click the Don't Have a Skype Name link and then enter a name and password to create a new account in the dialog that appears. Click Create to create the account. If the name you entered is already taken, a warning message advises you of this fact.

7. Click Sign In to sign in to Skype.

 The first time you log in to Skype, you may be prompted to update your account's personal information. Update the information as desired and click Apply to close the account profile window.

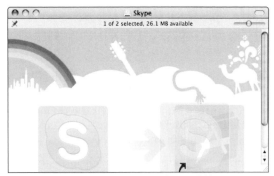

Figure 11-9: Dragging Skype to the Applications folder

Figure 11-10: Signing in to your Skype account

Place Calls Using Skype

1. Launch Skype from the Applications folder or Dock.

2. Type a Skype name or phone number in the text field at the top of the Skype window.

3. If the name isn't in your Contact list, click the Search for Skype Name button when it appears, as shown in Figure 11-11.

4. In the Skype search window that appears, wait for the search results to finish. When you see the listing for the person you want to call, click the name to select it and then click Add Contact. The person is added to the list of contacts in the main Skype program window.

5. To place a call, click the name of a person in your list of contacts and then click the Call button (it's green and looks like a telephone).

6. When the Call window appears, as shown in Figure 11-12, you're connected. Begin speaking.

7. To disconnect from a call, click the red Hang Up button in the lower-right corner of the Call window.

 You can also do text chats with Skype. Click the user's name and then click the Text Chat button (it's blue and looks like a cartoon speech balloon) next to the name. Text chat is a useful feature if a poor Internet connection or hardware troubles prevent one party from hearing or speaking.

 To set up a conference call with multiple parties, choose Call⇨Start Conference Call. Select members for the call in the Start Conference window that appears and then click Start. Conference calls work best if everyone on the call has a fast Internet connection.

Figure 11-11: The Skype search function for finding contacts

Figure 11-12: Making a free call over the Internet with Skype

Text Chat with Adium

1. Visit www.adiumx.com and follow the instructions on the Web site to download Adium.

2. After the download is complete, locate and double-click the disk image (.dmg) file for the installer and then drag the Adium icon to the Applications folder shortcut that appears in the Adium window.

3. Open your Applications folder and double-click the Adium icon to launch the program.

4. In the Accounts preferences pane that appears the first time you launch Adium, click the Add Account button (it looks like a plus sign in the lower-left corner) and choose an account type, as shown in Figure 11-13.

5. Enter the account name and password for your chat account in the window that appears and then click OK to create the account.

6. Close the Accounts preferences pane after you're done adding accounts and making other changes.

 To re-open the preferences pane later and add more accounts, choose Adium⇨Preferences.

7. Double-click a contact in your list of contacts and begin typing a message, as shown in Figure 11-14.

Figure 11-13: Choosing an account type to configure in Adium

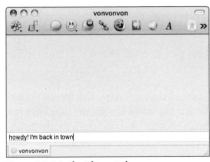

Figure 11-14: The Adium window

Part IV
Using Multimedia

The 5th Wave — By Rich Tennant

"We were just listening to Neil Young's
'Like a Hurricane' on iTunes."

Using iTunes, iPods, and iPhones

More than almost any other company in recent years, Apple has come to be identified with digital music. The iPod has emerged as the world's most popular and identifiable MP3 player, and iTunes revolutionized online music sales at a time when downloadable songs looked like they might be litigated out of existence. Apple's iPhone packages the best iPod technology into a full-featured mobile phone.

iPods, iPhones, and iTunes get along just fine with Windows PCs, but because you have a Macintosh, the integration couldn't be more simple. No matter what iPod you have — ranging from a tiny iPod nano to a full size (yet still compact) iPhone — it is recognized instantly when you connect the device to your Mac. And because iTunes is the program for synchronizing music and movies to an iPod or iPhone, it goes without saying that your Mac already has the necessary software to sync your device. This chapter shows you how to quickly and easily use an iPod or iPhone with your Mac.

Of course, you don't need an iPod to use iTunes. Even if you have no MP3 player at all, iTunes is a great program for storing, organizing, and playing songs, videos, audio books, podcasts, and other multimedia files. This chapter shows you how to manage and play your multimedia library with iTunes.

To ensure you have the latest version of iTunes, run Software Update, as described in Chapter 4, or visit www.apple.com/itunes or choose iTunes ⇨ Check for Updates.

Get ready to . . .

Import Music from CDs

1. Insert a music CD into the disc drive on your computer.

2. When iTunes opens, wait several seconds for iTunes to obtain data — which may include song titles, artist names, and album titles — about the music CD.

     If iTunes doesn't obtain song data automatically, choose Advanced⇨Get CD Track Names. Your computer must be connected to the Internet to obtain song data.

3. Remove the check marks next to the songs you don't want to import. In Figure 12-1, tracks 2 and 4 on the CD were deselected.

4. If you want to manually modify a data field (such as the song name or genre), click the field once to select it, wait about two seconds, and then click it again. Type a new entry.

5. Click the Import CD button in the lower-right corner of the iTunes window to import songs.

6. After all the songs are imported, click the Eject Disc button in the lower-right corner of the iTunes window or the Eject icon next to the CD's name in the Source List.

     When you start to import music, iTunes begins playing the imported songs. The import occurs slightly faster if you stop playback.

7. To locate the imported songs, click Music under Library in the iTunes Source pane and then browse the list of artists or albums to find the songs, as shown in Figure 12-2.

Figure 12-1: A list of tracks on a CD in iTunes

Figure 12-2: The iTunes Music library

Create a Playlist

1. Launch iTunes.

2. Choose File➪New Playlist. A new untitled playlist appears in the Source pane under Playlists.

3. Type a name for the Playlist.

4. Click Music under Library in the iTunes Source pane, and then browse to a song that you want to add to the playlist.

5. Click-and-drag a song from the Library window in the middle of the screen, and drop the song on the playlist name in the Source pane, as shown in Figure 12-3.

 You can also add movies, TV shows, and podcasts from your iTunes library to playlists. Simply click the appropriate Library category in the Source pane and then click-and-drag items from the Library to a playlist.

6. To start playing a playlist, double-click the playlist name in the Source pane. The playlist opens in a separate iTunes window, as shown in Figure 12-4. Click the Play button to start playing the playlist.

7. To change the order of songs in the playlist, simply click-and-drag songs up or down in the list, as shown in Figure 12-4. To remove a song from a playlist, select the song, choose Edit➪Delete, and then click the Remove button in the dialog box that appears. The song is removed from the playlist, but it remains in your iTunes library.

 If you send a playlist to your iPod, iTunes automatically synchronizes all of the songs and media in that playlist to your iPod. I show how to put songs and playlists on iPods later in this chapter.

Figure 12-3: Adding a song to a playlist

Figure 12-4: Organizing a playlist

Generate Smart Playlists

1. Launch iTunes.

2. Choose File⇨New Smart Playlist.

3. In the Smart Playlist dialog that appears, choose a category — such as Artist, Genre, or Comment — in the first pop-up menu.

4. Choose a condition — such as Contains or Does Not Contain — in the second pop-up menu.

5. Type a criterion in the third pop-up menu.

6. To add more criteria, click the plus sign to the right of the third pop-up menu. In Figure 12-5, a playlist is created by using songs in the Classical and Jazz genres.

 When using multiple rules, choose Any or All from the Match pop-up menu at the top of the Smart Playlist dialog, as appropriate.

7. Choose other criteria for the playlist and then click OK. For example, in Figure 12-5 I am limiting the size of the playlist to 25 songs.

8. After music that matches your criteria is selected and the playlist created, type a descriptive name for the playlist in the Source pane on the left, as shown in Figure 12-6.

9. To change a smart playlist (such as adding another genre), choose File⇨Edit Smart Playlist and repeat the preceding steps to add more songs.

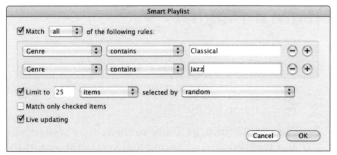

Figure 12-5: The Smart Playlist dialog

Figure 12-6: A smart playlist in iTunes

Buy Music from the iTunes Store

1. Launch iTunes, make sure your computer is connected to the Internet, and then click iTunes Store in the Source pane, as shown in Figure 12-7.

2. Type a song or artist in the search box in the upper-right corner of the iTunes window and press Return to begin your search.

3. Review the search results. To hear a preview, double-click a song. A 30-second preview of the song downloads and plays.

4. When you find a song that you want to buy, click the Buy Song link in the far-right column of the song list.

5. If you already have an Apple or AOL account, enter your ID and password in the login dialog, as shown in Figure 12-8.

    If you don't yet have an account, click the Create New Account button and follow the instructions on-screen to create an account. You need a credit card to create your account. After you're done creating the account and are logged in, you need to re-click the Buy Song link.

6. When you see the confirmation window, review the song or album you're about to buy and then click Buy. The status area at the top of the iTunes screen shows the progress of the purchase and download.

    The iTunes Genius feature analyzes your music library and listening habits, and then recommends songs to buy from iTunes. To start using Genius, click the Turn On Genius button in the Genius sidebar, or choose Store ➪ Turn On Genius.

Figure 12-7: The iTunes Store

Figure 12-8: Logging in with your Apple or AOL account

Copy Songs to an iPod

1. Connect the iPod to your Mac.

 Most iPods connect to your computer using a USB cable that comes with the iPod. Some models plug directly into your computer's USB port. Third-party iPod docks are also available for many iPod models.

2. If iTunes doesn't launch automatically, launch iTunes from the Dock or the Applications folder. iTunes might start to automatically fill your iPod with music from your iTunes library.

3. To set your iPod so that songs are not added automatically, click the name of the iPod under Devices in the iTunes Source pane. Click the Contents tab and then click the Settings button in the lower-right corner of the screen. Remove the check mark next to Choose Items Randomly in the Autofill Settings dialog that appears, and then click OK to close the dialog.

4. Locate songs in your library that you want to copy to the iPod, and then click and drag them to the iPod in the Source pane, as shown in Figure 12-9.

 To select multiple songs, hold down the ⌘ key while clicking each song you want to add. To select a series of songs, select the first song and then hold down the Shift key while clicking the last song. All songs between the first and last song are selected.

5. To automatically fill space on the iPod, click the iPod in the Source pane to open its contents.

6. In the Autofill From menu near the bottom of the iTunes window, select a folder or playlist from which you want Autofill to select songs, as shown in Figure 12-10.

Figure 12-9: Dragging songs to the iPod

Figure 12-10: Using Autofill to quickly copy to your iPod

7. Click Autofill. The iPod is filled automatically with songs from your iTunes library.

The steps listed here work the same whether you're syncing songs to an iPod or iPhone.

Adjust iPod Settings

1. Launch iTunes and connect the iPod to your computer.

2. Click the iPod in the Source pane, and then click the Settings tab in the main iTunes window.

3. Scroll down the Settings pane to the Options section, as shown in Figure 12-11.

4. If you're concerned about storage space, select the check box labeled Convert Higher Bit Rate Songs to 128 Kbps AAC.

5. Review other options and click Apply to save your changes to the iPod.

If your iPod is experiencing a lot of errors, click Restore on the Settings pane to restore the device to factory settings. This will erase all music and files from the iPod, but it can help you recover an otherwise non-functioning iPod.

Delete Media from an iPod

1. Connect the iPod to your computer and launch iTunes.

2. Click the iPod in the Source pane to display its contents.

3. Select a song or songs that you want to delete from the iPod.

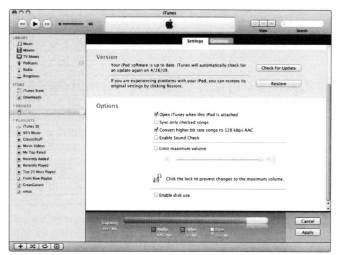

Figure 12-11: The Settings pane

Figure 12-12: Removing a song

4. Press the Delete key or choose Edit➪Delete, as shown in Figure 12-12. Click Remove in the dialog box that appears to confirm the deletion.

Create Custom iPhone Ringtones

1. Launch iTunes, and identify a song that you'd like to use as a ringtone. Play the song and determine whether you want the ringtone to begin at the start of the song or at another point. Make a note of the time (in minutes and seconds) at which you want the ringtone to start.

 If you don't mind spending a couple of dollars per ringtone, you can bypass the steps shown here and purchase ready-to-use ringtones directly from the iTunes Store. Purchasing ringtones from iTunes is a lot easier, but the steps provided here are free and give you more creative control over your iPhone's ringtones.

2. Click the song in your iTunes library once to select it and then choose File➪Get Info.

3. Click the Options tab and enter Start and Stop times for the song, as shown in Figure 12-13. The length of time between the Start Time and Stop Time must be 40 seconds or less.

4. Click OK.

5. Make sure the song is still selected in iTunes and then choose Advanced➪Create AAC Version. A second copy of the song now appears in your iTunes library. Make sure that the Time for the new copy is 40 seconds or less, as shown in Figure 12-14.

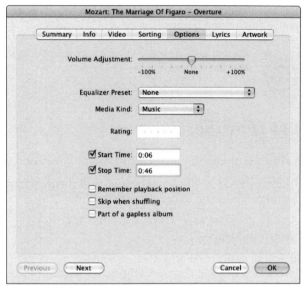

Figure 12-13: Setting start and stop times for the new ringtone

Figure 12-14: Making sure the AAC version is no longer than 40 seconds

6. Double-click the 40 second AAC song in your iTunes library to play it. Make sure the ringtone starts and stops when you want.

 If you aren't happy with the start or stop times of the ringtone, delete the AAC file you just created and go back to Step 2. Fine-tune the Start Time and Stop Time until you get it right.

7. Select the 40-second AAC song in iTunes and choose File⇨Show in Finder.

8. In the Finder that appears, click the song's filename once to make the name editable and then change the file extension from .m4a to .m4r, as shown in Figure 12-15.

9. Click Use .m4r when you're prompted to do so.

10. Double-click the .m4r file to open it in iTunes. The ringtone file is added to your iTunes library and starts to play.

 You may close the Finder now if you'd like.

11. Connect your iPhone to your computer if you haven't done so already.

12. Click and drag the ringtone to your iPhone, as shown in Figure 12-16. It will take a couple of seconds to sync the new ringtone to your phone.

13. On the home screen of your iPhone, tap Settings⇨ Sounds⇨Ringtone and then select your new ringtone.

 If the new ringtone doesn't appear on your iPhone, double-check the length of the ringtone in iTunes. If the song is longer than 40 seconds, your iPhone won't recognize it as a ringtone.

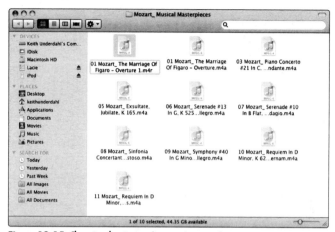

Figure 12-15: Changing the ringtone's extension to .m4r

Figure 12-16: Dragging the new ringtone to your iPhone

Store Data Files on Your iPod

1. Open your iPod's Settings pane, as described earlier in this chapter, and select the Enable Disk Use check box.

2. Adjust the Disk Use slider to determine how much space will be reserved for songs and data and then click OK to close the Settings window.

3. Use the Finder to click and drag files to the iPod, as shown in Figure 12-17.

4. Click and drag the iPod's Desktop icon to the Trash to manually eject the iPod.

 When the iPod's status light glows solid green, it can be safely disconnected from the computer's USB port.

Play Music Remotely with AirTunes

1. Install and configure an AirTunes-compatible AirPort Base Station (such as an AirPort Express), as described in Chapter 17. The Base Station's documentation will note whether it supports AirTunes. Connect powered audio speakers or another audio device to the audio output on the AirPort Base Station.

2. Open the Applications folder on your Mac, open the Utilities subfolder, and then double-click the AirPort Utility icon.

3. Click the Base Station name on the left, as shown in Figure 12-18, click the Continue button, and then choose Manual Setup in the message that appears.

Figure 12-17: Transferring data files to an iPod

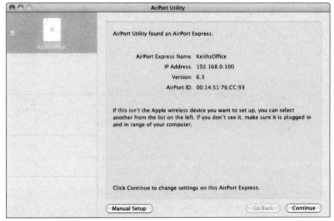

Figure 12-18: The AirPort Utility dialog

4. Enter the password for the Base Station and then click OK to log in to the Base Station.

5. Select the I Want to Change Some of the Settings for This AirPort option and click Continue.

6. Click Continue until you see AirTunes options, as shown in Figure 12-19. Select the Change These Settings option.

7. Select the Enable AirTunes check box.

8. Provide a descriptive name for the speakers that are connected to the Base Station in the iTunes Speaker Name field. Enter and confirm a password if you want to password protect the speakers.

9. Click Continue and then Update to upload your changes to the Base Station.

10. After the Base Station has restarted (its status light glows solid green), launch iTunes and find a playlist or songs that you want to play.

11. Choose the appropriate speakers from the Speakers menu at the bottom of the iTunes window, as shown in Figure 12-20.

 To play music to multiple speaker locations, choose Multiple Speakers and then place a check mark next to each set of speakers listed in the resulting window.

Figure 12-19: Enabling AirTunes on the Airport Express

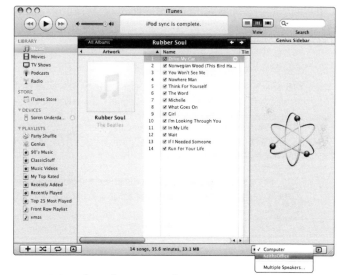

Figure 12-20: Selecting the AirTunes speakers

Listen to Internet Radio

1. Launch iTunes and click Radio in the Source pane.

2. Click an arrow next to a category to expand the listing, as shown in Figure 12-21.

3. Double-click a radio station to begin playing it.

 If the radio station broadcast frequently cuts out while the signal is buffered, choose a different station with a lower bit rate. For example, if you have a dial-up Internet connection, you probably can't listen to radio stations with a bit rate greater than 48 Kbps.

Subscribe to a Podcast

1. Launch iTunes and click the iTunes Store link in the Source pane.

2. Click the Podcasts category in the iTunes Store and browse to a podcast that interests you.

3. On the podcast's main page, click the Subscribe button, as shown in Figure 12-22, and then confirm your subscription when asked to do so.

4. To access a podcast, click Podcasts under Library in the iTunes Source pane.

 To get rid of a podcast in your iTunes library, click the podcast's title and then click the Unsubscribe button at the bottom of the iTunes window.

Figure 12-21: Internet radio stations

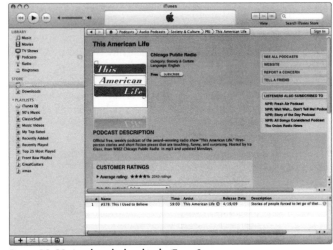

Figure 12-22: A podcast displayed in the iTunes Store

Working with Third-Party MP3 Players

When it comes to MP3 players, Macs and iPods seem to go hand in hand. But lots of MP3 players are made by companies other than Apple, and if you're reading this chapter, you probably have one of these third-party players.

Because you have one of these players, you may be wondering whether it's compatible with your Mac, especially if the player's instructions only tell you how to use it with a Windows PC. Fortunately, most MP3 players can be used with a Mac, although you probably can't use iTunes for copying media files and playlists directly to the player. Instead, you'll have to use the Finder. This chapter shows you how to

➡ Connect a third-party MP3 player to your Mac.

➡ Copy music files to the MP3 player.

➡ Create folders on the MP3 player in which to organize media.

➡ Delete music from the MP3 player.

The steps in this chapter apply to most third-party MP3 players, but it's possible that your particular player is uniquely incompatible with your Mac. Some players require proprietary software in order to access directories and copy files to the player. If you can't seem to follow the steps in this chapter with your MP3 player, check the manufacturer's Web site for special instructions or information regarding Mac compatibility. A few third-party players actually support iTunes. If you connect the player to your computer and it appears in the Devices list in iTunes, you should be able to use iTunes (see Chapter 12) to manage media on the player.

Connect the MP3 Player to Your Mac

1. Connect the MP3 player to your Mac's Universal Serial Bus (USB) port.

2. Look for the player's icon to appear on your Desktop as an Untitled disk volume, as shown in Figure 13-1.

 If the MP3 player doesn't appear, make sure the unit's power is turned on.

3. Before disconnecting the MP3 player from your USB port, drag its icon to the Trash icon on the Dock to unmount the volume. When the MP3 player's icon no longer appears on the Desktop, you can safely disconnect the MP3 player from the USB port.

Check for iTunes Compatibility

1. To see whether your MP3 player is compatible with iTunes, first check the player's documentation.

2. If the documentation is unclear, visit this Web site:

   http://support.apple.com/kb/HT2172

   This page lists some iTunes-compatible players, as shown in Figure 13-2.

3. Visit the manufacturer's Web site for OS X downloads for your MP3 player.

 Although some third-party MP3 players may work with iTunes, keep in mind that most non-iPod MP3 players can't play AAC files. This means that songs purchased from the iTunes Store won't work in most third-party MP3 players. For other music, convert it to MP3 format before copying it to a third-party MP3 player.

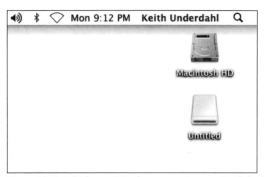

Figure 13-1: A third-party MP3 player appearing as an Untitled volume

Figure 13-2: A list of some iTunes-compatible players

Copy Music Files to the Player

1. Connect the MP3 player to your USB port.

2. Launch iTunes and find a song that you'd like to copy to the MP3 player. Select only one song for now. Click and drag the song to the MP3 player in the Source pane. If the file copies successfully, you're done. Otherwise, continue to the next step.

    If you're not sure whether a song's format is compatible with your MP3 player, select the song in iTunes and press ⌘+I. An Info window opens, showing you information about the song, including the file format. MP3 files should be compatible with any MP3 player, but AAC files are usually compatible only with iPods.

3. Choose File➪Show in Finder, as shown in Figure 13-3. Finder opens, showing the song you selected, as shown in Figure 13-4.

    iTunes usually organizes songs into folders and subfolders by artist and album. You may notice that other songs on the same album can be found in the Finder window when you open it from iTunes as described here.

4. Arrange the Finder so that both it and the MP3 player's icon are visible.

5. Click and drag the songs to the MP3 player's icon, as shown in Figure 13-4. A progress window displays the file copying progress.

    You can also use the Finder to copy files from your MP3 player to your hard drive; simply drag and drop files from the player to a hard drive folder to copy them. If some of the files are in WMA format, you must download and install Windows Media Player or Flip4Mac, as described in Chapter 14.

Figure 13-3: The iTunes File menu

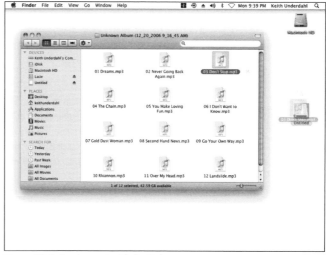

Figure 13-4: Copying music with the Finder

Create Folders on the Player

1. Connect the MP3 player to your USB port and then double-click the player's icon to begin browsing it in the Finder.

2. If the files are disorganized and scattered all over the window — which is especially likely if the MP3 player has been used on a Windows PC — choose View⇨Clean Up, as shown in Figure 13-5.

3. To create a new folder, press ⌘+Shift+N or choose File⇨New Folder.

4. Type a new name for the folder. In Figure 13-6, I created a new folder and named it VoiceMails.

5. Use the Finder to copy files into the new folder, as described in the preceding section.

6. Unmount the MP3 player and disconnect it from the USB port.

7. Test the MP3 player to make sure that audio files placed in subfolders are recognized and play properly. Some MP3 players may not be able to play files that are placed in subfolders.

 Many MP3 players can be used as thumb drives in a pinch. That is, if you have some files, such as PowerPoint presentations or Pages documents, and you need to quickly copy those files to another computer, you can copy the files to the storage area on an MP3 player and then connect the MP3 player to the other computer to retrieve the files.

Figure 13-5: Browsing your MP3 player

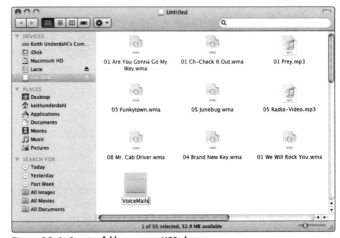

Figure 13-6: Creating folders on your MP3 player

Delete Files from the Player

1. Connect the MP3 player to your USB port and then double-click the player's icon to begin browsing it in the Finder.

2. Select a file or folder that you want to delete and then click and drag it to the Trash, as shown in Figure 13-7.

    To select multiple files or folders, hold down the ⌘ key and click each item that you want to select.

3. Press ⌘+Shift+Delete or choose Finder➪Empty Trash.

4. Click OK to confirm that you want to empty the Trash, as shown in Figure 13-8.

    Make sure you empty the Trash before unmounting the MP3 player. If you leave Trash items on the MP3 player, the player may not play music properly, and Windows users may have problems with the player's file system.

Figure 13-7: Dragging files to the Trash

Figure 13-8: Emptying the Trash before unmounting the MP3 player

Watching Videos and DVDs

A stroll around your local electronics store reveals a lot of cool digital gadgets, including TVs, stereo systems, and DVD players. Thankfully, you don't need any of those things because you have a Mac. Most new Macs come with built-in DVD player hardware and software.

Of course, DVDs aren't the only kinds of videos that you'll want to watch on your Mac. You can also download videos from the Internet, and you can watch videos recorded by a digital camera or camera phone.

This chapter shows you how to watch DVDs on your Mac as well as how to watch other types of video. This chapter focuses on three specific programs:

➡ **DVD Player:** As the name implies, this program allows your Mac to play movie DVDs.

➡ **QuickTime:** QuickTime Player is a popular program from Apple that allows you to watch videos in various formats, including MPEG and QuickTime video.

➡ **Flip4Mac:** This free program works as a plug-in for QuickTime and allows you to watch most Windows Media Video (WMV) on your Mac.

Get ready to . . .

Change the Default DVD Player

1. Choose Apple⇨System Preferences (or open System Preferences from the Dock) and then click the CDs & DVDs icon to open the CDs & DVDs preferences pane, as shown in Figure 14-1.

2. Choose an option from the When You Insert a Video DVD pop-up menu. The choices are

   - **Open DVD Player:** This is the default choice, and it's probably the best choice unless you prefer another third-party DVD player application.

   - **Open Front Row:** This is Snow Leopard's multimedia interface. If your Mac has an Apple Remote, the remote's Menu button activates Front Row for quick access to your music, movies, photos, and more.

   - **Open Other Application:** Choose this to select a different application; then browse to an alternative DVD player, as shown in Figure 14-2, and click the Choose button.

   - **Run Script:** Choose this if you have a DVD-related AppleScript that you want to run when you insert DVDs.

   - **Ignore:** If you don't want anything to happen automatically when you insert a DVD, choose Ignore.

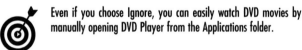 Even if you choose Ignore, you can easily watch DVD movies by manually opening DVD Player from the Applications folder.

3. Close System Preferences after you make a selection.

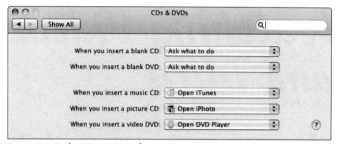

Figure 14-1: The CDs & DVDs preferences pane

Figure 14-2: Changing the default DVD player

Access DVD Features

1. Insert a movie DVD into your DVD drive. The DVD Player application starts automatically, and the movie plays.

2. If the movie opens in a small window, like the one shown in Figure 14-3, choose View⇨Enter Full Screen or press ⌘+F. Press ⌘+F again to leave Full Screen mode.

3. Move the mouse pointer to the bottom of the screen to reveal the DVD Controller, as shown in Figure 14-4.

     If the Controller doesn't appear, hover the mouse pointer near the top of the screen and choose Window⇨Show Controller in the menu bar that appears.

4. Use the Play, Stop, Forward, and Back buttons to control playback. Click Menu or Title to open the DVD menu (the exact menu that opens varies, depending on the DVD) and use the arrow buttons to navigate DVD menus.

     Unless you have a tray-loading DVD drive (found only on Mac Pros and some external drives), don't attempt to insert a 3.5" mini-DVD into your Mac's DVD drive. Mini-DVDs aren't compatible with the slot-loading drives found on iMacs, Mac minis, and portable Macs.

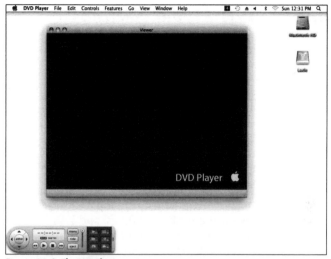

Figure 14-3: The DVD Player screen

Figure 14-4: DVD Player in Full Screen mode with the Controller open

Adjust DVD Player Settings

1. Open the DVD Player application.

2. Choose DVD Player➪Preferences. (If the menu bar is hidden, hover the mouse pointer near the top of the screen to make it appear.)

3. A preferences pane appears. Make sure the Player icon is selected at the top and then place a check mark next to Enter Full Screen Mode if you want DVD Player to open automatically in Full Screen mode and start playing when you insert a disc.

4. Click the Disc Setup icon at the top and select default languages for the Audio, Subtitles, and DVD Menu, as shown in Figure 14-5. If you're using external audio speakers, select the speakers in the Audio Output pop-up menu.

    If you're using System Sound Output on a laptop, *don't* select the Disable Dolby Dynamic Range Compression check box. Disabling this option could damage your laptop's small speakers.

5. Click the Full Screen icon at the top and choose how long you want to wait before the Controller disappears.

6. Click the Windows icon and change the appearance of Closed Captioning text if you want.

7. Click the Previously Viewed icon and select a default behavior for previously viewed DVDs.

8. If your Mac has a High Definition (HD) compatible DVD drive, click the High Definition icon at the top and, next to For High Definition, select a picture height that matches your display, as shown in Figure 14-6.

9. Click OK to close the preferences pane.

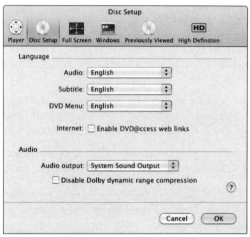

Figure 14-5: The Disc Setup screen

 If you see horizontal lines in the video during playback (especially on fast-moving subjects), choose Video➪Deinterlace to enable or disable interlacing. Deinterlacing is often necessary when watching video DVDs on non-interlaced displays, such as computer monitors.

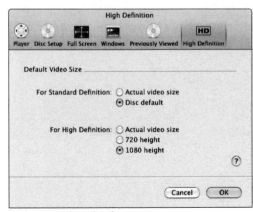

Figure 14-6: The High Definition screen

Watch Movies with QuickTime

1. Launch QuickTime by clicking its icon on the Dock or by double-clicking the QuickTime icon in the Applications folder.

    If you double-click almost any movie that's compatible with QuickTime — compatible formats include MPEG and QT — QuickTime launches automatically and plays the video.

2. To open a movie, choose File⇨Open File.

3. In the Open dialog that appears (as shown in Figure 14-7), browse to the movie you want to view.

4. Select the movie file and click the Open button. If the movie is in a format that isn't supported by QuickTime, an error message appears to advise you of this fact.

5. Use the playback controls to play the movie, as shown in Figure 14-8.

    To change the size of the video image, open the View menu and choose Half Size, Actual Size, Double Size, or Fit to Screen. You can also click and drag the bottom-right corner of the QuickTime window to dynamically resize it.

    You can use QuickTime to share movies with others using either iTunes or MobileMe. Choose iTunes or MobileMe from the Share menu to begin sharing. See Chapter 9 for more on using MobileMe, and check out Chapter 12 for more about iTunes. Chapter 16 shows you how to make and share movies using iMovie.

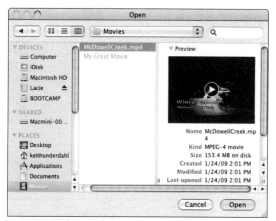

Figure 14-7: The Open dialog

Figure 14-8: The simple, friendly QuickTime interface

Install Flip4Mac

1. Visit `www.microsoft.com/windows/windowsmedia/` `player/wmcomponents.mspx`, to download the free Flip4Mac Windows Media Components for QuickTime.

2. When the download is complete, double-click the downloaded disk image. (The icon has `.dmg` at the end of the filename.)

    If you use Safari to download Flip4Mac, Step 2 is unnecessary because the disk image mounts automatically.

3. Open the disk image, double-click the Flip4Mac WMV installer package, and follow the on-screen instructions to install, as shown in Figure 14-9.

View Windows Media Video

1. If you've installed Flip4Mac and now want to open a Windows Media file, either

   • **Double-click a Windows Media file.** Windows Media Audio has the `.wma` filename extension, and Windows Media Video has the `.wmv` filename extension.

   • **Open QuickTime and choose File↪Open to locate a Windows Media file.**

2. Use the playback controls to play the Windows Media Video in QuickTime, as shown in Figure 14-10.

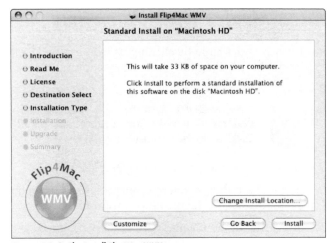

Figure 14-9: The Install Flip4Mac WMV screen

Figure 14-10: Viewing Windows Media in QuickTime with Flip4Mac

Viewing, Organizing, and Improving Pictures

*I*t's hard to imagine now how anyone ever got by without digital cameras. Back in the days of film cameras, photo processing was expensive and slow, and if you wanted to improve the quality of your photos, you had to just shoot a lot of (expensive) pictures and become a better photographer.

A digital camera won't make you a great photographer, but it will definitely make your life easier. Not only can you snap many photos without worrying about processing fees, but you can also quickly copy your digital images to your computer, where they can be easily reshaped, retouched, and shared with others via e-mail or the Internet.

This chapter shows you how to organize your photos with iPhoto, a program included free with your Mac. In addition to organizing photos, iPhoto can also make basic edits and improvements to photos. This chapter also introduces you to Adobe Photoshop, a more advanced photo editing program. The full version of Photoshop costs about $700, but Photoshop Elements is available for less than $100 and offers most of the photo editing features you'll need for day-to-day use.

Get ready to . . .

 If you need an online home for sharing your digital photos with others over the Internet, check out Chapter 9.

Download Photos from a Camera

1. To launch iPhoto, either click the iPhoto icon on the Dock (the iPhoto icon looks like a camera in front of a picture) or open the Applications folder and double-click iPhoto.

2. If you're launching iPhoto for the first time, you're asked if you want to use iPhoto when you connect a digital camera to the computer. Click a button to make a choice.

3. Connect your digital camera to your computer's Universal Serial Bus (USB) port and then turn on the camera. The camera should automatically appear under Devices in the iPhoto Source pane, as shown in Figure 15-1.

   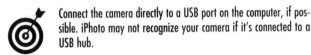 Connect the camera directly to a USB port on the computer, if possible. iPhoto may not recognize your camera if it's connected to a USB hub.

4. Click the name of the camera in the Source pane and then type a name and description for the Event, as shown in Figure 15-1.

   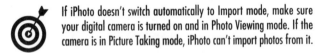 If iPhoto doesn't switch automatically to Import mode, make sure your digital camera is turned on and in Photo Viewing mode. If the camera is in Picture Taking mode, iPhoto can't import photos from it.

5. Select photos you want to import. Hold the Command key while clicking to select multiple photos.

6. Click the Import Selected button to begin importing selected photos from your camera. Alternatively, click the Import All button to import all photos on the camera.

7. When importing is complete, a dialog box asks if you want to delete the photos from your camera, as shown in Figure 15-2. Click the Delete Photos or Keep Photos button, as appropriate.

Figure 15-1: Selecting photos to import

 To import pictures that are already on your hard drive, choose File⇨Import to Library. Use the Import Photos dialog to find and import photos.

Figure 15-2: Choosing to keep or delete photos

Organize Your Photo Library

1. Launch iPhoto and then click a category under Library or Recent in the Source pane on the left side of the screen. Click Photos to view all photos, or click Events to view a list of events, as shown in Figure 15-3.

2. To create a new album in which to organize certain pictures, choose File➪New Album and then type a descriptive name for the album.

3. Click and drag photos from the Library window to the new album. In Figure 15-4, a new album named DC Trip was created.

 To copy multiple photos, first click and drag a box around all the photos you want to move. Alternatively, hold down the ⌘ key and click individual pictures that you want to select. When a group is selected, you can then click and drag that group to a new album.

4. Click the name of an album to view its contents.

5. To change the size of photo thumbnails, click and drag the Zoom slider in the lower-right corner of the iPhoto screen. In Figure 15-4, the thumbnail size was increased.

6. To display filenames for photos, as shown in Figure 15-4, choose View➪Titles.

 You can also choose to display keywords, event titles, and ratings from the View menu.

7. To delete a photo, simply select it and press the Delete key on your keyboard.

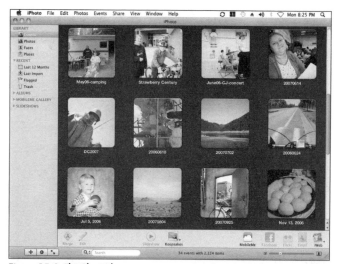

Figure 15-3: The iPhoto Library

Figure 15-4: The DC Trip album

Rotate Photos

1. Locate an image that you want to rotate and click it once to select it. If you want a better view, double-click the image to enlarge it, as shown in Figure 15-5.

2. Click the Rotate button at the bottom of the iPhoto window to rotate the image.

    You may need to click **Rotate** a couple of times to get the desired orientation.

3. Click in an empty area of the Source pane to return to the list of thumbnail images.

Resize Images

1. Select a photo that you want to export in a smaller size.

2. Choose File⇨Export.

3. Select either Small, Medium, Large, or Full Size in the Size menu, as shown in Figure 15-6.

    The Small size is 320 x 240, the Medium size is 640 x 480, and the Large size is 1280 x 960. Small is a good size for thumbnail preview images, Medium is a good size for email sharing, and Large is good for higher quality online sharing.

4. Click the Export button.

5. Enter a new filename, choose a location for the resized image, and click OK.

Figure 15-5: An image in need of rotation

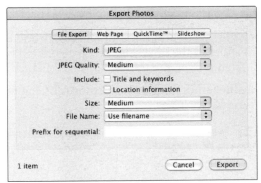

Figure 15-6: The Export Photos dialog

Crop Images

1. Locate the image you want to crop and click it once to select it. (*Cropping* an image means trimming off unwanted parts at the edges.)

    It's best to start with a relatively large image; if you crop smaller images, the resulting cropped image may be too small.

2. Choose View⇨Full Screen to enter full screen mode.

3. Hover your mouse pointer at the bottom of the screen so that the toolbar appears, as shown in Figure 15-7. Click the Crop button.

4. Click and drag the corners of the cropping box so that it only surrounds the area of the photo that you want to keep, as shown in Figure 15-8. Areas outside the rectangle will be cropped.

    You can fine-tune the crop area by clicking and dragging on edges or corners of the crop rectangle.

5. Click the Apply button to crop the image.

6. Hover your mouse pointer at the bottom of the screen to reveal the toolbar, and then click the Exit Full Screen mode button on the far right end of the toolbar.

    If you don't like the changes you've made to an image, select the image in your Library and choose Photos⇨Revert to Original.

Figure 15-7: Calling up the Crop tool

Figure 15-8: Setting the crop area

Create a Slideshow

1. Open iPhoto and select an event or album from which you want to base your slideshow.

2. Click the New Item button in the lower-left corner of iPhoto. The New Item button looks like a Plus sign.

3. Click the Slideshow icon, as shown in Figure 15-9. Type a descriptive name for the slideshow in the Name field.

4. Click Create to create a new slideshow. The slideshow contains all the images in the event or album you selected in Step 1, and it appears in the Source pane under Slideshows. Click the slideshow's name in the Source pane.

5. To remove an image from the slideshow, select it and press Delete on your keyboard.

 To change the order of images, click and drag their thumbnails left or right at the top of the Slideshow window.

6. Click the Settings icon at the bottom of iPhoto and change how long each slide should display using the arrow buttons next to "Play each slide for a minimum of," as shown in Figure 15-10.

7. Choose a transition to use between photos from the Transition menu. Review other options and then click the Close (X) button to close the Slideshow Settings window.

8. Click Play to play the slideshow. To stop the slideshow, simply click anywhere on an image during the show.

 To add a musical soundtrack to your slideshow, click the Music icon at the bottom and then choose a song or playlist from your iTunes Library.

Figure 15-9: Making a new slideshow

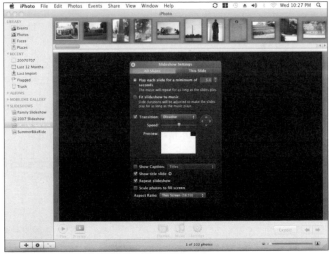

Figure 15-10: Working with slideshow settings

Resize an Image in Adobe Photoshop

1. Open an image file with Adobe Bridge.

    If you don't like using Adobe Bridge, open Photoshop and simply choose File⇨Open. You can then browse to files with the Open dialog instead of Adobe Bridge.

2. Choose Image⇨Image Size, as shown in Figure 15-11.

3. In the Image Size dialog that appears, select the Resample Image check box, as shown in Figure 15-12.

4. Enter a new size in the Pixel Dimensions area in the upper half of the Image Size dialog, as shown in Figure 15-12, or enter a new size in the Document Size area of the dialog.

    If you're resizing the image for Web or computer screen use, change the width and height in the Pixel Dimensions area. If you're resizing the image for later printing, use the Document Size area. If you plan to print the image, change the resolution to 300 pixels per inch before reducing the document size. This ensures the best possible print quality.

    In most cases, leave the Constrain Proportions check box selected. If you deselect this option, the image appears distorted after resizing.

5. Click OK.

    To crop an image, click and drag a box on the image and choose Image⇨Crop.

    When you crop or reduce the size of an image, make sure you choose File⇨Save As and save the file with a different filename. If you save the original file, you lose some of the original image and you can never get it back.

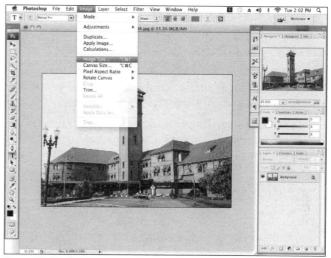

Figure 15-11: The Image menu

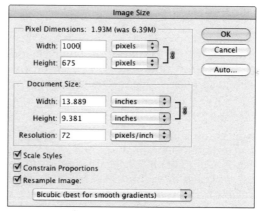

Figure 15-12: The Image Size dialog

Improve Color with Photoshop

1. Open the image that you want to improve.

2. Choose File➪Save As and save a copy of the image using a new filename. In the Save As dialog, choose Photoshop from the Format pop-up menu.

3. Choose Image➪Adjustments (open the Enhance menu in Photoshop Elements), as shown in Figure 15-13, and then choose something that you want to improve. Useful choices include

   - **Auto Levels:** Fine-tunes color, light, and contrast

   - **Auto Contrast:** Improves contrast and light

   - **Auto Color:** Adjusts and improves color

    No single enhancement improves every image. If you don't like the changes made by one enhancement, press ⌘+Z to undo the change and then try a different enhancement.

4. To fine-tune light and contrast, choose Image➪ Adjustments➪Brightness/Contrast (or Enhance➪Adjust Lighting➪Brightness/Contrast in Photoshop Elements). Use the sliders to make fine adjustments and preview the changes in the background. Click OK to accept your changes or click Cancel to reject them.

5. To fine-tune color, choose Image➪Adjustments➪ Variations (or Enhance➪Adjust Color➪Color Variations in Photoshop Elements). Click sample images to choose variations, as shown in Figure 15-14. Click OK to accept your changes or click Cancel to reject them.

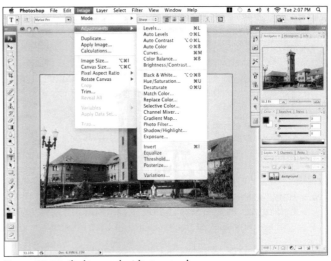

Figure 15-13: Checking out the Adjustments submenu

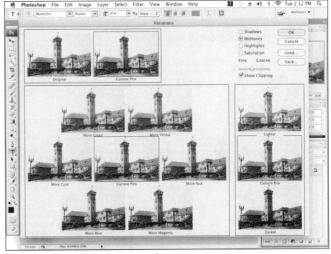

Figure 15-14: The Color Variations tool

Export a Photoshop Image for the Web

1. When you're done enhancing and improving an image, choose File⇨Save for Web & Devices, as shown in Figure 15-15.

2. In the Save for Web & Devices window that appears, as shown in Figure 15-16, choose a preset format in the Preset menu on the right.

    The GIF format is better for smaller images that have less color. Larger photos should be saved in JPEG format. The PNG format offers good quality but limited compatibility with some Web browsers (notably, Internet Explorer 6 and older).

3. Select options below the Preset pop-up menu, such as quality levels.

4. Enter a new size for the image in the Width and Height fields on the Image Size tab, as shown in Figure 15-16.

5. After entering a new size, click Apply.

6. Note the file size listed below the image preview on the right side of the preview pane. This will be the approximate file size of the image when you export it.

    Pay careful attention to the file size and estimated download time for the image, which is shown in the bottom left of the Save for Web & Devices window. Remember, many people still have relatively slow dial-up Internet connections, so they'll have a hard time viewing large image files.

7. Click OK.

8. Enter a filename and choose a location in the Save Optimized As dialog and then click Save to save the file.

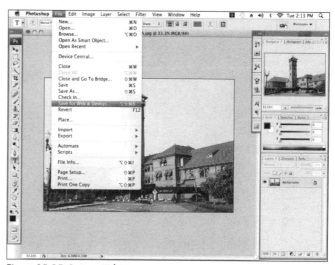

Figure 15-15: Saving a Web image

Figure 15-16: The Save for Web & Devices dialog

Making Movies

Apple has been a pioneer in digital video for over a decade. In the 1990s, Apple helped develop the *IEEE-1394 FireWire interface,* a high-speed data bus that allows high-quality digital video to be transferred quickly between digital camcorders and computers. Apple also pioneered software that helps you turn your raw video footage into a great movie with titles, music, and special effects.

Many new Macintosh computers come with a FireWire port, and all new Macs have iMovie pre-installed. The iMovie application allows you to import video from a digital camcorder, assemble a movie with only the scenes you want, add sound and video effects to your movie clips, and export your finished movie for viewing over the Internet. And if your Mac has a SuperDrive, you can also burn your movie straight to DVD.

This chapter shows you how to make movies with your digital camcorder and iMovie. I take you through tasks that show you how to create a new movie project, capture video from your camcorder, and turn your footage into a great movie. The tasks in this chapter also show you how to export your finished movie in a Web-friendly format or burn it to DVD.

 The latest versions of iMovie support most modern camcorders, including high-definition cameras and those that record video onto flash memory, hard drives, or DVDs. For more on making movies and working with iMovie, check out *Digital Video For Dummies,* 4th Edition, by Keith Underdahl or *iMovie and iDVD For Dummies* by Dennis Cohen (Wiley Publishing, Inc.).

Get ready to . . .

Launch iMovie

1. Click the iMovie icon on the Dock or double-click the iMovie icon in the Applications folder. When you see the Welcome screen shown in Figure 16-1, deselect the Show This Window When iMovie Opens check mark to bypass the welcome screen in the future.

    The first time you launch iMovie, you're asked whether you want to generate thumbnails for videos in your iPhoto library. Click Now to generate the thumbnails.

2. Choose File⇨New Project to start creating a new movie project.

3. Enter a name for your movie in the Project Name field, as shown in Figure 16-2.

4. Choose an option from the Aspect Ratio pop-up menu. In most cases, you want to match the aspect ratio of your source footage. Standard definition video is usually Standard (4:3), and high-definition video is usually Widescreen (16:9). iMovie also includes a special 3:2 format especially for viewing on iPhones.

5. Choose a theme for your movie from the Theme chooser, if desired. iMovie automatically generates menus, transitions, and effects based on the theme you choose.

6. If you want iMovie to automatically insert a favorite transition between each clip, select the Automatically Add check box and then choose a transition in the pop-up menu.

7. Click the Create button.

Figure 16-1: The Welcome to iMovie screen

 To open a previously edited project, click Project Library in the upper-left corner of iMovie, select a project, and click Edit Project.

Figure 16-2: Setting up a new project

Capture Video from a Camcorder

1. Launch iMovie and create a new project.

2. Connect the camcorder to your computer's FireWire or USB port and make sure that the camera is turned on to Player or VTR mode. iMovie automatically detects your camcorder.

    If iMovie doesn't detect your camera, double-check the cable connections and make sure the camcorder is turned on to the correct mode. You may also need to select a PC option on the camcorder's display screen. If you still have trouble, visit `http://support.apple.com/kb/HT3290` for a camcorder compatibility list.

3. In the capture window that automatically appears, choose a clip and then click Play to preview it.

    If your camcorder uses videotapes, use the playback controls in the capture window to play or rewind the tape to some video you want to capture. Click the Import button to start capturing video from the tape, and then click the Stop button when you finish capturing.

4. If you want to capture only certain clips, move the slider in the lower-left corner to Manual, as shown in Figure 16-3, and place check marks under the clips you want to capture.

5. Click Import All (or Import Checked).

6. If you're importing clips from a high-definition camcorder, an Import Setting dialog appears, as shown in Figure 16-4. Choose whether you want to import video using the Large or Full quality options, and then click OK.

7. In the dialog that appears, choose a location on which to save the files, review other capture settings, and click Import.

Figure 16-3: iMovie, ready and waiting to capture video

 If you share your movies on the Internet or on standard DVD, the Large setting is adequate. Choose Full if you plan to burn your movie to a high-definition Blu-ray disc.

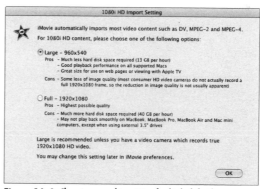

Figure 16-4: Choosing a quality setting for high-def video

Assemble Clips into a Movie

1. Open a movie project with captured video, as described earlier in this chapter.

2. Click an event in the Event library to see a list of clips. Imported clips are organized into events according to the date when they were originally recorded.

3. Hover over a clip in the Clip browser. Notice that the Viewer pane in the upper-right corner plays the spot over which you hover the mouse pointer. Click a clip and press the spacebar to play it.

4. Click on a clip to place a yellow border around it, as shown in Figure 16-5. Click and drag the edges of the border to choose how much of the clip you want to use.

5. Click and drag the clip from the Clip browser to the Project browser, as shown in Figure 16-6.

 If the clip takes up multiple rows in the Clip browser, simply click and drag down to select multiple rows.

6. Click and drag additional clips to the Project browser. To insert a new clip between two existing clips in the Project browser, simply drop the new clip between the two existing clips.

7. To remove a clip from the Project browser, click the clip to select it and press the Delete key.

Figure 16-5: Previewing clips in the Clip browser

Figure 16-6: Dragging a clip to the Project browser

Trim Clips in the Project Browser

1. Open a movie project in which you've already added some clips to the Project browser, as described in the preceding task.

    To adjust the zoom level of the Project browser, use the Zoom slider in the lower-right corner of the Project browser.

2. Click in the Project browser and then press the spacebar to play the clip.

3. When you identify a portion of a clip that you want to trim, pause playback so that the playhead is exactly on a spot where you want to trim.

4. Click and drag a yellow selection box around a portion of the clip, as shown in Figure 16-7.

5. Control+click on the selected area to open a shortcut menu, as shown in Figure 16-8. Choose one of the following:

   - **Delete Selection:** Choose this if you want to trim out only the portion of video that's selected inside the yellow box.

   - **Trim to Selection:** Choose this if you want to get rid of everything outside the yellow box.

   - **Split Clip:** Choose this if you just want to split the selection off and make it a separate clip.

Figure 16-7: Editing in the Project browser

Figure 16-8: Trimming a clip

Add a Soundtrack

1. Open an iMovie project that's been edited, as described earlier in this chapter.

     If the song you want to use for your soundtrack isn't already on your computer, use either a song you've purchased from the iTunes Music Store or one that you imported from an audio CD using iTunes, as described in Chapter 12. You can also add sound effects to your movie from the Sound Effects library that comes with iLife '09.

2. In iMovie, click the Music and Sound Effects button (it looks like a music note) below the Viewer pane.

3. Click iTunes in the Media list to view your iTunes Library, or choose another category. In Figure 16-9, the Jingles subcategory under iLife Sound Effects has been selected.

     Click the arrow next to a category to view subcategories.

4. Click a song or effect to select it and then click the Play button to preview it.

5. Click and drag a song or sound to the Project browser to add it to your movie. The song appears below the video clips. In Figure 16-10, an audio clip called Curtain Call Short has been added.

6. Double-click a clip in the timeline and then click the Audio tab in the Inspector window that appears. Adjust the Volume setting for the clip. In Figure 16-10, the Volume for a video clip has been set to 0% so that only the soundtrack music will be heard.

Figure 16-9: Browsing music and sound effects

Figure 16-10: The Inspector window, at your service

Apply Video Effects

1. Open an iMovie project that's been edited, as described earlier in this chapter.

2. In iMovie, double-click a clip in the Project browser to open an Inspector window, as shown in Figure 16-11.

3. On the Clip tab, click the Video Effect menu to reveal a list of video effects, as shown in Figure 16-12.

4. Hover the mouse pointer over an effect to preview it.

 When you preview an effect, the preview plays over and over in the Viewer pane.

5. Click the effect you want to use to select it.

6. Review the other video effects available to you. Important effects include

   - **Speed:** You can speed up clips using the Speed slider, or slow them down for a slow-motion effect.

   - **Stabilization:** Select the Smooth Clip Motion check box to stabilize shaky footage.

   - **Color and light:** Click the Video tab at the top of the Inspector and adjust the exposure, brightness, contrast, and color saturation for the clip. iMovie makes it easy to fine-tune the appearance of your clips.

7. Click Done to apply your changes.

 If you don't like the changes you made to the clip, double-click the clip to open the Inspector. Choose None in the Choose Video Effect pop-up menu, and click Revert to Original in the video color settings.

Figure 16-11: The Clip tab of the Inspector window

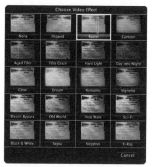

Figure 16-12: Choosing an effect

Insert Transitions between Clips

1. Open an iMovie project that's been edited, as described earlier in this chapter.

2. Click the Show/Hide Transitions Browser button, located under the Viewer pane on the right side of the screen (it's the second button from the right). The Transitions browser appears, as shown in Figure 16-13.

3. Hover the mouse pointer over a transition to preview it.

4. To apply a transition, click and drag the transition to a spot between two clips in the Project browser.

5. To adjust a transition, double-click it to open an Inspector window, as shown in Figure 16-14.

6. Change the length of the transition using the Duration field. The default duration for most transitions is half a second. In Figure 16-14, the duration has been changed to 1.0s, or one second.

 If you aren't happy with the style of the transition, click the Transition pop-up menu and choose a different transition.

7. Click Done to close the Inspector and apply your changes.

8. To remove a transition, click the transition in the Project browser and press Delete.

 For best results, use transitions sparingly and conservatively. Transitions should be used only between major scene changes, not between every single clip. Choose transitions that don't distract from the actual video content of your movie. Also, be aware that transitions sometimes add time to your movie, which can become troublesome if you have a carefully timed soundtrack.

Figure 16-13: The Transitions browser in the lower-right corner of iMovie

Figure 16-14: An Inspector window for transitions

Add Titles to Your Movie

1. Open an iMovie project that's been edited, as described earlier in this chapter.

2. Click the Show/Hide Titles Browser button (it has a T on it), located under the Viewer pane on the right side of the screen. The Titles browser appears, as shown in Figure 16-15.

3. Click and drag a title onto a clip in the Project browser, as shown in Figure 16-15.

4. Click the title in the Project browser to select it.

5. Click the text boxes in the Viewer pane, as shown in Figure 16-16, and type your own text.

6. Click Show Fonts in the Viewer pane to edit the text appearance.

7. Choose fonts, colors, and text sizes in the Choose Fonts dialog. You can also choose styles such as boldface and italics. Click Done to close the Choose Fonts dialog.

 In video, white text over a dark background usually gives the best readability. Make sure you preview your title to ensure that it's readable even as the background video image changes.

8. Click Done in the Viewer pane when you're done editing the title.

9. Click and drag the ends of the title in the Project browser to change the title's duration. Alternatively, double-click the title and change the duration in the Inspector that appears.

Figure 16-15: Choosing a title style in the Titles browser

Figure 16-16: Editing text using the Viewer pane in the upper-right corner

Burn the Movie to DVD

1. Complete all edits for your movie, as described earlier in this chapter.

2. Choose Share➪iDVD. iMovie prepares the movie for export, which may take a few minutes depending on the length of your movie and the complexity of your edits.

3. After iDVD launches, choose a DVD theme from the chooser on the right. (Clicking a theme opens it in the main screen, so you can be sure it's the one you want.) If you're asked whether you want to change the aspect ratio of your movie or keep it, as shown in Figure 16-17, click the Keep button.

Figure 16-17: Choosing a DVD theme and keeping your aspect ratio

 Use the pop-up menu at the top of the Themes list to view additional themes. Some themes include Drop Zones where you can drop pictures or video clips. Click Media in the lower-right corner of the iDVD screen to place photos from your iPhoto library into Drop Zones.

4. Double-click any placeholder text displayed by the theme in the main window to change the text.

5. Click the Burn button or choose File➪Burn DVD.

6. When you're prompted to insert a recordable DVD, as shown in Figure 16-18, insert a blank disc. The encoding and recording process may take several hours.

Figure 16-18: A prompt to insert a recordable DVD

Export the Movie for Web Viewing

1. Complete all edits for your movie, as described earlier in this chapter.

2. Choose Share⟿Export Movie.

3. Provide a filename for your movie in the Export As field and then choose a location in which to save it in the Where pop-up menu.

4. Choose a size for the exported movie, as shown in Figure 16-19. Notice the chart listing which sizes are best for various destinations, such as iPhone, MobileMe, and YouTube.

    Many Web users still resist downloading larger files. The smaller the file size, the more likely it is that more people will see your movie.

5. Click Export. The export process may take a few minutes, depending on the length of your movie and complexity of your edits.

    For online movies, don't use spaces in the filename.

Figure 16-19: Choosing an export size for your movie

Part V
Networking Your Mac

The 5th Wave — By Rich Tennant

ROCKET SOFT DESIGN AND CONSTRUCTION

"The feeling is, we may not have all the network security we should."

Networking Wirelessly with AirPort

*N*ext to the World Wide Web, few technologies have revolutionized personal computing in recent years as much as wireless networking. With Apple's emphasis on ease of use, it comes as no surprise that Macs were among the first computers to take advantage of networking with no strings attached.

AirPort is Apple's name for its wireless networking products. AirPort gear is fully compatible with most other Wi-Fi (also called 802.11Wi-Fi) networking technologies. Your AirPort-equipped MacBook can access the Internet through public hotspots and Wi-Fi–equipped Windows PCs can connect to your Apple AirPort access point.

This chapter shows you how to configure an AirPort access point to create your own wireless network. It also shows you how to connect various computers — Windows PCs, Macs, and even iPhones — to a wireless access point. This chapter even shows you how to create a wireless ad hoc computer-to-computer network.

The steps for connecting a computer (whether a Mac or Windows PC) to a wireless access point are the same regardless of whether the access point is an Apple AirPort unit or another type of Wi-Fi access point. See Chapter 20 for more on setting up wireless network security. For even more on wireless networking, check out Michael E. Cohen's *AirPort & Mac Wireless Networks For Dummies* (Wiley Publishing, Inc.).

Configure an AirPort Base Station

1. Connect an Ethernet cable between your broadband modem and the AirPort Base Station, if needed.

    See the owner's manual that comes with your Base Station for more information on cable connections. Whatever cables you connect, the power cord should be the last cable you connect.

2. Plug in the power cable for the Base Station and wait until the status light turns solid green.

3. Open the Applications folder on your Mac and then open the Utilities subfolder.

4. Double-click the AirPort Utility icon, as shown in Figure 17-1.

5. If your AirPort Base Station appears on the left, select it and then click Continue. Otherwise, click the Manual Setup button, as shown in Figure 17-2.

6. Enter a Base Station name and password. You'll use this password when you change Base Station settings.

7. Decide whether you want to create a new wireless network, replace an existing wireless router, or join the Base Station to your current network. Select the appropriate option, and then click Continue.

Figure 17-1: The Applications:Utilities folder

 If the Base Station isn't detected, click the AirPort icon on your Mac's Title bar and choose Turn AirPort ON in the menu that appears. Make sure that the status light on the Base Station is shining solid green. If the light is amber or flashing, wait a few more seconds. If after a minute it still doesn't shine solid green, unplug the Base Station for a few seconds and then plug it back in. When the light shines solid green, click Try Again in the AirPort Setup Assistant. You can also configure the Base Station by using an Ethernet-connected computer if the Base Station is connected to the same network.

Figure 17-2: Setting up a new AirPort Base Station

8. Enter a name in the Wireless Network Name text box, as shown in Figure 17-3.

 If you're adding the Base Station to an existing wireless network, the name of the wireless network should be the same as the rest of your network. If you're creating a new network, enter a unique, personalized name for the network.

9. Choose a security format and enter a network password twice. Computers that connect to the wireless network must use the correct name and password.

 WPA and WPA2 (Wi-Fi Protected Access) are the best types of security, but older computers and devices (such as game consoles) may support only WEP (Wired Equivalency Protocol). Use the highest level of security that's supported by the equipment you own. See Chapter 20 for more on wireless network security.

10. Click Continue and choose whether the AirPort Base Station connects to a router or modem. Select the first option (as shown in Figure 17-4) if your network already has a router or modem that uses Dynamic Host Configuration Protocol (DHCP). Otherwise, select the I Do Not Use DHCP option and accept the default DHCP settings.

11. Click Continue, verify the setup details, and click Update.

12. After the Base Station restarts and the Congratulations screen appears, click Quit. Setup is complete.

 The steps described here are the same whether you have an AirPort Express or AirPort Extreme Base Station.

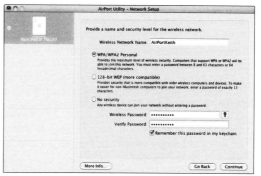

Figure 17-3: Entering a network name and selecting a security option

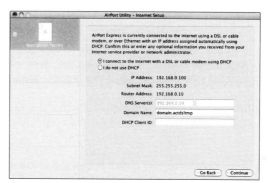

Figure 17-4: Determining the Internet setup

Connect to a Wireless Network

1. Click the AirPort icon on the menu bar and choose Turn AirPort On from the AirPort menu.

2. If an open network is detected, choose whether you want to connect to it, as shown in Figure 17-5.

    Don't connect to a network if you can't positively identify it. Connecting to unknown networks could expose your computer to data theft and virus infection.

3. To connect to a different network, click the AirPort icon and choose the desired network from the AirPort menu, as shown in Figure 17-6.

    If the desired network isn't listed, the network might be out of range, it might be turned off, or it might be closed. See the following section in this chapter for steps to access a closed network.

4. To disconnect from a wireless network, click the AirPort icon and choose Turn AirPort Off from the AirPort menu.

    If your computer routinely connects to the wrong network when multiple networks are available, open System Preferences, click the Network icon, click AirPort, and then select the Ask to Join New Networks check box. Click Advanced and then click and drag preferred networks to the top of the network list. Click OK and then Apply to save the changes.

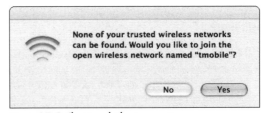

Figure 17-5: Choosing whether to connect to the new network

Figure 17-6: The AirPort menu

Access a Closed Wireless Network

1. Turn on AirPort if it isn't enabled already.

    Remember, you can use the AirPort menu to quickly turn AirPort on or off.

2. Click the AirPort icon on the menu bar and then choose Join Other Network from the menu that appears, as shown in Figure 17-7.

3. Enter the name of the network in the Network Name field.

    The network name is also sometimes called the Service Set Identifier (SSID). The network name is usually case sensitive, so make sure you enter it correctly.

4. If the network uses wireless security, choose the appropriate security method from the Security pop-up menu.

5. In the extra fields that appear, as shown in Figure 17-8, enter the network password and other details, as appropriate.

    The exact fields and menus that appear vary, depending on which security method you use. See Chapter 20 for more on working with wireless security.

6. Click Join to log on to the network.

    If you can't log on to the network, double-check that you entered the network name and any passwords or network keys with the correct case. Network names, passwords, and keys are often case-sensitive.

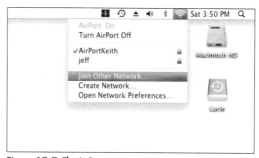

Figure 17-7: The AirPort menu

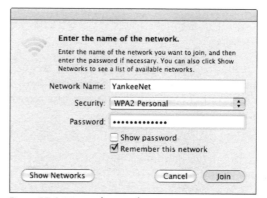

Figure 17-8: Entering the network name and login details

Connect an iPhone to a Closed Network

1. Closed networks must be manually configured. So, on the iPhone's home screen, tap Settings and then tap General.

2. On the General settings screen, tap Network and then tap Wi-Fi.

3. Tap Other.

4. Enter the network name, as shown in Figure 17-9.

 Remember, network names (also called SSIDs) are usually case sensitive.

5. Tap Security and choose the level of security used on the network. Tap Other Network to return to the Network Information screen.

6. Enter the network's password, as shown in Figure 17-9.

7. Tap Join. The network appears in the Choose a Network list, as shown in Figure 17-10.

8. Make sure that the Ask to Join Networks feature is turned on, as shown in Figure 17-10. This gives you control over which networks your iPhone can access.

9. Press the Home button to exit Wi-Fi settings and return to the home screen.

 You can disable Wi-Fi access by sliding the Wi-Fi control to Off. But if you need to temporarily disable all wireless features, tap Settings on the iPhone's home screen and turn on Airplane Mode. Airplane mode disables the cellular radio, Wi-Fi, and Bluetooth.

Figure 17-9: Configuring a closed network

Figure 17-10: Connecting to the right network

Create an Ad Hoc Network between Two Computers

1. Click the AirPort icon on the menu bar and choose Create Network from the menu that appears.

2. In the Computer-to-Computer window that appears, type a name for your ad hoc network, as shown in Figure 17-11.

    You can choose a specific wireless channel if you wish, but it's best to choose Automatic unless you encounter connection problems.

3. Select the Require Password check box and then choose either 40- or 128-bit WEP from the Security pop-up menu.

4. Enter a password twice. (The password must match the description shown in the dialog.) Then click OK to create the network.

5. On the other computer, click the AirPort icon and choose the desired computer-to-computer network from the list, as shown in Figure 17-12.

6. To access the other computer, open Finder and then click the name of a computer that you want to access under Shared in the Finder sidebar. Click the Connect button that appears, and log in to the remote computer.

7. When you're done using the computer-to-computer network, click the AirPort icon on the Title bar and choose Disconnect from Current Network.

    To quickly rejoin your primary wireless network, turn off AirPort via the AirPort menu, wait a few seconds, and then turn on AirPort again. AirPort logs on to your default preferred network, if it's available.

Figure 17-11: Naming your ad hoc network

Figure 17-12: Selecting an ad hoc network to join

Access an AirPort Base Station from Windows

1. In Windows, choose Start➪All Programs➪Accessories➪ Communications➪Network Connections.

2. In the Network Connections window, double-click the Wireless Network Connection icon.

3. In the Wireless Network Connection window, click the Set Up a Wireless Network for a Home or Small Office link under Network Tasks in the sidebar.

4. In the Wireless Network Setup Wizard that appears, click Next, choose Set Up a New Wireless Network, and click Next again.

5. Enter the network name, as shown in Figure 17-13, and choose the type of security (such as WPA or WEP) used on your network.

6. Select the Manually Assign a Network Key option and click Next.

7. Enter the *network key* (the password) and click Next.

8. Choose Set Up a Network Manually in the next screen and then click Next again.

9. Click Finish to complete the setup process and then make sure that your AirPort network appears in the wireless network list, as shown in Figure 17-14.

 To disconnect a Windows PC from your wireless network, double-click the wireless network icon in the Windows system tray (the area in the lower-right corner next to the clock) and then click Disable in the dialog that appears.

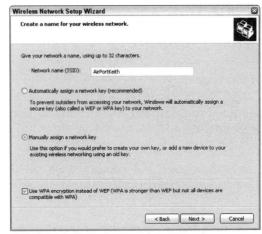

Figure 17-13: The Wireless Network Setup Wizard

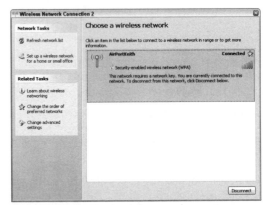

Figure 17-14: Checking the wireless network connection

Troubleshoot a Wireless Connection

1. Double-check that the AirPort Base Station is turned on, and that AirPort is enabled on your Mac, as described earlier in this chapter.

2. Check the signal strength by looking at the AirPort icon on the Menu bar. Four bars indicate a strong signal; fewer bars mean the signal is weak.

3. Check to see whether the network is closed. If it's closed, you need to manually enter the network name (also called the SSID) and select the security level, as shown in Figure 17-15. Network names are case sensitive. See the task called "Access a Closed Wireless Network," earlier in this chapter, for steps.

4. Connect an Ethernet cable between the AirPort Base Station and your computer and then follow the steps I describe in the "Configure an AirPort Base Station" task to make sure that the access point is configured properly.

5. Make sure that your computer is configured to work with DHCP, as I describe in Chapter 18.

6. Check that your DSL or cable modem is connected properly to the WAN (wide area network) or modem port on your AirPort access point, as I describe in Chapter 18.

7. If you're trying to network wirelessly with a Windows PC, check that your Mac's workgroup name is properly set, as I describe in Chapter 19.

8. Look for devices that may cause Wi-Fi signal interference, such as microwave ovens or 2.4GHz cordless telephones.

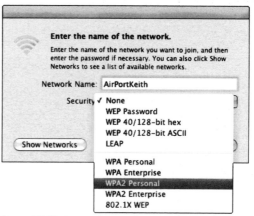

Figure 17-15: Entering the network name and security level for closed networks

 You might need to connect the modem to your computer to check its status.

 Rearrange your hardware so that interference sources aren't physically close to your AirPort access point or your computer.

Sharing Resources

*T*he number one reason to set up a network is to share stuff among your various computers. This "stuff" usually includes files, Internet connections, and printers. Sharing these resources is easy, as is accessing shared resources on other network computers.

Before you can share anything, your Mac must be properly connected to the network. Chapter 17 shows you how to connect your Mac to a wireless network, and this chapter shows you how to connect to a wired Ethernet network. Ethernet networks aren't quite as convenient as wireless networks, but they offer greater reliability, security, and speed. Most modern Macs include adapters for connecting to Ethernet networks. (Some models, such as the MacBook Air, require an external Ethernet adapter.)

This chapter shows you how to share printers, files, and Internet connections with the network after you set it up. The tasks in this chapter also show you how to access shared resourced on other networked computers. This chapter shows you how to network mainly with other Macintosh computers, although many of the principles apply to Microsoft Windows computers as well. See Chapter 19 for more on networking with Windows PCs.

 Sharing Internet connections, as I describe in this chapter, is usually necessary only if you have dialup Internet access. For example, if you access a dialup Internet service with the modem in your Mac, you can share that connection with the rest of your network if you want. If you connect to the Internet with a cable modem or digital subscriber line (DSL), the external modem for that service should be connected to the WAN (wide area network) port on your network's router.

Chapter 18

Get ready to . . .

Connect to an Ethernet Network

1. Connect an Ethernet cable between the Ethernet port on your Mac and a local area network (LAN) port on your Ethernet switch, hub, or router.

    If you need to buy new networking hardware, a router is the easiest to configure and provides the greatest flexibility.

2. Restart your Mac and then open System Preferences from the Apple menu.

3. In System Preferences, click the Network icon.

4. In the list on the left, select Ethernet, as shown in Figure 18-1, and then click the Advanced button.

5. On the TCP/IP tab, as shown in Figure 18-2, choose the Using DHCP option from the Configure IPv4 pop-up menu.

6. If a numeric IP address isn't listed next to IP Address (as shown in Figure 18-2), click the Renew DHCP Lease button.

7. Click OK and then Apply to apply your changes.

    To connect two computers together directly without using a hub or router, you might need to use a special Ethernet cable — a *crossover* cable. Crossover cables are available at most computer retailers. Keep crossover cables clearly marked because they don't work for connecting a computer to a hub or router. Many newer Macs can connect directly to each other with a regular network cable; check your Mac's documentation to see whether it has self-configuring ports.

Figure 18-1: The Network preferences pane

If you want to access an Internet connection that's shared by another computer (see the task "Share an Internet Connection," later in this chapter), follow the steps here to configure your network connection. The Internet sharing server behaves like a Dynamic Host Configuration Protocol (DHCP) server.

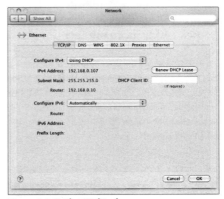

Figure 18-2: The TCP/IP tab

Set an IP Address Manually

1. Open System Preferences from the Apple menu and then click the Network icon.

2. In the list on the left, select Ethernet and then click the Advanced button.

3. On the TCP/IP tab, choose the Manually option from the Configure IPv4 pop-up menu, as shown in Figure 18-3.

 If your network uses a router or other DHCP server, but you still need to assign an Internet Protocol (IP) address manually, choose the Using DHCP with Manual Address option from the Configure IPv4 pop-up menu instead.

4. Type an IP address for your computer in the IPv4 Address field, as shown in Figure 18-4.

 On a typical home network, the IP address starts with 192.168.0. The final segment can be any number between 0 and 255. Each computer on the network must have a unique IP address. Check the documentation for your router or server software to see if the IP address should be in a specific range.

5. Enter a Subnet Mask, which in almost all cases is **255.255.255.0.**

6. In the Router field, enter the IP address for the router or server computer on the network. If you don't have a router, enter the IP address for the computer that connects to the Internet.

7. Click Apply and then close System Preferences.

 Usually you don't need to set an IP address manually. Only set it manually if a network administrator has instructed you to do so, in which case you should be provided with a specific IP address to use.

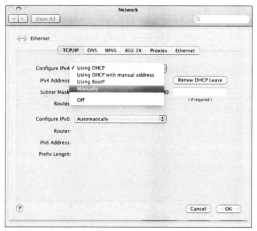

Figure 18-3: Selecting the Manually option

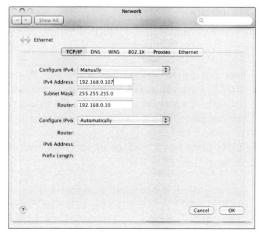

Figure 18-4: Entering the network addresses manually

Find the IP Address of a Mac

1. Open System Preferences from the Apple menu.

2. Click the Network icon.

3. Note the address listed in the IP Address field, as shown in Figure 18-5.

 The Network preferences pane shows the IP address for whichever network connection is currently active, be it Ethernet, AirPort, or another connection.

Find the IP Address of a Windows PC

1. On the Windows PC, open the Control Panel and click the View Network Status and Tasks link under Network and Internet.

 These steps are for Windows Vista. In Windows XP, choose Start➪My Network Places. Click the View Network Connections link in the Network window that appears and then click the active network connection to select it. The IP address is listed under Details.

2. Click the View Status link next to the active network connection, and then click Details.

 If the computer has multiple network connections (such as Ethernet and 802.11 Wi-Fi), make sure you choose the active connection.

3. Note the IP address listed in the Network Connection Details dialog, as shown in Figure 18-6.

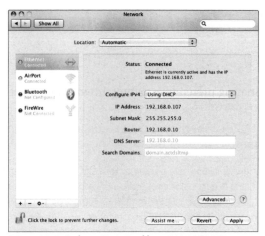

Figure 18-5: Finding a Mac's IP address (192.168.0.107)

Figure 18-6: Finding an IP address in Windows (192.168.0.104)

Share an Internet Connection

1. Open System Preferences from the Apple menu and then click the Sharing icon under Internet & Network.

2. In the Sharing preferences pane (shown in Figure 18-7), click Internet Sharing to open Internet sharing preferences.

3. In the Share Your Connection From pop-up menu, choose the network connection that connects to the Internet. If the computer connects via dialup, choose the Modem option. If you connect to the Internet with a DSL or cable modem, choose the connection to which the modem is attached. In most cases, this is the Ethernet connection.

4. In the To Computers Using list, place a check mark next to the connection that will be used to share the Internet connection with other computers. Your selection here should be a different connection than the one you selected in the Share Your Connection From pop-up menu.

    Make a note of the warning message that appears when you choose a connection and make sure that sharing your connection doesn't violate the service agreement with your Internet service provider (ISP).

5. If you're sharing the connection using AirPort, click the AirPort Options button. Select the Enable Encryption check box, enter a Wired Equivalency Protocol (WEP) password twice, and choose 128-bit from the WEP Key Length pop-up menu, as shown in Figure 18-8. Click OK.

6. In the list on the left, select the Internet Sharing check box to begin sharing your Internet connection.

Figure 18-7: The Sharing preferences pane

 The WEP password must be entered on all sharing client computers.

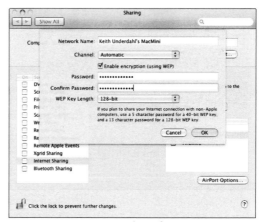

Figure 18-8: Securing Internet sharing for an AirPort

Share a Printer

1. Open System Preferences from the Apple menu and then click the Print & Fax icon.

2. Click the printer that you want to share to select it.

3. Select the Share This Printer with Other Users on the Network check box, as shown in Figure 18-9.

4. Click the Options & Supplies button and type a descriptive name for the printer in the Name field. Make sure that the Location field is descriptive and accurate and then click OK.

 The printer name and location appear on other network computers when the printer is shared, so make sure that the information adequately distinguishes the printer from other devices on the network.

5. Next to the warning message stating that Printer Sharing is turned off, click the Sharing button.

6. In the list on the left, select the Printer Sharing check box, as shown in Figure 18-10.

7. Close System Preferences.

 Remember, a shared printer can be accessed only when the computer to which it's connected is powered on (not asleep) and connected to the network. The printer must also be turned on and connected to the computer.

Figure 18-9: The Print & Fax preferences pane

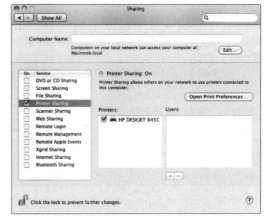

Figure 18-10: Making sure that Printer Sharing is enabled

Access a Shared Printer

1. Open System Preferences from the Apple menu and then click the Print & Fax icon.

2. Click the Add Printer button. It looks like a plus sign and is located under the list of printers on the left.

3. In the Printer Browser that appears, as shown in Figure 18-11, click the icon (located at the top of the browser) that fits your needs:

   - **Default:** Click this icon if the printer is connected to a Macintosh running OS X, as shown in Figure 18-11. Select the shared printer you want to access. Choose the correct model in the Print Using menu.

   - **Windows:** Click this icon if the printer is connected to a Windows PC. Select the shared printer.

   - **Fax:** Click this icon if you want to connect to a fax device.

   - **IP:** Click this icon if the printer is connected to your network by an Ethernet connection.

4. Click the Add button and then close System Preferences.

5. Open a document that you want to print and choose File⇨Print.

6. In the Printer menu, choose the shared printer to which you want to print, as shown in Figure 18-12, review other printing options, and then click Print.

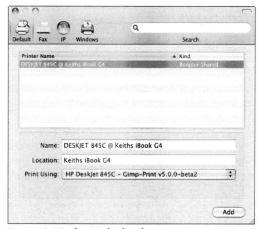

Figure 18-11: Choosing the shared printer

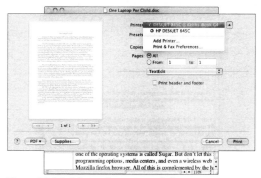

Figure 18-12: Selecting the printer to which you want to print

Enable File Sharing

1. Open System Preferences from the Apple menu and then click the Sharing icon.

2. In the Sharing preferences pane, select the File Sharing check box in the list on the left, as shown in Figure 18-13.

    Open the Sharing preferences pane and disable File Sharing whenever you access a public Wi-Fi hotspot or other network that isn't secure. This prevents unauthorized users from accessing your files.

3. Click the Add button (it looks like a plus sign) under Users to add a new authorized user.

4. On the left, select the Users & Groups option or the Address Book option to see a list of users. If you don't see the person you want to add, click the New Person button and enter a username and password in the window that appears.

5. Select the user, as shown in Figure 18-14, and click the Select button. The user now appears in the list of authorized users in the Sharing preferences pane.

    If the network user will access your computer from a Windows PC, see Chapter 19 for more on activating Windows file sharing.

6. Next to the user's name on the Sharing screen, use the menu to decide whether the user has Read Only, Read & Write, or Write Only access. Give Write Only access if you want the user to be able to drop files on your computer but not view or change other files.

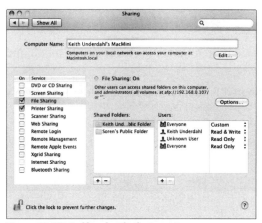

Figure 18-13: Enabling the File Sharing option

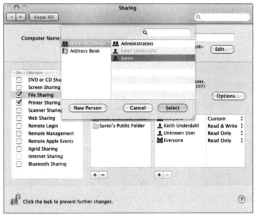

Figure 18-14: Controlling who can access your computer over the network

Share Files and Folders

1. Open System Preferences from the Apple menu and then click the Sharing icon.

2. In the Shared Folders list, select a folder for which you want to control sharing. If the folder you want to share isn't in the list, click the Add button (it looks like a plus sign) under Shared Folders and browse to the folder that you want to share.

3. Under the Users list, select a user, and then choose a level of access for the user in the menu that appears as shown in Figure 18-15.

4. Close System Preferences when you finish setting up shared folders and managing access.

5. Copy files into your shared folders to share those files.

 Items in your Public folder can be viewed or copied by anyone, so be careful what you put in that folder. Also, don't share other folders on your computer unless you know for sure that the folder's contents are safe for public consumption.

6. Open the Finder. Under Shared in the sidebar, click the name of a network computer containing shared items.

7. Click Connect As and then enter a valid username and password for the computer.

8. Use the Finder to browse the computer, as shown in Figure 18-16.

 Choose Guest to log in to the computer as a guest and access public items.

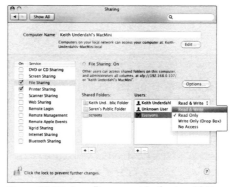

Figure 18-15: Controlling access rights for shared folders

Figure 18-16: Accessing shared folders with the Finder

Connecting to Windows PCs and Older Macs

*I*t's no secret that a majority of PCs in the world run Windows. You may even have some Windows PCs of your own. If so, there's no reason why your Macs and PCs can't live together. Setting up a network between Windows PCs and Macs takes only minutes; and after configuration, you can easily share files, printers, Internet connections, and other resources between the two. This chapter shows you how to network your new Mac with Windows PCs as well as with Macs running Mac OS 10.2 or earlier. Unless noted otherwise, the steps here assume that you have

➥ **Windows XP or later:** If you have an older version of Windows, you can follow the steps in this chapter to some extent, although some procedures might vary slightly. Windows XP or later provides easier, more secure networking.

➥ **An Ethernet router or wireless network:** For more on setting up Macintosh networking hardware and software, see Chapters 17 and 18. If you need to set up a Windows network, check out my book, *Wi-Fi Home Networking Just the Steps For Dummies* (Wiley Publishing, Inc.).

Get ready to . . .

Set Up Windows File Sharing

1. On your Mac, open System Preferences from the Apple menu and then click the Sharing icon.

2. Type a descriptive name in the Computer Name field, as shown in Figure 19-1. This is the name that other computers see on the network.

3. Select the File Sharing check box, as shown in Figure 19-1.

 File Sharing must be enabled, whether you want to share files with Windows PCs or other Macs.

4. Click the Options button.

5. Select the Share Files and Folders using SMB (Windows) check box.

6. Place a check mark next to those accounts that may access the computer from a Windows PC, as shown in Figure 19-2.

 Enable only the accounts that need file access from a Windows PC. Needlessly enabling file sharing for other accounts could compromise the security of your computer.

7. Click Done and then close System Preferences.

 If you no longer need to share files with Windows PCs, open the Sharing preferences pane and disable SMB sharing.

Figure 19-1: The Sharing preferences pane

Figure 19-2: Controlling which accounts can access the computer from Windows

Change the Workgroup Name on Your Mac

1. Open System Preferences from the Apple menu.

2. Click the Network icon to open the Network preferences pane.

3. In the list on the left, select the network connection you use to connect to the Windows network, as shown in Figure 19-3.

4. Click the Advanced button.

5. Click the WINS tab.

6. Type the name of your Windows workgroup in the Workgroup field, as shown in Figure 19-4.

7. Click OK and then click Apply to apply your changes.

 If you have OS 10.2, 10.3, or 10.4, setting the Windows Workgroup name is a little more complicated. Launch the Directory Access utility from your Applications:Utilities folder. Unlock the Directory Access Utility using your Administrator password and then select the SMB/CIFS check box. Click the Configure button next to SMB/CIFS and enter the Windows Workgroup name in the Workgroup field. Click OK and then quit the Directory Access utility.

 To determine a Windows workgroup name, open the Control Panel on a Windows PC and then double-click the System icon. The Computer Name tab of the System Properties dialog lists the workgroup name. The workgroup name should be the same on each computer on the network. The default workgroup name on most Windows PCs is MSHOME.

Figure 19-3: The Network preferences pane

Figure 19-4: Entering the Windows workgroup name

Connect to a Windows PC from Your Mac

1. Open the Finder and locate the Windows PC under Shared in the sidebar.

 Before you can connect to a Windows PC, both the Windows PC and your Mac should be powered on and connected to the network. File sharing must be enabled on the Windows PC (see *Wi-Fi Home Networking Just the Steps For Dummies* by me for more on enabling Windows file sharing), and you should set the workgroup name on your Mac, as I describe earlier in this chapter.

2. Click the name of the computer to which you want to connect. When you first click the name of the Windows PC, you'll probably see a Connection Failed message like the one in Figure 19-5.

3. Click the Connect As button.

 If you don't see the Connect As button, change the view setting in the Finder to view folders and files in columns. This should reveal the Connect As button.

4. Enter an account name and password, as shown in Figure 19-6. The account name and password should be valid on the Windows PC to which you want to connect.

 If you enter an invalid account name or no name at all, you can still connect as a Guest to the Shared Items folder on the Windows PC as well as other shared resources on that computer.

5. Click the Connect button.

Figure 19-5: Finding a Windows PC on your network

Figure 19-6: Entering an account name and password

Copy Files from a Windows PC

1. Connect to a Windows PC, as I describe in the previous task.

2. Use the Finder to locate files on the Windows PC, as shown in Figure 19-7.

3. To quickly copy a file from the Windows PC to the Documents folder on your Mac, simply click and drag the file to the Documents icon in the Finder sidebar, as shown in Figure 19-8.

 You can also click and drag items from the Windows PC to your OS X desktop, or you can open a second Finder and drag files to specific subfolders on your Mac.

4. To copy files from your Mac to the Windows PC, click and drag files and folders to the Windows folder in a Finder window.

 You can't copy files to any Windows folder showing a small lock icon on the folder image. You can copy only into folders for which you have write access.

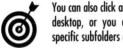 When you access a Windows hard drive from a Mac, the Mac OS leaves system file fragments called *resource forks* on the Windows hard drive. These files are unnecessary for the Windows operating system and can be deleted safely after the Mac has disconnected from the Windows PC. See the task on cleaning up resource forks later in this chapter for steps to get rid of resource forks.

Figure 19-7: Browsing Windows folders with the OS X Finder

Figure 19-8: Clicking and dragging files to copy them

Access Your Mac from a Windows PC

1. On your Windows PC, choose Start⇨My Network Places (Windows XP) or Start⇨Network (Vista).

   You can also access My Network Places in My Computer or Windows Explorer.

2. Under Network or Network Tasks on the left side of the window, click the View Network Computers link (if you see it).

3. Find the Mac to which you want to connect from the list of computers, as shown in Figure 19-9.

   If your Mac doesn't appear in the list, make sure that the Mac's workgroup name has been properly set (as I describe earlier in this computer) and double-check that the Mac is powered on and connected to the network.

4. Double-click the icon for the Mac to which you want to connect.

5. In the log in dialog that appears, as shown in Figure 19-10, enter a username and password that are valid on the Mac and then click OK.

   When logging in to a Mac from Windows, you must use a username and password that are valid on that Mac. The account must be authorized to log in remotely, and SMB sharing must be enabled on the Mac. If you're logging in from Windows Vista or later, you must enter the computer name of the Mac, followed by a backslash, and then the user account name.

Figure 19-9: The Network folder

Figure 19-10: The log in dialog

Copy Files from a Mac

1. Log in to the Mac from Windows, as I describe in the previous task.

2. Double-click the folder icon for the user account you used to log in to the Mac, as shown in Figure 19-11.

3. Browse to the files that you want to copy.

 Remember, you can access only the files owned by the user account that you used to log in to the Mac. Files owned by other user accounts aren't accessible.

4. Select the files you want to copy, as shown in Figure 19-12.

5. Open My Computer or Windows Explorer and then open the folder to which you want to copy the files. Arrange the windows so that both the Mac folder and the target folder are visible.

6. Click and drag files from the Mac to the folder on your Windows PC, as shown in Figure 19-12.

7. Repeat this procedure in reverse to copy files from your Windows PC to your Mac.

 You can also copy or move files in Windows by using the Ctrl+C (copy), Ctrl+X (cut), and Ctrl+V (paste) commands.

Figure 19-11: Accessing files from Windows

Figure 19-12: Copying files between Windows and OS X

Clean Up Mac Resource Forks on a Windows PC

1. On your Windows PC, use Windows Explorer or My Computer to open a folder that you know has been accessed by a Mac.

2. In the My Computer or Windows Explorer window, choose Tools➪Folder Options (Windows XP) or Organize➪Folder and Search Options (Vista).

3. Click the View tab to bring it to the front, as shown in Figure 19-13.

4. Under Hidden Files and Folders, select the Show Hidden Files and Folders option.

5. Click OK to close the Folder Options dialog.

6. Identify and select files that have ghost-like icons, as shown in Figure 19-14. These files have a filename that's similar to another non-ghosted file in the same folder. If you see a file named .DS_Store, select it as well.

7. Delete the selected files.

 If you aren't absolutely sure about a file's purpose, don't delete it. Except for the file .DS_Store, Mac resource fork files almost always share a filename with another, valid file.

Figure 19-13: The Folder Options dialog

Figure 19-14: Removing Mac resource forks, which aren't needed by Windows

Connect an Older OS X Computer to Your Network

1. If the older Mac doesn't have AirPort, select a network router or switch with extra LAN Ethernet ports and connect the Mac to one of those ports using an Ethernet cable.

2. Start the older Mac and open System Preferences from the Apple menu.

3. Click the Network icon. In the Network preferences pane, choose Built-in Ethernet in the Show menu.

4. Click the TCP/IP tab to bring it to the front and then choose Using DHCP in the Configure menu, as shown in Figure 19-15. Make a note of the number listed next to IP address. You might need this later.

5. Close the Network preferences pane, re-open System Preferences, and click the Sharing icon.

6. On the Services tab, select the Personal File Sharing and Remote Login check box.

7. Click the Firewall tab, select the Personal File Sharing and Remote Login check box, and close the Sharing pane.

8. With the Finder active, choose Go⇨Connect to Server.

9. Select the network computer to which you want to connect, as shown in Figure 19-16, and then click the Connect button.

10. Enter a valid username and password for the computer that you're logging in to and click OK.

11. Choose a volume to mount and click OK. A desktop icon for the mounted volume appears on the desktop.

Figure 19-15: The Network preferences pane

Figure 19-16: Choosing the computer to connect with

Networking Safely

Connecting your computer to a network brings added convenience to your electronic life. Networks let you share files and printers, and they allow you to connect easily to the Internet. The Internet is the world's largest network, so every time you connect to it, you're networking.

But with the added convenience of networking come some dangers. With networks, unsavory persons can steal your identity, violate your privacy, access your sensitive files, and infect your computer with viruses. You can avoid these dangers by taking some simple precautions, and this chapter shows you how. This chapter shows you how to

➡ **Create and use network locations.** Network locations allow you to quickly switch to a higher level of security when needed, such as when you connect to a public Wi-Fi hotspot.

➡ **Guard against intrusion with a firewall.** Firewalls block unwanted network and Internet intrusion into your computer.

➡ **Keep unauthorized users off your wireless network.** By changing and hiding your SSID (Service Set Identifier), setting up WEP (good) or WPA (better) encryption, and fine-tuning your wireless transmitter power, you can prevent neighbors and passers-by from accessing your network and using your Internet connection.

➡ **Encrypt files.** OS X includes tools to help you encrypt your most sensitive files for added protection.

Get ready to . . .

Create a New Network Location

1. Open System Preferences from the Apple menu and then click the Network icon.

2. From the Location pop-up menu, choose Edit Locations.

3. In the Edit Locations dialog that appears, click the Add Location button (it looks like a plus sign); type a descriptive name for the location, as shown in Figure 20-1; and click the Done button.

4. Make sure that your new location is selected in the Location pop-up menu. Then, in the list on the left, click the network connection that you'll use at this location (Ethernet, AirPort, Bluetooth, FireWire, or Modem) to select it.

5. If the location will use AirPort, select the Ask to Join New Networks check box, as shown in Figure 20-2.

6. Click the Advanced button.

7. In the Advanced settings pane that appears, click the AirPort tab and adjust network settings as needed for the connection. If you're configuring an AirPort location, click and drag network names up or down in the list. Names at the top of the list are preferred networks.

8. Select the Require Administrator Password to Control AirPort check box.

9. Select the Disconnect from Wireless Networks When Logging Out check box.

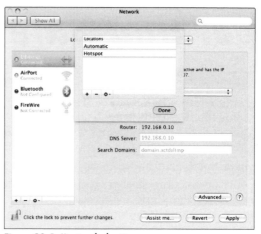

Figure 20-1: Naming the location

Figure 20-2: Making AirPort more restrictive in less secure locations

10. If the location has a wireless network that requires a specific login name and password, click the 802.1X tab.

11. Click the plus sign in the lower-left corner and choose Add User Profile. Type a name for the user profile, as shown in Figure 20-3.

12. Enter the User Name and Password; also enter the network's name in the Wireless Network field, as shown in Figure 20-3. The network name is the network's SSID.

13. Click OK to close the Advanced Settings pane.

14. Click Apply to apply your changes and create the new location.

Switch between Locations

1. Open System Preferences from the Apple menu and then click the Network icon.

2. From the Location pop-up menu, choose the desired location, as shown in Figure 20-4.

3. Click Apply to begin using the new location settings and then close System Preferences.

 To ensure your security, switch to your more secure location settings before joining a hotspot or other non-secure network.

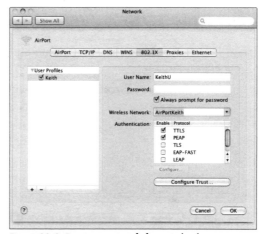

Figure 20-3: Entering security info for a wireless location

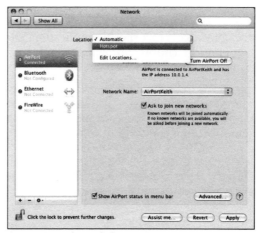

Figure 20-4: Selecting the location to use

Protect Your Mac with a Firewall

1. Open System Preferences from the Apple menu and then click the Security icon.

2. Click the Firewall tab to bring firewall settings to the front.

3. To block intruders from your computer, click Start to turn on the Firewall.

4. Click Advanced, as shown in Figure 20-5. If you want to block all possible outside access to your computer, enable the Block All Incoming Connections check box.

 If you block all incoming connections, iChat and other Internet-based programs may not work on your system. Enable this option only as a last resort. Services that are essential to proper network function such as DHCP will still work.

5. To grant or deny access to a specific application, click the plus sign button, choose a program from the Applications folder, and click Add.

6. Use the menus to the right of the name of a service or program listed to make changes. In Figure 20-6, for example, incoming connections are allowed for printer sharing, but incoming connections to Adium are blocked.

 To remove services or applications from the list, click the name of the application and then click the minus sign button.

7. Click OK.

8. Close System Preferences when you're done making changes.

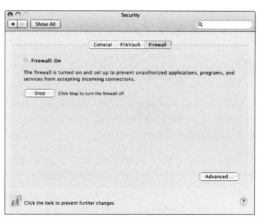

Figure 20-5: Toggling the firewall on and off

Figure 20-6: Controlling incoming connections

Encrypt Files with FileVault

1. Open System Preferences from the Apple menu and then click the Security icon.

    If you're not an administrator on the computer, you must get an administrator's help to enable FileVault because an administrator's password is required.

2. If System Preferences are locked, click the lock icon in the lower-left corner of the screen and enter an administrator password to unlock System Preferences.

3. Click the Set a Master Password button and then create a master password by filling in the Master Password, Verify, and Hint fields, as shown in Figure 20-7. Click OK.

4. Click the Turn on FileVault button.

5. Enter the password for your user account and then click OK.

6. Select the Use Secure Erase check box, as shown in Figure 20-8. This ensures secure deletion of files that are sent to the Trash.

7. Select the Use Secure Virtual Memory check box. This ensures that if virtual memory uses space on your hard drive, the data will be encrypted.

8. Click the Turn On FileVault button. The encryption process might take a while, especially if your home folder is large.

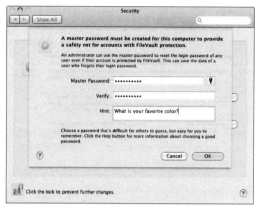

Figure 20-7: Creating a master password for FileVault

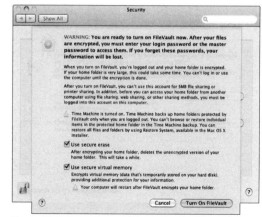

Figure 20-8: Ensuring secure deletion of trashed files

Set Up WEP Security

1. Open the Applications folder on your Mac and then open the Utilities subfolder.

2. Double-click the AirPort Utility icon to launch the utility.

 If the AirPort Utility isn't installed in your Applications:Utilities folder, you can install it from the AirPort setup disc that came with your AirPort Base Station.

3. Choose the network Base Station, and then click the Manual Setup button. In Figure 20-9, the Base Station is an AirPort Express device.

4. Enter the password for the Base Station and then click OK.

5. In the Base Station configuration pane that appears, click the AirPort icon at the top to bring AirPort settings to the front.

6. Click the Wireless tab.

7. From the Wireless Security pop-up menu, choose WEP 128 Bit, as shown in Figure 20-10.

 WEP 40 Bit may be required for some older wireless computers on your network.

8. Enter a password and verify it. A 128-bit WEP password is case sensitive and should be exactly 13 characters long.

Figure 20-9: The AirPort Utility pane at work

 Make a note of the password because you'll need it later to connect other devices to the network. Some devices support only hexadecimal WEP keys. In this case, the password should use only numeric digits 0–9 and letters A–F.

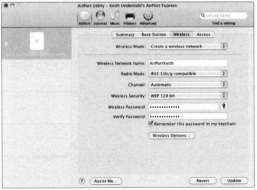

Figure 20-10: The Wireless tab of the configuration pane

9. Click Update to upload your changes to the Base Station.

10. When the AirPort Base Station has finished restarting (the status light glows solid green), quit the AirPort Utility.

11. On each wireless computer on your network, click the AirPort icon, as shown in Figure 20-11, and choose Join Other Network from the drop-down menu.

 If the name of your wireless network already appears in the AirPort menu, choose that network.

12. Fill in the Network Name field, as shown in Figure 20-12.

13. Choose WEP 40/128-bit ASCII from the Wireless Security pop-up menu.

14. Enter the 13-character password in the Password field.

 Hackers that are determined to access your network could easily defeat WEP passwords. Because of this, change your WEP password on a regular basis. Change it at least monthly, or weekly if your network is in close proximity to other potential users.

15. Click the Join button to join the network.

 WEP — Wireless Encryption Protocol — is less secure than WPA (Wi-Fi Protected Access), and WPA is less secure than WPA2. Use WEP only if your network includes hardware (such as wireless game console adapters or older computers) that supports WEP but not WPA.

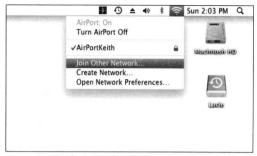

Figure 20-11: The AirPort drop-down menu

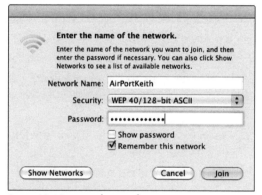

Figure 20-12: Joining the network

Configure WPA Encryption

1. Open the Applications folder on your Mac and then open the Utilities subfolder.

    WPA encryption requires Macintosh OS version 10.3 or later. For Windows PCs, handheld devices running Palm OS or Windows Mobile, wireless media players, wireless print servers, and other Wi-Fi devices, support for WPA depends on the manufacturer of the wireless networking adapter. Check the documentation for each respective device to make sure that WPA is supported. If any wireless device on the network doesn't support WPA, use WEP until you can upgrade the offending unit.

2. Double-click the AirPort Utility icon, as shown in Figure 20-13, to launch the utility.

    If the AirPort Utility isn't installed in your Applications:Utilities folder, you can install it from the AirPort setup disc that comes with your AirPort Base Station.

3. Select the desired Base Station in the list on the left and click the Manual Setup button.

4. Enter the password for the Base Station and then click OK.

5. In the Base Station configuration pane that appears, click AirPort to bring AirPort settings to the front.

6. Click the Wireless tab.

7. On the Wireless tab, choose either WPA or WPA2 Personal from the Wireless Security pop-up menu, as shown in Figure 20-14. WPA2 is more secure but it might not be supported by some older hardware.

8. Type a WPA password in the Wireless password field and verify it. The password should be 8–64 characters long.

Figure 20-13: The Applications:Utilities folder

 Longer passwords are better because they're less likely to be compromised.

Figure 20-14: Providing a WPA password for your network

9. Click the Update button to upload your changes to the Base Station.

10. When the AirPort Base Station has finished restarting (the status light glows solid green), quit the AirPort Utility.

11. On each wireless computer on your network, click the AirPort icon, as shown in Figure 20-15, and choose Join Other Network from the drop-down menu.

 If the name of your wireless network already appears in the AirPort menu, choose that network.

12. Fill in the Network Name field, as shown in Figure 20-16.

13. Choose WPA2 Personal from the Wireless Security pop-up menu.

 WPA2 is more secure than WPA, but some early WPA devices don't support WPA2. If you have some older computers or devices that can't connect to a WPA2 network, try using WPA instead.

14. Enter the password in the Password field.

15. Click the Join button to join the network.

 If you're joining a WPA-encrypted network at your workplace or other commercial location, you might need to follow different steps to connect to the site's RADIUS server. Contact your network administrator for details if you have trouble.

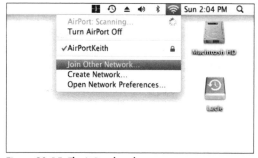

Figure 20-15: The AirPort drop-down menu

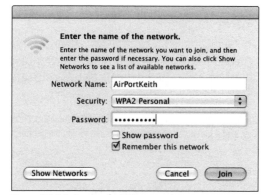

Figure 20-16: Entering the WPA password

Disable SSID Broadcast

1. Open the Applications folder on your Mac and then open the Utilities subfolder.

2. Double-click the AirPort Utility icon to launch the utility.

3. Select the desired network Base Station in the list on the left and click the Manual Setup button. Enter the password for the Base Station and click OK.

4. In the Base Station configuration pane that appears, click the AirPort icon to open AirPort settings, and then click the Wireless tab.

5. Click the Wireless Options button and then select the Create a Closed Network check box, as shown in Figure 20-17. Click Done and then Update to upload your changes to the Base Station.

 A closed network is one that doesn't broadcast the name or SSID, making it harder for unauthorized persons to join the network.

Reduce Transmitter Power

1. Open the AirPort Utility, as described in the previous task.

2. In the AirPort Wireless pane, click the Wireless Options button.

3. Choose a lower power from the Transmitter Power pop-up menu, as shown in Figure 20-18. Click Done and then Update to upload your changes.

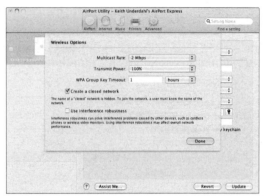

Figure 20-17: Creating a closed network, which disables SSID broadcast

 Reduce transmitter power when you're working in close proximity to others — such as in a hotel or apartment — and long range isn't important.

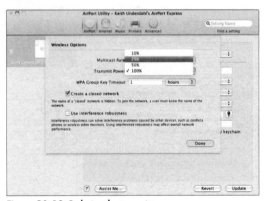

Figure 20-18: Reducing the transmitter power

Part VI
Extending Your Mac's Capabilities

Connecting to Bluetooth Devices

*I*f you've been using computers for a while, you're probably familiar with (and sick of) the resulting rats nest of wires when computers and peripherals are connected. These wires are messy, inconvenient, and prone to loss or breakage. *Bluetooth* is a technology that reduces the clutter and inconvenience of wires by connecting devices wirelessly. Wireless cell phone headsets are the most common Bluetooth devices, but other Bluetooth peripherals include keyboards, mice, handheld computers, GPS antennas, and more. You can even create wireless networks between computers using Bluetooth, although the short range of Bluetooth (usually less than ten meters) makes it best suited for peripherals.

All modern Macs come with Bluetooth technology built-in. (If yours doesn't, you can easily add an external Bluetooth adapter.) This chapter shows you how to

➠ Make your computer discoverable by other Bluetooth devices, an important step in connecting Bluetooth devices.

➠ Enable Bluetooth networking so that you can create a temporary Bluetooth network with another computer.

➠ Create and manage connections — called *partnerships* — between your computer and Bluetooth devices.

Although iPhones have Bluetooth, they work only with select Bluetooth headsets. As of this writing, iPhones don't support Bluetooth networking or file transfer.

Make Your Computer Discoverable

1. Open System Preferences and then click the Bluetooth icon.

2. Select the On check box if it isn't selected already.

3. Select the Discoverable check box, as shown in Figure 21-1.

 If the Show Bluetooth Status in the Menu Bar option is enabled, you can also click the Bluetooth icon on the menu bar to open the Bluetooth menu and enable or disable Bluetooth discovery.

 When working in a public area, disable Bluetooth discovery to hide your computer from unauthorized Bluetooth users.

Enable Bluetooth Networking

1. Open System Preferences and then click the Sharing icon.

2. In the Sharing preferences pane, select the Bluetooth Sharing check box, as shown in Figure 21-2.

3. From the Folder for Accepted Items pop-up menu, choose a folder that you want to allow Bluetooth users to access.

Figure 21-1: Enabling Bluetooth discovery

Figure 21-2: Turning on Bluetooth Sharing

 If your computer is operated within range of other potential Bluetooth users, avoid sharing private folders using Bluetooth.

Send a File via Bluetooth

1. Click the Bluetooth icon on the menu bar and choose Send File from the menu that appears.

2. In the window that appears, browse to the file that you want to send, as shown in Figure 21-3.

3. Click the desired file to select it and then click the Send button.

4. In the Send File dialog, look in the list of devices and click the device to which you want to send the file, as shown in Figure 21-4.

 If the desired device doesn't appear in the list, make sure that Bluetooth is enabled on the device and that the device is discoverable by other Bluetooth devices.

5. Click the Send button.

6. On the destination computer, click the Accept button in the Incoming File Transfer dialog that appears to accept the file.

7. Open the Documents folder on the destination computer to locate the transferred file.

 If the target device isn't a Macintosh computer, the procedure for accepting a file transfer will vary slightly from what is described here, although at some point you should be given a basic Yes or No choice. On computers running Microsoft Windows, Bluetooth-transferred files are saved in the My Documents folder.

Figure 21-3: Selecting a file to send via Bluetooth

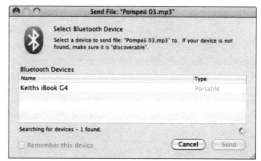

Figure 21-4: Selecting the device to which you want to send the file

Create a Bluetooth Partnership

1. Open System Preferences and then click the Bluetooth icon.

2. Click the Set Up New Device button. The Bluetooth Setup Assistant opens and starts searching for Bluetooth devices.

3. In the list of devices that appears, as shown in Figure 21-5, select the device to which you want to connect to, and then click the Continue button.

4. If the device requires a specific passcode (check the device's documentation), click the Passcode Options button, select the Use a Specific Passcode radio button on the Passcode Options tab that appears, as shown in Figure 21-6, and then click OK to close the tab.

 If the device is a computer and you want to set up a secure partnership, select the Automatically Generate a Passcode radio button. The Bluetooth Setup Assistant automatically generates a passcode and prompts you to enter that passcode on the device when you finish the setup process.

5. Click the Continue button and follow the instructions on-screen to complete the setup process. The remaining steps vary slightly, depending on the passkey options you chose.

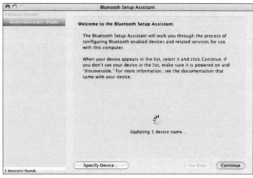

Figure 21-5: Selecting the device to which you want to connect

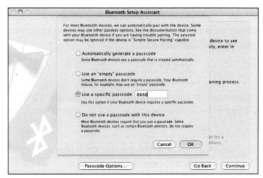

Figure 21-6: Checking the device's documentation for passkey options

Upgrading Your Mac

You've probably heard people scoff at the seemingly high price of new Macintosh computers. But Apple packs almost every new Macintosh with a lot of standard features that would be costly options on most Windows PCs. These features include built-in wireless networking, Bluetooth, IEEE-1394 FireWire, and enough RAM (random access memory) to ensure good computer performance. If you check the price of a Windows PC that contains all these features, you might find that the Macintosh is actually the better bargain.

Of course, no matter how full-featured your Mac is, you might want a little more storage space, screen real estate, or extra RAM to improve the performance and utility of your computer. This chapter shows you how to

➡ **Connect to a second monitor.** The second monitor may simply be another monitor to give you more on-screen Desktop space, or it may be a multimedia projector.

➡ **Add external storage space.** If you work with video or need lots of storage space, you can easily attach an external USB or FireWire hard drive to your computer. An external hard drive is especially useful as a backup location for Time Machine. (See Chapter 3 for more on using Time Machine.)

➡ **Upgrade your computer's memory.** The easiest way to improve the performance of your computer is to install more RAM. Upgrading the RAM in most Macs is easy, but adding RAM to the Mac mini does pose a bit of a challenge, which is why there's a separate task covering just that model.

Chapter 22

Get ready to . . .

Add External Storage

1. Purchase an external hard drive that's compatible with the Macintosh operating system.

2. Connect the external drive to your computer's FireWire or USB port, as appropriate.

> USB hard drives are more common, but FireWire (IEEE-1394) hard drives usually offer better performance. If you plan to use the external drive for video editing, choose a FireWire drive.

3. If the drive is formatted using the FAT32 file system (check the drive's documentation), but you don't plan to use the drive with any Windows PCs, open your Mac's Applications folder and then open the Utilities folder. Double-click the Disk Utility icon, select the external hard drive in the list of drives, and click Erase. Choose Mac OS Extended (Journaled) from the Format pop-up menu, as shown in Figure 22-1, and click the Erase button in the lower-right corner. Follow the instructions on-screen to erase and reformat the hard drive.

> Formatting erases all data on the drive. Reformatting the drive using the Mac OS Extended file system makes the drive perform more efficiently in OS X, but after you do this, you can't connect the drive directly to a Windows PC. Stick with the FAT32 file system if you plan to routinely switch the drive back and forth between your Mac and a Windows PC.

4. When formatting is complete, the drive's icon appears on your Desktop, as shown in Figure 22-2. Double-click the icon to browse the drive.

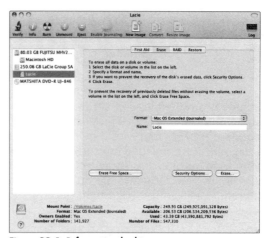

Figure 22-1: Reformatting the drive

Figure 22-2: An external drive's icon on the Desktop

> Before you disconnect an external hard drive from your Mac, drag the drive's icon to the Trash to properly unmount the drive from your computer.

Install More RAM

1. Shut down your computer, unplug it, and remove the battery (if applicable).

2. Purchase the correct type of RAM for your computer.

 The owner's manual for your Mac should tell you the exact format, capacity, and type of RAM that should be used in your computer. Only use RAM that's positively identified as being compatible with your specific Mac.

3. Locate the RAM slot on your computer:

   - **Intel-based laptops:** Remove the access panel and L-bracket inside the battery compartment.

   - **iMacs:** Open the RAM access panel on the back of the chassis.

   - **Mac Pros:** Remove the side cover for the computer case and locate the RAM slots on the motherboard.

4. Release the RAM module retention clips on the old RAM, as shown in Figure 22-3. Pivot the RAM module up and remove it from the slot.

5. Carefully insert the new RAM module, as shown in Figure 22-4, making sure that the connector pins and plastic guides line up perfectly.

6. Secure the retention clips and reassemble your computer.

Figure 22-3: A RAM slot under the keyboard

Figure 22-4: Seating the RAM and securing the retention clips

Upgrading RAM in a Mac mini

1. Shut down your Mac mini and unplug it from wall power.

    If your Mac mini is still covered by warranty, you should have the RAM upgraded by a professional. Opening the Mac mini is a complex operation, and if you damage anything, your warranty will be void.

2. Set the Mac mini upside-down on a clean work surface, and use a flat screwdriver or putty knife to carefully pry the white plastic bottom of the case away from the metal case surround, as shown in Figure 22-5. Work your way around the case, prying slowly and patiently.

3. When the base is loosened from the surround, turn the Mac mini over and lift off the case cover to expose the computer.

4. Disconnect the two-pin cable connector, as shown in Figure 22-6.

5. Remove a screw at each corner of the bracket that holds the DVD drive and hard drive. In Figure 22-6, a screwdriver is on one of the screws. Put the screws in a safe place so you don't lose them.

    One of the four screws is longer than the others. Make yourself a diagram of the computer and make notes to help you remember where the longer screw belongs.

Figure 22-5: Carefully prying the plastic base out

Figure 22-6: Unplugging the connector

6. Gently take off the AirPort antenna, as shown in Figure 22-7. Set the AirPort antenna out of the way but leave it attached.

 Be careful not to unplug the AirPort antenna wire from the motherboard. It's difficult to re-attach.

7. Carefully rotate the DVD and hard drive assembly up and set it down out of the way, as shown in Figure 22-8.

 It isn't necessary to disconnect the ribbon cable attaching the DVD and hard drive assembly to the motherboard, but take care not to put any strain on the ribbon cable.

8. Open the RAM module retention clips, as shown in Figure 22-8, and lift the old modules out of the computer. Handle the RAM modules only by the edges.

 Intel-based Mac minis use laptop-style 200-pin DDR2 PC5300 SO-DIMMs. For best performance in Intel-based Mac minis, use either a single RAM module or two matching modules of the same size and speed.

9. Insert your new RAM modules into the RAM slots. Make sure the modules are fully seated in the slots; press them down until the retention clips can be snapped back in place.

10. Replace the DVD and hard drive assembly and secure the four screws in the correct holes.

11. Reconnect the two-pin connector shown earlier in Figure 22-6 and put the AirPort antenna back in place.

12. Inspect the computer to ensure that everything else is still connected properly and then snap the cover back in place.

Figure 22-7: Removing the AirPort antenna

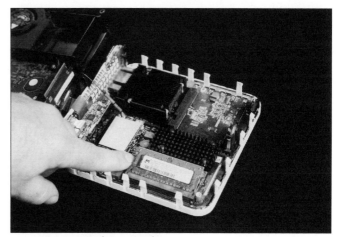

Figure 22-8: Opening the retention clips

Connect to a Second Monitor

1. Connect the appropriate display adapter to your computer, if necessary, and connect all displays to the computer. Make sure each display is powered on.

     Some Macs come with VGA adapters for installing a second monitor. These adapters connect to your Mac's DVI, Mini-DVI, or Mini Display Port (depending on your Mac's model). You can purchase display adapters as accessories, just make sure you buy one that is compatible with your specific Mac.

2. Open System Preferences and then click the Displays icon.

3. If a separate Preferences pane for each display doesn't appear, as shown in Figure 22-9, click Detect Displays.

4. Choose a resolution for each display in the Resolutions menu. Check the display's documentation for a recommended setting.

     Click the Menu button on your monitor and see whether the monitor's built-in menu provides resolution and refresh rate recommendations.

5. Choose a frequency in the Refresh Rate pop-up menu.

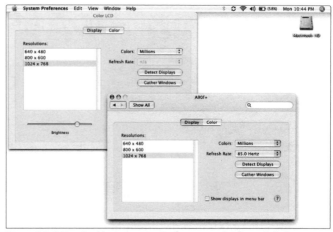

Figure 22-9: You should see a separate Preferences window for each display

Installing and Using Windows Programs

*N*ot so long ago, writing about Microsoft Windows in a book about Macs would've been like school on Saturday: no class. But OS X now includes a powerful feature called *Boot Camp*, which allows you to install and run Microsoft Windows on any Macintosh computer that has an Intel processor chip.

"Why would I want to install Windows on a perfectly good Mac?" might be your first question. In most cases, installing Windows will be a matter of *need* rather than *want*. Many software companies still develop products only for Windows, and you may need to run some of those programs for your work or personal needs. To install Windows on your Mac, you need

➡ **A Macintosh computer running OS 10.5 Leopard or better, and an Intel processor chip.**

➡ **A bare minimum of 10GB of free hard drive space for the Windows installation.** More space may be needed (I recommend at least 20GB), depending on the requirements of the Windows programs that you want to install.

➡ **A Microsoft Windows installation disc.** It must be a single disc full version (upgrade discs won't work) of 32-bit Windows XP (with SP2) or Windows Vista. As of this writing, 64-bit versions of Windows aren't supported by Boot Camp.

This chapter shows you how to install and run Windows on your Mac. Remember, even though you'll be running Windows on stable Macintosh hardware, the Windows installation will still be susceptible to Windows viruses and bugs.

Get ready to . . .

Install Windows

1. Open the Applications folder and then open the Utilities subfolder. Double-click the Boot Camp Assistant icon to begin running Boot Camp.

2. Click Continue to get to the Create a Partition For Windows screen, as shown in Figure 23-1; click and drag the slider left or right to change the size of the Windows partition.

3. Click the Partition button to start partitioning the hard drive.

4. When partitioning is complete, insert your Windows installation disc and click the Start Installation button.

5. Follow the instructions on-screen to install Windows.

    When you're asked to choose a partition, select the C: drive. The C: drive should be the same size as the Windows partition you create in Step 2. The C: drive should already be formatted with the FAT32 file system, so select the Leave the Current File System Intact option when you're asked whether you want to reformat the partition.

    If you have a problem during Windows installation and your Mac won't reboot, turn off the computer, hold down the mouse button, and turn on the power. The Windows installation disc ejects. Insert your Mac OS X installation disc, turn off the computer, and then turn the power back on while holding down the C key. The computer reboots using the OS X installation disc. Use the Boot Camp Assistant to delete the Windows partition and start over.

6. When Windows setup is successful, insert your Macintosh OS X Snow Leopard Installation disc and follow the instructions on-screen to install the hardware drivers, as shown in Figure 23-2.

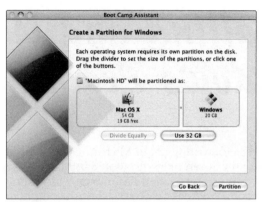

Figure 23-1: The Create a Partition for Windows screen

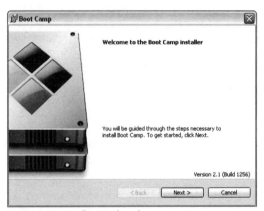

Figure 23-2: Installing Windows drivers

Configure AirPort in Windows

1. Boot up the computer in Windows and then choose Start⇨Control Panel.

2. If you see a list of categories, click the Network and Internet Connections category. Open the Wireless Network Setup Wizard icon.

3. When the wizard begins, click Next.

4. Select the Set Up a Wireless Network option and click Next.

5. Enter the Service Set Identifier (SSID) for your network, as shown in Figure 23-3. If you manually assigned a network key, select the Manually Assign a Network Key option. If your network uses WPA encryption, select the Use WPA check box at the bottom of the wizard.

6. Click Next, enter the network key, and click Next again.

7. On the screen that asks how you want to set up the rest of your network, select the Set Up a Network Manually option and click Next. Click Finish to close the wizard.

8. To join a wireless network or manage wireless connections, right-click the wireless connection icon in the Windows *system tray* (the area in the lower-right corner of the screen next to the clock), as shown in Figure 23-4, and choose View Available Wireless Networks.

9. Use the Wireless Network Connection window, as shown in Figure 23-4, to join or disconnect from wireless networks.

Figure 23-3: The Wireless Network Setup Wizard

Figure 23-4: Managing wireless networks in Windows

Adjust Display Settings in Windows

1. Boot up the computer in Windows and then choose Start⇨Control Panel.

2. If you see a list of categories, click the Appearance and Themes category and then open the Display icon.

3. In the Display Properties control panel, click the Settings tab to bring it to the front, as shown in Figure 23-5.

4. Adjust the Screen Resolution slider to change the screen resolution to fit your needs. Then click Apply.

    When you click Apply, a dialog appears, asking whether you want to keep the new settings. Click Yes if you do. If the resolution you choose isn't supported by your Mac's display adapter or monitor and the screen becomes unviewable, simply wait 15 seconds for the display to revert automatically to the previous setting.

5. If the display flickers undesirably, click the Advanced button.

6. In the dialog that appears, click the Monitor tab to bring it to the front, as shown in Figure 23-6.

7. Choose a higher setting in the Screen Refresh Rate menu and click Apply.

    Again, click Yes to accept the new setting or wait for the display to revert. A refresh rate of 85 Hertz or better reduces eye strain.

8. Click OK to close the dialogs when you're done.

    Use the Themes, Desktop, and Appearance tabs of the Display Properties dialog to change the cosmetic appearance of Windows.

Figure 23-5: The Settings tab of the Display Properties dialog

Figure 23-6: Choosing a higher refresh rate to reduce screen flicker

Change the Startup Disk in Windows

1. Boot up the computer in Windows and then choose
    Start➪Control Panel.

2. If you see a list of categories, click the Performance and
    Maintenance category. Double-click the Boot Camp icon.

3. In the resulting Boot Camp Control Panel, select the
    operating system you want to use as the default startup
    disk, as shown in Figure 23-7. If you select Macintosh
    HD, the computer starts in OS X by default.

 If you want to restart the computer in OS X immediately, make sure
that all other applications are closed and click the Restart button.

Change the Startup Disk in OS X

1. Boot up the computer in OS X and then open System
    Preferences.

2. Click the Startup Disk icon.

3. In the resulting Startup Disk preferences pane, select the
    operating system you want to use as the default startup
    disk, as shown in Figure 23-8. If you choose Mac OS X,
    the computer starts in OS X by default.

 If you want to restart the computer in Windows immediately, quit
all other applications and click the Restart button on the Startup
Disk pane.

Figure 23-7: The Boot Camp Control Panel

Figure 23-8: The Startup Disk preferences pane

Reboot the Computer

1. Save any open documents and close all applications.

2. Restart the computer by following these steps:

   - **OS X:** Choose Apple⇨Restart.

   - **Windows:** Choose Start⇨Turn Off Computer and then click Restart.

3. When the screen becomes black during the restart process, hold down the Option key (Alt key on Windows keyboards) and continue holding it until you see a screen like the one shown in Figure 23-9.

4. Use the arrow keys to select the desired operating system and then press Enter.

Eject a Disc in Windows

1. If your Mac doesn't have an eject button for the CD/DVD drive, choose Start⇨My Computer.

2. Right-click the icon for the CD/DVD drive and choose Eject from the menu that appears, as shown in Figure 23-10.

    Instead of right-clicking, you can also left-click the CD/DVD drive once to select it and then click Eject This Disk under the System Tasks heading in the upper-left corner of the My Computer window.

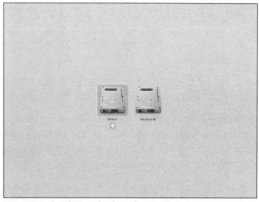

Figure 23-9: Selecting the desired operating system

Figure 23-10: Ejecting a disc

Index

David Matthews was born in London in 1967. His first book, *Looking for a Fight*, was shortlisted for the William Sports Book of the Year Award. He has written for several publications, including *GQ*, *Esquire* and *Observer*, and has worked as a broadcast journalist for the BBC and Channel Four. He also lectures in journalism at the University of Westminster. He lives in London.

Praise for *Man Buys Dog*:

'A fine definition of the British psyche, as well as a most entertaining read' *Sunday Times*

'A talented writer with a jaunty turn of phrase' *Sunday Telegraph*

'Matthews is a richly descriptive writer . . . [He is] superb at capturing the visceral thrill of seeing your own money racing round a track in pursuit of an artificial hare' *Time Out*

'A riveting read from beginning to end' *Scotland on Sunday*

'An intricately woven and marvellously modern investigation . . . [Matthews] has a pen that is often piercing in its sharpness' *Racing Post*

Also by David Matthews

Looking for a Fight

MAN BUYS DOG

A Loser's Guide to the World of Greyhound Racing

David Matthews

headline

First published in 2005
by HEADLINE BOOK PUBLISHING

First published in paperback in 2006
by HEADLINE BOOK PUBLISHING

1

0 7553 1172 8 (ISBN-10)
978 0 7553 1172 9 (ISBN-13)

Typeset in Cochin by Avon DataSet Ltd,
Bidford-on-Avon, Warwickshire

Printed and bound in Great Britain by
Clays Ltd, St Ives plc

Headline's policy is to use papers that are natural, renewable and
recyclable products and made from wood grown in sustainable forests.
The logging and manufacturing processes are expected to conform
to the environmental regulations of the country of origin.

HEADLINE BOOK PUBLISHING
A division of Hodder Headline
338 Euston Road
London NW1 3BH

www.headline.co.uk
www.hodderheadline.com

For Tunis Matthews and Bunmi Daramola

Acknowledgements

I would like to thank the following people for their help, support, encouragement and/or guest appearances: Juliana Foster, David Wilson, Helena Towers, Jane Butcher, Ian Marshall, and the Headline Syndicate; Julian Alexander and LAW; Linda Jones and everyone at Imperial Kennels; Corrina Faith; John Watt and Ray Jones; Big Al; Tamara Adair and Brian Coleman; Ann Aslett, Tracy Cooper and the staff at Walthamstow Stadium; Vince, Paul and John; Ginger and Romford Phil; Luca, Mum, Dr Paul, Wayne Jordash and Owen Clegg; Anna Lovegrove and Johanna Beumer deserve special praise for their commitment to the welfare of retired greyhounds; maximum respect is due to Danielle for putting up with me and my idiosyncratic behaviour.

And finally, to Kevin: thanks for the ride. It's been emotional.

chapter 1

I cracked open beer number four: just another day at the office. The traps flew open, and six scrawny-looking mutts sprang to life like a canine jack-in-the-box. The one dog, the four dog, the three, the five . . . Bleary-eyed I watched them scamper round the first bend through a hailstorm of sand in pursuit of a polyester bunny. Silly fuckers. They'd never catch that Day-Glo hare in a million years. Still, the dogs were not the only ones chasing a dream that night.

Ten feet away from me, lurking in the shadows, a man with pork pie fingers riffled through a thick wad of dirty cash. I rubbed my eyes, looked again and the dogs had passed the post, the crowd roaring its time-honoured approval like so many Romans. But empty vessels make the most noise. For every vocal, lucky winner, there are ten fated, muted losers. I wondered, in that moment of glory, how many fortunes had been won and lost; how many hopes and dreams had been flittered away in the night air; how many children would go without new shoes or pocket money thanks to a father's whim and £300 on a thing with four legs, two balls and no chance.

Soon enough I was introduced to Lennie Knell, a shifty trainer with a story to sell, albeit unintentionally. He seemed eager to please, eager for sleaze: a small-time cheat with a big mouth. 'You can't ever mention that however,' he muttered. Mention what exactly? 'I mean, obviously what I'm doing is illegal.' I was confused. I took a gulp of Red Stripe and crushed the can cos I could, cos I can. Ah . . . lager, lager, lager . . .

Suddenly, an equally indiscreet and well-fed character added with a cheeky grin, 'It's all a fix. It's all a twist.'

Hustlers hustle and rustlers rustle and so the world turns. Greyhound racing, by anyone's stretch, is a racket: man's best friend takes on man's second worst enemy,[1] i.e. greed, generating an electrifying £1.6 billion in revenue every year. Somebody somewhere is getting fat. Why, I wouldn't mind a lickle piece of that action myself. But if I was looking for an easy touch I had another think coming. It would not take long for me to find out that the only dead cert in greyhound racing is the hare. Everything else is a lottery. Or, as Winston Churchill had put it, 'animated roulette'.

Blindfolded by drink, tired and groggy, I was whisked away from the track on another diversion. I saw the shovels go to work. Bones were uncovered. A skull peered at me in the mist. Sweet Jesus, I'd been led to a mass grave. These old dogs, whose twisted remains lay rotting in the earth, had learnt a new trick all right: win or die. But how and where did this sort of thing go on? Where does a man kill a dog with a bullet to the back of the head: a farm, a clearing in the woods, the allotments up the road from Albert Square? Whatever. Location is immaterial at this point. I'd seen enough to be sucked in. Like an eighteenth-century duellist, I demanded satisfaction. I wanted more information, more dirt, more secrets and lies to satiate my lurid curiosity. I didn't have long to wait.

I could feel myself sinking. *Concentrate, concentrate*. I heard a voice say, with more than a touch of English relish, '*Tonight*, we chase down the criminals, *at the dogs*.'

Fade to black.

I came round, slowly. On the floor was half a can of beer. In my lap was a half-eaten pizza. In my mind was a half-baked idea.

---

[1] Fear is arguably man's greatest enemy but greed runs a pretty close second.

It was the usual tedious, suicidal winter night. December 2001. Slumped on a sofa in front of a portable TV in a dingy little flat in Paddington, west London, I had watched most of *Kenyon Confronts* – a BBC exposé on corruption in the world of greyhound racing – before drifting into the Witching Hour and then a 1a.m. resurrection. I call these moments of alcoholic, mindless inspiration 'research'. This is how I get all my best ideas, by eating pizza, getting trashed and crashing out in front of the telly.

From what I'd seen, or from what I thought I'd seen in the opening sixty seconds of the programme, the 'voice' a.k.a. eponymous hero Paul Kenyon, had managed to trip the light fandango through every conceivable stereotype and cliché of greyhound racing imaginable. Cheeky chappies, doping, snuffing out lame dogs, race fixing, you name it, the boy Kenyon had it all there bar the pencil line moustaches, camel hair coats and Arthur Daley.

But if you're born and raised in a place like the East End, which I was, and you'd had the odd, shall we say, 'run in with the authorities', which I had, then you take it for granted that a little bit of skulduggery is all part of life's rich tapestry. A bit of hooky gear here, a 'favour' there ... As Grandmaster Flash and the Furious Five broke it down on their seminal 1981 hip-hop anthem, *The Message*, '. . . you gotta have a con in this land of milk and honey'.

For instance, we all know that greyhound racing is bent, right? Like the man said, 'It's all a fix. It's all a twist,' is it not? How many times have you heard the one about a dog being fed a Mars bar or a bowl of porridge before a race to slow it down, or heard that greyhounds have mustard shoved up their choccy lockers to make them, literally, hot to trot? Then there are the puppy-dog tales of pumping a greyhound with gallons of water in order to bloat it to a standstill or 'ringing' – switching a slow dog for a fast one by disguising it with a false beard and moustache so that no one would recognise the poor bugger. Or how about putting a dog on roller skates with a nitrous oxide injection unit tied to its back so it could R-O-C-K-E-T its way to the finish line.

On a more serious note, in the summer of 2001 the Irish Greyhound Board, the Bord na gCon, had come down hard on doping in the sport by banning the use of Viagra. It had transpired that a number of unscrupulous trainers were using the love drug on their animals as a performance enhancer. Whether Viagra works on the track or not is debatable but I'm sure one or two dogs (and possibly trainers) have got more than they'd bargained for back at the kennels.

So there I am in my west London pad; still half-cut, still strung out on the sofa like a row of broken beads. I watched the tail end of Kenyon's investigation with heightened curiosity: he nailed Lennie Knell and his buddy Colin West offering to fix a race by over-feeding a dog at Catford track in south London; he also captured West on film boasting that the dynamic duo had once made eleven grand from a bent race. What a win-double! I had to take my baseball cap off to Kenyon for exposing these halfwits. Knell, West and their ilk had got their karma for being greedy little shits, for trying to cheat the system rather than beat the system.

An exposé by its very nature doesn't leave much room for balanced reportage. But to be fair to the thousands of honest Johns involved in greyhound racing, Kenyon had taken a cynical, one-sided angle, casting an even darker cloud over a much-maligned sport. I know all too well how easy it is to pull off a 'sting' or make a bad story fit a good headline. Muck-raking, stereotypes, clichés, demagoguery . . . this is my stock-in-trade. Heaven knows, as a journalist, I have fingered enough people in my time in pursuit of 'the truth'. Whatever that is.

As the old Fleet Street maxim goes, 'never let the truth get in the way of a good story'. I had a hunch there were many truths about the dogs that do not involve confectionery, cereals or amphetamines. Despite its bad press, greyhound racing is still Britain's second most popular spectator sport (football is number one) in terms of attendance. On any given day or night of the week, practically 365 days a year, there is dog racing at most of the 34 tracks licensed by the National Greyhound Racing Club (NGRC) – the sport's governing body – totalling around 68,000 races.

Either there are trailer loads of very gullible people out there, or these characters know something that the likes of Kenyon and I don't. Could there be another story to tell, another truth to reveal? Shock, gasp, horror: could it be that greyhound racing is not so bad after all? I suspected the dogs were a victim of the 'chav' witch-hunts of the early twentieth century, the marginalisation of the white-bread working classes and their associated 'end of the pier show' lifestyle. But there was only one way to find out for sure: it was time to put on the greasy trilby, the dirty raincoat and the cynical charm, and start sniffing around my local dog track.

chapter 2

After the festive season had crackerjacked its way out of sight and out of mind I trundled off to Wimbledon Stadium in south-west London to experience a night at the dogs. I badgered my woman Danielle and our friend Wayne into coming along with me. Danielle, who I affectionately nicknamed 'Margot' because of her penchant for the good life, knows more about foxhounds than greyhounds. That's not to say she's a toff. It's just that she was brought up with gymkhana, ponies and the thrill of the chase while I was dragged up with Jim Beam, Ford Escorts and the thrill of joyriding.

As for Wayne, he's a barrister and a 'brother' who, like me, had made his way 'across the tracks' in search of a career that didn't involve flesh-coloured pantyhose, a sawn-off shotgun and a getaway driver called Camp Freddy. Wayne is a cosmopolitan kind of guy and he leads a far from sheltered life; but it's fair to say that any relationship he was likely to have with the world of dog racing would be a vicarious one: i.e. via a character like me.

Anyway, as impromptu acid tests go, if a couple of left-leaning lounge lizards like Margot and Wayne could handle the simple pleasures of Wimbledon Stadium then maybe there was truth in the rumour that the trendy classes were now going to the dogs in their droves.

'Is this it?' said Margot frowning as the stadium came into view.

'I guess so,' I said.

Wayne looked at the pair of us and laughed. The Lady and the Tramp. I turned the corner into Plough Lane, passing a smattering of racegoers, then swerved Margot's Polo into a dimly lit car park. The exterior of Wimbledon Stadium is an unimpressive mix of crumbling brickwork and corrugated iron. It has the air of a makeshift penal colony. As we drove in, I noticed a sign dangling precariously on the wire perimeter fence advertising a car boot sale the following weekend. Class.

Apart from the dogs and boot sales, Wimbledon Stadium also doubles as a stock car and speedway venue. However, following the closure of White City Stadium in 1984 it has become synonymous with the English Greyhound Derby, the premier event in the dog-racing calendar. Sponsored by high-street bookie William Hill, the race runs every June and is now worth a cool £75,000 in prize money to the winner. The Derby is what 'dog people' dream of – be it breeding, owning or training a winner. But, on this particular night, the top prize was no more than 160 quid. Nevertheless, it was the start of the New Year and the dog-racing public, like the rest of us, was still nursing a headache after the excesses of the holiday season.

The three of us ambled up to the main entrance. A young couple were having a tiff in the car park. From the sounds of it, Boyfriend had spunked all his dough at the track already, so Girlfriend would have to settle for a video and chips, instead of The Ministry and a curry. Aw, young love . . .

'C'mon. It's not that bad,' I said, trying to humour Margot as we sashayed through the turnstiles. I gave her arse a squeeze.

'Can we get food in here?' asked Wayne.

'I'm sure you can,' I replied. 'Whether it's edible or not, I don't know.'

For a moment I felt like a mean old man, forcing his teenage children to get involved in some terminally boring adult experience while they whined, 'Do we have to?' I often took it for granted that despite my lofty pretensions as a hack writer and pseudo-academic, I inhabited for the most part an everyday world that many of my chattering friends were blissfully unengaged with: football, boxing, car boot sales, beanos, drug smugglers, ragamuffins, jerk chicken, pie and bloody mash and now, the dogs. If the truth be known, yeah I love slumming it, if only to reaffirm the fact that I still know how to cross the tracks every once in a while, and be comfortable with the view on either side.

Which was precisely why, theoretically, greyhound racing was something I could get into. Born in Hackney and raised in a mixture of E-numbered postal codes, I'm sociologically hardwired for such activities, much in the same way that I'm genetically hardwired for flat feet, baldness and a beer gut. But could the bourgeoisie 'get' into the dogs in the way that they had eventually 'got' football? As the comedian Frank Skinner once opined, 'Football's not the same since women and the middle classes got involved.' What Skinner meant was, to accommodate the fairer sex and the chattering classes, straight, predominantly white, working-class men have had to modify their behaviour at football matches to such an extent that they are now practically indistinguishable from Homo sapiens. Apart from football grounds, pubs and of course dog tracks, the British working class was running out of places to socialise en masse in, er, stereotypical working-class fashion. Political correctness had effectively banned smoking, boozing, belching, farting, swearing, fucking and fighting from public life. The personal freedoms of the common man were under threat. The only sanctuary regular Joes had these days was on the toilet seat at home with a jazz mag and a roll of Kleenex for company.

The way that I look at it, women and the middle classes have an appreciation for the finer things in life that blue-collar guys simply do not have. Fish knives, dental floss, keeping your elbows off the dinner table, yoga, getting in touch with your feelings, calling a napkin a napkin not a serviette, paying taxes ... this kind of stuff just isn't part of a working-class guy's remit. Now consider hunting knives, gold teeth, sticking your elbows in an opposing footballer's face, sex, getting in touch with your drinking buddies, calling a spade a spade not a bloody garden implement, paying your gambling debts . . . that's more like it.

For people like Margot and Wayne the dogs are . . . well, they were a couple of greyhound virgins, too sophisticated for such a Runyonesque pastime. But wait. What am I talking about? When I listen to myself waxing lyrical like this about class and race and blah blah blah I can hear distant voices echoing from the Dick Van Dyke School of Cockney. As a social chameleon I have become obsessed with class and race and blah blah blah. It tempers my view of everything I do and everyone I meet. I sound like a champagne socialist who's had one too many. What the fuck do I know about the sociology of greyhound racing? Before Wimbledon, I hadn't been to a dog track in nearly twenty years.

My initiation into greyhound racing came after I had started my first job, as an apprentice electrician. I'd left school with the bare minimum of qualifications, intent on earning a living and escaping the drudgery of a parochial existence. An awkward and gangly youth, apathetic yet highly excitable, I wasn't really interested in much of anything except my own teenage angst, scrapping, loafing around and getting laid, or more to the point, losing my virginity.

I worked with an old boy who (for the sake of a libel writ), I'll refer to as 'Monty Wright'. Monty was a compulsive gambler and a sociopathic liar. He was also very fat and very lazy. On Thursday afternoons, we would skive off work and head for Hackney Wick dog track, leaving broken central-heating systems, busted lights and dissatisfied tenants in our wake.

Monty was born and raised somewhere in Hackney but he'd done all right for himself so like anyone with half a brain, he moved out to the 'burbs in readiness for retirement. 'Fuck the council,' he used to say, trying to justify the paltry effort he put in for the maintenance department. 'What have they ever done for us, eh?' I could've told him that they'd given us a job and a steady income for starters but I didn't want to rain on his parade.

As an apprentice, I did as I was told, most of the time. I was at Monty's mercy. As much as I hated work, I wasn't into goofing off at a dog track. I wanted to learn how to be a sparks, make a few quid, do a few 'privates' now and again, buy a little gaff somewhere on the outer reaches of Zone 3, maybe shack up with some sister called Beverly or Sandra. Then I could goof off where I wanted to, like down the snooker hall on Leytonstone High Road or the Thai massage parlour in nearby Stratford.

Like most teenagers, I was narcissistic and vain. Going to the dogs was naff, especially at a dump like Hackney Wick Stadium. Once upon a time, it had been a prosperous dog track and speedway venue but now it was nothing more than a concrete wreck on the edge of Hackney Marshes. Its dog days had ended unceremoniously in 1994. Nowadays, for its sins, it was best known as a sprawling Sunday car boot sale, ringed by a phalanx of shifty pikeys who lived in unbelievably ostentatious caravans while dressed in tacky rags that were greasier than a mechanic's jockstrap.

Anyway, as Monty's protégé, where he went I went, which meant frequent trips to Hackney Wick Stadium. More often than not, I would sit in the smoky atmosphere of the main grandstand supping on half a lager and reading the *Daily Mirror* while Monty, as we like to say in the East End, 'did his bollocks' on the dogs. 'Fucking stupid mutt,' he would say, screwing up his fat face, before sticking it faithfully back into the race card in search of yet another loser. Not being a gambler, I'd snigger at his misfortune and amuse myself with the goings-on: loudmouthed bookies; irate losers; tic-tac men with white gloves and funny little hats, waving their semaphoric arms around like air traffic controllers on crack; old hags trying to double up on their pension money; care in the community cases having minor psychiatric episodes . . .

At the time, Hackney was reputedly the poorest borough in Britain, so there was never any shortage of toe-rags, skivers and dole bludgers hanging around the track. Where, and more importantly how, these people found the money to gamble I will never know. Did they not have jobs to go to, mouths to feed, and addictions to be treated?

Most of the punters at the track were small fry, Monty included. He was an habitual gambler but too stingy, or perhaps too smart, to wager meaningful amounts. There were other punters, however, particularly the hardcore professional gamblers, who bet with *real* financial conviction. They were all called Bill or Terry or George – the land of middle-aged likely lads who drove black cabs, owned pubs or 'businesses' that only handled cash and knew someone who knew someone who used to know the Kray twins. They would stroll up to the bookies, chests puffed out, shoulders back, barking shit like, 'A bottle on trap two,' or 'I'll have a monkey on the five dog.' A monkey: five hundred smackers! On a DOG?

The majority of these high rollers were thick as thieves with the bookies, so they never handed over their dough when they placed a bet. The bookie *trusted* the bet. Likewise, these punters did not need a ticket as proof of purchase, as the mugs did. Business was done on trust. Five hundred pounds *trusted* on a dog. In those days, back in the early eighties, £500 was a month's wages to me; or alternatively, twenty visits to that Thai massage parlour in Stratford . . .

Against this backdrop, I never saw the sense in greyhound racing. Put simply, like most forms of gambling, I considered it a waste of time and money. As a yoof I had played a little three-card brag or pool with my mates for shekels, but for the most part I thought gambling on the dogs was bullshit. The utter sense-lessness of it all seemed compounded by the fact that week in week out grown men and women wagered millions of pounds on an animal whose only talent was that it could outrun a Reliant Robin. Oh, and lick its own gonads: though unfortunately for the *Daily Sport*, not at the same time.

Two decades on and inside Wimbledon Stadium Margot and Wayne were as underwhelmed as I had once been. The track was too common for their liking. I tried to explain to them that its simplicity was part of the charm, the Zen if you like, of greyhound racing, but my argument was a waste of time. After walking through a carpeted façade, which offered a brief taste of style and modernity, we followed the signs to the bar through a grey, concreted anteroom. The interior of the bar was reminiscent of a bingo hall or a working men's club: hideous fluorescent lighting, a mishmash of primary colours splattered on the floor and the walls, enough plastic fittings to give Barbie and Ken hives, all scented with the stench of tobacco smoke and booze and dead things frying.

The poor weather had forced all but the headstrong into the bars and dining areas of the track. Corporate types and those going for the big night out headed for the relative glamour of the 'Broadway' and 'Star' restaurants or an executive box. We opted for the common or garden bar at the foot of the main grandstand. It was busy inside. Most of the patrons were men and white, many of them old enough to have lived through a couple of world wars. I ordered up two gin and tonics for Margot and Wayne, and a pint of Guinness for myself. A number of TV screens flickered with betting information on the Tote: forecasts and trifectas, theoretical wins, elusive promises of improbable prizes.

The next race was at least ten minutes away. Several overweight men and pallid old codgers were looking at replays of the previous race on a large screen, offering each other animated 'expert' analysis. I noticed Margot and Wayne scanning the bar, the punters and the décor, trying to reconcile their presence with this chavvy new environment. I could tell they were both wondering why they had agreed to go to the dogs with me. We found a table smeared with fag ends, half-eaten chips and empty plastic beer glasses and sat down.

Wayne grinned impishly, eyeing the posters of greasy burgers and meat by-product hotdogs at the takeaway concession. I spread out, pretending to study the form in the race card. Why does junk food smell so appetising? *I could murder one of those airbrushed quarter-*

pounders with chips. Well, the least I could do was have a nibble, in solidarity with Wayne of course.

So I bought a burger with chips. 'That looks *disgusting*,' said Margot, as I bit into the grease, meat, processed cheese and cardboard bun. It was *extremely* disgusting. Margot was right: women always are. My burger was so rare I thought it was going to eat *me*.

'I'm going outside to take in the atmosphere,' I said, picking my teeth, leaving Margot and Wayne at the bar.

On the track, several hurdles were wheeled out for the next race. The hurdles looked like giant wallpaper brushes turned up on end; they struck me as more of a novelty than a genuine obstacle. In front of the main grandstand was a narrow terrace with a series of steps that offered a decent view of the action. This was occupied by a number of coughing and spluttering old men, so I ventured over to the other end of the main grandstand where there was a small betting ring flanked by half a dozen or so bookmakers. It was just like I remembered Hackney Wick Stadium: suited and booted bookies in big dark overcoats with slicked-back hair and tangerine perma-tans, each with their own coterie of tic-tac men, clerks and tipsters helping to oil the machinery of bookmaking.

'I'll take 2–1 the favourite,' hollered one of the bookies in the far corner of the betting ring. 'TOODA-ONE!' The bookie's name was Tony Morris, the grandee of Wimbledon Stadium I learnt later. Tony M was real old school, a little guy with a big nose and an even bigger wallet. He was perched high on a stepladder or a stand of some sort, looking down at the throng of punters. He wore immaculately polished loafers, a well-cut single-breasted navy suit – bespoke I would say, none of that ready-to-wear muck – and a pair of gold-rimmed glasses.

'FIVA-TOODA-FIELD,' cried another bookie, this one with silver hair and a suit to match. The new market info sent the betting ring into a minor frenzy. Punters looking to back the favourite rushed from one side of the betting ring to the other to get the better price, pushing and barging each other like old girls at a jumble sale. While the punters waved their wads of cash at the bookie, he reeled off a series of numbers to his clerk sitting incognito in the background. Apart from the regulars, of course, when the bookie called the numbers, he handed out a ticket to each punter representing their bet: a simple yet effective system. Bingo for big boys. In sixty seconds these brightly coloured bits of card would be the difference between success and failure.

'Six dog: £175 for 50. Ticket 17,' cried the Silver Bookie. 'Two dog: £100 for 20. Number 18. Six dog: £120 for 40. Ticket 19. Six dog: £75 for 30. Number 20 . . .'

The bookie kept reeling off number after number as his clerk scribbled furiously, marking up each bet on a large ledger. Sweating, impatient, anxious men (for the betting ring is exclusively male, save for the most intrepid woman), continued to push and shove each other in order to place a bet. Prices moved constantly on each bookmaker's board, reflecting the intensity of the action in the betting ring. Suspending reality for a moment or two, here was a microcosmic futures market, a Stock Exchange for Joe Public.

No sooner had the punters gone crazy for the lengthened price on the favourite, than one competing bookie's flunky (who was keeping a beady eye on the proceedings) shouted, 'Johnny's gone a bottle on the bottom. You're out on your own.' With that, the bookie rubbed '5/2' off his board and marked up '2/1'.

And so the prices ebbed and flowed in the run up to 'the off' . . .

Added to their armoury of tic-tac, mobile phones and walkie-talkies, the bookies communicated with each other through a crude but unique nomenclature, which was utterly meaningless to the uninitiated, apart from the odd term that transcended the betting ring and made it into the cosmopolitan patois of modern Britain.

These gold-plated moneymen filled their leather satchels with a Noah's Ark of cash: 'monkeys', 'ponies', 'cockles' and 'bull's eyes'. In bookmaking parlance, words and phrases are an enigma and like any slanguage they act as a 'keep out' sign to those who aren't in the know. The bookies' lexicon is full of bent-out-of-shape, customised and redesigned words, which could be *converse* as much as conversed. 'Enin', for example, means nine (or alternatively 9–1) just as 'neves' stands for seven (or 7–1). There are expressions of etymological mystery like 'carpet' to express 3–1 (or 300 quid) or 'bottle' for 2–1 (or 200 quid).

There were now under thirty seconds to go before the next race. I had already missed half the card, but as I had no money I didn't intend to gamble anyway. Once again I looked at the race form, and once again, just as when I looked at the ever-changing Tote screens dotted around the track, the words 'arse', 'elbow' and 'don't know' sprang to mind. Form, statistics, the names and breeding dates of greyhounds meant nothing to me. I couldn't even pick a winner in a one-dog race.

I watched the kennel hands parade the dogs for the last time in front of the expectant crowd, and then load them into the traps, gently nudging them by their backsides into the tiny boxes, which were no bigger than the dogs themselves. No wonder they didn't hang around once the hare came calling. I was just thinking that the kennel hands probably earned less than the dogs did when Margot and Wayne appeared with another round of drinks.

'Aye, aye, Dave, what's the score?' said Wayne.

'I'd say bookies six, punters nil. Cheers.'

We headed through the betting ring for the stands to get a better view of the action. A wire mesh fence, some ten-feet high, ran along the perimeter of the track in front of the stands to stop the crowds from pelting the dogs with missiles. The lights around the stadium dimmed as though a 10,000-volt electric chair on Wimbledon's Death Row had been levered into action. A bell rang signalling the start of the race. A garbled voice over the PA announced, 'murmur murmur murmur, hare's approaching' and then *Pow!* six dogs exploded out of the traps, pounding their way down the home straight towards us, their paws drumming an allegro beat in the sand and gliding over the hurdles like they just weren't there.

The crowd followed the rapid progress of the dogs along the home straight with a Mexican wave of sound, the cheers climaxing then stalling as the tightly bunched mass of fawn, black, white and mottled coats, resplendent in their multicoloured satin jackets, hit the first bend at some 35mph. The two wide runners on the outside of the pack collided with each other leaving four dogs now with a clear run to the second bend some fifty metres away. They rounded the turn, galloping into the back straight, bounding effortlessly over the hurdles, then broke into Indian file as the lead dog, a big brindle machine, kicked on, racing to the third bend unopposed, leaving the field a tiring ragtag of also-rans.

The crowd roared again, urging on the lead dog, which took the fourth and final bend a good five lengths clear of its nearest rival. It flew over the last two hurdles and won comfortably. The winner, and the field, kept running until the kennel hands emerged from the other side of the track at the 'pick up' with the lure – a ragged cuddly toy used to compensate the dogs for not catching the elusive plastic hare. For just under thirty seconds of work I calculated that the winning dog had earned an hourly equivalent of £19,200, making it theoretically one of the highest paid breeds of athlete in professional sport.

Down in the betting ring the cabal of winners were having it large, back slapping, laughing, high on the rush of success. Meanwhile the losers, the silent majority, consoled themselves that they had nearly picked the winner, ripping up their tickets and throwing them into the air like confetti.

'Is that it?' asked Margot.

'Well, yeah,' I said. 'What were you expecting?'

'Well, it was over so quickly.'

'Yeah Dave, it was over so quickly,' said Wayne sarcastically. 'What you gonna do about it?'

The garbled voice returned to the PA announcing, 'uh, uh, wobble, wobble, rhubarb, rhubarb twenty-nine point wobble,

wobble seconds.' Strange. I could've sworn that I'd only had two pints. As the dogs were led off the track and through the entrance to the kennels under our enclosure, a small crowd gathered to congratulate the victor, not that he'd understand much, being a dog and all.

'Hey, let's have a butchers,' I said, beckoning Margot and Wayne. We went down to get a closer look at the winning animal, muscling our way past a group of small girls who were petting the panting, wistful creature. His name was Gift Trader. Not that this meant anything to most people. In horseracing, the gee-gees have names and personalities; in dog racing, greyhounds simply have numbers. Ordinary punters refer to dogs as 'the one dog, the two dog' and so on. For the average Joe, a greyhound is a commodity, a proposition, a living, breathing poker chip distinguishable only by the 1, 2, 3, 4, 5 and 6 of a red, blue, white, black, orange or monochrome jacket.

Up close and personal, Gift Trader did not seem as anorexic or yappy as I expected a greyhound to be; in fact he was poised, lean yet solid and muscular. Wide-eyed, frantic and muzzled when racing, they look psychotic, possessed, but as I stroked this dog's smooth Jaffa Cake coat and felt his tiny heart racing he was no more dangerous than any poodle. His tongue hung out of his head, dripping with saliva, as he caught his breath repeatedly. Even as the young girls mauled him, jockeying each other and giggling all the while, the dog remained impassive, majestic even.

'D'you wanna buy him? He's for sale you know.' I looked round and a nondescript middle-aged bloke was beaming at me.

'Really, what do you want for him?' I asked straightening up, not that I had money to burn on a greyhound.

'Ah, I'm only kidding,' said the man giving the dog a brisk rub. 'He's not for sale. I wouldn't sell him for the world.'

'Shame that. I was gonna make you an offer you couldn't refuse.'

'Ha. Beautiful dogs aren't they? I've got five of 'em you know. Got another one running here tomorrow.' The Dog Man leaned forward as though he had a great secret for sharing, but only with me. 'Her name's . . .' he whispered something like Tunbridge Cyclone or Maidstone Hurricane. ' 'Ave a few quid on her . . . she should win.'

'Cheers,' I said. 'Will do.'

'What was all that about?' asked Margot.

'I just got a hot tip from that bloke,' I said, hunching my back, giving it a touch of the Arthur Daley. 'I got connections here you know.' Margot looked at me sympathetically and laughed.

We went back into the stands, took in another race and stood there for a while shooting the breeze. A small tractor driven by a sullen man crawled round the track, smoothing the sand in readiness for the next race.

'I'm cold. Can we go now?' said Margot.

'What are you talking about?' I said. 'We've only just got here.'

'Don't look at me,' said Wayne, raising his arms in faux surrender.

Margot shrugged her shoulders and started walking towards the bar. 'Let's go back inside then.'

'Yeah, let's get another drink,' I said, throwing her the car keys. 'You can drive. I'm over the limit.'

I looked at Margot, gave her a cheesy grin and a gentle squeeze of her arse. We went back to the bar and I ordered another round of drinks. She looked bored.

Maybe the acid test had failed.

chapter 3

You get two things from a tip: small change and rubbish. Dog Boy said that Tunbridge Cyclone, Margate Tornado or whatever it was would win, but it didn't, did it? It came absolutely nowhere. Still, what did I expect? Relying on a tip from a stranger at a dog track was no smarter than Jack and that funny business with the beans. Which is why I did the right thing: I passed the information on to a buddy of mine and let him lose his shirt at the bookies instead.

Nevertheless, my descent into the wonderful world of greyhound racing had begun. Well, sort of. Perhaps it was inevitable that someone who has lived most of his life 'shooting from the hip', 'flying by the seat of his pants' and 'sailing close to the wind' would one day wind up as a human cliché by 'going to the dogs'.

It was actually a couple of months before the Wimbledon situation that my luck had really started to run dry. I had lined up in Sportspages, a pokey little bookstore off Shaftesbury Avenue with four other writers to contest the William Hill Sports Book of the Year Award, a.k.a. the 'Bookie Prize'. My entry, *Looking for a Fight* – the tale of how I'd transformed myself from a 15-and-a-half-stone slob into a 12-and-a-half-stone professional fighter – was drawn against a tome on sailing, the biography of a dead American horse, another book on boxing and the bookies' favourite, something about an Irish footballer nobody had ever heard of.

In the event, the dead horse won it: Laura Hillenbrand's *Seabiscuit: Three Men and a Racehorse* scooped the ten grand prize and all the bits and pieces that came with it. The book was later made into a movie that grossed over $100,000,000 within a couple of weeks of its release, which was of little consolation to me. For being pipped at the post by a necrobiotic nag I pocketed a grand in cash and a £750 complimentary bet from the sponsors. I didn't win the big one, or get a movie deal. But I wasn't bitter. Early retirement would just have to wait a while.

It didn't take me long to blow that grand, but the free bet voucher spent several weeks burning a hole in my pocket. Then the dog thing happened. I'm not sure how or why it happened. It just did. I know Paul Kenyon and that stupid bloody TV show had something to do with it; but the last time I saw *Only Fools and Horses* I didn't go out and buy a hundred and fifty remote control blow-up dolls, so I can't blame television for this one. Perhaps it was something I ate. Maybe it was delusions of grandeur or whispers in my mind. Who knows? Temporary insanity notwithstanding, for someone who is generally *compos mentis*, buying a greyhound was, er, an odd thing to do.

My previous 'hobby' of professional boxing had left me with a cauliflower ear, occasional dizzy spells, several pug-nosed enemies, and a libel suit from a well-known promoter. I was flat broke and fed up with being punched out for my art; fed up with all that struggling artist crap. There had to be an easier way out there to make a buck without actually doing any work. All I had left to my name was seven hundred and fifty smackers to wager on a dream – seven-fifty to parlay into a slot machine on legs. It seemed like *a good idea* at the time. Man buys dog. Man races dog. Man makes money for old rope. Man, I had taken too many punches to the head.

At the bottom end of greyhound racing, i.e. my end, I found out that I could buy a young unproven puppy for a monkey or a race-ready older one for around a grand. Kennel and training fees were about a fiver a day plus VAT, which could be covered in part by prize money. For a fraction of what a racehorse cost, I could get a dog that could run just as fast and would take up less space.

I had it all figured out: the costs, the benefits, everything. It's amazing how life always seems to work out right on paper. Finding a sure thing, however, was easier said than done. Picking a winner, even with someone else's money isn't easy. Bookies know the odds are stacked so much in their favour that free bets are nothing more than an act of fulsome generosity. So what do you do with a £750 free bet? In a moment of madness I considered whacking it on a 100–1 shot at Kempton but a one-off bet of such magnitude couldn't be staked on something as fleeting as a horse race, let alone a dog race.

In the final analysis, after careful consideration of football, cricket, athletics, snooker, darts, bowls and the World Shove-Ha'penny Championships in Billericay, I decided to go for England to win the Six Nations tournament. At 3–10 the odds were skin tight, but the market and the 'experts' suggested an England win was a *fait accompli*. Ireland, Scotland, Wales and Italy did not have a prayer, leaving France as the only viable threat. What did the French know about rugby anyway?

On January 31st I called William Hill and placed the bet: 750 sovs on England to win the Six Nations. I was about to learn my first painful lesson as an unprofessional gambler. Two days after I'd struck the bet England got off to a flyer: Scotland got whacked 29–3 at Murrayfield . . . *Swing low, sweet chariot*. One down, four to go . . . Two weeks later Ireland were annihilated at Twickenham 45–11 . . . *Coming fo' to carry me home*. Two down, three to go . . . Going into the game against the French at the Stade de France, England were still odds-on favourites. The French had creamed Italy 33–12 in their opening game, but the following week *Les Bleus* went to the wire with Wales, narrowly winning 37–33 in Cardiff. France v England was the match that would decide the eventual winners of the tournament.

As I watched the game at home on TV, the French in a methodical, disciplined fashion closed down England, chipping away at them like master stonemasons. If you don't want to know the score look away now: the French, everybody's favourite enemy, took England to school, winning 20–15. As the final whistle went, so did my £975 windfall. France now only had to overcome Scotland and Ireland to win the tourney. Even if you discounted the fact that the French were far superior to either team, history dictated that neither would do England any favours and actually try to win, even if it were humanly possible. France eventually beat Scotland 22–10 and battered Ireland 44–5 to complete the Grand Slam and lift the Six Nations trophy. *Merde*.

Having squandered my free bet, my dog days were over before they had even started. I had shot my big mouth off to all and sundry about my bright idea and was now in danger of winding up with ego all over my face. Professional sport, the bookies, the *system*, had all conspired against me, robbing me of what was rightfully mine. Mine, mine, mine, I tell you! To hell with England, William Hill and common sense. In the words of Iron Mike Tyson, 'I refuse to lose.' I *knew* I could beat the system. It was time to even the score, time to take on the big boys at their own game, time to score a blow for the little guy. So I went cap in hand to my publisher . . .

This was the deal: in return for salacious tales of dodgy deals, drugs, gambling, corruption, animal cruelty, celebrities and sex (I lied about the sex) my publisher would invest two grand and take a 50 per cent stake in the dog. Fair enough. They would also bankroll £1000 to cover initial expenses. OK. Of course, I would get a suitable advance for delivering a juicy manuscript in twelve months' time . . . Once the year was up I would get rid of the dog, for a profit, natch, and everything else would slot into place, including the Bookie Prize I had been so cruelly denied. With the money I earned I would go to Cuba and have a back-street plastic surgeon reconstruct my cauliflower ear for a hundred bucks and a year's supply of refried beans. Sorted.

A couple of months passed and the dough was in the bank. Damn. I was living large again. This was the easiest score I'd had in ages. My old man always said I had 'money counting hands'. It was now May and while the bulk of that fat cheque from my publisher marinated in its own juices at Lloyds TSB, I set aside two Gs and started looking in the obvious places for a bargain Derby prospect, chiefly the *Racing Post, Greyhound Star, Greyhound Monthly, Fiesta, Loot* and Battersea Dogs Home. The latter two turned up nothing of note, but I did get a great deal on a Sony Minidisc. *Fiesta* was simply a good read.

As you can imagine, the greyhound press was an oasis of dogs but without really knowing what I was doing, my lack of knowledge betrayed me every time I made an inquiry.

'What are you looking for exactly?' said the man in a thick Irish brogue.

'Er, a greyhound, er, that's, er . . .' I mumbled.

'Well, I know you're looking for a dog otherwise you wouldn't be calling would ya? What d'you want? D'you want an open racer, a grader, a sprinter, a stayer . . .? What d'you want? I got the lot you know.'

The ad in the paper said the man had 'Bitches For Sale'. I liked the sound of that. Bitches. Maybe he'd take one of my ex-girlfriends in part-exchange.

'I want something fast,' I ventured. Crackle crackle. It was a bad connection. 'How about . . .? Why don't I come and see what you've got?'

'What? What was that? Listen, this isn't a fekking car show-room you know! I got no time for timewasters!'

Brrrrrrrrrrrrrrrrrrrrrrrrrr.

'Hello? Hello? *Hel-lo?*'

Ignorant fucker. Subsequent calls were no more helpful. Breeders and dealers could spot a bullshitter a mile off, even down a phone line. One woman even said, with a mild hint of sarcasm, 'You're not that Paul Kenyon fella are ya?' after I intimated I was on a mission to find the 'inside track' on greyhound racing. I wasn't doing an exposé, so I wanted to be as upfront as possible with anyone I dealt with. Having been busted for ticket touting, spat at by tramps, hexed by a witch doctor and made to smoke crack cocaine, all in the name of investigative journalism, I'd long since given up on undercover reportage.

Sooner or later I had to get off my fat arse and spend some money, so I hit the road and headed for the greyhound sales at Perry Barr racetrack in Birmingham, which offered the discerning mug an unenviable selection of bargain-basement dogs. Over the years, regrettable purchases of clapped-out motors, snide antiques and job lots of salmonella foodstuffs have taught me that an auction isn't the best place to go shopping for quality goods. Buying a greyhound at a public sale was therefore a very risky business. Nevertheless, fortune occasionally favours the reckless as well as the bold so I decided to take a chance.

The Perry Barr sales were a treat for anyone brought up on Galton and Simpson sitcoms. Every fat, balding, incontinent, polyester-wearing, middle-aged man from the West Midlands seemed to be there, either propping up the bar and ruminating over the auction catalogue or gobbing scornfully at the track as the dogs went off in ones, twos and threes during the pre-sale time trials. It was a crisp spring day in Britain's second city, given lustre by a cinnamon glow of sunlight. But the punters weren't there for the weather. After a short nap in the Polo, I returned to the dark, dank atmosphere of the bar-cum-auction room to find the action underway.

'Eight hundred . . . eight hundred over there. Eight fifty, eight fifty, eight fifty . . .' The auctioneer was a chalky-white, elderly Irishman in a funereal suit. To the right of him on the dais was a weaselly little fella in his mid-forties clad from head to toe in synthetic sports leisurewear. Rub shoulders with him and sparks would fly. Throughout the bidding Synthetic Man whispered conspiratorially in the auctioneer's ear, to which the old man would utter some indistinguishable sales pitch such as, 'She's got bags of staying power, a gutsy little bitch,' or 'She was the 2002 All-Ireland Guide Dog Champion, trained at Barbara Woodlouse's Walkies School of Canine Excellence.' The crowd would grunt at every titbit of information then continue coughing and spluttering and murmuring their disdain as dog after bitch after mutt staggered on to the stage.

'Eight fifty, who'll give me eight fifty? Eight fifty. Nine hundred. Nine hundred. *Nine hundred* . . .' To the left of the stage, near the exit, stood a spotty-faced teenager with lot number something or other: a shivering, quaking mess of a dog, dazed and confused at his sudden fifteen seconds of infamy. I stood rigid by the exit door determined not to make any gesture that could be misconstrued as a bid. 'At nine hundred she's being sold. Nine hundred. *Nine hundred*. NIIIIIIINE HUNDRED POUNDS. Selling her away at nine hundreddddddd . . .'

A thousand pounds seemed to be as good as it got; many of the greyhounds on offer went for nothing more than chump change on a sliding scale of incontinence: the cheaper the dog, the weaker its bladder. For £200, you could buy a dog with its own aerodynamic colostomy bag; £100 bought you one with a year's supply of nappies; and for a score you got your very own Portaloo on legs. Some of the dogs were so old and piss poor they'd need a Zimmer frame to get round the track. This was not the place to find the next Mick the Miller or Scurlogue Champ, especially if you didn't know what the hell you were looking for. I decided that the only bid I would put in at this sale was a farewell one. As auctions went, ebay was more up my street.

For a chicken-shit greenhorn like me the safest route to take was to follow the advice of an advertisement I had seen in the Wimbledon race card. 'Why Not Become An Owner?' it said invitingly, with just the hint of a knowing wink. *Go on . . . Why Not Become An Owner, eh? Go on . . . you know you want to. Go on sucker . . .* The ad listed a number of trainers who would be 'pleased to advise' on buying a dog. This was more like it.

Aside from coursing greyhounds, which run round rural Britain terrorising hares, rabbits and city dwellers, there are basically two types of racing greyhound: open racers and graders. Open racers are the better class of dog. They travel from track to track (with the aid of a trainer and the obligatory white transit van) taking on allcomers for the best prizes, the ultimate being the Derby, followed by an array of Grand Prix and 'classics', many of which are named after famous horse races, such as the St Leger, the Oaks and the Grand National.

The majority of racing dogs however are graders, which compete on a sliding scale of ability based on recorded times and results. Graders are usually ranked from 1–9 with the A9 grade being for puppies and 'scrubbers' (or mediocre animals) to A1 for high quality dogs some of which may be good enough to moonlight occasionally as open racers.[2]

Another feature of professional greyhound racing is the use of selected or 'attached' trainers at each track. Major league promoters tend to have up to ten approved trainers under contract to provide a regular number of graders for race duty on a rota each week. Being attached is not an exclusive arrangement; it does not stop a trainer from taking his or her best dogs to other tracks. It just means the promoters can guarantee that their race cards are always full thanks to a revolving door of graded animals.

Race meets more often than not have a mixed ability of grades and distances. The first couple of races are usually for the lower grades and, as the card progresses, so the quality of dog improves. I was aiming for a good, young grader with bags of potential who could move up in class rapidly and then compete for the big money open prizes. I also hoped that the Easter Bunny, Santa Claus and the Tooth Fairy would give me six winning Lotto numbers. As the writer, Charles Bukowski once said before throwing up into a beer glass, 'Lack of hope makes a man discouraged.'

---

[2] Grade prefixes for greyhound races are as follows: 'A' for 475 metres; 'B' for 435 metres; 'D' for 275-metre sprints; 'S' for 640-metre stayers races; 'M' for 840-metre marathons; 'P' for puppy races; 'OR' for open races; 'H' for hurdle races; and 'HC' for handicaps. Trial races are denoted with a 'T'. Distances vary from track to track.

Now that I had a basic idea of what I was after – namely a dog that ran fast – I had to find a track from which to operate. Geographically, Wimbledon was the nearest track to my home so it would have been convenient to buy a dog through a trainer based there. Spiritually, however, Walthamstow Stadium, a.k.a. the Stow, was closer to my heart as I had spent much of my misspent youth on the streets in and around it.

In the early nineties, on the advice of the Pet Shop Boys, I decided to 'go west' and turn my back on Walthamstow and a life of sewing mailbags/drug addiction/insanity. Largely through my own recklessness, misfortune and bad company, at that point my twenty-five years as an East Ender had been a living horror movie rather than a cheery soap opera. In the event, the furthest west I had made it was Shepherd's Bush. Going back to Walthamstow after all these years would be like a homecoming of sorts, a way of rediscovering my darkened roots. I would become the Alex Haley of dog racing.

Sprawled across a drab, featureless part of the city and reclaimed from the surrounding marshes and encroaching forests, Walthamstow is a working-class area in the most traditional sense, one of London's last remaining hinterlands. To the north-east is Chingford, gateway to Essex and green pastures, and to the south is Hackney, a concrete cockney jungle. In some parts of Walthamstow, elderflower, rocket and fennel grow along with blackberries and wild strawberries; and in others, if you know where to look, you can also find magic mushrooms, khat and hydroponically cultivated strains of skunkweed.

Walthamstow has none of the gentrified 'artists' quarter' nonsense of Shoreditch or pretension of Islington; there's no Bo-ho Brixton or Hoxton hippy chick shit in these parts. Walthamstow is the original 'crap town', condemned in 1998 by *Midweek* magazine no less as 'one of the five worst areas in London'. Around the same time, a kangaroo poll voted the local football team, Leyton Orient, the worst for catering in the Football League. That is the worst out of *92 clubs* in the entire country.

In their greedy pursuit of virgin realty, estate agents have now dubbed Walthamstow and its environs 'the new Islington'. As if. Apart from being home to Europe's longest street market and the birthplace of nineteenth-century artist, poet, decorator, printer and socialist William Morris, Walthamstow has nothing going for it; it is little more than a conduit between sexier inner London and sassier Essex. It is a soulless dump. However, it does have one redeeming feature: the Stow.

On the border of Walthamstow and its relatively more salubrious neighbour Chingford, the Stow is an impressive venue, a suburban coliseum. Its façade, which is also the exterior to the track scoreboard, is a sight to behold: a white art deco monolith festooned in pink, orange and red neon and punctuated by a huge black illuminated greyhound leaping through a googolplex-megawatt sign that roars, **'WALTHAMSTOW STADIUM'.** At night, this larger than life slab of concrete and lights is a seductive beacon, a siren luring punters into an arena that harks back to the mythical good old days of greyhound racing. For over eighty years the dogs has been a quintessential part of British working-class life. God knows what it must have been like in the roaring thirties and forties, the sport's heyday, when crowds of up to 25,000 would be drawn to the stadium like pilgrims heading for Mecca.

A temple of glass and repro furnishings, the Stow's numerous bars and restaurants transcend the average night out in the East End. It even has a nightclub adjacent to the track called Charlie Chan's, a plastic plant and mirror ball throwback to the 1980s, replete with penguin-suited bouncers of the 'your name's not down, you're not coming in' variety.

The Stow is the vanguard of British greyhound racing. It has the largest attendance and gambling turnover of any of the NGRC tracks, with an on-course market turnover of around £50 million per annum and off-course bets generating nearly £300 million a year. On Saturday nights, it shifts over a thousand meals in its restaurants. No wonder the greyhound-racing community voted it the 'Racecourse of the Millennium'. From what I had seen so far of the competition, it would take a thousand years for them to catch up with Walthamstow Stadium. When media whores or movie directors want an archetypal dog track for their commercials and Brit flicks, this is where they come. There is no speedway or stock car racing here, mate, no car boot sales or caravan sites. The Stow is the Madison Square Garden of dog racing. This is the Big Time, baby.

chapter 4

I headed for the Popular Enclosure (the cheap seats) on the southern side of the stadium. It was a Tuesday night, warm enough to leave the jacket at home, cold enough to make you wish you hadn't. I was looking for a guy called Vince, an unassuming local in his early forties; we had met a couple of weeks earlier through an associate at the National Union of Journalists. Vince worked in the NUJ's accounts department, so he had a way with figures, which I guess was useful for an habitual gambler.

'I used to come here every night once upon a time,' said Vince, peering through his heavy specs over the smattering of grey faces in the stands. 'That was before the missus started getting the hump. I was so into the dogs at one point that buying a greyhound seemed like the natural thing to do.' Vince had once bought a greyhound for a few hundred quid with a couple of mates, which they had raced at the Stow. The dog had won a few and lost a few more but was forced into early retirement due to injury. The experience had left him somewhat jaded.

'Bloody thing,' he said ruefully. 'The others didn't want to know once it stopped racing. I was the mug who had to take it home. It sat around all day doing nothing. Most expensive pet I've ever had.'

'I'm after a greyhound myself,' I said. 'Got any advice?'

'Don't bother,' said Vince looking up from his race card. 'They're more trouble than they're worth.'

I laughed off this remark and allowed myself a temporary distraction from Vince's sermonising: the sight of the gleaming chrome and leather of a Harley Davidson perched behind the bar of the Classic Diner. It was the one concession to glamour in the otherwise dreary enclosure. Vince smiled and gave me 'the look'. You know the one I mean. The ocular tut tut tut. He carried on marking his race card. I carried on drinking and soaking up the over-familiar smell of fried food, second-hand tobacco smoke, BO and farts.

On Tuesday nights, entry to the Popular Enclosure is just £1 (including the price of a programme). Consequently, many old gits, misers, families, loners and Luddites hang out there in preference to the comparatively ritzier and more sociable Main Enclosure. Tuesday nights are strictly for graders and the top prize is usually no more than £120, which makes it a low-key event. On a quiet Tuesday night such as this one, the Stow would attract maybe a thousand or so punters.

Thursdays have a mix of graders and open racers, with top prizes running into several hundred pounds; it attracts a slightly livelier, pre-weekend crowd. Saturday nights, though, are the big money nights, where the top open racers can compete for several thousands of pounds in blue riband events. The atmosphere and timing of Thursday and Saturday meets pull in a lot of office parties, stag do and hen night types and the infamous 'six-packers'.

Six-packs are all-in-one deals consisting of, surprise surprise, six different elements: admission, scampi or chicken and chips, two alcoholic beverages and two £1 Tote bets, all for £13.50. The British Greyhound Racing Board (BGRB) had come up with the six-pack as a way of attracting casual punters to greyhound racing – the kind of people who see the dogs as just another night out rather than a means of supplementing their income.

Until the 1960s, greyhound racing only contended with football, the cinema, radio and the emerging goggle box. But in today's leisure-obsessed society, punters have an embarrassment of pastimes to titillate and amuse them. To keep the wheels from falling off the industry, race promoters, like all hucksters, need to get new blood through the turnstiles, so they have to offer more than packs of dogs running round a track and a free race card.

Like all modern leisure industries, greyhound racing is marketed as 'A fun day out for all the family'. Vince often took his two young daughters with him to the track, to give his wife a break. One of them was about five, the same age as my daughter, the other about ten years old. They would roam around the Popular Enclosure freely and hang out in the adjacent playground, occasionally bobbing up with requests for a Coke or a bag of crisps. Both were effervescent and playful; they seemed content to marvel in their own little world, blissfully disengaged from the adults around them. They reminded me of how self-contained children are, how the juvenile imagination can make magic of any situation. The older one ran in the 100 and 200 metres for her school. From the cradle to the grave, man and beast are always running after or away from something.

Apart from his kids, Vince went to the track with Paul, a work colleague and John, a giant of a man who worked behind the counter of a high-street bookie. Vincent, John and Paul. I called them 'the Saints'. It raised a giggle. However, they could hardly contain themselves at the thought of me buying a greyhound.

'Sounds like you've got brain damage,' said John, exploding with laughter.

Confessing you are an ex-fighter, regardless of status or intellect, is an invitation to ridicule. Pity the Frank Brunos and Michael Watsons of this world then, men who for different reasons lack the brainpower to parry the banana sharp wit of life's smartarses.

'Do yourself a favour,' implored Vince. 'Don't waste your money. Get yourself a car, go on holiday, anything. Just don't buy a greyhound, they're trouble, mark my words.'

I shrugged off his warnings. What did I care? Easy come; easy go.

For everyday punters the dogs isn't just about gambling and making money; it certainly isn't about partying hearty and pissing it up with your mates. Yes, it is a social activity, but more importantly, it's about the competition, the challenge of taking on the bookies and trying to *beat the system*. Aside from his own financial limitations, a punter is up against the promoters, the bookies, the race manager (whose job it is to handicap the races), the weather, the trainers and of course the dogs themselves. In this jungle of variables, gambling, as reckless as it seems to the abstainer, requires a lot of concentration. A punter has fewer than fifteen minutes between races to analyse each dog's form, permutate possible outcomes and scenarios, consider the odds and come to a conclusion from which a sensible bet can be made.

In the era of the ever-increasing short attention span the quick-fix dog race is a compulsive gambler's wet dream. During the course of a three-hour meeting of up to fourteen races, an habitual, but not necessarily high-rolling punter, like Vince, could easily stake the equivalent of week's wages or more. With such little time to play with you have to keep your eyes on the prize. Idle chitchat can cost a lot of dough. Hanging out at the track reminded me of how difficult it was as a kid to get my old man's attention on a Saturday afternoon when the gee-gees were running and he had one eye glued to the telly and the other ensconced in the *Daily Mirror* racing form.

Vince, Paul and John bickered with each other constantly over how the dogs would run. 'I told you the six dog wouldn't make it to the first bend in front,' Vince would say. Or 'That five dog will never stay the distance,' he advised. Of the three, Vince was undoubtedly the best judge. Six or seven times out of ten he got the pattern of the race right, if not the winner. He could predict the outcome of a race with frightening, almost clairvoyant, prescience. If I could learn what he knew about the dogs I'd be rolling in it; but at this stage I was more interested in the theory of gambling rather than the practice of it. It had been a while since my bank balance had been as flush as it was now. I wanted to keep it that way.

Nevertheless, Vince gave me a crash course in how to read the race card from an analytical perspective, i.e. a perspective I had previously ignored. Short of being 'in the know' with every trainer of every dog in every race, the race card is a punter's primary source of information.

The race card or programme contains information on each dog's last five starts (and at some tracks, six). It details the date and venue of races, distances, trap numbers, sectional times (i.e. the dog's recorded times at the crucial first bend), their positions at each bend, finishing positions, winning and/or losing distances, the name of each winner, winners' times, the going, weights, starting prices, grades and finishing times. It also gives an abbreviated review of each race, indicating for instance if a particular dog had been bumped, was slow or quick away, or ran lame in a previous race. These comments, coupled with the rest of the card's information, provide punters with vital clues as to what *might* happen in a future event.

The number one performance indicator in greyhound racing however is that most precious commodity: time. All things being equal, if greyhounds are made to race down a straight track, barring a mishap, the fastest one will win every time. But if you're aiming to pick winners based on time you have to make two assumptions: one, is the fastest dog on paper in a physical and mental condition to reproduce its best times; and two, what's the likelihood of some donkey impeding his run?

It is the fact that greyhound races run on an oval track (and always anti-clockwise) that makes the races competitive. It is also a fact that greyhound tracks, like the people who patronise them, are idiosyncratic. Walthamstow is known for its tight bends, which cause many dogs – particularly those unfamiliar with it – to baulk or 'check' when speeding into a turn. Whereas Hove, for instance, is a galloping track, characterised by longer straights and looser bends.

On such a tight circuit as the Stow, theoretically, dogs on the inside or the outside have a slight advantage over those in the middle. The middle traps are known as the 'coffin boxes' on account of the tendency for the middle runners to get boxed in and buried by traps one, two, five and six on either side, particularly at the first bend. Whatever happens at the first bend can make or break a race. If a dog has early pace and can get to the first bend in front and 'on the bunny' it stands a good chance of getting a clear run to the finish line by avoiding the scrimmaging and rough-housing the pack endures in the battle for the lead.

Conversely, a dog with a lot of 'early' pace might not necessarily have the stamina to maintain his lead over the distance, in which case a stayer or a finisher with a bad start, particularly a wide runner, can close the gap in the latter half of the race and steal a victory.

However, picking winners is not an exact science. All the data, indicators, inside info and *Daily Star* horoscopes may suggest a trap four win, but dogs are people too. Sometimes, they just do not perform to type; though an animal not known for its mental agility is generally easy to read. 'In most graded races there's only around thirty spots (30 tenths of a second) between the fastest dog and the slowest one,' said Vince. 'Greyhounds are very predictable animals. A railer's always gonna run on the inside and a wide runner's always gonna go wide.'

Some dogs only chase the tails of those in front, even if they have the pace to overtake them. Some dogs are simply prone to trouble and others are flyers, i.e. dogs that run and run and run. Greyhounds are simply creatures of habit. Unlike in horseracing, where a jockey can manipulate a horse's speed, save for a few rare exceptions, a greyhound does not hold anything back in a race. It will maintain an even speed, tiring only at the end of the race. Greyhounds buckle only from physical affliction, not emotional fatigue. This simple fact is probably the most important difference between man and dog. Dogs always try their best. They do not subscribe to work to rule, unions, cultural stereotypes, or laziness. This is why we love them, because they are dumb enough to keep on going regardless. Dogs have a level of tenacity that man often tries to facsimile but rarely achieves.

Apart from the odd occasions when something or someone is thrown on to the track, if you're going to nobble a greyhound race you've got to do it before the off. Another reason why punters like Vince prefer the dogs to horseracing is that the probability of human interference *during* the event is low. Every other sport that attracts a betting market, theoretically, is corruptible well in advance of the contest or during it; and in the case of professional boxing, given its history of dubious tinkering with scorecards, after the event too.

Just before the end of the evening, I decided to split and leave the Saints to spin the wheel of misfortune. 'How you getting on Vince, are you winning?' I asked. 'Getting there,' he mumbled. I was in no hurry to lose my shirt so I kept my money in its rightful place, i.e. my pocket. After all, I had bigger fish to fry. Vince gave me another warning about getting involved in the dogs. Perhaps it was to ease his conscience more than anything, as he seemed genuinely concerned for my financial well-being.

'Look, if you're serious about buying a dog, Linda Jones is the top trainer over here,' said Vince. 'She won the championship last year . . . top trainer in the country. I get a few winners from her dogs now and again. Then there's John Mullins – he's all right too. His mum used to train here but now he's taken over the business. Then there's . . .' Vince pointed to their numbers in the race card and suggested I call the ones he recommended. There were ten trainers under contract at the Stow including Jones, Mullins and Gary Baggs, who handled ex-footballer and Hollywood hard man Vinnie Jones's dogs. 'Good luck,' said Vince. 'See you again,' I said and left the track on the long journey back to west London, no richer or poorer but slightly wiser.

chapter 5

The following Tuesday I was back at the Stow in the Popular Enclosure with Vince and the Saints, trying my luck on the Tote. The Tote, short for 'totaliser', is a dog track's biggest earner. Punters stake their money in a pool from which the promoter takes a cut, which in the Stow's case is around 27 per cent. The balance is paid as a dividend to each winning punter, in proportion to their stake. Each dividend (to a ten pence stake) is displayed on the multitude of TV screens around the track. Ten pence is the minimum you can bet at the Stow. The low unit stake thus attracts punters in all financial shapes and sizes; the downside of the Tote however is that a few relatively large bets can change the odds dramatically.

Unlike with the bookies, whose minimum stake is a fiver, you don't know what price you're actually getting when you back a dog on the Tote as the computer-generated odds change rapidly in response to the market. The most popular bets are forecasts and trifectas. In the course of a fourteen-race card, even if you only have 'fun' bets of a few quid a race, your pockets soon empty if you hit a losing streak. As the rails bookies only take straight bets, even punters who favour fixed odds betting will have a flutter on the Tote if they fancy a forecast or a tricast, or the bookies' odds are too short for a bet on the nose. If you are only into small stakes of a couple of quid, the Tote is the ideal, affordable and accessible way to nurture a gambling addiction.

'Hello, love', I said, rummaging through the change in my pocket. 'I'd like a 50p reversed forecast on traps one, two and five please.'

'Three pounds please,' said the woman in the Tote kiosk punching away at a computer keyboard. She was chewing gum and nattering away with another old bird at the next counter. This is the Stow's equivalent of garden-fence gossiping.

The Tote kiosks are staffed mainly by women, young, old and in-between, the sort of disaffected checkout types, much like those who work in the high-street bookies. In between races they do their make-up, file their nails, gossip or simply stare at the ceiling. At no point do they ever seem the slightest bit interested in what is going on down at the track. They have a detachment that invites the uninitiated, the naïve and the clueless to gamble, which is probably a conscious marketing ploy on the Stow's part. The last thing they want is pseudo bookies behind the counter smoking cigars, swearing and putting off the six-packers and coach parties.

Once, I'd seen a Tote scam on *Derren Brown: Mind Control*, a TV show about this guy who walks around the streets hustling mugs with cod psychology and mental magic tricks. In one episode he went to the Stow and apparently managed to get money out of a Tote kiosk by banging on the counter and saying to the woman behind, 'This is the winning ticket.' I tried it twice. The first time the woman just looked at me and laughed. The second time another broad told me to stop acting like an idiot or she'd call security. So much for mind control.

Too much thinking leads to uncertainty and self-doubt. 'Paralysis by analysis,' my old boxing trainer Howard Rainey would say in response to my over-philosophising. I had to make a decision. Was I in or out, out or in? In out, in out, shake it all about . . . I had been shuffling around the dog track for a couple of weeks, trying to pick up scraps of information. One thing I learned was, while two thousand pounds seemed like lot of money for a dog, it was not excessive. Top dogs regularly change hands for up to £20,000 and more, but knowing this did not make me loosen my belt any quicker. I grew up in a household where everything was recycled; even the patches on my trousers had patches.

In the back of my mind, I knew owning a dog, let alone spending two grand on one, was an utterly ridiculous idea. Having signed on the dotted line, in Faustian fashion I had sold my soul, dear reader, for your delectation and my wallet. However, to get this freak show on the road I needed a dog, and I needed one fast. Time was marching on. Then fate, or should I say 'Faith' called on me . . .

Corrina Faith was a young, idealistic documentary filmmaker. Her latest project was a programme for ITV on men and plastic surgery and she had heard about my cauliflower ear. She got in touch with me and asked if I would be interested in being a contributor on her show. I thought if I played my cards right I could blag a free ear job. Howard Rainey called me a wimp for wanting rid of it. 'What d'you wanna get rid of it for?' he would growl. 'It's a fucking trophy!' To me this 'trophy' was fuel for my hypochondria, not an heroic souvenir. Corrina's boss however didn't think my ear was the right kind of prize meat for the show.

'Sorry, David, I'm afraid we've got someone who's keen on having a penile extension,' she told me. Alas, my lame lob had lost out to a shrivelled penis; nevertheless, Corrina and I met for coffee in one of those overpriced caffeine peddlers on Baker Street for a spot of 'relationship marketing'. Over a grande mocha with whipped cream she told me her ambition was to make programmes that meant something. I told her mine was to find a greyhound that made money.

'You should talk to Linda Jones then,' she said.

'Linda Jones, eh?' This sounded promising. 'Do you know her?'

'Yeah, I know Linda. I made a programme on her for *Pet Rescue*. She's a lovely woman, very sweet. She's the top greyhound trainer in the country.'

'Linda Jones . . . I've heard a lot about her . . .'

'She's really sweet and loves her dogs to pieces. I'll give you her number.'

I already had Linda's kennel number, along with those of several other trainers, from the Stow race cards. Now, armed with her mobile number and mutual friend Corrina, I felt more comfortable and 'in the know' which made taking the next step a lot easier . . .

Linda Jones is the queen pin of greyhound racing. She had been champion trainer in 2001 and was well on the way to doing the double in 2002. She had a column in the *Racing Post* every Wednesday and is one of the most respected figures in the game. I had no concerns about the animal rights lobby but I was mindful of the heat I was generating among my anti-racing friends and acquaintances, so I thought it best to do the right thing and find a kennel where the flies were on the dog shit, not on the trainer. I arranged to meet her at the Stow the following Thursday night, so that we could chitchat and check each other out.

I arrived at the track a couple of races into the card. A dour-looking security guard ushered me through the main entrance; a sharp right turn took me outside to the track and I made my way through a swamp of boozy wide-boys, peroxide blondes, big tits, cockney accents, office parties, stag dos and excited German tourists. Thursdays, particularly on balmy nights like this one, were the new Fridays – a night when short-sleeved and mini-skirted six-packers came out to play at the dogs, all of them ready, willing and able to lose their money in the name of 'entertainment'.

The race steward appeared in front of the traps in a white shirt, a pair of tight black jodhpurs and a black bowler hat. He looked as camp as a row of pink tents. A loud bell rang out: the muezzin called and the faithful scrambled frantically to pay their respects to Tote, God of Gambling. I noticed a sign by the finish line as I jostled my way through the betting ring: 'Flash photography strictly forbidden'. If only the same could be said for flash clothing.

Another bellowed: 'DANGER! KEEP OFF THIS RAIL!' I heard the track come alive as the hare went on its merry way. The lights dimmed. I stopped in my tracks and turned to face the traps. I knew the routine now. Programmed like Pavlov's dog, I responded instinctively to every sight and sound, smell and touch that this twilight world had to offer.

I could see Linda in the terraces in front of the Main Enclosure, surrounded by a group of largely overweight men. I recognised her instantly from her picture by-line in the previous day's *Racing Post*, where she beamed out of the page with an ear-to-ear smile. As I walked past the Main Enclosure through the betting ring, I saw her leap down from the terrace to the side of the track screaming frantically at the dogs. I neared her and could see the veins on her neck bulging, her face reddening as the crowd yelped and yawed behind her. She clenched her fists as though she were trying to squeeze a pip out of a grape. At one point, she looked like she was in a trance. Linda had the dog thing bad.

'Go on boy, go on, that's it, go on, go on, go on,' she cried. 'Yeaaaaaaaah!'

'Hello Linda,' I said, slipping through her coterie. 'I'm David.' She was breathing heavily, wide-eyed and grinning like a Cheshire cat; for a moment, she looked like a tranquillised housewife, but she was simply high on success. Having just notched up another winner, she had a right to be pleased with herself.

'Hello, David, pleasure to meet you. Come and join us up here.' I followed Linda up a few steps into the stands behind a row of Tote booths. 'These are some of my owners,' she said, waving her arm like the Queen Mum across a group of identikit thirty- and forty-something beer-bellied geezers, all of them a Gary, a John or a Steve. I was not a Gary, a John or a Steve, but as a Dave, I could still pass the Swinging Sixties name check. The complexion would take some work. As for the beer gut, that was coming along nicely. It wouldn't do for me to look too healthy: being slim at a dog track would make me stand out among the dog-owning set almost as much as being black did. Linda loved holding court. All the owners hung on her every word. Her 'larger than life' bonhomie was matched only by her figure. I noticed her work the owners very subtly with the odd coquettish glance or flirtatious comment. I guessed she was in her late forties, maybe early fifties, but her obvious love of the dogs was a natural anti-ageing agent both physically and mentally. To get myself into the conversation I asked the thinnest owner in the group if he had a tip for me.

'Yeah, don't gamble.' Cue: raucous laughter. The old ones are always the best.

'What about you, Linda?' I asked.

'Take it from me, David, gambling's a mug's game. Personally, I don't get involved in it. I don't know the first thing about it. The money, the gambling . . . it doesn't interest me one iota. It's the winning that counts.'

At that moment, a small party, including a photographer and a member of the track staff, interrupted our conversation by beckoning.

'OK then,' she said. 'Come on, David, you're not getting out of this.' Linda grabbed me by the arm and led me away with the group towards the winners' podium by the finish line. The winning dog was Sekopats Fancy. The owner was not at the track, so I had the honour of standing on the podium with Linda for the trophy ceremony and customary photo call.

'There you go,' said Linda, handing me the glass trophy, which had the Walthamstow Stadium logo carved into it.

'You what?' I said, slightly embarrassed by the gesture.

'Go on, have it,' said Linda, thrusting the trophy into my stomach. 'I've got plenty more where that came from.'

The optimist in me was impressed: here I was collecting trophies and having my photo taken on the podium and I didn't even own a dog. The cynic in me, however, figured this was a shrewd bit of marketing on Linda's part. *Kid the chump. Butter him up. Make him feel like a 'winner'.* Nevertheless, like a sucker, I bought Linda's spiel hook, line and sinker.

'I love my dogs more than I love people,' she said. 'That's the buzz for me: the dogs. I also love the excitement of the game, you know, pitting your wits against everybody else. When you look after the dogs day in day out – everything from picking up their mess to grooming 'em and feeding 'em – at the end of the day, when you take 'em racing and that dog wins, the feeling you get is like no other. It's better than sex, drugs and rock 'n' roll.'

Corinna was right. Linda was not just affable and easygoing, she was mad about her greyhounds. Moreover, she didn't smell of dog piss, which was an added bonus. Crucially though, she had drive, an addiction to success. I just hoped I wouldn't wind up being shafted by her. 'Don't worry, I think you'll be safe with me,' she joked, much to the amusement of her owners.

As the evening rolled on, I sensed Linda was getting itchy feet. Being the top trainer in the country meant there were always places to go, people to see. She had had an entry in ten out of fourteen races that night and picked up five winners and a place; not a bad success rate. I left her to her owners and glory and arranged to visit her kennels to talk business.

chapter 6

I left the Smoke early, ran the gauntlet of rush-hour traffic across London, and hit the M11 on my way to Linda's Imperial Kennels. Ninety-odd miles later I was in the sleepy village of Eriswell, Suffolk, a stone's throw from the US airbase at Lakenheath. Square-jawed GIs in Chevys, Cadillacs and Ray Bans flashed by as I crawled through the sleepy backwoods. The streets were deathly silent. England was about to kick off against Argentina in the World Cup. It was wet and miserable, a typical English summer. What a glorious day to go dog shopping.

I hung a left at the faded cardboard sign nailed to a tree, just as Linda had directed, and cruised slowly up a winding, leafy lane. The path was muddy and waterlogged in places. To the right were a riding school and fields with mounds of rotting, smouldering carrots and potatoes; to the left was a pig farm. I meandered along the path, pausing briefly to watch a stream of jets overhead as they broke the sound barrier, and the idyll with it. Wild rabbits darted in and out of the hedgerows in front of the car, inviting me to run them over. The landscape was flat, almost barren, and sparsely populated by distant faces that paid me no mind. Someone had dumped a car in a pond just off the lane, its rusty rear end sticking up in the air like a baboon's arse. Maybe the local yokels had run a pesky journalist off the road . . . Going into the country always gave me the creeps. The Fens, as they call these parts, seemed like the ideal place to snuff someone out.

About half a mile down the lane, I could see my final destination. Dogs were howling and yapping, vying for an audience over the sound of jet fighters in the distance. A long mesh fence ran along the side of the path to a set of heavy wrought-iron gates. Two sleek black greyhounds, barking furiously, chased the car as I cruised along the fence and then they tailed off in pursuit of an imaginary lure. A sign read: 'Beware, security dogs on guard.' All that was missing were entry posts, a watchtower and the cast of *Escape to Victory*. Welcome to boot camp for greyhounds.

I approached the gates and saw two burly fellas busying themselves inside the compound. One nodded grudgingly, the other said, 'All right mate.' The padlock to the gate was unlocked so I slipped inside. Neither man was going to open it for me. 'I'm looking for . . .' 'Down there on the right,' said the smaller, stony-faced one. I followed the wall of what looked like an elongated outhouse down to a grimy wooden door. Two lurchers leapt at me from behind the fence to an adjacent paddock. Startled, I opened the grimy door and went inside. For a moment, I thought I had stumbled into Denis Neilson's kitchen. Flies hovered round lumps of unidentifiable meat which were coagulating in several large plastic containers. Linda and a couple of kennel hands were preparing dinner for her hungry charges.

'Hello, Linda, what's on the menu?' I said.

'Ooh, you're just in time,' she replied, grinning. 'I've got some lovely beef here, succulent breasts of chicken, rice . . .'

The food looked very appetising . . . to a dog maybe. Linda fed her little darlings on meat from a commercial butcher, supplemented with dog biscuits or rice, for their dinner; breakfast was cereal with milk. I decided to take a raincheck on her offer and opted instead for a guided tour of the kennels and an insight into the world according to Linda Jones.

'David, I'm very competitive,' she said, as we trudged through paths separating the numerous paddocks. '*I* go out there to win. I want every *dog* that goes on the track to win. I don't enjoy coming second or third or last. I'm in it to win it. We all want to be top of the tree, don't we? It's *all* about winning . . . about getting the dog over the line first. At the end of the day, when you go home with the big trophy, it's absolutely wonderful.'

As we were walking through the kennels, in a little caravan next to Linda's modest detached house on the site, I noticed three of the kennel hands, Mark, Kelly and Peter (the stony-faced one), watching the big game. I poked my head round the door just in time to see David Beckham curl in the winning penalty against the old enemy.

'Yes, yes, yes,' screamed Peter. 'Get in there. Fucking Argies!'

Linda's spread was no Hilton hotel, nothing more than concrete huts built on farmland, but it was well equipped and maintained. She had 'around forty-five or so' dogs kennelled at any one time although she was deliberately vague about numbers as the neighbours weren't too keen on her being there, due to the dogs barking and all. Linda keeps most of her greyhounds in male and female pairs in 4ft × 4ft cubicles. They live in 'mixed' accommodation to stop the dogs from fighting each other, apart from when a bitch is in season, in which case she has private digs.

The greyhounds spend most of their time lolling around on mats and sawdust in their little bedsits, which suits their temperament. Contrary to popular belief, greyhounds do not need much exercise. At Imperial Kennels they get a couple of twenty-minute walks up the lane or gallops round a paddock each day; one after breakfast at 8a.m., and another in the afternoon following lunch. During their racing career, the last thing a greyhound needs is strenuous exercise. As sprinters they exert so much energy racing just once a week, they would burn out in no time if exercised vigorously on a daily basis.

'I can't run,' said Linda as we ambled along. 'I'm absolutely useless at running. I can just about walk! My dogs do the running for me. If you look after them, they'll do their best for you. I give 'em the best feed, I give 'em lots of attention . . . I've got lovely paddocks here . . . they're treated with kindness and love and that will make them win for you.'

Once again, Linda gave me her 'sex, drugs and rock 'n' roll' line. Sure, I was convinced (against to my better judgement) that I too could lose myself in dog racing; after all, my modus operandi is to immerse myself with autistic fervour into my work. However, the day I believe *anything* is better than 'sex, drugs and rock 'n' roll' is the day I cosy up inside a pine box.

I sussed that Linda was full of it; but instinctively I trusted her more than I could trust any male trainer. With men, you have to contend with all that macho ego crap. At 6ft 2in, with a 44in chest, a fair dose of testosterone, adrenaline, self-confidence and, most importantly, a brain, I am always deflecting weekend warriors, wannabe tough guys and plastic gangsters who feel threatened by me. *Grow up guys*. Men . . . we're our own worse fucking enemies.

'I'm a London girl,' said Linda proudly. 'But when I was a kid, at school we were factory fodder . . . and that's all we were.' Linda and I had a lot in common, that's why I trusted her. Like me, she too had been 'a bit of a tearaway' in her youth, on the streets of Plaistow in the East End, a stone's throw from the Stratford–Leyton–Leytonstone–Walthamstow axis where I grew up. After leaving school with few qualifications, she turned her hand to hairdressing among other things before landing her first job as a kennel hand in the late 1960s with 'a mad Irishman', Paddy Keane (RIP), at the now defunct Clapton racetrack in north-east London.

'Paddy would buy a big side of beef from the abattoir for the dogs, and he'd say to us kennel hands, "If any of you take a steak out of that beef I'll take a fucking steak out of you."' Paddy's 'bark was worse than his bite,' said Linda but that didn't stop him intimidating her on many occasions.

'Once, I had to give the bitches season-suppression pills and one of them fell pregnant. Paddy went ballistic,' said Linda, before going into one of the worst Irish accents I've ever heard. ' "I fucking told you to give dem pills to those fucking bitches, now

she's gone and got up the effing gut. She's fucking pregnant!"'
She explained how she had pleaded with Paddy, insisting she had
administered the pills; but the old boy was having none of it.
' "You fat fucking bitch, you silly cunt," he called me. I went to
Paddy's wife and his mum at the house, crying my eyes out.
"You'll be no good to me if that's how you're gonna behave,"
Paddy said. But it was thanks to him that I toughened up to the
sport. He taught me not to take any shit from no one. That's
where I got my gob from!'

Linda eventually left 'the fucking big crook' after he punched a
dog that lost a race on which he'd wagered heavily. She floated
around in odd jobs, worked at the Stow and Romford track in
Essex, before branching out there with a handful of her own dogs
and then landing a contract as an attached trainer. After nearly
three decades in the game, she eventually landed her dream ticket,
a contract at the Stow.

'I've had some good jobs in my lifetime, but this one I've
excelled at. I used to be a kennel maid at the Stow when I was
nineteen . . . I'm a little bit older now, but I'm back at the track
that I love, with the dogs I love. And I'm top of the tree, so I don't
see any reason why you can't be the same.'

Winning begets winning. I liked the idea of that. Maybe some
of Linda's boundless enthusiasm and optimism would rub off on
me. I *used* to be happy once upon a time too. Then I grew up.
Jesus. Where had this cynicism come from? I wore it like a cheap
t-shirt.

Badinage was easy with Linda. She spoke with an effusive mix
of old school cockney charm and wit. I like a woman with a sense
of humour, and an inbuilt ego massager. I knew I was being
reeled in, softened up. Linda beckoned one of the kennel hands
and asked him to fetch Twotone, a.k.a. 'Twoey'.

'Right, David,' she said, leading me towards one of the empty
paddocks. 'I want you to take a look at this dog: he's called
Twotone, which I think is quite apt for us as you're black and I'm
white.'

'Very apt,' I said, laughing along with Linda.

'I don't suppose you get many greyhound owners who are black, eh?' I asked.

'Do you know what?' said Linda, pausing for thought. 'In the eighteen years I've been a trainer I've had one black owner.'

We walked over to the wire fence surrounding the paddock where Twotone was and he took off like a rocket, covering the thirty or so metres of dirt in the blink of an eye. As his name suggests, he was dark brindle on one side of his coat and light on the other. If you squinted and took his head out of the equation, he looked like a sort of chimera – a cross between a cheetah and a wolf with a few other bits and pieces thrown in.

'He's an unknown quantity,' said Linda, watching Twotone keenly. 'He's a very young dog.'

'How old is he?'

'He's sixteen months old ... very well bred. He's by Mountleader Peer out of a bitch called Scotias Glen who's won several open races in Ireland.'

I nodded my head repeatedly in mock approval. I did not have the faintest idea about breeding dogs. It turned out that Mountleader Peer had been a runner-up in the 1996 Irish Greyhound Derby, which has a first prize of £100,000, making it the richest dog race in the world.

'He's a very nice dog but he's untried,' said Linda. 'We have to take him to Walthamstow for some qualifying trials. Now, I could take him to the track next week, and he doesn't chase; but on the other hand, I might take him to the track and he does a twenty-nine [seconds] dead, which would mean he'd be worth mega bucks to the owner.'

The 'owner' was an Irish outfit called 'The Dog Lovers Syndicate'. As their official agent, Linda would not give me any more details about them. 'They're very private,' she whispered, for dramatic effect. 'They like to keep themselves to themselves.'

Linda only sold dogs for 'trusted breeders' with whom she had a long-standing relationship. She said she was not in the business of selling dogs willy-nilly. Her reticence regarding the Dog Lovers fostered a belief in me that this syndicate was in fact a shadowy group of nameless, faceless men in suits, a spectral presence in the world of greyhound racing. Maybe they did not even exist. Maybe they were a front for Imperial Kennels?

'So what's your take then, Linda?' I inquired.

'I don't make a penny out of it, David,' she replied, looking me square in the eyes.

'C'mon. Ten, fifteen per cent . . .? You must get a drink out of it.'

'Not a penny.'

I didn't have a problem with her taking a cut from a sale. We all have to make a pound note somehow. I was just interested to know the *real* value of the animal, not the price I would have to pay as a sap.

'As you can see though he's an absolutely beautiful dog,' said Linda, still tracking Twotone's every move.

'Yeah, well, looks aren't everything, Linda. If they were, I'd be really successful.'

Linda laughed like a pantomime dame but the sound of yet another fighter plane overhead soon drowned out her cackling. There was a lot of activity in the gunmetal skies that morning. The word was Saddam Hussein was gonna get an ass kicking, so the military was busying itself, making sure Our Boys and the killing machines were well oiled and ready for action.

Back on the ground, Linda and I tiptoed towards the $64,000 question.

'Put it this way, if I take him to the track next week,' she said, 'and he doesn't run, the owners will more or less give him to ya. But if he goes and does twenty-nine seconds they'll want ten grand for him.'

'Ten grand?' I nearly swallowed my tongue. 'So what's the current asking price?'

'Four grand and he's yours now.' I checked my pockets. Nope, didn't think so, no four grand in there.

'Do you want to go in?' said Linda motioning towards the paddock gate.

'Sure, why not?'

I went into the paddock. Linda headed back to the kitchen, giving Twotone and me some quality time together. I went to stroke him, but he took off. A greyhound is officially a puppy until it's two years old, so I could forgive him the odd childish rebuke. 'Come on, boy. There's a good boy.' He sat at the end of the paddock, eyeing my every movement, waiting for me to move; then I as soon as I approached – whoosh – off he went again. 'Twoey, come on, boy. There's a good, good boy . . .' *Come on you little fucker*.

''Ere, try this,' said Linda strolling over with a handful of bone-shaped doggy biscuits. 'Twoey, *Twoey*,' I called out, intermittently whistling, but he would not take the biscuit. *Take the fucking biscuit*. After several attempts he sniffed my palm gingerly, looked up at me then bolted off to the other end of the paddock. Every time I went for him, he made a run for it. He even managed to scarper halfway through taking a shit before I could pet him.

I don't like rejection but I've learnt to live with it. However, if I were to buy this dog he would *have* to take the fucking biscuit. What was his problem? I had no idea what was going on in his head. He was nervy but Linda said he had the makings of a winner. Hmm . . . I respected his uncertainty, his caginess. He was a bit of a loner, a bit like me really. Did he know something I didn't? What utter nonsense. Humans are always projecting their bullshit ideas on to animals. You teach a dog to shake hands or roll over and all of a sudden he is qualified to be prime minister. Jesus. Any mutt with half a brain only does what you tell it to do because it's scared it'll get a kicking or, worse still, won't get fed.

Twenty minutes passed and Twotone stubbornly kept his distance. We were into a war of attrition. I liked his style: arrogant. If you want to make it in life you have to be an uncompromising sonofabitch. Maybe I was thinking all this because I was trying to convince myself that he was 'the one'. Self-delusion. I live for it.

'You been eating those biscuits?' said Linda, chuckling. 'It's all right, c'mon, boy.' Linda entered the paddock and Twotone went straight to her like a lapdog, no problem. Who was she, Dr Dolittle?

'David, good dogs are at a premium right now because the prize money's so good in Ireland,' said Linda. 'Trainers like Ian Greaves, the top man in Ireland, sell puppies for up to £6000 a time.'

Ninety per cent of all greyhounds racing in the UK are bred in Ireland. The wealth of available land for breeding, rearing and schooling, coupled with a long tradition of breeding dogs – and, of course, horses – and a greater cultural willingness to dispose of inferior litters, means that Ireland is indelibly linked with the best of the best. As an example of the Emerald Isle's dominance, the hundred fastest NGRC open race winners so far that year were all bred by Sean Dunphy at what the *Racing Post* called his 'greyhound empire' in Portlaw, County Waterford. As is the custom with many breeders, a Dunphy greyhound usually has a prefix to its name, as a mark of its bloodline. In his case, it is 'Droopys', as in Droopys Corleone, a contender for that year's Derby.

As with British cars, British engineering, British food and British weather, many experts see British greyhounds as duff. Along with most trainers in the UK, Linda does not have enough land for a track, so the majority of dogs she trains come from across the water pre-schooled. One punter at the Stow had told me that many dogs coming from Ireland were 'clued up' and suggested that they had already raced in unofficial meets as puppies before they got to the UK. Whatever happens in Ireland is anyone's guess; Imperial Kennels is more of a sort of prep school for greyhounds where the finer points of racing are honed.

Training a dog ain't rocket science: it is simply a matter of taking the athleticism that Mother Nature hath given the greyhound and programming it into a controlled activity. Pretty much as soon as a greyhound can walk, it is encouraged to chase squeaky toys and rags, which a trainer dangles provocatively in front of its nose, moving them backwards and forwards. Yes, this is a wind up for the dog and a crude one at that. The pup competes in these juvenile games with the rest of the litter and progresses to chasing a dummy lure in a gallop or paddock. Assuming it is not a runt, at around twelve to eighteen weeks old it heads off to a schooling track or racetrack where it is 'handslipped' i.e. released by hand behind a slow-moving lure, usually on a bend, to familiarise it with the sights, sounds and techniques of running round a track.

Once the trainer is satisfied the dog can or will chase the lure, the dog moves into the traps. Unfortunately, some dogs at this stage turn out to be either too smart or too stupid for their own good. If a pup susses out that the mechanical lure is a dummy, it can lose interest in the chase; and if it isn't interested in chasing . . . well, let's put it this way, it is in a puppy's *best* interest to chase the lure . . .

The next stage for our budding racer is to practise walking through the traps with the front and back gates open and a little gentle encouragement from its trainer. The claustrophobic atmosphere of the traps can freak a young greyhound easily, so this process continues until the greyhound is confident in the starting boxes and is able to exit the traps at speed and chase the lure.

After I'd moaned about Twotone's price Linda showed me what else was on offer. Like any salesperson, she had showed me the most expensive item first, clocked my reaction, and then set out an alternative stall.

'If you want something that's tried and tested I've got a couple of good racers for sale,' she said. Both were two-year-olds: a black and white dog called Ship of Dreams and a black bitch called Luck Sharp, both of whom were already running at the Stow. I wanted a dog with little or no form, something brand new and unspoilt that I could call my very own, so they were out of the frame.

Then there was a young bitch called Luscious and a couple of oldies in the twilight of their careers. For a moment, I contemplated the idea of buying an old dog as a charity case, to give it one last season around the track. What was I on? As for the bitch, Linda said that if I wanted to get the most out of a greyhound, a dog was a better proposition. Bitches tend to go off the boil when they are in season and are unable to race, which means they can't earn their keep. On the other hand, they often make better stayers than dogs – something to do with the female of the species being more dependable over the longer distance. That sounds familiar ... However, the trouble with stayers is getting the starts: there simply are not enough races over 640 metres at the Stow compared to 475 metres, which is the most common distance run.

'A lot depends on what sort of greyhound you're looking for,' said Linda. 'If you want the maximum amount of races at the Stow you want a 475 [metre] dog ... 435 dogs don't get much racing.'

Only heaven knew what I was looking for. Were big dogs better than small dogs, tall ones better than short? *Lonely Planet* didn't publish a guide to greyhounds so I had to have faith in Linda Jones and Dame Juliana Berners, prioress of Sopwell nunnery who, in 1418, became the first person to prescribe the 'points of a good greyhound'. In her *Booke of St Albans*, the great Dame wrote that a greyhound should have:

> A head lyke a snake,
> A neck lyke a drake,
> The feet of a cat
> A tail lyke a rat.
> A back lyke a beam,
> The sides of a bream.

Patience has never been a virtue of mine. I was getting dogged out. I had seen more tail than Bill Clinton. Despite the auctions, trailing through the greyhound press, making phone calls and mooching around the Stow, my total lack of knowledge on dog racing meant *any* purchase was going to be a gamble. Linda showed me round the rest of her pack of prospective mutts, bitches, stayers and sprinters. Nothing tickled my fancy. I was ready to call it a day, go home, and take up knitting or stamp collecting or something when a dog suddenly caught my eye. His name: 'Kevin'. Yes, Kevin. Well, that was his pet name. His race name was 'Zussies Boy'. He had a fawn-going-on-caramel coat and a savoury-sweet aroma, like freshly made scrambled eggs. His big, brown, soulful eyes melted when he looked at you. He also had what Linda called 'floaters', two extended ribs protruding from his coat like two chunks of Toblerone. Was this physical quirk an omen perhaps?

Kevin was a beautiful specimen, but he did strike me as a bit of a dumb blonde, in a manner of speaking. Yes, dogs can be dumb blondes too, you know. My folks once owned an Afghan hound, the most beautiful dog imaginable. He was sleek and gracious with long, flowing blonde locks. He was also as thick as two extremely short planks of wood.

Dog people put much stock on a dog's colour. For instance, blue dogs have a reputation for being suspect, perhaps only because they are rare and thus statistically amount to very little. Black dogs account for the largest distinct group and thus turn out many good runners. But there was such a kaleidoscope of markings amongst greyhounds I could not see how one colour trait was better than any other.

'Aw, everyone loves Kevin, don't they, sweetheart?' said Linda giving him a big hug. 'This one gets all the special treatment.'

Kevin was coy but not like Twoey. He shied away at first but it did not take much for me to bring him round. Like Twotone, the Dog Lovers Syndicate owned him too. Unlike Twotone, he did not have an attitude problem. He took biscuits, like a *proper dog*.

'So what's the score with Kevin then?' I asked.

'Well, he's out of Lakeshore Owney and Lakeshore Annie . . .'
Here we go again with that breeding stuff . . .

'Is he any good?'

'I'd say Twotone is the better of the two, but I'm putting my head on the chopping block here, cos I honestly don't know . . . I can't say for sure. Kevin could turn out to be the better dog. Who knows?'

Linda was hedging her bets. I told her I did not want to spend more than two grand on a greyhound; the asking price for Kevin was £2500. Buying a dog was now a matter of urgency for me, and she knew this, so she was bound to think I could be persuaded to find an extra £500 if need be. On the other hand, she knew that I knew that she knew that I knew deep down he was not in the same league as Twotone. Having spotted me coming up the M11 as a know-nothing, wet-behind-the-ears hack with more money than sense, natch, she would reason that, if I could find an extra £500 for one dog, why could I not find an extra £2000 for the other? If there's one born every minute, I had stumbled into Imperial Kennels on the stroke of sixty seconds. *Fuck it: you only live once.* I told Linda to inform the Dog Lovers Syndicate that I was interested in Kevin and Twotone, but they had to be flexible on price. 'I can't promise anything,' she said. Whatever. Linda, me, the Dog Lovers, Kevin and Twotone were now inexorably joined in a two-horse dog race. Let the games begin.

chapter 7

The going for the trial was −10, which meant that the track was running 10 hundredths of a second slower than normal. The going could run anywhere from −60 to +30 so it was an important factor when considering a dog's real times, particularly as around a quarter of a second generally separates the fastest dog from the slowest in the race and no more than a couple of a seconds separates a £40,000 Derby winner from a £200 scrubber.

Trials are held every Wednesday, from 10a.m. to just after lunchtime. Linda told me to see her in the paddock, so I walked the length of the home straight, through the empty betting ring to the far end of the stadium, stopping briefly to see what the competition had to offer. There was a small number of people dotted around the stands – their grey faces a counterpart to the overcast sky. Trials are a purely technical exercise, no-thrills racing. There aren't the distractions of a race meet. There was idle talk but on the whole the punters or aficionados kept one eye buried in their trial programmes (A4 sheets of photocopied paper with basic information about the day's 47 trials, a sort of simplified race card), the other on the track.

Twotone and Kevin were down to run against each other and a dog called Kinda Funny in trial number 39, over 435 metres, in traps three, five and one respectively. Recently Twotone and Kevin had both started their training off with a couple of 235-metre warm-up trials, before moving up to 435.

There were plenty of single guys sitting around, making notes and scratching their heads as the dogs came out in quick succession, some in single trials, others in twos and threes. One middle-aged couple filmed each trial with a camcorder; an old boy had a pair of binoculars; several people were scribbling notes on scraps of paper or the *Racing Post*. Something told me I should have brought my anorak.

The trials were a mixed bag: Doubting Thomas in the twenty-second trial bolted out of trap three, buckled and then head-butted the ground and rolled over, while his two competitors sailed by; two trials on, She's A Fantasy pulled up lame just before the third bend, yelping in agony; Balleric Sunrise decided to go walkabout after his trial, as did Blue Lad, who had the good grace to finish before leading his kennel hand on a Benny Hill-style chase across the track's central reservation. 'He's trying to get on the winners' rostrum,' joked one of the spectators. No one responded.

It was nearing Twotone and Kevin's trial, so like a child of Hamelin I followed the sweet sound of greyhounds yelping into the paddock, ignoring the clearly visible 'No Entry' sign. An embittered-looking fat bloke dressed in a white polo shirt emblazoned with a Cross of St George and blue track pants and trainers approached and confronted me immediately. By the state of him I guessed he'd never walked past a gym, let alone inside one.

'Have you got a licence, mate?' he asked.

'I'm here to see Linda . . .'

Before I could say Jones he said, 'Linda who?'

'Linda Jones,' I said.

'She ain't here, mate.'

'Well, I've been told she is.'

'Wait outside by the wall, mate, and she'll come out to see you.'

So she *was* there, stoopid. Was I becoming a misanthrope or was the world populated by unhelpful pricks? That's unfair. The guy was only doing his job. To get into the paddock you have to be a licence holder, which means you have to be a trainer, kennel hand, vet or track official, or have friends in high places. This is to stop unscrupulous characters from nobbling the dogs. A dog can be in the kennels or the paddock for anything up to four hours during a race meet, depending on the time it arrives and when it races.

Linda had twelve dogs on trial so she had her work cut out. We didn't chitchat for too long. 'Are they well?' I asked, which is dog people talk for, 'Has he got the shits/a club foot/eight Mars bars in his gut?' Linda said the pair were OK and scurried back into the yapping, yelping paddock in the kennelling area.

I took a seat in the stands and watched as Twotone trounced Kevin by four lengths, recording a time of 27.60 compared to 27.82. Given the difference in their prices every spot between the two dogs cost around £68, or £1500 to buy not even a quarter of a second's difference in speed. At the time the track record at the Stow over 435 metres was 25.71.

Even a novice like me could see that a novice like Twotone was patently better than a Kevin but at £4000 he was double my budget. Besides, he had a stinking personality, not taking that biscuit and all. Twotone cost £4000 and he couldn't even take a poxy dog biscuit from me. For four grand, he ought to dance for it. At least Kevin and I could get along. If I was going to pay four figures for a dog, he had to take the biscuit. Also Kevin was a truly beautiful animal. He was very docile, but fast enough to make the grade – just not as fast as Twotone.

The race manager grades the dogs initially on their performance during a trial, which presents a trainer with an opportunity to pull a fast one. Based on time the race manager will grade the dogs according to their relative speed. Slowing a dog down, or 'time finding' as it's known, is the best way to ensure a dog has an advantage when it eventually races for real. Time finding, while not punishable by death, is prohibited and could result in a fine or a trainer being suspended or banned from a track.

Before a trial or a race, each dog is weighed and has its particulars recorded in an individual identity book. As soon as they are processed, the dogs are kept in a kennel until their trial. Twotone had weighed in that morning at 35.5 kilos which was 1.5 kilos heavier than Kevin. If a dog lost or gained more than a kilo between races the alarm bells went off and the race manager would automatically disqualify the dog and question the trainer.

That night I called Linda to haggle.

'You sure you can't take two grand, Linda?' I said, pleading down the phone.

'No, sorry, David. I've had a word with 'em and they're not moving.'

'I'll make 'em famous.'

'They don't want to be famous, they're publicity shy.'

'All right, I'll make you famous then.'

'I'm famous already! Ha ha ha!'

I told Linda I'd have to think about it. I'd seen *Glengarry Glen Ross*. I knew how to close a deal. Yeah. The tables had turned. Now that she knew I was seriously keen she'd tell the Dog Lovers I was game and those little euro note signs would start rolling around their eyes. I cracked open a beer, kicked back and waited for the phone to ring.

Linda had me in her sights. If I wanted a dog that had more than three legs and wasn't called Satan and chained to a scrapyard fence in Bermondsey I'd have to fork out at least two-and-a-half grand, but my silent partner (i.e. my publisher) would only stump up £2000. I wanted Twotone but The Dog Lovers Syndicate would not budge on price. Despite my best efforts at begging, borrowing, stealing and blackmail the only way I could raise the extra £2000 was from my own coffers. If two-and-a-half 'large' seemed steep for Kevin, £4000 for Twotone was vertiginous. I could speculate to accumulate but this was business, baby. If I had learnt one thing during those tedious economics lectures at university, it was always get some other mug to invest in your daft enterprises. I did not have time to go traipsing around looking for more investors or another trainer and other dogs. I was down to a shortlist of one: Kevin. Nevertheless, I was still a monkey short of the asking price.

For some reason Margot had come round to the idea of me owning a greyhound. In fact, she even went so far as to throw her hat in the ring and offer to stump up the extra lolly. She said she simply wanted to 'help', which smelt fishy.

Anyway, I was all set to relieve her of the dough when we headed to the Glastonbury festival and a bunch of meddling hippies screwed things up. Margot and I were trudging around in the mud pretending to be on acid and talking about what fun she'd have as a fully paid-up member of the syndicate when out of the mud and marijuana haze appeared a shabby stall run by an outfit called Greyhound Action. A couple of do-gooders were handing out leaflets featuring the slogan 'You bet ... they die' and a picture of a skeletal greyhound that had been 'tied to a lump of concrete and drowned'. Like most animal rights organisations, Greyhound Action was low on subtlety and high on impact. Somehow I don't think Saatchi & Saatchi was running their ad campaign.

'Jesus fucking Christ,' I muttered under my breath.

'What was that?' said Margot as I tried to steer her away from the stall towards a mung bean burger bar.

'Support Greyhound Action!' came the cry. 'Thousands of innocent greyhounds killed every year!'

A jobless crusty wearing a t-shirt that looked like a used sanitary towel was working the crowd. I bet he lived in a converted Bedford van and had toenails like talons. The bloody soap dodger caught Margot's attention.

'Oh look, there's something about greyhounds over there.' Margot ambled over to the stall.

'Would you like to sign our petition?' asked Crusty.

'That's all I need,' I mumbled again. 'Fucking hippy wankers.'

'What was that?' said Margot.

'Nothing, sweetheart. I'm starving. Shall we get something to eat?'

Crusty butted in. 'Would *you* like to sign our petition?'

'Er, no thanks. I can't read.'

'Sorry?'

'So what's this all about then?' I feigned interest, hoping perhaps I could embarrass the poor fool behind the counter. Subterfuge and diversionary tactics had not worked. In fact, not only had they not worked, Margot was signing Crusty the Clown's petition! Traitor! Consorting with the enemy!

'Why the hell did you do that?' I scowled as we walked away.

'Aw, I felt sorry for him sitting there behind his little stand. No one was paying any interest.'

Let he who is without sirloin cast the first stone-baked vegetarian pizza. How dare they steal my thunder with their animal rights crap? And to think I was missing the 2002 FIFA World Cup third-place play-off between South Korea and Turkey for this nonsense. Margot was on the verge of giving me the money then this happens. Fucking hippies.

Greyhound Action claims that at least 40,000 greyhounds are bred every year in Britain and Ireland, with a similar number 'disposed of'. The consensus both inside and outside the industry is that at least 10,000 greyhounds retire from racing in the UK every year. According to the British Greyhound Racing Board, the sport's marketing arm, up to 2000 of these dogs find good homes, either with their owners or other individuals. For the other 8000 their fate is less clear. Refuges and charities save many but admittedly others are abandoned or put down by their owners, used for laboratory experiments or shipped to Spain and used as *galgos* or coursing dogs. This dark side of the sport means that Greyhound Action, along with several other animal rights organisations, including the League Against Cruel Sports, want to ban greyhound racing on the grounds that it is cruel. In a liberal democracy such a demand is fine. But if cruelty is the only criteria for banning stuff then let's ban Christmas. I'm still in therapy over December 25th 1974. I asked Santa for an Action

Man with gripping hands and got a box of fucking Quality Street instead.

I had always been too busy being an oppressed minority to bother with little things like animal rights, so I never really questioned the moral implications of racing dogs or keeping animals in kennels, cages, aquariums or little jars with a spicy marinade. Now the animal rights lobby was slowly crawling out from under its collective rock, getting on my case, getting in my face. Even my editor at the *Evening Standard* started getting heavy with me.

'If you buy a greyhound you'll never work for this paper again,' she said, with only a hint of irony.

'C'mon, Liz, that's a bit strong.'

'They do wicked things to greyhounds you know.'

'That's, er, a fallacy,' I replied, limply.

'What about what they do to them in Spain, eh? It's barbaric.'

'Tsch.'

To ram home the point Liz sent me some information about the poor state of the Spanish *galgos*, many of which are hanged from trees, stoned, thrown into wells and set on fire at the end of the coursing season every spring by their owners or *galgueros*.

I love animals, I really do. I especially love to eat them. Two-legged, four-legged, one-legged on a frigging pogo stick, I don't care. If it has a pulse and a three-second memory, I'll eat it. And if an animal exists that has a conscience or a soul, even better, I'll eat that too.

But something did disgust me when I saw those *galgos* hanging from trees like cured meat in a butcher's shop; and it wasn't the obvious graphic shock horror. Maybe I'm anthropomorphising dangerously here but the images were reminiscent of old photographs I'd seen of black people lynched in the Deep South, surrounded by proud grinning Klansmen: judges, policemen, farmers and other pillars of the community.

Still, I couldn't change the plight of the *galgos*, let alone the course of human history. Maybe I'd look into it when I went to

Spain in a couple of weeks. Yes, I had become a journalist because of a genuine desire to right wrongs, redress the balance and expose 'the truth'. And I tried, without preaching, to impart these same noble ideals to my bright-eyed and bushy-tailed students at the university where I moonlighted. But I had bills to pay, and the *galgos* and the truth and all that other stuff right now was just another awkward obstacle to overcome, a temporary setback, and an irritant that simply got in the way of me going about my bees' wax.

chapter 8

I shared a flat with a Jewish doctor named Paul. A friend had once described our place as 'very *Withnail and I*'. We lived like a pair of bums in that grotty little flat but our cohabitation did provide me with one essential luxury: a fat ride. Dr Paul had a metallic blue Mercedes E Class, or 'Jew canoe' as he liked to call it, fully loaded, with air con, heated seats, cruise control, the works. I was going to drive the canoe out to Imperial Kennels to close the deal, having talked my agent Julian into investing the extra £500 needed for Kevin's purchase. 'I don't know how I'm going to explain this to the accountant,' he had said. 'I don't think a greyhound is tax deductible.'

Tax, bills, commitments, responsibilities . . . I had to start cleaning up my act. I was thirty-six years old and still hustling. Clothes maketh the man, so from now on jeans and trainers were out; it was time to whistle up, don the camel-hair coat, the brogues and the Gucci watch. I hung out on the Portobello Road too much and the 'hood rat' look had rubbed off on me. Anyway, like most of my friends, Dr Paul thought my dog-racing idea was bullshit. When I told him I was about to buy a greyhound for £2500, he nearly fainted.

'If I told my old man I'd just spent two-and-a-half grand on a dog he'd say I was fucking mad!' he said.

❉   ❉   ❉

I collected the money in used £50 notes from the bank. I did my best to look 'respectable' but still encountered the usual pettifogging security checks. The bank teller pulled a wad of cash sealed in pink cellophane from a drawer and placed it in front of her VDU. 'Would you like it like this or would you prefer me to count it out for you?' she said, peering up at me. 'Let's count it, shall we? Just to be on the safe side.' The teller took umbrage and hastily counted the money. I lost track of the tally at £750. Whatever happened to the customer always being right?

As I left the bank a fat bloke in an Arsenal shirt bumped me. 'Easy,' I said, sneering. I felt empowered. I was the big man, in the big car with big cash in his pocket. I walked round the corner to McDonald's and got myself a Filet-O-Fish and a Coke and then crossed the Holloway Road, bouncing through the crowds of commuters and early risers. Sitting outside Barclays was a tramp, begging. I thought about the two-and-a-half grand in my pocket and how sacrificing a pound for this poor soul would make little impact on my bank balance but bring a whole lot of love to his heroin addiction. There are now more beggars on the streets of London than there are stray dogs. I walked on. I got in the car, pressed the central locking button and headed for Lakenheath.

I cruised down the lane towards the kennels. A voice on the car radio said the ban on hunting with dogs in Scotland would come into force that day. An old nag stood in a field, posing as though waiting for the sun to break through and the picture-postcard moment to arrive. The birds sang, frogs croaked, manure stank. God, I hate the countryside.

I reached the iron gates of hell, I mean Imperial Kennels, and steeled myself. Just as Paul Kenyon had infiltrated the world of greyhound racing posing as an owner, I too had infiltrated this murky subculture: posing as a complete idiot. This was not a hard act to pull off. Until I started swotting up on greyhounds my ignorance of the breed and dogs in general was blissfully mind-blowing. I thought a lurcher was a dog that leant to one side when it ran and that a whippet was a small breed of half-dog, half-ferret indigenous only to the north of England. I crossed myself – like I believe in that shit – picked up the brown envelope, put it inside my jacket and made my move.

'I think our path is mapped out for us the moment we're born, David,' said Linda as we strolled around the kennels, looking up towards the heavens as another jet streaked by. Greyhound racing *and* philosophy: an interesting combination. I was getting concerned about the noise from Lakenheath. Didn't it freak the dogs out?

'They don't pay it no mind,' said Linda.

I was really clutching at straws, setting up the fallout position, with that jet fighter thing: if Kevin proved to be a lemon I could blame it on the US military. We headed back to the kitchen for a cuppa and the last rites. I still had an opportunity to bail out. If I made a run for it I could be over the back fence, sneak round the side of the kennels, slip into the Merc and take off without anyone noticing. No, that isn't my style. My problem is I did not know how *or* when to give up.

The phone rang and Linda answered it, wheeling and dealing down the blower while her daughter Sarah, Mark, Kelly and a Belgian named Patrick (who had recently joined the kennels after working in Ireland) stopped carting around dog leads, bales of straw, bowls of water and food, buckets and spades, to join us for a celebratory cup of cha.

'He should've won,' said Patrick, referring to Kevin's last race, which I had missed. I was never big on homework. 'But at the third bend he was in second place and they tipped him out from behind. Somebody ran into his hind legs.'

Kevin wound up finishing third. Sarah jumped to his defence.

'They can be a bit green at first,' she said. 'But the more they run, the more they get used to what they're doing and then improve.'

'Twotone got off to a flyer, didn't he?' I said, still thinking about that arrogant little fucker and what could have been.

'Yeah, he won his first one,' said Sarah with a cheeky little giggle.

'But he's had a cut on his foot since,' said Linda, interjecting, 'so we've laid him off. He's had to have antibiotics, but he looks all right. You ain't changed your mind have ya?'

'No, no, no,' I said, unconvincingly. 'Unless you wanna change your mind and knock off that fifteen hundred quid.'

The small talk got smaller and smaller, moving from sexual innuendo, to the World Cup and on to food and holidays. Linda said she wasn't the holidaying type as she had 'too much work to do'. One of her owners however had recently treated her to a Caribbean cruise. 'I do like a man with a few quid in his pocket,' she joked. Jesus, there was nothing in the budget for *that* level of hospitality. The only Caribbean cruise Linda would get from me was a lift to the shops on Eriswell High Street.

' 'Ere, you've been on holiday, haven't you, David?' said Sarah.

'That's right. I've just come back from Ibiza. Can you tell by the tan?'

'I was just going to say, you've got a *bloody* good tan,' joked Linda.

Oh how we laughed.

'We've got one in the final tomorrow night at Hove and one in the final on Saturday night at the Stow,' said Linda, doling out lumps of meat and pouring vitamin B into dishes, 'so we're pretty busy at the moment. Actually, I've got a little job for ya.'

Linda passed me a container of potassium tablets and had me crush them, then sprinkle tiny measurements into the dogs' dinners. The greyhounds at Imperial get more nutrients in their three squares than probably 70 per cent of the world's population get on a daily basis. Apart from the moody types who give their dogs contraband, some trainers give their dogs an extra boost with perfectly legal supplements like creatine, a muscle-building metabolite. I had tried it myself many years ago but quit after reading stories about athletes dying on it. Vitamins, minerals and good food aside, Linda uses nothing suspect on her dogs. She does, however, have one 'secret ingredient'.

'People are always wondering why my dogs do so well,' she told me, 'so you always get one or two who think you're giving the dogs something dodgy to boost 'em up. I had a trainer approach me once at the track saying, " 'Ere Linda, what d'you use on your dogs, you know, to get 'em going?"' Linda starts hamming up the 'wanna buy a watch?' routine. 'I said to him, "Come over 'ere and I'll tell ya." He thought he was on to something . . . grinning his face off he was. I pulled him to one side and said "I've got this secret ingredient that I use." "Really, really, what is it?" he says, "It's called TLC." "What's that?" he says, thinking it's some new drug. "TENDER LOVING CARE, mate, now sling your hook!"'

The phone rings *again*, and Linda's back on the case. I chat to Sarah who tells me she couldn't imagine doing another job. 'The dogs are brilliant, they're lovely, they're happy. It's great to work with the dogs but it's also great to be outside. You've got no one breathing down your neck, saying "do this, do that". Everyone knows what they've got to do here. We all get on with it . . .' Sarah then whispers, 'When *she's* not cracking the whip.'

' 'Ere, you talking about me you little bitch?' jokes Linda. 'She's a little bitch, 'er.'

'I was just saying you like cracking the whip, Mum.'

'You're giving me a bad name,' says Linda. 'If he puts all that in the book you're sacked.'

We get through feeding and then knuckle down to business.

'I'm trusting that you're not going to shaft me, Linda,' I said, swatting flies.

'I think you're quite safe there.'

I reached inside my jacket and pulled out the brown envelope with the two-and-half gees. 'You drive a hard bargain, Linda.' Somehow it felt unreal, parting with £2500 for a dog.

'Aren't you gonna count it?'

'Why, shouldn't I trust you?' asked Linda.

'Well, yeah, you should, I guess.'

'Well I don't need to check it then, do I, David?'

'I guess not.' Linda put the envelope in her pocket.

'What about a receipt?'

'Do you want one?'

'Well, yeah. You know, tax and all that. Not that I ever pay any.'

Linda scanned the kitchen. I expected her to produce one of those WH Smiths receipt books but she started rummaging round for some paper. Then I noticed something strange on the shelf above her head.

'What's that?' I asked as she tore a piece of scrap paper in half and scribbled away.

'Oh that,' she said, looking at the stuffed hare mounted in a trophy cabinet set against a crudely painted rural scene. 'The staff at Romford presented him to me a few years ago when they stopped using real hares.' There was something spooky about that hare. He made my skin crawl.

'Lovely, ain't he?' said Linda wistfully.

'Charming,' I said.

Linda handed me the receipt:

Received on behalf of the Dog Lovers Syndicate, the sum of £2,500.00p in payment of a fawn greyhound named Zussies Boy.

L. E. Jones 31/7/02

IMPERIAL KENNELS
UNDLEY COMMON
LAKENHEATH, SUFFOLK
IP27 9BY

Deal done.

'What about insurance?' I asked.

'What about it?' she replied nonchalantly.

'Well, should I . . . I mean, can I insure him?'

'To be honest with you, David, no one bothers. It's very difficult to get insurance for a greyhound and the companies that do it charge astronomical premiums. Hopefully Kevin won't get injured. It's just one of the risks you have to take in this game.'

Linda told me a story about someone who had bought a greyhound that had made it to the quarter-finals of the Derby for something in the region of £18,000. It was out in the paddock early one morning, roaming around as happy as Larry. When feeding time came, one of the kennel hands went out to fetch the dog and noticed he was lying under a tree.

The kennel hand called out to him but the dog didn't respond. When he got to the dog he discovered it was stone dead. Apparently it had died of an aneurysm to the heart. I hoped Kevin was made of sterner stuff. I told Linda to make sure he lay off the booze, fags and fry-ups.

So now I owned a racing greyhound, a running machine. The training fees worked out at £7+VAT per day, a couple of quid dearer than I had bargained for. Then there were occasional vet's bills, de-worming, de-fleaing treatments and a physiotherapy service run by a former trainer called Ron Mills, which he did for Linda and only one other kennel.

Ron, who preferred the term 'sports massage therapist' to physio, visited the kennels once or twice a week and worked the dogs with massage and ultrasound in a little room next to the kitchen. He was in the process of completing on an apartment in Marbella. I was pleased that some of my kennel bills were going to an even better cause than Kevin. Ron had trained on humans and gave Linda a going over sometimes.

'Muscles are muscles however they're packaged,' said Ron, gliding his hands over his first patient, while Peter the kennel hand held the agitated mutt down. 'The drugs are the same as those given to humans, they're only marketed under a different name.

'This one's running on Saturday and he's got symptoms of a pulled hamstring.' Ron starts working the dog's hindquarter. It yelps and screams, whistling like a kettle on the boil. 'If you put pressure on the calf here, he comes up on it. I usually find these problems by touch. I start an examination with some basic stretching . . .' Ron trails off for a moment . . . '. . . He's got a bloody flea there. Dead though. That's the first one . . .' Then returns to the examination proper. 'Then I go over the body, checking the muscles. What we're dealing with is a tight muscle, so I'm going to massage it out.' The dog screams pitifully. 'No pain, no gain,' says Ron. 'I try and be as gentle as I can with 'em. They don't hold it against me.'

Within minutes Ron had broken down the adhesion in the dog's muscle, turning him to jelly. His tongue was hanging out and his eyes were glowing with almost post-coital satisfaction. 'There you go,' said Ron squeezing the muscle, 'gradually the pain goes . . .' The dog lay there, gaga. You could've picked him up and used him as a stole he was now that supple.

Kevin was certainly in the right place for five-star treatment: and at an average monthly cost of £250, boy, he'd better appreciate it. I've stayed in hotels that didn't offer the level of service Linda did. Kevin's prize money would go immediately to Imperial Kennels and I'd have the balance to pay. Linda wasn't cheap. Good women never are. In fact, she was probably the most expensive trainer in the country. But you can't put a price on quality. She wasn't the reigning champion trainer for nothing. Besides, providing he didn't turn out a lemon, Kevin's winnings would cover the bulk of his upkeep. And if he made it as an open racer, if he had a decent strike rate of, say, one-in-four wins, I'd be able to have a tasty little flutter on him from time to time.

'Have I got a decent dog then, Linda?'

'You think you're lucky, don't you? You said you think you are a lucky person, that you had a tough upbringing and all that.'

'Yeah, that's true. I'm lucky that I'm not six feet under or in jail, I guess.'

'Well then. If you're lucky, you'll be all right. Because it's luck more than anything else you need in this game.'

I was now officially 'dog people', although I didn't feel like it. Jesus. I owned a bloody greyhound. Well, half of one. No actually, a quarter to be precise. Whatever. Morally, if not technically, Kevin was mine, all mine. Maybe he could be the son I never had. And I could be the father I never had. And my father could be the grandfather he never had which would make me the illegitimate brother Kevin never had, which would be physically impossible because he's a dog and I'm a human and . . .

chapter 9

To celebrate my new acquisition I treated myself to a bottle of
Moet, a video and a lobotomy. I could not find anything along the
lines of 'How to Own a Greyhound III' at Blockbuster so I bought
a copy of *Steptoe and Son Ride Again* – not a particularly educational
film but hilarious to say the least. Just to refresh your memory,
it's the one in which Harold, using the proceeds from the sale of
the family nag, buys a greyhound from some dodgy geezer and
lives to regret it.

'Fear not, Dad, the family fortune is intact,' smirks a drunken
Harold, staggering into chez Steptoe. 'Meet Hercules the Second!'
Cue: mangy-looking dog.

'What's that . . . a greyhound? Oh my gawd!' The 'dirty old
man' could hardly believe it. 'A greyhound, a bleeding greyhound.
You want your head examined!'

Maybe I needed my head examined too. What had I done? I
had just bought a dog for two-and-a-half thousand bloody pounds.
Life had imitated art: I had become the dumber half of Steptoe
and Son. The following day, having just managed to prise my
head from my hands, I set off for the Stow to do the paperwork
on Kevin.

'Are you waiting to be seen?' said a buxom young sister from
behind the counter in the racing office. From her accent, I guessed
she was Bajan. Her name was Alfie. 'Uh?' I replied. I was
temporarily hypnotised by her heaving breasts. I had not seen tits

like that since I was eighteen months old. Four greying men draped in a variety of polyfibrous garments were standing around in the corridor. One had a hearing aid. The other was called Ron.

The sum of their ages would have taken you back to Moses and the Ten Commandments. My mobile rang.

'Sorry,' I said, giving Alfie an apologetic smile. 'I have to take this call.'

I noticed the codgers eyeing me as I yapped on my mobile. Ron had thick bifocal lenses in his glasses and a silly tartan hat. He looked like he fancied his chances: *in your acrylic dreams, old man*.

' 'Ere you are,' said Alfie to one of the codgers. 'Did you get a wage sheet?' Octogenarian bastards: why were they staring at me? I'm an owner. Respect is due. The old men shuffled off and I got down to business. Firstly, I had to re-register Kevin under my name. That cost £30. Then I had to transfer his paperwork from his previous owners to me. That cost £25. Then if I wanted to change his name from Zussies Boy to something, well, more interesting, that was £25 to the NGRC and £25 to the Irish Coursing Club (ICC), the official body for registering greyhounds bred in Ireland.

Linda had warned me that 'anything to do with the NGRC costs money'. *Hello?* It only cost £15 to change a human being's name by deed poll. I was already £2500 down and the till was still ringing. I decided not to change Kevin's name. Everyone was getting in on the act now. It was like I had a sign saying 'Insert Here' riveted to my arsehole.

The NGRC heads a tripartite group of private organisations that runs licensed greyhound racing in the UK. But the industry is ostensibly split into two groups: the tracks that are licensed by the NGRC are the major players, attracting off-course betting, and some of these are owned by the Big Three bookmakers – Ladbrokes, William Hill and Corals.

Private companies, leisure consortiums or family businesses however own the majority. On the other side of the industry, what you might call 'the dark side', are an estimated 27 independent or 'flapping' tracks which do not have off-course betting because the provenance and form of the dogs are uncertain.

Of the three organisations that run licensed greyhound racing, the NGRC regulates racing to control the integrity of betting. The British Greyhound Racing Board (BGRB) comprises primarily race promoters and bookmakers who 'promote the best interest of greyhound racing' in the UK. Finally, the British Greyhound Racing Fund (BGRF), also composed of promoters and bookmakers, collects a voluntary levy[3] from bookmakers of up to £4 million a year, which, unsurprisingly, many do not pay. The levy is spent largely on infrastructure and capital projects at tracks, such as restaurants and bars.

Under NGRC rules, an owner can change a greyhound's race name twice; were it not for the extra charge 'Zussies Boy' would have been history. I mean who or what the fuck is called Zussie? Moreover, surely Zussies Boy should have an apostrophe, as in 'Zussie's Boy'. For some reason race names do not have apostrophes. While I am at it, I may as well bitch about people always getting the bloody name wrong. I am sick of hearing 'Zessies Boy', 'Zassies Boy', 'Susies Boy' and 'Zossies Boy'. At least it wasn't the worst moniker around. There are animals on the circuit with all manner of crazy names. How some owners have the front to call their dogs Big Pockets, Potato Blight, Horseshoe Paddy, Vigilante, Jo King Only and Climb Max, I'll never know.

For a brief moment, standing in the racing office, I regained my social conscience and liberal sensibilities and thought about renaming Kevin, 'McDonalds Suck', 'Where's Osama' or 'You Sank My Battleship'. Stupid names are all part of this crrrrrrrraaaaaaaaaazzzzzzzzzy game. There is such a high premium on good names, creating something decent that hasn't been used already is beyond the imagination of most owners.

---

[3] In horseracing, the levy is mandatory.

Dog people usually lump any old shit together with a family member's name or breeder's prefix. It is also voguish to name dogs after minor celebrities and sportsmen, which has given rise to the likes of Fat Boy Slim, Louis Saha and Bomber Graham. Maybe one day, when I 'made it' someone might name a greyhound after me. I can see it now in the 19.30 at the Stow, trap one: 'Matthews' Turkey'.

I filled out a couple of forms and received a photocopy of Kevin's identity and race record book, containing details of the identification markings on his ears, his whelping date, sire and dam, anatomical marks (literally from his head down to his toenails), vaccination records and details of his trials and races to date. A few days later an envelope came in the post with four owners' passes providing free entry to the Stow and four half-yearly parking passes for the stadium car park. I had arrived.

Between Kevins first trial on June 12th and the beginning of August, he had had his first three professional races, coming fourth twice and third once over 435 metres. I had not seen any of these races as I had spent the better part of the month on holiday, raving in Ibiza and mainland Spain and indulging in other quaint 'sports'. At this point, it is worth using a little suspension of disbelief, while we go back three weeks, back back back in time to July 7th 2002 . . .

chapter 10

The early morning dew lay on the cobbled streets like gossamer. I'd been up since 5a.m. and was still feeling the effects of the previous night's bacchanal. It was now 7.30a.m.

'Here, get your laughing gear round this.' Scott lifted the goatskin, aimed it at my face and squeezed. Duck, dodge or drink? I opened my mouth and felt a jet stream of warm acrid wine hit the back of my throat. 'That'll sort ya,' said Afroman. I shook my head and grimaced as the wine kicked my palate. Men dressed in the traditional red and white outfit were jumping around necking bottles of cheap sangria and beers. The thought of alcohol at that time of the morning even rankled *my* thick skin.

Scott and Afroman (named so on account of his massive ginger hairdo) were a couple of Aussies I'd met on the way over from London. I had gone to Pamplona with my friend Owen for the *Fiesta de San Fermin* and the notorious *encierro* or 'running of the bulls', a tradition in these parts since 1591. After a twenty-four-hour red-eye drunken convoy of fifteen coaches, packed mainly with beer-swilling antipodeans, another twenty-four hours of partying in the city, and a couple of hours' sleep somewhere in between, I was ready for it. Owen came down to the City Square but bailed out of the *encierro* at the last minute. 'You know what? I think I'm gonna take a raincheck on it,' he said. At 6ft 6in he was worried that his height would make him vulnerable in the crowd. Owen had eaten snake in Cambodia and rat in Vietnam so I thought he'd have the stomach for the bull run. But I think his arsehole went at the last minute. Then again, if I had a brain I'd let my sphincter do the talking too.

Scott, Afroman, a bunch of other nuts and me followed the Big Man – an XXXL-sized Aussie tour leader – along the cobbled streets into the old city. Everyone was trying to laugh off the nerves and tension. As we walked through the crumbling citadel we passed the same stalls I'd revelled around the night before, bulging with calamari, *bacalao, paella* and *pollo y patatas*, a.k.a. chicken and chips. The Big Man gave us some rudimentary 'advice' on what to do in the race. He'd done the run once before. Once was enough for anyone he said. 'It's every man for himself out there boys,' said the Big Man. 'As soon as you see the bulls, run. Don't hang about. Don't wait for your mates. When it comes to the run you're on your own.' On the coach coming over from London they had shown a video of the previous year's run, but I had been too drunk to pay attention. I didn't have a clue what to do other than run, pray and keep my powder dry.

'We shouldn't run until we see the whites of their eyes,' said Afroman, grinning maniacally, as we reached the *Plaza Consistorial*, the City Hall Square. This was our starting point: 280 metres from the Santo Domingo corral where the six fighting bulls and two herds of steers were kept. The total length of the run from Santo Domingo to the bullring was 825 metres. I used to do a seven-minute-mile jog on a daily basis. I could run. I figured I could cover the 825 metres in four minutes without obstruction. A greyhound could do it in under 60 seconds. But I was no grader. A bull could cover the distance in around two minutes, which made me second favourite.

'Those who are about to die salute you,' I said punching the air. What a clown. I looked up at the City Hall clock. It was nearly eight. Large sections of the crowd started singing mournfully in Spanish. I think it was some sort of prayer.

I noticed a groundswell of bodies moving rapidly in my direction, up the inclined street and away from the corral. The first rocket or *cohete* went off dead on eight o'clock. This meant the corral gates were open. Half the crowd of two thousand or so runners, or *correadores*, took off instantly. 'Wait, wait,' I shouted. *You're not supposed to run until the second rocket. Uh?* I looked round and Scott had bolted. Afroman looked at me and smiled ruefully. The second rocket went off. This indicated that the bulls had now left the corral. I looked down the street towards the corral and saw a sea of freaks headed my way up the steep narrow street. As soon as I saw the bulls, I split. Fuck they were faaaaaaaaaaaaaass ssssssssssssst!!!!!!!! I'm running, I'm running, I'm running. Either I'll be gored to death by a ton of raging meat or crushed under the stampeding crowd. I'm running, oh Jesus I'm running. What was I doing here? This had *nothing* to do with greyhound racing. Shhhhhhhhhhhhiiiiiiiiiiiiiittttttttttt!!!!!!!!!!!!!!!!!!!!!!!!!!!

I'm running for dear life through the *Plaza Consistorial* and into the *Calle Mercaderes*, the only part of the course drenched in sunlight, as tall buildings overshadow most of the route. The bulls remain tightly bunched, steamrollering forward through the crowd. I reach the notorious *Calle Estafeta*, where there's a sharp right turn. Eight tons of muscle speeds down the cobbled street like a bovine tsunami. As the bulls hurtle past me in a cloud of dust I'm mesmerised, transfixed by the sight of such large animals moving effortlessly with force and grace.

I gather my senses and get going again, turning into the bend ahead of the last bull, which rounds the corner, skids on the wet cobblestones and careers into a wall, buckling under his own weight. There's a pregnant pause. For a moment he lays still, dazed and confused. As a herd animal a bull is most dangerous when separated from his *compadres*. Half of the remaining five hundred-strong crowd freezes, watching his every move; the other half pursues the herd into the distance. The bull rises, looks one way then the other. A Japanese photographer in full Nikon splendour, grappling with what looks like a mini tripod leaps out of the crowd and sets himself on the cobbled street for that Pulitzer Prize-winning shot. The bull rushes him, head down, like a 515 lb Jonah Lomu, and hits him full on in the solar plexus – BOOM!

– snapping his head back so that the terrified man cartwheels six feet into the air.

A roar goes up from the spectators as the photographer spins through the air, arms and legs wheeling like clothes in a tumble drier, and hits the ground. After a while, he springs to his feet and in that moment he and the bull share a common animal instinct: survival. The man clambers into the relative safety of the crowd, legs and arms flailing, and disappears with his pride bruised but his dinner party anecdote intact.

I'm frozen, gripped by the unfolding drama. I focus on the bull, awaiting his next gambit. A bull's balls are bigger than its brain so little wonder where most of its thinking comes from. I look to the side: no one is moving. The bull swings his powerful meaty head around again, searching for the next target. A bull has no concept of colour and very poor depth of perception. It goes for the biggest moving object it can identify. The average Spaniard is a 5ft 9in scrawny motherfucker. I'm 6ft 2in and not far off 200 lbs. I am the only black man in sight out of a crowd of several hundred runners. He can't see colour, right? Whether I'm the intended target or not, he heads in my direction.

I turn on a sixpence and make for the barriers around ten feet away, a distance I must've covered in two strides. Even with this generous head start the bull quickly narrows the gap with a chilling desire to maim or kill. Faced with, or more correctly, running away from, a creature that is equal in size and weight to a Ford Fiesta, and has a break horsepower to match, I make for the barricades but find every conceivable way is blocked by the frenzied crowd. I fall. I had been warned about this. Now I remember. The Spanish in their lust for blood and gore will do their level best to keep you in the game, even if it means you being gored in the process. It's nothing personal. If you've chosen to run with Pamplona's finest you stay in the race, *you little chicken-shit thrillseeker you*.

Jesus fucking Christ Almighty. I clamber to my feet, battling through the mass of spectators, my legs collapsing beneath me. I punch and kick my way along through the crowd, fighting desperately for a way out of danger. The only thing between the bull and me is tumbling bodies. The first person blocking my path I grab instinctively by the scruff of the neck and fling to the ground. I punch another in the kidneys, sending him careening away from the barrier. More space. I feel an elbow in my jaw. 'Motherfucker,' I yell and lash out. I feel the weight of the crowd behind me intensifying. I feel the bull's presence. No time to look back. *It ain't gonna be me*. Someone falls in front of me, screaming. I stumble again, caught in a human domino effect. I leap up, stick my right leg out and impale it in a runner's back, then bunk myself up with my left leg on his neck, crushing him underfoot, giving me the necessary leverage to leapfrog over a few more bodies. I trample one, two, three more runners in front and feel someone's spine crack, like treading on a massive cockroach. This is dog eat dog, man eat man. The most dangerous single exercise I have ever encountered. Never again. This makes professional boxing look like a tea dance. There is no time for the milk of human kindness. It's every mad fuck for himself.

I find myself in an orgy of screaming bodies but with just enough time and energy left to shimmy my way through a gap in the barricades. I dive in, meet resistance again from legs hard pressed against the wood, determined to keep the runners out. I have half my body through and can feel the weight of the spectators pushing me back, and the collapsing crowd of runners pushing me forwards. The bastards. Both sides are playing me like a fucking accordion. I continue to force my way through, kicking out behind me and punching out in front. I let rip a right hook into a standing spectator's crotch and hear him wince. He buckles long enough to fall off the barricade, creating a body-sized hole for me to smash through. I clamber to my feet, turn and hear a thud followed by a high-pitched 'zing' as the barricade vibrates under the bull's force. I have made it with inches to spare. The bull gives a contemptuous snort. Pandemonium. Perhaps it was an over-active imagination, the previous night's sangria or simply fear but I swear I saw smoke billow from his flared nostrils.

A sea of red and white sways in front of me, and a thick blue line of cops baton-charge. A small squat cop catches me on the shoulder with his truncheon. 'Fucking bitch,' I yell. I want back in the race. The police are trying to stop any spectators or surviving runners from crossing the barriers back on to the cobbled streets. The cops baton-charge again. The crowd reels backwards. I spot another gap in the barriers and make my escape as the bull tears off thirty feet ahead of me.

I make my way up the narrow, crowded *Calle Bajada de Javier* behind the bull. Spectators pack the balconies on either side. Still enraged and freaked by the crowd he indiscriminately attacks. I get complacent and slow down. The bull turns, heading in my direction once again. I do a 180 as the crowd dissipates to find huge barricades blocking my escape route back into *Calle Estafeta*. Shit. From where in God's name did they come? Sick Pamplonan motherfuckers! Did they erect the barrier to keep the bulls out or the runners in? This devious twist in the race sends the crowd fleeing; people try desperately to scurry up door shutters or clamber on to a balcony for sanctuary.

Corredores from the corral with long sticks and men with rolled-up newspapers try to beat the bull back on to the path to the bullring. The bull butts a cumbersome runner and takes off back up the street. Absolute mayhem. It's hard to say at this pace which presents the greater risk: the runners or the bulls. I pass through the *Teléfonica*, a causeway leading to a narrow channel of wooden fences that funnels straight into the bullring.

I reach the gates of the bullring panting and sweating. There's a backlog of people fighting to get to the bullring and their moment of glory. After storming the barricades with scores of runners, chanting 'Toro, toro', I come running out into the centre of a gladiatorial masterpiece: a two-tiered amphitheatre the size of a football stadium. People are going nuts, giving each other high-fives, hugging, crying, laughing, screaming. I spot two brothers and we connect instantly with an eerie sort of recognition. We indulge ourselves with a handshake. What a buzz.

The endorphins are starting to work their magic, but the Basques have one more trick up their sleeves. A final rocket goes off indicating that the last bull has entered the ring and the race is officially over, then, one by one, steers are released into the bullring for a five-minute workout with the few hundred remaining wannabe matadors. It's bad form to hit the bulls with anything other than a newspaper. Despite the debatable merits of the bull run, it is seen as disrespectful to touch or harm the bulls. A man wearing a cowboy hat puts this coda to the test by trying to rodeo ride one bull. He is quickly grabbed by a baying mob of Spaniards and punched to the ground. Another foreigner, dressed as a pantomime cow, narrowly escapes an impromptu mating with a steer, providing the morning's biggest belly laugh.

Dust and sand flies, vicars, nuns and assorted fancy-dress freaks run around making like El Cordobes and I get out of the ring as the third bull enters. My adrenaline is spent. A series of rockets go off, indicating the end of the event. At just over seven minutes, the first run of the *Fiesta de San Fermin* was nearly double the average duration. The longest ever bull run was on July 11th 1959, lasting thirty minutes when one of the bulls fell behind. Eventually a dog was used to bite the bull and drive it to the bullpen.

'You ought to be ashamed of yourself,' Linda had said, tut-tutting, when I told her of my 'holiday' plans just before I left for Spain. 'I hope those bulls give you what for up the you know what.'

Animal cruelty is a subjective business. One man's meat and all that. While Linda abhorred bullfighting, she wasn't averse to the odd spot of hare coursing in Ireland. 'But I'm not a fan of it,' she insisted. And despite my interest in Latino bullshit, I found more domestic activities like badger baiting, cockfighting, playing chicken and dogging pretty disgusting. Yes . . . one man's meat. I bet a few vegans would be happy to see the likes of Linda and me leathered. And given half a chance the anti-vivisectionists would have a piece of us too. Where did the buck stop? What about pet owners? Somewhere, a mob lay in wait for the owners of Polly and Fido. And what about insects? There are hardcore Jains whose religion requires total respect for any living, breathing organism and who wear facemasks to stop themselves from even breathing in bacteria, which they consider their spiritual equals.

Pamplona had given me an entrée into what it was like to be the hunted rather than the hunter. I'd given those bulls a chance to take a chunk out of me, which is more than can be said for your average fisherman, foxhunter or pheasant shooter, so I was square with the animal kingdom. In the local papers the following day the Spanish press was full of reportage and gory pictures of the bull run and the gored victims, many of whom were dumb foreign tourists seduced by *The Sun Also Rises*, the book that put Pamplona and Ernest Hemingway on the map.

Aw, I know all that Pamplona stuff was bullshit. Goddamn macho Hemingway crap even got me talking and writing like a Goddamn Yank, already. The good citizens of Pamplona erected a bronze statue in the old man's honour, right outside the bullring. For all that hard-drinking, beardy, bullfight stuff he never actually ran the *encierro* himself. Blew his fucking brains out cos he couldn't deal with being a fag though. I guess that's pretty macho. Well, goodbye Papa . . . and goodbye Pamplona. I had more important races to run, more pressing obstacles to overcome. The moment of truth had arrived. Er, almost.

chapter 11

'Your balls have got bigger,' said Margot when I got back from Pamplona. And so they had. I didn't put a ruler or a pair of callipers to them but with the strategic use of a shaving mirror I guessed that they'd grown by around 10–15 per cent. So with my new and improved, bigger, better balls I was ready to hit the track for the first time as a hotshot dog owner.

Tonight was the big night. Now I was finally going to see Kevin in action. I was sweating over a contentious piece about infidelity which I had just filed for the *Evening Standard* and was racing to meet another deadline. I had planned to go suited and booted to the track, maybe even wear a *boutonnière* to mark the occasion but I was pushed for time. I jumped into the Jew canoe and toed it across London, as Kevin was down to run in the second race of the night, a P8 scrubber's affair at 19.43.

I decided to make the trip on my own. This was my moment and I wanted it to be private. But more importantly, I didn't want to 'big up' the affair only to see him come last in front of all my friends. I'm sensitive like that.

I got to the track with about ten minutes to spare before the race. I had the runs, so I rushed to the toilets, clenching my butt cheeks like I was trying to crack a walnut. I managed to get inside the cubicle and pull my pants down moments before pebble-dashing the WC. Ah, Bisto . . .

There were a few minutes before the off. I turned to the side to reach for some toilet paper and . . . no toilet paper. Jesus. I was in such a hurry to get to the toilet I had left my bits and pieces – mobile, notebook and so forth – in the car so I had nothing to wipe my arse with. Not that I'd use a mobile phone for such a delicate exercise, mind you.

The only paper I had on me was the receipt for Kevin and a hundred quid in used notes. Wiping my backside with the receipt would have been a tacit admission that Kevin was shite and owning him wasn't worth the paper the receipt was written on. That left the money. I took a fiver out of my wallet. I heard the announcer say, 'There are three minutes before the off.' I stared at the fiver. What to do? I looked at my watch. I opened the cubicle door tentatively and noticed a group of lads chatting and rolling up a joint. In the cubicle next door, I could hear what sounded like an old boy honking up and letting a good one rip. Two minutes to go. I couldn't leave the cubicle like this, cack pouring out of my backside like a chocolate waterfall. I looked at the fiver again and turned it over. Elizabeth Regina. There goes the knighthood. I wiped my arse and threw the fiver into the WC. That would give the next patron something to think about. *Welcome to the high-rolling world of greyhound ownership.*

I got out and down to the heaving jungle that is the betting ring with just under a minute to spare.

The betting ring was the usual bear pit of machismo. The crowd was milling around to the strains of 'Golden Years' by David Bowie which was playing on the stadium's PA. I was woefully ill prepared for the event. I was dressed like a bum: crummy old running shoes, dirty jeans, baseball cap and a hooded sweatshirt with the logo 'CRIMINAL' emblazoned across the chest. This look *had* to go. I resolved to return wearing more suitable attire for a man of my new-found status. I also made a note to carry my own toilet paper in future.

Kevin left the kennels with his five fellow competitors, paraded fifty or so metres from the kennels to the betting ring and then went to the traps. The punters eyed the dogs as they pissed and shat themselves – the dogs that is, not the punters. I was mindful of a dog that relieved itself before a race, taking that as a sign they may well have been 'bunged up' with a Mars bar, porridge, a pint of lager, or what have you.

I craned my neck towards the traps to make sure everything was OK, no mustard jars around. The kennel hands then paraded the dogs back towards the boxes and started loading them up for the race. Kevin was in trap three, but it was too early in his career to say if this was a natural position for him. Nevertheless, for him to make it in a coffin box he had to show early pace and get to that first bend in front to stand a real chance of winning.

Kevin was up against Chrissys Charm in trap one; Baltovin Maid in trap two; his kennel mate Twotone in trap four; Bush Bill in trap five; and Miss Spartacus in trap six. 'Go on the three dog,' I cry, crunching the words out through tightened jaws. A couple of punters frown at me. 'The three dog . . . Zussies Boy . . . he's mine. I mean I own him.' The punters look at each other and go back to looking at the bookmakers' odds as the market starts buzzing.

'Seven a four the field.'

'Two elephant.'

'Two carpet.'

'Seven a four.'

'Shoulder the favourite.'

'Three bar one.'

'Top ching.'

'Three dog here.'

'Three to one bar one.'

'Three and a half, tenners.'

I look at my race card. I have thirty seconds to place a bet. The bookies are laying Kevin at 4–1 and Twotone at 7–1. Hmm. . . Perhaps the bookies knew something I didn't. Twotone had won his first race, a P8, on his maiden outing on Thursday July 4th 2002 at 8–1, beating the 4–7 favourite Knockard Terri to a pulp. I count out £50 in tens. And take a step forward. Hang on. I look at my race card again and look up at the bookies' prices. Twotone, 7–1? On current form, Twotone had the slowest times. All the so-called 'smart money' was going on Baltovin Maid. And the *Racing Post* had picked the trap one dog.

A little voice said, '*Put the fifty on Twotone. You know it makes sense.*' Nah, I can't bet against my own dog in my first race! '*But look at the INFORMATION.*' I recheck my race card. The Dog Lovers are still down as Kevin's owners. It'll be another week before the name's changed. *Steady on* . . . Suddenly there's a rush. I'm crowded from all sides. I lose my bearings for a second. I feel like a tourist on the Tokyo subway. I'm an owner, for Christ's sake, you can't manhandle me! I bowl over to the first bookie I see. 'Gimme a tenner on the three dog mate.' He snatches the money and hands me a ticket. The race steward in his tight black jodhpurs and bowler waves his magic flag. A bell rings, the lights dim. 'Hare's approaching . . .'

I hear the click and whir of the mechanical hare as it makes its way round the track like a miniature funfair ride, jolting and jerking as it hits each bend nearing the boxes. I can see Kevin's little face behind the bars. Aw . . . BANG! They're off!

Kevin's bumped at the off by the one dog and is last at the first bend. 'Oh you fucking Muppet.' They take the corner and he closes the gap going into fourth place at the second bend. 'Go on four, kick arse,' someone cries. *Fuck off four.* 'Go on Zussie . . . go on. Go on, boy.' Down the back straight he charges past Bush Bill, Chrissys Whatever and Miss Thing into second place. Nice. He's now up on Twotone's backside. 'Go on Kev, go on, my son!' I cry, stabbing a clenched fist at the air.

At the third turn he's still up on Twotone. 'Go on, boy, go on!' I'm throwing left and right hooks, shadowboxing, as Twotone and Kevin hit the fourth and final bend. 'Come on, come on, come on, keep coming, keep coming, keep coming keep . . .' And the winner is: Twotone, by 2¼ lengths. Shit. Fuck. Piss. 'Fucked up at that bend,' one of the bookies says to me. 'Yeah,' I say. I rip up my betting slip and head towards the kennels to congratulate my £2500 dog on bagging the £28 second prize. Ne'er mind. At least he'd set a personal best of 29.96 over 475 metres, which was, er, the first time he'd actually run *competitively* at that distance, so that was no mean feat.

'Dividends for race two,' says the announcer over the PA, *'win four, 22 pence; place four, 21 pence; place three, 24 pence. Forecast four and three pays 2 pounds and 75 pence. Trifecta four, three, one, pays 6 pounds and 67 pence.'*

The *Racing Post* had accurately picked Kevin for second place but curiously didn't rate Twotone to finish anywhere in the first three. I'd already figured out that the best average any newspaper tipster could hit on a card was one in three wins. Occasionally they did better, but more often than not they faired far worse. The moral of this: don't listen to tipsters. Dogs, horses, stocks and shares . . . Look, if these characters are so good at picking the next big thing they'd be making a tasty income from a beachside villa in the Caribbean, instead of eking out a living at a crummy desk.

Now, I could have had a forecast on Twotone to win and Kevin to place. Did I take the bet? No. More significantly, there were certain 'factors' I should have taken into consideration. But did I pay attention to these factors? Did I bollocks. In the end, I put a tenner on Kevin to win, purely out of loyalty. I could not bet against my own dog now, could I? Loyalty however means jack at the track. Such sentimentality is best left at the gates. To be a gambler, as opposed to being a mug punter, you have to be dispassionate about luck, coat colour, funny names, big cuddles and all that puppy-dog crap.

So Kevin was beaten into second place: story of my fucking life. He tried his best but his best wasn't good enough: the sequel to the story of my fucking life.

I went up into the bar and got myself a Jack D and Coke. It cost £2.55. Cheery ads appeared on the Tote screens in between the forecast and trifecta information. 'Happy twenty-first, Julie. Love from all of us.' Screw Julie. 'Goodbye Tom, good luck in

Leeds.' *Who cares?* 'This next one's 5–2–3,' says a punter at the table next to me. 'Nah, you want six in there,' says his mate. Everyone had moved on. Time waits for no man at the dogs. 'Sonofabitch,' I mumbled over the Jack D. I laid the race card out in front of me, smoothing the creases, and went over Kevin's form again, trying to make sense of a senseless enterprise. 'Sonofabitch.' There was no point trying to rationalise the race. Whatever way I looked at it, he hadn't won. Get over it. But he'd come so close; and his nemesis once again was Twotone, the Cain to his Abel. Seven-to-one he romped home at. I was starting to develop a grudge against that meddling dog. Kevin had now had four losses on the bounce compared with Twotone, the glory boy, who in the same period had won three out of five races. Something told me that the £1500 difference between them was going to prove very costly in the end.

chapter 12

The greyhound breed, including Salukis, Borzois and Afghans, is around eight thousand years old. Ancient Egyptians prized them for their speed, agility and hunting skills and kept them as pets. Although their exact origin is unknown, illustrations on Egyptian engravings and pottery dating back several thousands of years prove that greyhound-type dogs most certainly came from the Middle East. The Pharaohs used to bury themselves with their greyhounds, along with their wives, servants, liquid assets, tellies, videos, dishwashers etc.

In 800 BC, Homer became the first author to write about greyhounds in literature. Alexander the Great's and General George Custer's favourite dogs were greyhounds. In fact, Custer coursed his fourteen greyhounds the night before the Battle of Little Big Horn, although it did him little good the following day when Sitting Bull, Crazy Horse and the gang kicked his ass.

Britain and Ireland have the Romans to thank for the introduction of the greyhound, along with the hares that they coursed. Greyhounds have long been associated with hunting and nobility. For hundreds of years, right up until the nineteenth century, it was a crime in Britain for peasants to own a greyhound; such an animal was solely the property of royalty and lords and ladies of the realm. I could go on. To cap it all, the greyhound is the only dog referred to by breed in the King James Version of the Bible. In Proverbs 30, verses 29–31 Solomon says:

> There be three things which go well, yea
> Which are comely in going:
> A lion, which is strongest among beasts and
> turneth not away from any;
> A Greyhound; A he-goat also.

A common misconception about greyhounds is that their name has something to do with colour. In fact, grey greyhounds are quite rare. There are as many theories on the etymology of the word 'greyhound' as there are markings of the breed itself; the most popular notion is that the word greyhound comes from the Saxon 'grei' which means beautiful. Chaucer is the first writer recognised to have use the word 'greihound' in English literature. In *The Canterbury Tales* he writes, 'Greihounds he had as swift as fowl of flight.'

The first record of a greyhound race meeting in Britain dates back to 1876 in a field near the Welsh Harp, Hendon Way, in north London, when dogs chased a 'hare' dragged along by a hand-operated windlass. Nevertheless, the invention of a revolutionary mechanical dummy hare in 1912 by an American engineer named Owen Patrick Smith was the real genesis of modern greyhound racing. It would take another seven years before Smith's invention took off in America, while the British were reluctant at first to adopt the novel sport; most aficionados, rooted in romantic notions of tradition, the landed nobility, still viewed greyhounds as purely coursing animals.

Then in 1926 an American named Charles Munn, a retired chief constable called Sir William Gentle and a Canadian ex-pat, Brigadier-General A.C. 'Critch' Critchley, formed the Greyhound Racing Association (GRA) and invested £22,000 in Britain's first greyhound track at Belle Vue in Manchester. On July 24th of that year a dog with half a tail called Mistley flew out of trap two, to the delight of 1700 screaming spectators (half of them received free admission). Twenty-five seconds later, Mistley became the first winner of a greyhound contest run on a circular track over

440 yards in the UK, winning the race by eight lengths. Britain had finally gone to the dogs.

To get the ball rolling in those primitive days of racing, greyhounds were recruited from the world of hare coursing and trained to chase the dummy hare, which in the pre-animal rights days (and until relatively recently at many tracks) was a stuffed hare. In total, there were six races: one over 440-yard hurdles, two over 500 yards, and three over 440 yards. In the early days, eight dogs competed in each race; limiting races to a maximum of six greyhounds, which is unique to Britain, was not introduced until 1927.

The promoters of that first meet had captured the zeitgeist. By the third day of racing at Belle Vue 16,000 paying customers went through the turnstiles. The following year the GRA moved its headquarters to White City and attendance figures for greyhound racing in Britain reached 5.5 million. In 1930 this had risen to a phenomenal 13 million. The number of tracks in Britain would soon mushroom to 220, a number that exceeded professional Football League grounds by three-to-one. In 1936 the GRA floated on the stock exchange at a time when record numbers of 70,000 to 80,000 punters would flock to the Derby at White City, the epicentre of British greyhound racing.

Greyhound racing continued to thrive with little or no change. Apart from the odd technical innovation, such as new mechanical lure designs and faster traps, it remained true to its roots. There were one or two exceptions however.

In 1937, for instance, an old Harrovian and adventurer called Kenneth Gandar Dower introduced cheetah racing to Britain as an alternative to greyhound racing after importing eight big cats from Africa and promoting highly publicised races at Harringay and Romford stadiums. The cheetahs, however, showed little interest in racing each other and even less for the dummy lure. Their lack of competitive spirit meant that Dower's unique sport was soon consigned to history. Fortunately no spectators were eaten either.

In the early 1930s in America another bizarre variation of dog racing was launched. Trained as jockeys and dressed in silks, monkeys were made to ride on the backs of greyhounds. 'They are displaying exceptional skill,' the *New York Evening Journal* reported in 1933. 'You get a run for your money with these critters – and that's a lot more than you can say for bettors at the horse tracks.' The practice carried on into the 1950s at some tracks in the US. Once again, the British public was too discerning for the 'sport' to take hold in the UK.

By the 1950s and 1960s the dogs was the place to be and tracks continued to spring up across the country. Greyhound racing was now a sport in its own right. It was no longer an adjunct of hare coursing or 'the poor man's horseracing'. The dogs had become popular not only with the hoi poloi; the bug had bitten royalty, aristocrats, high rollers and movie stars too.

When the Stow opened in 1933, pioneer airwoman Amy Johnson was guest of honour. Hollywood greats like George Raft and Lana Turner were faces in the crowd long before Vinnie, Brad, Madonna, Guy and that bloke from *The Bill* got in on the act. Nowadays football has the upper hand on celebrity patronage. The tables have turned. Unlike greyhound racing, the nineteenth-century origins of football have no noble pretensions. Football was a resolutely working-man's game for over a century until courtship by the middle classes, pop stars and cynical politicians in the mid-1990s suddenly gave it bourgeois cred.

In the early days the dogs, like horseracing, the movies and radio, was a simple form of escapism. The public went for a night out, the excitement and the atmosphere, all of which was enhanced by the very presence of large numbers of people. But when in 1963 legislation was passed allowing bookmakers to ply their trade on the high street, suddenly punters didn't need to visit the track to make a bet. That's when the rot set in. The Stow had largely managed to buck the downward trend and escape the clutches of the developer's bulldozer, mainly by marketing itself more towards the 'six-pack' crowd, although like other tracks it had seen a disturbing fall in attendance. I decided it was time to ingratiate myself with the management at the track. 'Would you like a cup of tea?' said Ann. 'Oh yes, please.'

Ann Aslett is the marketing director at Walthamstow Stadium and, like most of the inner circle, a descendant of William Chandler, founder of the Stow. We first met in her little office, crammed with trophies and old photos, where she gave me a grilling about my journalistic exploits. 'I'm not doing a Kenyon,' I said, which seemed to satisfy her curiosity. However, it wouldn't be the last time she'd show concern about how dog racing, the Stow and, more importantly, the Chandlers, who owned the stadium, would be portrayed by me.

'Greyhound racing is great entertainment,' said Ann, offering me a biscuit. I took a Bourbon and a custard cream. 'It's a little bit different from the cinema or a club but I think that's why people enjoy it. It something *different*, isn't it?'

'Yes, very different,' I said.

Ann is a classy sort of broad, cultured, in her late forties or early fifties, I think. Her husband is a writer too. He has a yacht. He obviously knows something I don't. Ann gave me the deal about the Stow, but not in an oily, used-car salesman sort of way, which is what I expected from anyone connected to a dog track. As a director of the company she is forbidden from betting at the track, as is her right-hand woman Tracy Cooper, who is what a tabloid newspaper would call 'a pretty young blonde'. She's no dummy though. While it is Ann and Tracy's job to sell the merits of the Stow to anyone who'll listen, Tracy is as much an anorak as a PR. She knows her dogs and even has a tipster column in the local rag, imaginatively called 'Down the Dogs'. Ann is people people but Tracy is dog people.

'You've got your "dodge pot", that's a dog that doesn't know where it is on the track and runs all over the place,' said Tracy, 'or a "screw" which is one that lifts its tail in the air when it hits the bend, thinks "fuck that" and baulks. Or there are some trainers here,' she continued in a whisper, 'and I can't name names . . .

who put their dogs out then say "it's a fucking cripple" because they know it's carrying an injury. The trainers know the dog is good enough to run, so they won't pull it out, but they know it can't win.'

To be a tipster or to make a living out of gambling you have to know what's going on off the track as much as on it. Inside information is a very useful tool. 'If you're just a straight owner and pay your dough and go, you don't get a lot of info,' said Gillian, the Stow's resident photographer, who had just strolled into the office.

'I don't want to put a downer on things,' I said, changing the subject, 'but don't you ever wonder about the, you know, animal rights issue? I heard you've had a few demos down here.'

'They're entitled to protest,' said Ann. 'I don't have a problem with that. But we're *very* keen on the dogs' welfare. For instance, we work with the Walthamstow Greyhound Owners Association to make sure all dogs are re-homed. None of them are put down.'

To help fund the Stow's Retired Greyhound Fund their Directors matched every penny raised during their annual charity night 'pound for pound' which, according to Ann, was rapidly approaching £40,000.

Ann is an animal lover. Just like me. But we both share the same common duplicity when it comes to animal rights.

'Do you eat meat?'

'Yes, I do. Why do you ask?' said Ann, concerned.

'I'm just curious . . . you know . . . about our relationship with animals.'

'I'm sure that my dog has got a soul but I still eat steak for lunch. And if a dog has a soul then surely so does a cow. How do you explain that?'

'Hmm . . . I can't.'

'Biscuit?'

'Oh, thanks. So tell me about the Chandlers . . .'

Established in 1933 by the bookmaker William Chandler, and

still owned to this day by eight of his descendants, the history of the Stow is part of London's lesser-known urban folklore.

Bill Chandler, as the mercantile name suggests, was born into a poor working-class family in the East End of London in 1890. After starting out as an illegal bookmaker, with runners on street corners in and around his neighbourhood, Chandler quickly moved up in the world, went legit and became a bookmaker at horseracing tracks throughout the south of England. After a few years the pauper from Hoxton had done good, securing the No. 1 pitch at every racecourse in the South.

The next move was to become a rails bookmaker – a bookie operating in the Members Enclosure – alongside William Hill, Joe Coral and Max Parker, the founder of Ladbrokes. Chandler built a bookmaking empire and a reputation based on extravagant wagers and daring business ventures. As early as the 1920s he was known to take bets of £500, £800 or £1000 in his stride and barely a dog race went by at White City in which his book averaged less than five grand. On an eight-race card he would handle between £40,000 and £50,000 on a Saturday afternoon on top of income from his office and his own track. One evening at White City, he lost a reputed £120,000 on one race when a dog called Ribbon was beaten in the St Leger. Chandler's response was to casually turn to his clerk, open his book and start taking bets for the next race. Tall, dapper and charismatic, he was the archetypal old school bookie. One reporter once described him as, 'Loud-mouthed and loud-suited, cigar in mouth and two bottles on the bar, he exists now only in the imagination of the cartoonist.'

Chandler's interest in greyhound racing had started at White City. Aside from his bookmaking activity he owned a number of prize greyhounds including Peerless Call who beat the legendary double-Derby winner Mick the Miller in the London Cup in 1927.

When Chandler stopped betting at White City in 1931, he was approached by a wealthy dog owner called Gilbert, who had built the Regal Cinema in Marble Arch, about a piece of land in

Hackney. Chandler took one look at the land and bought it straight away. Chandler, Gilbert and another man named Wrightson invested £20,000 together and Hackney Wick Stadium was born. But within a couple of years Chandler had sold his £5000 worth of shares for a mere £500. Hackney Wick became one of east London's prosperous tracks and those same shares would've soon been worth £20,000. Despite the apparent gaffe Chandler described it as, 'Still the best day's work I ever did', for three weeks after selling his shares he had bought the Crooked Billet ground at Walthamstow, a small whippet racing and 'flapping' (unlicensed) greyhound track. A journalist at the time described the deal:

> He [Chandler] got out of his car, saw the owner standing on the track, asked him his price, agreed it, went around to the man's solicitors, and paid out the purchase price in cash on the spot.

When Bill Chandler died in 1946 aged just fifty-six, the dog man *par excellence* left a legacy with a long tail. Three grandsons, Charles, Jack and William, are respectively the Stow's chairman, managing director and secretary while a fourth, Victor, became one of the pioneers of offshore internet betting and a key figure in the introduction of tax-free gambling to the UK. Victor also lends his name and £15,660 in cash to the Victor Chandler Grand Prix competition every September and October, which along with the exotically named UK Packaging Arc in February and March are the Stow's biggest races. However, I had no chance of getting my hands on any of that Grand Prix lolly.

chapter 13

Twelve days after my debut at the track as an owner, Kevin was up against two of his old adversaries: Chrissys Charm and Baltovin Maid. This time he was evens favourite at the off. He trapped well but so did Baltovin Maid, who edged him to the first bend and maintained the lead. From then on in it was the same story as before: Kevin playing catch up right to the wire, beaten into second place by 2¼ lengths.

Perhaps it was a little late to start looking at bloodlines. But I thought I'd better pay closer attention to my 'investment' and look deeper into what I'd bought. Belgian Patrick knew a guy who ran a website (www.greyhound-data.com) listing all the details of every racing greyhound bred over the last four centuries.

Using this intriguing site, which listed the details of 873,640 greyhounds and nearly a million races from four continents, spanning four centuries, I traced Kevin's bloodline right back to Claret and Snowball the two nineteenth-century coursing dogs from which all modern greyhounds are descended.

Kevin's paternal great-great-grandfather was I'm Slippy, winner of the 1983 Derby. That was promising. Old Slippy sired at least 2623 offspring from a canine harem numbering scores of bitches, including Bangor Exchange, who begat Bangor Return, who in turn begat Bangor Jane, who in turn gave birth to Lakeshore Owney, Kevin's old man. In the line were Meadow Fescue, Miss Cinderella, Harmonicon, Husky Whisper II and

Brown Eyes III. I could name every one of Kevin's ancestors right back to the early nineteenth century yet I didn't even know my great-great-grandmother's name.

If only he had had that wonder dog Scurlogue Champ in his family tree, he may have inherited some balls. Scurlogue Champ was the Muhammad Ali of greyhound racing. A guy from the Fens called Ken Peckham, a double of Benny from *Crossroads*, had owned and trained him throughout a remarkable career. Between July 1984 and August 1986, he won a phenomenal 51 races from 63 starts, most of them marathons. His modus operandi would be to meander out of the traps and tail off for a circuit, giving the opposition a clear 15- to 20-metre head start before reaching remarkable speeds in the latter stages of a race, when he'd cut through the field like a hot knife through butter. He broke 20 records at the 23 different tracks and at one stage won 16 races on the bounce. He'd regularly run in front of ten to fifteen thousand screaming punters and won the big classic, the Cesarewitch, when it was staged at Belle Vue. He could cream a race by up to fifteen lengths. Bookies would not take bets on him. Managers and agents, in pursuit of some action, courted him like a pop star or Premiership footballer.

Peckham was offered up to £75,000 for the dog but he would not sell. Why should he? A dog with an 80 per cent strike rate was a walking, barking cash machine. The Champ was on course to beat the record for the most consecutive wins set by Westpark Mustard, Peruvian and Mick the Miller, when he stumbled on a stone on the track at Peterborough in an apparent betting coup (there'd been big money on the trap four dog, Sneaky Liberty). A punter then ran on to the track, right by the finish line, in an attempt to stop the race, and that was the end of that. He never amounted to anything at stud either.

A significant feature of Scurlogue Champ was his size: he was around 38 or 39 kilos, a good 10 to 15 per cent bigger than most dogs. Peckham had admittedly bulked him up, but as my flatmate Dr Paul noted when I showed him the video, 'That dog's moody.

If he were an athlete, he'd be drug tested every time. He's like Ben Johnson.'

Maybe they just don't make 'em like they used to.

Another dog I remember from blurred images on a TV screen was Ballyregan Bob. He too raced between 1984 and 1986 and became a racing legend, achieving a remarkable 32 successive wins over 695 metres, a world record that stood for Bob's overall record of 42 wins from 48 races, giving him an incredible 87.5 per cent strike rate. Remarkably, he never won a classic; never won the big one, the Derby.

But the granddaddy of them all, of course, was Mick the Miller. Mick raced between April 1928 and October 1931 and secured 15 victories from 20 races in his native Ireland before achieving another 46 wins from 61 races in England and Wales. He had a lower strike rate than his two modern rivals but, significantly, he won the Derby twice, in 1929 and 1930, plus a St Leger, a Cesarewitch and a Welsh Derby. He also broke five track records and notched up a British record of 19 consecutive wins. He was such a public icon that after his death he was stuffed and put on display in a glass cabinet at the Natural History Museum. I doubt David Beckham will ever get such star treatment.

On the face of it, any greyhound's historical breeding record can look rather impressive. However, this is often no more than smoke and mirrors, or at least a case of six degrees of separation. With a big enough laptop and a firm grasp of ancient language, I could probably trace my roots back to Shaka Zulu, Alexander the Great and Jesus. We all have to come from somewhere after all.

History, genealogy and all that is fine and dandy, but it doesn't pay the rent. I was in this business to make some moolah. According to the BGRB, British greyhound owners had won an estimated £11 million in prize money the previous year. So far, I had 'made' £56 from Kevin, but I had not even received my first kennel bill yet. That was bound to be £250. I had a long way to go to make a dent in the 2002 BGRB tally.

Kevin had had five races, including two under my ownership, now known as the 'Headline Syndicate', but was yet to win one. All of his races had been either P8 or A8 grade races, the lowest at the Stow. I was starting to get anxious.

'He's still a pup,' Linda kept saying. 'He's still learning, give him time.'

He had a lot to learn all right. Admittedly, he was still only seventeen months old. I was too impatient. Greyhounds hit their peak between two and three-and-a-half years old. No, what was I saying? He had to get a move on. At his level, a £68 first prize was chicken feed; after that, the money was derisory: £28 for second place and £25 for all other placings. I could not gamble on him to make up the shortfall in his kennel bills if he kept losing.

The boy had to toughen up his act. I would tell him as much after a race and then give the big lug a big hug. He had to stop being bullied out of the running. He was such a soft touch. If another dog so much as looked at him, he'd drop off the pace. Repeatedly he was bumped by more experienced opposition, usually at the first bend. He just did not seem to want to get on the bunny. His trapping skills were suspect too. Half the time he seemed to be asleep in the traps. What was he waiting for, Crufts? I guess, like his owner, he was simply a late starter.

Fortunately, he was still racing in the evenings. But if his performances didn't improve the race manager would soon stick him on the BAGS circuit – the 'Bookmakers Afternoon Greyhound Service', which pipes daytime races into the high-street betting shops via the Satellite Information Services (SIS) system.

BAGS started in the 1960s when the bookmaking industry negotiated contracts with track promoters to provide greyhound racing during betting shop hours. This novel idea was a ruse to keep punters spending whenever horseracing was cancelled due to bad weather. Greyhounds ran whatever the weather and the standard of BAGS dogs was ropey so nobody gave a shit if the odd dog was busted up due to bad track conditions. Add pitiful prize money to the equation and BAGS racing soon proved a cheap and convenient alternative to the gee-gees. All this is good news for the bookmakers, promoters and compulsive gamblers but bad news for small-time owners like me. If your dog winds up being a regular on the BAGS the chances are that is where it will stay. Consigning a dog to BAGS racing is like contracting herpes: you keep that shit like luggage. And if that happened, Kevin and I were both doomed.

chapter 14

The following Sunday I was heading for the kennels when I saw dark clouds looming overhead. In another half an hour or so it would be pouring with rain and the clouds went on and on and on. I'd just hit the M11 and could see that by the time I got to Lakenheath the kennels would be a mudbath, so I decided to do a U-turn and head for home.

On my way back into London I drove through Hackney Wick, dodging hordes of greedy shoppers, traffic and double-parked cars. People were scuttling around with bedding, tellies and videos, carpets, food processors and a variety of consumer goods. It was like the LA Riots all over again. Hackney Wick car boot sale was in town.

Hackney Wick Stadium had been host to one of the country's biggest car boot sales on the site long before the dogs had stopped running. In fact, an old acquaintance of mine used to manage it; his brother had done a deal with the owner and old family friend, George Walker, and had started using the site as a market in the early nineties. The stadium had been redeveloped in 1995 at a cost of £18 million but Walker's company had slipped into receivership while the party celebrating its opening was still echoing round the stadium.

Since the dog track ceased operating the stadium had provided the great unwashed of the East End with countless tacky, cheap and often dubious goods. The site was bought in early 2003 by the London Development Agency and the word was they would use it as the platform to mount a bid for the 2012 Olympics. Perhaps if the Olympics introduced greyhound racing, darts, snooker, bowls and shove ha'penny – you know, sports the British are actually good at – then maybe we'd win some medals.

I pulled up and found a parking space by the side of Hackney Marshes, a good quarter of a mile from the action. A gang of police officers and parking attendants were busying themselves, issuing tickets with the usual contempt. Drivers were remonstrating with them, failing to see the problem in parking on the kerb on a double yellow line with an out-of-date tax disc.

I hadn't been to the market in years. When I rounded the bend into Waterden Road, where what was left of the old dog track stood, I hit a gauntlet of street peddlers and hustlers: Romanians, Somalians, Turks, pikeys, beggars, fakers, fakirs, fences, muggers and thieves – the market offered a snapshot of neo-Dickensian Third World London.

I wheeled my way through the crowd, surfing the waves of half-cooked jerk chicken vendors, takeaway outlets of questionable provenance, bootleg CDs, asylum-seekers, pickpockets and assorted electrical goods, until I was inside the track. I contemplated one man's offer of a snide Rolex watch. 'Twenty-five pounds, you have.' 'Thanks but no thanks,' I said and moved on.

A couple of weeks earlier the British anti-piracy organisation Federation Against Copyright Theft (FACT) and the police had raided the market, making seven arrests and seizing a 'large quantity' of bootleg CDs, videos and PC software.

An impressive grandstand, which had apparently been built at huge expense without planning permission, lines one side of the track. By the time it had gone up the company running the show, Brent Walker Entertainment, had gone down and it was never used. The iron rails on which the hare once ran are still visible in sections of the stadium. I could see the ghosts of the dogs, the punters, and the bookies weaving their way through this colourful sea of faces, strangers to what had once been.

'You from the council, mate?' A tall likely lad in his forties approached me as I slipped out of a doorway that led to the track's scoreboard. 'No, I'm just taking a trip down memory lane,' I said. 'But it looks like Memory Lane is now a cul-de-sac.' The man, a stallholder, laughed and peered through the doorway at the rubble and mess. The guts had been ripped out of the place. It stank of piss and shit. 'People use it as a toilet,' he said. 'This place has gone downhill big style.'

Hackney had gone the way of so many other London tracks before it. In the 1950s and 1960s the Greyhound Racing Authority had bought several tracks and continued to do so until the property boom of the early 1970s when the company renamed itself GRA Property Trust and started redeveloping many of its sites for residential and commercial use. West Ham and Clapton were early casualties, followed by White City in 1984 and Harringay in 1994?

Once upon a time, even a hippie haven like Glastonbury had a local unlicensed or 'flapping' track as they're commonly known. But in less than ten years, eleven NGRC tracks had closed down in the UK, mainly for financial reasons: Bolton, Bristol, Canterbury, Cradley Heath, Dundee, Hackney, Middlesbrough, Powerhall in Edinburgh, Ramsgate, Swaffham and Wembley are gone and others are earmarked for the chop.

The first innovation in gambling to hit the dogs was the legalisation of off-course gambling, which started the high-street betting shop revolution. Then in 1966, betting tax was introduced, which dealt a further blow to the dogs. The advent of television didn't help either, which seems ironic given the reliance sport now has on TV revenue, advertising and PR. By the mid eighties the industry was in turmoil and attendances had dropped to an all-time low of 3.7 million in 1985. In 1993 the high-street bookies introduced evening opening hours, once again putting the squeeze on the beleaguered track promoters.

The death of the London dog track in many ways ran parallel to the slow, grinding demise of the traditional working-class in the capital. Huge swathes of north, south and west London had yielded to the juggernaut of gentrification. Once upon a time you couldn't *pay* folk to move to Islington, Brixton or Notting Hill – nowadays a lock-up garage in these parts will set you back telephone numbers. But the property boom hit the east of the city first and hardest. Thatcher's fabricated eighties boom turned the Docklands into a yuppie citadel and spawned a generation of chinless wonders. It was out with the fishwives and in with the fish knives.

A decade later, much of what remained of the Old East End proletariat, with their two-up two-down accents, foreign tongues and exotica, was giving way to a New East End elite of artists' quarters in Hoxton and Shoreditch, writers' ghettoes in Stepney and Whitechapel, and actors' enclaves in Bethnal Green and Hackney. And as we all know, shit comes in threes. Where the workers and immigrants had blazed a trail for the artists and dilettantes, the corporates and moneyed classes would follow. The heart of cockney London was being priced out to the Far East End of Tower Hamlets, Waltham Forest and Redbridge to make way for the rich. The East End of the Cable Street Riots, the Blitz, the Krays, the Swinging Sixties and the Melting-pot Seventies was over. All that was left in its place was a soap opera.

The fate of the dog track in many ways mirrors the demise of many parts of my personal history. For instance, where I was born, the Mothers' Hospital in Lower Clapton, Hackney (E8), is now a private housing estate; my old secondary school Ruckholt Manor in Leyton (E10) is a car dealership; and my former primary school, an Edwardian edifice on the border of Leyton and Stratford (E15), is now scheduled for demolition too. And what would become of that? A shopping centre, a hypermarket? I bet Eton or Harrow never wind up as a fucking Tesco superstore.

But things are looking up, in some ways at least, for the dogs. According to the BGRB up to four million punters are going through the turnstiles each year, gambling an estimated £1.6 billion. Throughout Europe, the US, Australia and the Far East greyhounds race competitively and the explosion of internet betting means that a punter in Kuala Lumpur can now, in real time, lose his shalwar-qamiz on a dog running over 6500 miles away in Nottingham, Swindon or Sunderland. And Wembley plc has confirmed plans to build a £7 million stadium in Liverpool – one of the few new tracks in the UK for thirty years.

The government kept banging on about how it was going to liberalise the gaming laws to the extent that soon you'd be able to open a crap shoot in an infants school. It seemed pretty obvious to me that once gambling licences became easier to get than TV licences, and the archaic rules surrounding table and card games were deregulated, more casinos would open up. But what offered the infrastructure, gambling know-how, equipment, staff and space to invest in such a cash-intensive, growth business like a casino? A dog track of course. In typically schizoid fashion I was back to thinking I had made a smart move with this greyhound lark. With the expertise I was amassing, a couple of years down the line I would be making money hand over fist.

chapter 15

I lived in a rough neighbourhood. Two doors down from my flat was a knocking shop, crack heads and junkies fixed up in doorways nearby and on Friday and Saturday nights there was always some creep beating up his old lady. A couple of poxy-looking local drunks had taken up residency on the front doorstep of the flat. Throughout the summer, on sweltering days when the tarmac on the stoop would melt, the drunks would freak out as their beer cans, cigarettes and pants stuck to the steps. Leaning out of the sitting-room window, cursing, I'd shoo them away like flies as they looked up with their dirty, rodent faces, before skulking off down the street, scratching and sniffing. I was waiting, just waiting, for the opportunity to get medieval on 'em and throw a bucket of hot steaming piss all over their mangy heads. Man, I was born in the wrong fucking century.

The streets of Paddington were not paved with gold but littered with the detritus of human failure and misery. Sometimes I would look out my window and grieve for humanity. In another, virtual, movie life, I'd be Travis Bickle. *Some day a real rain will come and wash all this scum off the streets*. But on other brighter days, usually when I was sleepwalking or stoned, I'd look out the window at those same scumbags and go all Oscar Wilde: 'We are all in the gutter, but some of us are looking at the stars.' How quaint.

Now it was nearly time to say goodbye to all that. I was on the move again, the seventh time in four years. If I had had a tent, a top hat and juggling balls I'd be a circus. This nomadic lifestyle had to stop. Margot and I were going to try living together in a few weeks' time. Her father owned a swanky pad on the Thames, in Battersea. He agreed to let us stay there for a while, as a social experiment, to see if we could handle each other 24/7. If it worked out, maybe one day we'd buy a place together, settle down, have kids and go insane.

Kevin was running in the 19:30, the opening race at the Stow. Many punters never bother with the first or second race on the card, as it's always puppies and scrubbers at the start of the show. As you move down the card the quality of the dogs gets better, with the real triers and form dogs making up the meat of the schedule.

Anyway, Kevin was due a win. I was having a party at the flat that night so I couldn't make it to the track. Instead, I popped over the road to the bookies to watch the race on SIS. Seeing him up there on the screen for the first time was like seeing my daughter in a nativity play. I was filled with a goose-pimply pride as the kennel hand paraded him in front of Britain's compulsive gambling public. He opened out at 2–1. I had a score on him. Aw, fuck it. I stuck another tenner on the nose. He went to 7–4, then 6–4. The way the price was moving suggested he had 'connections' at the track. At the off he was evens. The boy was turning into a little steamer.

'*Hare's approaching* . . .' yakked the TV commentator. Kevin fell out of trap four like a drunk leaving a club on New Year's Eve. Jesus. He then clattered into the one dog like a 'screw' at the first bend but managed to make up ground down the home straight. 'Go on, boy, go on.' My fist clenched, as per, I willed him on as he closed in on the leader, Brickfield Fox. 'Oh, for fuck's sake Kev . . .' He finished second, three-quarters of a length behind the winner. If he'd trapped, i.e. had a good break at the start, he would've won. He ran on and was first to the pick up (the cuddly toy used to calm the dogs down after a race), which meant he had a bit left in the tank. Lazy sonofabitch.

That was six defeats on the bounce, three under my ownership. So much for him being a one in four dog. If he were a professional boxer, a human athlete with the same record, he'd be finished by now. Some dude with a big mouth, electroshock hair and sovereign-ringed knuckles would've turned him into a human punch-bag by now.

That night I put defeat behind me and partied like it was 1999. I'd hired a 1000-watt rig, busting speakers and decks – the works. A few friends spun some tunes and we drove the rats out from under the floorboards for a night. There was plenty of booze, good music and other shit to distract me. Around 4a.m. two Environmental Health officers from Westminster Council arrived and served me with a noise pollution notice. 'We've had complaints about the noise,' they said. 'Thank you,' I said, slamming the door in their faces. It hadn't been a bad day after all.

chapter 16

At the track, interaction with your dog is brief and usually immediately after its race. Once Kevin had done his thing, i.e. lost, I'd go over to the paddock and beckon one of the kennel hands to bring him out after he'd been cleaned up, given a rub down and a drink of water. He'd mince over to me, tongue hanging out as he caught his breath, and he stare at me with those doleful eyes as if to say, 'Who the fuck are you?' I'd pet him and chat with the kennel hand about his performance, or lack of, and for a moment I'd forget about the £2500 and the reality that, like a basketball team of pygmies, he'd never amount to anything.

Our post-race love-ins were very short. I'd get three, maybe five, minutes tops with him. The atmosphere in the paddock was always frenetic and the kennel hands were usually too busy to hang around; besides, security and safety are always an issue. The Stow will not, cannot, allow a greyhound to be out of the paddock while a race is underway. In fact, apart from Kevin and the other track fodder, pet dogs or animals of any description are strictly verboten on the premises. But on Sundays you can visit the kennels and hang out with your dog for a couple of hours. Here was an opportunity for Kevin and me to bond. I could take him for walks, give him a bit of cheese or some other treat, maybe some coke or PCP to perk him up, and generally act like I actually had something going on with him.

Going to the kennels was a bit like visiting a sick relative or a friend in a mental institution. Initial contact was always a bit clumsy. One of the kennel hands would fetch Kevin from his hutch, present him to me while I cooed, 'Come to Daddy,' with my arms outstretched. Kevin would give me that dumb look again, trying to figure out who the hell I was, stick his tail between his legs, and scurry behind the kennel hand, shitting himself, literally. However, as soon as I got hold of the reins, stuck that muzzle on, and gave a few reassuring rubs, baby we were flying, off down the lane into the Suffolk sticks.

'Don't overdo it now, David,' Linda would say if Kevin was racing within the next day or two. The dogs love to break free from the confines of the kennel and stretch their legs but too much exercise is not good for a greyhound. Being a sprint animal they need to conserve their energy so, technically speaking, giving a greyhound long walks is the easiest way to nobble it. 'In *theory*,' Linda told me, 'all you've got to do to slow a dog down is overwork it. But don't you go doing that, David.'

But why slow down your own dog?

Well, to speed a dog up *significantly* in the short term you have to blatantly break the rules: you have to dope it. Some form of amphetamine would work. But the problem with that is: (a) it's wrong; (b) it's wrong; and (c) it's wrong. Doping harms the animal, cheats the system, the punters and your competitors and, to be really officious, it 'undermines the integrity of greyhound racing'.

As for slowing down the other dogs in a race, well, even if you were that way inclined, pulling it off would require such sophisticated subterfuge that you'd probably be putting your Machiavellian skills to profitable use in some other field like politics or organised crime. That's not to say it didn't use to go on. I know a petty crook who claimed that back in the Sixties he was paid to break into kennels and dope dogs. These days people are too clued up and security is too tight at most kennels to get away with that sort of thing on the regular at all but the most provincial tracks. But overworking your own dog, now that is another matter. Alternatively, as one old boy I knew in Sheffield used to do when he owned greyhounds, you can 'lay it up', i.e. have it lie around for days on the sofa doing absolutely nothing, so it becomes listless and apathetic and ready for the fix.

Once you had slowed it down sufficiently, for say two or three races, its odds would lengthen with the bookies and maybe the race manager would drop it down a grade too. The most anyone who wasn't 'in the know' would think was that the dog was a bit peaky. After all, even a greyhound is entitled to have the odd off day. You would then start shaping it up, exercising it and massaging it in readiness for a big hit. When the right race came along you'd have a big punt and clean up with the bookies. All this of course is *theory*. Anything can happen in practice.

One trainer I met on my travels told me that he had slowed a dog down on the repeated insistence of a rich owner who had several dogs at his kennels. The trainer felt pressured by the owner and against his better judgement he overworked the dog for him. After a week of long, hard walks the dog raced . . . and won! The owner and his cronies lost several thousand pounds after backing another runner in the same race. To make matters worse the dog went on a losing streak despite being put back on a normal training schedule, costing the owner even more money.

To keep a dog or bitch in tiptop shape you can't let them shag either, unless you're into the mating game, in which case you let 'em have it plenty. The chances of Kevin getting his end away however were pretty slim. It would take a miracle for him to reach stud dog status. Only the best of the best dogs ever get their groove on. In the meantime he could only dream of getting his end away. Whenever I took the little virgin out for a walk down the lane, I would remind him of the carnal delights that awaited him if he bucked up his ideas and actually won something, anything.

'Hey, Kevin. I might be able to fix it for you to get a little, er, you know, *action*. But you have to help me out here. You have to *win* boy, *win*. Hey, Kevin? Kevin? I'm fucking talking to you.'

Kevin would just amble along the lane, sniffing, the ground, the air, my crotch. I'm speaking to the dog, trying to give him a pep talk and all he does is look at butterflies, flowers and shit. Belgian Patrick had dubbed him 'The Poet' due to his acute sensitivity and introspective airs and graces. I had gone in search of a Linford Christie and come back with a Linton Kwesi Johnson. Did he not realise I had competing interests on a Sunday? By rights, Kevin was at the bottom of a dominical food chain. Sundays were generally the only days I got a chance to spend time with my daughter. Then, as a season ticket holder at Spurs, many of their home games were on a Sunday. Moreover, I had to do the lovey-dovey picnic in the park routine, shopping, art galleries and all that girly shit with Margot.

Sundays, don't you just love 'em? Kevin and I would always take the same route: right out the compound's gates and down the lane, following the same path I took driving into Imperial Kennels. I never strayed into the adjoining fields for fear of giving some farmer a bit of target practice. I was also concerned about Kevin walking into sheep-dip or manure or eating a festering morsel of dead rat or badger pooh.

For safety's sake I'd usually keep Kevin muzzled while out walking. The common sight of muzzled greyhounds has helped foster an erroneous belief among the public that they are a vicious breed, but on the whole they're harmless. The muzzle is only there to stop them taking a nip out of each other while racing and eating crap off the ground.

So I'm walking Kevin. Maybe if he tried to take a chunk out of me he'd show a little gumption. When the odd wild rabbit darted out of the bushes more often than not he'd be indifferent. Sometimes he'd strain on the leash, I'd hold it tight and we'd chase after it. Other times, at the sight of a rabbit, his ears would prick and then flop down again as if to say, 'What, you again? Please!'

Despite being a sight hound Kevin could sniff like the best of them. He would walk the lane, burrowing his shiny little nose into the undergrowth, sniffing out a variety of scents from bundles of little critters. His ritual was to make a series of sniffs followed by a quick leak, so that the sequence would go something like: sniff-sniff-sniff-sniff-piss-sniff-sniff-sniff-piss and so on for more than an hour. And of course he'd keep snuggling in there, looking for love.

'See, this is your problem, Kevin,' I'd say. 'You're too soft. You need the killer instinct, boy.' He'd stop, look up at me with those puppy dog eyes and snuggle his schnozzle right in my schnitzel. 'Aw, you soppy little fucker.' I'd give him big hugs, rubs, cuddles and fuss. He loved that shit. So did I. But listen, I drew the line at that dog-licking-your-face nonsense though. Think about it. Even the fattest, most unwieldy mutt is capable of munching the living daylights out of its gonads, which is why you never see a dog renting a porno movie, reaching for the top shelf at Smiths or buying Kleenex. The fact that a dog spends 50 per cent of its every waking moment licking its crotch, usually after it's just relieved itself (which it spends most of the other 50 per cent of its time doing), means that at any given moment it could paste the Sistine Chapel with enough cack to keep *Location Location Location* busy for years.

We would walk down the lane, Kevin and me, me and Kevin, like a couple of old swells: one man and his dog. Sundays being a day of rest and reflection and all, whenever I took Kevin for a walk, I would often ruminate, meditate and philosophise and ask myself, *what in God's name, does he think about?*

'So, what are you thinking about, Kevin, you know, in general?' Blank look. Nose in crotch. Sniff of the air. Kevin did not really say much in response. In fact, he didn't say anything at all. Greyhounds hunt silently, which means they seldom bark. It also means they speak even less. This preoccupation with non-verbal communication and an apparent lack of emotion has also fostered a notion that greyhounds are aloof, unfeeling and detached from reality – a bit like the Royal Family.

The truth is, Kevin probably could not think further than his next meal, so psychoanalysing him was a waste of time. As one old Jewish proverb goes, 'What do hens dream of? Of Millet.' Alternatively, as the poet Rupert Brooke pondered, do fish believe in Heaven? 'Fish say, they have their stream and pond; but is there anything Beyond?' The answer is: no. For man nor beast, there is nothing out there except nothing. Zilch, nish, nitto. There is no heaven; there is no hell. God told me so in a vision I once had on acid.

My conclusion then was that greyhounds did not think in a logical, stream-of-consciousness way. It was important for me to come to accept that Kevin was a thoughtless, soulless mutt – nothing but a cuddly running machine, a 35 mph teddy bear. I needed to come to this conclusion to prepare myself for the time when he made the journey away from me, into the unknown, and possibly the Kitty Kat factory.

Apart from taking Kevin for a walk, Sundays at the kennels also gave me an opportunity to get the odd titbit of information or idle gossip from the other owners over a cuppa. One of Linda's favourite owners and close friends was Big Al. His daughter Kelly had worked for Linda at Imperial since the 1990s. Big Al was a twenty-stone retired copper and fulltime Yorkshireman who had a number of dogs at the kennels. 'I wanted to be a teacher when I was at school,' Big Al told me, 'but I thumped a prefect and was gonna be thrown out. I saw an ad for the Met on the careers board . . . wound up being a protection officer for twenty-eight years out of thirty-four years service.' As a young man, Big Al had obviously shown the requisite qualities of a copper.

After a stroke in 1983, he lost his 'licence to kill', switched to other duties and retired in 1996. Now he did driving for the military. When I say Big Al was big, I mean *very* big. Big Al was so big he could have had his own seat at the UN. His somewhat more petite wife, Mavis, made exceedingly good cakes and biscuits, which she would bring every Sunday to the kennels for Linda. No wonder Big Al was so big.

Big Al got into the dogs in 1993, via a circuitous route, after his youngest son bought a greyhound with a bunch of college buddies, who, just as I had, thought it would be a 'good idea'.

'They ended up with a hefty bill which I eventually squared up. We then went in at the deep end and bought two three-month-old pups from a litter but unfortunately one developed a hip disorder when he was only a babe so he went to the great man in the sky. Eventually I acquired his sister. Then my son decided he and another mate wanted a dog, so they bought Ridgefield Millie. And it went from there. My son knew more about greyhound racing than most of the trainers did, certainly about the breeding. He could name the dams and sires of every dog out there. He was only eighteen at the time. He studied greyhounds and got into it. He didn't gamble. He used to have a bet but nothing special. Eventually we went to Linda in '97.

Big Al regaled me with tales of alleged abuse, and he was not the first person to tell me about dogs being ill-treated or neglected, but I had not seen any cruelty at first hand, either by owners or trainers. The odorousness of animal abuse that trailed greyhound racing like a bad case of flatulence however was inescapable.

'There was a demo last night at the Stow,' boomed Big Al as Linda doled out another round of teas. 'Some old bag and around half a dozen of the great unwashed were outside, ranting about cruelty and that. They had a poster with a greyhound on it lying on the ground . . . dead I suppose, with a brick tied round its neck. They pull the same old pictures out every time and blow 'em up out of proportion. Bloody rent-a-mob.'

'We've heard it all before, David,' said Linda, shaking her head. 'Two sugars?'

'Yes please,' I replied.

'Talk of cruelty, banning racing and all that . . .'

'Go on. Go for a walk with your dad,' said Linda's mum, a.k.a.

'Nan'. One of the kennel hands had brought Kevin over to me for his afternoon stroll. 'When you get round the corner you can show him all those bruises I gave ya!' Nan was a sprightly silver-haired old bird, eighty-six going on sixty-eight. She was always at the kennels on a Sunday, mucking in and wisecracking. Her and Linda were a regular double act. Nan had a habit of often asking Linda a question she'd already given her the answer to. Linda would tut and roll her eyes while Nan carried on gassing. I don't think it was senility, just a sly wind up. 'Yeah, I had to give him a right good kicking this morning, right in the gut,' Nan added, playfully squeezing Kevin.

'Did you have your hobnail boots on when you did it, Mum?' piped Linda, 'cos it ain't the same with trainers on.' OK, I get the picture. Such is the sensitivity surrounding the constant charges of cruelty levelled at greyhound racing that dog people have to make a joke of it else they'd never stop flipping their lids.

'I wouldn't have a problem having a horse or a dog put down rather than send it to a bad home,' said another owner who cruised in and out of the conversation as Linda, Nan and me loitered by the kitchen doorway. She was a matronly woman who said she had once worked with 'unruly boys' and had met Frank Bruno as a fifteen-year-old. I was just about to find out how unruly Bruno had been as a kid when Kevin started straining on his lead, heading for the gate. All the talk of beatings and euthanasia finally was too much for his sensitive little soul, so I took him off up the lane to marvel at the Suffolk countryside, its pig farms, its piles of manure . . .

When I got back to the kennels Big Al was still there, this time with a little silver-grey Italian greyhound, no bigger than a shoebox. He was called Eric. Eric belonged to Big Al's son. The dog was a handful, lithe and slippery. They made quite a contrast – Big Al and Little Eric. For an ex-copper, Big Al was OK. And to think, there was a time when the only way I'd be in the same room as a cop was to have my fingerprints taken. Now I was being invited round for tea and biscuits. How times had changed.

chapter 17

Margot looked anxious. 'I think I'm going to freak out,' she said, grabbing my arm. 'Look at them: they've all got big ears and bald patches with crazy clumps of hair coming out of their heads.'

'Calm down, babe,' I said, almost reassuringly. 'Everything's cool.' The crowd was swelling rapidly, squeezing us in, pushing us forward towards the track. I downed my drink with the aid of someone's elbow and pulled Margot closer to me. Then I made a face and took a snapshot with my camera. I loved this cultural safari shit.

I needed to earn some Brownie points after a run of writing some 'controversial' material for the *Evening Standard*. My shit hadn't gone down too well with the ladies, especially Margot. Chicks are always blabbing about empathy and honesty and shit like that but when it comes to affairs of the heart most women I know prefer well-crafted white lies to brutally dark truths. Consequently, my self-confessional brand of journalism re women was interpreted as an anthology of misogyny. I guess with features entitled 'Giving Birth Turned Me Off' and 'I Could Never Be Faithful' what did I expect?

So I had to appease the woman. I thought a romantic weekend away would do the trick, so I booked a couple of flights and a room at the swanky Morrison hotel in Dublin. The interiors were designed by the fashionista John Rocha; and at £180 a night minimum for a double, I knew it would be somewhere approaching the lifestyle that Margot was accustomed to. As luck would have it, it just so happened that the romantic weekend coincided with the Paddy Power Irish Greyhound Derby, the world's richest greyhound race. Yeah, yeah, I know what you're thinking. Just call me Mr Lover Man, OK?

I looked at my watch: 9.15p.m. It was fast approaching the big race. Margot and I had been cruising around Ireland for a few days in a, er, Hyundai, and had reached the end of our road trip, Shelbourne Park Stadium, via the Ring of Kerry, the National Stud and the Irish St Leger at the Curragh. I'd landed a couple of modest winners on the gee-gees that afternoon and felt confident. Whether it was horses or dogs I didn't know one race from another to be honest. Betting on an animal still seemed absurd to me, regardless of a race's history, prestige or the prize money at stake, but a little flutter never did anybody any harm.

Three months earlier, even at the English Derby, I would've prided myself on being able to watch every race on the card and not bet a penny. But as a fully paid up disciple of the dogs it now felt irreligious not to have the odd punt, especially in a gambling Mecca like Ireland. In the run up to the Derby, Shelbourne Park bookie Ted Hegarty had laid one of the biggest bets ever at the track: €30,000–€4000 resulting in a winner, Fast Kodiak. The same punter who had that touch landed €16,000 for a €1000 stake. I could only dream about such gambles. I wouldn't even stake that kind of dough in a game of Monopoly.

I left Margot in the teeming crowd of *Father Ted* look-alikes, 'blown-ins' and Saturday night punters and headed for the bar. It was six or seven deep. Arms crawled over arms, people guffawed, multiple orders went in, cash tills rang as reams of newly adopted euros went back and forth across the bar. 'Who d'you have to sleep with to get a drink round here?' Wisecracks and asides flowed with estuaries of Murphys, Guinness and whiskey and cokes. Unlike the English Derby at Wimbledon, where people feel suffocated by the burgeoning crowds and scuffles break out, at Sherbourne Park, a far smaller track in comparison, punters hold their own, and their drink, in the cramped inebriated atmosphere. And love every minute of it.

'Where are ye from, big man?' asked a chap at the bar, his broad shoulders squeezed into a tight double-breasted blazer. 'I'm from London,' I said, craning. 'The East End originally. I'm about to move to Battersea, but now I live not far from Kilburn. D'you know it?' He had to know it. Kilburn was the Irish quarter of London, Little Dublin you might say.

'Ah Kilburn. I know it, I know it. I lived there for a while a few years ago. I was working in London you know. Not a bad place . . .' Then he leant into me and whispered. 'If you discount all the fucking Paddies! Ha ha ha . . .'

I have a lot of time for the Irish. In fact, I am something of an honorary Irishman. A year earlier, just for the hell of it, I had followed the Republic of Ireland to Iran for a crucial second-leg World Cup qualifier. There was no beer for love nor money in Tehran, all the women were dressed as Ninjas and you couldn't piss without some state security monkey inspecting your foreskin but it was great to hang out in a foreign country with a bunch of football fans who spoke your language but weren't into Nazi salutes and killing the locals.

I admire the Irish sense of positive cultural identity, pride and respect. When I was around sixteen or seventeen a big pikey paid me a tenner to smash his right hand with a paving slab, just so he could avoid a bare-knuckle fight with some meathead in a pub car park. 'As God is my witness,' he had growled, 'if I have to fight that man I'll fucking kill 'im.' I'd never met Big Pikey before – he just stopped me in the street. But I had no reason to disbelieve him. He had a face carved out of granite and fists of stone. He was built like Old Trafford. If he was a bottle job, what the beejaysus did the *other* guy look like? Big Pikey explained that it was bad form to back out of a fight for no good reason; it had something to do with the didicoy code of honour. A serious injury was a legitimate excuse not to scrap though. So I smashed his right hand with a 2ft × 2ft, inch-thick paving slab. And he gave me a tenner ... with his left hand. The right one was now completely fucked. Now I know what you're thinking, but look, £10 was a lot of money to a delinquent teenager back in the early eighties. Besides, it was an act of humanity. I'd saved one man's life and another from fifteen years in jail. Yeah, yeah, I know. I'm a regular Good Samaritan.

Of the many things I like about Ireland – the scenery, the hospitality and the easy-going pace of life – I particularly like the way the Irish have subverted the English language. For instance, if I am having a quiet pint in a pub in Skibbereen and someone asks, 'Are ya here for the craic?' this is not an invitation to free-base cocaine hydrochloride. See, us blacks and the Irish are on a level: we go back a long, long way – right back to the plantations of slavery, where the Micks held the whip and the niggers did all the fucking work. OK, let's forget that one. But there is an affinity between these two tough breeds of men, a shared earthiness and a collective 'soul'. We had both had our languages, land and culture raped, pillaged and plundered by successive English tyrants. Ordinary blacks and Irish had shared the same itinerant path for centuries, working like slaves, treated like dogs. As Mark Lamarr lookalike Jimmy Rabbitte reflected in *The Commitments*, 'The Irish are the blacks of Europe,' which is a touching, empathetic sentiment. The only fly in the ointment or 'nigger in the woodpile' with this concept is that *black people* are the blacks of Europe. But, hey, why be pedantic.

It was nearly the appointed hour of the final – 9.42p.m. I eventually got to the bar. Negotiating the crowd with a bottle of Moët, two flutes, a packet of dry roasted peanuts and a bag of ready salted would be too much, so I grabbed a pint, a G&T, forgot the snacks and headed back to the stands by the track.

I got back to find Margot still looking bemused. We had a modest punt on the final and waited for the bell. The stadium lights dimmed, the crowd exploded, the traps flew open and an almighty roar nearly lifted me off my feet.

Bursting out of trap five, the 11–8 favourite Bypass Byway was first to the bend, his sleek black frame a blur as Droopys Agassi challenged on the outside at the turn, a neck behind. By the second bend Bypass Byway had stretched his lead to a length over Droopys Rhys, with Droopys Agassi in third and Tyrur Bello, Heavenly Hero and Tamna Rose trailing into the back straight. POW! Bypass Byway put the pedal to the metal and kicked it down the back straight like he was on rocket-fuelled roller blades. Within nanoseconds he'd gone four or five lengths clear of the chasing pack with half the course blitzed. I'd never seen a dog move that fast. Correction: this wasn't a dog it was a goddamned Kawasaki 1100 in a dog suit. The pace was unbelievable. By the third bend the pack seemed to implode as they scrambled to make the turn, bouncing and checking their way out of the running, leaving Bypass Byway to romp home, smashing the track record, clocking 29.42 seconds over the 550-yard race and shaving 15 spots off the previous record. Now remember, Kevin was just about clocking 30.00 seconds at 475 metres. When I say that Bypass dog was fast I mean he was *fast*. (28 metres further in 0.20 seconds faster than Kevin's best time to date. Every dog certainly has its day.)

I had burned a score on Droopys Rhys, the second favourite, but in a way it was a pleasure to lose money to see such a display of speed and agility. It's not every day that you get to see some of the fastest creatures on the planet in full flight without the threat of them taking a chunk out of you. Cheetahs and impala just do not play ball the way greyhounds do.

When it came to handing out the trophy and cheque for a hundred big ones to the winner, there wasn't just some corporate lackey on the podium doing the honours. No sir. They had Bertie Ahern, the *Taoiseach* handing out the prizes. Bertie Ahern. The fucking Prime Minister! Can you imagine Tony Blair standing in the pissing rain at Wimbledon Stadium handing out the goods at the English Greyhound Derby? Admittedly, as my Irish connections later stated, Bertie Ahern would 'go to the opening of a car door' to get his ugly mug in the papers. He had had problems with the construction of an Irish national stadium, so he needed all the good PR he could muster. Across the pond, Tony Blair was facing his own problems in Parliament over the ban on hunting with dogs, a ban which incidentally could have serious repercussions on greyhound racing.

However, given that the Bord na gCon is a commercial quango, established in 1958 under special legislation by the Irish government, Bertie's appearance was not out of the ordinary. Irish greyhound racing is as much a state institution as a national obsession.

Ireland had embraced greyhound racing in 1927, a year after it had been introduced in England. The Irish too had fallen truly, madly, deeply in love with the sport from its inception and although the love affair was waning on the Sceptred Isle it was going from strength to strength on the Emerald one.

While prize money in Britain had hardly changed in twenty years, in Ireland it had grown progressively from €2.4m in 1995 to €7.4m in 2002. Right across the board the industry was booming. The number of race meetings was increasing annually and attendances had nearly doubled in seven years to over a million punters. Sponsorship was up and total betting turnover had gone from €28.9m in 1995 to a staggering €105.8m in 2002.

Having embraced the EU and all the lovely little euros that went with it, Ireland was undergoing a boom. Property prices were up, wages were up and many good old boys who had made big dough in America and Australia were coming back to the homeland with a lot of hard currency, further bolstering the economy. These factors combined with increased sponsorship and promotion meant the future looked bright for Ireland's greyhound industry.

However, this boom wasn't without its costs. Sadly, in Ireland, greyhounds are often treated like disposable dogs. The kindest trainers leave them in dog pounds to be put down on the cheap, but many are not so kind. The dominance of Irish breeding is a numbers game: the more dogs you breed, the higher quality you will produce; but you'll also produce more runts, dogs who just won't chase.

Some former racing dogs are used as resident 'blood donors' for other breeds at the Veterinary School in University College Dublin. What a transmogrification: from dice on legs to walking blood banks. An estimated fourteen greyhounds are dissected every year there so student vets can learn about animal anatomy.

I was biting into my toast in the Morrison dining room, thinking about how much Kevin would be worth as vet scrap when I had an eureka moment. *Why not buy another dog at an auction here in Ireland for, say, 200 quid, take him to Britain, change Kevin's race name to something like Electric Lovebox, change the new dog's name to Zussies Boy, sell Kevin (I mean, Electric Lovebox), recoup the £2500 I paid for him and pocket the difference.* My sleeping partners in the Headline Syndicate would never know the difference.

Then another thought occurred to me: not only was this idea ridiculous, it was also conspiracy to commit fraud. I could go to jail for just *thinking* about this shit. I'd lose my publishing deal, my livelihood and ruin what was left of my crumbling reputation. I'd never work in this, or that, town again. Aw, it was just the hangover talking. To assuage my guilt for thinking so *crudely*, after breakfast I decided to call Linda to see how Kevin had performed the night before. The news was shocking.

'He won,' said Linda. 'He ran really well.'

'Bloody Nora,' I said.

The result was typical of my role as his absentee father. There he goes, making his debut in the school play, scoring his first goal for the team, losing his virginity, and where's Pops? Knocking 'em back like an eedjit in Dublin. On the night that Bypass Byway won the Irish Greyhound Derby and pawed £100,000 into owner

Michael Kearney's pocket, Zussies Boy, at his ninth attempt of asking, won his first race. Things were looking up. I had just earned £65. Smashing . . .

chapter 18

Thanks to Kevin's first win and the few bob I had pocketed in Ireland I started to grow in confidence with my betting. Big mishtake. But I could only heed Linda's advice not to gamble for so long. I didn't want to stand on the sidelines like a kibitzer. I lived by the maxim 'experience teaches wisdom' and given that Kevin wasn't going to earn his keep in prize money I had to find alternative ways of financing his future. Gambling was the way forward. As long as I kept my stakes small I'd be safe. I just needed to earn enough to pay the kennel bills.

If I was going to be serious about gambling I needed to get myself organised. First up, I decided to set aside a modest bankroll of £500, from which I'd reinvest half of any winnings, gradually increasing my roll and stakes accordingly. As a safety precaution I'd only ever take £100 to the track with me to gamble, that way I could limit my losses at any given meeting. Furthermore, to be a dedicated punter you need a system. Any dummy knows that. So having bought myself a couple of idiot's guides to gambling I got down to work with a notepad, a calculator, the *Racing Post*, and a pen behind my ear.

The easiest thing in the world to do, if you want to call it a system, is to back the favourite. According to Tracy Cooper the Stow had the highest strike rate for favourites in the country – at least 35 per cent. In one of the books I'd recently purchased on 'betting systems that win' the author claimed that around 32 per cent of favourites win on average at every meet, with second favourites winning 22 per cent of the time. More tellingly, the underdog or rank outsider wins little more than 5 per cent of races on a card. Or put another way, he loses 95 per cent of the time. But you have to judge these percentages against the odds. While a good number of favourites indeed win at the Stow, many of them are short-priced. On a Saturday night there is so much action in the betting ring that open-race favourites will come in at evens, 1–2, 4–7 ... crazy odds. Backing favourites indiscriminately is a false economy.

One way to overcome this problem is to be discerning about your favourites and second favourites or find a good source of tips and use a staking method, like the Martingale, which is designed for roulette and requires you to double your stake after a loss. The idea is, statistically speaking, if you stick rigidly to one selection, i.e. favourites or a trap number, eventually it must come up. Also, to always be in profit you have to back a selection at evens or greater. Betting odds-on doesn't work in your favour. Still awake? Right. Now all this is great on paper but in reality if you double a £1 stake over the course of a 12-race card, always backing the favourite, and no favourite wins you'll be £5595 out of pocket. Do the math.

Then there is the Fibonacci progression system in which you increase your stakes in units of 1, 1, 2, 3, 5, 8, 13, 21, 34, 55, 89, 144, 233, 377 ... and so on after every loss; the Labouchère or cancellation system; the O'Hare Straddle or Ronnie Biggs – an alternate doubling scheme that works by borrowing a large amount of cash on a short-term basis, setting aside enough money for a ticket on the next plane to South America. Bet the rest on one favourite at even money. If you win, return the principal and retire on the rest. Otherwise, use the plane ticket. Or how about backing the second favourite with the field in a forecast? Alternatively you can 'play the numbers', i.e. bet the same two trap numbers religiously in a reverse forecast. Or what about working the win percentage of each trap?

The world and its aunt are full of sure-fire betting systems. The internet is the worst culprit. What a treasure trove of useless betting systems, strategies and techniques designed to separate the fool from his money with as little effort as possible it is. One example is the P=MCR system, which was either dreamt up by an acid-dropping twit or is an April Fool's Day joke that won't go away. This is how it works: (1) watch the first race at any given meeting; (2) subtract the smaller trap number from the larger one, i.e. 1 beats 3, 3–1 = 2; (3) back the resultant trap number in the next race; (4) if it loses, repeat: i.e. 5 beats 4, 5– 4 = 1, back the one dog next race, double your initial stake. The inventor claims that the system is 'so simple, I challenge you to find ANY meeting on the dogs where the system loses in any 12-race run'. What the numskull failed to mention was: (5) lose your bollocks. Such a system is illogical and financially suicidal. There are countless clowns out there peddling systems of one description or another and many more red noses buying into them. In the end I decided to stick to the basics and rely on good old intuition and inside information. Oh, and luck.

Whenever I went to the track in daylight hours I always felt like I was goofing off, like I should be somewhere else, doing something more productive, more important, more . . . grown up. The track affords adults the opportunity to act like children, to indulge in the bizarre, mindless, selfish and often unexplainable pastime that is greyhound racing.

One afternoon I was in the toilets at the Stow and overheard two punters bitching about the facilities. It turned out that the Stow was set to receive £100,000 from the BGRB to renovate their loos. Meanwhile there were plenty of broke-arse tracks in the country without air-con who had their dogs locked in kennels for up to six hours on long hot summer's days. It is amazing the kind of shit you pick up in a public toilet at a dog track. It is the sort of place where you might overhear someone plotting to have his factory burnt down or his missus bumped off.

I was starting to really obsess about this game now.

Eavesdropping on conversations in public toilets? Did I really hate my own company that much? Was there such urgency to get out of the house? Initially I'd go to the dogs only when Kevin was running but now I was hitting the track three or four meets a week. I'd also nip into the bookies when I couldn't make it to the Stow and have a punt, sometimes even on the gee-gees, which I knew absolutely nothing about. Then there were other bets . . . nothing much, a bit of football, draws, home wins, away wins, half-time results, correct scores, yellow cards, indignant arm waves and theatrical goal celebrations, that sort of thing. I'd do a few quid on the lottery too, no scratch cards though – didn't have that itch. I didn't bet in big hefty chunks of cash like the high rollers. I tended to make many smaller bets, parlaying my wins until, in snakes and ladders fashion, the cash went spiralling down to zero. I'd always had very little respect for money but I was nonetheless frugal. Now I was starting to slowly lose control.

In 1933 the Royal Commission defined a bet as thus: 'A promise to give money or monies worth upon the determination of an uncertain or unascertained event in a particular way. It may involve the exercise of skill or judgement.' What the Commission failed to add was that it usually involves luck. Luck or the belief in it is central to the notion of gambling. 'Chance governs all,' Milton said in *Paradise Lost*. And ever since the ancient Romans invented gambling with dice, luck has been a prerequisite of betting. I was running out of luck, fast. So I needed a system, a new system. And preferably one that worked.

My last visit to the kennels had been a week before the Irish Derby, the night Kevin had notched up his first success. He hadn't raced between that visit and his win, so was it possible that he had responded to my pep talk after all? It was a long shot, wishful thinking perhaps, but had positive energy, peace, love and all that happy hippy shit had a marked effect on his performance? Maybe he didn't need the killer instinct at all. Maybe all he needed was lurvvvvvvvvvvvve . . .

To test my hypothesis I returned to Imperial Kennels that Sunday. This time, however, I went doubly armed. I took my daughter with me.

'Ooh isn't she lovely?' crowed Nan. 'Ooh she's beautiful. Got lovely hair, ain't ya?'

Luca did her shy thing; we got Kevin and took him for a stroll up the lane. At first he was reticent about the little 'un, even more so than with me. But he soon changed his tune. Within minutes he was ignoring me and was all over Luca like a cheap suit. 'Hey, what about me?' I said. Kevin really got into Luca, snuggling and nuzzling. 'That's it, love him up,' I said. Oh boy, if he came good again after all this fuss I could really be on to something. I could see it now: a street, a ship, a Cambridge college named after me. 'That's it, give him a big cuddle . . .'

The following day at the BAGS meet Kevin flew out of the traps and pissed the race, recording a personal best of 29.84. That dog *ran*! Uncharacteristically he managed to stop licking his nuts and trapped well, bursting out of the boxes like a dog possessed. I couldn't believe it. The boy runs for *love*. Holy guacamole. This was a miracle. If Kevin ran within forty-eight hours of a visit he did the business. I had to test my hypothesis once more.

I went out to the kennels. The gang was all there, pottering about. It's a funny thing, training a dog, because ostensibly, once you figure out it's a goer, a chaser, all you do is feed it, walk it, massage it, pamper it, let it rest and that's it. If I'd had a garden of my own I could've saved myself £250 a month and kept him at home and done the self-same thing. It wasn't like he had to do ten miles a day on a treadmill or needed to bench press 250lbs or do pilates or the lotus position or jujitsu. He just needed to run and that's what he did naturally. Training. Bah! I was starting to feel a bit hard done by.

'These owners are always going on like they know what's best,' said Linda 'That's what I like about you, David. You keep your mouth shut and let us get on with it.' Little did Linda know I only kept my mouth shut because I didn't have a clue what I was doing.

'I've had owners in the past trying to tell me how to run my dogs or even try to 'influence' me, but I won't have it. One fella wanted me to a slow a dog down for him, cos he wanted to back him later and I told him I wouldn't do it. He insisted but I said 'no'. I put the dog out and it won. He didn't back it and was gutted. A few days later he came by and took all of his dogs out of the kennel. I won't have owners tell me how to run my dogs.'

Thanks to Kevin's improved track time the race manager, I think unfairly, penalised him for winning. Despite losing his next race, he was moved up a grade from A8 to A7. The supposed justification for this was that his times had improved: he'd managed to break through the 'psychological' thirty-second barrier.

When Kevin was in full flight, striding, leading, *winning*, he was a joy to behold. Of course such joy was rare, which made the win-seeking all the more addictive. He notched up three more mediocre runs before winning, as luck would have it, his thirteenth race. Kevin blasted out of the traps and won by a length and a half, having led right from the off. This was the shortest stretch he'd had to date between wins: two out of his last five starts, including a win early in October, as a 7–4 favourite, in which he scored a personal best of 29.80.

At the kennels I loved him up as usual, gave him some cheese and a good talking to. The following day he came third. Well, I was really clutching at straws. To make matters worse, in my haste to get back to the safety of London, I was tagged by Five-O doing 98 mph on the M11. Three points on your licence and sixty sheets, thank you very much. The following week Kevin came fourth. Then fourth again. The week after that, just for a bit of variety, he came last for the first time in his career. Fortunately I wasn't at the track to savour that little slice of history. I must've spunked a couple of hundred in between. The wins never seemed to amount to anything but the losses always did. Maybe someone was trying to tell me something . . . Anyway, Kevin then follows his dismal run with a win. The dog was a fucking yo-yo. There was no figuring him out, no determining what he would do from one race to the next.

Some three hundred dogs are contracted to run at Walthamstow. I'd come across dogs who hadn't had a win in sixteen races, so Kevin wasn't the worst. He was just, well, not very good. If a dog ever reaches a point where it can't get round the track without hailing a cab first, its racing days are over. There are no Eddie the Eagles or Eric the Eels at the Stow.

The strain of actually winning something must've taken its toll on Kevin as he lamed out of his next race, which earned him a three-week lay up. Fortunately it was nothing more than a little muscle strain, something that physiotherapy and some TLC from Linda cured. It did, however, put him out of circulation which, given his meagre earning capacity at the best of times, cost me money I could ill afford. I'd been struggling workwise and my bank balance was going down faster than a Bangkok whore on the Titanic. When things weren't going my way, which was most of the time, being a minor greyhound owner was a costly business. It was just disaster after disaster . . .

One time I was simply standing by the track rail, offering Kevin some words of encouragement while he was being paraded. 'Hey, hey. All right, boy,' I said with schoolboy enthusiasm. 'Go on, my son.'

One of the punters looked at me disapprovingly. Kevin came fifth, or second from last as we optimists like to say. 'You spooked him,' said Margot. 'Oh shut up will ya,' I said. 'Come on, let's go.' I stormed out of the track, sulking. It's surprising how much of your own ego you can invest in something as meaningless as a dog. If the dog wins, you win. But if the dog is shit, you are shit.

Despite the overall improvement in his times Kevin was still languishing in BAGS hell. This meant the opportunities to amaze my friends and family at the dogs had become virtually nonexistent. It was a struggle getting them there on a balmy Saturday night in the summer, let alone a wet Monday afternoon in the bleak of mid-winter when Kevin was getting caned by five or six lengths.

chapter 19

Over in the Popular Enclosure, which I'd avoided since my coronation as an owner, Kevin had barely registered on Vince's radar. 'Susie's Boy?' he asked quizzically when I told him of my new acquisition. 'Never heard of him.' Vince knew every dog at the Stow by name. All serious punters keep a mental intelligence file on every runner. 'No, *Zussies Boy*,' I said, 'trained by Linda Jones.' Vince thought for a moment. 'Oh, *Zussies* Boy. I know the dog you're talking about. Bought it from Linda Jones, did ya? Hasn't done much yet, has it?' 'He had a result a few weeks back,' I counter. 'You picked a winner there,' he said with a toothy grin and a soupçon of sarcasm. Then, in a feeble attempt to mitigate my obvious failure, I blabbed, 'I *could've* had Twotone for four grand.' Vince raised an eyebrow. 'Like I said. You picked a winner.'

It had become apparent that Kevin wasn't going to set the world alight. Whether through my own sheer ignorance, a good old-fashioned bit of salesmanship by the Dog Lovers Syndicate via Linda Jones or a combination of the two, I'd been well and truly Tango'd. Kevin was a lemon, and as such the only place he was gonna get a squeeze was the BAGS circuit. Linda, like all trainers contracted to the Stow, had to provide her fair share of dogs for the BAGS. Kevin's name was now firmly in the frame. The man with the electroshock hairdo was moving in.

The dogs on the BAGS tend to be the more inconsistent or inferior performers at the track, which means betting on the BAGS is more of a lottery than evening meets. I'd often watched BAGS races and seen the favourite repeatedly blown out of the water. Some BAGS meetings, particularly at provincial or northern tracks can produce few or no winners at short odds, making me highly suspicious about the grading systems that were in operation.

As a sop to us poor minnow owners and to entice the feckless hordes and pensioners away from Oprah, Kilroy, Tricia and all that makeover shite on telly, entry to BAGS meets is free and the drinks are half price. Which is just as well because I needed a stiff shot or six at the end of an afternoon.

For Kevin to escape BAGS hell and save me from perdition his times and performances would have to improve and remain consistent. But on current form this didn't look likely. Greyhound racing is not a sport where one can say, 'It's not the winning that counts, it's the taking part that matters.' Bargain basement racehorse owners may get a buzz seeing their 1000–1 donkey ridden by a part-time milkman crawl home in eighty-ninth place at Aintree. But at thirty seconds a pop, a greyhound race is too fast, intense and expensive to cheer your dog home for anything other than a win.

As one owner told me, 'For small-time owners like you to stay interested, the race manager's got to get you an average of one win in six races. You get that and you're happy. But if you have longer losing streaks, there's no money in it, is there?'

Since its inception in 1967, BAGS racing has grown in popularity with high-street punters and now accounts for 27 per cent of off-course turnover, which at the last count was around £6.2 billion. But the BAGS isn't so popular with owners, trainers or independently owned tracks. Many fear that the Big Three bookmakers, who have a tasty 60 per cent of the off-course market share, exert too much influence over the dogs but few will speak out on record for obvious reasons. However, former Hove trainer

Bob Young once wrote in the *Racing Post*, 'Trainers live on the edge when supplying runners for BAGS racing, [and] fear being sacked if a greyhound wins and has been backed although no rule of racing has been broken.'

Like most stereotypes, the image of the swindling, money-grabbing bookmaker is largely founded on a few overblown myths. And the fact that the high-street bookmakers have the dogs by the balls. Approximately 8500 betting shops receive the BAGS service, of which the Big Three own almost half, and they also own 40 per cent of SIS. Of the £15 million the bookmaking industry paid to greyhound racing in 2001 the majority was for the BAGS service. Crucially, the bookmaker-controlled tracks supply anywhere between 40 and 50 per cent of the BAGS racing. Get the picture?

Every week the *Racing Post* groans with tales of woe from owners, trainers, promoters and concerned members of the public slamming the BAGS cartel for screwing the dogs. However, the tracks not owned by the Big Three bookmakers, owners and trainers have formed a shaky alliance under a BGRB initiative called the New Deal and are fighting back for a significant increase in the voluntary levy of 4 per cent from bookmaker profits and to stop them from recycling funds into their fat coffers. The points of the disputed, debated and protracted New Deal campaign are:

1. To ensure that only the highest standard of integrity exists throughout greyhound racing.

2. To raise prize money to levels where any greyhound that races once a week, and wins one race in four, is able to cover its owner's training costs.

3. To properly reward greyhound trainers for their expertise, dedication and commitment.

4. To provide the necessary funding for the Retired Greyhound Trust to enable it to strive to find a good home for every former racing greyhound.

5. To pay kennel hands a fair living wage that represents their

importance to the greyhound industry and offers a viable long-term career path.

6. To provide a platform for head kennel hands and assistant trainers to become professional trainers.

7. To take all necessary measures to ensure the wellbeing and welfare of every NGRC registered greyhound.

8. To ensure the race managers are free to provide fair and safe racing without undue pressure or influence from third parties or outside sources.

9. To ensure any conflict of interest in bookmaker track owner-ship does not prevent racecourses and betting-shop punters from betting on greyhound racing with total confidence.

10. To end bookmaking control forever, so that greyhound racing has the freedom to move forward independently and un-influenced for the sole benefit of those who are within or support it.

The problem, ostensibly, is about money. But the wrangling over percentages and slices of pies had turned political, which was my cue to go watch some paint dry. It was a complicated, messy and confusing issue but as Geoffrey Thomas, Chief Executive of the BGRB[4] put it, 'It has become increasingly clear as the New Deal has gained momentum that this deal is no longer just about money or politics but also about securing a future for the people who work in and support greyhound racing that is free from bookmaker control.'

Everyone in the game appreciates that bookmakers are a necessary evil. But, just as McDonald's has given the burger a bad name and Starbucks has taken the sting out of coffee, the chain bookmakers have fostered an image of corporate greed and faceless bean counters in suits. On-course bookies on the other hand enjoy a far different reputation. They are seen as

[4] Thomas eventually resigned over the New Deal issue after seven years as BRGB chief, following controversial comments made about the bookmaking industry which led to a £5000 fine from the NGRC.

lovable rogues, gentlemen hustlers, sly old dogs who could rob you blind but do it in a style that invited your willing acquiescence.

Dougie Tyler is one such character. He'd been at the Stow for years and was the granddaddy of the track's rails bookies. People showed Dougie respect. He drove a Bentley with a personalised number plate.

'I've been here since 1946,' said Dougie in a clipped cockney accent as he stood next to his pitch. If you squinted, you could mistake him for Arthur Daley's non-biological twin. 'I'm owed a fortune. I'll never get it. 'Ere, this is Gary but I call him Long Tongue,' said Dougie, introducing me to a deceptively youthful-looking character who acted as his floor man, giving him nuggets of information, starting prices and his take on how the market would develop in the ante-post betting ring frenzy. 'Very popular with the ladies is Long Tongue.

'Back in the old days there were loads of characters with funny nicknames: you had Odd Eye, One Arm Lou, Dead Body, Oily Rag . . . all of 'em used to work for the bookies. When I first started under the board in 1946 there used to be this tearaway where I used to bet. One day he says, "Give us three quid." "Got no money," I said. He looked at me . . . I could see he was dangerous. He had a knife in his jacket. "I'll cut your fucking ears off," he said. "I'll make you a dwarf." My heart was going bang bang. Anyway, he scarpered. But years and years ago there were some very nasty gangs and bookies. Them Krays never used to bother us; for others it'd be a £100 a week or turn it in. They'd blow your legs off.'

To be a trackside bookie you have to have charisma and a touch of the showman about you. Apart from Gary Long Tongue, Dougie ran the pitch with his two sons, a couple of new school characters who looked more like accountants than bookmakers. While his sons balanced the books and Long Tongue fed Dougie his information, the old master chalked up the odds and enticed the punters with his vaudeville banter.

'Too many favourites winning today,' said Dougie thoughtfully. 'I'm doing a lot at the moment. Normally, if the favourites win the bookies lose. Years ago people used to come just for the gambling. Now it's socialising.'

So how do the Dougies of this world make their money? Well, the statistical probability of a dog winning in a six-dog race is 5–1, which seems obvious on paper. But not all dogs are created equal. Acting on information, a bookmaker will calculate probabilities of each dog winning based on a number of factors. The starting point is time. Which is the fastest dog in the race? Then there's the health, fitness, age, running style and other variables to consider. Once he has an idea of how a race is likely to pan out he creates a book – a list of probabilities that he then converts into odds. In order for him to make a profit these odds must total more than 100 per cent probability. Why does the total come to more than 100 per cent? So the bookie can make a profit, stoopid.

Scientifically, it's impossible to have a greater than 100 per cent certainty of an event occurring. But bookies are mathematical magicians. A bookmaker *artificially* shortens the odds for a particular race outcome or, conversely, increases the estimated probability of a race outcome. Consequently, the odds offered for a race by a bookie are not true odds or fair odds. You can't bet on all six dogs in a race and expect to win. The difference in price between fair odds and the bookmaker's odds or mark-up is called the over-round: and that's how he makes money. The over-round can be anywhere from 116 to 128 per cent, depending on the size and location of the betting market and the greed of the bookmaker.

'You're always trying to guess what they wanna back,' said Dougie of the punters. 'Sometimes you're right, sometimes you're wrong. See that fella up there,' Dougie gestured towards a guy up in the stands dressed like Indiana Jones in a leather flight jacket, chinos and a trilby. 'He's an excellent, excellent judge. Professional punter. Very very clever. He turns a handsome profit every year. Some people you'd love to play against all day cos you'd finish up with all their money. But if you played against him every day you'd end up penniless. If there were ten more like him in the stadium I'd walk away.'

Probability is an interesting science. For instance, it's thought that if an endless succession of monkeys were set before a typewriter with limitless paper, eventually they'd create the complete works of Shakespeare, by chance of course. Now if there are fifty keys on a typewriter, the probability of a monkey getting Shakespeare's name correct for starters is raised to the power of the number of characters (letters and spaces) in 'Shakespeare' plus the adjustments of the typewriter needed for capitals and punctuation. On this basis the chance of the monkeys typing 'Hamlet' correctly is 1 in 15,625,000,000. To quote the probability of our simian cousins typing the Bard's complete works then involves an extremely large number. And a lot of patience. And coffee. And . . .

Christ. What had I become? I was approaching my very own John Nash/*A Beautiful Mind* moment, i.e. paranoid schizophrenia, characterised by delusions, hallucinations and bipolar manic freak-outs. I never was one for maths.

Anyway, against the pros, bookies like Dougie will protect themselves by putting a cap on their stakes. 'You've got to cut 'em down sometimes. When they come in for a grand you give 'em 200 quid.' Indiana Jones was part of a crew of big punters who I'd often see at the BAGS meetings, all of whom bet nothing less than a bottle, and often a grand, on most races on the card. They strutted around like they owned the place. In some ways, they did.

'Nobody in this world has seen more greyhound races than me,' said Dougie from behind his pitch. 'I've seen hundreds of thousands of races. I'm eighty-five years old.'

'No!' I said, with genuine disbelief.

'Well, eighty-four-and-a-half actually. I'll never retire. I wanna be carried out.'

'The thing about the game is,' said Gary, 'with people like Dougie once they give the game up . . .'

'They die,' said Dougie.

'They die,' repeated Gary. 'They just give up on life.'

'I don't drink, I don't smoke,' said Dougie, 'I can't handle women . . . well, I can't get no movement, can I? There's no movement!'

'He was actually on the front page of the *News of the World* years ago,' said Gary.

'I was definitely the Don Juan of the greyhound tracks in my younger days, but not now. Like I said, I can't get no movement. There could be a woman here stark bollock naked. Wouldn't make no difference to me!'

One of the other bookies trudged over, a fat, ruddy-faced old codger. ' 'Ere, this man's a personality in the game,' said Dougie, introducing me to 'Billy'. 'He's been about a long time . . . acts a bit stupid sometimes . . . but deep down he's quite a nice chap.'

'When I was in the army,' said Billy, 'I saved two hundred soldiers . . .'

'He did, yeah, he did,' chipped in one of the floor men.

'Yeah, I shot the cook!'

'This is a very big area for gambling,' said Gary. 'Chingford, Walthamstow, Leyton, Leytonstone . . . I think the game was a lot better years ago. It was crammed out here, d'you know what I mean? You just couldn't move, mate. But now it's a lot weaker. It's still holding it's own at the moment. There's been talk of William Hill taking over. How true it is, I don't know. But it's more than just speculation. What you have to remember is the Chandlers aren't getting any younger. They're all in their sixties.'

'But Thursday and Saturday nights are a licence to print money,' I ventured. Dog tracks are full of rumours. Why would the Chandlers want to sell such a cash cow? Gary played the 'bookies lose money too' card, claiming that while the Chandlers made money the bookies often took a hit. But I can't say I've ever seen a poor bookmaker. He said there was some confusion among many punters about the difference between the high-street bookies, many of whom owned their own racetracks, and the smaller, family-run operations like Dougie's.

'The game here for bookmakers isn't as easy as you'd think. Look, as far as punters and trainers are concerned bookmakers are the scum of the earth, the enemy, which is not the way to look at things. Some of it's tongue-in-cheek. But we're all human beings, we all have to earn a crust. They're out there to do as best they can to beat the book and you're out there as a bookmaker to try to beat them. That's what it's all about. You can't characterise people by thinking what you *think* they are.'

This view came from a justifiable cynicism towards the big bookmaking chains as opposed to the independents. 'We're not here for our amusement or theirs; this isn't charity, it's business. We're all here to make money so a lot of the criticism bookies get is unfair.'

A voice from the stands cried, 'Four minutes'. 'Right, business must prevail now, gentlemen.' No sooner had Dougie's son said the word than the old man turned his attention to preparing for the next race, chalking up odds on the board. Gary, ever the scout for information, started probing me about Kevin, who had come second two races earlier.

'So, what did you pay for him, if you don't mind me asking?'

'What would you say?' I said, feeling a lump of embarrassment forming at the back of my throat.

'I wouldn't pay no more than . . . he's only a puppy . . . I wouldn't pay no more than five or six hundred pounds.'

'Jesus fucking . . . Oh, I won't tell you what I paid. But it was a little bit more than that.'

'He's only an A5 or A6 dog,' said Gary. 'What did you pay for him? Over £1000?'

'Yeah, over a thousand.'

'You've paid a lot of money for him,' said Gary, euphemistically. 'I'm not being funny but he's nothing special. You've paid a hell of a lot of money for him.'

'Yeah, er, ah . . . tell me about it . . .'

With thirty seconds to the next race the usual organised chaos was well underway. The small band of big boys, the Premiere League of punters, who were too lazy, established and loud-mouthed to cover the twenty-odd feet from the stands to the bookmakers' pitches and physically place their bets, were barking out their wagers as the lower divisions of workshy, feckless, semi-pros and compulsive gamblers battled it out on the floor. Dougie worked the crowd like a snake oil salesman as the other bookies used their own spiel to liberate we band of fools from our money.

'Top, fifteen hundred quid, Doug,' cried one punter from the stands, a Bobby De Niro lookalike in regulation slacks and short-sleeved shirt. Dougie seemed otherwise occupied. Perhaps it was the size of the bet that made him turn his attention elsewhere. 'Fifteen, Doug. Doug! You switched the hearing aid on again or what?'

'No it was off,' said Dougie nonchalantly. 'Did you shout?'

'Fifteen hundred quid on top,' said De Niro, finally getting his bet on.

'To win a monkey,' replied Dougie, confirming the bet.

In the seconds leading up to the off things can get desperate in the betting ring. Punters want to 'get on' but the bookies can't or won't always play ball. Once that bell goes and the dogs are out the traps betting ceases and in the mad scramble to make a wager some punters get lost in the mêlée.

'That's fucking out of order.' The Indiana Jones man was remonstrating with Billy the bookmaker after failing to register his bet. In the event, the dog Indiana Jones fancied won.

'I've been coming to BAGS meetings here for donkey's years and I can't get on?' said Indy, his face reddening. 'There's fellas been here five minutes and you take their money, Bill. What's your problem?'

'No problem, Terry.' Billy looked embarrassed. He offered some lame excuse about not hearing Indy's, a.k.a. Terry, bet before the off, but Indy wasn't having it. Now it was handbags at ten paces. Billy, head down, rummaged through his moneybag and paid out a handful of lucky punters, ignoring the increasingly agitated Indy.

'That's out of order, Bill. Bang out of order.' As Dougie had said, if a bookie doesn't fancy the odds against a big-spending punter he won't accept his bet. But for the sake of business and gambling etiquette at the very least the bookie should offer to take a reduced bet. But bookies love a bit of gamesmanship with punters and if there is a way of wriggling out of an awkward situation by playing dumb, they'll take it.

'Terry, I didn't hear you, mate.' said Billy, repeating his defence.

'Didn't hear me? You must be fucking joking.' Indy had lost out on around £500 or so in winnings. As the wheels of the betting ring started turning again in readiness for the next race, having taken enough stick from Indy, Billy finally had a crack at his expense.

'Yep, *you've* got plenty of time to get on, John,' he joked as one of his regulars stepped up to place a bet. A ripple of laughter went round the betting ring. Indy was incensed.

'You're making yourself look a right cunt in front of all these people, Bill,' snapped Indy.

'Watch it.'

Ooh! A collective groan went round. And greyhound racing was meant to be fun? Maybe there were too many negative ions in the air or something. Tempers were running high. I was starting to feel pretty pissed off myself after yet another loss-making day at the track and Gary Long Tongue's revelation that I'd been stung over Kevin.

I slipped up to the bar to have a quick one, and then headed for the kennels to see the Boy Blunder, but his handler Kelly had already gone. Just as I was slinking out of the stadium, licking my wounds, Dougie spied me walking through the betting ring.

' 'Ere, if you wanna buy any more dogs, you better come and ask us first,' shouted Dougie.

'I think my dog-buying days are over. The dog-selling days are coming though . . .'

Gary had evidently told Dougie about our earlier conversation. 'Tell me the truth, what d'ya pay for the dog? C'mon, tell me the truth. What was it?'

I made a finger-twisting gesture, indicating an unspecified amount.

'*Sixteen hundred quid?*' whispered Dougie, before shaking his head. I think I may have said, 'Yeah'. Well, if I had told him the real price he'd have had kittens. And I'd feel like an even bigger schmuck.

'Still . . .' and Dougie took the words, to add to the money he'd earlier taken from my pocket, right out of my mouth. 'You learn by experience.'

'Exactly,' I said.

'You won't do anything silly again.'

'Exactly, that's for sure. That's for sure.'

The word had really gone round that a sap was in the house.

' 'Ere, if you're looking for something, he's got some lovely dogs,' said Billy, nodding towards a wide-boy floor man leaning against the rails.

'I got one for sale *at the moment*,' the fella said, his voice lifting at the end of the sentence, as if to suggest it was *my lucky day*.

'Oh *really*?' I said, putting on my best mug-punter air of optimism. Like I needed to fake it.

'He runs at Romford. He's running tonight.'

'What's his name?'

'Car Car Kid.'

'Car Car Kid?' I said.

'Car Car Kid. He's in the second race tonight. He's up for sale for *three grand*.' The wide boy put the stress on the end of the sentence this time to emphasise that three grand *was not a lot of money*.

I asked a few more bullshit questions about Cack Cack Kid's form, just to string the guy along. What did they take me for? A mug, I guess. Wide boy's mobile rang, he answered it sheepishly, turning his back on me, so in the time-honoured tradition of a journalist, I made my excuses and left.

chapter 20

December 2002. I had given up keeping any serious record of my bets. Well, what was the point? For one, there were too many to record, but more importantly it was too depressing looking in my little black book and seeing all that red ink and minus signs. Most of my 'odd flutters' these days were at the bookies as opposed to the track. With Kevin stuck on the BAGS circuit it was becoming harder to see him race, in the flesh at least. It was easier to pop into the bookies and see him 'live' on SIS.

One afternoon I was in my local bookies waiting for Kevin to make his grand appearance. I felt confident. He looked in good shape. When I had asked Linda a couple of days ago, 'Is he well?' she'd given me the nod. He was favourite for the race, so I decided to have a score on him at 5–2. He soon moved to 2–1 and stayed there at the off. BANG! He's out of the traps like Linford. An old brother standing next to me was 'riding the betting shop pony', making like Frankie Dettori, clicking his fingers in a whipping motion and urging on the one dog, who was bumped by Kevin at the first bend.

'Go on, my son!' I shouted in retaliation. 'Go on, you little beauty.' The sonofabitch led all the way, baby. I collected my £70 from the cashier. 'Pleasure doing business with you,' I said sarcastically. Getting one over on the bookies, particularly William Hill, was something to savour. As they showed a re-run of the race I turned and said to the old brother, 'See that? That's *my* dog that is.' 'So why ya na give me a tip then?' he said, looking me up and down. 'I didn't want to jinx him.' I walked out of the door clutching my £50 profit. Nice. When Kevin won I was a winner and basked in his reflected glory. But when he lost I was a loser.

Things just hadn't gone the way I planned. Correction: I hadn't planned anything and things had gone the way you'd expect when you don't have a plan. I'd always prided myself on being a bit of a smart cookie but I'd been had. Fucking dogs. I wanted out. This business didn't make sense: a bunch of dogs chasing a windsock, and I'm doing my bollocks on it? The 'winnings' barely covered half the expenses. I spent more on that stupid dog than I did on my daughter. This was bullshit. People just didn't 'get me' any more. I suspect my friends thought I'd really lost it this time. I used to joke about being a loner, an outsider. Now I had become one. I could float in and out of circles, networks, crowds and worlds and feel no attachment. I was a chameleon. I was an invisible man.

We took off after Christmas for Barbados, Margot and I, for some much-needed winter sun. Boy did I need a holiday. I'd been writing some heavy shit for the *Evening Standard* and was now on the hit list of every fascist, feminist and black power organisation in the country. I'd been keeping a low profile for a month or so, slowly going stir crazy.

While in Barbados I tried to forget about work, money and the dogs – all the things I was meant to enjoy but invariably had conspired against me. Then, one evening, while pondering the meaning of life over a margarita, I came up with the smart idea of importing greyhound racing to Barbados. They had a lovely little mile-long track on the edge of Bridgetown called the Garrison. It was a simple oval turf course with a shorter sand track on the inside, which could easily be modified for dog racing. Barbados was the perfect place for it: a sporty, outdoors culture with lots of well-heeled ex-pats and locals. All I needed was a couple of mil, a few dozen dogs, some trainers, kennel hands, bookmakers and I was in business. I then woke up, ordered a rum punch and let sleeping dogs and mad ideas lie for a while.

When I got back from Barbados at the end of January, Britain had come to a standstill. For a change, it wasn't the wrong kind of leaves on railway lines that was responsible, or petrol protestors, or baying mobs hounding paediatricians mistaken for paedophiles but simply Mother Nature. Substantial bands of snow had shut down the south-east counties, East Anglia, Essex, Bedfordshire and Hertfordshire, lying between 5 and 12 cm deep in most places. North and north-west suburbs of London also experienced a late period of heavy snow. There was major disruption and gridlock on motorways in Essex and Hertfordshire; some tube networks were also affected.

After nearly eighty years of dog racing there is still no safe, uniform all-weather surface. In days gone by, many tracks were grass, others were a combination of grass and sand and now most were just sand. At Peterborough dog track the wrong type of sand had once led to greyhounds suffering blisters on their paws. A mix-up meant the sand used to fill in gaps and cover bare patches was too gritty, so the track's managers had to stump up £9000 for 530 tonnes of the right type of sand.

The Stow had the right kind of sand but the wrong kind of weather for a lightweight like me, just back from the Caribbean. The heavy snow meant conditions on the track were ranging from minus 30 to minus 60. Apart from the very severest of conditions the show always goes on regardless. But even when the show can't go on there are alternatives.

Computers, robots and the machines, like H.G. Wells had predicted, are taking over the world. Sports leisure is no exception. The machines are taking over greyhound racing. Some bright spark had ignited a forest fire of fantastical high-street bookmaking the previous year with the invention of 'virtual' racing. Along with BAGS, the gee-gees, 49s, Heads or Tails and a bunch of other garbage, computerised horse and dog races, producing apparently randomly generated results are being piped into the high-street chains via SIS. While the gee-gees have the fictitious 'Portman Park' and 'Steepledowns' racetracks, the dogs have 'Millersfield' and 'Brushwood', where the yapping, pixel-fixed greyhounds bound 'over the sticks'. Like the ad in my local bookies said, 'There's nothing virtual about a winner.' Of course the same could be said about a loser – in fact, more so. Virtual racing is gambling for the Playstation generation.

In virtual racing the odds are fixed before the race, so the market never changes. But people do make big scores playing it. Ladbrokes once took a £10,000 bet on a virtual 6–4 favourite which won, while Hill's have taken bets of up to £4000 on totally fictitious animals, which just goes to prove there's one born every minute. That said, I've actually won a few quid on virtual dogs, obviously by sheer luck. Only the odd fiver or so, but my hit rate at predicting virtual winners was actually higher than with real dogs.

In my eternal quest to find an 'edge' and avoid ever having to work again I came across a variety of software programs available for the 'professional punter', most of which were utter rubbish. One intriguing innovation was the 'Greyhound Predictor', a computer program that promised to simulate the running of a greyhound race after you input data into it. Using the results from old copies of the *Racing Post*, I tested the software. And every time I punched in the necessary info, using my historical data – dog weights, best record times, running style and so on – the results never matched the outcome.

Then there is that other ruse, internet betting, which is as virtual as virtual gambling in the sense that, by using a computer screen and a credit card the bookies hope you won't realise you are actually gambling or, more accurately, losing your money. All these gimmicks are aimed at people just like me: the computer-literate, pre-middle-aged punter. The old school gamblers and technophobes wisely don't have time for such nonsense, preferring good old cash to credit cards and computer chips.

Internet bookies entice you with the offer of free bets, just like the £750 one that reeled me into this mess in the first place. For one, you never get the complimentary stake back and as the odds are always against you, the chances are the free bet will fizzle out like a damp sparkler. Even if you win, you'll plough the winnings back in. And that is how they get you.

chapter 21

The city droned in the winter. All that grey concrete, the traffic, the fumes and the bad manners were in stark contrast to the azure sea, golden sands, palm trees and post-colonial civility of Barbados. One of the many long-dead white men that I'm fond of often quoting once said something about, 'When a man is tired of London, he is tired of life.' I needed to get out of the Smoke urgently, before London ground me down and into a slipknot of rope slung over a balustrade. I needed to see green fields, go rambling on towpaths, bird watching, or maybe even hunt small defenceless creatures with packs of scavenging dogs.

An old boy called Brian Coleman had asked me to join him as a 'foot follower' on the Puckeridge Hunt in Hertfordshire, to give me a flavour of what country life is like. Brian was a retired terrier man, which is an adjunct assisted by terriers who rides on horseback or on a quad bike with the hunt in order to sniff out a fox if it goes to ground. An old mutual friend called Tamara, whose family had long been into foxhunting and various equine pursuits, had introduced me to Brian, who worked as a steward at the car boot sale at Hackney Wick Stadium.

It was a cold, misty morning, and drizzly, which was apparently bad news for the hunt but good news for the fox. Around twenty-five to thirty brace of hounds were 'speaking', not barking, as they jockeyed their way round the courtyard of the Barclay spread. The Barclays ran the Puckeridge Hunt. They had proper dough. 'See him over there,' said Brian casually, nodding towards a character who looked like he'd just rode out of a Stubbs. 'If I tapped him for £100 million he'd still be a billionaire.'

'But people have got hunting wrong,' chipped in Tamara. 'It's not all toffs and la-di-da.' Tamara was always at pains to explain that hunting is not an elitist activity. She had recently dragged me off to a Countryside Alliance demo in Parliament Square and insisted that I couldn't get involved with greyhound racing without looking at hunting. 'Yeah, yeah,' I'd said, at first dismissing the links between city sport and country sport as tenuous. But there were links.

Despite living not far from central London, Tamara was a big supporter of the Countryside Alliance. Her family hailed from Chigwell but like many people in that part of London they had made the exodus eastwards from Bethnal Green decades earlier. I knew Tamara's dad George pretty well too: salt of the earth geezer and all that. George had done the whole East End rites of passage thing, from being an amateur boxer to running a stall and grafting at Billingsgate fish market, with a few scrapes and adventures in between. He was also godfather to the actor Ray Winstone and knew the boxing promoter Frank Warren in the days when he was just starting out with characters like Lennie 'the Guv'nor' McLean.

All of this cockneyology is intriguing but largely irrelevant to greyhound racing, I agree. But it just illustrates that you don't need six degrees of separation to join the dots between town and country. It is the people and their attitudes rather than the physical environment that has created a new spin on what Disraeli called Britain's 'Two Nations'. Nowadays the barriers between people are not just economic, cultural or racial; there is a huge divide between town and country. Tamara had taken me to demos where police had baton-charged protestors dressed in plus-fours and anoraks and men with thick Cornish accents had looked me square in the face and declaimed the genuinely held belief that they were 'ethnic minorities' being oppressed by the state.

Like country folk and city folk, foxhounds and greyhounds are two different branches of the same species. While foxhounds are bred to hunt by smell, greyhounds, of course, chase by sight and with silent stealth too. One of the reasons a fox can outsmart a sixty-strong pack of bloodhounds is because, like all dimwits, they blow a lot of hot air and make a lot of useless noise. Greyhounds use guile and agility to nail their prey while foxhounds rely simply on brute force and numbers. They're mangy, semi-feral creatures, oafish and clumsy – a good few notches down the food chain from greyhounds.

Standing around a pack of hounds or, more correctly, twenty-odd brace of hounds, helped me to develop a degree of superiority as a greyhound owner. Greyhounds aren't known for being smart like Alsatians or mongrels, but there was always the outside chance that Kevin could be taught at the very least to sit, fetch and heel. Judging by his results, rolling over and playing dead already came naturally to him. Foxhounds on the other hand are beyond domestication once they've hunted. As Tamara kept telling me, 'If foxhunting is banned every hunting dog in the country will have to be put down. Where are the animal rights in that?'

Indeed, what little intelligence a foxhound has is devoted to its stomach and how to line it. 'I've had to pull hounds out of restaurants, clubs, even a pet shop, to get 'em away from food,' said Brian, pointing out that when they get loose they head straight for the catering. I felt there was something sinister about foxhounds. Maybe it was just what I thought they symbolically stood for. Or perhaps it was because two or three of them sauntered over to me and sniffed at my crotch while I was drinking my mulled wine and eating my fruity biscuit. 'You'll be all right,' whispered Brian, 'as long as you don't make a sudden move. If one of 'em goes for ya the pack will follow, and that's it. They'll rip you to pieces.'

I kept still, sipped my mulled wine and nibbled the biscuit. The

Barclay matriarch eventually saved my bacon by announcing it was tally-ho time. Despite Tamara and Brian's insistence that foxhunting was a people's sport, the red tunics, rat-catcher tweeds, jodhpurs and odd billionaire gave the event a decidedly toffee-nosed air. I'd dressed like a hunt saboteur for the occasion, you know, to get a reaction, but none of the forty or so riders and followers gave me a second glance. Snobs. I wondered what would happen if little Emily or Charlotte took me round to mummy and daddy's for Sunday lunch? I'd wind up as fucking desert, that's what would happen. I thought of England, knocked back another glass of mulled wine, pocketed two biscuits and set off for the hunt.

We trudged through mud and grass for half an hour. It all seemed like a harmless jolly until I made the mistake of being the first person to spot the fox. 'Here, what's that over there?' I said quizzically, peering some three hundred metres into the distance. 'That's it, isn't it?' Bounding across the horizon was a bushy clump of crimson and brown. At first I was excited. Here was a proper, well-fed, Disney-coloured fox not a manky urban critter like the ones I'd see lurking around the bins of my local Tesco. But my excitement soon waned. Without batting an eyelid, Brian let out an almighty cackle that sounded like an emu having its nuts crushed in a vice. 'Aaaaaaaaaaarrrrrrrrrk . . . Aaaaaaaaaaa aaaaaarrrrrrrrrrrrrk . . . aaaaaaaaaaaaarrrrrrrrrrrk!!!!!!!'

A bugle sounded. The field emerged from some woods far off in the distance, headed by the master of the hunt. Brian waved his arms frantically and pointed to a dell into which the fox had seemingly disappeared. We headed over to the dell, where the master of the hunt and the whip master met us. 'Have you chaps been here long?' the hunt master asked Brian, while Tamara explained to me that the field was kept out of sight of any potential kill, which I thought was rather civilised. There were a couple of young teenagers in the field and a boy no older than eight on what looked like a seaside pony. 'Very few people see a kill,' said Tamara. 'The RSPCA kill more animals each year than all the hunts put together. Most people go for the chase, because it gives them a chance to put some air in their horses' lungs. Riding over fences and hedgerows is better than beating tarmac at two miles an hour.'

I felt crummy. I'd fingered the fox. For the first time in my life I'd been an informer, a grass, a rat. I had turned Queen's Evidence on one of Aesop's little chums. The hounds went into the copse, turning over the joint like Feds on a manhunt. The master of the hunt mentioned something about the holes in the ground being bunged up the night before to stop the fox from going to ground, you knew, just to make it a fair hunt. But after ten minutes or so they gave up looking in the copse and rode off into the distance. From that point on I spent the next eight hours traipsing around the Hertfordshire countryside, praying the fox would get away, while Tamara extolled the virtues of country life as yet more foot followers, cars, quad bikes and of course funny-looking people on horseback galloped around the countryside in search of that sly old Mr Fox. As luck would have it, by the end of the day they still hadn't caught the little fella, so I was in the clear. Phew. The fox, the man and the guilty conscience. Aesop would've dug that one.

chapter 22

I just couldn't get enough of rural Britain and charming cunt'ry folk these days. Taking Kevin for idle walks in Suffolk, meandering through the rolling hills of County Kerry and badgering foxes in picture-postcard Hertfordshire had renewed my faith in nature. For the first time in years I felt comfortable venturing out into the sticks without fear of odd stares, harassment or a starring role as wicker man at ye local village witch-burning fête. Why, I even started buying the odd copy of the countryside bible *The Field*. But only for the sport, mind you.

I felt it was time to go further afield. It was time to go back to my roots – well, Kevin's roots really – in search of the ancient origins of greyhound racing, that soon-to-be-outlawed forerunner of the track and quaint county ritual: hare coursing.

It's 8.30a.m. and the final of the one hundred and fifty-sixth Waterloo Cup is due to kick off in an hour's time on the late Lord Leverhulme's estate at Great Altcar, a misty plain on the outer regions of bleakest west Lancashire. An enterprising Liverpool hotelier named William Lynn inaugurated the annual three-day event in 1836 as a way of promoting his establishment, the Waterloo Hotel. In the late 1800s crowds of up to 75,000 flocked to the Waterloo Cup, earning it a reputation as the Grand National of hare coursing. These days it was more widely recognised as the most controversial event in the British sporting calendar.

Mingling in the crowd of early risers I could feel the tension wafting through the dawn air. My initial attempts to make idle conversation with the locals were met with grunts, groans, and general indifference. People were eyeing me suspiciously. I was the only black man in a crowd of four thousand-odd rednecks; and I was talking into a Dictaphone and scribbling in a notebook. And I was dressed in a black leather jacket, black woolly hat, shades and combats, rolling like one of the Panthers. I knew I should've brought wellies and an Ian Duncan Smith rubber mask. Now was not a good time to stand out in a crowd.

The opening day of the event had been marked by around two hundred placard-waving animal rights protesters crying 'murderers' and 'scum' at the coursing fans; consequently, a number of surly looking cops were on standby in riot vans parked on the site. The news media had had a field day with the city v country, civilisation v barbarism narrative of the Waterloo Cup. Depending on which paper you read, what you ate or who you voted for, hare coursing is either a quaint English tradition essential to the fabric of rural culture, or an a evil, mindless, oafish, barbaric act of cruelty. If the hunting bill, which had been debated in the Commons the previous day, became legislation, the Waterloo Cup and all forms of hunting with dogs would be consigned to the knacker's yard.

Hare coursing is one of the world's oldest field sports, dating back to the time of the Pharaohs. The Greeks introduced it to the Romans who in turn introduced it to England. Then in 1014, King Canute enacted the Forest Laws, which decreed that only noblemen could own and hunt with greyhounds. However, it wasn't until Tudor times that it became popular in England.

Lord Orford, the same chap who bred the modern greyhound, founded the country's first coursing club towards the end of the eighteenth century. So this wasn't some fly-by-night badger-baiting cult. The advent of greyhound racing in 1926 saw a decline in the numbers of coursing spectators, particularly from the cities; but the pro-coursing lobby still had history on its side. Coursing, they argued, was an English tradition, like the Changing of the Guard, dancing round the maypole and noncing. But as Marx had said, 'The traditions of the dead weigh like a nightmare on the living.' People are too caught up in tradition, defending it, fighting for it, dying for it. Sometimes you just have to move with the times.

I kept circulating. Half an hour had passed and nothing much had happened. A small contingent of rails bookies was taking odds on the first course. Punters were digging into hampers in car boots – some with champers from buffed-up Range Rovers, others with cider from beat-up Escorts. Kids darted in and out of the crowd and old men in flat caps and oilskins chatted idly.

'Number seventeen, South Shore, is withdrawn,' came an announcement from a stuffy voice over the PA. 'We remind you that we will be *ruthless* with any member of the public having a dog on a lead, in their coat or in any other fashion,' continued the voice à la *1984*. 'They will be either removed or the dog will be put in the car. It'll be your choice. Can I also remind the public that when the hares are getting close to the dogs, please do not impede any escape routes. Yesterday, er, there were a couple of times when the enthusiasm of the crowd might well have turned a couple of them. Please let the hares escape through any gaps.'

If a hare could out-manoeuvre the dogs for more than forty seconds, chances are they'd run out of steam and give up, leaving the hare to escape into the thicket at the other end of the course or through refuges called 'soughs'. However, if the dogs caught the hare, it'd be turned into a Christmas cracker faster than you could say 'Jack Rabbit'.

I walked along a row of stalls of country apparel and dog paraphernalia thinking I might find a wee present for Kevin. Trophies, leads, collars, jackets and all sorts were on sale. As I was fondling a rather fetching leather riding crop I thought of Margot and then noticed an old pikey, dressed in a cheap two-piece suit, leaning against a low wire fence behind me. He seemed in distress. 'You all right?' I asked. 'Urggggghhhhh .... Urrrggg gghhh . . .' came the response as the man threw up on to the grass. A bunch of spotty-faced lads no older than fourteen strolled by swigging cans of beer, laughing. 'Urgggghhhh .... Urgggh hhh . . .' *Sod him. He'll live.* I left the old duffer straining to regurgitate what looked like a cross between half a pint of pina colada and a tin of pea soup and headed for the heart of the action.

Sixty-four greyhounds had started the knockout competition in pursuit of the Waterloo Cup and the £5,000 first prize, now down to the last sixteen on the third and final day. The runner-up would receive £1500 and a trophy, the next two £650 each, the next four £200 and the last eight £100, pretty shite prize money if you ask me.

As I got nearer to the course, I noticed the judge of the competition, a short fat stump of a man with a gammon ham face dressed in full hunting pink, having trouble mounting his horse. 'Give him a swift kick in his fookin' knackers,' cried a wrinkly old mare to the assembled crowd, as a stable hand gave the judge a face-saving bunk up. 'I'll give ya a fiver he falls off.' The assembled crowd roared with laughter as he finally worked his ample girth into the saddle. It was the judge's job to award the dogs points for speed and agility. Thankfully no one was judging him.

It was fast approaching 9.30a.m. The crowd seemed restless. I jostled my way deeper into the mass of bodies towards a gully separating the course from the southern bank of spectators. I felt increasingly uncomfortable, surrounded by hordes of Jacobean runts in flak jackets, khakis, combat pants, oilskins and fatigues. It was like dress-down Friday at a Ku Klux Klan convention. No surprise, then, that Lancashire was the heartland of the British National Party's 'political' activity. In 2003, of the seventeen council seats held by the BNP, ten were in Lancashire. This was not my kind of country. I caught a few choice stares and saw in some of the dark eyes of those rednecks an ancient truth: once upon a time the ancestors of these self-same characters would've hunted *my* ancestors through the rain forests of Africa and the plantations of the West Indies.

'They're now in slips, now in slips,' said the announcer. 'On the red collar, More Harry and on the White Collar, Judicial Best.' The crowd had swollen above five thousand and it felt as though every one of them was standing behind me, peering over my shoulder and watching my every move.

More Harry and Judicial Best were the first brace, in the first 'slip' or race of the day. They were competing in the Waterloo Purse, one of two warm-up acts before the Waterloo Cup final. The wind was picking up across the field. I rubbed my hands and felt my feet tighten with cold. The crowd grew ever more expectant and agitated. It was a long waiting game.

It passed 10a.m. My feet had frozen. My balls were as hard as brass. One scrawny hare appeared but was given free passage across the field and the dogs, chomping at the bit, weren't let loose. I asked a man standing next to me if he knew why the hare hadn't been coursed and he ignored me but for a shrug of the shoulders. The bookies were trying to work up the crowd: 'treble the field' and 'six to four the red collar', they kept calling, but the action was lacklustre. I was about to throw a tenner to the wind when *Henry V* got in on the act:

> I see you stand like Greyhounds in the slips,
> Straining upon the start. The game's afoot:
> Follow your spirit; and upon this charge
> Cry 'God for Harry! England and Saint George!'

Distraction. The spectators at the far end of the course caught sight of the hare first. The beaters had driven it from out of the surrounding bushes and on to the course. Game on. A ripple of anticipation went through the crowd, then a breaker, and then a tidal wave. I was standing in front of a group of old yokels who reeked of either very cheap scotch or cough syrup. 'Here we go, boys!' yelled one of them, a Welshman. The hare came into view, its feet a blur, its marble eyes bulging with utter panic. 'That'll do us, that'll do us, that'll do us,' squawked a ruddy-faced stoat in a deerstalker, followed by an enthusiastic cry of, 'Go on, pussy.' As the hare fizzed past the small screen in the middle of the course, behind which the slipper held the dogs, voice after voice barked, 'Let 'em off, let 'em off.'

The hare was given the requisite eighty-odd-yard head start ahead of the screen before the slipper let loose the baying dogs. Within seconds they'd closed in on the hare but it then made a sharp right turn, losing More Harry in the process. 'He's in bother, he's in bother,' hollered a Cornishman. 'He's on line, he's on line,' came back an Irishman as More Harry corrected himself and rejoined Judicial Best in the chase. 'He's up and turned him,' said the Cornishman behind me. The hare bobbed and weaved as the dogs fought to keep track of him; he had too much in the way of guile, speed and technique for the dogs and bolted off towards the thicket at the other end of the course, leaving the greyhounds trailing behind. 'All right, pussy, all right, lovely,' mumbled the Deerstalker Man, cryptically, as handlers rushed on to the field to retrieve the dogs.

The announcer pronounced Judicial Best the winner. Clearly the hare should've got the decision. The next course was equally, if not more, barbarous than the first, as this time the hounds gained on the hare much faster than their predecessors had. One of the dogs buckled as he made a wide turn in pursuit of the arcing hare. In such an instance, a hare can literally run rings round a greyhound as its lower centre of gravity, lighter weight and smaller frame make it easier for it to negotiate tight bends, which is why, I guess, they always pass the finish line first at the track. The hare disappeared into the thicket and survived, but only just. Hares 2, Greyhounds 0.

Just as I was debating whether to stay for the inevitable slaughter of one hare my mobile rang. It was Dr Paul. Dr Paul wanted to know what had gone down. I gave him an appraisal of the last slip.

'So what happened to the hare?' asked Dr Paul.

'Oh, it's probably being ripped to shreds right now,' I said jokingly, to which Deerstalker Man interjected, 'Na, na, na, na, no, no, no, no, don't say things like that. That hare went straight away, straight away.' What was it with these inbred freaks, repeating word, after, word, after, word, after word?

'That doesn't happen, that doesn't happen at all,' continued Deerstalker Man, now supported by a small mob of equally touchy-filthy friends. 'Don't give the wrong impression,' he added. 'Forgive me,' I mocked, barely able to conceal the cry of 'wankers' in a forced cough. The mob gave me the eye. I gave them the eye back. *Go on, make a move, you freaks.* The first half a dozen or so wouldn't be a problem: a left hook here, a straight right . . . it'd be fun. The other four thousand would be a bit of a handful though. Now they were all piling in. 'Ripping it to fucking pieces?' moaned one. 'Attacking hare coursing again, eh?' said another. 'For fuck's sake . . . unbelievable,' groaned another still.

'What's up?' I said, shrugging my shoulders as I made my way through the gauntlet of angry yokels, keeping a watchful eye on their fists, just in case someone fancied their chances. The cops weren't far away but they'd probably pile in too if the crowd turned nasty.

'If you don't like hare coursing, why don't you fuck off?' said one banjo-playing specimen as I walked by.

'Make me,' I snapped, stopping to glare at him. As Sophocles, or perhaps Chris Eubank, might have said, 'A short saying oft contains much wisdom,' so I told Banjo Boy to 'fuck off' for good measure. He gave an embarrassed grin, glanced round, looked me up and down and disappeared into the crowd. I could hear murmurs, words of disquiet: the prelude to action. I edged along at a skewed angle so I could keep an eye on my back and simultaneously keep an eye on the local pond life, in case they fancied giving me the bum's rush. I passed through the crowd, bumping a few shoulders and exchanging sneers and snarls, playing up to the sort of big bad black bogie man stereotype that freaks the shit out of white folks. Well, if you've got it, flaunt it.

I decided that two courses of wild hare à la frustrated grey-hounds was enough and split before I became dessert.

Most of the time greyhounds are docile, passive creatures. But they have a dark side to their character, a vicious mean streak essential to their pathology which is easy to ignore on the racetrack or when out for walks. Thousands of years of progressive breeding, crossbreeding, rearing and schooling have made them fundamentally highly trained assassins. That's why they race. The only reason they race. For a greyhound, chasing a plastic hare round a track is like a sniper taking pot shots at tin cans. Once faced with live bait, something tangible to aim at, the temptation to kill is overwhelming.

As for the hares, the National Coursing Club, in its glossy promotional literature, argues that the little buggers enjoy nothing more than a good day's coursing:

Opponents of coursing admit that the sport ensures the preservation of the hare and that few are killed, but claim that the hares are terrified. Research carried out on behalf of the RSPCA by Dr Stoddart has shown that the flight of the hare is a natural, instinctive and routine response to danger. Dr Stoddart concluded that the hare would've become extinct years ago if it was not capable of escape from pursuit. For the hare, it's all in a day's work.'

I particularly love that last line about it being 'all in a day's work', as though dodging the snapping, salivating chops of two 34-kilo greyhounds is something a bad-ass hare's just gotta do to make it in the hood.

The seventeenth-century philosopher Thomas Hobbes could've been referring to hare coursing when he said famously, 'Life in an unregulated state of nature is solitary, poor, nasty, brutish and short.' It was precisely this idea, according to Hobbes, that caused humans to enter into social contracts, gladly accepting the moral constraints of civilisation to its alternative, the law of nature.

Morality, as an extension of that contract, is a way of protecting ourselves from the brutality of living in a world where people simply do what comes naturally, i.e. kick the living shit out of anything that moves.

A hare or a greyhound can't change its spots. But with the use of Oxy 10 a man can. To the uninitiated, coursing hares just for a lark was sadistic. Sure, farmers kill or cull foxes, hares, crows and other pesky critters all the time – but that's to protect their livelihood, which ultimately is in the food-buying public's interests. Animal husbandry is one thing; hunting for sport or, more accurately, to stiffen an erectile problem, is something else. Just because some weird practice has been around for centuries doesn't make it morally justifiable. Man will always try to rationalise bad behaviour by making a cultural virtue of it, especially if he gets a hard on to boot.

By the end of the day, Heneritta, a three-year-old greyhound bitch trained by Irishman Joe Walsh, had beaten Goodbye Joe to become the Waterloo Cup Wonderdog. No sooner had the rosettes, laurels and crowns of thorns been awarded than a war of words erupted between the RSPCA and the event organisers. The RSPCA said that in the last four events, 76 hares had been killed and claimed that one in 3.6 slips – the highest ratio since the charity had started keeping records – had resulted in a kill. But the National Coursing Club hit back, accusing the RSPCA of 'concocting the statistics' in order to boost opposition to the event. Liz Mort, spokeswoman for the National Coursing Club, told anyone who'd listen that the RSPCA's figures were 'pure fantasy'.

'These statistics are all wrong,' said Mort. 'There were a total of 109 slips and under 20 hares were caught.' The RSPCA was appalled at the suggestion that their officers had lied. There had been demos and counter-demos by outraged opponents and supporters alike. The Countryside Alliance claimed only one in eight hares was killed and said the crafty little buggers, much like the fox, had a good chance of escaping the hounds. The

International Fund for Animal Welfare (IFAW), on the other hand, insisted the death rate was nearer to one in five and said that one of its undercover investigators had witnessed Waterloo Cup organisers shipping in at least seventy hares two nights earlier. A few tweeds cried, 'Hear, hear!' and a few crusties yelled back 'Fuck off' and so the debate ding-donged in time-honoured fashion until all was forgotten, at least for another year.

Like *The Mousetrap*, the hunting issue was set to run and run. The day before the final, Westminster's Politburo had ended its consideration of the hunting bill, which was aimed at bringing about an effective ban on foxhunting and hare coursing in England and Wales. The rural affairs minister, Alun Michael, condemned hare coursing as an 'unnecessary and cruel activity' that failed the utility test set by the hunting bill. It was widely expected that when the bill returned to the Commons the following month many MPs would get tough and seek an amendment calling for a total ban outlawing *all* hunting with dogs. But why stop there? Having smelled blood, the animal rights lobby, spearheaded by the League Against Cruel Sports, was clawing for a ban on greyhound racing too, effectively outlawing the hunting of plastic bunnies and smelly old rags.

The abolitionists talked a good fight. But I had little faith, and less money, to back on New Labour coming to the rescue and actually standing by one of its manifesto commitments; there'd never be a ban on hare coursing and fox hunting, let alone greyhound racing without a bunch of limp-wristed provisos and get-out clauses attached.

To paraphrase John Gray, Professor of European Thought at the London School of Economics and author of *Straw Dogs: Thoughts on Humans and Other Animals*, for much of human history and all of prehistory, we did not see ourselves as different from any other animal. In fact, hunter-gatherers, to which hare coursers may claim a relation, saw their prey as equals, if not superiors. Ancient peoples worshipped greyhounds, like many animals. 'The humanist sense of a gulf between ourselves and other animals is an aberration,' says Gray.

I had tried to go hare coursing with an open mind. I'd seen *Snatch*. But fuck it. I was glad I hadn't seen a hare pulled apart at the seams. If greyhound racing was anachronistic, hare coursing was positively antediluvian. Lacking the high drama and brutal aesthetic of, say, bullfighting or boxing, and the genuine competitiveness of greyhound racing, it was hard to accept any argument in favour of hare coursing. This poor excuse for a 'sport' was a cheap and nasty little pastime that appealed to graceless drunken oafs who had nothing better to do than stand around a soggy field all day dressed up like toy soldiers, waiting with baited breath for the odd rodent to be devoured by hungry dogs.

We put animals in zoos and goldfish bowls and ring-fenced fields because we want to play God. We imagine that somehow we are subverting the Universe through such acts. We can peer, meddle, feed, love, withdraw love at our mercy. The animal looks up at us and prays in its silent way that today we are benevolent. A dog wags its tail and hopes we'll just carry on drinking, smoking, dancing away in our semi-detached Pantheons and not deliver an avalanche of hate or a psychological earthquake into its little world. When man hunts, he trades in God for the Devil. In such instances we still command divine control but we do so with a sadistic edge. There is the theoretical possibility of escape. Of course, like a bookie, we have adjusted the odds so that the experience is over-round: one way or another we can't lose. If the quarry has the good fortune to escape, we have still derived pleasure from the 'thrill of the chase', the foreplay *and* in-out, in-out of the act. If and when the kill comes, so much the better, for herein lies that essential ejaculatory moment.

The Devil gets all the best lines because of his unpredictability. This is what hunting is: a set of pre-arranged factors wrapped up in the fancy dress of apparent randomness. The 'laws of nature' apparently even things out. Trouble with that axiom is there are at least six billion people on the planet. Even if all the lions, tigers, cheetahs, crocs, black widows etc. formed their own G7 or NATO and massed ranks to take on the global enemy that is mankind, we'd take them out in no time. Gnashing teeth and a good line in stingy tails are no match for weapons-grade plutonium and Stealth bombers.

That said, what the hell do I know? While I found hare coursing and the people who practised it repugnant, my disgust didn't give me the moral ammunition to join the prohibitionists. I'd sit this one out and maintain the best position a journalist can ever occupy: smack bang on the fence. Rural Britain was another country and one that I felt I had no business troubling. Let them eat cake. Or as the nineteenth-century essayist William Hazlitt put it, 'There is nothing good to be had in the country or if there is, they will not let you have it.' Too fucking true. I hit the dirt road out of Great Altcar, did a wheel spin, turned left on to the B5195, left on to the A565, then the A5207, the M6, the M1 and kept right on driving with my foot to the floor, back to the relative civilisation of Londinium.

chapter 23

'Once upon a time you had White City, Wimbledon, Hackney, Wembley . . . and punters came in their droves.' Gary Long Tongue scanned the stadium mournfully. 'Now look at it.' It was a damp, listless Thursday night. I was down to my last score and searching the Stow for life. Drained of the chattering, raucous bodies that had been its lifeblood during the summer, the Stow had the ghostly air of an out-of-season seaside resort. There was still a crowd, still action, a few 'kiss me quick' revellers, but the greying cynical diehards had the run of it, not the party hearty six-packers.

'Greyhound racing's going down the toilet, mate,' said one punter, another lonely fool who was evidently eavesdropping on my conversation with Long Tongue. 'In the summer you'd be fooled into thinking the game's healthy but it's fucked. Once the weather turns it's empty here. Many owners don't race their dogs any more . . . same with trainers. Can't make it pay, can they?'

I certainly couldn't make it pay. But that didn't stop me coming back again and again. How had I become hooked by such a godforsaken, grimy, low-rent pastime like the dogs? Why is it so easy to become addicted to crap? Whether it's smack, crack, junk food, dogging, booze or tobacco, man's addictions have one thing in common: they're all based on a predilection for utter rubbish. Gambling is addictive because it's bad for you. And gambling is bad for you because, get this, *you lose*. And the more you lose, against all reason and better judgement, the more you're sucked in. Why? Well, apart from the subconscious need to beat yourself up, there are a number of reasons, but one other major factor is ego. Every time you lose, someone, somewhere has taken your money. They've bent you over a counter, pulled your pants down and given you a right good seeing to. And you want to get your own back. Gambling preys on the need for men to get their own back, to get even. One thing that boxing taught me is that you learn a lot more about life as a loser than as a winner.

We losers love gambling because it tempts us with the prospect of being a winner, a prospect that ultimately is never fulfilled. We always lose more than we win. Which reinforces the fact that we're losers. Which makes us feel good. Cos that way we wind up knowing we were right all along. We get *validation* through losing. Many gamblers are losers because they are addicted to gambling, not making money. If they were addicted to making money they'd engage in an activity that could yield them a greater profit, like a job, a rich wife or a career in the porn business. Unless you can turn gambling into something other than gambling, i.e. bookmaking, you're on a hiding to nothing.

A dictum of philosophy is that anything taken to an extreme turns into its opposite. I thus spent many hours, days, weeks and months pondering the probability of turning my increasing debt into a profit . . . with little success.

Having come through two hard races third and second, the formbook suggested that Kevin should've been a good bet as an 11–4 favourite in the previous day's BAG'S meeting. Just as well I didn't run the A406 gauntlet to see him race in the flesh. Instead I opted for the relative comfort of a smoke-filled betting shop in Portobello Road. As craggy-faced punters hacked their way through several tons of B&H, Silk Cut and Lucky Strike, I saw fifty quid on the nose sail down shit creek as Kevin feebly weathered the storm of another rocky race to finish fourth. That dog was a weed. He was over two years old now; he should've been bullying his opponents by now, instead he was still acting like the runt.

The BAGS was killing it for me, like it had killed it for a lot of small-time owners. Where was the joy, the pleasure, the excitement of watching your dog limp around on a freezing Friday afternoon while you ate a soggy meat pie and drank warm beer? So much for the glamour of racing. As far as I was concerned the little guy was getting shafted left, right and centre. Not only did we provide a service for the Big Three bookmakers to get fat, we had to do so at a time of day that was not conducive to us. I had a lot of time on my hands but I couldn't afford to spend it wiling away the daylight hours at a dog track.

On a lighter note, while Kevin was slumming it with his fellow scrubbers, his old buddy Twotone was in the UK Packaging Arc, second round, heat three, at the Stow. Second round, heat three! I could've owned that mutt. The top prize was £15,000. If he got to the final and won it I'd ring his little brindle neck! But I wasn't bitter.

'You would've been better off buying a dog from a sale than a trainer,' said Ginger, his eyes darting from me to the race card to the track. 'If it's any fucking good the trainer won't sell it to you, he'll sell it to one of his big owners, do you know what I mean?' Ginger laughed. My height decreased an inch per swipe, as he told me at a rate of knots what I'd known the moment I'd got knee deep into the dogs: I'd mugged myself off. 'And you went in at the deep end, didn't ya, with Linda Jones? You could've gone to someone small and got a cheap dog. I'd never buy a dog from any trainer. Ever. I don't see it run, I don't wanna buy it, simple as that. 'Ere, let's watch this race. I think six might lead five up. I make it a match five and six.'

What did Ginger know? He was currently lying third from bottom in the Tipster Challenge out of 25 tipsters, on minus £155, way behind 'The Fox', 'I Used To Wear Trousers' and 'Manface.' The Tipster Challenge was a monthly competition that cost £100 to enter but paid 80 per cent of the pool to whoever picked the most naps and next best selections on the evening cards. (The other 20 per cent went to the Owners Association.) With a payout of £800 to £1500 a month, it was a nice little earner and as a pool competition it didn't cost the Stow a penny.

What *did* Ginger know? A damn sight more than me, that's for sure. I'd come to know him through Tracy Cooper. He was one of the bigger punters I'd met at the Stow. Ginger always sat in the same seat in the main stand, usually with the same bunch of lads. And always had the same expectant look on his face. A youthful forty-five, he was more strawberry-blonde than ginger, well-fed but not a cholesterol factory like many punters I'd seen.

Ginger didn't get the forecast but he still picked another winner. Five beat one. 'One of the biggest owners at the Stow owns this,' he said, pointing to the five dog's form in the next race. 'Mr Correll. He's got about fifty-two dogs . . . about half a million pounds' worth. And he pays MONEY. Never mind two-and-a-half grands. He pays twenty grands for his dogs. I saw him here earlier so I knew it was a runner.'

Ginger wasn't big like Correll but he had money invested in 'a few bits and pieces' of dogs scattered around and a promising pup at the Stow. 'It's had four runs, we bet it three times and it's won three times.' Ginger grinned. 'It won six-and-a-half on Tuesday – first time over the distance . . . Patience is a virtue in this game. You've got to be patient.

'Me and the boys went to Ireland a few weeks back, just for a weekend of racing, and we picked up two young dogs there. They've both come out and both won twice for us. If they were with a big trainer, they'd be dear. You wanna buy something from Linda Jones, you're talking telephone numbers. But if you go to a little trainer in Ireland you can buy quite cheap. About ten years ago we bought twelve dogs for a £1000, took the whole lot. And every one of them dogs won.'

Ginger had been in the game since he was four, so you could say the dogs was in his blood. I was getting the feeling I was thirty-something years behind the competition. 'Me mum used to work at the dogs,' he told me. 'Me dad left when I was small so me mum used to take me across in the pushchair. I've been to nearly every track in England.

'I grew up with the dogs. Some people like to go discoing, drinking . . . I just like the dogs. I love the dogs. I *study* the dogs. When I finish the card tonight, I'll go home and I'll be studying till three, four in the morning for Saturday's meeting. I'll have people ring me up saying, "What d'you fancy, Ginge, what d'you fancy?" I know all the races already. I've read 'em so many times . . . I mean there's a dog running tonight, it'll be a big, big price, 33–1. I was gonna bet this next time up in an A7 but they've thrown it in an open race now – much too hot for it. Sometimes they do ya like that. But the dog'll come out *flying* and go straight for the rail. Could cut one off: 33–1? Maybe I'll have a few quid on it, take a chance.

'Once those traps open, mate, you're on your own. But horses are harder. You've got to get the horse to be right, the jockey to be right . . . Ain't no jockey pulling up a dog. Dogs run more to form than horses. A dog can only make its own mistakes but a horse can make a mistake *and* a jockey can make a mistake. You get much more value in a dog. I don't play the horses much. I might have a bet if I'm at home on a Saturday but I wouldn't go out of me way to bet a horse.'

Ginger had all the moves, all the ideas, all the lingo. He'd call Maxi Rumble, the darling of the Stow, a 'fucking aeroplane' but if a dog was a dead duck it'd be 'a fucking screw'. 'Dodge pot' or 'cripple' were others.

Punters throw insults at the dogs as a means of expressing anxiety or frustration rather than genuine malice. 'It's fucking paralysed,' they'll scream when a dog fails to make the turn or 'Die you fucking mutt,' they'll holler at any dog that's gaining on their selection, which does sound a bit strong. I even indulged in a little sledging myself but I never thought ill of a dog, no matter how useless it was. Linda, however, didn't care about the intent. To her, people who dissed dogs were scumbags.

'I hate it when people insult and swear at the dogs. It's not on. They do their best for these people and all they can do it slag 'em. There was a fella over the Stow recently started having a go at a dog. I said to him, "Why don't you fucking get down there, then, and see if you can do any better?" He shut right up. Ooh, it makes me mad.'

Still, dog people are dog people. They are entitled to their little grunts and gripes; after all, they've served their time. But the more dog people I met the more I felt like an outsider.

'I've been everywhere,' said Ginger, now clearly on a roll. 'I've had dogs on the flaps, Silver Salver, er, Aldershot, Derby, everywhere. I can do the tic-tacking, I can do it all, look.' Ginger started waving his arms around, wheeling and turning, just like a pro. 'One, two, three, four, five, six . . .' Clap, click, clop, click . . . '. . . Evens, eleven-a-ten, five-a-four, eleven-a-eight . . . Cos you grow up with it. Once you grow up with it you get used to it.

'This is racing. Everything's a challenge. You're always out to see if you can beat 'em. This geezer here is one of the best grading managers there is. He's *mustard*. He's mustard. But every now and again you think, I've got him. You won't find a better geezer at grading dogs up. The boys here buy videos of every meeting. I never bother with 'em. I believe what I see with me eyes, don't watch the telly. I see what I see in the race and I remember it. Cos if you start relying on the video you start seeing loads of things and doubting yourself. But that race manager is mustard.'

Not all race managers got the kind of respect Chris had. I heard many punters at the bookies grumble about the standard of grading at other tracks, particularly in the provinces. I usually avoided backing dogs at northern tracks for this reason. At many BAGS meetings I had watched on SIS, plenty of races produced finishes where the dogs came home in Indian file, indicating poor handicapping.

The race manager holds all the aces at a dog track. He has the power to disqualify, fine or ban a dog or its trainer or kennel staff for anything suspicious, he records track times, does the weighing in and officiates over disputes. He also has to keep an eye out for dogs with an attitude problem. Fighting is frowned upon and the NGRC operates a two-strikes-and-you're-out rule. If a dog is caught twice for biting another dog it is banned from racing, end of story. 'Aggressive interference' they call it. Some banned dogs invariably fall into the twilight world of flapping, where such rules and regulations are not enforced. Others that have been sanctioned just once or been a bit unruly in the kennels are put into hurdle races. Hurdling gives a dog something else to concentrate on rather than its competitors' jugulars. That's not to tar all hurdlers with the same brush. Many hurdlers have switched from flat racing for a number of reasons.

The race manager knows all the dogs at the track and as such allocates their races and trap numbers in accordance with their times and running styles. The last thing punters want is a wide runner in an inside box, careering all over the place. The race manager is to dog racing what a handicapper is to horseracing. His job is to match six dogs so that the statistical probability of a dead heat is raised. That's the theory at least. In practice this doesn't happen, simply because greyhounds have their own minds and occasionally, just occasionally, like to do their own thing. But punters want to see properly graded races where every dog is given at least a theoretical chance of winning.

Ginger could talk dogs until the cows came home. He'd had chunks on dogs here, lumps on them there. Three, four, five hundred quid straight bets were the norm. He liked the forecasts and tricasts too. He said there was hope for me yet, that knowing sweet FA wasn't a barrier to making a few quid.

'If you come here every meeting and you watch the dogs run and don't listen to people and do your own thing, you'll pick winners. But if you wanna be like me and bet every race, you can't do it. If you stick to a couple of races you can make this game pay. But never bet a dog odds on. Never. Even if it's first past the post I won't bet it. Quickest way to the poor house.'

And boy was I on my way there.

chapter 24

Today was the moment of truth, the day of judgement, the day of reckoning, the eleventh hour . . . The war in Iraq was on its way; but I had more important things to think about, namely would Kevin win the 4.18 that afternoon at Walthamstow. If he didn't win that was it, it would be over. I'd be out of the dogs, for good.

'I didn't want him to see me,' I said to Felix, as we strolled back from the traps. I had cajoled Felix, an old college buddy, into taking snaps of Kevin with his swanky digital Nikon camera. 'He might catch sight of me, you know, recognise me. Well, I'm easy to spot, aren't I? You don't get many black people at the dogs, do you?' Felix murmured, then carried on taking pictures of the crowd and the sun-kissed track, impervious to my armchair sociology.

' 'Ere, that's right,' said one of the floor men in the betting ring, sidling up next to me. 'One in five, I'd say . . . less probably. But at the bookies it's at least 50–50. I wonder why that is?'

'I've got no idea,' I said. I did have an idea but it was pointless trying to explain it with under thirty seconds to go to the race.

Once again, Kevin flopped. Fourth. It was his twenty-ninth race and the twelfth time he had come fourth. He did a 30.21, his slowest time in eight weeks. Whatever. The numbers didn't add up.

'Silly fucker.' A fella in the betting ring was whining about the five dog, a.k.a. Kevin. He ripped up his ticket and threw it on the floor dismissively. 'If it'd trapped instead of shitting itself it'd have had half a bloody chance.'

'Hey, that's my dog you're talking about,' I said, trying to make light of what was a shitty situation for me too.

'It could be your missus for all I care,' said the punter, walking away. 'I just lost fifty quid on that mutt.'

That mutt. How dare they talk about my Kevin like that! This was the problem with owning a loser. You became a de facto loser yourself. Loser, loser, loser. I went over to the paddock for the customary slap on Kevin's back. Belgian Patrick was cleaning him up. He brought him out and Felix started snapping away again. Kevin was panting and giving me a forlorn, dare I say, hangdog look.

'Eh, you could've bought Twotone, couldn't you?' said Patrick as I commiserated with Kevin. Not another one. Why bring that up? If I heard any more about Twotone I swore I'd head for Imperial Kennels and slip him a Mickey. Twotone this, Twotone that. I was sick of hearing about that damn dog. When I had told Tracy Cooper that I had had the opportunity of buying him her face had lit up like a Christmas tree.

'Really,' she said. 'For how much?'

'Four grand.'

'Four grand. Really?'

'Four grand. Why, what do you think he's worth now?'

'Oh . . . I'd say about . . . twelve to fourteen thousand pounds.'

I nearly choked. That dog was earning more money than I was. I had been monitoring him over the months, measuring and comparing his performances against Kevin's. The results did not make happy reading.

At this point in their careers Kevin had just run his thirtieth race and Twotone had twenty-six starts under his belt. Kevin had secured a mere four wins compared to Twotone's ten but I took some sadistic consolation in the fact that Twotone hadn't had a win in nine races. This was down to the increasingly competitive races he had to compete in. But where his form had started to dip in recent weeks, Kevin's had remained mediocre for months. My boy was consistent if nothing else.

When Twotone was on the up I had imagined him dressed in a smoking jacket and cravat back at Imperial Kennels, sipping on fine wines, chugging on a Cohiba, eating caviar and regaling the other keen-eyed greyhounds with his stories of derring do at the track, while Kevin sat in a corner, brooding, jealous, sensitive. At various points in his career Twotone had had an impressive 50 per cent strike rate compared to Kevin's 1 in 7.5. For the sake of 1500 measly pounds my fortunes could've been radically different.

I didn't need this. I had spent a small fortune in this game and for what? I had to stop this life-imitating-art-participatory-gonzo-journalism bullshit. The previous night I had been at the Stow and blown £150, after going £75 up on my roll. In a good week I could recycle several hundred pounds in bets yet I felt inadequate, totally out of my depth compared to most punters. The only time I felt equal to the guys at the track was when they lost. Vince had offered me some kind words to stem the tide of my growing cynicism. 'Once he gets the sun on his back, a shine to his coat, he'll come good,' he said reassuringly. God I hoped he was right.

'What d'you fancy?' Vince had asked as I peered dreamily at the race card.

'I dunno,' I replied.

'It'd help if you look at the right race,' said Paul, turning the page of my card. Jesus. Where was my head at?

As a visiting university lecturer, with an MA, I was practically an academic. I was a man of letters, a published author and award-winning journalist. The previous week I had given a speech at the Mansion House in front of the Duke of Edinburgh. I was *this* close to the fucking king of England! Last year I'd met Bill Clinton. Damn. That dirty ol' dog has one big-ass Cro-Magnon man-sized head. I had the mobile phone numbers of at least two D-list celebrities.

And I knew Vinnie Jones.

Ann from Marketing had introduced me to Vinnie one night

in the Paddock Grill, the Stow's 'prestigious restaurant'. The Chandlers, Dougie Tyler and all the big-time owners and corporate types hung out there. 'Hi, Ann, how are ya?' Vinnie gave Ann a warm kiss. He was wearing a white open-necked shirt and grey slacks. He looked like any other white boy wide boy with money rather than an ex-footballer turned Hollywood hard man.

'I'm fine, thanks,' said Ann. 'Vinnie, this is David. He's writing a book on greyhound racing.'

'Hello, David,' said Vinnie, giving me a soft handshake. I appealed to Vinnie's vanity and told him we shared the same publisher. He liked that. Without giving him the pitch, he knew the score.

'Get my number from Ann and we'll sort something out,' he said, giving me a knowing nod. 'I gotta go, see you later.' Vinnie was in a hurry. Ann gave me a wink. Nice PR.

Vinnie had been into the dogs since he was ten or eleven. He famously introduced Brad Pitt to greyhound racing when the pair were filming *Snatch*. At the last count he had 53 racing greyhounds and puppies, including a brood bitch named Smoking Barrels, twenty of which he raced at Hove under Derek Knight as well as the Stow with Gary Baggs. Jones had a dog that had come fourth in the Derby. Not bad out of 143 original entrants. He also had a horse called Sixty Seconds.

The Vinnie Joneses of this world were unofficially mandated with the responsibility of taking greyhound racing to the trendy masses, making it more attractive for a younger, funkier audience. Celebrities, always keen to get in on the next big thing, had followed the former Wimbledon hard man into greyhound racing like he was the Pied Piper. Brad Pitt, Damon Albarn, that geezer from *The Bill*, they all got in on the act. But rather than reinventing the wheel, this new generation of faces had only followed a long-established tradition. Outside the Paddock Grill was a rogue's gallery of celebrity photos: Mike Reid, Raymond Chandler, that geezer from *The Bill* again . . .

Following my brief encounter with Vinnie I called his people. I spoke to his agent's assistant, Cecilia. As her name indicated, she was posh totty.

'Vinnie's in Atlanta, then he's off to Prague for two weeks. May's chock-a-block and I can't commit to anything after that, sorry.' This is known in the business as the executive brush off.

But so what? I had better things to do than star gaze . . .

chapter 25

Chrome, plastic, synthetic fibres and a kaleidoscope of gaudy colours spewed together like a Saturday night pool of vomit; fruit machines, soggy chips, OAPs smoking for England; flat beer, flatter cola, chewing-gum stuck on the seats, translucent faces and empty heads . . .

Sitting in a bingo hall is like dropping acid without the threat of permanent psychosis. Not only is it a mind fuck, the cumulonimbus of carcinogens wafting through the room doesn't do much for your lungs either. The public didn't come here to play games; they came to smoke. If 80 per cent of the cost of a packet of fags went to the government in tax, I wanted a rebate. I must have got through 20 tabs just walking to the lavatory. Smoke and be damned.

My eyes were aching from looking at the carpet and wallpaper, let alone from staring at page after page after page of random numbers, while dabbing at them furiously with a marker pen. Never had the mundane required so much concentration. 'Seven and three . . . seventy-three. Number twelve, one and two. One and three, thirteen. Number four on its own, number four. Sixty-six, all the sixes . . .'

'Oussssse!'

'Sixty-six. A line one sixty-six . . .' Bollocks. So near and yet so farcical.

My mum had invited Margot and me to the Mecca bingo

hall on Hackney Road for a chance to win thousands and thousands of pounds, but the certainty of winning fuck all. We were also there to bond. When most parents want to meet their son with their 'partner' they invite them over for Sunday lunch or a night out to a bijou restaurant. But such niceties didn't happen in the Matthews family. No sir. When my mum wants to check out her next ex-daughter-in-law, she takes her to the bingo.

The old girl treated us to the festivities: about thirty-three quid on an assortment of bingo games, including the National, the Link and the American – potentially paying out from £20 for a line to £95,000 for the national game, which was linked to Mecca's cross-country bingo network.

'You've got to move faster, faster,' my mum kept saying as the caller reeled off digits like Mecca had just bought a job lot of prime numbers, odds, evens and 'fat ladies'. 'Christ. I can't keep up,' I said. 'How the hell do you do this at your age?'

'You gotta move, move.'

The game is surprisingly fast, and strangely addictive. If you can handle being used as a human beagle for cancer research, smoke-filled location aside, bingo is quite a compelling game. The addiction comes from the repetition, the knowing that the same thing will happen repeatedly. In essence, this is what addiction is all about: the need to repeat. The predictability of doing something until your fingers fall off is reassuring for many people. And occasionally, just occasionally, ye gods shine on you and hand over some moolah. Just like at the dogs.

The losing is the predictable bit, the meat and drink of gambling. It's also part of the working-man's philosophy that 'Everything else is a bonus,' which is a bit like contracting lung cancer and thinking, *hmm, well at least it wasn't testicular*. It was slowly dawning on me that *I didn't have to be a loser all my life*.

Winners, many of whom I have had the privilege and misfortune to know by the truckload, don't think that 'Everything else is a bonus.' To a winner, losing is the bonus or, put another way, it is the *slim* possibility of defeat that gives their calculated odds of winning the necessary zest to make the game interesting.

Since the introduction of the Lotto, née National Lottery, in 1997 ('It Could Be You' but it sure as hell won't be), it was now beyond doubt that Britain was a nation of losers, for to gamble excessively is to lose excessively. The Lotto, as Billy Connolly pointed out in an aggressive ad campaign, is, for a paltry pound coin, an easy tease. Why live on a rundown council estate existing on month-old bread and rusting tins of Spam when you can take your 14,394,367–1 chances and pocket a few mil?

In all my days of growing up, my dear mother had never been a gambler, unlike my father. But lately even she had joined the bandwagon, thanks to the convenience of the modern gaming industry. Twice as many women in Britain as men play bingo. It's the only gambling proposition where female punters outnumber males. Chicks love it, probably because it gets them out of the house and away from their grumpy old men, the screaming kids and the barking dogs. Judging by the 'talent' in the hall, though, I think many a husband and boyfriend appreciated the space too.

The dogs may be a guy thing and bingo a chick thing, but everyone is playing the wheel of misfortune these days: geriatrics, teenagers, black, white, rich, poor ... no, scrub the rich ... compulsives, impulsives, repulsives, everyone has a game of choice. Millions are hooked on scratch cards, text competitions, pools, sports betting, spread betting, bingo, bookies, dice, cards, quiz machines, fruit machines, one-arm bandits, two-horse races and three-card Monty, all of which amount to a massive five-knuckle shuffle for the punter. Britain is in the grip of gambling fever.

In Las Vegas, they have slot machines in the backs of cabs, just in case you get withdrawal symptoms travelling between the crap tables at Caesar's Palace and the poker room at the Sands. And you know that we're twenty years behind America. Actually, that's not strictly true. We're twenty years behind them in terms of the shitty stuff but fifty years ahead on everything else, like fashion, art, culture, civilisation, that sort of thing.

Soon, Britain's gaming laws would be liberalised and then it'd be open season on gambling. And the dog tracks were better placed than most to capitalise. Unlike racecourses, dog tracks tend to be in or around big cities and towns, have ample capacity for man and car alike, are easily accessible and have the gambling experience and floor space to accommodate their own casinos, just like Sheffield's dog track, Owlerton Stadium, who helpfully note in their programmes that, 'No strippergrams will be allowed on these premises.' Very post-*Full Monty*.

Just as I was getting into the swing of things my flow was interrupted by a commotion a few tables away from us. A greying old man in his sixties had collapsed with a suspected heart attack. Mum reckoned it was the stress of playing bingo. Margot thought it was to do with the oppressive heat in the hall and the result of the scores of high-wattage lamps designed to help people see the cards. I thought it was simply because he was old, as that's what old people do: they roll over and die and SPOIL YOUR BLOODY EVENING.

'Can someone call an ambulance?' said a fishwife sitting across from the heart-attack man. A small crowd flapped round him and one woman kindly dialled 999 from her mobile, as emergency calls don't cost anything, even on Pay-As-You-Go. But as soon as the caller started up again with, 'Eyes down,' they fled back to their bingo cards, leaving the man propped up against his table, wheezing like a semi-deflated blow-up doll. People are so selfish. Of course *I* would have helped the guy out but I needed 'one and four, fourteen' for a full house and I was damned if some bird with no teeth called Eileen was gonna beat me to it.

chapter 26

Spring came late as usual, or perhaps summer had come early. Winter stood at the new season's gates, shaking its fist like a miserable old git. The winter months at the track had been bleak, and made bleaker by Kevin's mediocre form. He'd had something like thirty races to date and five wins. There you go: the magical 'one-in-six'. I hoped that the fair weather might improve Kevin's chances.

I was spending an unhealthy amount of time at the track. Every opportunity I had I was down there. My problem, apart from not being able to pick any winners, was that the frequency of my betting had increased steadily over the months. The most I'd bet on a single wager was £100, but nevertheless all those little bets were starting to mount up.

When I had cash in pocket (ha!) I'd have straight win bets. When I was on my uppers I'd chance my arm with a few quid on reversed forecasts and tricasts. But I had to have a bet in some form. I needed that fix. However, I only ever seemed to recycle my money. If I were up £200 one week, I'd be down £300 the next. My form was as unpredictable as Kevin's.

Thanks to an epiphany of 'professional integrity' I had decided to stop writing rubbish for the tabloids. However, not writing rubbish and concentrating on serious issues reduced my income by about, oh, 100 per cent. My outgoings were killing me. The payments on the Porsche, the yacht and the villa in the South of

France would, er, have to wait while I concentrated on paying parking fines, rent and utility bills. I knew I'd spunked a few grand but was unable to account for any of it.

The sum of my gambling was a bunch of old betting slips, illegible notes of results and bets and systems scrawled over race cards, envelopes, red letters and sundry bits of paper, a stack of dog-eared copies of the *Racing Post* and a spiralling kennel bill. Oh, and I did have an over-the-top overdraft and half a dozen credit cards on meltdown too.

Over the weekend Baghdad had taken a pounding in Gulf War II: Return of the Fuckwits. I hadn't done much better at the track. I asked Dougie's sons what odds they'd give me on an Iraqi victory. Yeah, I'm a sucker for the underdog. They looked at me apologetically. Perhaps the joke was in poor taste. But it could've been worse. I once tried to get odds from William Hill on the Queen Mum and the Pope dying within twelve months of each other. Unsurprisingly they didn't take the bet. Thorstein Veblen wrote in *The Theory of the Leisure Class* that, 'We have a need to have entertainment during times of crisis.' I had a need for entertainment in my time of crisis. But as my crisis was financial I couldn't afford any bloody entertainment.

'So, are you going to open a casino here?' I asked Ann, dunking a digestive biscuit into my tea. I could always be guaranteed a cuppa in her office if I'd spunked my beer money at the track.

'I don't know. I couldn't say yes or no really. Why do you ask?'

'Well, it's just I'd heard a rumour that you guys were thinking of selling up, which seemed odd because this place is a licence to print money.'

'Selling up, eh? Where did you hear that?'

'Oh, just some fella at the track. You know, the usual gossip.'

'We get these rumours surfacing from time to time . . .'

There were always rumours going around, rumours about dogs, hot tips, the war. Most of them were bullshit. But if you were 'in the know' you might get wind of something special. I'd become so accustomed to people listening in or inviting themselves into my conversations at the track that I too was now in the habit of eavesdropping on every little piece of chitchat I could. If you were lucky you might get a tip or hear someone in the toilets talking about fake Rolex watches, hot mobiles or bank jobs.

I hung around the track until that evening's meet. Dog tracks are great places to simply hang around. I'd become good at that these days, hanging around. I often felt I was bringing up the rear in a futile race against time, despite harbouring a constant, nagging fear that I was wasting my time, my life, through disorganisation and poor 'time management', i.e. laziness. I popped over to the Popular Enclosure, hoping to catch Vince. I hadn't seen him for a while. I had a present for him.

'Sorry, I've been meaning to give this to you,' I said, handing over a video of Scurlogue Champ's greatest hits which Vince had lent me eight months earlier. He grinned, took the video and carried on looking at his race card. Neither he nor the Saints were having a good night.

'I'm going to see Chris Page in a minute,' I said.

'Oh really?' said Vince, animatedly. 'Ask him what's happened to the traps. They had three false starts last week. One of 'em even did a U-turn and started running in the opposite direction . . . never seen anything like it.'

Most punters would give their back teeth to get into a race manager's head, as his most important role as far as they are concerned is grading. On my way to see Chris, dark thoughts entered my mind. Maybe there was some way I could change his direction? No, not get him in a Ron Davies type moment of madness. I mean exploit his human frailties. What was his weakness? I wondered. What was his Achilles heel? Even a straight guy like him had to have a kink in his character some-where. Financial inducement would be far too tacky. That sort of move is best left to wealthy Arab shopkeepers and Tory MPs. Besides, I was skint. I couldn't afford the brown paper envelope, let alone the dough to put inside it. No, what I had in mind was more along the lines of the journalist's trusty manoeuvre: bad publicity. Maybe if I slipped into the racing office and caught them at it, whatever 'it' was, I could get an edge, maybe get Kevin dropped a grade or two or, better yet, matched against three terrapins, a tortoise and a dead cat.

During race meetings, once he had done the preliminaries, Chris lived up in the gods, in a little office high above the spectators, overlooking the finish line. From this vantage point he could see each race in its entirety and along with his two colleagues and a computerised timing and video recording system he compiled the necessary data that was circulated to the betting results services and used in future race programmes.

As fascinating as it was watching Chris spot minor infractions and incidences on the track and punch numbers into a computer, I didn't get any juice. Chris was so straight he was liable to snap in half. There were no drunken orgies going on up there, no lines of Coke on mirrors or gimps. Without the necessary leverage for blackmail I decided to let Chris and his fellow Honest Johns get on with it and took off. On my way downstairs I passed through the rather elegant Goodwood Lounge when someone cried out to me, 'Oi, Dave, over 'ere.'

His name was Michael Marks, David Stephens, Matthew Richards or some such doubled-up apostolic name. I had drunk too much that evening to think or care. Did we used to work on a building site somewhere together? Then it started coming back to me. I used to call him Rottweiler, because he looked like one and had a short temper.

'You don't remember me, do you?'

'To be honest, John, no.'

Rottweiler laughed. He didn't care that I couldn't remember him. Being a nobody was an occupational hazard. I knew that from experience. I didn't remember him at first because I guess it was easier to forget. Here's a tip: if you're ever in the East End and you bump into a fella but you can't remember his name, call him John. It's such a common name that at least 50 per cent of the time you'll guess right. And if you're wrong, keep calling him John anyway. It's a bit of an East End thing; like calling someone 'mate', 'china' or 'slag'.

'I heard that you're a journalist these days,' said Rottweiler.

'Yeah, for my sins. I'm actually writing a book on greyhound racing. I own a dog that I race over here.' Rottweiler looked at me dumbfounded, and laughed. I found it embarrassing meeting people from the past, people I had nothing to say to.

'Anyway, I've to go upstairs and interview someone right now. I'll see you on the way down.'

Got out of that one. Once upon a time I had another life, one not so far from the Stow. But despite my frequent visits to the track I seldom looked in on my old mates. A few were in jail, incoherently nuts or dead, so unless I found myself a good rope ladder, a lot of patience and a time machine, they were off the Sunday visit list. Most of my old school mates though I only saw at weddings, funerals and stag dos, which was just as well because we seemed to have so little in common these days. Many of them equated journalists with police informers and a few had actually grown to distrust me simply because of the (justifiably) bad reputation hacks have for selling their grannies to get a story.

Since the publication of my first book and the critical acclaim I got for it (ahem!) as far as the old school were concerned operating in the public domain meant exposure, and exposure was something many of my boys could do without. I felt sad at times that I had moved out of the loop and couldn't relate to people I'd known intimately since childhood. But times change and people move on. My idea of a great night out isn't smuggling ten kilos of coke in a camper van on a cross-channel ferry, thank you very much; and while I like a good drink as much as the next bad boy I like to keep my blood-alcohol levels with the balance on the blood side of the scales.

'I've got to go, mate. Got winnings to collect and all that. Be lucky.'

'Yeah, all the best.' John put his hand out. I shook it. It was clammy. Like he'd just been playing with himself.

I went back down to the betting ring. I had no winnings to collect, only thoughts. Why return to Walthamstow after all these years? What was the point in going back? I'd done so much to get the hell out of this crummy neighbourhood and a dog had dragged me back, and dragged me down too.

Down in the betting ring I ran into Ginger and his mate Phil. Phil had a touch of the Dirty Den about him. He was middle-aged, with slick, dark hair, lean and sharp features, always the geezer in slacks, loafers and open-necked shirts and leather jackets and jewellery, but nothing too ostentatious. He owned a mini-cab company. He turned over a lot of bread. 'They all know me down there,' said Phil, nodding towards the bookies, 'either as Phil or Romford Phil or Romford.'

Phil was a big punter. A thousand pound a race was nothing to him. Consequently, the bookies would run shy of him at times. 'It's all about beating them at their own game,' Phil would say. 'To beat the bookies you've got to think like them, bet like them.'

Like all big punters, Romford Phil had a system. Back in the main stand he explained it: it's what's known as 'hedging' or 'dutching'. 'What I do is play the bookies at their own game,' said Phil, 'it's the only way you'll get anything out of them. See, I don't like to have big single bets like these fellas.' He cast his eyes over Ginger and his pals and frowned. 'They think I'm mad doing it this way . . . too complicated for 'em. But the way that I look at it is, rather than put big single lumps on a dog, I'd rather spread the same amount of money across three dogs and increase my chances of winning. Look, this is how it works . . .'

Phil started scribbling figures on his *Racing Post*, outlining the level of stake to put on each dog according to its odds. The idea was to scrub out the two rank outsiders in the field and from that work out the likely winner from the remaining three or four runners. Phil would then hedge his bets by putting say £150 on one dog, £300 on another and £250 on a third, depending on the odds. Occasionally he'd back a fourth dog against the bookies.

'A punter doesn't have to bet on every race,' said Phil, pulling out a brick-sized wad of notes, 'but the bookies have to take bets, they have to take a risk or they won't make money. So you work the odds to your favour. You bet on what *you* want, not what they want. Patience is a virtue in dog racing.'

Like Ginger, Vince and every serious punter I'd come across, Phil had a highly developed level of mental arithmetic. But none of these guys were mathematical geniuses or even enjoyed maths at school. Many punters didn't even finish formal education. Even the larger than life John McCririck, ex-bookie and Channel 4's eccentric and bejewelled racing pundit, had said he 'couldn't even pass my Elementary Maths O-Level'. Being a mathematical whiz was not a prerequisite to being a bookie or gambler so there was hope for me yet.

What kind of cultural values are at play in a society where a largely working-class and moderate to poorly educated band of gamblers and dog fanciers can work out statistics, form and complex betting permutations that would challenge the average accountant but are incapable of going beyond comprehensive school education?

I had a degree in business, scored an A in my statistics finals and couldn't understand half the shit these guys spoke about.

But of course it didn't always go their way. Ginger lost £300 on a mutt called Toosey Magic in the last race of the evening. He'd waited all night for this opportunity. The others were so convinced by Ginger's predictive powers that they too laid several hundred pounds on the dog. Ginger had slipped down to the bookies and wagered what looked like a couple of grand in total. These guys could lose more in one night, individually, than I could *win* in a year. When I asked Ginger how he felt about losing big lumps of cash he simply shrugged his shoulders and said, 'Win some, lose some.'

The wads of cash that people handled at the track always

intrigued me: bulging doorstops of tens, twenties and fifties, thick juicy wedges of cash to be touched, to be won and lost. Forensic examination of the notes doing the rounds at the Stow would uncover traces of cocaine, carbon deposits from spent shotgun cartridges, blood . . . At a dog track there is enough dirty cash in circulation to make a Nigerian oil minister's eyes pop out. The obligatory wad of cash is always kept in mini wads of a hundred, preferably with four twenties back to back with another folded across like a money clip; that way one hundred pound batches can be conveniently removed from the pocket without the need to rifle through loose cash or count. Similarly, wads are always kept in the pocket, never a wallet, as nothing short of a handbag can accommodate £1000 plus in cash.

Of course, I didn't have the disposables to front it like Ginger, Romford Phil and the like, although I would occasionally, when I was flush, stuff several hundred pounds in my pockets, just so I could *feel* like a high roller in the betting ring.

According Dr Rebecca Cassidy, an anthropologist at Goldsmiths University, men, specifically, gamble because gambling evokes a sense of 'being a good bloke'. You are in essence defined by your wad. I could appreciate this notion, coming from a background where cash is king. Whether down the pub or the snooker hall, in the East End you are always armed with a wad of cash, good old working-class currency. Back in the day, credit cards were for fags. Real men eat cash, not quiche.

I think our relationship with cash comes from those afternoons way back in childhood spent playing Monopoly or 'shops', toying with wads of fake money as we dreamed of one day doing the same with the Real McCoy. 'Gambling money is play money,' Dr Cassidy told me. 'You don't use gambling money for practical purposes, such as paying the rent or the gas bill.' No, gambling money is special money, money for treats like booze, a good curry and more gambling.

Everybody's trying to beat the system somewhere, somehow. In boxing, beating the system means not being killed. Winning comes into it somewhere but the manner in which you win is more important than the pure statistical record of success. In greyhound racing, beating the system for the punter is beating the bookies and, given the state of my finances, it was time to start accepting that the system had perhaps beaten me.

chapter 27

Joy and love and carbon monoxide were in the air. Looking out of the window on to the Thames I had the kind of vista I had always dreamed of. Suddenly, to paraphrase Tony Montana in *Scarface*, London was 'one big pussy waiting to get fucked'. According to the *Sunday Times* my local Sainsbury's on the Cromwell Road sold more bottled water than any other supermarket in Britain. Look Ma, top of the world! All I needed now was a Volvo, a set of golf clubs, and a prolonged course of psychotherapy and my embourgeoisement would be complete. Some money would help too. In fact, *a lot* of money would help.

One day, I pulled up to the front gates of the apartment block. I had never lived in a gated community before, well, not one that was as easy to walk out of as it was to walk into. I had left my remote control for the gate in the apartment so I idled in front of the gate, waiting for it to open. One of the concierges approached me. 'Good afternoon, Sir. Can I help you?' 'Er, no,' I said. 'I live here.' 'OK, right, er, that's that then. Have a nice day.' Bet he wasn't expecting that in his cheap suit.

'Getting on is the opium of the middle classes.' Walter James, b. 1912. If this was the case then gambling was the crack cocaine of the working classes . . . I had Spanish lessons and occasional massages and pedicures. I had membership to a private club and an exclusive health resort. I took black cabs instead of mini cabs

. . . I'd moved further from Walthamstow, Paddington and Harlesden both physically and metaphorically. If I migrated any further westwards I'd be chewing tobacco, wearing a ten-gallon hat, chaps and riding a bucking bronco.

On the surface I had moved up in the world. This had had a temporary effect on both Kevin's and my fortunes. Within days of moving into my new, riverside, gated home, I'd won a few quid on the old dog in a trifecta at the track. He then won the following Monday, his first victory in eight outings followed by a couple of second places.

After a succession of nothing but grey BAGS meetings I finally hit the track on an afternoon when the sun was out. Life was so much more bearable in the spring and the summer.

'He's got two chances,' said Billy, chalking up 7–2 next to *Zussies Boy*.

'Don't start,' I said. 'I was about to have a punt.'

'I'm kidding. He's a good dog, that Zussies Boy,' said Bill. I waited for the punchline but none came. 'Yeah, a good dog. Not bad. I've seen worse.'

'In that case I'll have a score on him.' I pulled out a twenty and handed it over. If Kevin didn't win it was a long way back to Battersea. In the event, I didn't need the exercise. The boy trapped real sharp, bumped the one dog but recovered to romp home in a personal best of 29.55. You beauty. When I went to congratulate him on his success, Kelly said she thought that perhaps he didn't like the cold weather and now the sun was out maybe, just maybe, he'd perform.

'Well done, mate.' Some guy called Pete introduced himself to me by the paddock and gave me a pat on the shoulder. 'Well done.' Pete kept on walking, going about his business, smiling. I'd never met the guy before. My win, Kevin's win, *our* win had put a smile not just on my face but also on somebody else's. In a world where praise is scant and recognition fleeting, being the best for most is never a prospect. At the coalface of society simple pleasures count. To win at something, anything was an achievement when the most you'd ever won before was a plastic gimcrack or a goldfish with a seven-day shelf life at the fair.

Maybe there was the outside chance that Kevin could turn the corner and make it. The statistics seemed to prove that he was a fair-weather runner. Out of forty-two starts he had won seven races, which meant he was maintaining his hit rate of one-in-six; not fantastic but not utterly hopeless.

After the BAGS meeting I took off for Walthamstow High Street to celebrate Kevin's success with plate of double pie and mash. Flicking through the *Racing Post* I noticed there were further BAGS meets at Monmore Green that evening so I finished up, went to the nearest cash till and strolled into Ladbrokes up the road.

'Hello, is that David Matthews?' You know you're in trouble with an introduction like that.

'Yes it is. What can I do for you?'

'Hi, my name's Mark. I'm calling from MBNA bank. You have an outstanding . . .'

'Hang on a second. Go on, my son, go on . . .'

'Yes, you have a payment overdue and . . .'

'Sorry. Yes, yes, yes . . .'

'You need to make a payment before . . .'

'Look, I'm kind of busy at the moment trying to win back that outstanding payment. Now if you just leave it with me I'll take care of business.'

'But . . .'

Who did these people think they were? Calling you up like that in the evening. There was no respect for time any more. The 24-hour society meant that banks, credit card companies and the like could call you after office hours and at weekends, hassling you for cash. Away with you! My attitude was, debt is a commercial thing and thus it only counts during nine-to-five office hours. The rest of the time I'm a debt-free citizen.

Two hours later I emerged, £75 lighter than I had been when I entered. The 10 to 20 per cent of the time that I actually won money the cash would slip into the shadows of my back pocket without a trace, then creep out moments later like a teenager on heat. Maybe I didn't want to win at all? Or had I formed an unhealthy relationship with losing? In Bill Bryson's charming book *Mother Tongue*, he wrote that dogs go '*ouâ-ouâ* in France, *bu-bu* in Italy, *mung-mung* in Korea and *wan-wan* in Japan'. For some strange reason when I backed them they seemed to go 'last-last'.

It was approaching time for me to start thinking about Kevin's future or, more importantly, how I was going to get rid of him. I'd been a real April Fool. What a month. I was approaching a grand in arrears over my kennel bill and had blown several thousand pounds more in betting. How I had amassed such a loss I couldn't tell but I seemed to be haemorrhaging money. I was living so far beyond my means we were in different time zones. Kevin had come second twice, third and fifth that month. He was going backwards. Soon he wouldn't bother coming out of the kennels, just kick back with a fag and say, 'Nah, don't fancy this one. I'm staying put.' As seasons changed I'd suffered my heaviest losses to date. Perhaps it was a sense of optimism that kept me going. But the gambling was starting to get out of hand. Perhaps I was giving my troubles too much thought.

I could feel the threads of life's rich tapestry slowly coming apart at the seams. It was Margot's birthday and cash was running low. At this rate the only present she'd get from me was a hard luck story. Still, it was a convenient excuse not to spoil her. She never appreciated my fucking presents anyway. I now had a budget of just fifty quid for presents and another fifty to keep me going. The plan was to go to the bookies and win her birthday present. I'd try Corals on Battersea Park Road for a change. I'd been lucky the last time I popped in. Yes, lucky. I'd managed to walk out with my shirt *and* pants intact. As soon as I doubled my money I'd walk away and go buy Margot a bag full of goodies.

Conveniently, where I lived was ringed by a number of bookies, enough to keep a compulsive gambler happy. There was the

Tote on Battersea Bridge Road, then Corals, William Hill and Ladbrokes on Battersea Park Road.

I thought I'd try out Romford Phil's hedge betting system, so I spread forty quid in the bookies on the 3.07 at Monmore by placing £10 on trap 1 at 4–1, £10 on trap 2 at 4–1 and £20 on trap 6 at 5–2. None of them came in. Stupid fucking hedge betting. Bollocks. So much for the *Racing Post* nap selection too. I should've stuck with my own bad judgement. I screwed up the slip and threw it dejectedly across the shop floor, hitting a guy in the side of the face. I then spunked another score or so on piddling forecasts, tricasts and video roulette. This didn't leave much for presents. I wound up buying Margot a dodgy picture frame and a book she's never read. It was after this maddening afternoon in the bookies that I decided to go to Gamblers Anonymous. Life had started to imitate art with treacherous consequences. All I had for chronicling the underbelly of British society were empty pockets and a stomach ulcer. In fact, as cliché no. 167 goes: if it weren't for bad luck, I'd have no luck at all.

What bullshit. Gambling to buy birthday presents. This was almost as absurd as gambling to pay my bills. What next, gambling to pay my gambling debts? It was getting so bad that I'd be in the pub and when one of those charity cases came in, you know, with the fake ID and the plastic egg-timer-shaped ponce box I'd say, 'I can't make a *donation*. But I bet you I can guess how much money you've got in there to the nearest pound. If I win I keep the money. If I lose I'll give you double the amount you've got.'

Of course they never went for it. They'd always say that it was 'illegal' or some silliness like that. Still, at least it got me out of a donation without ignoring the poor bastard or uttering some student union line about 'not believing in charity and it being the government's responsibility and nah, nah, nah-nah-nah . . .'

Margot had become concerned at my increasing interest in betting and my mood swings. 'You're not turning into a compulsive gambler, are you?' she asked one evening. 'No, of course not,' I replied. 'I bet you even money I don't have a problem with gambling.' She didn't laugh. Margot had seen me pouring over bits of paper and betting slips, scribbling notes and making various miscalculations night after night and I had acquired various books on gambling and statistics in the past few months. I'd got into this game for sport, comically thinking I could make a fast buck out of it: now I was on the brink of financial meltdown.

It almost goes without saying that greyhound racing, while an amusing pastime for the casual onlooker, is rooted in gambling. I was mad to have thought all those months ago that I could get into the dogs without gambling. Having something to lose, be it your pride, reputation or shirt, transcends the sport into another realm. It was the same thing I had found with boxing – what psychologists call the 'rollercoaster syndrome', the need to always be on the edge of potential or impeding catastrophe.

I needed the fix so instantly I couldn't waste time travelling to the track. I'd just go straight to the local bookies, another cauldron of testosterone, just like the betting ring at the Stow. Bookies stink of masculine deceit. The macho posturing and aggression in these environments partly explain why women are virtually non-existent in the betting ring, other than as curious onlookers to the antics of their menfolk; and the women in betting shops, a significant minority drawn largely from the white bread, twenty Silk Cut and a scratch card classes, are the kind of bints that used to give the January sales a bad name. In the bookies you get a few little old ladies wagering their pension books and the odd one or two on the fruit machines accompanying their compulsive partners, but it's certainly no pick-up joint.

If I were a new-age, born-again, revisionist, new-man psychologist I'd probably make a connection between cruising and men hanging around in betting shops, tracks, five-a-side football pitches and prison cells. Men like hanging out with each other, I suspect, more than women like hanging out with women. Men like hanging out with women when they're after something, nominally sex or food. The rest of the time we can amuse ourselves with a vast array of toys, inventions, machinations and the like. Women, by drawing attention to our anally retentive desire for such distractions, do not make convenient playmates in such games. Their need to probe, to investigate the statistical absurdity of the Goliath, the Heinz or the ITV Seven, to highlight the overstated importance of the off-side rule (a rule so simple to comprehend a marmoset could figure it out in thirty seconds yet a woman feels duty bound to 'not get it') embarrasses most men.

Men that have had the macho-guy hardwiring removed, or at least modified, tend to find female company easy. In essence those men have been feminised. Feminisation makes things work. The world doesn't work better through the masculinisation or retarda-tion of women. You only have to look at Africa and Islamic states to realise that 'keeping women in their place' creates fascism and mayhem. Having only 49 per cent of the world's population, i.e. men, running the show is not the way forward. Britain would've been wiped out during the Second World War had women not gone to work in industry.

I had amassed a library of bits of paper with stats, facts and figures thrown together in the fantastical belief that somehow this information would lead me to the pot at the end of the rainbow. But to a gambler, the pot would only present another opportunity to test the boundaries of his failure.

'Go on trap two,' said the man, tapping the TV screen as if to gee on the dog. 'Go on, ya blood claat!'

What a clown; riding the betting shop pony was an exercise in dismay. The few spare coins I had left I threw into a video roulette machine. Clunk. Clunk. My money was gone. The screen seemed to turn black, as if to say, 'I don't play with broke-ass losers,' and I noticed my reflection in the glass. I looked pained, haggard. And all along there was I thinking I was having a great time shovelling fives, tens and twenties into the betting industry's coffers.

I had a problem. Not a major one, but a problem nonetheless. I had the Chinese water torture version of gambling addiction, a daily, constant drip drip of fives, tens, twenties, small change, credit card transactions, milk tokens, gift vouchers, anything. I had been consumed by my own artifice, exposed by reckless conceit. I had to do something about this before I was sunk. Something in the region of £15,000 had disappeared in under a year and I had nothing to show for it other than a collection of torn betting slips, sob stories and a dog that was worth more in cat food than kennel bills. Kevin was spoilt. A useful amount o' fleas is good for a dog – keeps him from brooding over bein' a dog.

I got some information about Gamblers Anonymous, just out of curiosity. The flyer said: 'Most compulsive gamblers will answer YES to at least SEVEN of these questions:

1. Do you lose time from work due to gambling?
2. Is gambling making your home life unhappy?
3. Is gambling affecting your reputation?
4. Have you ever felt remorse after gambling?
5. Do you ever gamble to get money with which to pay debts or to otherwise solve financial difficulties?
6. Does gambling cause a decrease in your ambition or efficiency?
7. After losing, do you feel you must return as soon as possible and win back your losses?
8. After a win do you have a strong urge to return and win more?
9. Do you often gamble until your last pound is gone?
10. Do you ever borrow to finance your gambling?
11. Have you ever sold anything to finance gambling?
12. Are you reluctant to use gambling money for normal expenditures?
13. Does gambling make you careless of the welfare of your family?
14. Do you gamble longer than you planned?
15. Do you ever gamble to escape worry or trouble?

16. Have you ever committed, or considered committing, an illegal act to finance gambling?
17. Does gambling cause you to have difficulty in sleeping?
18. Do arguments, disappointments, or frustrations create an urge within you to gamble?
19. Do you have an urge to celebrate any good fortune by a few hours' gambling?
20. Have you ever considered self-destruction as a result of your gambling?

I answered YES to eleven of the above questions.

chapter 28

The more I got into gambling, the less I saw the dogs as living, breathing creatures. Just as brokers do not care much for the physical, spiritual or philosophical nature of what they trade in, a gambler does not think too deeply about the welfare of the greyhounds he backs. I am not suggesting that gamblers wish harm on a dog, or any animal for that matter; gamblers are not necessarily barbarians. If anything, they believe deep down that good animal welfare is essential for the sports to survive and for them to have sufficient gambling opportunities. Ill-treatment of dogs also gives the sport a bad name and by implication gamblers too, which is why perhaps gamblers tend to be very charitable outside of the money markets of the races.

While I was at the track I ran into Ginger, who kindly reminded me what the root of my problem was.

'Yeah, get rid of him now while he's still winning. You'll get your money back that way. You keep him any longer, mate, and he'll be worth nothing, nothing, mate. Stick 'im in there.' Ginger pointed to a copy of the *Racing Post* on the table. I felt a bit sentimental. To people like Ginger racing dogs were just a commodity, a gambling chip. I told Ginger what a dead loss Kevin had been. ' 'Ere, Dave got into the dogs to write a book about it and now he's a compulsive gambler,' he joked with Romford Phil that night.

'Yeah, put an ad in there,' repeated Ginger, stabbing again at the *Racing Post*. 'He'll get two and a half for him, won't he, Phil?' Phil nodded his agreement. 'There's worse dogs going for more money at the moment,' added Ginger.

What to do now? I couldn't afford to keep Kevin racing, so I had to look at other options. Firstly, I could sell him for chump change, or chump meat. Secondly, I could do a deal with another owner and give him away on licence, as it were, to keep racing until his days were over. I'd retain ownership of him but I wouldn't have to maintain him. Nah, that would involve too much hassle. Thirdly, I could reform a syndicate and sucker some friends into financing his training fees, but given my friends' apathy in the first place it was highly unlikely they'd go for it now. Finally, if I couldn't sell him or give him away, I could offer him up for adoption. Short of shipping him off to Spain for the dreaded hare-coursing death sentence, there was one last option: I could keep him.

Somehow, though, this just didn't seem feasible. I didn't live in a home conducive to owning a dog. I should've had my exit strategy worked out a year ago when I first got into this mess. A greyhound can live to around fourteen years of age, which is ninety-eight in dog years, if you accept the notion that a human year is equal to seven dog years. That is a long time to be saddled with an animal. I couldn't even contemplate spending that long with a woman.

I started slowly, tentatively, asking friends if they knew anyone who might be interested in him. Margot implored me not to 'turn my back on him'. She pestered me constantly about Kevin's future, like a child nagging for a new toy. Or a pet. I told her that he had always been a commercial consideration, a movable asset, an investment. I didn't see anything intrinsically wrong with using animals as moneymaking tools. Margot and her friend Liz had met someone walking a retired racer in Battersea Park and she had told them that over nine thousand greyhounds are put to the sword each year. Here we go again . . .

'It'd be bad PR for you if you got rid of him,' she said. 'What you gonna do when people start asking what happened to him?'

'All right, all right.'

'Supposing he gets into the wrong hands? It could come back on you and your publisher.'

'But I can't afford to keep him and we can't have him in the flat.'

'But . . .'

'But what? I'll deal with it. Jesus. Give me a break.'

chapter 29

It was like a prison waiting room: sweaty, frowsy, the aroma of rancid hard-luck stories wafting through the air. Thirty compulsive gamblers, all men, no women, all fucked. This was the bad time. This is what they don't tell you about in the glossy promo brochures and the betting-shop posters. This is hell.

'My name's Terry and I'm a compulsive gambler. It's been six days since my last bet.' A smattering of applause and salutations greeted Terry, a weaselly cabbie in his mid-forties, as he sat in the hot seat in front of the group. Terry explained that he'd do endless night shifts to fund his gambling but would get so skint he couldn't put any diesel in his cab.

'Horses, football, dogs . . . anything . . . I'd bet on anything,' said Terry. Several members of the group nodded sagely. One or two rocked in their chairs. I could see a sliver of spittle running down the side of one old boy's mouth as he sat there agape. Young and old, rich and poor, what a band of brothers, what a fraternity of hard knocks and misery. One by one they sat in that rickety old chair and spilled the beans on a life of false expectations and failure. Jesus, this was so depressing. It was like being teleported into *One Flew Over the Cuckoo's Nest*. What a bunch of basket cases. I'd been to funerals that were more upbeat.

The methods of Gamblers Anonymous are simple. The programme of recovery is taken from Alcoholics Anonymous. The steps of recovery are read at weekly meetings and the chairman, one of the members, invites each punter to speak of his own experiences. This is called his therapy. He describes something of his gambling days and how great his life is now that he's addicted to group therapy rather than scratch cards or bingo.

As a new member I was meant to have an epiphany through self-recognition. The meeting, they say, is your 'mirror'. Christ, what a reflection. There was plenty of talk of new lives, sin, repentance and 'the truth'. The truth? *You can't handle the truth!* Another side of the evangelical nature of these twelve-step programmes is the, I feel, false supposition that once an addict, always an addict. Where is the hope in that? The line is that there is no cure for addiction so you come to the meeting to stop you from going to the dog track, amusement arcade or whatever tickles your fancy. I refused to believe that a twelve-month moment of madness slumming it at the dogs could result in a lifetime of addiction.

Tim broke down in tears, saying that he was lonely and that playing the slot machines in an amusement arcade in King's Cross helped him cope with his loneliness. Yeah, go Tim! Around a quarter of all GA members are addicted to fruit machines. Fucking fruit machines! Christ, if you are going to be addicted to something make it worthwhile, like cocaine or rich women. But fruit machines? These days you can be addicted to anything. You can even be addicted to being addicted to something. Now where was the goddamn help for these people? Since the introduction of the Lotto GA has seen a 17 per cent increase in calls, not just for Lotto, but across the board. What a sad bunch. Surely it hadn't come to this? I was here for research purposes only. Research. I heard awful stories of men rifling through their elderly mothers' handbags, lying, cheating and stealing in order to get cash to gamble with.

Halfway through the session I started to feel guilty; not just because the line between research and reality had blurred indistinguishably but because I was in an environment where, as the chair of the meeting had said, 'Anything that's said in here stays in here, so feel free to speak openly.' I had baulked at secretly recording the meeting but I still felt like a plant and I knew at some point I would regurgitate selected sufferings of the gamblers present on to the page. The only way forward was to protect the identities of those present by using pseudonyms. Everyone was referred to strictly by first name only and I don't doubt that some of those were *nom de plumes* anyway. But to be on the safe side I decided to change the identities of anyone who had a distinctive name and or stated occupation. So Ezekiel, the forty-something advertising exec and George Clooney look-alike from Kew, became 'John' just as Chad, the openly gay QC who I also noticed drove an aquamarine Aston Martin DB5, simply became 'Steve'. So that puts everyone in the clear.

Along with GA one man said he was also attending two NAs, an AA and Freudian psychotherapy. Such permutations of therapy gave me another blistering idea: how about an Anon Anon, or AA2 if you like – Anonymity Anonymous. *Hi. My name's David and I'm a compulsive group therapy attendee. My last meeting was two hours ago.*

What the GA meeting told me was that compared to the other patrons I had it easy. In fact, I didn't have a gambling problem at all. And to prove it, two nights later, I went to the track and duly lost £120.

'Mo' had got in the hot seat and compared gambling to taking narcotics, which he had also done. 'You start slowly, with small stakes, but you soon need a bigger fix to get you off. So you make more bets, for bigger stakes and it just goes on and on until all you can do is think about where to get money to gamble. Gambling is bullshit. It's fucking hell. That's all I've got to say.' Rapturous applause.

More than one gambler mentioned, in an aside, that at the height of their addiction they found gambling better than sex. Linda had said the same thing about racing greyhounds which prompted me to think what kind of sex were these people having?

I was intrigued at how so many of the guys could remember their first punt, as your first gamble isn't as memorable as, say, losing your virginity or passing your driving test. But nonetheless, it was eerie how many gamblers could remember their first bet, as though they were conscious at the time that they were undergoing some kind of initiation or rite of passage. Once you got on the bandwagon, it seemed, you were fucked. The bookies were in a win-win position: if you started your gambling career a winner you started believing you were lucky. If you started out a loser, then your ego made you want to start chasing your losses; you'd become obsessed with beating the bookies and they'd grind you slowly into the ground. And if you won a bit and lost a bit, on the dogs or the horses, well that just made you obsess about provenance, streaks, biorhythms and other superstitious claptrap.

It's easy to look at pathological gamblers as greedy, lazy, stupid. Because so many of them are. But what came out of my informal relationship with the gambling fraternity was that here are people, real people, who manifest the kind of compulsive behaviour that seems to be all-pervasive in Western society. It could be argued that our pathological behaviour only becomes a problem when money or other people are involved. But take away money and people from Western culture and what are you left with? Nature? Thin air?

At the very least gambling had greatly improved my powers of mental arithmetic.

And then *I'm* in the chair.

'Hi. My name's David. It's been forty-eight hours since my last bet. Jesus. I can't believe I just said that.'

I spent the next *twenty minutes* talking absolute bollocks about myself. I spilled my guts on how I had an ego problem, I over-estimated my talent, I was arrogant, selfish, deceitful, conceited, disorganised, moody . . .

'Thank you for sharing that with us, David,' said the chairman before I'd even finished my monologue. I returned to my chair to several nods and screwed-up faces of encouragement.

As my father used to tell me, 'Experience teaches wisdom.' But was losing all of one's money necessary to learn the lesson that gambling doesn't pay?

My father. It was his fault. Well, you have to blame someone. And I was fed up of dumping it on Kevin. The most illuminating thing to come out of that balding fart of a poet Philip Larkin was 'They fuck you up, your mum and dad.' New research has found a genetic/hereditary rather than an environmental link in addiction between parents and offspring. Cackling round me like a group of harridans several GA members repeated the line that it was not gambling that was the problem but something in their nature – a pathological addictive or compulsive personality, laying dormant like a cancer, waiting for a trigger, the catalyst that would spur them into action. All addictions follow the same pattern and all have a human *and* financial cost. Even if the only financial cost is paying a Harley Street shrink to get you over your addiction to apathy, it costs somewhere down the line. So what was eating me; what was the root of my compulsive behaviour? Was it hereditary, something constructed or a combination of the two.

My father had, at various stages, been a heavy gambler. I wouldn't go as far as saying he had a problem, but then like most personal problems, if well concealed, they usually manifest themselves in an indirect fashion. For me this meant having Dunlop Greenflash instead of Adidas SL80s as a kid.

Having grown up watching my father slip-slide into hypertension, in part through thrombotic Saturday afternoon rituals like horseracing, I understand that gambling can seriously damage your wealth and your health. How can any activity that makes the veins on your neck bulge like mutant black pudding be any good for you?

'Go on, son, go on, son, go on, my boy . . .' the old man would yell at the TV while making like Lester Piggot with a severe case of whip fever. In between races he'd nip round the corner to the conveniently located bookies (next to the conveniently located off-licence) to place a bet, collect his paltry winnings and, more often than not, lose his mind.

Sometimes I'd look into his yellowing eyes as he worked himself into a lather in front of the goggle box, transfixed by the 3.15 at Kempton Park, and wonder what could possess someone to get so worked up about a financial proposition which they knew ultimately was doomed to failure. Usually the old boy lost. Not big money, but enough to deny me a pair of Levis or a Meccano set.

Other times he would despatch me to the bookies to lay a bet on for him. A bookmakers is a strange, intimidating place for a shy adolescent. I was always struck by the foul, manly smell of the place. The air thick with cigarette smoke and BO, the punters with their stinking alcoholic breath – it insulted my frail sensibilities. A bookie is one chronic case of halitosis. And thus I learnt that gambling, especially on animals, was bullshit. Nevertheless, we don't always act on what we know . . .

At the end of the meeting I hung around drinking tea and eating stale biscuits. One of the guys said if the gaming industry didn't get its act together and stump up an extra £2.2 million to fund treatment for gambling addicts, it faced a possible levy on its profits. The industry had failed to educate people about the dangers of gambling. Funding treatment was a key condition of the proposed deregulation of the UK's gambling laws.

Richard Caborn, the Minister for Sport and Tourism had warned gaming companies that they had to find £3 million to pay for care for addicts or the Government would introduce a levy on gross profits. So far the industry had raised only £800,000 to fund GamCare, which promoted 'responsible attitudes to gambling', and Gordon House, the country's only residential treatment centre for gamblers.

More than one of the speakers at GA spoke of walking into the bookies 'feeling confident'. What did this mean? Confident about what? I'd used this line before. Bullshit. We're kidding ourselves. See, that was the problem with us mugs, the ill-informed and feckless fools who spent too much time at the track and the bookies: we got off on *gambling*, not making money.

Statistically speaking, if you're serious about making money from gambling the best odds are to be found at a blackjack table. An astute player can average out a 10–15 per cent profit in the long term. Blackjack is the only game in town where you can consistently fix the 'edge' in your favour. Trouble is, to be good at blackjack, as I once learned to my cost in Las Vegas, you have to card-count, concentrate on sequences of numbers and percentages of high and low cards, alter stakes according to probability outcomes and all that bollocks, which is too much work for the average mug punter.

One punter once even said to me, 'If the dogs was so bent, people wouldn't bet millions on it, would they?' This kind of self-delusion is common amongst gamblers. It has to be to keep the wheels turning.

'If you ever fancy going to the dogs, I've got passes,' I said to the merry men gathered outside the meeting hall. They looked at me blankly.

'There's another meeting on Thursday,' said one character. 'You should come.'

'I'll think about it,' I said and walked off into the night.

chapter 30

Kevin was lagging. He came in fifth over the 640 trip, which was the second time he'd run the distance. He was simply making up the numbers. I didn't have a single bet. I decided to deal with my addictions and afflictions myself. Besides, I didn't have any money. I hung around for the last race, looked down at my watch to check the time and clocked the date. It was May 12th, my father's birthday. Where art thou, old man? I hadn't seen him in nearly three years. He'd just upped and gone. The last I had heard of him was a rumour that he had gone back to Guyana to sort out a retirement home and had been mugged and beaten to the ground by a couple of hoodlums. Jesus, why hadn't we spoken in all this time? He had my mobile number; it had been the same for ten years. All he had to do was dial and there I'd be. And even if he'd lost my number he could find me, it wouldn't take much. After all, I made enough of a cock of myself in the papers or on TV to get spotted. Surely someone who knew him would've said, 'I read some piece of shit by that no good son of yours . . .'

A slightly disconcerting recent observation was how I had started to become more like my father and less like myself. Age has a way of playing such tricks on you, like the way that as you get older your parents become proportionately less older than you, creating the illusion that if you keep on ageing *ad infinitum* you would both wind up the same age one day. (For example, when I was eight years old my father was forty, i.e. five times my age. When I turned sixteen, my father was forty-eight, i.e. three times my age. Now that I was thirty-six and he was sixty-eight, he wasn't even twice my age. The age gap between us was narrowing and so was the difference between us.)

Not speaking to my father had done me some favours. It made me feel a hell of a lot easier about being a shit dad to my own kid. It made me realise that being a 'good father' is not all it's cracked up to be. Being good at anything isn't all it's cracked up to be.

After a run of bad form at 640 metres Kevin finally returned to winning ways at 475 metres, leading from the off to record another decent time of 29:56. At 4–1 he would've made someone reasonably happy. As I was on the betting wagon I had to content myself with the knowledge that I had bagged the princely sum of £65 as owner.

For Kevin's arch nemesis, Twotone, things were also looking up.

So I'm slopping out the dog food at the kennels – the usual mix of hard biscuits, diced beef, chicken and minced lamb. Maybe Linda could give me a job to work off my kennel bill. She's looking at the weekly feeding schedule that outlines the weights of each dog and reels off their names as we hang around waiting to ferry an aluminium bowl to each hungry hound.

'Stinky,' she cries. 'Mary and Kevin . . .'

'Sounds like a good Catholic couple,' I say.

'Blackie.' Linda looks up at me. 'No offence meant.'

'None taken.'

'He's all right,' says Nan. 'He don't mind, do you, love?'

'To be honest with you I hadn't even given it any thought.'

'He's all right, Linda. He's one of us.'

What did she mean by that. One of us? What, was I a white man all of a sudden?

I hadn't even thought about the implications of a black dog named Blackie. It wasn't like calling a fawn dog 'Chinky' or a brown dog 'Paki'. And it certainly wasn't like the RAF hero (played by Richard Todd) Wing Commander Guy Gibson's Labrador in *The Dam Busters*, who was affectionately known as 'Nigger' which friends of pensionable age inform me was a common name for black cats and dogs in the 1940s. Every time I see that movie I can't help but marvel at the scene where the dog kicks the bucket after being run over by a car bringing Gibson, squadron leader of the historic bombing raid on the Ruhr dams in Germany in 1943 and wannabe Tory MP, to tears. (Gibson, incidentally, had requested that 'Nigger' be buried at midnight, the time of the unsuccessful raid, and that the word 'Nigger' be used as the codeword for the breaching of the Möhne Dam.) Some film historians and critics cite Nigger as being the conscience of the film. (ITV famously edited references to 'Nigger' from the film thus incurring the wrath of anti-censorship goons. And US TV networks even replaced the epithet with 'Trigger' when the film was shown across the Atlantic.)

'Right. This is Twotone's,' said Linda, giving me the eye. 'And watch it, you. No funny stuff in his food.'

'Don't worry.'

When I got back to the kitchen Linda was on her high horse.

'Someone ought to do something about what they're doing in Europe to the cats and dogs,' she said.

'Why, what's happened to them?'

'Didn't you see that programme on telly the other night? Oh, it was terrible. People are stealing them for their fur. Making Alsatian fur coats they were. Terrible business.'

Linda told me she had been on a disciplinary charge at Walthamstow Stadium for 'time finding', i.e. deliberately slowing a dog down for a trial in order to have it downgraded so it can run against inferior opposition. Was the old girl a bit tricky after all? Maybe her luck was changing too. She was down to third place in the Greyhound Trainers' Association rankings and the winners weren't coming in like they used to. Ultimately, she beat the time-finding rap. 'They couldn't prove anything one way or the other at the inquiry,' she said. 'I've been a good girl, David. It's just one of those things. They just gave me a slap on the wrist and said don't let it happen again. What can you do, eh?'

I told Linda I was wondering what to do with Kevin. I didn't want to tell her outright that I was planning to get rid of him. I managed, through circumlocution, to get round to the subject. 'So, er, ha . . . Twotone, eh? Be worth a few quid if he gets into the Derby?'

'That's right, David. Bundles.'

'Ha, dogs, eh? Who'd have 'em? So, er, what do you reckon, you know, I'm thinking about getting a few more people on board on the syndicate. Er, what do you . . .'

'If you wanna tell 'em what he's worth, say £500. That's what you'd get for him.'

Linda cut me a knowing glance and carried on divvying up lumps of beef and chicken. Five hundred pounds. Five hundred pounds for a life. It would hardly cover his kennel bill. Extricating myself from her and Kevin would not be easy without being mercenary. Since I'd had a child, and now a dog, I'd gone soft. Perhaps I could take Kevin on to the dog show circuit . . . after all a greyhound had won 2003's best of breed for hounds or Crufts.

Five days later Twotone entered the Derby trial at Wimbledon, his defining moment. He'd been saved for over a month for his big shot. A win would put him into the next round and ever closer to that £75,000 prize.

Before that, he'd won six out of his last ten races, an incredible strike rate. But then his luck changed. He was beaten into third spot. Only the first two from each trial could qualify for the heats. Ha! I never liked that dog's attitude from the off. That'll learn him for not taking a biscuit from me. Boy, did I know how to hold a grudge. What *Schadenfreude!* But look at it from my point of view: if Twotone had gone on to run and, heaven forbid, win the Derby I would've lost £75,000 for the sake of an extra 1500 quid.

In all honesty I wasn't crowing. One should never bask in others' misery. I'd heard too many punters cussing dogs in the stands, blaming their lack of judgement or just fate on a dumb animal. For all my lip, I did believe in the Corinthian ideal, fair play, being a good sport, 'it's the taking part that counts' and all that tosh.

Winning is great, but it's rare, a fleeting moment to be savoured, a dream. Losing on the other hand is a perpetual grind; it is the commute to work, the credit card bills, the failed exam, the wife walking out with the kids. It's the reality of everyday life. Four days earlier Kevin had come fifth; a week after that he won and I pocketed £65 in prize money. But the results didn't matter any more. They really didn't.

chapter 31

It was time to organise a 'testimonial' so the other silent partners of the Headline Syndicate could see the Boy Blunder run one last time before I sold him into medical research. It would be one last roll of the dice, his last opportunity to shine. If he impressed, maybe my friends and acquaintances would finally realise what they'd been missing and buy a share in him, that way I could keep him running until I figured out his fate, otherwise it was curtains. The expense of running a greyhound was more than I could shoulder on my own. I owed Linda so much in training fees, if I didn't get a handle on the money situation, I'd be washing dishes and slopping out at Imperial Kennels for the rest of my life. I would call the dog track, tell them I wanted to put on a bit of a do on a forthcoming Thursday night, sponsor a race and that'd be that. But there were complications, like rules.

'You'll have to talk to Chris about that,' said Ann. 'I can't get involved in all that. It could be a bit . . . tricky.'

'OK. By the way, I'd like to call the race the Zussies Boy Memorial Stakes.'

Ann wasn't too keen on the idea.

'David, please don't call it the Memorial Stakes,' she said, 'as they only do that when someone's dead!' There I go again. Thinking too far into the future.

Allowing owners to sponsor races in which they have a canine stake creates a clear conflict of interest. Imagine the hullabaloo if

I sponsored a race that Kevin actually ran in ... and won? Questions would be asked. Eyebrows would be raised. In the event, I, I mean the Headline Syndicate wound up sponsoring, *for one night only*, the 'Headline Stakes' for the cost of a trophy and £290 in prize money.

A problem was the grade of Kevin's race. It was Chris Page, the Race Manager's responsibility to grade races according to ability, not wallet size, and Thursday nights were open race nights, which meant ordinarily Kevin would have no chance of running. However, as a one-off, Kevin was appearing in the following Thursday's 20:49 race – the Eric Burgess Retirement Stakes. On paper he wasn't the slowest dog in the field but the grade was a notch or two higher than he was generally used to and the competition was much more consistent with their times. All I could hope for was that he didn't embarrass himself or me in front of his new fans.

Come the night, I felt mildly nervous. For the first time in months, in fact ever, a substantial number of friends, acquaintances and colleagues had turned up at the Stow to see Kevin in action.

'The toffs get Ascot and we get Walthamstow,' said my friend Tam, looking round at the clientele. But so what? So what if the toffs had 'the season'? I had the 'counter-season'. Who needed Henley, Royal Ascot and Glyndebourne when you had the English Greyhound Derby, the National Lawnmower Championships and the All England Hod Carrying Finals?

But enough of the social commentary. Let's cut to the chase. When Kevin's race finally came around half my crew were too pissed to even notice. Having made a conscious effort to curb my gambling habits I made a concession for the Boy Blunder and stuck a token £10 on him at 10–1. Having studied the form in the race card I may as well have set a match to the money. By the time he came out the traps most were so far into their scampi and chips they didn't even see him get fried at the first bend. He didn't have a chance. Come the second turn he'd been well and truly muscled out of the game by the pack. At the third bend he was lagging, unable to contend with the superior opposition. Boy, the Stow had covered its arse all right. Unless he pulled a kalashnikov from out of his jacket and went postal on the other dogs he had no chance of winning. Coming down the home straight I could feel a year's work going down the toilet.

Kevin came last.

Not only did he lose, he lost spectacularly, crawling home last by at least six lengths. I felt sorry for the boy. Nobody gave a toss about him really. He was just a dog. All that stuff about us being a nation of animal lovers is romantic fantasy. People don't give a shit about animals. Like Ann had said, she loved her dogs but still ate steak. As if on cue, at a time when I assemble a decent crowd of people and after pulling strings to get him on the Thursday night card, Kevin comes last for only the second time in his career. At least everyone had a laugh at our expense.

But hey, if you are going to lose, lose in style baby. Everyone remembers Eddie the Eagle and Eric the Eel because they came last. Can you remember who won the 2000 Olympic downhill or 100 metres breaststroke? Exactly. Case closed. And what about that freak Tony Bullimore who tried to row across the Pacific in a bath tub or something? Everyone remembers that nut because he got within a hundred metres of the shore in Australia after an epic 900-odd-mile journey only to capsize the fucker. *Winner!*

Plucky Brits, just as we know it will rain at Wimbledon, know not to complain or try too hard or change things too fast. In this sense the plucky Brit has something of the Zen master about him, always guided by the middle way.

In the final analysis I could always console myself that I was simply following in the tradition of the Great British loser. Basil Fawlty, Rigsby, Steptoe and Son, Ian Duncan Smith . . . After all, there is a lot more to be said for being a loser than being a winner. Winning leaves little room for reflection other than the usual protestations of thanking God, Mum and the Academy. You only have to witness the fawning, gushing yak of Oscar winners, podium-traipsing Olympians and obsequious politicians to deduce that there is something vaguely tacky, slightly oily, about winning and winners. The conscious loser on the other hand is the second-rater's philosopher, the master of mediocrity, doyen of the dropout.

Well that's one way of looking at it.

After the race I led some of the troops over to the kennels. This caused a bit of a stir. I could see Patrick, Kevin's handler, doing the post-race honours, washing his feet and giving him a rub down. Eventually he brought him out to the expectant crowd. Kevin was panting heavier than I'd ever seen him. 'Aw, poor Kevin, you're such a loser,' came a voice from the crowd.

'No he's not,' I said, trying to stay cool and not take the slight personally. *It was aimed at the dog, not me.* I started babbling on again about him being overmatched and out of his depth etc. but my words fell on deaf ears. I carried on but the group just melted away into the mass of spectators in the stands with their beers and thoughts of dancing the night away at Charlie Chan's. Everyone was laughing. When I went to join the group in the club, the doormen stopped me and my friend Damian, who was dressed in an Hawaian shirt, khaki shorts and trainers. 'Not tonight, lads,' said one of them, looking at Damian's attire. I felt like a chump.

This had been Kevin's forty-third race and he'd won seven. He was the epitome of mediocrity. The little fella had really pulled the stops out in the race. And came last. Once again he'd tried his best. That's all a greyhound can ever do. But his best simply wasn't good enough.

chapter 32

'We've got a saying up here in Yorkshire,' said Old Man Dennis, leaning back in his chair. 'If you don't like someone, give 'em a greyhound.' Boy, did I know what he was talking about.

I ran into Dennis after dropping Margot off at her parents' house in Cheshire and heading across the Pennine Way to Sheffield to see some of my boxing cronies. Dennis owned the gym I used to train at in my bad old days as a boxer. He claimed to have been the first man in Sheffield to own a Rolls Royce Silver Shadow and was a bit of a character. Now in his mid-sixties he was still stocky, still pugnacious, but a 'lovable rogue'. These days he ran a modest scrap-metal business, a couple of cafés and a sauna and massage parlour, among other business interests.

'I'd say I've done over a million pounds gambling over the years, Dave,' said Dennis, as we pulled up outside his old friend Walter Hesselwood's scrap-metal factory. Dennis had been a compulsive gambler with a bizarre set of superstitions to match. There was the usual stuff, like lucky socks and jumpers, but he'd also make his ex-wife wear any item of clothing she'd worn when he'd last had a big win. 'I even used to ask her where she was standing when such and such a dog or horse won,' said Dennis. 'And she'd say, "Over there" and point to a corner or other part of a room. I'd then tell her, "Go and stand in that fucking corner; the race is on in a minute and he's running again." I were fucking insane, Dave.'

Superstition had started to get the better of me too. I was convinced that Kevin was jinxed. For one, whenever I backed him he lost. OK, admittedly more often than not he lost regardless of whether I backed him or not. But he had, after all, brought me nothing but bad luck. I knew that protruding ribcage of his was an omen. Well, I couldn't put my failure purely down to my own incompetence, could I? Gamblers and dog owners are a superstitious bunch. Superstition gives you a sense of control by making you think you can work out what's going to happen next, a sort of adjunct to the 'locus of control' – the belief that you can control your destiny.

I didn't want to believe in luck any more. But somehow I couldn't help but think luck had played a massive role in my life of late . . . all of it bad. My foray into greyhound racing had been cursed from the start. Why hadn't I taken Vince's advice and bought a car?

Dennis eventually gave up gambling for four years following a course of hypnotherapy with a mutual friend called Paul Dorking. Paul had worked with me on mental techniques I had used in boxing training. But just as I'd started to pile on the pounds and lose the six-pack through lack of mental conditioning, Dennis had returned to his gambling ways.

'A million pounds. Lot of money innit, Dave?'

'It is, Den.'

'You think I would've learnt my lesson.'

'But you haven't, have ya?'

'I'm a fucking shit gambler as well. Waste of money. You know I used to have thirty-odd greyhounds.'

We strolled into Walter Hesselwood's office, an old school joint locked in a 1970s vacuum, and met the old boy sitting behind his desk. His secretary was shuffling files around and stapling bits of paper together. Walter had 'pillar of the community' written all over him. He greeted us and wasted no time with the nostalgia.

'Tell Dave how many dogs you had, Walter,' said Dennis.

'Oh, I couldn't say, Den. Loads. Loads. I used to buy 'em from a farm in Ireland. One week I bought forty different dogs for different trainers and I had up to thirty dogs running at any one time.'

Walter, now aged seventy-four, had owned the Duke of Alva who won the St Leger in 1957, which he said was one of the first greyhounds to earn appearance money 'without even putting a paw on sand'. The St Leger was the first ever televised greyhound race. Alva won every heat and then of course the final. He won seventeen consecutive four-dog races.

'I had so many dogs,' reminisced Walter. 'Tinryland Snowball . . . he were a winner at Hull, Bradford and Leeds in the *News of the World* Inter Track Competition 1956. Trained by Jack Brennan. I sold Newdown Prairie to Paddy Keane for stud in Australia. He had a hairline fracture and went lame. Then I had Shepherds Gold. He were a good hurdler, but he were vicious. Greyhounds are lovely animals but when they turn they don't bite, they chomp. Vicious . . . Jimmy Jowette was walking six dogs when one turned on him – never said which one it was – two hundred stitches he needed.'

Walter dropped names like they were out of style. His time had been about names, faces, big wins and championships. Mine had been about . . . well . . . fuck all really. We couldn't have been further apart on the greyhound scale.

'It were exciting in them days. It were good to take a dog anywhere, you know, and take on all comers. I suppose the kick were gambling. But I haven't had a bet in twenty years.'

Old boys make me laugh. They have the kind of patience I envy. Like a lot of the 'younger generation' I want everything yesterday, which means I often fall short today. Age slows you down for a reason; it forces you to stop wasting your time. My old man used to say, 'Youth is wasted on the young.'

'I've got some advice for you,' said Walter, leaning across his desk. 'Find someone you don't like, give that bloody dog you've got to 'em as a Christmas present, cos there's no future in it.'

Chance would be a fine thing. I couldn't even give Kevin away. There was always one last resort however.

'Aye, there's flapping near Barnsley,' said Dennis as we headed back into Sheffield city centre. 'I don't go any more but there used to be some right scams in the old days, Dave. People would rub Vaseline in dogs' eyes, dope 'em, dig holes in front of boxes, anything to nobble a race. A fella once got pulled for putting Formica in traps at one track.'

Flapping is the arse end of greyhound racing, the lowest of the low. Part sport, part fairground attraction, flapping is the bare-knuckle fighting of dog racing. One of the last surviving flapping tracks near Sheffield is Highgate Greyhound Stadium in a village just outside Barnsley called Thurnscoe. Thurnscoe is England's fortieth worst employment area. It's one of only four council wards in the Yorkshire and Humber Region which are in the top hundred of the most deprived out of 8500 wards in England. The unemployment rate is double the national average. This is a hidden Britain of burnt-out cars, a forgotten Britain of potholed roads and scallies on stolen mopeds.

The high street of boarded-up shops and smashed windows had had the guts ripped out of it and what was once a thriving community based on industry, coal and steel was now a wasteland. On the corner of Tudor Street, just off the main drag, was the Spit and Whisper, the Officials Club which promised 'New Members Welcome'. I bet if I went in and tried to get membership I'd be made welcome all right. In Thurnscoe it was an occupation for scrawny Reebok-clad youths to loiter on street corners and prepubescent girls to dress like whores. Kids without helmets or ambition raced up and down the high street on snarling motor-bikes. Everywhere I turned I was stared at. This was real white-boy territory. For many years I had embraced the spirit of multiculturalism but this was a bridge-building exercise too far. I'd ventured out into the sticks enough to know that feeling like a foreigner in your own supposed country was a damn sight more uncomfortable than feeling like a foreigner in a foreign country.

While the origins are unclear, I've heard it said that the term 'flapping' comes from the sound that the rag lures used to make in the old days. Regardless of historical pretensions, people in the BGRF/NGRC community take a dim view of the unregistered flapping track scene. The lack of regulation and casual philosophy of many flapping folk mean that, rightly or wrongly, it attracts the kind of bad press the mainstream industry is working hard to eradicate.

There are 27 unsupervised flapping tracks like Highgate in Britain, but since 1985 some 28 had closed, many of them in the north of England. Aldershot, Ashington, Barnsley, Barrow, Berwick, Bideford, Bolton, Carfin, Chasewater, Chester, Chesterfield, Clacton, Cleethorpes, Coatbridge, Deeside, Doncaster, Falkirk, Glastonbury, Hawick, Huntingdon, Preston, Skegness, Skewen, St Helens, Stanley, Westhoughton, Wisbech and Workington were all names consigned to the dustbin of greyhound racing. Maybe it was simply the case that public tastes and attitudes had become too sophisticated for the gritty reality of standing in a field with a pint of Smiths and a roll-up watching your sixteen seconds of fame whiz round a sodden field.

I paid my £3.50 entry fee and passed through a rickety turnstile. The track, situated in the middle of a field and surrounded by corrugated iron, was even grimier than I had imagined. The dogs weren't actually kennelled on site; people kept them in their vehicles – white vans, Astra estates, trailers or some just on the back seat of a car.

As soon as I set foot inside Highgate, typically, all eyes were on me. Every note I took, every observation I made, someone, somewhere was monitoring my actions. I felt uncomfortable, unwelcome even, although there was no open hostility.

I got myself a pint of Guinness from the bar, hung back and watched the goings on.

A black and white dog came out of the paddock reluctantly with its owner, a walking meat pie of a man. It was straining its lead as it stopped, shivering with fear, to take a shit on the sand.

'C'mon there,' said Meat Pie Man. The dog was a nothing more than a rasher of skin and bone. The crowd at the stand-side rails looked on dismissively.

I overheard an old boy giving a fella next to me some advice. I think his name was Alf. He was the only man in all the time I'd been to the dogs that I saw actually wearing a flat cap. Alf had a face like a fist, all gnarled and calloused. I asked him if he had a tip.

'Yeah, keep ya money in ya pocket. There's now't but rubbish here t'day.'

The last straw came when a black dog named 'Darkie' was paraded in the paddock. Its name was called out and I heard a few sniggers followed by furtive glances in my direction. Time to get the fuck out of there and get back to civilisation. Time to get back on the beaten track, forget about the dogs and end this cultural safari once and for all.

chapter 33

Weeks passed, then months and Kevin's performances got worse and worse. His stock value was nil. Selling was no longer an option. Apart from a small knock in December of 2002 which laid him up for three weeks, he'd been fit and healthy and a loyal, if mediocre, servant and was still running, but if he had ever had a best he'd long passed it. I had exploited him. That was the name of the game. But what could I give him in return? A home? The property company that managed the Norman Foster des res where I lived had other ideas. In a memorandum that was sent to all residents they reiterated *inter alia* their policy of 'no pets or animals allowed' in the building. Screw them and Foster anyway. Living in a million-pound pad overlooking the Thames wasn't all it was cracked up to be.

Margot and I returned to Barbados for our annual dose of winter sun. We paid a trip to the Garrison racecourse, had a great day out and a modest flutter. I'd managed to wean myself off compulsive gambling, not through group therapy or hypnosis but sheer willpower, which meant avoiding the Stow and my local bookies long enough to escape the lure. I had given up gambling, just as I had once given up smoking, being fat, lazy and a scallywag, simply by recognising the futility of what I was doing. It felt good being clean again, being free of an irrational compulsion.

Barbados was crying out for a dog track but I certainly wasn't going to measure it up for one. No, my days in the greyhound business were about to come to an abrupt end. Halfway through the holiday, one evening, while spraying mosquito repellent on my legs and knocking back an ice-cold beer, I got a voicemail message. It was Linda Jones. 'Can you call me, David?' she said. 'It's very important.' It was Thursday night, a race night, and around 11.30p.m. UK time. *My God. Something's happened to Kevin.* Linda and I hadn't spoken for a while, but not through a falling out. I just owed her a chunk of change in unpaid kennel fees. I had the matter in hand. I'm no deadbeat: I always pay my debts . . . eventually. But I was embarrassed at not sorting it out sooner and was caught in the ninety-day invoice trap by one of my paymasters. I called her back straight away.

'Hi, Linda, how's it going?' I said, fearing the worst. We talked small for a bit, about the kennels, performances etc. She'd been trying to contact me for some time she said. The bills never failed to get through though. I apologised profusely for my flakiness. Linda was cool. I felt better, temporarily. Getting into greyhound racing had always been a big risk. Not just financially but because a life was involved, a dog's life. For all my macho posturing, Kevin, in a small way, combined with my fumbling experiences in town and country, track and field, had taught me to give animals a bit of a break.

'OK. Give me the bad news.'

'Well, Kevin's been carrying a bit of an injury,' said Linda.

'His hock?'

'That's right,' she said. 'And he's not been doing too well. To be fair to him we put him out last week and he won.'

'That's great,' I said.

'But he's been struggling. We put him out again tonight and . . .'

He's dead.

'Well, he could hardly get round, David. I'm afraid we're gonna have to retire him. I think it's for the best.'

He's not dead.

'He's OK? I mean, he's all right in himself?'

'Oh yeah, he's fine. He's just struggling to make the grade.'

'But he's OK?'

'Yes, David.'

'Thank Christ. I thought you were going to tell me he'd snuffed it.'

'No, no. Don't be silly.'

Linda told me that she would make the necessary arrangements for him to go into the Stow's greyhound retirement scheme. All I had to do was pay a registration fee of £100 and they'd kennel Kevin until a suitable home for him was found.

'That's fine. I'll sort it out when I get back to London. And, er, I'll, er, take care of my bill too.'

'Don't worry, David. I know you won't let us down. And by the way . . .'

'Yes Linda?'

'Don't forget to bring us back some sunshine. The weather's terrible over 'ere.'

I put the phone down. Margot looked across the room at me, sympathetically. 'What's up, babe?'

I peered at the floor and shrugged my shoulders. What an anti-climax. 'It's all over, sweetheart. Kevin's done his hock in and Linda reckons it'd be best if we retired him now before it gets worse.' Kevin's career was effectively over. If ever I needed an ending to the story, it was now.

Epilogue

It was nearly noon, early spring, but the charcoal sky and driving rain betrayed the time of year. After four frustrating hours on the road I finally reached the tiny village of Lydney in the Forest of Dean, Gloucestershire, and my appointment with Ray Jones, a small-time trainer I had met through a tax exile from Barbados called John Watt. John, his estranged wife, their son, his wife's brother (also called John) and their cousin Ray had formed a syndicate in the late 1990s with a view to breeding and training open racers and perhaps, one day, an elusive Derby winner.

I pulled into the farmyard adjacent to Ray's kennels, over-steered, skidded, and then coasted into an iron gate. *Why me?* I got out of the car. *No damage, thank God.* I got back in the car, drenched, called Ray from my mobile and waited.

A minute later he appeared, all eighteen stone of him, dressed in waterproofs and a woolly hat, trudging through the mush. Ray, who had not long turned 40, had more than a passing resemblance to the former England cricket captain Graham Gooch, insofar as he had a thick handlebar moustache, dark hair and darker eyes. I wound down the window and a backhand of rain slapped me in the face. 'Hello Ray,' I spluttered, drying myself off. 'All right Dave,' he replied in his West Country twang. 'You'd better stay in the car cos these dogs go mad when they see a stranger. I'll give you a shout when I've finished sorting 'em out.'

I sat in the car, listening to the rain drumming on the roof. *Why me? Why the cats and dogs whenever I ventured into the countryside? What had I done to Mother Nature?* Gradually, the rain and sleet subsided and I could hear barking and empty buckets being tossed around outside. Ray soon reappeared with his cousin John, a wiry, unobtrusive character, and we all traipsed off to the kennels, the bulk of which had been fashioned out of a rusting corrugated transport container, home to a dozen or so dogs.

'Most of 'em are locked up now,' said Ray as we made for the rickety old caravan that served as his office. John mumbled something about pups and then scuttled off. 'I bet this ain't like Linda Jones's place, eh?' said Ray, laughing. 'It's not . . .' I said, looking round at the array of leads, collars, muzzles, bowls, grooming equipment and sundry crap. 'But it's not far off.'

Ray's 'home' track was Reading, a shack of a place compared to the Stow. He charged £2.50 a day in kennelling fees as opposed to Linda's £7 plus VAT. I had tried on more than one occasion to palm off Kevin on Ray, just for a couple of months, so I could buy some time and figure out what to do with him. But Ray wasn't having any of it. 'I ain't got the room, Dave,' he said, pottering around the caravan. 'I got too many here as it is.'

I sat in the caravan shivering. *Damn the countryside and everything in it.* 'Haven't you got a garden shed you could put him in, or a car boot, anything?' I pleaded. Ray laughed. With four retired greyhounds living at home he was already doing his bit for the greyhound welfare state. 'They put in the effort for us so we owe it to them to do the right thing,' he said, giving me a knowing look. 'I suppose we've got a duty to them.'

Now I felt even more guilty. I had failed in my 'duty' as an owner and now I was paying the price for it.

'Look, for a small outfit like us we've got to go for open racers,' explained Ray. 'If we don't get open racers, we sell them [the graders] and breed another litter. The first litter we bred, three of them were good open racers out of five and the other was an A1 track champion. When you get used to having good dogs, having mediocre ones after that isn't the same. I've sold pups to people who've been in racing 25 years with the aspiration of getting an open racer and they've never had one. We were in it a few years and got three in our first litter so you can see we were a bit fortunate.'

Ray showed me a litter of eighteen-week-old puppies that he had bred. They lived in their own private kennel, fenced off at the end of a field backing on to the main enclosure. *How cute. The little bastards . . .*

'There's a bias against English dogs,' said Ray as the little nippers jumped up excitedly at the wire mesh separating them from us. 'If you took an English dog to the sales you'd get laughed at.' Despite the prejudice, Ray only trained and raced dogs bred by his loving hand. This was mainly for the sense of personal achievement but also to protect the integrity of his bloodlines. Greyhound racing is certainly not a free-for-all when it comes to breeding – one cannot pair up any two mutts without the right official paperwork. But it is not controlled as rigidly as thorough-bred racing where, for instance, artificial insemination is banned. Thanks to the wonders of the internet, it is possible to buy frozen greyhound semen from a variety of sources. Take one bitch and a pipette and you're in business. *Now there's an idea.*

As I toyed with Ray's puppies, teasing out their natural instinct to chase, I thought of the thousands of animals that are culled every year because they'll never make the grade. I had to ask the obvious question.

'So what do you do if you breed a dog that's duff?' I said.

'Luckily we haven't been in that situation yet, but I have had one in a litter that wouldn't chase. Well, he'd chase, but he went after the lure and then started looking at me at the side of the track. I'd never seen anything like it. The Great White Hope he was called. If they do that . . . well, if you try 'em a couple of times and they're still not chasing you've got your work cut out. I gave him away I did. He was a beautiful puppy.'

After a greasy breakfast we headed to a schooling track in Kidderminster, Worcestershire to trial four of Ray's older puppies.

When we got there, several other owners, trainers and dogs were queuing at the side of the track, waiting their turn to pit their wits and bloodlines against the clock. A grey-haired trap steward in green overalls was standing on the track ready to hand slip a slightly bemused looking pup. His chubby owner stood on the sidelines with another pup, watching keenly as the hare came clackety clack round the track, travelling at half-speed to make pursuit that bit easier.

As an added touch, the trap steward made a point of showing the dog the hare until it rounded the bend and reached them, upon which he gave the dog a gentle push, as though releasing a dove from cupped hands, urging it to give chase. 'Go on boy,' cried the steward, but the dog remained motionless. It then sniffed the air nonchalantly before turning to the steward and jumping up, attempting to lick his face, leaving the hare trundling off into the distance.

'We've got no fucking chance with these two, have we?' said the chubby man to the steward in a broad west Midlands accent. *How did I ever get into this comedy of a business?*

'You see how that guy slipped that dog,' said Ray gesturing toward the steward, 'I don't like doing that, cos that's encouraging the dog to look behind for the lure. As soon as it comes by it's gotta be pretty dumb not to see it anyway.

'A lot of trainers will take pups for a walk to chase rabbits,' continued Ray, as we slowly advanced in the queue, waiting our turn to trial. 'The trouble is, the more kills they've had the more they figure out the lure is a dummy. I was talking to a trainer yesterday who has a ferret. He lets it run around free and gets the dog to sight it, just to liven it up. Anyway, the dog ran and won. But you can only do that once in a while.'

There are so many tricks and dodges in greyhound racing and even though I'd probably learnt more than the average punter I had only scratched the surface. To make it in this game, like any business, you need dedication. You have to live and breathe, eat, shit and sleep the dogs. You needed patience, money to burn and time on your hands. I had none of this left to offer. I was nothing more than a dilettante, and a failed one at that.

'At the end of the day they wanna get to that lure first,' said Ray, gazing at the conveyor belt of dogs going round the track in pursuit of a rag and a stupid cuddly toy thrown in for good measure. 'That's what it's all about – that's what the competition is. You do get some dogs that, after they've raced a while, get a little bit cunning and realise that they're just there for the night out!' *That'll be Kevin.* 'But they enjoy it . . .' Ray seemed almost hypnotised by the cyclical goings on. He is a dog man, all right. And I am a fraud. 'You see these,' he said, looking at the queue of dogs, 'when that hare comes round they wanna get on it. They're bred to do that, that's their instinct.' As if on cue, as an illustration of Sod's Law, at that point one of the next dogs to trial came to an abrupt halt halfway round the track and started sniffing the ground, the air and listening to the spring chorus of birds tweeting in the nearby woods. And to think I paid £2,500 for one of these idiot animals.

'We're up next anyway,' said Ray. 'This one's a bit nervous, the fawn one. She doesn't take to it.' The bitch was yelping and squeezing her tail firmly between her legs. Ray took her and a black dog through a small gate leading onto the track, where a steward was on hand to help them into the traps. 'This is the second time they're going in the boxes,' said Ray. 'As you school 'em, you do it a little different every time. First off, when you bring 'em here you start 'em just where that dog wouldn't run, straight around to the pick up over here – that's the first time. Then the second time you slip 'em by that tower further on and time 'em, so you've got half an idea then. Then the third time, hand slip 'em from here; fourth time out of the boxes for the first time; fifth time out of the boxes for the second time but with a muzzle on. And the next week, everything being OK, you start two dog trials and . . .'

Back in London, I still flirted with the idea of bringing the Boy Blunder home. Ever the nomads, Margot and I had recently moved to a modest but spacious new build opposite Battersea Park. Without a garden, the park nevertheless offered ideal dog walking territory.

'I could build a kennel and he can live on the balcony,' I'd suggested, trying like a desperate, bogey-nosed child to convince Mummy that I could, I would, I *should* have a dog of my very own. *Grow up man.* Margot almost bought the idea until a meddling French polisher and know-it-all ex-greyhound owner showed up one day to do some work and pointed out that a big dog could easily jump off the balcony if a passing cat took its fancy. Well, I guess he had a point. A thirty-two-kilo dog falling thirty feet would make a bit of a mess.

At one stage, an ex-girlfriend agreed to re-home Kevin, then changed her mind, then changed again on the basis that she would have him for a trial period, then reconsidered, then re-reconsidered and then . . . *whatever.* In the end I gave up and paid the £100 as Linda had suggested and Kevin went into the lottery that is the Walthamstow Stadium Homefinding Scheme.

Eventually, Kevin wound up in Whittingham Kennels near Waltham Abbey, on the edge of Epping Forest in Essex, where up to 48 retired dogs are cared for. As he bided his time here hoping that some poor sap, I mean *animal lover*, would come along with a new lead, a rubber bone and a cosy home, I all but gave up on him. I had become the epitome of the wretched, embittered, failed owner. *Why should I care anymore?* He was out of my hands and had served his purpose, albeit miserably. The retirement people could take care of him from now on. *Stuff him.*

Yeah, go on: boo and hiss and paint me the pantomime villain. But let's get it into perspective: I am a grown man and he a *dog*. I had other shit to deal with. For instance, in the time that Kevin had joined the retirement home, I had learned that my father, aged 69, had died the previous summer in Guyana. It had taken seven months for me to be informed. *Seven months*. But that's another story. Suffice to say, in the most anticlimactic way possible, the gambler, the raconteur, the drinker, the arrogant sonofabitch who had forged me was gone. There was no 'closure', no reconciliation, no Hollywood ending to the Great Man's demise. I felt empty for a long while. Empty.

I had to move on. I had to draw this chapter to a close. The time for wallowing in self-pity was over. And I'm talking about Kevin here, not my old man! On the page, if not in life and death, I *could* find reconciliation, I could be the architect my own destiny. Resolution: this was the key. Maybe I did have a heart after all.

'Zussies Boy?' said Johanna, who runs the Whittingham Kennel. 'Kevin . . . hmm . . .' Down the telephone line I could hear her flicking through the pages of a ledger. 'Kevin . . . that's right. He's with a lovely woman called Anna down in Surrey. Hang on a minute I'll give you her number.'

I arranged to meet Anna one Sunday afternoon near her home in Mogador, Surrey at the 'dog friendly' Sportsman – an archetypal isolated country pub on the edge of a snow-covered moor. I felt uncharacteristically nervous, like a father about to meet his long-lost son for the first time. As I crossed the threshold every one of the dozen or so patrons, to a tee, stopped talking, turned, gave me a cursory look, and then carried on with their business.

Having survived the entrance test, I scanned the bar for Kevin. I couldn't see him. I did a double take. *Am I in the right pub?* Suddenly, I clocked him snuggled up on a jacket on the floor next to Anna, who by this point had got up to greet me with a wide grin and a handshake, introducing herself and her younger brother, James. 'Hi Anna, James,' I said, beaming, before turning my attention, somewhat rudely, to Kevin who was now on his feet attempting to sniff my balls. At first he seemed apprehensive. Cowering ever so slightly, unsurprisingly with his tail between his legs, he gave a few more sniffs and calmed down. 'I think he remembers you,' said Anna. 'Maybe he thinks I've come to take him back to the track,' I said. I got myself a drink, sat down and couldn't shake him off.

We were like old swells again, Kevin and me, snuggling and cuddling. Anna, a petite twenty-six-year-old occupational therapist, explained that she had got Kevin six months earlier from Johanna after seeing several other greyhounds at a retirement home in Gravesend, Kent. 'A friend of mine has got one and it's such a beautiful, gentle dog I thought I'd get one,' she said. 'I purposefully went for a big dog because I know they're harder to home; and I like the fact that he's mature. He's already got his personality, so there are no shocks. He's so laid back he'd sleep for twenty-four hours if he could.'

Living at home with her family meant there were always people around to look after him, and he even got on with her two cats, although at a distance. Many patrons came up to pet Kevin. He was obviously a star in the local. A middle-aged couple in particular, who were sitting next to us getting slowly sloshed, were all over him. 'Ooh, he soooo beautiful,' cooed the woman. 'Do you wanna sell him? Only joking! No, I couldn't have another one. We lost a greyhound a few years ago.'

'Lost?' I enquired. 'What happened to him?'

'Died . . .'

'Oh, that sort of lost,' I said.

'Lovely dogs, lovely,' continued the woman. 'Custer we called him. Greyhounds are the Gerald Hadley of the dog world: cool, calm, self-assured. They've got a posh face, haven't they? They've got *class*.'

The couple were so fixated with Kevin and reliving their greyhound memories that it was becoming increasingly difficult to have a conversation with Anna without them butting in. This was my big reunion and they were screwing it up.

'So, Anna.' I said, trying to squeeze a word out through gritted teeth.

'He lived to about fourteen, didn't he love?' said the man, returning to the bar with what looked like a couple of double malt whiskeys. 'We used to dress him up at Christmas in a Santa outfit.'

'With little reindeer horns,' added the woman. *Oh the laughter!*
'Beautiful dogs, beautiful.'

Behind my bravado and insouciance and sneering cynicism I
was genuinely happy that Kevin had found a good home. Seeing
him leading a dog's life and not busting his balls on a track
assuaged any guilt I had felt for exploiting such a graceful,
peaceful animal for such a frivolous pastime as dog racing. In
truth, I felt mildly jealous of Anna and Kevin as an 'item'. But at
least I could take satisfaction in knowing that some good had
come of my adventure, even if it was at my expense.

As we left the pub for a quick country walk and last goodbye,
it started snowing again. 'He *loves* the snow under his feet,' said
Anna, removing Kevin's lead. Unshackled and unrestrained I
waited eagerly for him to take off into the distance at speed with
gay abandon, chasing powdery snowflakes and dancing shadows.
But he simply took a few steps, cocked his leg against a tree,
relieved himself and ambled along sniffing the ground. Such is
life.

LOOKING FOR A FIGHT

DAVID MATTHEWS

Shortlisted for the
William Hill Sports Book of the Year

'Huge vitality, beguiling characterisation,
authentic dialogue and a fine evocation of
time and place . . . We have lost a boxer,
but gained a writer' *Sunday Times*

'Unexpectedly intriguing' *Spectator*

When journalist David Matthews wanted to write
a piece on what makes boxers tick, he found the
way barred. So he decided the only way really
to understand their life was to join them,
at first hesitantly then wholeheartedly, by
training to become a professional fighter himself.
After two years of self-sacrifice, loss, blood, sweat
and self-discovery, he got himself into shape,
learned how to box and finally climbed into
the ring for one bout. He emerged having
found out much about himself, and about
the true nature of the fight game.

NON-FICTION / SPORT 0 7472 6235 7

FATHERS, SONS AND FOOTBALL

COLIN SHINDLER

The fascinating story of one unique family,
the Summerbees, whose trade for seventy years
has been professional football.

This book is a remarkable account of the changing
nature not only of football but of society itself.
From the depression in 1930s Preston
where George struggled to make ends meet,
through Mike and the Swinging Sixties in
Manchester, and on to Nicky, the modern star
and tabloid target, this is in turn a moving and
funny account of the ups and downs of a career in
football. Shindler brilliantly portrays not only how
the players struggle to cope with their changing
circumstances, but how those closest to them
are affected by it all.

'Amusing and candid' *Evening Standard*

NON-FICTION / SPORT 0 7472 3225 3

More Non-fiction from Headline

1966 AND ALL THAT

GEOFF HURST

'Stands out from the standard ghosted
autobiographies . . . the period detail gives it
huge charm' Simon Barnes, *The Times*

Geoff Hurst's unique hat-trick in the 1966 World
Cup final catapulted him to international
superstardom and changed his life forever. Now,
in this updated edition of his long-awaited and
bestselling autobiography, he recalls England's
greatest sporting moment, and reveals the inside
story of what it was like playing with and against
some of the finest footballers in history –
Pele, Moore, Beckenbauer and Charlton.

His assessment of today's superstars, packed with
insight from one of the game's true legends,
must be read, as England look to the future
with an exciting young squad.

NON-FICTION / AUTOBIOGRAPHY 0 7472 4187 2

Now you can buy any of these other bestselling non-fiction titles from your bookshop or *direct from the publisher*.

FREE P&P AND UK DELIVERY
(Overseas and Ireland £3.50 per book)

Manchester United   *Colin Shindler*   £6.99
   Ruined My Life
A wonderfully evocative, bestselling account of a childhood spent in sixties Manchester as a City fan when all were turning to United.

A Lot of Hard Yakka   *Simon Hughes*   £6.99
The William Hill prize-winning insider's account of the ups and downs, the lifestyle, practical jokes and sheer hard yakka of county cricket.

Midnight Rugby   *Stephen Jones*   £7.99
An award-winning writer provides the inside story of the rugby revolution since the arrival of professionalism in 1995.

The Wildest Dream   *Peter and Leni Gillman*   £7.99
A powerful and affecting portrait of doomed hero George Mallory, assessing the motives and goals of this inspirational yet complex figure and including previously unpublished family papers.

TO ORDER SIMPLY CALL THIS NUMBER
AND QUOTE REF *50 SPORT*

01235 400 414

or visit our website: www.madaboutbooks.com

Prices and availability subject to change without notice.